Directory A–Z

THIS EDITION WRITTEN AND RESEARCHED BY

Sandra Bao,
Brendan Sainsbury, John Lee, Becky Ohlsen

› Washington, Oregon & the Pacific Northwest Top Experiences ›

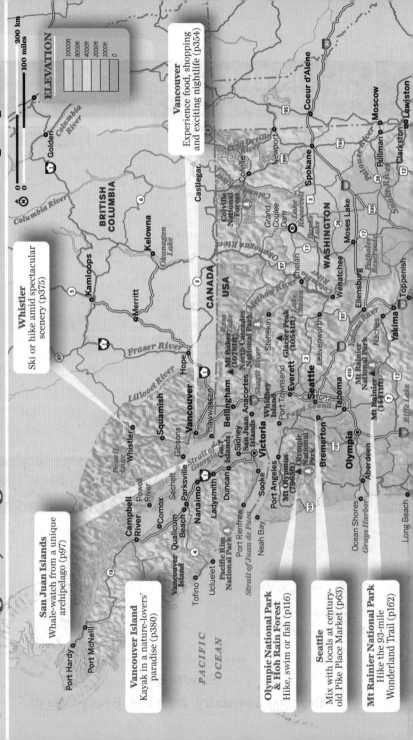

Whistler
Ski or hike amid spectacular scenery (p375)

Vancouver
Experience food, shopping and exciting nightlife (p354)

San Juan Islands
Whale-watch from a unique archipelago (p97)

Vancouver Island
Kayak in a nature-lovers' paradise (p380)

Olympic National Park & Hoh Rain Forest
Hike, swim or fish (p116)

Seattle
Mix with locals at century-old Pike Place Market (p63)

Mt Rainier National Park
Hike the 93-mile Wonderland Trail (p162)

ELEVATION

10000ft
8000ft
4000ft
2000ft
1000ft
0

200 km
100 miles

BRITISH COLUMBIA

CANADA
USA

WASHINGTON

PACIFIC OCEAN

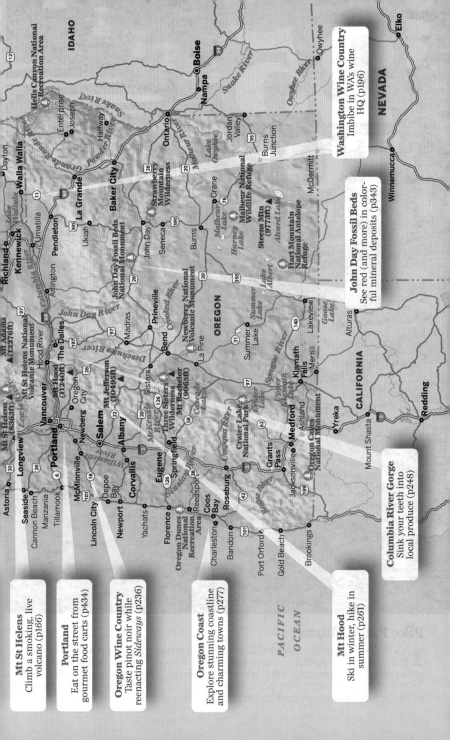

Pike Place Market

1 It's Seattle's biggest tourist attraction, and with great reason. Stuffed full of fun, funky shops, this old market (p63) has been selling a wide variety of wares – from produce to crafts to antiques and more – for more than a hundred years. Time your visit early on weekdays to mix with locals and avoid the tourist crowds (you've been warned!). Once you've gotten your fill of flying fish, go explore the mazes below – there are plenty of surprises waiting to be discovered.

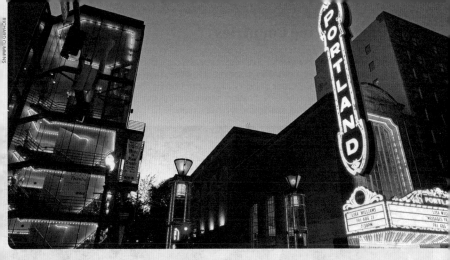

RICHARD CUMMINS

Portland

2 It's easy to brag about PDX (p200), but no one will hassle you for it – after all, everyone loves this city. It's as friendly as a big town and home to a mix of students, artists, cyclists, hipsters, young families, old hippies, ecofreaks and everything in between. There's great food, awesome music and plenty of culture, plus it's as sustainable as you can get. Come and visit, but be careful – like everyone else, you might just want to pack up and move here.

GLENN VAN DER KNIJFF

Vancouver, BC

3 As big cities go, it's hard to get more sophisticated, international or beautiful than Vancouver, BC (p354). Fresh from the 2010 Winter Olympics, this metropolis has it all – awesome food, trendy shopping, cool neighborhoods and exciting nightlife. There's so much to do, from visiting museums and art galleries to cycling and kayaking, that it'll make your head spin. And it's all framed by glorious mountains, forests and waterways, so there's always beauty in the background.

Washington Wine Countries

4 Washington is the second-largest wine-producing US state. Although its vines are relatively young, the terroir (environmental qualities) of Walla Walla – the most famous grape-growing region here – is excellent, with rich layers of sediment from the long-ago Missoula floods. It's Washington's equivalent of California's Napa Valley, with a historic downtown and upscale tourist services. For a less primped-up wine destination, head out to Yakima or Spokane, making sure to try the specialty reds of cabernet sauvignon, syrah and merlot.

YAKIMA VALLEY VISITORS & CONVENTION BUREAU

San Juan Islands

5 For something completely different, hop on a ferry to the San Juan Islands...and go back in time. Out of the more than 450 'islands' (p97; most are only rocky promontories), only about 60 are inhabited, and just four are regularly served by ferries. Nature is the main influence in this archipelago and each island has its own personality, both geographic and cultural. What can you do here? Start with cycling, kayaking and spotting orcas – then just sit back and relax.

TOM BOYDEN

ANN CECIL

Oregon Coast

6 Cruising along Oregon's stunning coast (p277) is an unforgettable experience any time of year. Lofty headlands reach out to the ocean, offering spectacular views, while steep mountains of rock jut offshore like giant sentinels. There are beaches to walk on, dunes to explore and charming small towns to check out. And if you like camping, tide-pooling or whale-watching, you'll be in heaven. Just remember to bring your camera...and a sense of adventure.

Mt Rainier National Park

7 When the skies are clear, Mt Rainier looms high over Seattle, creating an amazing backdrop to the emerald city. Still very much a live volcano, the 14,411ft peak is the shining centerpiece of the national park (p159), which offers a rare inland temperate rain forest, hikes through alpine wildflower meadows and the famous 93-mile Wonderland Trail. If you're fit and adventurous enough, attempt to climb the peak itself; just be ready to traverse some of the largest glaciers outside Alaska.

Whistler

8 Love to ski? Then you'll adore Whistler (p375), a top-notch resort adored by celebrities and the jet set. This Canadian hot spot hosted a good chunk of the 2010 Winter Olympics, including the heart-stopping alpine skiing events. Boasting 200 runs, it's one of North America's largest ski areas (the slopes are open from November to June). But the mountains here aren't just for snow sports. In summer you can hike, mountain bike, raft and rock climb among some of the most spectacular scenery in Canada.

Microbreweries

9 Love beer? Welcome to paradise. The Pacific Northwest has some of the best microbrew in the world, and plenty of it. In fact, Portland (aka 'beervana') holds the distinguished record of 'most microbreweries of any city in the world.' And it shows – you can hardly cycle down any trendy street and not pedal past a bar serving the stuff. Seattle and Vancouver are no slouches, either; you'll find plenty of great choices there. So raise a pint and toast to 'buying local' – and feel good in more ways than one.

Portland Food Carts

10 Eat at a Portland food cart! They're good, cheap and locally owned, and the choices are endless: sandwiches, pizza, pasta, waffles, pies, crepes. And they're international: Indian, Japanese, Peruvian, Thai, Cuban, Czech, Hawaiian...there are even Jewish and gluten-free carts. Don't think you'll be getting run-of-the-mill grub – expect creations such as duck confit sandwiches, beef goulash, chicken-coconut curry, vegan barbeque, kimchee quesadillas and fried risotto balls. Intrigued? Keep an eye out for these mobile trailers, and stop by for a quick, delicious bite (p218).

Ecola State Park (& Twilight Film Locations)

11 Swaddle up your lovely neck and hope this lessens the temptation for whichever lustful vampire might be lurking in the woods. Despite the fact that Twilight was based in Forks, Washington, this rabidly popular movie (and its sequels) was actually filmed mostly in Oregon – around Portland and the Columbia River Gorge. Indian Beach, at Ecola State Park on Oregon's coast (p284), was the stand-in for La Push, Washington – home to werewolves. It's not the first time Ecola has seen superstars on its shores; it was also used to film The Goonies and Point Break.

Oregon Wine Country

12 Pinot noir was Oregon's specialty grape long before the film Sideways pushed it into the limelight. Cruise the roads around the towns of Newberg, Dundee and McMinnville, at the heart of Oregon's wine country, and sample chardonnay, Riesling and pinot gris, along with the star grape. If you'd like to stay longer than a day there are plenty of B&Bs, along with some gourmet restaurants – all of which offer even more opportunities to sample the Dionysian nectar.

JOHN ELK III

Olympic National Park & Hoh Rain Forest

13 One of Washington state's premiere tourist attractions, Olympic National Park (p116) takes up a huge chunk of the Olympic Peninsula and boasts its own mini rain forest. Hike through old-growth forests draped with moss, waltz through meadows filled with wildflowers, swim in pure mountain lakes or try to summit Mt Olympus. You can even go trout fishing, beachcombing, hot-springs soaking and cross-country skiing, all within the park's official boundaries, which includes a thin coastal strip along the Pacific Ocean.

AARON MCCOY

Space Needle

14 Many visitors can't leave Seattle without heading to the top of the needle (p64), the city's most distinctive symbol and landmark. Why? From more than 500ft up you'll get views of everything, from downtown to Puget Sound to the Cascades and Mt Rainier. You can even break the bank at the rotating restaurant up top, but don't fool yourself – the best thing here is that 'I'm at the top of the world' feeling you get as the city slowly spins around you.

Mt St Helens

15 Having recently celebrated the 30th anniversary of its 1980 eruption, Mt St Helens (p166) still occasionally billows out plumes of smoke. But this recent activity is nothing like the catastrophic event that killed 57 people, flattened 230 sq miles of forest and blew nearly 1300ft off its top. Today, you can hike to the edge and peer down into the mile-wide caldera, but if you're against strenuous exercise (and believe us, it's not easy) then just drop by one of the visitor centers for some history, and a faraway look at this amazing volcano.

Hot Springs

16 With its volcanic geography, you'd think the Pacific Northwest would have some good hot springs – and you'd be right. There are springs in BC, and Washington has its popular Sol Duc resort, with decent services and family-friendly pools. Oregon, however, has many more popular hot springs. Try Bagby or Umpqua for rustic, free soaks; Breitenbush, Belknap or Crystal Crane for more services without being too fancy; and Bonneville Hot Springs Resort & Spa for the ultimate in luxury. And don't forget your rubber ducky.

JIM WARK

CHRIS CHEADLE/ALAMY

Mt Hood

17 Oregon's highest peak, Mt Hood (p261; elevation 11,240ft) is a recreational wonderland. In winter there's skiing at four resorts (including one with the longest year-round season in North America), while in summer glorious hiking trails and campgrounds abound. Or test your climbing mettle and head to the top – Mt Hood is the second most climbed peak over 10,000ft in the world. Whatever you do, stop in for a drink or meal at Timberline Lodge, whose facade was the star of the movie The Shining.

Columbia River Gorge

18 Carved out by the mighty Columbia as the Cascades uplifted, the Columbia River Gorge (p248) is a geologic marvel. With Washington State on its north side and Oregon to its south, the state-dividing gorge offers countless waterfalls and spectacular hikes, as well as agricultural bounties of apples, pears and cherries. And if you're into windsurfing or kiteboarding, then head straight to the sporty town of Hood River, ground zero for these extreme sports. Whether you're a hiker, fruit-lover or adrenaline junkie, the gorge delivers.

Crater Lake National Park

19 Beautiful doesn't begin to describe Crater Lake (p321). It's serene, sublime, transcendent – in other words, it might just blow your mind. A 6-mile-wide caldera created when Mt Mazama erupted nearly 8000 years ago, this amazingly blue lake is filled with some of the purest water you can imagine. It's also America's deepest lake at nearly 2000ft, and so clear you can easily peer a hundred feet down. Camp, ski or hike in the surrounding old-growth forests while enjoying unforgettable, jaw-dropping views.

ROBERTO GEROMETTA

Vancouver Island

20 The largest populated landmass off North America's west coast, Vancouver Island (p380) is ready-made for a nature lovers. Its diverse ecosystems include mountains, rivers, lakes, rain forests, marshes and beaches – a paradise to the island's many wildlife species, both on land and in water. Fish for salmon, go bird- or whale-watching or just explore the many nature reserves and parks. And when you get tired of all that green, stop off in lovely Victoria, where the historic architecture might just make you believe you're in Europe.

Coffee

21 You're unlikely to find better coffee anywhere in the world than in the Pacific Northwest. A huge number of coffee shops brew up rich espressos, creamy lattes, frothy cappuccinos or chocolate-y mochas. But it's the specialty roasters you shouldn't miss – be sure to try Stumptown Coffee in Portland (p224). And do hang out in some coffee shops; it's the perfect Pacific North-westerly thing to do here, whether you're sitting at a sunny sidewalk table or keeping warm inside when the rain pours down.

Native American Culture

22 Evidence of once-thriving Native American groups can be seen throughout the Pacific Northwest, but some of the best-known sites are Seattle's Pioneer Square and Vancouver's Stanley Park (including the iconic totem poles). For exceptional exhibits, check out Vancouver's UBC Museum of Anthropology; Seattle's Burke Museum; Spokane's Northwest Museum of Arts & Culture; Eugene's University of Oregon Museum of National History; and the Warm Springs Museum in Central Oregon.

Oregon Shakespeare Festival

23 The Shakespearean plays at this famous festival (p311) run from February to October, but this doesn't mean you shouldn't hurry to snag a ticket – performances sell out weeks in advance. There are three venues, but try for a play at the outdoor Elizabethan theatre stage, which has to be the most dramatic setting in town; it's a replica of London's 17th-century Fortune Theatre. You might just feel like the bard himself is nearby, overseeing the actors performing his masterpieces.

John Day Fossil Beds

24 It's hard to believe that hillsides can be so colorful, until you visit this amazing site (p343). Kaleidoscopic layers of red, gold, orange, beige and brown mineral deposits decorate the landscape, and the hues can change dramatically with the light. There are fossils, too – the bones of small horses, rhinos, primates and sabertooth-like cats have been (and still are being) uncovered. It's like an eerie moon surface, all created by volcanic eruptions and erosion over millions of years, and named after a man famous for getting robbed and stripped naked by Indians.

Orcas

25 Spotting a pod of majestic killer whales, also known as orcas, can make your day! And there's hardly a better place to do it than around Washington's Puget Sound. Take a boat tour from Friday Harbor, on San Juan Island (p98), where resident pods (totaling about 90 whales) frolic and hunt for salmon. Here, sightings are nearly guaranteed in summer. Landlubbers can plant themselves at Lime Kiln State Park (p99) and get lucky from the shoreline. On Vancouver Island, Telegraph Cove (p401) is another exceptional jumping-off point from which to spot these great beasts.

Welcome to the Pacific Northwest

Microbrews, killer coffee, lush forests, a pristine coastline, eco-minded locals, and music and art galore – Pacific Northwesterners have it good and they don't mind sharing.

Outdoor Adventures

You can't escape the natural world in these parts. Even the big cities are peppered with verdant parks and punctuated by looming, snowy peaks: Seattle's Mt Rainier, Portland's Mt Hood and Vancouver's North Shore Mountains. And that's not to mention the raging rivers, rolling deserts, dense old-growth forests and hundreds of miles of glorious public beaches that are never too far from any urban landscape here.

The great outdoors offers endless opportunities to get into nature – think camping, hiking, cycling, climbing, skiing and mountaineering. And while it does rain aplenty, all that moisture translates into a perfect storm of water sports; you can raft down white water, surf gnarly waves, navigate a kiteboard through ripping winds, fish for everything from sturgeon to salmon, and watch majestic whales migrate up and down the coast.

Land of Locavores & Beer Lovers

The varied climates of the Northwest produce an abundance of locally grown, raised and harvested food, from berries and hazelnuts to wild mushrooms, seafood, cheese and grass-fed beef. This bounty has spawned a serious movement to eat locally by practitioners known as 'locavores.' They get their fix at specialty grocery stores, community gardens and restaurants that source ingredients locally – as well as at farmers markets, where farmers often sell their own fresh, seasonal crops.

In these parts, beverages hold equal clout. The nation's gourmet coffee scene may have started in Seattle, but dozens of artisan microroasters across the Northwest now produce some of the best espresso in the world. Microbrewing became famous here, within a stone's throw of the nation's highest concentration of hop farms. Today, all kinds of craft brewers pump out fragrant, delicious India Pale Ales (IPAs) and more. And don't forget wine; grape vines cover many Pacific Northwest hills, producing a harvest of intriguing reds and whites.

Art & Culture

While the region's outdoors largely define how Northwesterners recreate, there's no shortage of urban entertainment and culture. Think indie garage bands, world-class symphonies, jazz bars and an abundance of public art. There are offbeat film houses and art galleries tucked into even the smallest towns around the region, and nearly everyone seems to be making homemade crafts. Pacific Northwesterners pride themselves on being open-minded and accepting of all kinds of self-expression.

Seattle, Portland and Vancouver all support symphonies, operas, vibrant dance troupes (both modern and ballet) and all sizes of theater companies. Galleries and museums display visual work by locals, including Native American artists, wood- and metal-workers, ceramicists and painters, and glassmakers inspired by Tacoma's Dale Chihuly. You'll always have more than enough art and culture to appreciate in this region, the supremely creative Pacific Northwest.

need to know

Currency

» US dollars ($)

» Canadian dollars (C$)

Language

» English

When to Go

Whistler
GO Dec-Mar to ski; May-Oct to hike

Vancouver
GO Jun-Sep

Seattle
GO Jun-Sep

Eastern Washington
GO May-Oct

Portland
GO Jun-Sep

Eastern Oregon
GO May-Oct

Oregon Coast
GO mid-Dec-Jan & Mar-Jun for whale watching, Jun-Sep for the beach

- Desert, dry climate
- Warm to hot summers, mild winters
- Mild to hot summers, cold winters

High Season
(Jun–Sep)

» Sunny, warm days throughout the region

» More crowds and higher prices for accommodations and sights

» For ski resorts, busiest times are December to March

Shoulder
(Apr–May & Oct)

» Crowds and prices drop off

» Temperatures remain mild

» Services are more limited, but there's less competition for them

Low Season
(Nov–Mar)

» Colder days, less sunlight, more rain

» Some services may close along the coast, and high passes can be blocked by snow

» Indoor activities such as theater and music are at their best!

Your Daily Budget

Budget less than
$100

» Inexpensive motel room/dorm bed: $75/$25

» There are many supermarkets for self-caterers, or look for food carts in larger cities

» Some sights have free-admission days

Midrange
$100–$175

» Hotel room: $100 a night

» Meal in a good restaurant: $15–$20

Top End more than
$175

» Upscale hotel room: $150

» Fine-dining meal: $25

Money

» ATMs widely available. Credit cards accepted at most hotels, restaurants and shops.

Visas

» Visa requirements vary widely for entry to the US. For information check http://travel.state.gov/visa/visa_1750.html.

Cell Phones

» The US and Canada use GSM-850 and GSM-1900 bands. SIM cards are relatively easy to obtain in both countries.

Driving

» Drive on the right; steering wheel is on the left side of the car.

Websites

» **Lonely Planet** (www.lonelyplanet.com/usa/pacific-northwest)

» **Seattle Tourism** (www.seattle.gov) The city's official website.

» **Oregon Tourism Commission** (www.traveloregon.com) Travel planning site.

» **Travel Portland** (www.travelportland.com) Portland info.

» **Tourism British Columbia** (www.hellobc.com) Official tourism website of BC.

» **Washington State Tourism** (www.experiencewa.com) Washington State Tourism's official website.

Exchange Rates

Australia	A$1	$0.97
Canada	C$1	$0.97
Europe	€1	$1.38
Japan	¥100	$1.22
New Zealand	NZ$1	$0.75
UK	UK£1	$1.58

For current exchange rates see www.xe.com.

Important Numbers

The following numbers apply to both the USA and Canada.

Country Code	☑1
International Access Code	☑011
Ambulance, Fire and Police	☑911
Local Directory Assistance	☑411

Liquor Laws

The legal age for drinking in British Columbia is 19 (with photo ID). In Oregon and Washington you have to be 21. In bars throughout the Pacific Northwest, alcohol is served until 2am. In Oregon and Washington, you can buy beer and wine at supermarkets, convenience stores or private outlets (ie specialty wine shops). When buying liquor in these states, however, you'll have to seek out state-approved liquor stores. In BC, you can only buy beer, wine and liquor from government-sanctioned liquor stores.

Arriving in the Pacific Northwest

» **Sea-Tac Airport** (p81)

» Link Light Rail – connects to downtown Seattle in 30 minutes

Bus – Metro buses stop outside baggage carousel 5

Shuttle – frequent services from $11 one way

Taxi – $35; about 25 minutes to downtown

» **Portland International Airport** (p228)

Max Light Rail – connects to downtown Portland in 40 minutes

Shuttle – frequent services from $14 one way

Taxis – $30; around 20 minutes to downtown

» **Vancouver International Airport** (p373)

SkyTrain – connects to downtown Vancouver in 25 minutes

Taxi – C$35; around 30 minutes to downtown

what's new

For this new edition of Washington, Oregon & the Pacific Northwest, our authors have hunted down the fresh, the revamped, the transformed, the hot and the happening. Here are a few of our favorites. For up-to-the-minute reviews and recommendations, see lonelyplanet.com/usa/pacific-northwest.

Twilight Fever

1 We've all heard of it, some of us admit to having read the books, and even fewer of us admit to having seen the movies – but the *Twilight* phenomenon can't be denied. The unlikely love story between a peace-loving vampire and a clumsy teenage girl has turned the drizzly little town of Forks, Washington, into a serious destination. Tourism has grown by 600%, and the hordes are still thick as blood – so to speak (p132).

Vancouver's Museum of Anthropology

2 Twice as big and shinier than ever, this revamped world-class museum houses amazing collections, including spectacular Native American artifacts. Snag a spot on a free tour to take it all in (p362).

Long Beach Discovery Trail

3 Officially inaugurated in September 2009, this interpretive trail – which runs from Ilwaco to Long Beach – commemorates the final 8 miles of Lewis and Clark's journey along the Pacific (p415).

Turtleback Mountain Preserve

4 Fragile wetlands and savannah are now under protection in this new nature preserve on Orcas Island, Washington. Two hiking trails take you to spectacular viewpoints, and horseback riding is possible (p105).

Washington's Paradise Inn

5 After a two-year, 30-million-dollar facelift, this historic lodge re-opened. Not to worry, however – its Great Room looks better than ever, highlighted by an unforgettable grid of massive timbers (p162).

Seattle and Vancouver: new rapid transit to the airport!

6 Seattle's Sound Transit boasts a new light-rail service to Sea-Tac, while Vancouver's SkyTrain now goes to the airport from downtown. What does this mean to you? Cheap, fast transport from airplane to hotel (p81 and p373).

Oxford Hotel

7 Bend's slick new boutique hotel is fashionably decked out in earth-tone colors, contemporary Zen-like designs and cutting-edge techno-gadgets – all the while exuding a superior, ecosustainable ethos (p271).

Hot Lake Springs

8 Just outside La Grande, Oregon, is this unique hotel complex six years in the making. Sleep in the lovely historic rooms, take a bronze-foundry tour or soak in the hot springs nearby (p333).

if you like...

Wildlife

Lions and tigers and bears, oh my – well, maybe not the tigers. And the lions are the mountain kind. But if you're looking for wild critters, there's plenty of them here in the Northwest. Gray whales, seals and orcas frolic in the ocean, while Roosevelt elk, pronghorn antelopes and black bears scamper over land. And raptors, such as bald eagles, often soar overhead, along with sandhill cranes, downy woodpeckers and many corvid family species.

San Juan Islands Ground zero for spotting orcas; several pods live here year-round (p97)

Oregon Coast In winter and spring, gray whales migrate from Mexico to Alaska – and back (p277)

Hart Mountain National Antelope Refuge Pronghorn central, but keep a sharp eye out – they're the second-fastest land mammals in the world (p350)

Klamath Basin National Wildlife Refuge You're nearly guaranteed a bald eagle sighting; up to a thousand gather here in winter (p326)

Hiking

In the Pacific Northwest, it's hard to throw a rock without hitting a hiking trail. Stomp around the volcanic cones, including Mt Rainier, Mt St Helens or Mt Hood; explore the far reaches of the Wallowas, the Columbia River Gorge or Olympic National Park; and go crazy figuring out which of BC's trails are the most gorgeous. In short, this region is heaven on earth for hikers.

Wonderland Trail Circumnavigate Mt Rainier's lofty peak – it's 93 miles of spectacular nature (p162)

West Coast Trail BC's famous 47-mile ribbon of adventure is for those truly serious about their outdoors (p397)

Oregon's Coast Neahkahnie Mountain, Cape Lookout, Saddle Mountain – whether you're after wildflower meadows or stunning views of the Pacific Ocean, you won't be disappointed (p277)

Columbia River Gorge Tread up the easy Eagle Creek Trail (p252) for a waterfall wonderland, or sweat up Dog Mountain (p252) for unbeatable vistas.

Beaches

Ah, those waves lapping the shore, salty wind on your face and warm sand squishing between your toes. What says 'vacation' more than a day at the beach? Head to Oregon's coast for 360 miles of fun, while Washington has a beautiful shoreline within a national park. The Pacific Northwest has plenty of beaches to check out, whether you want to party at a resort or just be alone.

La Push beaches Come here for beauty and adventure – the beaches offer kayaking, surfing, hiking and sublime scenery (p132)

Long Beach Miles and miles of beachcombing, awesome breakers and even an old-growth forest to explore (p135)

Cannon Beach With its photogenic Haystack Rock looming just offshore, Cannon Beach is about as scenic as it gets (p284)

Oregon Dunes Explore this National Recreation Area on foot or in a dune buggy; the sandy mountains tower up to 500ft and spread 3 miles inland (p297)

GREG GAWLOWSKI

>> South Sister, the tallest and youngest of the sisters in Three Sisters Wilderness (p269)

Microbrews

If you appreciate the rich, complex flavors of a lovingly microbrewed beer, then you'll find nirvana here. And while the Pacific Northwest didn't actually invent the stuff, it certainly raised the fermentation of hops to a fine art. In fact, there's so much great beer in these parts that a cold glass of suds will never be far from your lips – we promise.

Fish Tale Brew Pub, Washington Olympia's oldest brewpub pours more than two dozen handcrafted brews, including organic beer and fruit ciders (p115)

Green Dragon, Portland A huge variety of microbrews, with nearly 50 beers on tap – including its own concoctions (p223)

Belmont Station, Portland Both a bar and large beer store, this spot boasts more than 1000 local and international brews (p223)

Alibi Room, Vancouver This tavern pours 25 diverse taps, with a rota of local selections; try the beer flights (p370)

Wine

Pinot noir lovers unite! It's Oregon's most famous grape, finicky as a superstar and the foundation for some very exceptional wine. But Washington produces more wine than nearly any other state, and it's of a very high quality too. Just head to the Walla Walla Valley for a taste of cabernet or syrah, and you'll be tipping your glass in agreement.

Walla Walla Washington's hot wine-growing region, with its namesake town as a very pretty centerpiece (p196)

Yakima Valley More than 50 wineries, most of them family-run, highlight this backbone of Washington's wine industry (p179)

McMinnville The heart of Oregon's grape land; base yourself here and your pinot noir glass will never run dry (p235)

Cowichan Valley If you can't make it to BC's prime Okanagan Valley, Vancouver Island's boutique vineyards are a worthwhile alternative (p392)

Shopping

Love to shop? How does zero sales tax sound? That's Oregon for you – the price is what the price is. But there's plenty of fabulous shopping in Washington and BC as well, from funky bohemian shops to fancy boutiques to farmers markets galore. So load up the bank account and bring your reusable shopping bags – mama needs a new pair of shoes.

Pike Place Market Seattle's famous market boasts fruit, vegetable and seafood stalls above, while everything else lies in the maze below (p63)

Oregon's outlet malls Discount shopping malls are conveniently located near tourist destinations (see http://web.oregon.com/shopping/outlet_shopping.cfm). In Portland, both Columbia Sportswear and Nike have factory stores (p226).

Portland's 23rd Ave Also called 'trendy-third' for its hip boutiques and upscale chains such as Gap, Banana Republic and Restoration Hardware (p207)

Granville Island Public Market More than just a covered farmers market with luscious delis and bakeries – countless stalls of arts and crafts await discovery (and your wallet) in Vancouver (p361)

If you like... beach camping
Oregon's Coast (p277) is paradise – more than a dozen coastal state parks with campgrounds
If you like... caves
Oregon Caves National Monument (p317) offers guided cave trips

Great Food

Perhaps it's no longer a secret, but the Pacific Northwest offers nearly limitless gourmet experiences. From Vancouver's world-class Chinese food to 'northwest cuisine' to fancy vegan offerings, this region boasts enough eating options to make your stomach spin – but in a good way. See our food chapter (p432) for more.

Granville Island Public Market A tasty bite for everyone, from luscious pastry treats to a top international food court (p361)

Pike Place Market Seattle's grand old market sells ripe fruit, fresh vegetables and gleaming fish – among many other things (p63)

Portland's Food Carts Trendy, cheap and oh-so delicious, Portland has turned the lowly food mobile to a cutting-edge movable feast (p434)

FareStart Restaurant Seattle restaurant with great food, good value and an even better cause; definitely one of a kind (p72)

Jaw-Dropping Landscapes

This region is pretty much made up of amazing landscapes, from scenic shorelines to snow-dusted volcanic mountain ranges to desolate but beautiful desert panoramas. Lofty Cascade peaks can even be seen from the big cities of Seattle, Portland and Vancouver, making great natural backdrops to the urban bustle.

North Cascades National Park Stark landscapes highlighted by formidable mountaintops, all in a national park known for its isolation (p146)

John Day Fossil Beds An almost unbelievable palette of colors layer the sedimentary hills of this geological wonder (p343)

Three Sisters Wilderness A string of peaks with striking character, from Broken Top's jagged edges to South Sister's dimpled dome (p269)

Cape Scott Provincial Park Some of the most rugged and wild coastline you'll ever see or experience (p402)

Live Music

Creative musicians just love the Northwest, and it shows – Portland, Seattle and Vancouver claim some of the hottest new bands on the indie circuit, though small towns such as Olympia have their own talent. Venues run from intimate rooms to quirky spaces with floating floors to large, loud clubs. For more on indie music, see the Music & Arts chapter (p425).

Doug Fir A hip haven with a great sound system, attracting cutting-edge talent for near-nightly shows (p224)

Mississippi Studios Former recording studio turned 300-seat venue with great atmosphere and up 'n' coming bands (p224)

Crocodile Cafe Seattle's historic music venue, which first saw grunge emerge from the shadows. Everyone from Cheap Trick to Yoko Ono has rocked here (p78)

Commodore Vancouver institution with art-deco atmosphere, unique dance floor and soon-to-be-famous local bands (p371)

If you like... funky public sculpture
Seattle's bohemian Fremont neighborhood (p66; aka 'Center of the Universe') is famous for its concrete bridge troll – and more

If you like... gardens
Sniff flowers from Victoria's Butchart Gardens (p390) to Portland's International Rose Test Gardens (p205) – with plenty of others in between

Skiing

Strap on those skis – there are some great downhill slopes here in the Pacific Northwest. With plenty of precipitation, the snow pack can really add up to create some exceptionally deep powder. And, for some, the cross-country skiing is even better; there are endless scenic trails winding through lovely hills and forests.

Whistler The mother of all ski resorts, or close to it; huge area with plenty of powder (p375)

Mt Hood Availability is this mountain's appeal – you can ski here every month of the year (p261)

Crystal Mountain Located on the flanks of Mt Rainier, this is Washington's largest ski resort, with more than 50 named runs (p165)

Methow Valley A cross-country skier's paradise, boasting more than 125 miles of groomed trails (p151)

Hot Springs

If you're looking for a hot, therapeutic mineral soak, there's lots to choose from in this volcanic region. Everything from desolate water holes in a desert to rustic and unpretentious springs with a few services to luxury soaks in fancy resorts are on tap, so to speak. Nudity is – unsurprisingly – *de rigueur* at the more remote and free locations.

Sol Duc Well-established springs with good services and family-friendly appeal (p121)

Breitenbush Lovely springs near the forest, with vegetarian food, yoga and accommodations (p246)

Bagby Free but surprisingly developed, with hollowed-out tubs and even private 'rooms' (p246)

Umpqua Free springs with an unbeatable location; they're perched on a cliff above the Umpqua River (p319)

Famous Drives

With all the fantastic scenery in the Pacific Northwest, sometimes you need a great drive to take it all in. After all, there's a lot of ground to cover – snowy mountains to skirt around, lush forests to whiz past and rocky shorelines to cruise by. So fill up the tank, strap on your seatbelt and let the road trip begin.

North Cascades Highway Strikingly diverse and scenic highway that passes North Cascades National Park into the Methow Valley (p146)

Historic Columbia River Highway Forget busy Hwy 84 and take the long way around – a winding and beautiful byway also known as Hwy 30 (p249)

Three Capes Scenic Drive Visit three dramatic headlands on this 40-mile side road along the gorgeous Oregon coast (p288)

Sea to Sky Highway Connecting Vancouver with Whistler, Hwy 99 offers breathtaking vistas, from the Pacific Ocean to lofty mountain peaks (p374)

month by month

Top Events

1. **Oregon Shakespeare Festival**, February
2. **Pendleton Round Up**, September
3. **Whale-watching**, March–June
4. **Oregon Brewers Festival**, July
5. **Bumbershoot**, September

January

One of the quieter, greener months in the lowlands and on the coast, where the rains fall. Mountain resorts bustle with skiers and boarders taking advantage of the white stuff, especially around New Year.

Truffle Hunting in the Cascade Mountains

The Northwest's best native edible truffles are ripe for the picking this month. Eugene and Corvallis become truffle hubs, and many restaurants serve the expensive fungi.

Polar Bear Swim

Hundreds of shivering, brave souls plunge into the icy waters of the Burrard Inlet in Vancouver, BC, on January 1 to celebrate the New Year.

February

A good time to visit the three metro areas, which become the territory of locals during these gray days. Book ahead for snow-related activities though; resorts and mountain cabins fill up quickly.

Chinese New Year

Vancouver's large Chinese population celebrates with parades, activities, prizes, dragon dances, traditional art and – of course – plenty of great Chinese food.

Oregon Shakespeare Festival

In Ashland, Oregon, tens of thousands of theater fans party with the Bard at this nine-month-long festival (that's right!) highlighted by world-class plays and Elizabethan drama.

March

Early blooms are harbingers of the region's long spring and upcoming fruit bounty. Major destinations on the coast and in the mountains become crowded with local families during spring break; book early.

Spring Whale-Watching Week

Spot the gray whales' spring migration anywhere along the Pacific Coast. Around Oregon's Depoe Bay it's semi-organized, with docents and special viewpoints. The northward migration happens through June.

St Patrick's Day in Seattle

Head to some of the city's best Irish pubs for some green beer and jolly celebration.

Moisture Festival

Seattle embraces its humidity with vaudeville, circus and burlesque acts that appeal to the whole family.

Victorian Festival

Port Townsend, Washington's Victorian jewel, dresses up in frilly costumes. Tours of period homes, carriage rides and craft workshops are offered.

April

Even though the rains continue, warmer temperatures and spots of sun inspire more outdoor activities, especially in the drier, eastern part of the region. Easter weekend can be crowded everywhere.

 Skagit County Tulip Festival

Acres of red, purple, yellow and orange tulips bob in the breeze as visitors partake in wine tastings, bike tours and helicopter rides over the expansive fields surrounding La Conner, Washington.

Hood River Valley Blossom Festival

Celebrates the fruit bounty of Oregon's fertile Hood River Valley, with food, wine, crafts and a 47-mile agricultural tour route known as the Fruit Loop.

Spring Arts Walk

Olympia, Washington, celebrates the coming of spring with visual arts and performances. The highlight is a 'Procession of the Species' parade, which honors Earth Day and involves creative and colorful plant and animal costumes.

May

Spring has sprung, but don't leave the rain gear at home. Memorial Day weekend can be busy at campgrounds and parks despite the occasional drizzle.

Northwest Folklife Festival

This Seattle festival is celebrated with hundreds of musicians, artists and performers from all over the world.

Victoria Day

Originally honoring Queen Victoria's birthday, this Canadian holiday now celebrates the current sovereign's birthday (and unofficial start of the summer season) with parades and fireworks.

Seattle Cheese Festival

Meet local artisan cheesemakers, and learn how to make your own mozzarella, pair wine with cheese and more.

June

Blooming roses and outdoor celebrations mark the beginning of summer. Hotels fill up fast in the cities and on the coast.

Portland Rose Festival

Music concerts, floral parades, children's events, carnival rides, tall ships, dragon-boat races, the naval fleet, fireworks and a half-million spectators.

Britt Festival

An outdoor summer music celebration in Jacksonville, Oregon, featuring world-class jazz, folk, country and classical-music artists – including some mighty big names.

Bard on the Beach

A season of four Shakespeare-related plays take place in the Vanier Park tents in Vancouver, BC. Runs through September.

Sandcastle Day

Cannon Beach becomes ground zero for art created with...sand. Expect stunning creativity and execution – these aren't your typical sand-bucket castles.

July

Soak up the sun during the region's summer peak. Farmers markets are going strong this month, and the coast and mountains (and everywhere in between) are flooded with visitors.

Oregon Brewers Festival

Enjoy Portland's summer weather at this fun beer festival, where more than 50,000 microbrew-lovers eat, drink and whoop it up on the banks of the Willamette River.

Seattle's Seafair

Three-week party that includes a torchlight parade, hydroplane races, plenty of music and the arrival of the naval fleet.

da Vinci Days

Kinetic sculpture and home-built electric-car races happen at this funky arts-and-science celebration in Corvallis, Oregon.

Berry Picking
Walk the rows of local farms and fill your bucket with boysenberries, blueberries, strawberries and raspberries.

August
While the greener parts of the region may brown a bit this month, it's still a great time to be outdoors. Book early in the major cities, on the coast or at campgrounds.

Pacific National Exhibition
Family-friendly shows, music, concerts and a fairground in Vancouver, BC.

Washington State International Kite Festival
Huge kite festival on the sand at Long Beach, Washington. Look for new world records, including the largest kite flown and the most kites aloft at one time.

Garlic Festival
Chehalis, Washington, celebrates this aromatic bulb with crafts, music and garlic-laden food.

September
Cool nights but reliably sunny days make this one of the best months to visit. Kids are back in school, and fall harvests begin for wine grapes, mushrooms and more.

Pendleton Round Up
Country music, dances, art shows, a Native American powwow, bronco-breaking and Western pageantry preside here, at one of the country's most famous rodeos.

Bumbershoot
Seattle's biggest arts and cultural event boasts two dozen stages and hundreds of musicians, artists, theater troupes and writers.

Vancouver International Fringe Festival
Wild and wacky theatricals at both mainstream and unconventional Granville Island venues.

October
Even though the weather begins to get wet this month, hearty Northwesterners still head outdoors for bike races, coast visits and beer fests.

Oktoberfest
Oktoberfest in Leavenworth, Washington, where men in boyish shorts and vests eat, drink and dance.

Vancouver International Film Festival
Highly regarded film festival screening some 300 international films and documentaries from more than 50 countries.

Fresh Hop Beer Festivals
As soon as the year's fresh hop beers are ready the festivals begin, along with a chance to try unique seasonal brews. Look for the biggest ones in Yakima, Hood River and Portland.

Cross Crusade Race Series
Competitors ride intense laps through mud and over barriers in the largest cyclocross race series in the country, in Portland, Astoria and surrounding areas. Spectating is just as fun, with beer, cowbells and *frites*.

November
Book early for Thanksgiving weekend lodging. The most avid skiers and boarders will take to the slopes for early snows, while city shoppers hit the streets.

Eastside Culture Crawl
An open studio art event, which takes place over three days in Vancouver, BC.

Wine Country Thanksgiving
The Willamette Valley's 150 wineries open their doors to the public for three special days. Hit some of the small, family-owned wineries usually closed to visitors (www.wilamette wines.com).

December

The holidays mean larger crowds at mountain resorts and in cities. Find solitude on the coast and in rural areas.

Victorian Christmas

A Christmas past; witness a community tree lighting, Victorian ball, Father Christmas parade, carolers and town criers in Jacksonville, Oregon.

New Year's Eve in Seattle

Washington's ground zero for the new year is the Space Needle, where revelers dress up, count down and drink champagne as fireworks go off.

Ski Season

Skiers and snowboarders hit the slopes in search of powder and fun, from Eastern Oregon to Whistler, BC.

itineraries

Whether you've got six days or 60, these itineraries provide a starting point for the trip of a lifetime. Want more inspiration? Head online to lonelyplanet. com/thorntree to chat with other travelers.

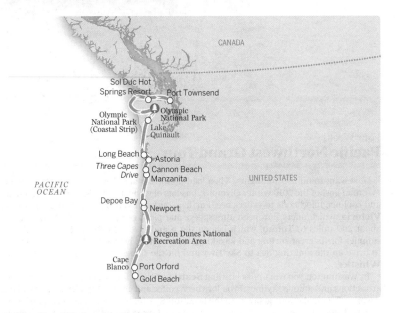

One to Two Weeks
Along Highway 101

❯ From the California border to **Gold Beach** – renowned for its Rogue River fishing – is some of Oregon's most magnificent coastal scenery. Heading north, **Port Orford** has art galleries and great restaurants, while **Cape Blanco** offers exhilarating views. Check out the sandy hills at **Oregon Dunes National Recreation Area**, and don't miss Newport's first-rate **Oregon Coast Aquarium**. If it's the season, take a whale-watching excursion at **Depoe Bay**. Enjoy the awesome scenery of **Three Capes Drive**, then relax in laid-back **Manzanita**. Upscale **Cannon Beach** is great for people-watching, while cute **Astoria** features historical attractions.

Cross into Washington via the long Astoria-Megler Bridge. Like to drive on sand? Go to **Long Beach**. Further north, beautiful **Lake Quinault** has good fishing and a great lodge. In **Olympic National Park**, be sure to visit the Hoh Rain Forest, with its short but magical Hall of Moss Trail. The **Olympic Coastal Strip** boasts 57 miles of wild, isolated coastline. Heading inland, **Sol Duc Hot Springs Resort** is great for a long soak. End your travels at the Victorian hamlet of **Port Townsend**.

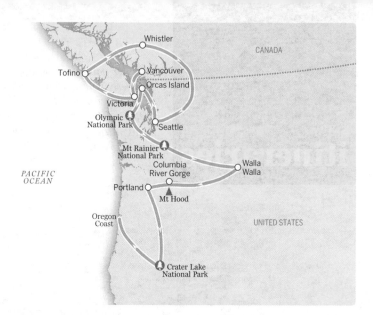

Four Weeks
Pacific Northwest Grand Tour

〉 Just want to hit the highlights? Then load up the car and drive this way. **Vancouver**, proud host of the 2010 winter Olympics, has lots of wonderful parks, ethnic attractions and cool neighborhoods to experience. Further south, on Vancouver Island, is charming **Victoria**, which offers European atmosphere and picture-perfect scenery. Now head up about 200 miles to **Tofino**, which lies on the island's western coast and is popular in summer for its great surfing and kayaking. If it's winter, however, ski-hounds will want to drive up the amazing Sea to Sky Hwy and hit the slopes at the world-class resort of **Whistler**.

In Washington you can't miss bustling **Seattle**, with its funky neighborhoods, myriad attractions and unique skyline; if you love beer, coffee and gourmet food, you'll be staying a while. Then make your getaway to the beautiful San Juan Islands, perhaps spotting an orca pod along the way. Speaking of which, woodsy **Orcas Island** makes a great destination – you can bike around, climb Mt Constitution (the archipelago's highest point) or just find a quiet spot to relax. Back on the mainland, **Olympic National Park** is the jewel of the Olympic Peninsula, boasting a unique rain forest ecosystem. For more of the state's gorgeous landscapes, **Mt Rainier National Park** is a must; plenty of stunning hiking trails, some with views of glaciers, abound. And wine aficionados shouldn't pass up the chance to taste the goods in Eastern Washington's **Walla Walla**, an attractive, laid-back town.

There's no escaping the attractions in **Portland** – from its landmark Powell's bookstore to its many microbreweries to tax-free (and hip) shopping. Just east are the grand vistas of the **Columbia River Gorge**, laden with dozens of gushing waterfalls and great hiking trails. Nearby **Mt Hood** is unbeatable for camping and hiking, and the historic Timberline Lodge begs a visit – this hotel starred in the movie *The Shining*, after all. There's also skiing on Mt Hood – not just in winter, but every month of the year! Much further south, **Crater Lake National Park** is a geologic wonder with supreme scenery; you can drive around its rim only in summer, when the snow has melted. Finally, if you have time left over, there's the grandeur (and seafood cuisine) of the beautiful **Oregon Coast**.

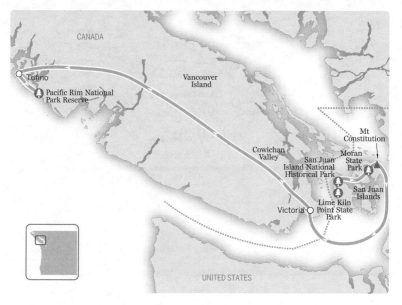

One to Two Weeks
Island Hop

❯ Washington's San Juans is an archipelago of hundreds of islands covering some 750 sq miles. Only about 60 are inhabited, and just four are accessible by public ferry. Three of these islands bring thousands of vacationers every year, but each has managed to keep a serene atmosphere and distinct character.

San Juan Island has the best tourist facilities of the islands, along with the archipelago's only sizeable town, Friday Harbor. **Lime Kiln Point State Park** has prime whale-watching shores; in June, keep a lookout for killer or minke whales feasting on salmon runs. To the north is **San Juan Island National Historical Park**, with old British military facilities and earthwork fortifications and – on clear days – great mountain views.

The largest of the islands, **Orcas Island** is probably the most beautiful – and the poshest. It's dotted with fancy homes, and the lack of a central town gives it an exclusive neighborhood feel. Check out **Moran State Park**, which offers camping, fishing, hiking and mountain biking. **Mt Constitution**, the highest point in the archipelago, is also here, and features some of the finest views in Washington.

Lopez Island is the most peaceful island, with friendly locals and pastoral charm. Don't expect too many tourist services – agriculture and farming are the main focus here. The mostly flat island is made for cycling, and there's little vehicular traffic.

If you're not pressed for time, a much larger island to explore is British Columbia's **Vancouver Island**. Start in lovely **Victoria**, a cosmopolitan city with a variety of ethnic cultures, along with a touch of old Britain. Can't-miss attractions include the world-famous **Butchart Gardens**, a few miles north of town, and high tea at the grand **Empress Hotel**. Wine-lovers and foodies should head about 40 miles northwest to the **Cowichan Valley**, home to boutique wineries and organic farms. Further west, on the coast, is the town of **Tofino**, where you can go kayaking and spot marine life including gray whales. Nearby is **Pacific Rim National Park Reserve**, home to rain forests, crashing coastal surf, islands to explore and amazing hiking opportunities. Finally, head to land's end at **Cape Scott Provincial Park** to explore remote and pristine beaches; outdoor lovers have miles of challenging trails and backcountry camping opportunities – plus the chance to get away from it all.

Two Weeks
Seattle & Washington

❯ The Pacific Northwest's largest city, **Seattle** has plenty going for it – a great location on Puget Sound, a myriad of dynamic neighborhoods, interesting sights and attractions, lots of first-rate coffee and beer, and – looming over it all – the lofty peak of majestic Mt Rainier. Must-sees include Pioneer Square, Pike Place Market, the Seattle Aquarium and the Space Needle, but there's plenty more to keep you busy.

Get out of town by hopping on a ferry to Bainbridge Island, then heading north to **Port Townsend**. With its Victorian architecture and location on the Strait of Juan de Fuca, this picturesque little town is a magnet for artists and eclectic personalities. From here you can take a bicycle on a ferry to the San Juan Islands, though if you want to drive you'll have to access them via Anacortes (more on this later). Work your way east along the Olympic Peninsula, perhaps stopping in Port Angeles for a quick day trip to Vancouver Island's pretty capital, **Victoria**.

Olympic National Park can't be missed. Its coastal strip includes 57 miles of remote beaches with pounding waves and wild scenery; visit Rialto Beach for amazing views. Inland, the Hoh Rain Forest is a prime destination with its famous Hall of Moss Trail. Now head further south to **Lake Quinault**, a gorgeous glacier-fed lake boasting a historic grand lodge. This is the place to go fishing, boating or swimming. Then pack it up and drive to **Olympia**, Washington's lively capital that's full of music culture.

If you like volcanoes, **Mt St Helens** will be on your itinerary. The 30th anniversary of its 1980 blast recently passed – and a new dome is forming. Not to be outclassed, Mt Rainier is another can't miss geologic landmark. Hope for good weather and go hiking among glaciers, alpine meadows and old-growth forests in **Mt Rainier National Park**.

Looping back to Interstate 5, drive up to Anacortes and take a ferry to the beautiful **San Juan Islands**. There are three distinct main islands to explore. San Juan Island has undulating hills and a scenic west coast where you can spot whales; upscale Orcas Island claims the area's highest peak; and Lopez Island is flat, laid-back and great for cycling.

Two Weeks
Portland & Oregon Loop

❯ Start your Oregon adventure in **Portland**, well known for its roses, bridges, beer and progressive politics. Be sure to visit downtown's landmarks and the Pearl District's boutiques; Powell's City of Books is one of the world's largest independent bookstores. Over on the east side of the Willamette River are several distinct and fun neighborhoods including Hawthorne, Mississippi and Alberta. Take frequent breaks in the city's excellent coffee shops or microbreweries.

Now drive west towards the coast to **Astoria**, the first permanent US settlement in the west. Today it's a pleasant port city with a restored downtown, historic museums and Victorian houses. Further south are plenty of beach resorts, fishing towns, state parks and scenic promontories that jut out to sea. If it's summer and you like to camp, there are endless opportunities along the Oregon coast – just reserve ahead. Just south of Florence is the **Oregon Dunes National Recreation Area**, the largest expanse of coastal sand dunes in the US.

Heading inland, you'll soon hit **Eugene**, a liberal and fun-loving city famous for founding Nike and putting out track-and-field champions. Drive further south on mountainous Route 58 to **Crater Lake**, Oregon's only national park, offering supreme views of an old volcanic caldera; the water here – fed only by rain and snow – is some of the clearest and purest in the world. Going north on Route 97 will bring you to **Bend**, a city tailormade for outdoor lovers. Close by you can go hiking, skiing, fishing, golfing, kayaking, rafting and rock-climbing, among other things. Located on the dry east side of the Cascade Range, Bend also boasts 250 days of annual sunshine – not your stereotypical drizzly Oregon destination.

Driving north you'll branch off onto Route 26, ending at **Mt Hood**, the state's highest peak at 11,240ft. While summiting the volcanic cone is only for hardy mountaineers, there are countless beautiful hikes on Mt Hood's flanks, along with plenty of campsites. Be sure to stop in for a drink (or meal) at the historic Timberline Lodge. Now head north again on Route 35 and you'll come to the **Columbia River Gorge**. Cruise through this amazing geologic feature, stopping for lovely waterfalls and hikes along the way, and you'll eventually finish your loop back where you started – Portland.

Pacific Northwest Outdoors

Best Experiences

Hiking The West Coast Trail in Pacific Rim National Park and the forests around Mt Rainier and Mt Hood are all super.
Skiing Whistler-Blackcomb boasts world-class facilities.
Rock Climbing Smith Rock State Park is stunning, both for its routes and vistas.
Cycling For road trips, Washington's San Juan Islands are prime time. Oakridge, outside Eugene, has top-drawer mountain biking.

Best Times to Go

July to September The summer months are best. for outdoor activities such as hiking, camping or cycling.
December, February and March These months produce the finest powder for skiing.
February to May Winter rains mean waterfalls are at their fullest.
November to June Whale-watchers can bark 'Thar she blows!'.

Armed with kayaks, crampons, fly rods, mountain bikes and full racks of climbing gear, adventure-loving people who migrate to the Pacific Northwest come to experience its world-famous great outdoors. There's a huge diversity of landscapes, and it's all reasonably accessible from the nearest town or city; within a day you can be on a river, coast, mountain, high-desert canyon, alpine lake, lava field, rain forest or wetland. You can carve fresh tracks in the champagne powder of world-class ski resorts or cling to your kiteboard as you hurl across the water at ferocious speeds. You can spin around 360 degrees on the summit of Mt Rainier or pedal your heart out going up and over the breathtaking Cascades. And if it's solitude you crave, set off with a backpack into the wilds – the hardest part will be choosing where to go.

The Pacific Northwest is paradise for those who worship Mother Nature. If you're one of her followers, let the area unroll her carpet of snowy mountains, desert panoramas and wildflower meadows – and welcome you to her world.

Hiking

The Pacific Northwest is blessed with some of the most sublime hiking landscapes and terrain imaginable. You can spend anywhere from a couple of hours to a couple of years exploring waterfall gorges, mountainside trails, verdant forest paths or backcountry tracks. Summertime sees hot weather and crowds at their peaks, but the warming spring is the perfect time to witness gushing rivers, while fall is a splendor of foliage colors with temperatures remaining perfectly mild. In winter you'll practically be by yourself.

Ranger stations and visitor centers are excellent information resources for permits, fees, safety and trail conditions. Below are lists of the most spectacular hikes, but there are tons more mentioned in the appropriate destinations of each regional chapter.

For camping information, see p446.

Washington

In the Olympic Mountains you can hike deep canyons and alpine meadows, and the glacier-carved valleys and towering ridges of Washington's North Cascade Mountain Range offer dramatic and unforgettable landscapes. For spectacular views of glaciers and peaks head up 3.7 miles to Cascade Pass, and either return by the same route or continue 19.3 miles on to High Bridge, where a shuttle bus runs to Stehekin (a tiny settlement at the head of Lake Chelan with no road links to the rest of state). There are many other wonderful hikes in North Cascades National Park.

In the Southern Cascades, you can explore the foothills of Mt Adams and smoldering Mt St Helens. To leave the crowds behind, try Glacier Peak, which offers a sparkly lake and alpine goodness to satiate your inner hiker. The classic Wonderland Trail circumnavigates the snow-capped behemoth Mt Rainier, but takes a commitment – it's a seven- to 10-day hike.

Oregon

The Oregon coast's windswept beaches and rocky bluffs offer rugged and grandiose beauty. Check them out from the tip of Cape Falcon or from the top of Neahkahnie Mountain – both in Oswald West State Park. The challenging hike up Saddle Mountain also offers unbeatable views. Further south, Cape Lookout has a magnificent coastal panorama.

Just east of Portland, you can hike in the Columbia River Gorge among lush fir forests and dramatic waterfalls. Multnomah Falls is the hallmark, but there are other knockout hikes nearby, such as the Eagle Creek Trail or Dog Mountain (which is actually in Washington). South of the gorge, the popular 40-mile Timberline Trail Loop circumnavigates Mt Hood through alpine forests, and offers outstanding views. Ramona Falls is another awesome area hike.

In the Cascades, the challenging South Sister hike offers spectacular views from Oregon's third-highest peak. For exceptionally lofty views of Crater Lake – that turquoise phenomenon – hike up Mt Scott, high above the rim. In remote Northeast Oregon, the Wallowa Mountains, Eagle Cap Wilderness and Hells Canyon are other outdoor paradises.

British Columbia

Nothing short of a hiker's paradise, BC has hundreds of out-of-this-world parks and innumerable trails. On Vancouver Island, trails such as the 47-mile West Coast Trail in Pacific Rim National Park wind through ancient rain forests and gorgeous shorelines. Or take one of Whistler's gondolas and enjoy wandering on high alpine trails without making the high alpine climb. For a stellar coastal hike, you can do an extensive trip or a day hike on the Juan de Fuca Marine Trail.

Rock Climbing

With its wide variety of geology – think high granite cliffs and colorful volcanic rock – there's some world-class climbing in the Pacific Northwest. Anyone from beginner to expert should find excellent, fun routes, many with views of surrounding mountains, forests or even bodies of water.

Washington's top climbing mecca is Leavenworth, which refers to both the Bavarian-themed tourist town and its surrounding climbing area. You'll have hundreds of single and multipitch routes to choose from among the highly featured granite crags, and there's some great bouldering as well. Climbing here is best in spring or fall, as summertime can be very hot.

Just an hour's drive northeast of Seattle are the thin, clean cracks of Index Town Wall. The granite faces here rise up to 500ft from a verdant forest below. As most routes are 5.8 or higher, this area is best for advanced climbers. And close to the Oregon border is Beacon Rock, offering technically demanding multi-pitches. Other good destinations in Washington include Darrington, Mt Erie, North Bend and

PLAN YOUR TRIP PACIFIC NORTHWEST OUTDOORS

PARK	LOCATION	FEATURES	ACTIVITIES	BEST TIME TO VISIT	PAGE
Crater Lake	Oregon	ancient volcano, deepest lake in North America	sightseeing, cross-country skiing	Jul-Oct	p321
John Day Fossil Beds	Oregon	technicolor landscape of prehistoric ash flows, one of the world's foremost fossil sites	sightseeing	year-round	p343
Mt Rainier	Washington	alpine peaks, wild-flowers; black bear, mountain goat, elk	hiking, climbing	Jul-Sep	p159
Mt St Helens	Washington	spectacular volcano; elk, black bear, deer	hiking, sight-seeing	Jun-Oct	p166
North Cascades	Washington	alpine peaks, remote wilderness; mountain goat, grizzly bear, wolf	climbing, fish-ing, backpack-ing	Jul-Sep	p146
Olympic	Washington	alpine peaks, lush rain forests, wild coasts; black bear, elk, spotted owl	backpacking, climbing, fishing	year-round	p116
Oregon Dunes	Oregon	vast dune field, remote coastlines; bald eagle, osprey	off-road ve-hicles, hiking, horseback rid-ing, canoeing, swimming	year-round	p297
Pacific Rim	British Columbia	wild coast, giant rain forest trees, world-famous Coast Trail; bald eagles, black bear, cougar	hiking, kayaking	Jun-Sep	p396
Strathcona	British Columbia	remote wilderness, solitude, highest Canadian waterfall; wolf, black-tailed deer, elk	backcountry hiking & adventure	Jul-Sep	p402

Vantage. For more information see www. climbingwashington.com.

Smith Rock State Park is Oregon's premiere rock climbing destination – and a gorgeous place to visit even if you don't climb. Eroded from an old volcanic vent, the high canyon walls here are home to more than 1000 sport and traditional routes of all levels. The views are spectacular, especially from multi-pitch routes, and bouldering is also possible. As with Leavenworth, spring and fall are the best times to climb, as summertime sees high temperatures.

Other hot Oregon climbing spots are French's Dome near Mt Hood, Broughton Bluff near Troutdale and Horsethief Butte in the Columbia River Gorge. Also note that Beacon Rock is very close to Portland.

BC spoils its climbing community with places such as Squamish, located about 40 miles north of Vancouver. Featuring high-quality granite often compared with Yosemite's, this destination boasts more than 200 diverse routes including the Chief, a 2000ft-high granite dome with world-class multi-pitches.

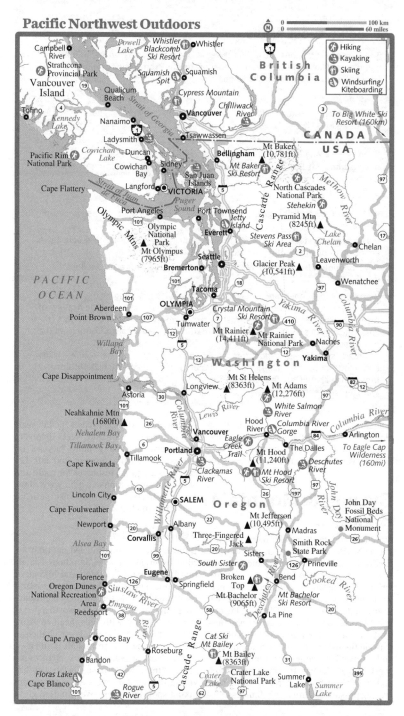

Legend: Hiking | Kayaking | Skiing | Windsurfing/Kiteboarding

Campbell River
Strathcona Provincial Park
Vancouver Island
Tofino
Kennedy Lakes
Qualicum Beach
Nanaimo
Ladysmith
Pacific Rim National Park
Duncan
Cowichan Lake
Cowichan Bay
Cape Flattery
Langford
VICTORIA
Sidney
San Juan Islands

Powell Lake
Whistler Blackcomb Ski Resort
Whistler
Squamish Spit
Squamish
Cypress Mountain
Vancouver
Chilliwack River

British Columbia
CANADA
USA
To Big White Ski Resort (160km)

Strait of Georgia
Tsawwassen
Bellingham
Mt Baker (10,781ft)
Mt Baker Ski Resort

Olympic Mtns
Port Angeles
Olympic National Park
Mt Olympus (7965ft)
Port Townsend
Jetty Island
Everett
Seattle
Bremerton

North Cascades National Park
Stehekin
Pyramid Mtn (8245ft)
Stevens Pass Ski Area
Glacier Peak (10,541ft)
Leavenworth
Lake Chelan
Chelan
Wenatchee

PACIFIC OCEAN

Aberdeen
Point Brown
Tacoma
OLYMPIA
Tumwater
Crystal Mountain Ski Resort
Mt Rainier (14,411ft)
Mt Rainier National Park
Naches
Yakima
Yakima River

Willapa Bay

Washington

Cape Disappointment
Longview
Mt St Helens (8363ft)
Mt Adams (12,276ft)

Cape Blanco

Astoria
Neahkahnie Mtn (1680ft)
Nehalem Bay
Tillamook Bay
Cape Kiwanda
Tillamook
Columbia River
Lewis River
White Salmon River
Hood River
Columbia River Gorge
Vancouver
Eagle Creek Trail
Portland
Clackamas River
The Dalles
Mt Hood (11,240ft)
Mt Hood Ski Resort
Deschutes River
Arlington
To Eagle Cap Wilderness (160mi)

Lincoln City
Cape Foulweather
Newport
Alsea Bay
Corvallis
SALEM
Albany
Oregon
Mt Jefferson (10,495ft)
Three-Fingered Jack
Sisters
Madras
Smith Rock State Park
Prineville
John Day Fossil Beds National Monument

Florence
Oregon Dunes National Recreation Area
Reedsport
Eugene
Springfield
South Sister
Broken Top
Mt Bachelor (9065ft)
Mt Bachelor Ski Resort
Bend
Crooked River
La Pine

Cape Arago
Coos Bay
Bandon
Roseburg
Cascade Range
Cat Ski Mt Bailey
Mt Bailey (8363ft)
Crater Lake
Crater Lake National Park
Summer Lake

Floras Lake
Cape Blanco
Rogue River
Siuslaw River
Umpqua River
Willamette River
Deschutes River
John Day River
Columbia River

BAGGING THOSE PEAKS

The Cascade volcanoes and jutting spires in Oregon, Washington and BC present climbers with an unprecedented number of choices, from easier day-long up-and-backs to multiday technical challenges.

Washington

» **Mt Rainier** – the imperial landmark of the region is also the highest mountain in the contiguous US (14,411ft)

» **Mt St Helens** – noted for being one of the more geologically interesting climbs; sometimes blows smoke from its newly forming crater

» **Mt Adams**, **Mt Baker**, **Mt Olympus** and **Glacier Peak** – other popular climbing destinations in the state

Oregon

» **Mt Hood** – Oregon's highest mountain and one of the most climbed peaks in the world

» **The Three Sisters** – just west of Bend; each is over 10,000ft; hard-core climbers do all three in one day (the 'Three Sisters Marathon')

» **Mt Bachelor**, **Broken Top**, **Mt Jefferson** and **Three-Fingered Jack** – other lofty peaks

Inexperienced climbers should seek out guide services, as bagging these peaks can be a hazardous proposition. Professional guide companies include **American Alpine Institute** (www.aai.cc) in Washington, **Timberline Mountain Guides** (www.timberlinemtguides.com) in Oregon and **Canada West Mountain School** (www.themountainschool.com) in BC.

Oregon's Mazamas is a nonprofit mountaineering organization that offers hikes and climbs for both members and nonmembers. In BC, the **British Columbia Mountaineering Club** (www.bcmc.ca) also offers climbs, courses and programs for members and nonmembers.

Fleming Beach, Mt Wells, Mt MacDonald, East Sooke Park and Strathcona Provincial Park are all good climbing destinations on Vancouver Island.

Cycling & Mountain Biking

A cyclist could hardly ask for more than the Pacific Northwest has to offer. Big cities including Seattle, Portland and Vancouver are some of the most bike-friendly on earth, offering safe bike lanes, a supportive bike network and endless shops for parts and advice. Even smaller cities such as Olympia, Eugene and Victoria (which even has a cycling festival) are well known for their bike culture. Outside the urban centers there are diverse and spectacular cycling opportunities on the coast, in high deserts, up alpine mountains and through lush rain forest. And the bike touring possibilities are nearly limitless.

Though hard-core cyclists pedal year-round through rain and sleet, there are (unsurprisingly) many more bicycles on the road in spring, summer and fall. Local shops are great resources for route and back-road suggestions, while www.dbmechanic.com/biking has trail/bike path information and links.

Washington

You can have an unparalleled multiday cycling experience in the San Juan Islands that incorporates kayaking and hiking, or you can just cycle for the day. Lopez Island is known for its flat terrain and bike-friendliness, but all the islands are worth a pedal. If you're cycling with kids, head to Bainbridge or Vashon Islands. For a challenge, cycle the scenic loop around Mt Rainier.

The Yakima Valley offers picturesque wine country, while Lake Chelan also has vineyards – but is more of a mountain-biking spot. In eastern Washington, go to

Moses Lake for the loop around Potholes Reservoir.

Near Mt St Helens, the Plains of Abraham/Ape Canyon Trail and the Lewis River Trail provide top-notch mountain biking in staggering Cascade scenery. The Wenatchee Lake and Leavenworth areas also attract riders; here you'll find Devil's Gulch, which boasts the smoothest, fastest single track in the state.

Closer to Seattle is easy Rattlesnake Lake, along with more challenging trails such as Black Diamond Coal Mine and Tiger Mountain's Poo Poo Point. Expert mountain-bike riders should head to Galbraith Mountain and Phillip Arnold Park.

Oregon

The Historic Columbia River Hwy and mellow Sauvie Island loop are two classic rides near Portland. Around the Cascade Range there are magnificent cycling destinations: the Cascade Lakes Hwy (Hwy 46) is stunningly beautiful, as is the Diamond Lake to Crater Lake challenge. On the coast, the Three Capes Drive near Tillamook has brilliant scenery and burly climbs. In the remote northeast, Hells Canyon Scenic Byway weaves more than 200 miles through dramatic landscape, and you can take side trips along the Snake River.

For mountain biking near Portland there's Forest Park's Leif Erikson Drive, Powell Butte and Hagg Lake. Mt Hood's Surveyor's Ridge Trail has tremendous scenery (and makes you work for it), while Post Canyon (near Hood River) has gnarly free riding with big jumps and extensive wood features.

Oakridge, east of Eugene, has premier mountain biking. Also relatively nearby, the McKenzie River Trail is some of the best single-track trail in Oregon; it takes you past scenic lakes, streams, waterfalls and lava fields.

Bend is the unofficial mountain-bike capital of the state, with ecosystems such as alpine forests, old-growth and high desert canyons. Fine trails here include the Deschutes River, Phil's and Riverside.

British Columbia

This whole region is full of roads begging to be cycled. Vancouver Island's Saanich Peninsula is definitely a highlight, as are the rolling hills and pastoral scenery of the Cowichan Valley wine country. For short island rides with picturesque seascapes, take a couple of days and hop around the Gulf Islands. Right in Vancouver, both tourists and local cyclists frequent the beautiful 1000-acre Stanley Park – especially its 5.5-mile Seawall Trail.

Mountain biking is everywhere in BC, both free riding and cross-country. Whistler and Squamish are both famous for their diverse, world-class mountain trails, while North Vancouver and the Sunshine Coast have extensive trail systems.

Skiing & Snowboarding

A legion of mountainsides dusted with prime powder translates into top-drawer skiing or snowboarding in the Northwest. Add a down-to-earth, casual and family-

---

BIKE TOURS

Don't want to deal with the logistics? Try a tour company.

Adventure Cycling Association (www.adventurecycling.org) Guides supported and self-contained tours. It also sells good cyclist-specific maps for extensive touring.

Bicycle Adventures (www.bicycleadventures.com) Runs tours in Oregon, Washington and BC, among other places.

Cascade Huts (www.cascadehuts.com) Offers mountain bikers hut-hopping, self-guided, multiday trips in Mt Hood National Forest.

Randonnée (www.randonneetours.com) Self-guided tours in BC's Gulf Islands.

Smith & Miller Productions (www.rollingpubcrawl.com) Tours Oregon by day and microbreweries by night.

Womantours (www.womantours.com) All-women company featuring a Northwest route.

For more information go to www.bikingbis.com.

friendly regional vibe – without the pretensions of many uber-fancy resorts (except for perhaps Whistler) – and you're sure to have a great, laid-back time on the slopes.

The peak season runs from about December to March, with shoulder seasons offering fewer crowds and the possibility of discount tickets. On Mt Hood you can ski any month of the year; it's the only resort in the US that offers year-round skiing (though two weeks in September are closed for maintenance). If you want to avoid waiting in long lines, go midweek.

Backcountry skiing is very popular in the Pacific Northwest. Obviously, you will need to be skilled in backcountry travel, know how to ski out of an avalanche and be trained in wilderness first aid (and carry a kit). A couple of books with great information are *Backcountry Ski! Oregon* by Christopher Van Tilburg and *Backcountry Ski! Washington* by Seabury Blair Jr. Local mountain shops might have recommendations on where to go, based on the latest weather conditions.

If you're willing to take the financial plunge, there's also heli-skiing/boarding. The North Cascade mountains are the place to go in Washington. In BC there's a wide variety. Check out www.heliskiguide.com.

Cross-Country Skiing & Snowshoeing

In the Pacific Northwest, snowy winters make for a diversity of wonderlands to explore on cross-country skis or snowshoes. And these sports are easy, accessible and appealing to almost anyone. You can tool around groomed trails for a couple of hours, or head off on multiday backcountry adventures. Renting equipment is affordable but not always available on site, so you may need to snag your gear before reaching your destination. Local mountain-sport shops and ranger stations are a great source of local information.

Washington's premiere destination is the Methow Valley, the second-largest cross-country ski area in the USA, which boasts more than 125 miles of groomed trails. You can also break trail through alpine meadows and evergreens in Olympic National Park. The Mt Baker area also offers many spectacular jaunts, with especially good trails around Silver Fir campground and at Heather Meadows. Meanwhile, Wenatchee National Forest holds some prime trails with mountains vistas, ice caves, ancient forests and solitude.

Oregon's Mt Hood area has fantastic spots including Teacup Lake, Trillium Lake and White River Canyon, all with great views of the mountain. Around Bend there's Mt Bachelor, a world-class Nordic center with extensive groomed trails, and Dutchman Flat, offering panoramas of the surrounding peaks. Further south you can ski around serene Odell Lake and through pristine snow along the rim of Crater Lake, which is gorgeous in winter – and devoid of crowds. And in Eastern Oregon, near Baker City, is the Anthony Lakes Mountain Resort.

In BC, cross-country skiing and snowshoeing are hugely popular, and there are endless possibilities all over the region. Ski resorts such as Big White and Whistler have tremendous trail systems.

White-Water Kayaking & Rafting

Water gushes down from ice-capped volcanoes and spires in the Pacific Northwest, creating a play-land for white-water enthusiasts. The region's diversity of world-class river landscapes is amazing; there's high desert, steep canyons or old-growth forest. Whitewater crazies run rivers year-round, but most people come out from May until September. Whether you spend half a day playing on a stream or embark deep into wilderness on multiday trips, there is a river for you.

Washington's rivers are prime time. The Upper Skagit River has great rafting opportunities, along with a chance to spot bald eagles. The Klickitat flows through remote wilderness canyons, while the Tieton boasts the state's fastest white water. The White Salmon River is known for its smorgasbord of rapids and for hosting competitions for the extreme white-water elite. And let's not forget the Wenatchee and the Skykomish – both roaring, popular rivers – while the Hoh and Elwha offer milder, scenic adventures.

There are worthy rivers relatively close to Portland, such as the Clackamas and North Santiam (a locally known jewel). The Deschutes is another river very popular with Portlanders, and often boasts sunny warm weather. The Rogue is a classic – a premiere

To a kayaker, the Pacific Northwest is an oasis. It offers intricate and protected waterways, abundant marine life, coastal splendor, campsite access, alpine lakes and plentiful public parks. Sea or lake kayaking is more relaxed than white-water kayaking, inspiring quiet exploration of the natural world rather than rampaging through it with a big dose of adrenaline.

Paddling on the ocean requires some technical knowledge and close attention to tides and currents, so be prepared. On a lake you can paddle around knowing just the basic safety fundamentals. In temperate regions sea kayaking can be a year-round activity, but summer is really when sea kayakers luxuriate in their sport.

In Washington there is world-class kayaking on the Olympic Peninsula, the San Juan Islands and in Puget Sound (don't miss the Cascadia Marine Trail, one of the best places in North America to sea kayak; see p98). In BC, the Pacific Rim National Park Reserve's Broken Group Islands is kayaking heaven, but there are also great spots in the Southern Gulf Islands and around Victoria and Tofino. Oregon has plenty of coastal bays and inland lakes to explore, along with excellent rivers including the McKenzie, Deschutes and North Umpqua.

Nearly all outdoor towns and cities near large bodies of water have kayaking outfitters; tours and renting gear are both possible.

run protected by Congress and offering beauty, wildlife, history and amazing rapids. Other excellent rafting rivers include the North Umpqua (great forest scenery), John Day (longest free-flowing river in Oregon), McKenzie (with great hot springs and fishing nearby) and the Owyhee (in a remote but stunningly beautiful canyon).

You can live it up rafting the tumbling white water of Campbell River on Vancouver Island. Travel just over an hour outside of Vancouver, and you can be in the Cascade foothills rafting the Chilliwack River. If your visit is during May, check out Vancouver Island's **Paddlefest** (www.paddlefest. bc.ca), a major kayaking event held each year in Ladysmith.

Windsurfing & Kiteboarding

The Columbia River Gorge is the gusty superstar of wind sports in the Pacific Northwest. Unlike any other river in the US, you can windsurf or kiteboard with the eastbound winds and float back on the westbound current. People pilgrimage to Hood River (ground zero for these activities) from all over the world to take on the gorge's famously strong and consistent winds.

There are other first-class wind-sport sites, especially on the Oregon Coast. These include the South Jetty at Fort Stevens

State Park (in Astoria), Flores Lake (outside Port Orford) and Pistol River State Park (between Gold Beach and Brookings); the last hosts the Pistol River Wave Bash, a windsurfing competition that takes place in June. Sauvie Island, near Portland, is a great place to learn.

In Washington, Jetty Island in the Seattle area has world-class kiteboarding and is one of the top places for beginners, as is Lake Washington. Other outstanding places are Lake Wenatchee and Bellingham Bay.

The beaches of Kitsilano in Vancouver are popular launching points for urban windsurfers, while breezy Squamish Spit, 40 miles north, is BC's favorite spot to catch some kiteboarding wind. Tofino, on Vancouver Island's west coast, is the province's surf central, with dozens of operators.

Fishing

If you're an angler visiting the Pacific Northwest, you might not leave. The region abounds with countless lakes, rivers, bays and a whole coastline (of course), all waiting for anglers to cast their line. For state information on fish and fishing in Washington, Oregon and British Columbia, see www. dfw.state.or.us, wdfw.wa.gov and www.env .gov.bc.ca/fw.

The waterways of the Olympic Peninsula, such as the Hoh, Queets and Elwha, are regarded as some of the best salmon rivers in

TOP SKI RESORTS

Washington
Crystal Mountain (☑360-663-2265; www.skicrystal.com) Beautiful views of Mt Rainier plus lift-accessible backcountry tours. Washington's largest ski area and a less commercial alternative to Whistler.
Mt Baker (☑360-734-6771; www.mtbaker.us) Deep powder and fabulous backcountry; some think Washington's best downhill skiing is here. Also great for snowboarding.
Stevens Pass (☑206-812-4510; www.stevenspass.com) Lift-accessible backcountry and a huge variety of terrain for all skill levels.

Oregon
Cat Ski Mt Bailey (☑800-733-7593, ext 754; www.catskimtbailey.com) Backcountry tours only. Acclaimed powder is accessed via snow cats that seat up to 12. Very close to Crater Lake.
Mt Bachelor (☑800-829-2442; www.mtbachelor.com) Very boarder friendly, with colder, drier snow. Located just outside Bend.
Mt Hood (☑503-337-2222; www.skihood.com) Consists of three main resort areas: Meadows, the biggest and most renowned; Timberline, with year-round skiing; and Ski Bowl, the largest night-ski area in the US.

British Columbia
Big White Ski Resort (☑800-663-2772; www.bigwhite.com) Deep, dry powder combined with terrain that pleases both skiers and snowboarders. Plenty of backcountry options.
Cypress Mountain (☑604-419-7669; www.cypressmountain.com) Home to the freestyle snowboard park of the 2010 Winter Olympics, with great night skiing.
Whistler-Blackcomb (☑866-218-9690; www.whistlerblacomb.com) Gigantic, powder-laden resort that hosted the alpine events of the 2010 Winter Olympics. A new gondola (over 4km long) connects the peaks of Whistler and Blackcomb Mountains.

the world. North of Seattle, Sauk and Skagit Rivers are famous for winter steelhead. Saltwater fishing in Puget Sound is revered by anglers, as are Westport and Ilwaco.

The Deschutes River near Bend is famous for its trout and steelhead. Close to Roseburg, the North Umpqua – with 33 miles of river set aside for fishing – is touted for summer steelhead and smallmouth bass, along with its fall salmon runs. Other steelhead rivers are the Rogue, Sandy and Clackamas, while the McKenzie is home to trout and salmon. The John Day is great for small-mouth and large-mouth bass, and the mighty Columbia is hard to beat for its salmon and sturgeon.

On the coast, Tillamook Bay is a prime spot for salmon because several large runs converge here. Up and down the coast, however, are opportunities to cast a line and hook some albacore tuna, rockfish and halibut.

The Thompson and Skeena Rivers have made names for themselves with their plentiful salmon and steelhead. Near Vancouver, the Pitt River is known for its trout varieties. Over on the Sunshine Coast, the fruitful lakes and inlets are popular with anglers.

Whale-watching

The Pacific Northwest is one of the world's premiere spots for whale-watching. Gray and humpback whales have the longest migrations of any mammal in the world – more than 5000 miles from the Arctic to Mexico, and back again. Most pass through from November to February (southbound) and March to June (northbound), but a few hundred resident whales can be seen nearly year-round. Since the Pacific Northwest's shoreline is so long, if you want to see whales at their peak, pick a particular coastal spot – then find out when most whales will be passing through. And don't forget your binoculars!

ACTIVITY	WHERE?	WHAT?	MORE INFORMATION PLEASE
horseback riding	Washington Cascades, WA	reasonably priced day rides out of Easton	www.happytrailsateastonwa.com
	Methow Valley, WA	day rides with cowboy barbecue	www.sunmountainlodge.com
	Pasayten Wilderness, WA	multiday llama-trekking	www.delillama.com
	Long Beach, WA	guided rides on beach & dunes	www.longbeachhorserides.com
	Oregon Cascades, OR	lava flows, lakes & forests	www.lhranch.com
	Florence, OR	romantic beach rides	www.oregonhorsebackriding.com
	Vancouver Island, BC	panoramic island scenery	www.woodgatestables.com
diving	Puget Sound, WA	notoriously clear water, diverse marine life (giant octopuses!)	www.underwatersports.com www.pugetsounddivecharters.com
	east coast of Vancouver Island, BC	wolf eels, octopuses, navy ships	www.divenanaimo.travel
paragliding & hang gliding	Lake Chelan, WA	soar nearly endlessly; 100-mile flights are not uncommon	www.chelanflyers.com
	Lakeview, OR	warm thermals, towering cliffs & conditions for all levels	www.lakecountychamber.org/hang www.cascadeparaglidingclub.org/pages/lakeview.php
	Fraser Valley, BC	wide rivers, rolling farmland & verdant valleys	www.flybc.org www.westcoastsoaringclub.com
surfing	Westhaven State Park, Half Moon Bay & the Groins, all near Westport, WA	extreme tides & rugged surfing conditions – especially outside summer	www.steepwatersurfshop.com www.surfwa.org
	short sands near Oswald West State Park, OR	friendlier than most, good for all levels, great scenery	www.oregonstateparks.org/park_195.php www.oregonsurf.com
	Otter Rock near Depoe Bay, OR	great for beginners & longboarders	magicseaweed.com/Otter-Rock-Surf-Report/317
	Tofino, BC	dramatic waves, long sandy beaches & spectacular forest backdrop	www.coastalbc.com

Oregon

Oregon's long coastline offers many opportunities for whale watching, but Depoe Bay and Newport are especially dedicated to the activity. Here you'll find several tour-boat companies willing to take you out, but if you'd rather stay on land that's fine too. An organization called 'Whale Watching Spoken Here' rallies hundreds of trained volunteers to assist visitors in spotting whales at various sites all along the Oregon Coast. Check their website (www.whale spoken.org) for details on the best locations.

And in Depoe Bay, be sure to check out the **Whale Watching Center**, offering exhibits and sea views.

Washington

You can spot gray and humpback whales from Washington's coastline, especially from Long Beach (near the Oregon border), Westport and Ozette. The most famous kind of whale in this state, however, is the killer whale or orca.

About 90 resident orcas in several pods live in the Puget Sound and San Juan Islands area, feeding on fish. The San Juan Islands in particular are the best place for spotting orcas, since they often swim close to shore. You can take boat tours from the islands or spot them from land – Lime Kiln Point State Park on San Juan Island is an especially good place. And while you're here, be sure to visit the **Whale Museum** in Friday Harbor.

The best time to spot orcas is from April to September; numerous charter companies run cruises from the San Juans, Puget Sound and Seattle. You might be able to spot orcas from a ferry too.

Out on the coast, any orcas you might see are part of transient pods that can roam from Alaska to California. These killer whales don't interact with resident pods, and their diet includes seals, sea lions and even small whales.

British Columbia

Every March, Tofino and Ucluelet – the communities surrounding Pacific Rim National Park Reserve on Vancouver Island – put on the **Pacific Rim Whale Festival** (www.pacificrimwhalefestival.com). This special occasion celebrates the northbound travels of the gray whale during its spring migration. With an estimated 20,000 whales passing through, you're likely to spot a few blowholes around here from March to May.

Another good place on land to try spotting whales is Telegraph Cove, where orcas can often be seen. If you'd rather go for a super close-up, however, there are several boat-tour companies in Victoria that head out.

Travel With Children

Best Regions for Kids

Seattle
Kids will love the interactive Pacific Science Center and the Children's Museum. Tacoma's Point Defiance Zoo & Aquarium boasts sharks *and* elephants.

Northwestern Washington
Bellingham's Whatcom Children's Museum offers imaginative activities and workshops.

Washington Cascades
For warm-weather fun head to Slidewaters Water Park at Lake Chelan.

Portland
Frolicking fountains, the world-class Oregon Zoo, and hands-on museums, including the Children's Museum.

Oregon Coast
Miles of beaches, plus the Oregon Coast Aquarium in Newport, the less flashy Seaside Aquarium, and Port Orford's dinosaur-filled Prehistoric Gardens.

Vancouver, Whistler & Vancouver Island
In Vancouver, Stanley Park, Science World and the Vancouver Aquarium are highlights. And what could be better than BC's Victoria Bug Zoo, home to millipedes and tarantulas?

From aquariums teeming with sea life to cowboys riding bucking broncos, the Pacific Northwest will spark any child's imagination. Whether you head to the coast, the mountains or rolling farmland, you'll be greeted with kindness and patience – this is a culture that loves kids and knows how to treat families right, whether they're giving wee ones a glimpse of rural life (who doesn't like to milk goats?) or showing them public art that was designed to be scaled by the younger set.

Pacific Northwest for Kids

From the sun, sand and surf along the coast to the snow-covered slopes further inland, the Pacific Northwest is a fun and exciting destination for families. Kids love exploring the many child-oriented museums, amusement parks, zoos and animal safaris. National and state parks often organize family-friendly exhibitions or activities, and whale watching can be a big hit. There are also plenty of kid-friendly hotels, restaurants, shops, playgrounds and even skateboard parks in the region. Finding things to do with your kids won't be a problem, but dragging them away from all that fun might be.

For general information, advice and anecdotes, read Lonely Planet's *Travel with Children*. And for city-specific suggestions, see the children's sections for Seattle (p69), Portland (p215) and Vancouver (p364).

Children's Highlights

Sun, Sand & Sea

» Long Beach and La Push (teenagers and *Twilight* connection!) in Washington.

» Sea Lion Caves and Oregon Coast Aquarium in Oregon.

History & Science

» Lewis & Clark National Historic Park, Evergreen Aviation & Space Museum, Eugene's Science Factory and Ashland's Science Works in Oregon.

» San Juan Island National Historic Park and Fort Vancouver in Washington.

» Fort Langley and Museum of Mining in Vancouver.

Snow Sports

» Crystal Mountain and Stevens Pass in Washington.

» Mts Hood and Bachelor in Oregon.

» Grouse Mountain and Whistler-Blackcomb in Vancouver.

Fun Food Frolics

» Portland's Saturday Market, Seattle's Pike Place Market, Vancouver's Granville Island Public Market.

» Baked goods, produce and cheese samples from any of the region's hundreds of farmers markets.

Planning

Kids often get discounts on such things as motel stays, museum admissions and restaurant meals; the definition of child, however, can vary from age zero to 18 years old.

The choice of baby food, infant formulas, soy and cow's milk, disposable diapers (nappies) and other necessities is great in supermarkets throughout the Pacific Northwest. In urban areas you'll find all manner of organic and dietary-restricted kids food in restaurants and natural markets. If you don't want to lug cribs, strollers or car seats around for your whole trip, head to a baby equipment rental company, such as www. tinytotstravel.com in Seattle, www.rent 4baby.com in Portland or www.weetravel.ca in Vancouver. Diaper-changing stations can be found in many public toilets, including ones inside the multitude of rest areas along highways and interstates. When in need of a babysitter, online services including www. sittercity.com and www.care.com can help you find someone to meet your needs.

When crossing the border from the US into Canada, be sure to bring birth certificates or passports for each child; if a child enters the country with only one parent, she/he must have a letter from the other parent saying it's OK for the child to enter Canada.

In this guidebook, very family-friendly destinations have been marked with a ⊕.

Sweet Dreams

Most hotels accept children without any problems; a few may even offer babysitting services. Motels are even more family friendly, sometimes boasting a pool, playground or kitchenettes. Larger campsites often cater to families with many services – including play structures – and yurts (or even teepees!) in state parks are a great way for families to camp in some luxury.

Places that aren't as good for kids are youth hostels and B&Bs, which often don't take children under a certain age. To make sure you know what you're going to get when you arrive, consider asking some questions when booking. Do kids stay free? Do you offer playpens, cribs or rollaway beds? Is your pool indoor/outdoor? How far to the nearest park or playground?

WHAT TO PACK

☐ Raingear and galoshes – important gear for the drizzly Pacific Northwest.

☐ Extra dry socks – whether you're camping or hiking, it's good to prepare for wet feet.

☐ Extra water and towels – muddy hikes and sandy beaches can make car rides messy.

☐ Binoculars for wildlife viewing – the region is filled with cool birds and other animals.

☐ Outdoor toys, including kites, Frisbees and beach things.

☐ Water gear – swimsuits, sunblock, safety vests and waterproof sandals.

☐ Bicycle helmets – smaller-sized helmets can be hard to come by at rental stores.

Whine-Free Dining

In general, restaurants in the Pacific Northwest welcome children of all ages and are prepared with highchairs and booster seats. Many have children's menus and some even supply crayons. If you're planning a special, high-end meal, especially one that requires reservations, ask if children are welcome. Most places will gladly serve older, well-behaved children.

While most eateries in Seattle qualify as kid-friendly, some excel at welcoming little ones, including Ivar's Acres of Clams (p74) and Molly Moon's (p75). Portland is also considered particularly kid-friendly, and some restaurants – such as Old Wives' Tales (p215) – have a playroom. Even a few brewpubs welcome children, such as the Laurelwood Public House (p215). In Vancouver, families love Little Nest (p364).

Group Play

Parks with water features, coffeehouses with playrooms and a variety of classes are all ways that parents and kids can meet new people. Seek out activities through websites such as www.urbanmamas.com, which has a calendar listing all kinds of events in Portland as well as weekly summer camps (a good way to entertain kids during longer stays). Similar websites in Seattle and Vancouver are www.seattleparentsnetwork and www.kidsvancouver.com. Also, look for city pool classes and programs in larger towns and cities, or head to specialty children's stores, which will have fliers and advice about organized events.

regions at a glance

The Pacific Northwest boasts everything from crashing surf along its spectacular coastline to the gorgeous, scenic peaks of Mt Rainier and Mt Hood, creating a varied outdoor playground for hikers, climbers, campers and skiers. And its rich agricultural lands offer a diverse array of year-round seasonal produce that has inspired chefs, winemakers and beer brewers throughout the region.

The major urban centers of Seattle, Portland and Vancouver are also shaped by the natural world, with parks and outdoor sculpture gardens. But indoor culture rivals any outdoor fun, especially during the gray days of winter; think coffee bars, brewpubs, art museums, theater, music and great restaurants.

Seattle

Nightlife ✓✓
Food ✓✓
Art ✓✓✓

Bars & Pubs
Find a mixture of cocktail bars, dance clubs and live music on Capitol Hill. From grungy to upscale, these watering holes serve up local craft brews and fruity cocktails to the perennially thirsty. And the city that was home to grunge won't disappoint live-music lovers.

Seafood
Few cities are so inter-twined with the ocean. If Seattle's waterfront isn't proof enough, head to Pike Place Market for its slip-pery fish throw-and-catch show. Then pick a nearby restaurant to taste the sea-sonal oysters and catch of the day.

Visual Expression
Begin to understand the city's fascination with art at the Olympic Sculpture Park, then visit the notable Asian Art Museum and the Henry Art Gallery. And don't ignore the skyline: the Space Needle juts skyward as artistic proof of historic innovation.

p56

Northwestern Washington & the San Juan Islands

Whales ✓✓✓
Cycling ✓✓
Landscapes ✓✓

Thar She Blows
Whales frequently populate waters near the coastline and around the islands of this verdant region. From the rocky coast at Lime Kiln Point State Park, scan the Haro Strait for signs of a whale's blow, or pop into the Whale Museum in Friday Harbor to learn more about orcas – aka killer whales.

Pedal Power
Bicycles rule the landscape of the San Juans. Island-hop with your two-wheeler to enjoy rolling paved roads that reveal stunning vistas overlooking the sea. Don't forget to detour at coffee shops and juice bars for fuel.

Sweet Scenery
Heavy rains make this a lush place, with fir-covered islands and green mountain foothills. But the sparkling sea provides the most impressive backdrop, especially on the jewel-like San Juan Islands.

p84

Olympic Peninsula & Washington Coast

Forests ✓✓✓
Beaches ✓✓
Vampires ✓✓✓

Lush Forests
Declared a national park in 1938, the 1406-sq-mile Olympic National Park holds some of the country's most pristine forests. Back-packers, cyclists, climbers, fishermen and campers flock to these parts to see abundant wildlife and enjoy trails, rivers and lakes.

Sand & Surf
Washington's coastline stretches from Ocean Shores to the edge of the Columbia River, offering hundreds of miles of smooth kite-flying areas, sandy dunes and crashing surf. Don't miss local oyster farms, which can supply a feast on the half shell.

Twilight Madness
The popular *Twilight* books and movies have inspired fans to flock to places such as Forks, La Push and Port Angeles to see where Edward, Bella and Jacob lived out their fictional dramas. Be prepared for shrouds of mist and squealing tweens.

p111

Washington Cascades

Volcanoes ✓✓✓
Scenic Drives ✓✓
Hiking ✓✓✓

Explosive Geology
Five potentially lethal volcanoes punctuate the Washington Cascades. Part of the Pacific Ring of Fire, these peaks showed their stuff in May 1980, when Mt St Helens erupted with devastating consequences. Visit the trails or crevasse-covered glaciers traversing their flanks.

Rewarding Roads
Roads here wind between wilderness areas and two national parks – creating the ideal conditions for a road trip. Take your time and enjoy the views of glacier-draped peaks and the rolling ridges of the Cascades, making scenic memories that will last a lifetime.

Mountaineering
All levels of mountaineers bag peaks in these parts, although Mt Rainier rules as the most challenging summit. Even so, beginners can hire experienced guides and make the ascent during the wee hours of the morning.

p141

Central & Eastern Washington

Wine ✓✓
Culture ✓✓✓
Outdoors ✓✓

Vines
The parched desert hills of southeastern Washington are helping to produce some stellar grapes, the prima donnas of the state's burgeoning wine industry. Head to Walla Walla for a high concentration of tasting rooms, wineries and wine-friendly restaurants.

Bavarian Transplant
Dust off your lederhosen and prepare to belt out a German drinking song in Leavenworth, Washington's very own Bavarian village. The quirky theme town sits within easy reach of the picturesque North Cascade peaks, a good place to take a picnic of brats and gingerbread.

Natural Solitude
Don't cross this remote area off your list for outdoor recreating. National forests, tiny ski areas and pockets of alpine splendor offer quiet, off-the-beaten-path spots for great outdoor fun.

p171

Portland

Food ✓✓✓
Cycling ✓✓
Nightlife ✓

Locavore Nation
What happens when young, expressive chefs collide with some of the nation's best locally grown produce, hazelnut-finished pork and fresh cheeses? Portland's food scene. Even the food carts here have become outlets for culinary expression, as the city's top restaurants take Northwest cuisine to new heights.

Human-Powered Movement
With the highest percentage of bicycle commuters in the US, this town celebrates all things bikey through costume theme rides, races, the Zoobomb, handcrafted bike shows, and a slew of bike delivery businesses.

Brewpubs & Bars
While Portland's not known for its late-night discos, beer rules the night-time social scene. New tasting rooms offer a chance to try barrel-aged beers, while many bars and pubs feature expansive European, local and regional beer lists.

p200

The Willamette Valley & Wine Country

Wine ✓✓✓
Hot Springs ✓✓
B&Bs ✓✓✓

Pinot Production
The valley's mild summers and long, wet winters foster the delicate, thin-skinned pinot noir grape, the variety that's become famous in these parts. Try various vintages at winery's tasting rooms, B&Bs and wine bars, which are popping up even in small towns.

Steaming Soaks
One of Oregon's best free soaks, Bagby Hot Springs, is a few hours' drive east of Salem. Climb into hollowed-log tubs here or head down the road to the Breitenbush Hot Springs resort, a rustic, laid-back experience with yoga, massage and vegetarian food.

Small-Scale Lodging
As wine country grows, so do its lodging options, and tiny, well-run B&Bs provide the perfect base for navigating the vines. Look for historic inns, working farms with rooms in grain silos, and vineyard homes with tasting areas and cozy rooms for guests.

p230

Columbia River Gorge

Waterfalls ✓✓✓
Hiking ✓✓
Fruit ✓✓✓

Central Oregon & The Oregon Cascades

Mountains ✓✓
Water ✓✓✓
Beer ✓

Oregon Coast

Beaches ✓✓✓
Cycling ✓✓
Weather ✓

Raging Waters

The massive Columbia River is fed by hundreds of waterfalls, many of which flow year-round. Hike to and around some roaring giants that soak the surrounding mossy forests with a perpetual sprinkling.

Take a Hike

The Gorge is a prime destination for hikers and backpackers, especially those who like to gain vertical. But well-maintained trails usually come with a gentle criss-cross of switchbacks, making any Gorge trail doable at the right speed. Look for spring wildflowers and fall foliage.

The Fruit Loop

Just outside Hood River, a 35-mile driving loop will take you through dozens of orchards and farms, selling everything from lavender and pumpkins to pears and cherries – depending on the season. There are even a few wineries on the way, and many orchards offer u-pick opportunities.

p248

Steep Slopes

Starting with the glaciers of Mt Hood and stretching down through the Three Sisters Wilderness area, some of Oregon's steepest slopes translate to prime skiing, snowboarding and mountain biking. As a general rule, resorts outside Bend offer fluffier powder than their Mt Hood counterparts.

Lakes & Rivers

While Crater Lake – down south towards Ashland – is the best-known lake in the Cascades, you can't ignore other serene waters. Visit Waldo and the Cascade Lakes, and waterways such as the Deschutes and Metolius rivers – prime spots for white-water rafting, kayaking and fishing.

Bend's Craft Brews

In the past few years, Bend's brewing scene has exploded. Today, eight breweries in town pump out exceptional beers; stop by the tasting rooms (and maybe 'hop' on a tour!) to sample sudsy and delicious creations.

p260

Public Access

Thanks to some serious forward thinking, every inch of Oregon's 362 coastal miles is public land. Since the early 1900s the state has created more than 70 parks and protected areas along this exceptionally beautiful shoreline.

Riding 101

Cyclists everywhere dream of riding this stretch of Hwy 101, a windy road that rises and falls between bluffs and cliff-side overlooks. It can get busy with cars and RVs, so nerves of steel are a must. But those who've made the journey know it's worth sharing the road.

Storm Watching

The coast can be a dramatic place, defined by brilliant sunbursts followed by pounding hailstorms, rainbows or lightning. Delight in the drama, especially during the winter months when empty beaches create the chance to commune with the boastful weather gods.

p277

Ashland & Southern Oregon

Wine ✓✓✓
Theater ✓✓
Lodging ✓✓

Rising Vines

A warmer, sunnier climate down south has helped create some of Oregon's fledgling wine regions. Grapes in the Umpqua and Applegate Valleys, and around Jacksonville, Grants Pass and Medford, are transformed into everything from big reds to oakey whites.

Shakespeare

Any festival that runs for nine months of the year shouldn't be ignored, but Ashland's Oregon Shakespeare Festival will grab your attention more for quality than quantity. Topnotch productions, including plays, readings and concerts, honor the Bard and his vast body of work.

Sweet Sleeps

Maybe it's the nearby Shakespeare Festival that inspires such charm, but this region boasts exceptional lodgings, including the landmark Crater Lake Lodge, Wolf Creek Inn (near Grant's Pass) and Ashland's Country Willows B&B.

p308

Eastern Oregon

Wilderness ✓✓✓
Hiking ✓✓
Geology ✓✓✓

Desert Solitude

If you think wilderness is defined by how many people you don't see on any given day, this region is pure bliss. Hard to reach and bare of national parks or huge attractions, this is the place to slip into forests, mountains and especially deserts – and find peace.

Twisting Trails

Hikers can find amazingly scenic trails here. Backpackers should spend multiple days in the Eagle Cap Wilderness, while day hikers will find plenty of scenic options in the Wallowa Mountains. Or walk the mellow trails in the colorful John Day Fossil Beds National Monument.

Ancient History

Discovered in the 1860s, the John Day Fossil Beds were laid down between six and 50 million years ago – a span that's captured everything from dung-beetle balls to the bones of pint-sized horses and saber-toothed, feline-like animals.

p328

Vancouver, Whistler & Vancouver Island

Skiing ✓✓
Coastline ✓✓✓
Food ✓✓

Olympic Opportunities

In 2010, snow-sports fans gathered at Whistler-Blackcomb to witness awe-inspiring feats. Sports lovers can take advantage of excellent snowfalls and a long resort season (November to June) by skiing and boarding famous Olympic race runs and half pipes.

Waterways

The geography here is defined by water – abundant rivers, miles of island inlets and dramatic coastline. Stroll the seawall at Stanley Park or kayak the Sunshine Coast to experience its waves. Then there's Vancouver Island's Pacific shoreline, wild and rugged, with a wonderfully primordial feel.

Authentic Asian

Rub shoulders with Asian-language students, immigrants and fanatical foodies who flock to Vancouver's Asian restaurants. Think dim sum, sushi bars and creative Asian fusion and prepare your taste buds for a spicy adventure.

p351

Look out for these icons:

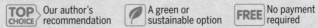

TOP CHOICE — Our author's recommendation

A green or sustainable option

FREE — No payment required

See the Index for a full list of destinations covered in this book.

On the Road

Seattle

Best Places to Eat

» Dahlia Lounge (p74)

» Steelhead Diner (p73)

» Coastal Kitchen (p75)

» Tilth (p76)

» Salumi (p72)

Best Places to Stay

» Moore Hotel (p69)

» College Inn (p72)

» Edgewater (p70)

» Ace Hotel (p70)

» Sorrento Hotel (p69)

Why Go?

The largest city in the Pacific Northwest also happens to be a perfect distillation of all the great things the region has going for it. Known as the Emerald City, it's a lively, progressive urban center, lush with parks and surrounded by natural beauty, home to about 3.3 million people (an estimated 602,000 in the city proper). People here are fond of getting out into nature, and they're serious about protecting the environment. The live-music scene that lifted Seattle to pop-culture prominence in the '90s continues to thrive. Seattleites love good beer; the city is a cornerstone of the microbrew revolution. And it does coffee well enough to have launched an espresso empire.

It's a bookish, erudite place, but also a dynamic and inventive urban center, with thriving technology industries (high-tech, biotech, Boeing) and a growing population – an exciting entry point to an exploration of the Pacific Northwest.

When to Go
Seattle

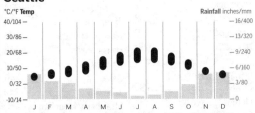

June–August
Perfect weather and some of Seattle's best festivals – be sure to book ahead.

September
Bumbershoot, the annual music, arts and culture festival, is a big draw.

October–May
Seattle's long winter adds to the appeal of its many coffee shops and good pubs.

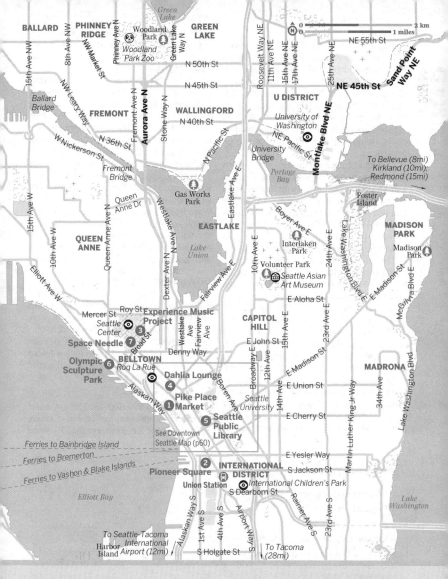

Seattle Highlights

1 Wander the maze of shops and restaurants in historic **Pike Place Market** (p63)

2 Soak up old-town atmosphere in **Pioneer Square** (p60), then explore tunnels under the city's surface

3 Ride the monorail to a rock and roll adventure at the **Experience Music Project**

(p64), where you can record your own video or kneel at the altar of Hendrix and Cobain

4 Treat yourself to a slice of foodie heaven at the Northwest-cuisine landmark **Dahlia Lounge** (p74)

5 Ogle the stunning, Koolhaas-designed **Seattle Public Library** (p59); be sure

to ride up the green escalator inside for the full effect

6 On a fair day, scope some top-notch sculpture and an awesome view of the Olympic mountains from the **Olympic Sculpture Park** (p63)

7 Look out from the heights of Seattle's ultimate landmark, the **Space Needle** (p64)

History

Seattle was named for Chief Sealth, leader of the Duwamish tribe of Native Americans that inhabited the Lake Washington area when David Denny led the first group of European settlers here in 1851. The railway came through in 1893, linking Seattle with the rest of the country. For a decade, prospectors headed for the Yukon gold territory would stop in Seattle to stock up on provisions.

The boom continued through WWI, when Northwest lumber was in great demand and the Puget Sound area prospered as a shipbuilding center. In 1916 William Boeing founded the aircraft manufacturing business that would become one of the largest employers in Seattle, attracting tens of thousands of newcomers to the region during WWII.

The city has spawned some major business success stories and international brands – Microsoft and Starbucks are loved and loathed in equal measure. Boeing relocated its headquarters to Chicago, though it's still a major presence in Seattle.

The city is currently about to be reshaped yet again. The Alaskan Way Viaduct – which takes Hwy 99 along the waterfront and is generally considered to be structurally unsound as well as an eyesore – is being replaced with a bored-out tunnel alternative. Meanwhile, light-rail and streetcar transit have expanded to serve the airport as well as a hub of biotech companies and residences in south Lake Union. Seattle anticipates a 40% population growth in the next two decades.

◉ Sights

Most of Seattle's attractions are concentrated in a compact central area. The historic downtown, Pioneer Square, includes the area between Cherry and S King Sts, along 1st to 3rd Ave. The big-name shopping area is downtown, along 4th and 5th Aves from Olive Way down to University St. Just north of downtown is Seattle Center, a World's Fair relic, home to the Space Needle and Experience Music Project. Across busy Alaskan Way from the Pike Place Market is the Waterfront, Seattle's tourist mecca. As long as you account for the hilly terrain, it's easy enough to walk back and forth among all of these areas. Public transport serves the outlying neighborhoods; see p81 for details.

DOWNTOWN & FIRST HILL

What most people mean by 'downtown' is the collection of office buildings, hotels and retail shops between 2nd and 7th Aves. It's home to much of the city's most important architecture. The jungle of high-rises teetering on the steep streets makes for an imposing skyline. In fact, though, the core is quite compact and walkable.

Seattle Art Museum MUSEUM
(Map p60; ☎206-654-3100; 1300 1st Ave; adult/child $15/free, admission free 1st Thu of month; ☺10am-5pm Wed-Sun, 10am-9pm Thu & Fri) Since

---

WASHINGTON FACTS

» **Nickname** Evergreen State

» **Population** 6.5 million

» **Area** 71,342 sq miles

» **Capital city** Olympia (population 44,600)

» **Other cities** Seattle (population 602,000, estimated), Spokane (population 198,000), Yakima (population 82,800), Bellingham (population 75,150), Walla Walla (population 30,900)

» **Sales tax** 6.5%

» **Birthplace of** singer and actor Bing Crosby (1903–77), guitarist Jimi Hendrix (1942–70), computer geek Bill Gates (b 1955), Denver Broncos quarterback John Elway (b 1960), saxophonist Kenny G (b 1956), music icon Kurt Cobain (1967–94)

» **Home of** Mt St Helens, Microsoft, Starbucks, Nordstrom, Evergreen State College

» **Famous for** grunge rock, coffee, *Grey's Anatomy*, *Twin Peaks*, *Twilight*, volcanoes, apples, wine, precipitation

» **State vegetable** Walla Walla sweet onion

» **Driving distances** Seattle to Portland 174 miles, Spokane to Port Angeles 365 miles

its 2007 expansion, the Seattle Art Museum has twice as much gallery space and a lot of new art to show off – to the tune of about $1 billion worth of gifts and 1000 new acquisitions. The original Robert Venturi–designed building of limestone and ornamented terracotta – with Jonathan Borofsky's enormous moving sculpture, *Hammering Man,* at its front door – contains 150,000 sq ft of space. Architect Brad Cloepfil's design expanded the museum into the adjoining Washington Mutual building, adding 118,000 sq ft, including a number of new spaces that are free to the public.

The sense of excitement is palpable from the museum's entrance up to the main floors. Above the ticket counter hangs Chinese artist Cai Guo-Qiang's *Inopportune: Stage One,* a series of white cars exploding with neon. Moving up into the galleries, you'll see Andy Warhol's painting of Elvis and an enormous sculpture by Korean artist Do-Ho Suh, *Some/One,* a cloak made of thousands of dog tags. Nearby is a room dedicated to the work of Harlem Renaissance painter Jacob Lawrence, who spent his last 30 years in Seattle, and to Gwendolyn Knight, his wife and fellow painter. There are also now dedicated spaces for the

museum's impressive collections of masks, canoes and totems from Northwest coastal Indian tribes, as well as collections of Australian Aboriginal art and American and Native American textiles.

TOP CHOICE **Seattle Public Library**   LIBRARY
(Map p60; ☎206-386-4636; 1000 4th Ave; admission free; ◷10am-8pm Mon-Thu, 10am-6pm Fri & Sat, noon-6pm Sun) There's not much chance you'll miss glimpsing the Seattle Public Library, but it's worth going inside for a closer look. The $165.5 million sculpture of glass and steel was designed by Rem Koolhaas and LMN Architects to suit the functions it would need to serve: a community gathering space, a tech center, a reading room and, of course, a whole bunch of book storage. The main room, on Level 3, has especially high ceilings, a teen center, small gift shop and coffee stand. There's an underground level for parking ($9, $6 Saturday to Sunday). Near the top is the Seattle Room, a 12,000-sq-ft reading room with 40ft glass ceilings. It has amazing light, nice views of downtown and seating for up to 400 people.

But the importance of function hasn't cost anything in the form department. In short, the building looks awesome, as striking as any other building in the city including the Space Needle. The overall style is sort of like when that sexy librarian finally takes her spectacles off. Lemon-yellow escalators, hot-pink chairs and zippy wi-fi connections make for a modern, tech-friendly experience. There are also 132 research computers available in the 'Mixing Chamber,' where librarians in teams help with in-depth research. And the Book Spiral, spanning several floors, holds most of the library's nonfiction books organized by the Dewey Decimal System with numbers marked on small mats on the floor. Guests can take free one-hour group tours (for a schedule see www.spl.org) or a self-guided podcast tour.

FREE **Frye Art Museum**   MUSEUM
(Map p60; ☎206-622-9250; 704 Terry Ave; ◷10am-5pm Tue, Wed, Fri & Sat, noon-5pm Sun, 10am-8pm Thu) This small museum on First Hill preserves the collection of Charles and Emma Frye. The Fryes collected more than 1000 paintings, mostly 19th- and early-20th-century European and American pieces, and a few Alaskan and Russian artworks. If this inspires a stifled yawn, think again. Since its 1997 expansion, the Frye has gained a hipness that it once lacked; fresh ways of presenting its artwork, music performances, po-

DISCOUNT PASSES

If you're going to be in Seattle for a while and plan on seeing its premiere attractions, consider buying a **City-Pass** (adult/child $59/39). Good for nine days, the pass gives you entry into the Space Needle, Experience Music Project, Pacific Science Center, Seattle Aquarium, Argosy Cruises' Seattle Harbor Tour, the Museum of Flight and the Woodland Park Zoo. You save about 50% on admission costs and never have to stand in line. You can buy one at whichever of the venues you visit first or online at www.citypass. com/city/seattle.html.

Another option is the **Go Seattle card** (www.goseattlecard.com; adult $45-134, child $28-89), which offers free or discounted admission to a long list of sights and entertainment. Available in one-, two-, three-, five- and seven-day versions, the cards get you in free to a number of the city's top attractions.

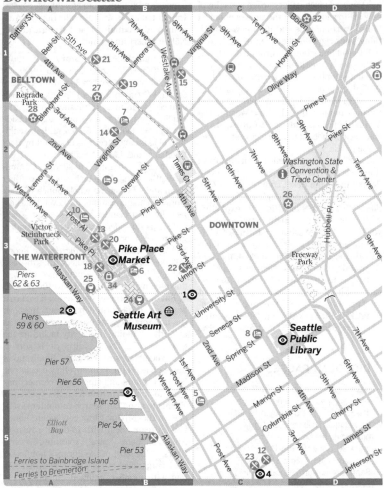

etry readings and interesting rotating exhibits from traveling painters to local printmakers, make the museum a worthwhile stop.

Benaroya Concert Hall CONCERT HALL
(Map p60; 200 University St) With a hefty bill of almost $120 million in construction costs, it's no wonder the Benaroya Concert Hall, Seattle Symphony's primary venue, oozes luxury. From the minute you step into the glass-enclosed lobby of the performance hall you're overwhelmed with views of Elliott Bay; on clear days you might be lucky enough to see the snowy peaks of the Olympic Range far in the distance. Even if you're

not attending the symphony, you can walk through the foyer and marvel at the 20ft-long chandeliers, specially created by Tacoma glassmaker Dale Chihuly.

PIONEER SQUARE
This enclave of redbrick buildings, the oldest part of Seattle, languished for years and was almost razed to build parking lots, until a wave of public support led to Historic Register status followed by an influx of art galleries, antique shops and cafés. It can be seedy at night, but these days trendy nightclubs perpetrate more crimes than individuals do.

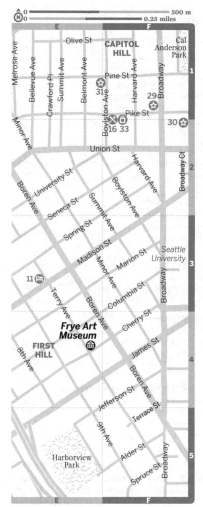

trees that marked Seattle's first industry. Known officially as Pioneer Square Park, the plaza features a bust of Chief Sealth (Seattle), an ornate pergola and a totem pole. Some wayward early Seattleites, so the story goes, stole the totem from the Tlingit natives in southeastern Alaska in 1890. An arsonist lit the pole aflame in 1938, burning it to the ground. When asked if they could carve a replacement pole, the Tlingit took the money offered, thanking the city for payment of the first totem, and said it would cost $5000 to carve another one. The city coughed up the money and the Tlingit obliged with the pole you see today.

The decorative pergola was built in the early 1900s to serve as an entryway to an underground lavatory and to shelter those waiting for the cable car that went up and down Yesler Way. The reportedly elaborate rest room eventually closed due to serious plumbing problems at high tide. In January 2001, the pergola was leveled by a wayward truck. It has been restored and was put back where it belongs the following year, looking as good as new.

FREE Klondike Gold Rush National
Historical Park   MUSEUM
(☑206-220-4240; 319 2nd Ave S; ⊙9am-5pm) In an early example of Seattle civic boosters clamoring to put the city 'on the map,' the Seattle *Post-Intelligencer* trumpeted the news that a ship full of gold had arrived in town on July 17, 1897. Masses of gold-fevered unfortunates swarmed the city on their way to the Klondike River area in the Yukon Territory, and local merchants made a killing. Seattle's seminal position as the outfitting and transportation hub for the Alaskan and Yukon Gold Rush is recognized at Klondike Gold Rush National Park, one of the USA's few indoor national historical parks. It's easy to miss, but worth seeking out. Exhibits, photos and news clippings document the era and give an idea of how much gear, food and true grit were necessary to stake a claim in the Klondike. Gold panning is demonstrated by park rangers, and you can sit down and view a slide presentation about the gold rush.

Smith Tower   HISTORIC BUILDING
(☑206-622-4004; 506 2nd Ave S at Yesler Way; observation deck adult/child $7.50/5; ⊙10am-dusk May-Sep, 10am-5pm Apr & Oct, 10am-4pm Sat & Sun Nov-Mar) You can't miss Seattle's first skyscraper. For half a century after its construction in 1914, the 42-story Smith

Yesler Way was the original 'skid road' – in Seattle's early days, loggers in a camp above town would send logs skidding down the road to Henry Yesler's pier-side mill. With the slump in the timber industry and resulting decline of the area, the street became a haven for the homeless. The nickname Skid Road (or 'Skid Row') eventually came to mean the opposite of 'Easy Street' in cities across the US.

Pioneer Square Park   PARK
(Cherry St & 1st Ave) The original Pioneer Square is a triangular cobblestone plaza where Henry Yesler's sawmill cut the giant

Downtown Seattle

Top Sights

	Frye Art Museum	E4
	Pike Place Market	B3
	Seattle Art Museum	B4
	Seattle Public Library	C4

Sights

1	Benaroya Concert Hall	B4
2	Seattle Aquarium	A4

Activities, Courses & Tours

3	Argosy Cruises Seattle Harbor Tour	B5
4	Bill Speidel's Underground Tour	C5

Sleeping

5	Alexis Hotel	C5
6	Green Tortoise Hostel	B3
7	Hotel Ändra	B2
8	Hotel Monaco Seattle	C4
9	Moore Hotel	B2
10	Pensione Nichols	A3
11	Sorrento Hotel	E3

Eating

12	Bakeman's	C5
13	Café Campagne	A3
14	Dahlia Lounge	B2
15	FareStart Restaurant	B1
16	Honeyhole	F2
17	Ivar's Acres of Clams	B5
18	Lowell's Restaurant	B3
19	Palace Kitchen	B1
20	Steelhead Diner	B3
21	Top Pot Donuts	A1
22	Wild Ginger	B3
23	Zaina	C5

Drinking

24	Pike Pub & Brewery	B4
25	ZigZag Cafe	A3

Entertainment

26	A Contemporary Theater	D3
27	Cinerama	A1
28	Crocodile Cafe	A2
29	Neighbours	F1
30	Neumo's	F2
31	R Place	E1
32	Re-Bar	D1
	Seattle Symphony	(see 1)

Shopping

33	Babeland	F2
34	Pure Food Fish	B3
35	Sonic Boom	D1

Tower was well known as the tallest building west of Chicago. The distinctive tower was erected by LC Smith, who built his fortune on typewriters (Smith-Corona) and guns (Smith & Wesson). Smith died during the building's construction, so he never got to see the beauty that still bears his name. Walk into the onyx- and marble-paneled lobby, step aboard one of the brass-and-copper manually operated elevators and let it whisk you up to the 35th-floor observation deck for a great view of Seattle's Waterfront. The ride up is as exciting as the view.

Occidental Park PARK

(Occidental Ave S & S Main St) Notable in this cobblestone plaza are the totem poles carved by Duane Pasco, a nationally respected Chinookan carver and artist from Poulsbo on the Kitsap Peninsula. The totems depict the welcoming spirit of Kwakiutl, a totem bear, the tall Sun and Raven, and a man riding on the tail of a whale. Heading south toward Jackson St, the park turns into a tree-lined pedestrian mall bordered by galleries, sculptures and coffee shops.

INTERNATIONAL DISTRICT

A lively neighborhood that's home to various Asian cultures, 'the ID' has all of the trappings of a multi-ethnic neighborhood, from bustling markets to fun import shops to amazing places to eat.

Wing Luke Museum of the Asian Pacific American Experience MUSEUM

(☎206-623-5124; www.wingluke.org; 719 S King St; adult/child $12.95/8.95; ⏲10am-5pm Tue-Sun, 10am-8pm 1st Thu & 3rd Sun each month, closed Mon) This Pan-Asian museum is devoted to Asian and Pacific American culture, history and art. Named after the first Asian elected official in the continental US, it examines the often difficult and violent meeting of Asian and Western cultures in Seattle. Particularly fascinating are the photos and displays on Chinese settlement in the 1880s and the retelling of Japanese American internment during WWII. The museum's new home, in the historic East Kong Yick Building, housed many immigrant workers from China, Japan and the Philippines; a typical first apartment is re-created here.

The intimate 2nd-floor Community Portrait Galleries tell the stories of the various Asian-American communities in the Seattle area, and the George Tsutakawa Art Gallery houses exciting contemporary work by Asian artists from around the country. Opt for a guided tour (included with admission) if possible. The museum also coordinates guided tours of the rest of the ID (adult/child $17.95/10.95), based around various themes – call to make arrangements, or ask at the ticket counter.

International Children's Park   PARK
(Map p57; S Lane St & 7th Ave; 🛝) If the kids aren't up for exploring the Asian markets or sitting still for a dim sum brunch, bring them here to work off some energy by playing on the bronze dragon sculpture, designed by George Tsutakawa, a Seattle native who spent much of his childhood in Japan, then returned to become an internationally renowned sculptor and painter and a professor at the University of Washington.

PIKE PLACE MARKET & WATERFRONT
The first stop for many visitors to Seattle, this area of town rewards early birds. It's particularly important to get to the market early if you want to avoid that cattle-truck feeling. Weekdays and before 10am on weekends are best. The Waterfront is more weather-dependent – it will be swarming with people on a sunny weekend afternoon, while on a misty weekday morning you'll have the place pretty much to yourself.

Pike Place Market   MARKET
(Map p60) The heart of downtown Seattle is Pike Place Market, on Pike St between Western and 1st Aves. The buzzing warren of fruit stands, cafés and little shops is excellent street theater, although it gets claustrophobically crowded on weekends. Go early on a weekday morning to avoid the crush – and go hungry, as you'll find endless opportunities to snack while you explore the market maze. The Main and North Arcades are the most popular areas, with bellowing fishmongers, arts and crafts, and precarious stacks of fruits and vegetables. Don't miss the oddball shops on the lower levels.

Seattle Aquarium   AQUARIUM
(Map p60; ☎206-386-4300; 1483 Alaskan Way at Pier 59; adult/child $17/11, with Argosy harbor cruise $30/19.25, free with CityPass; ⏰9:30am-5pm; 🛝) Probably the most interesting site in the Waterfront area, this well-designed aquarium offers a view into the underwater world of Puget Sound and the Pacific Northwest coast. In 2007 the pilings that support the building were found to be rotten, so they were replaced and the aquarium added a café, gift shop and two new exhibits. 'Window on Washington Waters' is a look at the sea floor of the Neah Bay area, where rockfish, salmon, sea anemones and more than 100 other fish and invertebrate species live. 'Crashing Waves' uses a wave tank to show how marine plants and animals cope with the forceful tides near shore.

Other exhibits include re-creations of ecosystems in Elliott Bay, Puget Sound and the Pacific Ocean, including tide pools, eelgrass beds, coral reefs and the sea floor. The centerpiece of the aquarium is a glass-domed room where sharks, octopi and other deepwater denizens lurk in the shadowy depths. The passages eventually lead outdoors to a salmon ladder and a pool where playful sea otters and northern fur and harbor seals await your attention.

Victor Steinbrueck Park   PARK
(Map p60; Western Ave & Virginia St) When you've had enough of the market and its crowds, wander out the end of the North Arcade and cross Western Ave to Victor Steinbrueck Park, a grassy area designed in 1982 by Steinbrueck and Richard Haag. You'll find benches, a couple of totem poles designed by Quinault tribe member Marvin Oliver, a few shuffling vagrants and great views over the Waterfront and Elliott Bay. Rallies and political demonstrations are often held here.

BELLTOWN
North of Pike Place Market is Belltown, famous as the birthplace of grunge music. A few of the original clubs are still here, but the area shifted upscale, with fancy restaurants and designer boutiques alongside the rowdy bars and noodle shops. It's one of the best parts of town for nightlife, and the Olympic Sculpture Park provides an anchor for daytime visits.

FREE Olympic Sculpture Park   PARK
(Map p57; 2901 Western Ave; ⏰30min before sunrise-30min after sunset) Hovering over train tracks in an unlikely oasis between the water and busy Elliott Ave is the 8.5-acre, $85 million Olympic Sculpture Park. Worth a visit just for its views of the Olympic Mountains across Elliott Bay, the park has begun to grow into its long-range plan. Among the highlights is the 'Eagle,'

Alexander Calder's 39ft-tall red steel creation from 1971, which crouches along the horizon of the park. The thing probably weighs about a ton, but from where it's positioned, it looks like it's about to launch itself off the top of the hill and into the distant mountains.

The sculpture park is an excellent lesson in how to make the most out of limited urban space. Its Z shape slinks back and forth between Belltown, busy Elliott Ave and the edge of the bay, rescuing three parcels of land and filling them with art and plant life. Starting from the bottom, Tony Smith's *Wandering Rocks* zigzag up the hill in the Ketcham Families Grove, described on signs as 'a deciduous forest of quaking aspen' – well, eventually. It's just beginning to sprout now, but it's still pretty. More than 20 large pieces of sculpture dot the landscape, including Claes Oldenburg and Coosje van Bruggen's *Typewriter Eraser, Scale X*, with its weird blue sprouts bristling over Elliott Ave.

The glass building at the top of the park contains a small café, restrooms, a gift shop and visitor information.

Roq La Rue
GALLERY

(Map p57; ☏206-374-8977; 2312 2nd Ave; ⊘1-6pm Wed-Sat) This Belltown gallery has secured its reputation by taking risks: the work on view here skates along the edge of urban pop culture. Since opening in 1998, the gallery, owned and curated by Kirsten Anderson, has been a significant force in the pop surrealism field, frequently featured in *Juxtapoz* magazine. It also has an entertaining blog about the undercurrents of Northwest art at http://roqlaruenews.blogspot.com/.

SEATTLE CENTER

In 1962 Seattle hosted a summer-long World's Fair, an exhibition that enticed nearly 10 million visitors to view the future, Seattle-style. The vestiges, which 45 years later look simultaneously futuristic and retro, are on view at the Seattle Center.

Space Needle
MONUMENT

(☏206-905-2100; www.spaceneedle.com; adult/child $17/9; ⊘9am-midnight) Seattle's signature monument, the Space Needle (originally called 'The Space Cage') was designed by Victor Steinbrueck and John Graham Jr, reportedly based on the napkin scribblings of World's Fair organizer Eddie Carlson. The part that's visible above ground weighs an astounding 3700 tons. The tower takes advantage of its 520ft-high observation deck – offering 360-degree views of Seattle and surrounding areas – to bombard visitors with historical information and interpretive displays. On clear days, zip to the top on the elevators (43 seconds) for excellent views of downtown, Lake Union, Mt Rainier and the Olympic Range mountains way across Puget Sound; don't bother spending the cash on cloudy days. If you're coming up to take aerial photos, be forewarned that there's fencing around the observation deck's perimeter, making clear shots impossible. Its revolving restaurant, Sky City, is overpriced for the quality, but reservations in the dining room do give you a free ride up the elevator.

Experience Music Project
MUSEUM

(☏206-367-5483; www.empsfm.org; 325 5th Ave N; incl Science Fiction Museum adult/child $15/12; ⊘10am-7pm Jun–mid-Sep, 10am-5pm mid-Sep–May; ⊕) The Experience Music Project (EMP) is worth a look for the architecture alone. The shimmering, abstract building – designed by Frank Gehry – was inspired by Microsoft cofounder Paul Allen's passion for Jimi Hendrix's music and was initially intended as a tribute to Hendrix alone. It now houses 80,000 music artifacts, including handwritten lyrics by Nirvana's Kurt Cobain and a Fender Stratocaster that Hendrix demolished. There's also Janis Joplin's pink feather boa, the world's first steel guitar and Hendrix's signed contract to play at Woodstock. Appropriately, the best exhibits are the **Hendrix Gallery**, a major tribute to Jimi; the **Northwest Passage**, displaying everything from Ray Charles' debut album (recorded in Seattle) to Heart's stage apparel; and a long hallway that details the evolution of grunge. Upstairs is the **Sound Lab**, a futuristic studio that lets you lay down vocal tracks and play guitars, drums and keyboards. Kids will love it, as will anyone obsessed with Northwest music, but others may find themselves yawning. If you're sitting on the fence about paying, the Sky Church theater and Revolution bar are accessible free of charge.

Science Fiction Museum
MUSEUM

(☏206-724-3428; www.empsfm.org; 325 5th Ave N; incl Experience Music Project adult/child $15/12; ⊘10am-7pm Jun–mid-Sep, 10am-5pm mid-Sep–May) Barnacled onto the hull of the EMP is this nerd paradise, a collection of costumes, props and models from various sci-fi movies and TV shows. Highlights include the actual alien queen from the movie *Aliens* (1986) – never fear, she's behind Plexiglas in the cargo bay – and the only 3-D model of the Death Star made for *Star Wars: Episode 4*. Lowlights include a bedraggled Twiki costume from the *Buck Rogers* TV series. Rare books and manuscripts – including Neal Stephenson's handwritten *Baroque Cycle*, stacked as tall as the ET figure next to it – lend the display credibility. But mostly it just makes you want to go rent *Blade Runner* again.

Children's Museum   MUSEUM
(206-441-1768; www.thechildrensmuseum.org; 305 Harrison St; adult & child/grandparent $7.50/6.50; 10am-5pm Mon-Fri, 10am-6pm Sat & Sun;) In the basement of Center House near the monorail stop, the Children's Museum is an anachronistic learning center that offers activities and displays seemingly imported from an earlier time; it's a museum that might itself belong in a museum. But it's all very charming, if lacking in modern-day bells and whistles. The play area includes a child-size neighborhood and an area dedicated to blowing soap bubbles. Also nearby is the **Seattle Children's Theater** (206-441-3322; www.sct.org; tickets $10), a separate entity with summer performances in the Charlotte Martin and Eve Alvord Theaters.

Pacific Science Center   MUSEUM
(206-443-2001; www.pacsci.org; 200 2nd Ave N; adult/child $14/9, Imax Theater & Laserium with general admission $4 extra, without general admission $9/7; 10am-6pm;) This interactive museum of science and industry once housed the science pavilion of the World's Fair. Today, the center features virtual-reality exhibits, a tropical butterfly house, laser shows, holograms and other wonders of science, many with hands-on demonstrations. Also on the premises is the vaulted-screen **Imax Theater**, a laserium and a planetarium.

Monorail   RELIC
(206-905-2600; www.seattlemonorail.com; adult/child $4/1.50; 9am-11pm) A 1.5-mile experiment in mass transit, the Monorail runs every 10 minutes daily from downtown's Westlake Center right through a crumple in the smashed-guitar hull of the Experience Music Project.

CAPITOL HILL
This stylish, irreverent part of town displays all the panache and vitality you'd expect from Seattle's primary gay-and-lesbian neighborhood. The junction of Broadway and E John St is the core of activity, with restaurants, bars, shops and plenty of interesting characters to watch.

Capitol Hill is about 1.5 miles northeast of downtown. Take bus 7 or 10 and get off at Broadway. Continue north to find stately **Volunteer Park**, on E Prospect St, which was originally Seattle's main cemetery.

Seattle Asian Art Museum   MUSEUM
(Map p57; 206-654-3100; www.seattleartmuseum.org; 1400 E Prospect St, Volunteer Park; adult/child $7/free; 10am-5pm Wed & Fri-Sun, 10am-9pm Thu) For almost 60 years the Seattle Art Museum occupied a prestigious Carl Gould–designed space in Volunteer Park. When it moved downtown in the early 1990s, the Seattle Asian Art Museum moved in. The museum now houses the extensive Asian art collection of Dr Richard Fuller, who donated this severe art moderne–style gallery to the city in 1932. Admission is free on the first Thursday (plus 5pm to 9pm on the second Thursday) of each month. Also in Volunteer Park is the glass-sided Victorian **conservatory** (admission free), filled with palms, cacti and tropical plants.

Jimi Hendrix Statue   STATUE
(1600 Broadway) Jimi Hendrix, guitar genius and Seattle's favorite son, rocks out eternally in this bronze sculpture by local artist Daryl Smith, made in 1997. Hendrix fans have been known to leave flowers, candles and notes at the base of the kneeling statue.

Richard Hugo House   COMMUNITY CENTER
(206-322-7030; 1634 11th Ave) Established in honor of the famed Northwest poet, the 1902 Victorian Richard Hugo House, a former mortuary, is now the center of an active segment of the city's literary life. The house contains a library, conference room, theater and café with a small stage. It hosts readings and performances, writer-in-residence programs, reading groups and writing classes.

U DISTRICT
The University of Washington's 700-acre campus sits at the edge of Lake Union in a commercial area about 3 miles northeast of downtown. The main streets are University Way, known as the 'Ave,' and NE 45th St, both lined with coffee shops, restaurants, bars, cinemas and bookstores. The core of campus is **Central Plaza**, known as Red Square because of its brick base. Get information and a campus map at the **visitors center** (206-543-9198; 4014 University Way; 8am-5pm Mon-Fri).

Burke Museum — MUSEUM

(206-543-5590; 16th Ave NE & NE 45th St; adult/student $9.50/6, 1st Thu of month free; 10am-5pm, 1st Thu of month 10am-8pm) This museum of natural history and anthropology is located on the University of Washington's campus. There's a good collection of dinosaur skeletons, but the real treasures here are the North Coast Indian artifacts, especially the collection of cedar canoes and totem poles. On the ground level of the museum is the pleasant **Museum Café**, a high-ceilinged, atmospheric place with warm pine paneling and wooden tables. If you pay $1 extra for a ticket here, you can get into the Henry Art Gallery on the same day for free.

TOP CHOICE Henry Art Gallery — MUSEUM

(206-543-2280; 15th Ave NE & NE 41st St; adult/student $10/free, Thu free; 11am-4pm Wed, Sat & Sun, 11am-9pm Thu & Fri) The university's sleek fine-art gallery, also on campus, mounts some of the most intelligent exhibits and installations in Seattle and serves as a touchstone for the arts community. There are dedicated spaces for video and digital art, and a small permanent collection, as well as rotating shows (35 a year). Part of the permanent collection is Skyspace, by James Turrell, an artist whose medium is light. Turrell's installation over the sculpture garden will alter the way you look at the ever-changing Seattle sky. For an extra $1 you can visit the Burke Museum on the same day for free.

UW Suzzallo Library — LIBRARY

Those architecturally minded will be interested in the University of Washington's Suzzallo Library. Designed by Carl Gould around 1926, this bibliophile's dream was inspired by Henry Suzzallo, UW's president at the time. Suzzallo wanted it to look like a cathedral, because 'the library is the soul of the university.' Unfortunately for him, his bosses disagreed; on reviewing the building, they deemed it too expensive and fired Suzzallo for his extravagance. Gould was the founder of the university's architecture program; he created the plans for 18 campus buildings.

FREMONT, WALLINGFORD & GREEN LAKE

These three residential neighborhoods are all fun to explore for a sense of everyday life in Seattle. Green Lake is centered on a lake-filled park circumnavigated daily by hundreds of walkers, bladers, cyclists and strollers. Wallingford is a quiet little neighborhood that branches out from NE 45th St.

And Fremont, about 2 miles north of Seattle Center, is known for its lefty vibe, farmers market and wacky public sculpture, including a rocket sticking out of a building and a statue of Lenin shipped over from Slovakia. People come from all over town for the **Fremont Sunday Market** (www.fremontmarket.com; 10am-5pm Sun Jun-Aug, 10am-4pm Sun Dec-Feb), which features fresh fruits and vegetables, arts and crafts and all kinds of people getting rid of variable-quality junk.

FREE Gas Works Park — PARK

(Meridian Ave at N Northlake Way;) Urban reclamation has no greater monument in Seattle than Gas Works Park. The former power station here produced gas for heating and lighting from 1906 to 1956. The gas works was thereafter understandably considered an eyesore and an environmental menace. But the beautiful location of the works, with stellar views of downtown over Lake Union, sailboats and yachts sliding to and from the shipping canal, induced the city government to convert the former industrial site into a public park in 1975. Rather than tear down the factory, landscape architects preserved much of the old plant. Painted black and now highlighted with rather joyful graffiti, it looks like some odd remnant from a former civilization. It also makes a great location for shooting rock album covers and music videos. Be sure to climb the small hill in order to see the sundial at the top.

Woodland Park Zoo — ZOO

(206-684-4800; 5500 Phinney Ave N; adult/child $11/8 Oct-Apr, $16.50/11 May-Sep; 9:30am-4pm Oct-Apr, 9:30am-6pm May-Sep;) In Woodland Park, up the hill from Green Lake Park, the Woodland Park Zoo is one of Seattle's greatest tourist attractions, consistently rated as one of the top 10 zoos in the country. It was one of the first in the US to free animals from their restrictive cages in favor of ecosystem enclosures, where animals from similar environments share large spaces designed to replicate their natural surroundings. Feature exhibits include a tropical rain forest, two gorilla exhibits, an African savanna and an Asian elephant forest. Parking costs $4.

Fremont Troll — SCULPTURE

(N 36th St & Troll Ave) Beware the scary-eyed *Fremont Troll,* a mammoth cement figure devouring a Volkswagen Beetle beneath the Aurora Bridge. The troll's creators – artists Steve Badanes, Will Martin, Donna Walter and Ross Whitehead – won a competition sponsored by the Fremont Arts Council in 1990. The 18ft figure is now a favorite place for late-night beer drinking.

Waiting for the Interurban   STATUE
(N 34th St at Fremont Ave) A much-discussed piece of public art, *Waiting for the Interurban* is a cast-aluminum statue of people awaiting a train that never comes: the Interurban linking Seattle and Everett stopped running in the 1930s (it started up again in 2001 but the line no longer passes this way). Check out the human face on the dog – it's Armen Stepanian, once Fremont's honorary mayor, who made the mistake of objecting to the sculpture.

Theo Chocolate Factory   FACTORY
(206-632-5100; www.theochocolate.com; 3400 Phinney Ave N; tour $5; 10am-6pm, tours 1 & 3pm daily plus 11am Sat) What, perhaps you wondered, could possibly take the place of the free beer that came at the end of a Redhood Brewery tour? How about free chocolate? That's right – the old Redhood Brewery, empty for years since the company moved operations to Woodinville, has been re-opened as the Theo Chocolate Factory, and it does tours. Enough said.

BALLARD & DISCOVERY PARK
Ballard, despite its hip veneer, still has the feel of an old Scandinavian fishing village – especially around the locks, the marina and the Nordic Heritage Museum. The old town is a nightlife hot spot, but even in the daytime its historic buildings and cobblestone streets make it a pleasure to wander through.

Nordic Heritage Museum   MUSEUM
(206-789-5707; www.nordicmuseum.org; 3014 NW 67th St; adult/child $6/4; 10am-4pm Tue-Sat, noon-4pm Sun) This museum preserves the history of the northern Europeans who settled in Ballard and the Pacific Northwest, as well as bringing in special exhibits of new work by contemporary Scandinavian artists. It's the only museum in the USA that commemorates the history of settlers from all five Scandinavian countries. A permanent exhibit features costumes, photographs and maritime equipment, while a second gallery is devoted to changing exhibitions. The museum also offers Scandinavian language instruction, lectures and films.

To get here, take bus 17 from downtown at 4th Ave and Union St, get off at 32nd Ave NW and walk one block east on NW 67th St.

FREE Hiram M Chittenden Locks   LOCKS
(3015 NW 54th St; 24hr) Northwest of Seattle, the waters of Lake Washington and Lake Union flow through the 8-mile Lake Washington Ship Canal and into Puget Sound. Construction of the canal began in 1911; today 100,000 boats a year pass through the Hiram M Chittenden Locks, about a half-mile west of Ballard off NW Market St. On the southern side of the locks, you can watch from underwater glass tanks or from above as salmon navigate a fish ladder on their way to spawning grounds in the Cascade headwaters of the Sammamish River, which feeds Lake Washington. To get here, take bus 17 from downtown at 4th Ave and Union St.

Daybreak Star Indian Cultural Center   COMMUNITY CENTER
(visitors center 206-386-4236; 3801 W Government Way; 8:30am-5pm Tue-Sun) In 1977, Native American groups laid claim to the land in this area, now Discovery Park, and 17 acres of parkland were decreed native land on which now stands the Daybreak Star Indian Cultural Center, a community center for Seattle-area Native Americans. Discovery Park has over 7 miles of hiking trails, several of which lead to the Daybreak Star Center. Except for a small art gallery, there are few facilities for outside visitors. The vista point in front of the center affords beautiful views of the Sound, and several steep trails lead down through the forest to narrow, sandy beaches.

Activities
Seattle's location lends itself to hiking, cycling and all kinds of activities on the water. Cyclists shouldn't miss the 16.5-mile **Burke-Gilman Trail** meandering from Ballard to Seattle's Eastside.

Recycled Cycles   CYCLING
(206-547-4491; 1007 NE Boat St; bike rental half/full day $20/40; 10am-8pm Mon-Fri, 10am-6pm Sat & Sun) This U District shop has a friendly, unpretentious vibe.

Counterbalance Bicycles   CYCLING
(206-922-3555; www.counterbalancebicycles.com; 2943 NE Blakeley St, U District; bike rental per hr/day $10/30; 7.30am-7pm Mon-Fri, 10am-6pm Sat & Sun) The Burke-Gilman Trail runs right past the front door; rentals include Breezer 3-speed commuter bikes.

Agua Verde Paddle Club   PADDLING
(206-545-8570; 1303 NE Boat St; s/d kayak per hr $15/18; 10am-dusk Mon-Sat, 10am-

SKI SEATTLE

The variety of terrain in Washington ski areas is such that just about any level of skier or snowboarder can find a good fit. Resorts here are down-to-earth and unpretentious. They're also notably friendly toward snowboarders and backcountry Nordic skiers.

Daily adult lift-ticket prices range from the mid-$40s to low $60s. Hours of operation and ticket prices vary by season. Always check conditions online or by phone before setting out.

Not technically on its namesake, **Mt Baker** (☎360-734-6771; www.mtbaker.us) ski area is located on the adjacent Shuksan Arm, east of Bellingham on Hwy 542. It blows the mind with an average annual snowfall of 647in and holds the unofficial world record for seasonal snowfall at an established ski area (1140in during the 1998–99 season). Rightly famous for powder, expert runs and backcountry, Baker is also home to the Legendary Banked Slalom every February. The Slalom started in 1985 and was the first organized snowboarding competition in the world. Baker is about three hours' drive from Seattle, but is worth the trip.

Just off the eastern flank of Mt Rainier National Park, **Crystal** (☎360-663-2265; www.skicrystal.com; 33914 Crystal Mountain Blvd, Hwy 410) offers unparalleled views of Mt Rainier, Washington's highest mountain, and some of the best skiing on the West Coast. Located 80 miles from Seattle, Crystal is the largest of the ski areas with the most accessible peak skiing, a solid variety of terrain and a reputation for powder.

Stevens Pass (☎206-812-4510; www.stevenspass.com; Summit Stevens Pass, US Hwy 2) is some 80 miles east of Seattle. It is known for its variety of terrain; everything from glades to bowls to bumps to an elaborate terrain park. Throw in a huge lift-accessible 'backside' area that gives a backcountry experience without the danger or extra effort and you can't go wrong. Stevens is also good for families and groups that vary in skill level.

The Summit at Snoqualmie (☎425-434-7669; www.summitatsnoqualmie.com; 1001 State Route 906, Snoqualmie Pass) is a network of four ski areas 50 minutes east of Seattle on Interstate 90. Alpental is a smaller mountain best for advanced and expert skiers. It is known for its steeps, extensive backcountry and limited but challenging tree skiing. Summit West is the main area of the Summit; it's for beginners and families and has gear rentals and the most developed lodge and dining facilities. It is possible to ski from Summit West over to Summit Central, which is for beginners and intermediates and is home to the Summit's largest terrain park. Summit East is the smallest of the areas and is good for intermediates. It's the location of the Nordic ski center.

6pm Sun Mar-Oct) Rent kayaks from this friendly place on Portage Bay.

Center for Wooden Boats   SAILING
(☎206-382-2628; www.cwb.org; 1010 Valley St; sailboat rental per hr weekday/weekend $25/30, rowboat $20/25, beginner sailing course $375; ⊙12.30pm-dusk Sat & Sun & by appointment Oct-Apr, 12.30pm-dusk Tue-Sun May-Sep) Sailboat lessons and rentals on Lake Union, including a beginner course with eight to 12 lessons. Seasoned sailors who are a little rusty can take a one-on-one lesson for around $50 per hour.

Moss Bay Rowing & Kayak Center
    PADDLING
(☎206-682-2031; www.mossbay.net; 1001 Fairview N; ⊙8am-8pm summer, 10am-5pm Thu-Mon winter) Rentals, lessons and tours on Lake Union.

Northwest Outdoor Center   PADDLING
(☎206-281-9694; www.nwoc.com; 2100 Westlake Ave N, Lake Union) A vast selection of rentals, guided tours and instruction in sea and white-water kayaking.

Underwater Sports   DIVING
(☎206-362-3310; www.underwatersports.com; 10545 Aurora Ave) Diving courses in an on-site pool.

UW Waterfront Activities Center PADDLING
(☎206-543-9433; canoe & rowboat per hr weekday/weekend $8.50/10; ⊙approx 10am-7pm, closed Nov-Jan) Rent canoes or rowboats with a current driver's license or passport.

Sierra Club   HIKING
(☎206-378-0114; cascade.sierraclub.org; Suite 202, 180 Nickerson St) A busy and active group, with offerings from

SEATTLE FOR CHILDREN

The whole of Seattle Center will fascinate youngsters, but they'll get the most out of the **Pacific Science Center** (p65), which entertains and educates with virtual-reality exhibits, laser shows, holograms, an IMAX theater and a planetarium, and the **Children's Museum** (p65). Downtown, the **Seattle Aquarium** (p63) is a fun way to learn about the natural world of the Pacific Northwest. Seattle's numerous parks are all good places to let the tykes run free, and **Gas Works Park** (p66) is particularly good for flying kites.

beachcombing and botany walks at Alki to weekend day-hiking and car-camping trips along the Pacific Crest Trail.

☞ Tours

Argosy Cruises Seattle Harbor Tour BOAT
(Map p60; ☎206-623-1445, 800-642-7816; www.argosycruises.com; adult/child $22/9.75) Argosy's popular Seattle Harbor Tour, departing daily from Pier 55 year-round, is a one-hour narrated tour of Elliott Bay, the Waterfront and the Port of Seattle.

Bill Speidel's Underground Tour
WALKING, HISTORICAL
(Map p60; ☎206-682-4646; 608 1st Ave; adult/child $15/7; ☉departures roughly every 30min 11am-5pm) This famous 'underground' tour, though corny at times, delivers the goods on historic Seattle as a rough-and-rowdy industrial town.

See Seattle Walking Tours WALKING, THEME
(☎425-226-7641; www.see-seattle.com; per person $20; ☉10am Mon-Sat) See Seattle runs a variety of theme tours, from public-art walks to scavenger hunts.

Chinatown Discovery Tours
WALKING, HISTORICAL
(☎425-885-3085; www.seattlechinatowntour.com; 90min tour adult/child $17.95/12.95; ☉10:15am & 2pm Tue-Fri, 10:15am, 1 & 3pm Sat) This tour group leads travelers through the International District with stops at historic sites, a fortune-cookie factory and various shops. Options include a daytime tour with a dim sum lunch.

★☆ Festivals & Events

Northwest Folklife Festival MUSIC
(www.nwfolklife.org) Memorial Day weekend in May. International music, dance, crafts, food and family activities at the Seattle Center.

Seafair WATER
(www.seafair.com) Late July and August. Huge crowds attend this festival on the water, with hydroplane races, a torchlight parade, an air show, music and a carnival.

Bumbershoot MUSIC, LITERATURE
(www.bumbershoot.com) Labor Day weekend in September. A major arts-and-cultural event at Seattle Center, with live music, author readings and lots of unclassifiable fun.

🛏 Sleeping

Many downtown hotels participate in **Seattle Super Saver Packages** (☎800-535-7071; www.seattlesupersaver.com), a program run by the Convention & Visitors Bureau. Room prices are generally 50% off the rack rates from November through March, with substantial discounts all year, and they come with a coupon book that offers savings on dining, shopping and attractions.

DOWNTOWN & FIRST HILL
Moore Hotel HOTEL **$**
(Map p60; ☎206-448-4851, 800-421-5508; 1926 2nd Ave; s/d $74/86, with shared bathroom $59/71, ste from $117; ☎) Excellent value for its location, the once grand Moore Hotel offers 120 rooms of varying sizes and configurations, including some suites set up for business travelers and families. The building is no longer fancy but has been refurbished with an understated elegance. The early-20th-century lobby, with its molded ceiling and marble accoutrements, speaks of the Moore's long history, which is echoed in the better rooms (ask for one with a view of the Sound). Wi-fi is free but unreliable; it works best in the lobby. Children under 10 stay free.

Sorrento Hotel HOTEL **$$$**
(Map p60; ☎206-622-6400, 800-426-1265; www.hotelsorrento.com; 900 Madison St; d from $269; ☎🅿☎) William Howard Taft, 27th US president, was the first registered guest at the Sorrento, an imposing Italianate hotel known since its birth in 1909 as the jewel of Seattle. The combination of luxurious appointments, over-the-top service and a pervasive sense of class add up to a perfect blend of decadence and restraint. The hotel's award-winning

restaurant, the Hunt Club, is worth a stop whether you're staying here or not. Continental breakfast ($11) and a shuttle to the airport ($65) are among the extras on offer.

Hotel Monaco Seattle HOTEL $$$
(Map p60; ☎206-621-1770, 800-945-2240; www.monaco-seattle.com; 1101 4th Ave; r from $259; ✿❋❀✿) The hip, gay-friendly Hotel Monaco is housed in the old Seattle Phone Building, which sat vacant before the Kimpton group from San Francisco converted it. The suite-style rooms have stripy wallpaper and heavy curtains; a friend described it as 'like sleeping inside of a clown.' Leopard-print bathrobes are part of the deal. If you're lonely for your pet, you can borrow a goldfish for the length of your stay. The hotel's restaurant, Sazerac, is a popular New Orleans–style joint with a following of its own.

PIONEER SQUARE

Alexis Hotel HOTEL $$$
(Map p60; ☎206-624-4844, 888-850-1155; www.alexishotel.com; 1007 1st Ave; r from $249, ste from $284; ✿❋@❀) Each of the 109 rooms in this gay-friendly Kimpton hotel is decorated with original artwork. Some suites include fireplaces and jetted tubs. Ask about the 'Miles Davis Suite,' which contains art, biographies and CDs by the jazz legend. There's wine tasting in the lobby each evening. Even your dog gets distilled water in its bowl on arrival, along with a complimentary doggie bed and the canine equivalent of a pillow mint. The attached Library Bistro and Bookstore Bar are cozy nooks. You can also get room-service facials from the nearby Aveda spa.

Best Western Pioneer Square Hotel
HOTEL $$
(☎206-340-1234, 800-800-5514; 77 Yesler Way; r from $159; ✿❋❀) Rooms and common areas at this historic hotel feature period decor and a comfortable atmosphere. Right smack in the historic heart of Seattle, it can't be beaten for location – as long as you don't mind some of the saltier characters who populate the square in the off hours. Nightlife, restaurants and shopping are just steps from the door.

PIKE PLACE MARKET & WATERFRONT

Edgewater HOTEL $$$
(☎206-728-7000, 800-624-0670; www.edgewaterhotel.com; 2411 Alaskan Way, Pier 67; r with city/water views from $289/349; ✿❋@❀) Perched over the water right in Elliott Bay,

the Edgewater is one of the few places that lives up to its storied past. The timber-lodge theme, with its rock fireplaces and rough-hewn pine furniture, is pure Pacific Northwest, but a seriously classed-up version. Half of the 223 rooms have bay views and the rest overlook the Seattle skyline; many contain gas fireplaces. OK, so you can't fish out the windows anymore, but that's probably just about the only wish this place won't fulfill.

Pensione Nichols B&B $$
(Map p60; ☎206-441-7125; www.pensionenichols.com; 1923 1st Ave; s/d/ste $110/140/255; ❀) In a town with few lower-priced hotels and hardly any B&Bs right downtown, Pensione Nichols is a treat. Right in the urban thick of things between Pike Place Market and Belltown, this charmingly remodeled European-style pensione has 10 rooms that share four retro-cool bathrooms, two large suites and a spacious common area that overlooks the market. Rooms come with a complete and tasty breakfast. Parking is in a nearby garage.

Green Tortoise Hostel HOSTEL $
(Map p60; ☎206-340-1222; www.greentortoise.net; 105 Pike St; 8-/6-/4-bed dm $28/30/32; ❀) This hostel is one of the few budget options in the city and has an unbeatable location right across the street from Pike Place Market. Once pretty crusty, the place has moved to the Elliot Hotel building and now offers 30 bunk rooms and 16 European-style rooms (shared bathroom and shower). Free breakfast includes waffles and eggs. The hostel offers a free dinner three nights a week and there are weekly events such as open-mic nights.

BELLTOWN

Ace Hotel HOTEL $
(☎206-448-4721; www.acehotel.com; 2423 1st Ave; r with shared/private bathroom $99/195; ❀) Each of the Ace's 28 hospital-tidy rooms is unique and so stylish you quickly get the feeling you're the star of an art film. Ranging from European style with shared bathrooms to deluxe versions with private bathrooms, CD players and enough mirrors to make you paranoid, the rooms are stocked with condoms and, where your average Midwestern motor inn would place the Gideons Bible, a copy of the Kama Sutra. Obviously this isn't the place for the uptight – it's also bad for light sleepers, as the always-hopping Cyclops bar and restaurant is just downstairs. Barflies and night owls have it made.

Hotel Ändra
HOTEL $$$

(Map p60; ☎206-448-8600, 877-448-8600; hotelandra.com; 2000 4th Ave; r from $229, ste from $279; ❄✳⬡) Wild fabric patterns and vivid colors combine with sleek Scandinavian-influenced design to give this hotel (formerly the Claremont) a calming yet sharply modern feel. Its 119 rooms have a sense of luxury without being claustrophobically overfurnished with the usual trappings of decadence. The trappings here, in fact, are quite unusual: alpaca headboards, anyone? There are blue-glass wall sconces, brushed-steel fixtures, gigantic walnut work desks – even the fitness room has spartan prints and flat-screen TVs on the walls. Some of the suites have plasma-screen TVs. Bathroom toiletries come from Face Stockholm. The hotel is attached to chef Tom Douglas' Greek-via-Northwest restaurant, Lola.

City Hostel Seattle
HOSTEL $

(☎206-706-3255, 877-846-7835; www.cityhostelseattle.com; 2327 2nd Ave; dm $35-38, r with shared/private bathroom $79/99, incl tax; ❄@⬡) This fun, friendly hostel is a great budget option right in the midst of Belltown. It's an 'art hostel,' which means work by local and regional artists decorates every available surface in dorm rooms and common areas, and the hostel is part of the Belltown 2nd Friday Art Walk. The owners' welcome speech conveys their irrepressible enthusiasm for what they do. The place is spotless, down to the tile floors in the large bathrooms. There are three guest kitchens, a nice outdoor garden, a fastidiously maintained hot tub and a 20-seat theater where guests can watch free DVDs. Breakfast and bedding are included in the nightly rate.

SEATTLE CENTER & QUEEN ANNE
MarQueen Hotel
HOTEL $$

(☎206-282-7407, 888-445-3076; 600 Queen Anne Ave N; r from $175; ❄✳⬡) A classic old-school apartment building (built in 1918), the MarQueen has hardwood floors throughout and a variety of rooms, all with kitchenettes left over from their days as apartments. The neighborhood is an undervisited gem, handy to various attractions. If hill-walking isn't your thing, a courtesy van will take you to nearby sights. Children 17 and under stay free with a parent. Note that there are no elevators in the three-story building.

Travelodge by the Space Needle
HOTEL $$

(☎206-441-7878, 800-578-7878; 200 6th Ave N; r from $140; ❄✳@⬡) It looks a bit grim from the outside, but rooms in this motor lodge are larger and nicer than you'd find in some of the pricier downtown hotels, and equally convenient. There's a seasonal, outdoor pool and a year-round Jacuzzi, exercise room, in-room coffee or tea and a free continental breakfast.

Best Western Executive Inn
HOTEL $$

(☎206-448-9444, 800-351-9444; 200 Taylor Ave N; r from $144; ❄✳@⬡) In the shadow of the Space Needle, the Executive Inn has a terrifying, almost brutalist facade, but is perfectly decent inside. Pillowtop beds, in-room coffee and tea, microwaves and refrigerators, room service, a fitness room and a sports lounge are available, and there's a complimentary shuttle to downtown.

CAPITOL HILL
Bacon Mansion
B&B $$

(☎206-329-1864, 800-240-1864; www.baconmansion.com; 959 Broadway E; r $99-179, Capitol Suite $159-234; ⬡) A 1909 Tudor mansion with an imposing exterior that belies the quirky charm of its friendly hosts, this four-level B&B on a quiet residential street just past the Capitol Hill action has a grand piano in the main room that guests are invited to play. The 11 rooms come in a variety of configurations, including a carriage house that's wheelchair-accessible, and include TV and voice mail. One large suite has a view of the Space Needle, one has a fireplace, and one has an Italian fountain as a backdrop.

Gaslight Inn
B&B $$

(☎206-325-3654; www.gaslight-inn.com; 1727 15th Ave; s $98-128, d $118-168; ❄⬡) The Gaslight Inn has 15 rooms available in two neighboring homes, 12 of which have private bathrooms. In summer, it's refreshing to dive into the outdoor pool or just hang out on the sun deck. No pets; the B&B already has a cat and a dog.

Salisbury House
B&B $$

(☎206-328-8682; www.salisburyhouse.com; 750 16th Ave E; r $125-195; ❄⬡) Salisbury House, in a quiet, tree-lined neighborhood near Volunteer Park, is a 1904 home with four elegant corner rooms and one suite, all equipped with private bathrooms, phone with voice mail, and wi-fi. It's comfortably modern, without the floral overload of a typical B&B. The full breakfast is vegetarian and served family-style. Downstairs there's a library with a fireplace. Children over 12 are welcome.

U DISTRICT

College Inn
B&B $

(☎206-633-4441; www.collegeinnseattle.com; 4000 University Way NE; s/d from $60/80; ⊖☎) The College Inn is a great budget option. Built for the 1909 Alaska-Yukon Exposition, the building has 27 European-style guest rooms with shared bathrooms down the hall. There's no TV, but there's a ton of atmosphere, and some of the rooms have a view of the Space Needle through big bay windows. South-facing rooms get the most light. Rates include a continental breakfast served in the communal lounge. Downstairs there's a coffee shop that serves full meals, a convenience store and a lively pub. Note that the building lacks elevators, and the 'front desk' is four flights up a narrow stairway.

Chambered Nautilus B&B
B&B $$

(☎206-522-2536, 800-545-8459; www.chamberednautilus.com; 5005 22nd Ave NE; d $139-164; ⊖✳☎) The 1915 Georgian-style Chambered Nautilus has six guest rooms that are decorated with authentic British antiques, as well as an annex with one- and two-bedroom suites. All B&B rooms have private bathrooms, down comforters, handmade soaps and a teddy bear. The communal living room has a welcoming fireplace, and the full gourmet breakfast is reason enough to stay here. It's in a handy but quiet location, tucked into the forested hillside that lies between the university and Ravenna Park.

University Inn
HOTEL $$

(☎206-632-5055, 800-733-3855; www.universityinnseattle.com; 4140 Roosevelt Way NE; r from $120; ⊖✳@☎≋) What pushes this spotless, modern, well-located place over the edge into greatness is, believe it or not, the waffles served at the complimentary breakfast. They're amazing. The hotel is three blocks from campus, and its 102 rooms come in three levels of plushness. All of them offer such basics as a coffee maker, hair dryer and wi-fi; some have balconies, sofas and CD players. There's a Jacuzzi, an outdoor pool, laundry facilities and a guest computer in the lobby. Attached to the hotel is the recommended Portage Bay Café, and there's a free shuttle to various sightseeing areas.

✗ Eating

Possibly the most fun way to assemble a meal in Seattle is by foraging in Pike Place Market for fresh produce, baked goods, deli items and take-out ethnic foods. But Seattle has an embarrassment of riches when it comes to restaurants – without much effort, you can find everything from an Argentinean steak to a vegan cupcake.

DOWNTOWN & FIRST HILL

Aside from old-fashioned oyster bars and cavernous steak houses, downtown is home to two places that seem particularly characteristic of Seattle.

TOP CHOICE FareStart Restaurant
NORTHWEST $$

(Map p60; ☎206-443-1233; http://farestart.org; 700 Virginia St; soups & salads $2.50-9.50, lunch mains $8-12, 3-course dinner $25; ⊙11am-2pm Mon-Fri, dinner Thu) FareStart serves substantial meals that also benefit the community. The constantly changing lunch menu is pretty darn gourmet for the price – try the veggie Reuben, or a flatiron steak in blue-cheese sauce. All proceeds from lunch and the popular Thursday-night Guest Chef dinners – when FareStart students work with a famous local chef to produce outstanding meals – go to support the FareStart program, which provides intensive job training, housing assistance and job placement for disadvantaged and homeless people. Reservations are strongly recommended for dinner.

Wild Ginger
ASIAN $$

(Map p60; 1401 3rd Ave; satay $3-6, lunch $8-16, dinner mains $14-28; ⊙lunch Mon-Sat, dinner until 11pm Sun-Thu, midnight Fri & Sat) Seattle was more or less introduced to the satay bar by this popular Indonesian fusion restaurant, where throngs of diners sit and sample bite-size, skewered bits of fiery grilled chicken, vegetables or scallops, luscious soups and daily specials. More substantial dishes include Burmese curry crab and cinnamon-and-anise-spiced duck. The bar is a happening place, and there's a live-music venue, the Triple Door, downstairs.

PIONEER SQUARE

The historic core of the city has a surprising number of good budget-friendly dining options scattered amid its atmospheric old saloons and steak houses.

Salumi
SANDWICHES $

(309 3rd Ave S; sandwiches $8-12, plates $12-15; ⊙11am-4pm Tue-Fri) Sure, you'll have to wait in line. This is Mario Batali's dad's place, after all. But the line to get a Salumi sandwich is like its own little community. People chat, compare notes, talk about sandwiches they've had and loved...it's nice. When you

finally get in the door of this long, skinny storefront, you're further teased by display cases of hanging meats and cheeses. Sandwiches come with any of a dozen types of cured meat and a handful of fresh cheese on a hunk of bread – you can't go wrong. There's only a couple of seats, so be prepared to picnic. On Tuesday, family members hand-roll gnocchi in the window.

Bakeman's
DINER $

(Map p60; 122 Cherry St; sandwiches $4-7; ☻10am-3pm Mon-Fri) Legendary for its theatrical counter service and its roasted-fresh-daily turkey-and-cranberry sandwich, this subterranean diner demands that you know what you want and aren't afraid to ask for it.

Zaina
MIDDLE EASTERN $

(Map p60; 108 Cherry St; gyros $8-11; ☻10am-9pm Mon-Fri, 11am-9pm Sat) This friendly café, bejeweled with a mishmash of sparkly decorations and pulsing with Middle Eastern pop, dishes out juicy falafel sandwiches stuffed to overflowing, as well as shawarma, tabbouleh, hummus, great baklava and freshly squeezed lemonade. On weekend nights the vibe goes clubbish, with hookahs and belly dancers in the house.

Grand Central Baking Co
SOUP & SANDWICHES $

(214 1st Ave S; sandwiches $4-10; ☻7am-5pm Mon-Fri, 8am-4pm Sat) This artisan bakery in the Grand Central Arcade builds sandwiches on its own peasant-style loaves and baguettes, with soups, salads, pastries and other treats. Breakfast sandwiches made with cage-free eggs and Beecher's artisan cheese are also a great deal.

INTERNATIONAL DISTRICT

The International District is a great neighborhood for cheap eats, or you can go all-out on a sumptuous eight-course dinner banquet. Don't miss a chance for a dim sum brunch – or dinner, or midday snack – if you're in the area.

Pho Bac
VIETNAMESE $

(1240 Jackson St; pho from $6.50; ☻7am-9pm) You can get three sizes of *pho* (noodle soup) at this well-established restaurant on the edge of 14th Ave and Jackson St, with its huge windows gazing onto Little Saigon, as well as excellent salad rolls wrapped in fresh herbs and other classic Vietnamese dishes. Bonus: iconic Seattle chef Tom Douglas famously loves the place.

House of Hong
CHINESE $

(408 8th Ave S; dim sum per item $2-3, mains $12-15; ☻9am-11pm) This huge mainstay of the neighborhood serves dim sum from 10am until 4:30pm every day – handy if your craving hits you in the middle of the day.

Purple Dot Cafe
CHINESE $

(515 Maynard Ave S; mains $7-14; ☻breakfast, lunch & dinner, until 3:30am Fri & Sat) The Purple Dot looks like the inside of an '80s video game (it is actually purple) and draws a late-night drunken-disco crowd on weekends, but most of the time it's a calm, quiet place to get dim sum and Macao-style specialties (meaning you can feast on baked spaghetti and French toast along with your Hong Kong favorites).

China Gate
CHINESE $

(516 7th Ave S; starters $4-12, mains $8-15; ☻10am-2am) Like House of Hong, the China Gate now has all-day dim sum. The Hong Kong–style menu offers a couple hundred choices, and the building is interesting in its own right – it was built in 1924 as a Peking Opera house.

PIKE PLACE MARKET & WATERFRONT

Explore the market on an empty stomach and commit to a few hours of snacking – you'll be full by the time you leave, and it doesn't have to cost much. If you're looking for serious dining, you can find that here too – some of Seattle's favorite restaurants are tucked into mysterious corners of the market.

Steelhead Diner
SOUTHERN, DINER $$

(Map p60; ☎206-625-0129; http://steelhead diner.com; 95 Pine St; starters $9-14, sandwiches $12-13, mains $15-28; ☻11am-10pm) 'Highbrow diner' sounds like an oxymoron, but the Steelhead does it right – hearty, home-style favorites like fish 'n' chips, buffalo meatloaf or pork rib chops become fine cuisine because they're made with the best of what Pike Place Market has to offer and paired with cleverly chosen sides. 'Sequimbled Eggs' (named after Sequim Bay, known for its crab and oysters) come poached over Dungeness crab on toast; a fried-chicken sandwich is fall-apart moist and lemony; and the crab cakes make local foodies swoon. The place is all windows, which is great as it's perched right over the market and Elliott Bay, and decorations include tied flies in glass. Reservations recommended.

Café Campagne
FRENCH $$$

(Map p60; ☎206-728-2233; 1600 Post Alley; breakfast menu $9-18, lunch menu $19, French

101 dinner menu $29; ☻breakfast & lunch Mon-Fri, brunch 8am-4pm Sat & Sun, dinner daily) At this casual younger sibling of the upscale Campagne, the quality of the French-style cooking is what you'd expect from such a talented kitchen; the prices are more manageable, and you don't have to dress up for dinner. The weekend brunch is a treat.

Lowell's Restaurant   DINER $
(Map p60; 1519 Pike Pl; mains $6-9; ☻breakfast, lunch & dinner) If you want a sit-down meal but nothing fancy, head to Lowell's, well loved by shoppers, businesspeople and fellow market operators for its classic, eye-opening breakfasts and cheap-and-cheerful lunches. Order up eggs Benedict, salmon omelets or fish 'n' chips from the chalkboard menu, lunch cafeteria style, then take it over to a window seat and enjoy the view.

Ivar's Acres of Clams   SEAFOOD $
(Map p60; Pier 54, 1001 Alaskan Way; fish & chips $8.29; ☻lunch & dinner; ⛵) Ivar Haglund was a beloved local character famous for silly promotional slogans ('Keep clam!'), but he sure knew how to fry up fish 'n' chips. Ivar's is a Seattle institution that started in 1938. Forgo the dining room for the outdoor lunch counter; the chaotic ordering system involves a lot of yelling, but it seems to work, and then you can enjoy your clam strips or fish 'n' chips outdoors on the pier.

BELLTOWN
A hodgepodge of dining options, Belltown has everything from chic to sushi, with plenty of casual noodle houses, pizza joints and cafés thrown into the mix.

Dahlia Lounge   NORTHWEST $$$
(Map p60; ☎206-682-4142; 2001 4th Ave; lunch $10-22, dinner starters $9-15, mains $22-38; ☻lunch & dinner Mon-Fri, dinner until 11pm Sat & Sun) Owner Tom Douglas started fusing flavors at this Seattle institution in the late 1980s and singlehandedly made Seattleites more sophisticated; his empire has grown a lot since then, but the flagship restaurant remains a local favorite. There's a bakery next door where you can pick up one of the Dahlia's fabulous desserts to go. Reservations are recommended.

Palace Kitchen   NORTHWEST $$
(Map p60; 2030 5th Ave; starters $9-15, mains $15-26; ☻dinner until 1am) Owned by the Dahlia's Tom Douglas, the Palace is a see-and-be-seen hot spot that really picks up for the late-night cocktail scene. Daily dinner

specials present such wonders as spaetzle-stuffed pumpkin or traditional pork loin. Snack on appetizers – including a smoked-salmon-and-blue-cheese terrine or a sampler plate of regional cheeses – or go for the whole shebang with grilled trout, leg of lamb or roasted chicken with blackberries and nectarines. There's a late-night happy hour starting at 11pm that includes barbecued short ribs and other awesome deals ($4 to $5), plus drink specials.

Black Bottle   NORTHWEST $
(☎206-441-1500; blackbottleseattle.com; 2600 1st Ave; mains $5-12, flatbreads $9; ☻4pm-2am) The huge crowd congregating outside the front door of this new Belltown restaurant is your first clue that something interesting is happening inside. The menu has a lot more clues: octopus carpaccio, lemon-caper-squid salad, saffron risotto cakes, eggplant-mozzarella flatbread. It's a spartanly decorated but warm-looking space, with friendly service and a chic atmosphere. Reservations are accepted, and might be a good idea if you want to avoid a wait.

Belltown Pizza   PIZZA $
(2422 1st Ave; starters $6-8, sandwiches $9.99, pizzas $12-17; ☻dinner, bar until 2am) Pizza and beer is great, but pizza and liquor works quicker. Started as a tiny bar serving New York–style pizza, Belltown Pizza has expanded a lot since then but maintains its original mission of good food and good fun at grown-up hours (the bar's open until 2am). A large pie is enough to feed four hungry people. You can also get salads, pasta and sandwiches.

Shiro's Sushi Restaurant   JAPANESE $$
(2401 2nd Ave; starters $5-8, mains $8-15, sushi dinner $26.75; ☻dinner) Kyoto-born sushi master Shiro Kashiba ran Seattle's first sushi restaurant, Nikko, for 20 years. He spends a lot of time shopping for the freshest ingredients, hence his reputation as the go-to guy for raw fish in Seattle. He's a cheerful-looking fellow but takes his sushi very seriously – get a seat at the bar if you can, and watch him work.

Top Pot Donuts   DOUGHNUTS $
(Map p60; 2124 5th Ave; doughnuts $1-3; ☻breakfast, lunch & dinner) At Top Pot it's all about the doughnuts, and no, it is not wrong to eat them three meals a day. The doughnuts here are hand-forged as quickly as the little Seattleites can gobble them up. They're also available at various coffee shops around

town, but it's best to go to the source. Krispy what?

SEATTLE CENTER & QUEEN ANNE

Queen Anne's 5 Spot is a favorite for a casual, homey meal, and Canlis is perhaps the most frequently recommended place in Seattle for special-occasion dining.

Canlis   NORTHWEST, AMERICAN $$$
(☑206-283-3313; 2576 Aurora Ave N; starters $18-28, mains $36-96; ☺dinner Mon-Sat, plus Sun Dec) This place is old-school enough for either prom night or your grandma's birthday dinner. The traditional, classic food and service are both top-notch, and you can rest assured that none of the style is affected. Canlis has been around since 1950 and its authenticity shows. The view is lovely, too. Reservations are recommended, especially for weekends.

5 Spot   NORTHWEST $
(1502 Queen Anne Ave N; breakfast scrambles $9-10, lunch $8-12, dinner mains $10-16; ☺breakfast, lunch & dinner until midnight, closed 3-5pm Sat & Sun) In Upper Queen Anne, everyone's favorite breakfast and hangover diner is the 5 Spot. Good strong coffee keeps the staff ultraperky. Try a local legend, like the red flannel hash ($9.50), or get crazy with the wild-salmon cakes. On weekend mornings, go early to avoid the lines snaking out the door – or go for lunch or dinner; this is an excellent place for a quiet meal featuring good American cooking.

CAPITOL HILL

The scene on Capitol Hill is almost as much about style as food. It's no use enjoying a fabulous dinner if no one can see how chic you look while you're eating. Then again, ambience hardly detracts from a fine dining experience, so who's complaining?

Café Presse   FRENCH $
(1117 12th Ave; croque monsieur $6, half chicken $14; ☺7am-2am) This dreamy new café specializes in unfussy dishes the likes of which you'd find once upon a time in a terrace café around Saint-Germain-des-Prés. The *croque monsieur* and *madame* are huge, thick slabs of creamy goodness; steak *frites* are perfectly cooked and filling; and the vegetables are fresh and crispy. There's a handful of outdoor tables outside the beautiful café-bar; a long list of aperitifs and digestifs adds to the classy Euro feel. The café's adorable servers seem to have been hired based on their resemblance to Jean Seberg in *Breathless*.

Molly Moon's   ICE CREAM $
(917 E Pine St; ice cream $3-5; ☺noon-11pm; ☝) The lines out the door start to make sense once you get your first taste of Molly Moon's salted caramel ice cream. The boutique creamery gets its ingredients locally, including hormone-free dairy from Washington cows, and specializes in improbably brilliant flavors like garlic, cardamom and strawberry balsamic, as well as old reliables like chocolate and vanilla.

Coastal Kitchen   NORTHWEST $$
(☑206-322-1145; 429 15th Ave E; lunch mains $7-12, starters $6-8, dinner mains $9-19; ☺breakfast 8am-3pm, lunch & dinner until 11pm) This longtime favorite turns out some of the best food in the neighborhood – it has an eclectic mix of Cajun, Mayan and Mexican inspirations, and an Italian-language instruction tape running in the bathroom, if that gives a clue toward influences. Menus rotate by theme, but constant favorites include roasted chicken, pork chops and all-day breakfast. Fish dishes are startlingly fresh and always interesting. Pasta lunch specials are also highly recommended.

Bimbo's Cantina   MEXICAN $
(1013 E Pike St; tacos $2.95, burritos $5.50-7.50; ☺lunch & dinner, until 2am Fri & Sat) It's moved, but not so far that you'll get lost trying to find it when you need it. Bimbo's slings fat tacos, giant burritos and juicy quesadillas until closing time. The space is less crammed now, but still has its kitschy knick-knacks, including velvet matador portraits, oil paintings with neon elements, and a hut-style thatched awning. The best feature of the restaurant is still the attached bar, the Cha-Cha Lounge.

Honeyhole   SANDWICHES $
(Map p60; 703 E Pike St; sandwiches $5-12; ☺10am-2am) Cozy by day, irresistible at night, the Honeyhole has a lot to recommend it: big stuffed sandwiches with cute names (the Luke Duke, the Texas Tease), greasy fries, a full bar, DJs and a cool cubbyhole atmosphere at night.

Cafe Flora   VEGETARIAN $$
(☑206-325-9100; 2901 E Madison St; starters & sandwiches $4-12, mains $13-18; ☺brunch Sat & Sun, breakfast & lunch Mon-Fri, dinner daily; ☝) Just beyond Capitol Hill in Madison Park is this longtime favorite for vegan and vegetarian food. Flora has a gardenlike feel and a creative menu, with dinner treats like seitan spring rolls and breaded coconut tofu

dipped in chili sauce, a portobello French dip, caprese (tomato, mozzarella and basil) pizza and black-bean burgers. Or go for the hoppin' john fritters or tomato asparagus scrambles at brunch.

U DISTRICT

This is one of the best neighborhoods for authentic, inexpensive ethnic food and inventive vegan menus. Don't be put off by unappetizing-looking storefronts – some of the most interesting food comes from places that have the outward appearance of run-down five-and-dime stores. The adventurous will be rewarded.

Agua Verde   MEXICAN $
(✆206-545-8570; 1303 NE Boat St; starters $2-6, 3 tacos from $9.75; ☺11am-9pm Mon-Fri, 9am-8pm Sun, 9am-9pm Sat, takeout window 7.30am-2.30pm Mon-Fri) On the shores of Portage Bay at the southern base of University Ave, Agua Verde is a little gem that overlooks the bay and serves fat tacos full of lemony cod, shellfish or portobello mushrooms, plus other Mexican favorites. There's usually a wait for a table, but you can have a drink and wait on the deck, or order from the walkup window. You can rent kayaks in the same building, in case you want to work off your dinner.

Flowers   ECLECTIC $
(4247 University Way NE; lunch buffet $8, mains $7-15; ☺lunch, dinner until 2am; ☑) One of the most stylish places in the U District, Flowers has a vegetarian buffet served until 5pm, and dinners include meat choices. The lunch menu includes 20 sandwiches, each around $5. After hours, it becomes an inviting place to sip a cocktail, munch on an appetizer and 'do homework' with a promising study partner.

Ruby   ECLECTIC $
(4241 University Way NE; sandwiches $6; ☺breakfast, lunch & dinner until 2am) This attractive space next to Flowers had just been remodeled when we visited, but it still has a Casablanca feel, and the core of the menu is built around fragrant jasmine rice bowls ($8 to $12), in just about any combination you can imagine. The bar is hopping at night, and drinks are large and well crafted.

Cedars Restaurant   INDIAN, MIDDLE EASTERN $$
(4759 Brooklyn Ave NE; starters $6-8, lunch mains $7-12, dinner mains $8-15; ☺11:30am-10pm Mon-Sat, 1-9pm Sun) Cedars serves enormous curries and vindaloos so smooth and creamy you want to dive into them. Eat here just once

and you will dream about it later. There's also a great selection of Mediterranean specialties like shish kebabs, falafel and gyros, much of which is vegetarian. The covered wooden patio is a cool hangout in nice weather.

FREMONT, WALLINGFORD & GREEN LAKE

These residential neighborhoods have a number of well-loved restaurants, old and new.

✒Tilth   ORGANIC $$$
(✆206-633-0801; 1411 N 45th St; small plates $7-21, large plates $13-30, brunch plates $5-15; ☺brunch Sat & Sun, dinner daily) The only ingredients on chef Maria Hines's menu that aren't organic are those found in the wild, like mushrooms and seafood. Everything else, from asparagus to cheese, is carefully selected to meet certified-organic standards and prepared in a manner that preserves its essence. Try the mini duck burgers, made with the first organically raised ducks in Washington. Servers in the small restaurant are unpretentious and friendly, and will gamely answer any questions about the food or wine. Reservations are recommended; there's also a small bar in the corner.

Bizzaro   ITALIAN $$
(✆206-545-7327; 1307 N 46th St; starters $8-12, mains $14-20; ☺dinner) With a name like Bizzarro you'd never guess that this Wallingford hotbed is an excellent neighborhood Italian café. When you learn that it's actually someone's garage crammed with kitschy art and weird antiques, the name makes sense. Deliciously buttery pasta dishes, a good wine list and frequent live music add to the experience.

BALLARD & DISCOVERY PARK

Ballard boasts an ever-changing restaurant scene, so don't hesitate to ask around and check local papers for the latest recommended places.

La Isla   PUERTO RICAN $$
(✆206-789-0516; 2320 NW Market St; starters from $4, mains $12-17; ☺11.30am-2am) What started as a food stand at Fremont Sunday Market has become this always-packed little café, offering possibly the only Puerto Rican cuisine in the area. As a starter, try the empanadillas ($3.99), little fried dough pockets filled with your choice of shrimp, pulled pork, garlicky potatoes, cheese, tofu, chicken or beef. Better yet, go for the appetizer platter

($9.99), which lets you also sample the salted cod fritters and the *alcapurria,* made with plantains and green bananas. The enormous *pernil* (pulled pork) platter ($14.99), with a huge pile of juicy meat alongside saucy rice, beans, avocado and cheese, plus a couple of piquant sauces, is hard to beat – you'll be eating it for days and still be sad when it's gone.

La Carta de Oaxaca
MEXICAN $

(☎206-782-8722;www.lacartadeoaxaca.com;5431 Ballard Ave NW; mains $7-12; ⊙lunch Tue-Sat, dinner Mon-Sat) This lively place near the Ballard Locks serves the cuisine of Oaxaca, particularly black mole sauce – try the *mole negro Oaxaqueno,* the house specialty. You can sample the same stuff on tamales, or go for a combination of various small plates. Seating is mostly picnic-style, and there's a full bar – handy considering there's usually a wait for a table.

🍷 Drinking

You'll find cocktail bars, dance clubs and live music on Capitol Hill. The main drag in Ballard has brick taverns old and new, filled with the hard-drinking older set in daytime and indie rockers at night. Belltown has gone from grungy to fratty, but has the advantage of many drinking holes neatly lined up in rows. And, this being Seattle, you can't walk two blocks without hitting a killer coffee shop.

Shorty's
DIVE

(2222A 2nd Ave, Belltown; alco-slushies $5.50; ⊙noon-2am) A comfy oasis in a block of *très chic* lounges, Shorty's has cheap beer and hotdogs, alco-slushies and a back room that's pure pinball heaven.

Zig Zag Cafe
COCKTAIL LOUNGE

(Map p60; 1501 Western Ave; cocktails from $8; happy hour 5-7pm Mon-Fri $5; ⊙5pm-2am) For serious cocktails, this is the unmissable destination in town. Classic and inventive drinks are made with precision by handsome and nattily attired alchemists – including Murray Stenson, widely acknowledged as the best bartender in Seattle, and the charming Erik, who vaguely resembles *Twin Peaks'* Agent Dale Cooper. These fellows know how to sling a bottle of chartreuse; sitting at the bar on a quiet night and watching them command the stage is a treat. You'll see all manner of potions behind the bar, most of which you've probably never heard of (and if you're nice, you might get a taste).

King's Hardware
BAR

(5225 Ballard Ave NW, Ballard; ⊙4pm-2am Mon-Fri, noon-2am Sat & Sun) King's Hardware has a hunting-lodge-meets-Old-West-gameroom feel. There's pinball and skeeball toward the back, big wooden booths, and taxidermied jackalopes propped between bottles of liquor behind the bar. The spacious hangout also has a good jukebox and, in case you're feeling shaggy, easy access to Rudy's Barbershop (it's attached).

Blue Moon
DIVE

(712 NE 45th St, U District; pints $2-4) Legendary haunt of literary drunks, the Blue Moon rewards a high tolerance – not just for drink but for oddballs, gregarious bums and all manner of salty characters.

Brouwer's
BEER DUNGEON

(400 N 35th St, Fremont; ⊙11am-2am) This dark cathedral of beer has rough-hewn rock walls and a black metal grate on the ceiling; a replica *Mannequin Pis* statue at the door and the Belgian crest everywhere clue you in to the specialty.

Copper Gate
BAR

(6301 24th Ave NW, Ballard; ⊙5pm-midnight) Formerly one of Seattle's worst dives, the Copper Gate is now an upscale bar-restaurant focused on meatballs and naked ladies. A Viking longship forms the bar, with a peepshow pastiche for a sail and a cargo of helmets and gramophones.

Pike Pub & Brewery
BREWPUB

(Map p60; 1415 1st Ave; pints from $4, growlers $6; ⊙11:30am-2am) This Pike Place Market pub serves great burgers and brews in a funky neo-industrial multilevel space.

B&O Espresso
COFFEEHOUSE

(204 Belmont Ave E, Capitol Hill; ⊙7am-midnight Mon-Thu, 8am-1am Fri, 7am-2am Sat, 8am-midnight Sun) Full of understated swank, this is the place to go for Turkish coffee – if you can get past the pastry case up front.

Zeitgeist
COFFEEHOUSE

(171 S Jackson St, Pioneer Square; sandwiches $6-8, salads $5-6; ⊙6am-7pm Mon-Fri, 8am-7pm Sat & Sun) A lofty, brick-walled café, the pretty Zeitgeist has great coffee and sandwiches.

Panama Hotel Tea & Coffee House
COFFEEHOUSE

(607 S Main St, International District; nanpaste sweets $3.25, cup/pot of tea $3/8; ⊙8.30am-11pm Mon-Sat, 9am-9pm Sun) The Panama, a historic 1910 building that

contains the only remaining Japanese bathhouse in the USA, doubles as a memorial to the neighborhood's Japanese residents forced into internment camps during WWII.

Hale's Ales Brewery   BREWPUB
(4301 Leary Way NW, Fremont; ☉11am-10pm Mon-Thu, 11am-11pm Fri, 9am-11pm Sat, 9am-10pm Sun) Hale's makes fantastic beer, notably its ambrosial Cream Ale. Its flagship brewpub feels like a business-hotel lobby, but it's worth a stop. There's a self-guided tour near the entrance.

☆ Entertainment

Live music is still a huge draw in Seattle; clubs come and go, but the scene thrives. Consult the *Stranger* and *Seattle Weekly* for listings.

Cinephiles shouldn't miss the **Seattle International Film Festival** (SIFF; ☏206-464-5830; www.seattlefilm.org; tickets $5-10, passes $300-800). The festival uses a half-dozen theaters but also has its own dedicated theater, in McCaw Hall's **Nesholm Family Lecture Hall** (321 Mercer St, Seattle Center), and starts in mid-May.

Crocodile Cafe   LIVE MUSIC
(Map p60; ☏206-441-5611; 2200 2nd Ave) A beloved institution in Belltown and famous as a launching pad for the grunge scene, the Croc still hosts great local and touring bands.

Neumo's   LIVE MUSIC
(Map p60; ☏206-709-9467; 925 E Pike St) The 'new Moe's' fills the big shoes of its long-gone namesake in booking some of the best local and touring rock shows in town.

Chop Suey   LIVE MUSIC
(☏206-324-8000; 1325 E Madison St, Capitol Hill) Chop Suey is a dark, high-ceilinged space with a ramshackle faux-Chinese motif and eclectic bookings.

Tractor Tavern   LIVE MUSIC
(☏206-789-3599; 5213 Ballard Ave NW, Ballard) This spacious, amber-lit venue in Ballard mainly books folk and acoustic acts.

Cinerama   CINEMA
(Map p60; ☏206-441-3653; 2100 4th Ave) One of the very few Cineramas left in the world, it has a fun, sci-fi feel.

Northwest Film Forum   CINEMA
(☏206-329-2629; www.nwfilmforum.org; 1515 12th Ave, Capitol Hill) Impeccable programming, from restored classics to cutting-edge independent and international films.

A Contemporary Theatre   THEATER
(ACT; Map p60; ☏206-292-7676; www.actthe atre.org; 700 Union St) One of the three big companies in the city, ACT fills its $30 million home at Kreielsheimer Pl with performances by Seattle's best thespians and occasional big-name actors.

Intiman Playhouse   THEATER
(☏206-269-1900; www.intiman.org; 201 Mercer St, Seattle Center) The Intiman Theatre Company, Seattle's oldest, takes the stage at this theater.

Seattle Opera   OPERA
(☏206-389-7676; www.seattleopera.org) The Seattle Opera features a program of four or five full-scale operas every season, including a summer Wagner's *Ring* cycle that draws sellout crowds. They perform at McCaw Hall in the Seattle Center.

Seattle Symphony   SYMPHONY
(Map p60; ☏206-215-4747; www.seattle symphony.org; 200 University St) A major regional ensemble; plays at the Benaroya Concert Hall, downtown at 2nd Ave and University St.

Pacific Northwest Ballet   BALLET
(☏206-441-9411; www.pnb.org) This is the foremost dance company in the Pacific Northwest and does more than 100 performances a season from September through June at McCaw Hall in the Seattle Center.

Seattle Mariners   SPORTS
(☏206-628-3555; www.mariners.org; admission $7-60) The beloved baseball team plays in Safeco Field just south of downtown.

Seattle Seahawks   SPORTS
(☏425-827-9777; www.seahawks.com; admission $42-95) The Northwest's only National Football League (NFL) franchise plays in the 72,000-seat Seahawks Stadium.

Gay & Lesbian Venues

Re-Bar   DANCE CLUB
(Map p60; ☏206-233-9873; 1114 Howell St) Storied dance club where many of Seattle's defining cultural events happened (Nirvana album releases etc); gay, straight, bi or undecided revelers fill its dancefloor.

Neighbours   DANCE CLUB
(Map p60; ☏206-324-5358; 1509 Broadway Ave E) Always-packed dance factory for the

gay club scene and its attendant glittery straight girls.

R Place
DANCE CLUB
(Map p60; ☏206-322-8828; 619 E Pine St) Three floors of dancing to hip-hop/R&B DJs and plenty of sweaty body contact.

🔒 Shopping

Downtown dominates Seattle's retail scene with big-name shopping malls. But take a look in the corners of Pioneer Square for art and antique shops, or in the many nooks and crannies of Pike Place Market for everything from embroidered tea towels to lollypop condoms. Make the Waterfront your stop for obligatory souvenirs. For fashion or novelties, browse on Capitol Hill.

Note: a 9.5% sales tax is added to all purchases except food to be prepared for consumption (ie groceries). Unlike the European VAT or Canadian GST, the sales tax is not refundable to tourists.

Elliott Bay Book Company
BOOKS
(☏206-624-6600; 1521 10th Ave, Capitol Hill) In its new home on Capitol Hill, the venerable Elliott Bay Book Company has gone from creaky and labyrinthine to vast and soaring-ceilinged. At first everyone worried about the relocation, but the new space has an open, energetic vibe – maybe even better than the original. (Sacrilege!) Still one of the best bookstores in the Northwest, Elliott Bay is also the local leader in author appearances, with writers appearing at a reading or signing almost nightly – pick up a schedule near the entrance to see who's coming up.

Easy Street Records
RECORDS
(☏206-691-3279; 20 Mercer St, Queen Anne; ◷9am-midnight Mon, 9am-11pm Tue-Sat, 9am-9pm Sun) An awesome selection of new and used vinyl and CDs in a huge variety of genres makes it tempting to spend entire afternoons browsing the endless shelves of this record store. There's also a pretty good magazine rack, and on a recent visit there was a whole section devoted to music from the Northwest.

Archie McPhee
NOVELTY
(☏206-297-0240; 1300 N 45th St, Wallingford; ◷9am-8pm Mon-Sat, 11am-6pm Sun) No longer in Ballard, but still crammed to the gills with all manner of wacky goodies you probably didn't even know you needed, Archie McPhee is a Seattle tradition and a lot of fun, whether you're buying or just marveling at the selection. Inflatable meatloaf, anyone? Maybe some Cthulhu mints?

Pure Food Fish
SEAFOOD
(Map p60; ☏206-622-5765; 1511 Pike Pl) Perhaps the gift that says 'I heart Seattle' the most is a whole salmon or other fresh seafood from the fish markets. All the markets will prepare fish for transportation on the plane ride home, or you can just call and have them take care of the overnight shipping; Pure Food Fish has the best reputation locally for quality and value.

Babeland
ADULT
(Map p60; ☏206-328-2914; 707 E Pike St; ◷11am-10pm Mon-Sat, noon-7pm Sun) Opened in 1993 as Toys in Babeland, this sex-positive toy store – inspired by the riot grrl aesthetic and staffed by possibly the friendliest and least judgmental people on earth – has since abbreviated its name and expanded its business to include shops in New York and Los Angeles.

Also recommended:

Sonic Boom
RECORDS
(Map p60; ☏206-568-2666; www.sonicboom records.com; 1525 Melrose Ave; ◷10am-10pm Mon-Sat, 10am-7pm Sun) A local institution, Sonic Boom has moved from 15th Ave to this arguably more handy spot, and also has a location in **Ballard** (2209 NW Market St). Sells new and used vinyl and CDs. Ask about in-store performances by bands coming through town.

Gregg's Cycles
BICYCLES
(☏206-523-1822; 7007 Woodlawn Ave NE) This is Seattle's largest bicycle dealer. Near Green Lake, it has a huge stock of all kinds of bikes and accessories and a very helpful staff.

Uwajimaya
GROCERIES, IMPORTS
(☏206-624-6248; www.uwajimaya.com; 600 5th Ave S, International District; ◷9am-10pm Mon-Sat, 9am-9pm Sun) All you need to prepare an Asian feast – fresh and frozen meat and fish, produce, canned and dried and intriguingly labeled treats of all kinds, as well as cooking tools, spices, cookbooks, toiletries and gift items.

ℹ Information

Emergency & Medical Services
45th St Community Clinic (☏206-633-3350; 1629 N 45th St, Wallingford) Medical and dental services.

Community Information Line (☎206-461-3200) Information on emergency services, housing, legal advice etc.

Harborview Medical Center (☎206-731-3000; 325 9th Ave, First Hill) Full medical care, with emergency room.

Seattle Police (☎206-625-5011)

Washington State Patrol (☎425-649-4370)

Internet Access

Practically every bar and coffee shop in Seattle has free wi-fi, as do most hotels. For laptop-free travelers, internet cafés include:

Cyber-Dogs (☎206-405-3647; 909 Pike St, Downtown; first 20min free, then per hr $6; ☺10am-midnight) A veggie hot-dog ($2 to $5) stand, espresso bar, internet café and youngster hangout/pickup joint. Note the initial limited free access.

Online Coffee Company (☎206-328-3731; www.onlinecoffeeco.com; 1720 E Olive Way, Downtown; internet use first 30min free, then per hr $1, 1hr free for students; ☺7am-10pm) A cozy former residence on Olive Way. Also has a second, more utilitarian-chic branch at 1404 E Pine St, Capitol Hill.

Media

KEXP 90.3 FM Legendary independent-music and community station.

KUOW 94.9 FM NPR news.

Seattle Gay News Weekly.

Seattle Times (www.seattletimes.com) The state's largest daily paper.

Seattle Weekly (www.seattleweekly.com) Free weekly with news and entertainment listings.

The Stranger (www.thestranger.com) Irreverent weekly edited by Dan Savage of 'Savage Love' fame.

Money

American Express (☎206-441-8622; 600 Stewart St, Downtown; ☺8:30am-5:30pm Mon-Fri)

Travelex-Thomas Cook Currency Services Airport (☎206-248-6960; ☺6am-8pm) Westlake Center (☎206-682-4525; Level 3, 400 Pine St, Downtown; ☺9:30am-6pm Mon-Sat, 11am-5pm Sun) The booth at the main airport terminal is behind the Delta Airlines counter.

Post

Downtown (☎206-748-5417; 301 Union St; ☺8:30am-5:30pm Mon-Fri)

Tourist Information

Seattle's Convention and Visitors Bureau (☎206-461-5840; www.visitseattle.org; 7th Ave & Pike St, Downtown; ☺9am-5pm Mon-Fri,

plus Sat & Sun Jun-Aug) Inside the Washington State Convention and Trade Center.

Websites

hankblog.wordpress.com Insider art-related news and views from the folks at the Henry Art Gallery.

slog.thestranger.com A frequently updated blog by the staff of the *Stranger*.

www.historylink.org Loads of essays and photos on local history.

www.lonelyplanet.com/seattle For planning advice, author recommendations, traveller reviews and insider tips.

www.seattlest.com A blog about various goings-on in and around Seattle.

www.visitseattle.org Seattle's Convention and Visitors Bureau site.

 ## Getting There & Away

Air

Seattle's airport, **Seattle-Tacoma International Airport** (Sea-Tac; ☎206-431-4444; www.port seattle.org/seatac), 13 miles south of Seattle on the I-5, has daily services to Europe, Asia, Mexico and points throughout the USA and Canada, with frequent flights to and from Portland and Vancouver, BC.

Boat

Victoria Clipper (☎800-888-2535, 206-443-2560; victoriaclipper.com; round trip adult/child from $145/72.50, under 12yr free) operates several high-speed passenger ferries to Victoria, BC (from two to six daily), and to the San Juan Islands. It also organizes package tours which can be booked through the website.

The **Washington State Ferries** (☎206-464-6400, in Washington 888-808-7977, ferry traffic info 551; www.wsdot.wa.gov/ferries; Seattle-Bainbridge adult/child/car & driver $6.90/5.55/14.85, bicycle surcharge $1) website has maps, prices, schedules, trip planners, weather updates and other news, as well as estimated waiting time for popular routes. Fares depend on the route, size of the vehicle and duration of the trip, and are collected either for round-trip or one-way travel, depending on the departure terminal.

Bus

Greyhound (☎800-231-2222, in Seattle 206-628-5561, baggage 206-628-5555; www.greyhound.com; 811 Stewart St, Downtown; ☺6am-midnight) connects Seattle with cities all over the country, including Chicago ($203 one way, two days, two daily), Spokane ($39, eight hours, three daily), San Francisco ($116, 20 hours, three daily) and Vancouver, BC ($32, four hours, five daily).

Train

Amtrak (☎800-872-7245; www.amtrak.com)
serves Seattle's **King Street Station** (303 S
Jackson St; ⊙6am-10:30pm, ticket counter
6:15am-8pm). Three main routes run through
town: the *Cascades* (connecting with Vancouver,
BC, Portland and Eugene), the *Coast Starlight*
(connecting with Oakland and Los Angeles) and
the *Empire Builder* (connecting with Spokane,
Fargo and Chicago).

Sample one-way fares include Seattle–
Chicago ($341, 40 hours, daily), Seattle–Port-
land ($37 to $42, three to four hours, five daily)
and Seattle–Vancouver, BC ($37, three to four
hours, five daily).

❶ Getting Around
To/From the Airport

The options for making the 13-mile trek from
the airport to downtown Seattle have improved
drastically with the completion of the airport
light-rail line. It's fast, cheap and takes you
directly to the heart of downtown, as well as a
handful of other stops along the way.

Dial ☑55 from any of the traveler information
boards at the base of the baggage-claim escalators for transport information. There's also an
information booth on the 3rd floor of the parking
garage.

Taxis and limousines (respectively about $35
and $40) are available at the parking garage on
the 3rd floor. Rental-car counters are located in
the baggage-claim area.

Gray Line's Airport Express (☎206-626-
6088; graylineseattle.com; adult/child $11/15
one way) Fetches passengers in the parking
lot outside door 00 at the south end of the
baggage-claim level.

Shuttle Express (☎800-487-7433; shuttle
express.com; $10-55) Pickup and dropoff point
on the 3rd floor of the airport garage; ask about
the $10 Sea-Tac airport special, which applies
to certain locations.

Sound Transit (☎206-398-5000; www.
soundtransit.org) Light-rail service to the
airport goes every 15 minutes or better between 5am and midnight. Stops in town include
Westlake Center, Pioneer Square and the
International District. The ride between the two
furthest points, Westlake and Sea-Tac, takes 37
minutes and costs $2.50.

Car & Motorcycle

Seattle traffic has been among the worst in the
country for years and isn't improving. If you do
drive, take a friend: some Seattle freeways have
High-Occupancy Vehicle Lanes for vehicles car-
rying two or more people. National rental agencies have offices at the airport and around town.

Public Transportation

Buses are operated by **Metro Transit** (☑sched-
ule info 206-553-3000, customer service
206-553-3060; metro.kingcounty.gov; fares
$2-2.75), part of the King County Department of
Transportation.

Taxi

All Seattle taxi cabs operate at the same rate,
set by King County; the current rate is $2.50 at
meter drop, then $2.50 per mile.

Graytop Taxi (☑206-282-8222)

Orange Cab Co (☑206-522-8800; www.
orangecab.net)

Yellow Cab (☑206-622-6500; www.yellowtaxi.
net)

AROUND SEATTLE

Blake Island

An easy way to get from Seattle onto the
Sound is with **Tillicum Village Tours** (☑20
6-443-1244; Pier 55, Seattle; tours adult/child
$79.95/30; ⊙daily summer, Sat & Sun only Oct-
Mar). The four-hour visit to Blake Island,
the birthplace of Seattle's namesake Chief
Sealth, includes a salmon bake, a native
dance and a movie at an old Duwamish Native American village.

Bainbridge Island

The island is a popular destination with locals and visitors alike. It's the quickest and
easiest way to get out on the water from Seattle, and the ferry ride provides stunning
views of both Seattle and the Sound. Prepare
to stroll around lazily, tour some waterfront
cafés, taste unique wines at the **Bainbridge
Island Winery** (☑206-842-9463; ⊙tastings
11am-5pm Fri-Sun), 4 miles north of Winslow
on Hwy 305, and maybe rent a bike and cycle
around the invitingly flat countryside.

Washington State Ferries (☑206-464-
6400, in Washington 888-808-7977, ferry traffic
info 551; www.wsdot.wa.gov/ferries) run several times a day from Pier 52 (adult/car and
driver $6.90/14.85, bicycle surcharge $1).

Vashon Island

More rural and countercultural than Bainbridge, Vashon Island has resisted suburban-
ization – a rare accomplishment in the Puget

Sound area. Much of Vashon is covered with farms and gardens; the small community centers double as commercial hubs and artists' enclaves. Cascade views are great, with unencumbered vistas of Mt Rainier and north to Baker.

Vashon is a good island to explore by bicycle or car, lazily stopping to pick berries or fruit at a 'U-pick' garden or orchard. There's also the option to plan a hike in one of the county parks.

An accommodations option for budget travelers in summer is **AYH Ranch Hostel** (☑206-463-2592; www.vashonhostel.com; 12119 SW Cove St; tent/dm/r $13/23/65; ☺May 1-Sep 30).

From Pier 50 in Seattle, a passenger-only ferry leaves eight times each weekday for Vashon Island ($9, 25 minutes). However, the ferry deposits you far from the centers of Vashon commerce and culture, so you'll need to bring a bike ($1 extra charge) or have a lift arranged. From Fauntleroy in West Seattle, a car ferry leaves over 30 times daily for Vashon (passenger/car and driver $4.45/19, 15 minutes). Fares are collected only on the journey to the island.

Bremerton

Seattle's other ferry destination is Bremerton, the largest town on the Kitsap Peninsula and Puget Sound's principal naval base. The main attractions here are the **Puget Sound Navy Museum** (☑360-479-7447; 251 First St; ☺10am-4pm Mon-Sat, 1-4pm Sun, closed Tue Oct-Apr) and the historic destroyer **USS Turner Joy**, right next to the ferry terminal.

The car ferry to Bremerton makes frequent daily trips from the terminal at Pier 52 (passenger/car & driver $6.90/14.85, one hour). Passengers are charged only on the westbound journey; those with vehicles pay both ways.

Boeing Factory

Near the city of Everett is the facility where most of Boeing's wide-bodied jets – the 747, 767 and 777 – are produced. Tours of the **factory** (☑360-756-0086, 800-464-1476; adult/child $15.50/8; ☺8.30am-5pm), the world's largest building by volume, include views of planes being built. No photography is allowed. Reservations are recommended; tickets sell out quickly June through September.

To reach the Boeing factory, follow I-5 north to exit 189; turn west and drive 3 miles on Hwy 526.

Museum of Flight

Aviation buffs wholeheartedly enjoy the **Museum of Flight** (☑206-764-5720; 9404 E Marginal Way S, Boeing Field; adult/child $15/free, free 5-9pm 1st Thu each month; ☺10am-5pm Fri-Wed, 10am-9pm Thu), while others traipse through suppressing yawns, so be choosy about who you bring. The museum presents the entire history of flight, from da Vinci to the Wright Brothers to the NASA space program. More than 50 historic aircraft are displayed. The restored 1909 Red Barn, where Boeing had its beginnings, contains exhibits and displays. The six-story glass Great Gallery has 20 airplanes suspended from its ceiling. Vintage fliers reside on the grounds outside the buildings. There's also a hands-on area where visitors get to work the controls and sit in the driver's seat. Films about flight and aircraft history are shown in the small theater, and there's a gift shop and café.

The museum is about 10 miles south from downtown. To get there by car, take I-5 south to exit 158, turn west and follow East Marginal Way north, or take bus 174 from downtown.

Eastside

Bellevue, on the eastern shores of Lake Washington, is an upscale burg with high-income housing, attractive parks and some interesting shops and boutiques. Civic and social life centers on Bellevue Sq, at Bellevue Way NE and NE 8th St, the shopping mall that sets the tone for the downtown and the surrounding communities. Across from the mall is the **Bellevue Art Museum** (☑425-519-0770; 510 Bellevue Way NE; adult/student & senior $10/7; ☺11am-5pm Mon-Thu, 11am-9pm Fri, noon-5pm Sat & Sun), featuring changing exhibits of contemporary Northwest art. Admission is free the first Friday of each month.

To reach Bellevue from downtown Seattle, take I-90 east and exit on I-405 northbound. By bus, take 550 from Convention Pl or any of the 3rd Ave tunnel stations ($2.25).

North of Bellevue on I-405 is **Kirkland**, known for its lakefront business district, marinas and antique shopping malls. Some of the best public access to Lake Washington is along Lake Ave W. Lots of waterfront restaurants are found here, some with docks for their boat-transported customers. East of Kirkland is **Redmond**, a sprawling suburb and the center of Seattle's high-tech industry. To reach Kirkland and Redmond from central Seattle, take Hwy 520 over the Evergreen Point Bridge or catch bus 251 along 4th Ave.

Tacoma

Tacoma gets a bad rap as a beleaguered mill town known mostly for its distinctive 'Tacom-aroma,' a product of the nearby paper mills. Its nickname, 'City of Destiny,' because it was the Puget Sound's railroad terminus, once seemed like a grim joke. But destiny has started to come through for Tacoma. A renewed investment in the arts and significant downtown revitalization make it a worthy stop on the Portland–Seattle route.

Find information at the **visitors center** (⌨800-272-2662; www.traveltacoma.com; 1516 Pacific Ave; ⊙8am-5pm Mon-Fri).

Tacoma's tribute to native son Dale Chihuly, the **Museum of Glass** (⌨866-468-7386; 1801 Dock St; admission $12; ⊙10am-5pm Wed-Sat, noon-5pm Sun, 10am-8pm 3rd Thu each month), with its slanted tower called the Hot Shop Amphitheater, has art exhibits and glassblowing demonstrations. Chihuly's characteristically elaborate and colorful **Bridge of Glass** walkway connects the museum with the enormous copper-domed neobaroque 1911 **Union Station**. Some huge pieces by Chihuly greet visitors to the city's **Federal Courthouse** (1717 Pacific Ave). For smaller-scale work, don't miss Chihuly's permanent collection at the **Tacoma Art Museum** (⌨253-272-4258; 1701 Pacific Ave; adult/student $9/8; ⊙10am-5pm Wed-Sun, 10am-8pm 3rd Thu each month).

Take Ruston Way out to **Point Defiance** (⌨253-591-5337; zoo admission adult/child $13.50/11.50; ⊙9:30am-5pm), a 700-acre park complex with free-roaming bison and mountain goats, a logging museum, zoo, aquarium and miles of trails.

The **Antique Sandwich Company** (⌨253-752-4069; 5102 N Pearl St; sandwiches $6-11) is a funky luncheonette and coffee shop near Point Defiance.

Moderately priced hotels are scattered south of the center between I-5 exits 128 and 129.

Sound Transit bus routes 590 and 594 (Seattle $3) use the station behind the **Tacoma Dome** (510 Puyallup Ave). **Amtrak** (⌨253-627-8141; 1001 Puyallup Ave) links Tacoma to Seattle and Portland.

Northwestern Washington & the San Juan Islands

Includes »

Best Places to Eat

» Seeds Bistro & Bar (p94)
» Pepper Sisters (p88)
» Adrift (p91)
» Bilbo's Festivo (p106)

Best Places to Stay

» Willows Inn (p90)
» Wild Iris Inn (p93)
» Rosario Resort & Spa (p105)
» Hotel Bellwether (p87)

Why Go?

Spread between Seattle, the Cascade Mountains and Canada lies Washington's most archetypal region, a 'greatest hits' of the Pacific Northwest with all the sights and sounds outsiders traditionally associate with the land of pure air and West Coast hedonism. There's the skyline-hogging volcano (Mt Baker); the wilderness-flecked natural parks (everywhere); the liberal, collegiate city (Bellingham); the antiresort ski 'resort' (Baker, again); innumerable islands (the San Juan archipelago), and even a small stash of credible vineyards.

The Northwest's urban hub is laid-back Bellingham, while its rural highlight could be any one of the 200-plus islands that speckle the northern reaches of Puget Sound. Cultural life tends to be influenced by the fast-developing metropolises of Vancouver and Seattle, ensuring that the music's electric, the microbreweries are abundant, and the coffee is aromatic.

When to Go
Bellingham

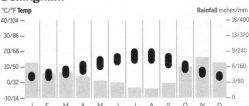

March–April
Vibrant flower displays at the Skagit Valley Tulip Festival

June Dutch-inspired 'Holland Days' festival in Lynden

September–October Avoid summer crowds and enjoy fall colors in the San Juan Islands

NORTHWEST COAST

Bellingham

POP 80,000

Imagine a slightly-less-eccentric slice of Portland, Oregon, broken off and towed 250 miles to the north. Welcome to laidback Bellingham, a green, liberal and famously liveable settlement that has taken the libertine, nothing-is-too-weird ethos of Oregon's 'City of Roses' and given it a peculiarly Washingtonian twist. Mild in both manners and weather, the 'city of subdued excitement,' as a local mayor once dubbed it, is an unlikely alliance of espresso-supping students, venerable retirees, all-weather triathletes and placard-waving peaceniks. Publications such as *Outside Magazine* have consistently lauded it for its abundant outdoor opportunities, while adventure organizations such as the American Alpine Institute call it home base.

Historically, Bellingham is actually four different towns – Fairhaven, Sehome, Whatcom and Bellingham – that amalgamated into a single metro area in the late 19th century. Despite vestiges of an ugly industrial past along the waterfront, and a flirtation with out-of-town 1980s mall development directed mainly toward bargain-hunting Canadians, Bellingham's downtown has been revitalized in recent years with intraurban trails, independent food co-ops, tasty brunch spots and – in genteel Fairhaven – a rejuvenated historic district.

Bellingham is 18 miles south of the Canadian border crossing at Blaine and 89 miles north of Seattle on I-5. The current city center is west of I-5; exit 253 leads to Holly St, a major downtown artery and one of the few streets to cut through the area without getting caught up in conflicting street grids.

If one event sums up the essence of modern Bellingham it's the annual Ski to Sea Race, held in May. It's a seven-leg team relay from the top of Mt Baker down to Puget Sound that involves skiing, cycling, running and kayaking, and enshrines the eccentric combination of magic and madness that make this great city tick.

Sights

Whatcom Museum of History & Art
MUSEUM

(www.whatcommuseum.org; 121 Prospect St; adult/child $10/8; ☉noon-5pm Tue-Sun; ⌖) This revamped museum is spread over three buildings: historic Whatcom City Hall (built in 1892), the adjacent Syre Education Center, and the innovative new Lightcatcher building, which opened in 2009. The last incorporates a spectacular 37ft glass wall and is Leadership in Energy and Environmental Design (LEED) certified. A rich array of exhibits includes historical material, Northwest art and Native American basketweaving. There's also a small shop and a special Family Interactive Gallery with exhibits and art for kids.

The Whatcom Museum has formulated an **Old Town Bellingham Walking Tour** that starts close to the museum and incorporates 20 sites in and around West Holly St. Pick up a map and leaflet when you visit the museum.

American Museum of Radio & Electricity
MUSEUM

(www.amre.us; 1312 Bay St; adult/child $5/2; ☉11am-4pm Wed-Sat, noon-4pm Sun) This museum showcases more than 2000 exhibits relating to the early days of electricity and the golden age of radio. It houses the largest collection of its kind in the US.

Western Washington University
ART GALLERY

Founded in 1893 as a teacher training institute, WWU was redesignated as a university in 1977. Environmental Studies is a popular specialty here. The **WWU Visitors Information Center** (☉7am-5pm Mon-Fri) at the end of South College Dr can provide details of a self-guided tour of the campus' two dozen outdoor sculptures, and you can also pop into the **Western Gallery** (www.western gallery.wwu.edu; ☉10am-4pm Mon-Fri, until 8pm Wed, noon-4pm Sat) to view the art exhibits. The gallery is closed for summer recess.

Whatcom Falls Park
PARK

Have you wandered unwittingly into the North Cascades? No. Instead, Bellingham's eastern suburbs are bisected by a wild region that stretches from Lake Whatcom down to Bellingham Bay. The change in elevation is marked by four sets of waterfalls, including **Whirlpool Falls**, a popular summer swimming hole. There are numerous trails in the park as well as picnic tables and recreational facilities.

Activities

Wedged precariously between mountains and sea, Bellingham offers outdoor activities by the truckload. Lakes Whatcom,

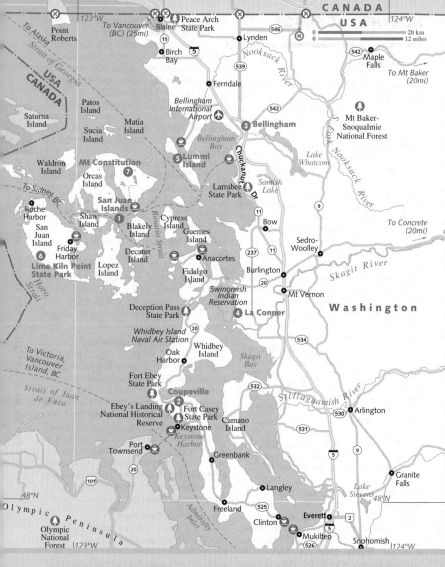

Northwestern Washington & the San Juan Islands Highlights

1 Propel yourself by human-powered transport around the **San Juan Islands** (p104)

2 Eat mussels in **Coupeville** (p96) on Whidbey Island

3 Browse all day in Bellingham's bookstores and grab lunch in the **Colophon Cafe** (p88)

4 Stay in a La Conner B&B during the **Skagit County Tulip Festival** (p93)

5 Switch off your phone, Blackberry and computer on **Lummi Island** (p90)

6 Whale-watch from **Lime Kiln Point State Park** (p99) on San Juan Island

7 Take in the view from the top of **Mt Constitution** (p104) on Orcas Island

Samish and Padden, all within a few minutes of town, make for great picnicking and boating, while walkers and hikers can trace the well-paved trail through Fairhaven to Larrabee Park.

Climbing

Bellingham is a mini Katmandu for the ever-active Northwest climbing community and home to the highly regarded **American Alpine Institute** (www.aai.cc; 1515 12th St, Fairhaven; ⊙9am-5:30pm Mon-Fri), which organizes everything from Everest ascents to guided trips up Mt Baker and a slew of other North Cascade peaks.

Cruises

Bellingham also offers a number of scenic and wildlife cruises; pick up brochures at the visitors center or the Bellingham Cruise Terminal and shop the options. **Victoria/San Juan Cruises** (www.whales.com; 355 Harris Ave) runs sunset cruises (with dinner) around Bellingham Bay ($49) or further afield to the San Juan Islands (from $58) and Victoria, BC (from $99). Enquire about the whale-watching add-ons.

Other Activities

If you're interested in renting kayaks, try **Moondance Sea Kayak Adventures** (www.moondancekayak.com; ⊙Apr-Sep) which runs a full-day trip in Chuckanut Bay, launching from Larrabee Park, for $95.

Fairhaven Bike & Mountain Sports (1103 11th St) rents bikes from $20 a day and has all the info (and maps) on local routes. This is one of the most bike-friendly cities in the Northwest, with a well-maintained intra-urban trail going as far south as Larrabee Park. The shop also rents out cross-country skis and snowshoes (per day $22/14) in the winter.

✯✯ Festivals & Events

The unique and utterly crazy **Ski to Sea Race** (www.skitosea.com) runs 94 miles from Mt Baker's ski slopes down to Fairhaven Marine Park. It takes place in late May. The seven relay disciplines are cross-country skiing, downhill skiing, running, cycling, canoeing, mountain biking and kayaking.

🛏 Sleeping

[TOP CHOICE] **Hotel Bellwether** BOUTIQUE HOTEL $$$
(☎360-392-3100; www.hotelbellwether.com; 1 Bellwether Way; r $156-272, lighthouse from $473; ❇❈❅) Bellingham's finest and most charismatic hotel is positioned on a re-

developed part of the waterfront and offers views over toward the whale-like hump of Lummi Island. Billing itself as a European hotel on the basis of its Italian furniture and Hungarian down duvets, the Bellwether advertises 66 luxury rooms, none of which are exactly the same. Its crowning glory is the celebrated 900-sq-ft lighthouse condominium, an old converted three-story lighthouse with a wonderful private lookout.

Fairhaven Village Inn HOTEL $$$
(☎360-733-1311; www.fairhavenvillageinn.com; 1200 10th St; r with bay/park view $179/199; ❇❈) Downtown Bellingham lacks a decent number of well-appointed independent hotels, but one good alternative option is this prime place in genteel Fairhaven. Well in keeping with the vintage tone of the historic district, the Village Inn is a class above the standard motel fare, with prices to match. In this instance, they're probably justified.

Guesthouse Inn MOTEL $
(☎360-671-9600; www.bellinghamvaluinn.com; 805 Lakeway Dr; s/d $81/91; ❇❈) The secret of a good 'chain' hotel is that it doesn't seem like a chain. To see the theory in practice, check out the clean, personable Guesthouse Inn, just off I-5 and an easy 15-minute walk from downtown Bellingham. The Vancouver–Seattle Bellair Shuttle (p89) stops here, making it an ideal base for overnighters who want to explore the Bellingham area.

Larrabee State Park CAMPGROUND $
(☎360-676-2093; Chuckanut Dr; tent/RV sites $21/28) Seven miles south of Bellingham, along scenic Chuckanut Dr, these campsites sit among Douglas firs and cedars with access to Chuckanut Bay and 12 miles of hiking and biking trails.

Birch Bay Hostel HOSTEL $
(☎360-371-2180; www.birchbayhostel.org; 7467 Gemini St off Alderson Rd; dm/d $25/55; ⊙May-Sep) If you're on your way to or from the BC/Washington border, you can stay at this HI hostel at Bay Horizon County Park in Blaine, just south of the 49th parallel. Clean dormitory beds and private rooms for up to four are housed in old military barracks with a cozy social space. At breakfast, eat your fill of pancakes for free at weekends. Nearby are the beach, waterfront restaurants and Canada.

🍴 Eating

Strict vegans, visiting Californians, and parents sick of stuffing their kids with hot dogs will all find solace in Bellingham, where the reverence for good food has an almost San Francisco–like aura about it. Railroad Ave is a good place to start looking.

TOP CHOICE **Pepper Sisters** SOUTHWESTERN **$$**
(www.peppersisters.com; 1055 N State St; mains $9-13; ⊙from 5pm Tue-Sun; 🚻) People travel from far and wide to visit this cult restaurant with its bright turquoise booths. The food is hard to categorize; let's call it American southwestern cuisine with a Northwestern twist. Try the cilantro-and-pesto quesadillas, blue corn rellenos and potato-garlic burritos. There's even a chicken-strip-free kids' menu.

Colophon Cafe INTERNATIONAL **$**
(www.colophoncafe.com; 1208 11th St, Fairhaven; mains $7-10) Linked with Fairhaven's famous literary haven, Village Books, the Colophon is a multiethnic eatery for people who like to follow their paninis with Proust. Renowned for its African peanut soup and chocolate brandy cream pies, the café has indoor seating along with an outside wine garden and is ever-popular with the local literati.

D'Anna's Café Italiano ITALIAN **$$**
(www.dannascafeitaliano.com; 1317 N State St; mains $11-19) Bellingham does a fine job in transporting you gastronomically to other parts of the world. For D'Anna's read Sicily, meaning fresh homemade pasta, authentic chicken marsala and a Mt Etna–like portion of linguini and clams. The wine list mixes Italian favorites with some up-and-coming Washington cab savs.

🌿 **Mallard** ICE CREAM **$**
(1323 Railroad Av; www.mallardicecream.com; ⊙10am-11pm Sun-Thu, 11am-11pm Fri & Sat) Bellingham's date-night central is a lurid '50s-style ice-cream parlor with a zillion different flavors – many of them weirdly exotic. Come here before or after a show and sample the vanilla-and-pepper or green tea varieties – all organic, of course!

Old Town Cafe BRUNCH **$**
(316 W Holly St; mains $6-8; ⊙till 3pm) This is a classic bohemian breakfast haunt where you can get to know the locals over fresh pastries, espresso and a garden tofu scramble. Wandering musicians sometimes drop by to enhance the happy-go-lucky atmosphere.

🌿 **Swan Café** CAFÉ **$**
(http://www.communityfood.coop; 1220 N Forest St; sandwiches $5-7; 🚻) The Swan Café is pure Bellingham: a community food co-op with an onsite café-deli that sells fresh, organic, fair-trade and guilt-free food. It's also a vegetarian and vegan's heaven, offering such items as vegan muffins, organic beer and a delicious daily selection of fresh, interesting salads. Takeout or eat on-site in a bright, airy seating area that offers plenty of decent snacks.

🌿 **The Bagelry** BAGELS, CAFÉ **$**
(1319 Railroad Av; bagels from $5) Who knew that (outside of New York) there were this many varieties of bagel? Your second dilemma will be what to put in them.

🌿 **Mount Bakery** CREPERIE, BRUNCH **$$**
(www.mountbakery.com; 309 West Champion St; brunch $6-12; ⊙8am-3:30pm) This is where you go on Sunday mornings with a Douglas fir–sized copy of the *New York Times* for Belgian waffles, crepes and organic eggs done any way you like.

Dirty Dan Harris STEAKHOUSE **$$**
(www.dirtydanharris.com; 1211 11th St, Fairhaven; mains $16-20) Named after Fairhaven's notoriously unhygienic founder, Dirty Dan's has been knocking out excellent steaks, ribs and seafood from this historic Victorian tenement for more than 35 years.

🍷 Drinking

Boundary Bay Brewery & Bistro BREWPUB
(www.bbaybrewery.com; 1107 Railroad Ave) Perennially popular Boundary Bay crafts its own ales and serves hearty Northwest-influenced fare for lunch and dinner. The smoked-salmon chowder hits the spot on a rainy night.

Copper Hog Gastro-Pub GASTRO-PUB
(www.thecopperhog.com; 1327 N State St) A new downtown pub with a strong food bias, the Copper Hog styles itself as 'European,' meaning you get a dozen ales (including IPA) and soccer on the big screen.

☆ Entertainment

Pickford Cinema CINEMA
(www.pickfordcinema.org; 1416 Cornwall Ave) If you can't face getting in the car to catch the latest blockbuster at a satellite mall, check out the latest arthouse movie at the 88-seat Pickford, run by the Whatcom Film Association. Plans are afoot to move the venue to a refurbished historic downtown theater at 1318 Bay St in 2011. Check the website for details.

Mt Baker Theatre
THEATER

(www.mountbakertheatre.com; 106 N Commercial St) With its minaret-like tower and elaborately designed interior, this grand old historic theater, built in 1925, has become one of Bellingham's signature buildings. Showcasing everything from live music to dance to plays, the theater regularly draws in top-name acts.

WWU Performing Arts Center
THEATER

(www.pacseries.wwu.edu; 516 High St) WWU's performing arts center usually features an intriguing line-up of international music and dance figures. See the website for the current program.

Wild Buffalo
MUSIC VENUE

(www.wildbuffalo.net; 208 W Holly St) Bellingham's 'house of music' is hidden in this inviting century-old building and is bereft of the traditional pub foibles of cigarette smoke, games machines and unsubtly positioned TV sets. Come here to enjoy local and national acts play jazz, blues, funk, salsa, rock and roll, and much more. Microbrew ales are served and dancing is de rigueur.

🔒 Shopping

Bellingham is a genuine readers' haven, with at least a dozen great bookstores. Music collectors will be equally enamored by a clutch of offbeat record stores, many of which stock old vinyl.

Village Books
BOOKSTORE

(www.villagebooks.com; 1210 11th St) This is a real community resource in Fairhaven, with lots of literary activities, to say nothing of being the home of the popular Colophon Cafe.

Henderson Books
BOOKSTORE

(116 Grand Ave) A veritable warehouse, this place stocks an estimated quarter million titles, both new and used. You could spend the better part of a day browsing the well-organized shelves.

EM Everyday Music
MUSIC STORE

(www.everydaymusic.com; 115 E Magnolia St; ⊙9am-midnight) Late-night vinyl browsing available until midnight 365 days a year. Plenty of time to search for that rare New Order 12-inch.

ℹ Information

There's a downtown **Visitor Info Station** (www.downtownbellingham.com; 1304 Cornwall

St; ⊙9am-6pm) and another **office** (905 Potter St; ⊙8:30am-5:30pm) close to I-5.

ℹ Getting There & Away

Air

Bellingham International Airport is northwest of town off I-5 exit 258 and is served by **Horizon Air** (www.horizonair.com) with regular flights to Seattle. **San Juan Airlines** (www.sanjuanair lines.com) flies daily from Bellingham to the San Juan Islands and BC.

Boat

Bellingham is the terminal for the **Alaska Marine Hwy Ferries** (www.dot.state.ak.us/amhs; 355 Harris Ave), which travel once a week up the Inside Passage to Juneau, Skagway and other southeast Alaskan ports. Passenger fares to Skagway start at $363; add a small car (up to 15ft), and the fare jumps to $1183. Cabins for the three-day trip cost an additional amount and can be hard to come by, so reserve well in advance.

The **San Juan Islands Shuttle Express** (www. orcawhales.com) travels daily (March to October only) from the Fairhaven ferry terminal to San Juan and Orcas Islands (one way/round trip $20/33). Bicycles are welcome on board with a $3/5 surcharge.

Ferries run by **Victoria San Juan Cruises** (www.whales.com; Bellingham Cruise Terminal, 355 Harris Av, Ste 104) run between Bellingham's Alaska Ferry Terminal and Victoria (Canada) Inner Harbor daily between May and September at 9am (one way from $49.50, three hours).

Bus

Greyhound buses serve Bellingham on the Seattle–Vancouver run, with four heading north to Vancouver ($16.50, two hours) and another four going south to Seattle ($17, 2½ hours). The **depot** (Harris Ave) is in the same building as the Amtrak station in Fairhaven.

The **Bellair Shuttle** (www.airporter.com) runs around the clock to Sea-Tac airport ($34), Burlington ($5) and Anacortes ($11). You can also reserve Ferndale and Blaine pick-ups/drop-offs. It stops at the Guesthouse Inn, just off I-5 exit 253; and at Bellingham airport. **Quick Shuttle** (www.quickcoach.com) runs comfortable buses with free onboard wi-fi between downtown Vancouver and Bellingham airport five times a day (one way/round trip $22/40).

Train

Daily **Amtrak** (www.amtrak.com) trains from Vancouver, BC (from $13, one hour 50 minutes), and Seattle (from $20, two hours 25 minutes) stop at the train depot at the end of Harris Ave, near the ferry terminal.

ℹ Getting Around

The city has a fairly extensive local bus system run by **Whatcom Transportation Authority** (www.ridewta.com). Bus 15 connects downtown Bellingham with the Bellis Fair shopping mall, buses 105 and 401 run to Fairhaven and the Alaska ferry terminal, and bus 50 runs out to Gooseberry Point and the ferry embarkation for Lummi Island. Fares start at $1 for local trips.

Around Bellingham

LUMMI ISLAND

POP 822

Not technically one of the San Juan Islands, but with them in spirit, Lummi – a five-minute ferry ride from the mainland at Gooseberry Point – acts as a bucolic buffer to the fast-spreading tentacles of American outlet-mall culture further east. A slender green finger of land measuring approximately 9 miles long by 2 miles wide and supporting a population of just under 1000, this tranquil dose of rural realism is home to the world's only reef-net salmon-fishing operation, a pioneering agritourism project, and an unhurried tempo of life best epitomized by the island maximum speed limit – a tortoise-like 25mph. Often described as a state of mind rather than a physical entity, Lummi is sprinkled with enough simple diversions to consume a weekend of quiet serendipity. Pencil in cycling around the 7-mile road loop, hiking 1664ft Baker Mountain (the second-highest point in offshore Washington); picking up composting tips at organic Nettles Farm, and counting whales in nearby Rosario Strait.

The uphill slog to the top of **Baker Mountain** starts just south of the junction of Suncrest Dr and Sunrise Rd and traverses a protected preserve managed by the Lummi Island Trust. Call in for a pass first at the small hut in Sunrise Rd. The hike is steep for the first 15 minutes and then flattens out for peek-a-boo views of the San Juan Islands from an elongated ridge. There's parking at the trailhead.

TOP CHOICE ⭐ **Willows Inn** (☏360-758-2620; www.willows-inn.com; 2579 West Shore Drive; r from $135; ✳🐾) reigns supreme over Lummi's other accommodation option. The 100-year-old inn has a variety of compact but cozy rooms poised above the Rosario Strait. It also has a creative restaurant where pretty much all the ingredients are plucked from nearby Nettles Farm or the island's unique reef-net fishing operation (the owner is an experienced reef-net fisherman).

CHUCKANUT DRIVE

Chuckanut Dr (SR11) is one of the West Coast's most spectacular and historic coastal back roads, a thin ribbon of winding asphalt that provides a refreshing alternative to the cars speeding along busy I-5. Running 21 miles from Old Fairhaven in Bellingham down to Burlington in Skagit County, the route takes in the craggy coastline overlooking the San Juan Islands, protecting hidden beaches and a 2500-acre state park, and offering such myriad diversions as hiking, cycling, beachcombing and fine dining along the way.

Defying steep oceanside terrain, the 'drive' was first laid out in 1896 to link Whatcom County with Mt Vernon and Seattle to the south. In 1912 a railcar was added on the northern part of the route and in 1915 local entrepreneur Charles Larrabee donated 20 acres of Chuckanut Mountain to make Washington's first state park. But in the 1920s, as traffic demands between Seattle and Vancouver exploded, Hwy 99 (now I-5) was constructed further east to ply an easier route through the coastal lowlands, leaving Chuckanut as something of a rural road relic.

If you're ambling by, be sure to pull over at the spectacularly located **Oyster Bar** (2578 Chuckanut Dr; ⏱11:30am-10pm) for a laid-back lunch.

Anacortes

POP 16,300

Travelers striking out for the San Juan Islands have been known to thank the odd summer ferry delay. Without it they would never have uncovered the latent joys of ferry port Anacortes. Linger in town for an hour or three and you'll quickly find that Anacortes is more interesting than it first appears, with a main street embellished by arty murals, an expansive waterfront park, a yacht-filled marina, and good-enough-to-write-home-about seafood (check out the crab cakes and oysters in particular). What the heck, there goes another ferry!

Anacortes is on Fidalgo Island, separated from the mainland by a narrow channel, 17 miles west of I-5 on Hwy 20. The downtown harbor skirts the edge of the business district, giving the town a detectable maritime air.

LYNDEN

'Welkom to Lynden,' reads the greeting on a shop wall in Front St. In any other town the unconventional spelling would be the work of an academically challenged graffiti artist; but here in the state's dyke-fortified, tulip-embellished northwest corner it's the proud expression of the region's Dutch culture. While Leavenworth embraces more than one million annual visitors with its Bavarian bonhomie, Lynden, a small town of 9000 people located 5 miles south of the Canadian border, wears its less-heralded Low Countries credentials with a little more understatement.

First settled in the 1850s, Lynden received its first wave of Dutch settlers in the early 1900s – a steady trickle of Calvinist farmers who arrived from the Netherlands via brief stopovers in the Midwest. United by raspberries (the town produces 60% of the US crop), they formed a Christian Reform Church and set up mixed farms on the kind of flat pastoral fields that would have had Van Gogh grasping for his paint palate.

As well as competing for the prize of 'cleanest town in the US,' Lynden also excels in historical preservation. Handsome Front St includes a 72ft windmill, a mall with a canal, various Dutch eateries and the inspired **Lynden Pioneer Museum** (www.lyndenpioneermuseum.com; 217 Front St; admission $7; ☉10am-4pm Mon-Sat).

Providing a great prologue/epilogue to any Canada-US border crossing is **Dutch Mothers** (405 Front St; ☉6am-4pm Mon-Thu, 6am-8pm Fri & Sat) where clog-wearing wait staff serve up pot pies, Dutch pea soup and famously good desserts (try the strawberry and rhubarb pie). Rumor has it that people from as far away as California plan pie sorties to **Lynden Dutch Bakery** (421 Front St; ☉7am-4pm Mon-Thu, 7am-5pm Fri & Sat) a few doors down. Accommodation can be found in the aforementioned windmill that doubles up as the **Dutch Village Inn** (☏360-354-4440; 655 Front St; r from $75). Rooms are comfy B&B-style if a little dated. The check-in is in the adjacent gift shop.

For real Dutch immersion, come to Lynden in early June for the ecstatic **Holland Days Festival** or visit the similarly jubilant **Holland Happenings** in Oak Harbor (p95) on Whidbey Island.

◉ Sights & Activities

Anacortes History Museum MUSEUM
(8th St & M Ave; ☉11am-5pm Jun-Aug, Sat & Sun only Apr, May, Sep & Oct) Has photo exhibitions showcasing the area's maritime history.

Snagboat Heritage Center MUSEUM
(713 R Ave; admission $2) Contains the restored hulk of the *WT Preston* Snagboat that operated on Puget Sound between 1929 and 1981, removing navigational hazards from the waterways.

For prime picnic spots and attractive oceanside hiking and biking trails make your way over to **Washington Park** just west of the ferry terminal.

🛏 Sleeping

Majestic Inn & Spa HOTEL $$
(☏360-299-1400; www.majesticinnandspa.com; 419 Commercial Ave; r from $169; ❀❀❀) Once home of the oldest store in Skagit County (1890), the Majestic was restored as a hotel after a fire in 2005. Its plush modern amenities offer the best of both worlds and add character to a building of longstanding historical significance. Expect bathrobes in your closet and whirlpool tubs in your bathroom. If you're fresh from a muscle-wrenching outdoor adventure in the San Juan Islands, the in-house spa could be an appropriate tonic.

Islands Inn MOTEL $
(☏360-293-4644; www.islandsinn.com; 3401 Commercial Ave; r $79-99; ❀@) The coziest of the cluster of motels on Commercial Ave, this well-equipped inn is run by a Dutch couple from Amsterdam and offers a wide variety of spacious rooms, some with whirlpool tubs. **Cameron's Living Room Restaurant** is also onsite.

🍴 Eating

Adrift INTERNATIONAL $$
[TOP CHOICE] (506 Commercial Ave; ☉8am-9pm Mon-Thu, 8am-10pm Fri & Sat) Warm service and high-class food without high prices will satisfy all levels of taste in locally rated Adrift, where you can get everything from a hearty

WORTH A TRIP

GUEMES ISLAND

Spend an hour skimming pebbles across the bay on Guemes Island (population 700) and you'll quickly realise that things are a little different in this corner of the state. Situated five minutes by ferry from Anacortes, this 8.3-sq-km slice of bucolic bliss is the San Juans' resident contrarian. Shunning tourist celebrity, Guemes has only one store (the dependable **Anderson's**), bevies of munching sheep and cows, and a tourist infrastructure that begins and ends at the rustic and decidedly unresortlike **Guemes Island Resort** (☏360-293-6643; www.guemesislandresort.com; 4268 Guemes Island Rd; yurts/d cabins $71/225; ⊛) right in the water.

Most travelers bound for the San Juan Islands don't even know Guemes exists (it uses a different hard-to-find ferry dock in Anacortes). Indeed, part of its innate attraction is the fact that it isn't really an attraction at all. Guemes visitors can't whalewatch or hunt for antiques like other San Juan vacationers; but they *can* go crabbing, circumnavigate the island by kayak, contemplate life without an iPhone, or sit on the deck outside Anderson's with a glass of Anacortes beer listening to the local folk band serenade the sunset.

The 22-car **Guemes Island Ferry** (500 I Ave, Anacortes; ⊗half-hourly btwn 6:30am & 7pm, hourly until 11pm) costs $9 round trip. The crossing from Anacortes takes seven minutes.

soup bowl to a fancy fish meal. The interesting decor features a small library (books do furnish a room), chairs on wheels and a classic long bar with high stools. There's regular art exhibitions, and music some evenings.

Rockfish Grill/Anacortes Brewery

SEAFOOD, PUB $

(320 Commercial Ave; fish & chips $7) If you're in the area, this place is worth a visit in its own right on two counts: firstly, the local brew beer, and secondly, the hearty pub grub. Try the halibut and chips washed down with a pilsner, or plump for the Aviator Doppelbock, in which case you'll probably want to skip lunch.

❶ Information

Visitor Information Center (www.anacortes -chamber.com; 819 Commercial Ave; ⊗9am-5pm Mon-Fri, 10am-3pm Sat & Sun).

❶ Getting There & Away

The **Bellair Shuttle** (www.airporter.com) offers eight runs a day from Burlington to Anacortes and the San Juan ferries (one way/round trip $6/10). The shuttle picks up passengers from the Ferry Terminal and the Texaco station on 14th St and Commercial Ave (no reservations required). Connections can be made in Burlington to Bellingham and Sea-Tac airport.

Skagit Transit (www.skat.org) bus 410 travels hourly between Anacortes (10th St and Commercial Ave) and the San Juan ferry terminal.

Bus 513 connects Anacortes with Mt Vernon's Skagit station four times a day.

Lower Skagit River Valley

Exiled Hollanders from Amsterdam and Utrecht have been known to double-take in the Lower Skagit, a flat, fertile river delta backed by the imposing Cascade Mountains, where hardworking second-, third- and fourth-generation farmers (many of them with Dutch ancestry) grow daffodils, tulips and copious amounts of vegetables, including 100% of the nation's parsnips and Brussels sprouts.

MT VERNON
POP 22,059

A former and rather unlikely winner of the 'Best Small City in America' prize, Mt Vernon is a place that most people only see the back end of as they race through on their way to Seattle or Vancouver on I-5. And, despite its prominence as a local agricultural nexus and headquarters for Skagit County's annual tulip festival, they're not missing much. Aside from a summer farmers market and a rather quaint theater (the Lincoln), Mt Vernon's attractions are limited. Far more alluring are La Conner to the west or Mt Baker to the east.

For a cheap stopover try the **Tulip Inn** (☏360-428-5969; www.tulipinn.net; 2200 Freeway Dr; r from $66; ⊛ @), just off I-5, a comfortable motel that was renovated a couple of years ago. For a potent tipple check out the **Skagit River Brewery** (www.skagit brew.com; 404 S 3rd St), an atmospheric pub that sells its own homebrew beers including Dutch Girl lager, IPAs and the famous Trumpeter stout. You can also load up on savories here, including fine pizza.

LA CONNER
POP 760

Celebrated for its tulips, wild turkeys, erudite writer's colony, and (among other culinary treats) enormous door stop–sized cinnamon buns; La Conner's myriad attractions verge on the esoteric. Abstract writer Tim Robbins lives here if that's any measuring stick, along with about 760 other creative souls, many of whom devote much of their time and energy to tourism. Jammed with gift shops, classy B&Bs and – in April, at least – long lines of cars, once-decrepit La Conner has undergone a post-1970s renaissance, transforming itself from forgotten Northwest port into out-of-the-box artist's community

Aside from three decent museums, the zenith of La Conner's cultural calendar is the annual tulip festival, when the surrounding fields are embellished with a colorful carpet of daffodils (March), tulips (April) and irises (May). It's either the best or worst time to visit, depending on your traffic tolerance levels.

Sights & Activities

La Conner's three small yet interesting museums are highly informative and well maintained.

Museum of Northwest Art   MUSEUM
(www.museumofnwart.org; 121 S 1st St; admission $5; ☺10am-5pm Tue-Sun) This gallery endeavors to portray the 'special Northwest vision' through the works of representative artists. The ground floor is dedicated to changing shows by regional artists, while the upstairs space houses pieces from the permanent collection.

Skagit County Historical Museum MUSEUM
(501 S 4th St; adult/child $4/3; ☺11am-5pm Tue-Sun) Perched atop a hill that affords impressive views of Skagit Bay and the surrounding farmlands, this place presents indigenous crafts, dolls, vintage kitchen implements and other paraphernalia utilized by the region's early inhabitants.

La Conner Quilt Museum   MUSEUM
(☑360-466-4288; 703 S 2nd St; admission $4; ☺10am-4pm Wed-Sat, noon-4pm Sun) Of more specialized interest, the quilt museum displays examples of quilt art from several generations. The museum is housed in the old Gaches mansion, which has stood here since 1891.

Roosengaarde Display Garden   GARDEN
(www.roosengaarde.com; 15867 Beaver Marsh Rd, Mt Vernon; admission $5; ☺9am-6pm Mon-Sat, 11am-4pm Sun) Halfway between La Conner and Mt Vernon, this renowned 3-acre garden plants 250,000 tulip bulbs annually and, with Mt Baker and a Dutch-inspired windmill glimmering in the background, photo opportunities abound. Bring a camera!

⚑ Festivals & Events

La Conner finds its pulse in spring when the annual **Skagit County Tulip Festival** (www.tulipfestival.org) lights up the surrounding countryside with shades of red, purple, yellow and orange. Events include wine tasting, bike tours and bird's-eye helicopter rides over the expansive fields.

⌂ Sleeping

TOP CHOICE Wild Iris Inn   B&B $$
(☑360-466-1400; 121 Maple Ave; www.wildiris.com; r $119-169; ☎) La Conner's B&Bs have the swank of boutique hotels and the homeyness of your gran's house. As a consequence, you'll never feel like you're kipping in someone else's property. Take the Wild Iris for instance, where you can sit back and enjoy fluffy bathrobes, a crackling fireplace, Jacuzzi baths, a stellar breakfast and complimentary homemade cookies.

La Conner Country Lodge   HOTEL $$
(☑360-466-1500; 205 N 1st St; r $149-289; ❄) Though of recent vintage, this handsome luxury lodge does its best to look in keeping with the rest of old La Conner. Large and airy rooms have fireplaces and decks facing the channel and a polished grand piano adorns the lounge. A few hundred yards away, the **La Conner Channel Inn** (☑360-466-3101; 107 S 2nd St), run by the same company, offers similar facilities and prices.

Hotel Planter   HOTEL $$
(☑360-466-4710, 800-488-5409; 715 S 1st St; d $75-129) This refurbished hotel offers a decent blend of c 1907 charm and modern amenities, including a covered hot tub in the courtyard. Children are allowed on weekdays only.

✕ Eating

TOP CHOICE **Seeds Bistro & Bar** MODERN $$$
(☑360-466-3280; 623 Morris St; mains $18-25) If you needed a single reason to visit La Conner, here it is. Situated in the old Tillinghurst Seed building, Seeds Bistro offers that rare combo of classy food and brunch-café-style friendliness. The key lies in harnessing the fresh flavors of the surrounding farmland and mixing it with equally fresh fish plucked from the nearby ocean. The result: unparalleled ling cod, off-the-ratings-scale crab cakes, and a raspberry and white chocolate bread pudding you'll still be talking about months later.

Calico Cupboard BAKERY, CAFÉ $
(720 S 1st St; mains $7-12; ☺7:30am-4pm, until 5pm Sat & Sun) The size of the cinnamon buns here beggar belief, and their quality (there are four specialist flavors) is equally good. Factor in a 10-mile run through the tulip fields before you tackle one and you should manage to stave off instant diabetes. The rest of the goods – if you ever get round to viewing them – are, not surprisingly, highly addictive. Try the bread pudding, flans, omelets or light lunches. There's seating inside. There's another branch in Anacortes.

La Conner Brewing Co BREWPUB $
(117 S 1st St; pizzas $8-9, sandwiches $7-8; ☺11:30am-10pm, until 11pm Fri & Sat) A polished pine pub that manages to combine the relaxed atmosphere of a café with the quality beers (including IPA and stout) of an English drinking house. Bonuses include wood-fired pizzas, fresh salads and eight home brews on tap.

ℹ Information

La Conner Chamber of Commerce (www.laconnerchamber.com; Morris St) Pick up helpful maps to orientate yourself here.

Whidbey Island

Whidbey Island is an idyllic emerald escape beloved of stressed-out Seattleites. While not as detached or nonconformist as the San Juans (there's a bridge connecting it to adjacent Fidalgo Island at its northernmost point), life is certainly slower, quieter and more pastoral here. Having six state parks is a bonus, along with a plethora of B&Bs, two historic fishing villages (Langley and Coupeville), famously good mussels and a thriving artist's community. Of less interest to travelers is the US Naval-Air base that

dominates Oak Harbor. At 41 miles long, Whidbey is the longest island on the US west coast. A free weekday bus service provides a useful way of getting around.

ℹ Getting There & Around

BOAT Services from Washington State Ferries run between Clinton and Mukilteo (car and driver/passenger $8.60/$3.95, 20 minutes) and between Keystone and Port Townsend ($11.15/$2.60, 30 minutes).

BUS The **Bellair Shuttle** (www.airporter.com) offers frequent bus service to Oak Harbor from Sea-Tac (one way/round trip $34/60) or from Bellingham ($12/22); transfer in Burlington for the Whidbey-bound connection. Prepaid reservations are required to ensure a seat.

☑**Island Transit** (www.islandtransit.org) is a community-financed scheme offering the ultimate encouragement for people to get out of their cars and onto the buses. Buses run the length of Whidbey daily except Sunday, from the Clinton ferry dock to Greenbank, Coupeville, Oak Harbor and Deception Pass. Other routes reach the Keystone ferry dock and Langley on weekdays. Service is hourly and free – yes – FREE!

DECEPTION PASS STATE PARK

Captain George Vancouver originally supposed Whidbey Island to be a peninsula. Eventually Joseph Whidbey – who set off in a small boat to explore and map Puget Sound – found this narrow cliff-lined crevasse churned by rushing water and Whidbey's insularity was confirmed. Deceived no more, the spectacular narrow passage got a name – though even today it remains a challenge to navigate with a motorized boat.

Emerging from the flat pastures of Fidalgo Island, **Deception Pass** leaps out like a mini Grand Canyon, its precipitous cliffs overlooked by a famous bridge made all the more dramatic by the sight of the churning, angry water below. The bridge consists of two steel arches that span Canoe Pass and Deception Pass, with a central support on Pass Island between the two. Visitors to the 5.5-sq-mile **park** (41229 N State Hwy 20) usually introduce themselves to the spectacular land and seascape by parking at the shoulders on either end and walking across the bridge. Built during the 1930s by the Civilian Conservation Corps (CCC), the bridge was considered an engineering feat in its day. The park also spans the channel, with facilities – including campgrounds – on both the north and south flanks of the passage.

More than 3.5 million visitors per year visit Deception Pass, which makes it Washington's most popular state park. Besides the dramatic bridge overviews, the park's attractions include more than 15 miles of saltwater shoreline, seven nearby islands, three freshwater lakes, boat docks, hundreds of picnic sites and 27 miles of forest trails. Scuba divers and sea kayakers can explore the area's reefs and cliff-edge shores. Organized kayak tours (per person from $30) depart from Bowman Bay; contact the **Deception Pass Adventure Center** (☑360-293-3330) to reserve.

The park sports three **campsites** (☑888-226-7688; tent/RV sites $21/28) with more than 300 spaces nestled in the forests located beside a lake and a saltwater bay. Facilities include running water, flush toilets, hot showers and snack concessions. Reserve well ahead for summer weekends, as competition can be fierce.

OAK HARBOR
POP 19,795

There are two main distinctions between the San Juan Islands and Whidbey Island. First, Whidbey has a mainland bridge connection (via Deception Pass) and second, it has Oak Harbor, a modern mishmash of boxlike chain stores and recent urban development that looks rather like a Seattle suburb, relocated and shunted 70 miles to the north. Dominated by Naval Air Station Whidbey Island, completed in 1942, Oak Harbor is a military town with a distinguished Irish and Dutch heritage dating back to the late 19th century. Today it accommodates the island's largest marina, a notable playhouse and – surprise, surprise – plenty of indigenous Garry oak trees.

Ever keen to shake off its lackluster image, Oak Harbor has embarked upon a major charm offensive in recent years, with a redevelopment plan emphasizing its nautical heritage and waterfront amenities. The helpful **Oak Harbor Visitor Center** (32630 State Rte 20; ☉10am-5pm Mon-Fri), situated on the main drag through town, should be able to put you straight on the town's not-so-obvious attractions. **Holland Happenings** is held during the last week in April when the tulips are still in bloom.

Oak Harbor's most striking and culturally distinctive lodging has to be the **Auld Holland Inn** (☑360-675-2288; 33575 State Rte 20; r $49-149; ☒☺), an admirable nod at the town's Dutch heritage that dominates SR-20

with its long timber-beamed frontage and towering old-fashioned windmill. Run by a family from Holland, the rooms and service here live up to their European promise, and extra bonuses include an outdoor swimming pool, a gym, a children's playground and a gift shop that sells authentic clogs. The hotel also has an excellent onsite restaurant.

COUPEVILLE
POP 1723

Going to Whidbey and not visiting Coupeville is like going to Italy and not visiting Rome. This picturesque fishing community is what the island is all about: fresh mussels and clams, old-world B&Bs, historic clapboard shopfronts, and instant access to a National Historic Reserve (the village actually sits on the eastern edge of Ebey's Landing National Historical Reserve). For those who thought Whidbey Island began and ended at Deception Pass (and there are quite a few), think again!

◉ Sights & Activities

Island County Historical Society Museum
MUSEUM
(908 NW Alexander St; admission $3; ☉10am-5pm May-Sep, 10am-4pm Fri-Mon Oct-Apr) The island's most comprehensive museum has plenty of local historical testimonies showcased in meticulous and well-presented display cases. Also on offer are self-guided walking-tour maps of Coupeville's vintage homes. The helpful staff can also enlighten you on the highlights of Ebey's Landing National Historical Reserve.

Whidbey's Greenbank Berry Farm
BERRY FARM
(www.greenbankfarm.com; Hwy 525 off Wonn Rd; ☉10am-5pm) Go 10 miles south of Coupeville to find the world's largest producer of loganberries, a sweet, blackish berry rather like a black raspberry. The winery-style farm is open daily for touring, tasting and picnicking.

⎚ Sleeping

Coupeville Inn
MOTEL $$
(☑360-678-6668; www.coupevilleinn.com; 200 Coveland St; d $90-120; ☒@) It bills itself as a motel, but with its French architecture, oak furniture and rather plush interior this is far from your standard highway sleepover. Situated close to Coupeville's tiny town center, this plush place is a bargain, given its fancy furnishings and substantial complimentary breakfast.

Captain Whidbey Inn
INN $

([image]360-678-4097; www.captainwhidbey.com; 2072 W Captain Whidbey Inn Rd; incl breakfast s/d $85/95, cabins $175, cottages $275) They don't come any more outlandish than this. The Captain Whidbey is a 1907 inn built entirely out of rust-colored madrone (arbutus) wood. With its low ceilings, creaky floors and cozy lounge strewn with faded copies of *National Geographic*, it feels more like something out of a medieval forest than a 21st-century tourist island. Lodging is in 12 sea galleon–style guest rooms (with shared bathrooms) in the main lodge, as well as wood-heated cottages and a more modern building with verandahs facing a lagoon.

Anchorage Inn
B&B $$

([image]360-678-5581; www.anchorage-inn.com; 807 N Main St; r $89-149) Continuing the Northwestern penchant for Victorian-style B&Bs, this place comes up trumps with plenty of lace curtains, patterned wallpaper and old-fashioned upright chairs. Seven rooms with private bathrooms are encased in a turreted house overlooking Penn Cove; the owners even run a course on inn-keeping. With so much fine china on display, children under 14 aren't permitted.

✖ Eating

Christopher's
MODERN $$$

([image]360-678-5480; 103 NW Coveland St; mains $17-26) Go where the locals go and bring a good appetite. Christopher's does exciting and creative modern cooking in huge portions. The mussels and clams are the best in town (no mean feat in Coupeville) and the seafood alfredo pasta is wonderfully rich. Then there are the desserts – anyone for chocolate mousse?

Toby's Tavern
SEAFOOD, PUB $$

(www.tobysuds.com; 8 Front St; mains $7-13) A quintessential Coupeville pub housed in a vintage mercantile building dating from the 1890s, Toby's historic setting is personified by its polished back bar that was originally shipped here around Cape Horn in 1900. These days the attention to detail is no less fastidious, with home-produced microbrews and a menu spearheaded by such local classics as beer batter onion rings, clam strips, and halibut and chips.

ⓘ Information

Visitor Information Center ([image]360-678-5434; www.centralwhidbeychamber.com; 23 NW Front St) ([image]10am-5pm) Right in town.

EBEY'S LANDING NATIONAL HISTORICAL RESERVE

This unique National Historical Reserve was the first of its kind in the nation when it was created in 1978 in order to preserve Whidbey Island's historical heritage from the encroaching urbanization that had already partly engulfed Oak Harbor. Ninety percent privately owned, **Ebey's Landing** (admission free; ⊘8am-5pm Oct 16-Mar 31, 6:30am-10pm Apr 1-Oct 15) comprises 17,400 acres encompassing working farms, four historic blockhouses, two state parks and the town of Coupeville itself. A series of interpretive boards shows visitors how the patterns of croplands, woods (or the lack of them) and even roads reflect the activities of those who have peopled this scenic landscape, from its earliest indigenous inhabitants to 19th-century settlers.

The Island County Historical Museum in Coupeville distributes a brochure on suggested driving and cycling tours through the reserve. Highly recommended is the 3.6-mile **Bluff Trail** that starts from a small parking area at the end of Ebey Rd. The energetic can walk or cycle here from Coupeville (approximately 2.5 miles along a quiet road), thus crossing the island at one of its narrowest points.

At the reserve's southern end is **Fort Casey State Park**, with facilities for camping and picnicking. Fort Casey was part of the early 1900s military defense system that once guarded the entrance to Puget Sound. Visitors can investigate the old cement batteries and underground tunnels that line the coast. Other recreational activities here include scuba diving, boating and bird-watching – best along Keystone Spit on the southwestern tip of Crockett Lake. **Admiralty Head Lighthouse**, built in 1861, houses the park's interpretive center. From here, it's a 4-mile walk north along the beach to **Fort Ebey State Park**, a wonderfully secluded spot with eroded cliffs and old WWII-era coast defenses, where further trails meander off into the surrounding woodland.

Fort Casey State Park offers 38 **campsites** overlooking Keystone Harbor, and Fort Ebey has 53 sites ($21) plus four with RV hookups ($28). Facilities include flush toilets and running water.

A unique lodging option is **Fort Casey Inn** ([image]360-678-8792; www.fortcaseyinn.com; 1124 S Engle Rd; r $165). The inn consists of a series of five c 1909 houses that served as WWI officers' quarters and are now rented as overnight accommodations (the rooms sleep up to four guests). Perched on a bluff overlooking the lighthouse at Fort Casey, the houses have restful porches with oak armchairs.

LANGLEY
POP 959

Langley, like Coupeville, is a tiny seafront community that is little changed since the late 19th century. Encased in an attractive historic center are small cafés, antique furniture shops, funky clothing boutiques and a couple of decent B&Bs. While there's little to do here activity-wise, Langley provides a perfect antidote to the hustle and bustle of nearby Seattle and is a great place to relax and unwind, after numerous hours packed bumper-to-bumper on I-5.

Langley is 8 miles north of Clinton and the ferry service from Mukilteo, making this the closest of the Whidbey Island communities to the urban areas of northern Seattle.

🛏 Sleeping & Eating

Eagles Nest Inn　　　　　　　B&B **$$**
(✆360-221-5331; www.eaglesnestinn.com; 4680 E Saratoga Rd; r $150-195) A unique octagonal house located on a forested hill, the Eagle's Nest is a veritable B&B gem even by Whidbey Island's high standards. Four lovingly furnished rooms blend perfectly with their natural surroundings, while luxurious extras such as locally roasted coffee, aromatherapy shampoos, private lounge (with piano) and well-stocked cookie jar add a memorable touch. The property is adjoined by 400 acres of public trails.

Inn at Langley　　　　　　　　INN **$$$**
(✆360-221-3033; www.innatlangley.com; 400 1st St; r incl breakfast $290-595; ❈🐾) This contemporary, condo-esque inn is the trendsetter in style and expense. The 26 beautifully furnished waterfront rooms have large windows, whirlpool tubs and fireplaces. A full-service spa provides Swedish massage and seaweed body masks, plus there's a fine-dining restaurant serving six-course meals. There's just the small matter of the cost.

Cafe Langley　　　　　　MEDITERRANEAN **$$**
(www.cafelangley.com; 113 1st St; lunch under $10, dinner $11-17) Ah, at last: some choice Mediterranean cuisine, with a few deft Northwest seafood infusions (eg mussels) thrown in for good measure. There are some amazing lamb options here (at least

five), an Andalusian steak, Italian pasta, Greek moussaka and a memorable sweet, sticky baklava for dessert. Delicioso!

SAN JUAN ISLANDS
POP 12,400

Leafy hedgerows, soporific settlements and winding lanes jammed with more cyclists than cars. Where the heck are you? Not in continental America, surely. The answer is both 'yes' and 'no.' The San Juan Islands, a nebulous archipelago of approximately 172 landfalls, islets and eagle perches that lie splayed between the mouth of Puget Sound and Vancouver Island, conjure up images of a sleepy American throwback where the clock last chimed in the 1970s, '60s or even '50s, depending on where you dock. Sharing a jagged watery border with Canada, it's also where the 'special relationship' between Britain and the US got distinctly tetchy in 1858 over a ridiculously overblown dispute about a dead pig (the two countries nearly went to war). These days peace, not war, is the archipelago's greatest hallmark in communities where cars are left unlocked, motorists offer salutary waves, and shopping malls remain a ghostly mainland apparition. Don't come for the Starbucks and casinos (there aren't any); come instead for the fishing, whale-watching, beachcombing, hiking, cycling, paddling, crabbing, clamming, philosophizing and memorable, psychedelic sunsets.

ℹ Information

For general information about the San Juans, contact the **San Juan Islands Visitors Bureau** (www.guidetosanjuans.com; The Technology Center, 640 Mullis St, Bldg A, Ste 210/215, San Juan Island; ⊙10am-2pm Mon-Fri). Its website provides links to numerous San Juan businesses and organizations. In addition, the chambers of commerce of San Juan, Orcas and Lopez Islands maintain their own visitor walk-in information centers – see those sections for details.

ℹ Getting There & Away

AIR Two airlines fly from the mainland to the San Juans. **Kenmore Air** (www.kenmoreair. com) flies from Lake Union and Lake Washington to Lopez, Orcas and San Juan Islands daily on three- to 10-person seaplanes. Fares start at $75 one way. **San Juan Airlines** (www. sanjuanairlines.com) flies from Anacortes and

On paper it sounds like an oxymoron (unless you've mastered the art of walking on water) but, in practice, it's one of the most unique long-distance odysseys in the United States.

The Cascadia Marine Trail (CMT) is a 160-mile saltwater sailing/paddling route starting in Olympia and finishing at the Canadian-US border that links more than 50 specially designated campsites and 30 or more waterside inns in a spectacular aquatic journey through Washington's sheltered inland seas. Conceived in 1993 by the Washington Water Trails Association (WWTA), a group of avid kayakers from the Seattle area, the trail is designed to be used by wind- or human-powered water craft making use of myriad campsites en route, spaced approximately 5 to 8 miles apart.

The San Juan Islands make up one of the most popular segments of the trail, with many of the archipelago's outlying state parks sporting rustic CMT campsites (maximum capacity 16 people) equipped with landing areas, picnic tables, toilets (usually 'compost-style') and official CMT signs (the sites are checked regularly by volunteer stewards). Other popular stop-offs are Whidbey Island, Port Townsend and Blake Island near Seattle.

For a comprehensive trail guidebook you'll need to become a member of **WWTA** (www.wwta.org).

In 2000 the CMT was chosen by the White House as one of only 16 'National Millennium Trails' reflecting 'defining aspects of America's history and culture.'

Bellingham to the three main islands (one way/return $53/106)

BOAT The majority of people who visit the San Juans arrive on **Washington State Ferries** (WSF; www.wsdot.wa.gov/ferries), which runs a fleet of comfortable and efficient car ferries. The main port on the mainland is Anacortes; ferries for the four principal islands of Lopez, Shaw, Orcas and San Juan depart from here. From April to December, two Washington State Ferries a day continue on to Sidney, near Victoria on Vancouver Island, before returning in the opposite direction. There is no US–Canada service from January to March.

You can pick up an easy-to-decipher WSF timetable at any ferry outlet or access it on the website. The timetable varies depending on the season, but follows a standard route of Anacortes–Lopez (45 minutes), then Shaw (one hour), Orcas (70 minutes), Friday Harbor (80 minutes) and Sidney (three hours). Four or five ferries a day are inter-island, in that they don't call at either Sidney or Anacortes.

Fares are collected on west-bound ferries only. They are $12.15 for foot passengers to any destination except Sidney, which is $16.14. Car fares range from $33.15 (Lopez) to $55.10 (Sidney). Bike passengers pay a $4 surcharge. Foot passengers and cyclists can ride inter-island ferries for free in either direction.

You can only reserve tickets for the Sidney sailing. All other ferries operate on a first-come, first-served basis. In winter, drivers are advised to arrive 45 minutes before sailing; in summer, two hours.

There are three additional privately owned passenger-only ferries (no cars) that travel to the San Juans:

Puget Sound Express (www.pugetsound express.com) Runs from Port Townsend to Friday Harbor from March to September.

Victoria Clipper (www.victoriaclipper.com) A Seattle–Friday Harbor link, with service on to Victoria, BC. It only runs from late June to late September.

Victoria San Juan Cruises (www.whales.com; 355 Harris Ave, ste 104, Bellingham) Operates between Bellingham, San Juan Island, Orcas and Victoria from May to September.

San Juan Island

POP 6894

The most exciting aspects of the archipelago's history have been preserved on San Juan Island (how does a near war between Britain and the US grab you?) in a couple of old military camps. It is also the only island to register anything approaching a town; compact Friday Harbour acts as the archipelago's unofficial capital. Other San Juan Island highlights include sheltered Roche Harbor and blustery Lime Kiln Point State Park, where you can whale-watch from the shoreline overlooking deep Haro Strait.

The ferry terminal is at Friday Harbor, on the eastern side of the island. The main route south from here is Cattle Point Rd, while Beaverton Valley Rd heads to the west coast. To get to Roche Harbor, take 2nd St to Guard St, then turn right on Tucker Ave; from there it's a 10-mile drive to the resort.

◎ Sights

San Juan Island National Historical Park
HISTORICAL PARK

More known for their scenery than their history, the San Juans nonetheless hide one of the 19th century's oddest political confrontations, the so-called 'Pig War' between the USA and Britain. This curious 19th-century cold war stand-off is showcased in two separate historical parks on either end of the island that once housed opposing American and English military encampments.

On the southern flank of the island, the **American Camp** hosts a small **visitors center** (admission free; ◎8:30am-4:30pm daily Jun-Sep, Thu-Sun Oct-May) and is a good place to start your historical excursion. Among the remnants of an old fort are the officers' quarters and a laundress' house, while a series of interpretive trails lead to earthwork fortifications, a British farm from the dispute era and desolate South Beach. The 1.8-mile hike along the ridge of Mt Finlayson makes for a pleasant hike with splendid views and unlimited bird-watching potential.

At the opposite end of the island, **English Camp**, 9 miles northwest of Friday Harbor, contains the remains of the British military facilities dating from the 1860s. A path from the parking area leads down to a handful of restored buildings that lie in an attractive setting overlooking Garrison Bay. Hikes from here lead to an old British cemetery and the top of 650ft Young Hill.

Lime Kiln Point State Park
STATE PARK

Clinging to the island's rocky west coast, this beautiful park overlooks the deep Haro Strait and is, reputedly, one of the best places in the world to view whales from the shoreline. There is a small **interpretive center** (🕿360-378-2044) in the park open from Memorial Day (last Monday in May) to Labor Day (first Monday in September), along with trails, a restored lime kiln and the landmark Lime Kiln lighthouse, built in 1919. Orca and minke whale sightings are more common in summer after the June salmon run. Offering exceptional views of Vancouver Island and the Olympic Mountains, the park is best enjoyed at sunset.

With a population of approximately 2000 people, Friday Harbor is the San Juan's only real town, with restaurants, shops and a couple of interesting museums providing enough diversions to fill a good morning's exploration. In recent years a growing contingent of realty offices has added disquiet. But realtors aside, Friday Harbor is still a low-key, pedestrian-friendly kind of place where the worst kind of hassle you're likely to face is an uneven paving stone.

If you've only got time for one sight, be sure to pop into the **Whale Museum** (www. whale-museum.org; 62 1st St; adult/child $6/3; ◎10am-5pm; 🖝), a small but cleverly arranged display space dedicated to the life of the orca (killer whale), which has become something of a San Juan Island mascot. Among whale skeletons and life-size models of orcas, there are eloquent DVD presentations, interactive maps and details of local research projects, all of which will teach you everything you need to know about these magnificent but cruelly misunderstood sea mammals.

In an 1890s farmhouse on the outskirts of town, the **San Juan Historical Museum** (www.sjmuseum.org; 405 Price St; adult/child $5/3; ◎10am-4pm Thu-Sat, 1-4pm Sun May-Sep) commemorates early pioneer life on San Juan Island. While the building itself is interesting for its vernacular architecture, the displays of kitchen and parlor furnishings – like the pump organ and massive wood range – are also worth checking out. Open afternoons only in the winter.

San Juan Vineyards   WINERY
(www.sanjuanvineyards.com; 3136 Roche Harbor Rd; ◎11am-5pm) Washington's unlikeliest winery has a tasting room in an old schoolhouse built in 1896. Open-minded tasters should try the Siegerrebe and Madeleine Angevine varieties.

🏃 Activities

For kayaking and cycling information, see p104.

Fishing

Fishing trips for black bass and tiger rockfish can be arranged through **Trophy Charters** (www.fishthesanjuans.com), which does half-day fishing tours aboard a 29ft sport fisher from $95 per person.

Whale-Watching

Western Prince Cruises (www.orca whalewatch.com; 1 Spaing St, Friday Harbor) is

San Juan Islands

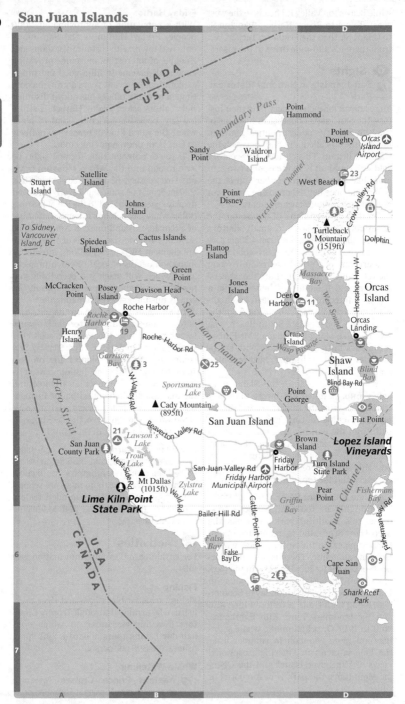

CANADA
USA

Boundary Pass

Point Hammond

Point Doughty

Orcas Island Airport

Sandy Point

Waldron Island

West Beach 23

27

Stuart Island

Satellite Island

Johns Island

Point Disney

President Channel

8

To Sidney, Vancouver Island, BC

Spieden Island

Cactus Islands

Flattop Island

Green Point

Jones Island

10

Turtleback Mountain (1519ft)

Dolphin

Massacre Bay

Orcas Island

McCracken Point

Posey Island

Davison Head

Deer Harbor 11

West Sound

Horseshoe Hwy W

Roche Harbor

Roche Harbor

19

Henry Island

Roche Harbor Rd

San Juan Channel

Crane Island

Wasp Passage

Orcas Landing

Garrison Bay

3

25

4

Shaw Island

Blind Bay

W Valley Rd

Sportsmans Lake

Point George

6

Blind Bay Rd

Haro Strait

Cady Mountain (895ft)

San Juan Island

5

Flat Point

21

Lawson's Lake

Beaverton Valley Rd

Brown Island

Lopez Island Vineyards

San Juan County Park

Trout Lake

San Juan Valley Rd

Friday Harbor

Turn Island State Park

Mt Dallas (1015ft)

Zylstra Lake

Friday Harbor Municipal Airport

Pear Point

Fisherman Bay

West Side Rd

Wold Rd

Lime Kiln Point State Park

Bailer Hill Rd

Cattle Point Rd

Griffin Bay

San Juan Channel

Fisherman Bay Rd

CANADA
USA

False Bay

False Bay Dr

18

2

Cape San Juan

9

Shark Reef Park

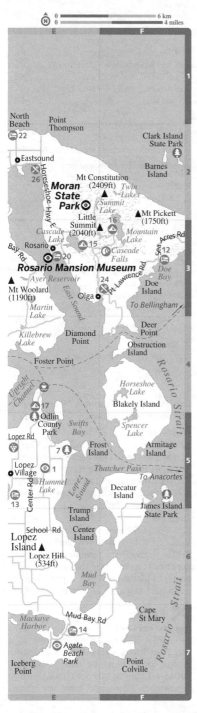

the San Juan Islands' oldest whale-watching tour company and its year-round ecofriendly excursions keep an eye out for eagles, seals and porpoises as well as the formidable orcas. Tours on the *Western Prince,* which accommodates up to 30 people, depart daily from June to August (adult/child $76/49), less often and less expensively in spring and fall. You can make reservations via its website or visit the office right next to the ferry dock in Friday Harbor.

🛏 Sleeping

TOP CHOICE Earthbox Motel & Spa

BOUTIQUE MOTEL **$$$**

(☑360-378-4000; www.earthboxmotel.com; 410 Spring St; r from $197; ❄📶) Reaching out to retro-lovers, Earthbox styles itself as a 'boutique motel,' a hybrid of simplicity and sophistication that has taken a former motor inn and embellished it with features more commonly associated with a deluxe hotel. The result: a variety of funky, cleverly designed rooms with iPod docking stations, comfy beds and colorful yet minimalist undercurrents. Other bonuses include a pool, spa, fitness room, bike rental and fine gardens. The only downside is the prices – which aren't very motel-like.

Roche Harbor Resort

RESORT **$$**

(☑800-451-8910; www.rocheharbor.com; Roche Harbor; r with shared bathroom $139, 1-3 bedroom condos $269-379, 2-bedroom townhouses $499; ❄📶🐾) Located on the site of the former lime kiln and country estate of limestone king John McMillin, this seaside 'village' is a great getaway for all budgets. The centerpiece of the resort is the old world Hotel de Haro, where the pokey rooms and shared bathrooms are enlivened by the fact that John Wayne once brushed his teeth here. Brand-new townhouses are stacked up behind the harbor, and modern condominiums are discreetly tucked behind a stand of trees. Waterfront restaurants, a 377-berth marina with boat rentals, a new spa and an old dockside general store make the place pretty self-contained.

Olympic Lights B&B

B&B **$$**

(☑360-378-3186; www.olympiclightsbnb.com; 146 Starlight Way; r $150-160) Once the centerpiece of a 320-acre estate, this splendidly restored 1895 farmhouse now hosts an equally formidable B&B that stands on an open bluff facing the snow-coated Olympic Mountains. The four rooms are imaginatively named Garden, Ra, Heart and

Olympic; sunflowers adorn the garden and the hearty breakfasts include homemade buttermilk biscuits. The wintertime room rates are a relative bargain at $105.

Friday Harbor House HOTEL $$$
(☑360-378-8455; www.fridayharborhouse.com; 130 West St; r without/with view $215/300; ❄☎) The town's most exclusive lodging is a modern boutique hotel with great views over the harbor. All 20 rooms have a fireplace, open-plan bathroom/Jacuzzi tub and other upscale niceties, and the whole place exudes a surgical level of cleanliness.

San Juan County Park Campground
CAMPGROUND $
(☑360-378-1842; 380 West Side Rd; hiker/cyclist sites per person $10, campsites $32) San Juan's best campground is beautifully located in a county park on the scenic western shoreline. The site includes a beach and boat launch, along with 20 pitches, flush toilets and picnic tables. At night the lights of Victoria, BC, flicker theatrically from across

the Haro Strait. Reservations are mandatory during peak season.

Wayfarer's Rest HOSTEL $
(☑360-378-6428; 35 Malcolm St; dm/r $30/70) The archipelago's only backpacker's hostel is a short hike from the ferry terminal. Budget travelers will love its comfortable dorms and cheap private rooms but beware – it gets busy.

Orca Inn MOTEL $$
(☑877-541-6722; www.oracinnwa.com; 770 Mullis St; r $84-99; ❄) Seven blocks from Friday Harbor ferry terminal, the budget Orca is more motel than inn, with a barracks-like atmosphere. If price is your main parameter, it's an acceptable option.

✕ Eating

Market Chef DELI $
(225 A St; ☉10am-6pm) Welcome to a San Juan Island legend that's well known among locals plus the odd in-the-know outsider. Eat-in or takeout options such as sandwiches, salads and tacos are rustled

up rapidly and come with unusual infusions. All are made with local ingredients. The only downside is that you might have to fight for a place to sit – it's that popular.

Duck Soup Inn
FUSION **$$$**

(📞360-378-4878; www.ducksoupinn.com; 50 Duck Soup Lane; mains $32-35; ⊙Apr-Oct) It ain't cheap, but it's good. Situated 4 miles northwest of Friday Harbor amid woods and water, Duck Soup offers possibly the best island fine dining using its own herb garden to enhance menu items such as oysters, scallops and – best of all – Blueberry Habanero Chicken. The extensive wine list includes an island-produced chardonnay... if you dare.

McMillin's
SEAFOOD **$$$**

(📞360-378-5757; Roche Harbor; mains $18-26; ⊙5-10pm) Set in the former house of lime and cement entrepreneur John McMillin, this intimate dining room offers the best of Pacific Rim cooking. Favorites include hazelnut-crusted halibut, local spot prawns and Dungeness crab ravioli.

Doctor's Office
CAFÉ **$**

(www.do-café.com; 85 Front St; ⊙4:30am-10pm; @🛜) Break up the boredom of a long ferry line-up in the portside Doctor's Office, where the best 'prescriptions' are locally roasted coffee, hot soups, sandwiches and – best of all – homemade ice cream. And where else opens at 4.30am 365 days a year?

Lime Kiln Cafe
DINER **$**

(Roche Harbor; mains $6-10; ⊙8am-2pm) Perched on the end of the Roche Harbor marina wharf, this simple but pleasurable establishment serves up mouthwatering American breakfasts that feature organic eggs in a hearty San Juan scramble with avocado and sour cream. The lunch menu offers deli sandwiches. Even better, fresh home-cooked doughnuts are served all day.

Golden Triangle Thai Kitchen
THAI **$$**

(42 1st St; mains $13-19) Thai food? On an island? Sure it's not Ko Samui? Living proof that San Juan can go ethnic; the casual Thai Kitchen is where huge portions go a long way.

Hungry Clam
SEAFOOD **$**

(130 1st St; seafood baskets $6-9; ⊙11am-7pm) A good option if you've got a long wait for your ferry ride but, while the fish 'n' chips here aren't bad, they're not really worthy of their 'world famous' boast.

🍸 Drinking

Front Street Ale House & San Juan Brewing Company
BREWPUB **$$**

(1 Front St; mains $10-17; ⊙11am-11pm Mon-Thu, 11am-midnight Fri & Sat) The island's only brewery serves up British-style beers, including Royal Marine IPA, in a real spit-and-sawdust–style pub. Traditional pub grub features shepherd's pie and bangers and mash, and it ain't 'arf bad (as they say in London).

ℹ Information

Chamber of Commerce (Spring St) Inside a small arcade; a good place to pick up free maps and other information.

ℹ Getting Around

From May to October, **San Juan Transit** (www. sanjuantransit.com) shuttles visitors from the ferry landing to Roche Harbor, plus points along the west coast, including Lime Kiln Point State Park and the English Camp. Buses run hourly between 10am and 6pm (round trip $8, day pass $15). Otherwise, call **San Juan Taxi** (📞360-378-3550).

Susie's Mopeds (125 Nichols St), just up from the ferry dock, rents mopeds at $25 an hour or $62.50 a day, or Geo Tracker jeeps from $96 a day.

Orcas Island
POP 4593

Orcas is a special island. More rugged than Lopez yet less crowded than San Juan Island, it has struck a delicate balance between friendliness and frostiness, development and preservation, tourist dollars and priceless privacy – for the time being at least.

Lying in the dry rain shadow of the storm-lashed Olympic Mountains, the island was once an important trading post for the North Straits Salish Native Americans, who maintained a permanent settlement in present-day West Sound. The first European homesteaders arrived in the 1860s and within a couple of years they had set about clearing the old-growth rain forest for crops and fruit orchards. Another early industrial project was lime production, and by the early 20th century 35 lime kilns dotted the island, burning huge amounts of local wood.

The growth of tourism is a distinctly modern development and an inevitable consequence of Orcas' refreshing get-away-from-it-all location. Former Seattle mayor, Robert Moran, opened the doors to the deluge in the early 1900s when he constructed

THE SAN JUANS BY HUMAN-POWER

From 1-acre Posey Island to 57-sq-mile Orcas Island, the San Juans aren't large, meaning you don't need a 210 horsepower V6 engine to get around. Instead, a leg-powered bicycle or an arm-powered kayak will easily do the job.

The biking is memorable on all three main islands (and Shaw if you're up for a short circuit). Lopez Island is the most popular with cyclists thanks to its flat-ish terrain and salutation-offering local motorists (there are bike racks outside almost every shop and business). San Juan Island's roads are a little busier but no less alluring, while hilly Orcas offers the biggest challenge for aspiring cyclists, with the 5-mile-long drag to the top of 2406ft Mt Constitution worthy of a miniature 'King of the Mountains' competition. All three islands have bike rentals that can deliver cycles to the ferry terminal during peak months. Hire fees are approximately $7.50/30 per hour/day. Contact:

Island Bicycles (www.islandbicylces.com; 380 Argyle Ave) Friday Harbor, San Juan Island.

Lopez Bicycle Works (www.lopezbicycleworks.com; 2847 Fisherman Bay Rd; ☺May-Sep) Lopez Island.

Wildlife Cycles (www.wildlifecycles.com; 350 North Beach Rd, Eastsound) Orcas Island.

Off-land the islands are navigable via the complicated web of sea channels that lie between them. Kayaking away from the coast can be challenging, with strong winds, riptides and ever-changing weather; join an organized trip or stick to the sheltered shorelines and coves if you're unsure. More experienced kayakers can progress along the Cascadia Marine Trail (see p98). Kayak rentals and organized trips (three hours from $65) can be organized at the following:

Cascadia Kayak & Bike (www.cascadiakayakandbike.com; 135 Lopez Rd) Lopez Island.

San Juan Kayak Expeditions (☑360-378-4436; www.sanjuankayak.com; Friday Harbor) San Juan Island.

Shearwater Adventures (☑360-376-4699; www.shearwaterkayaks.com; 138 North Beach Rd, Eastsound) Orcas Island.

a Xanadu-like mansion, the Rosario (now a hotel), overlooking the shimmering waters of East Sound. He subsequently donated large tracts of his private land to create Moran State Park.

◉ Sights & Activities

TOP CHOICE **Moran State Park** STATE PARK
(☺6:30am-dusk Apr-Sep, 8am-dusk Oct-Mar) In 1911, Moran donated 7 sq miles of his property to create this park on the island's eastern saddlebag. The park, which has enough attractions to consume the best part of a day, is dominated by 2409ft **Mt Constitution**, the archipelago's highest point and a mountain with the grandeur of a peak twice its size. To say that the view from the summit is jaw-dropping would be an understatement. On a clear day you can see Mt Rainier, Mt Baker, Vancouver's north shore and a patchwork of tree-carpeted islands floating like emerald jewels on a blue crystalline ocean. To see above the lofty firs a 53ft **observation tower** was

erected in 1936 by the Civilian Conservation Corp.

For drivers, the mountain has a paved road to the summit, though the view is infinitely better if you earn it via a 4.3-mile hike up from Cascade Lake's North End Campground or a 5-mile cycle that begins just past Cascade Lake. Beginners beware: the grade is a persistent 7% (7ft vertical rise for every horizontal 100ft) with frequent hairpin turns.

The park's two major bodies of water, **Cascade Lake** and **Mountain Lake**, offer campgrounds, good trout fishing, rentable paddle boats and rowboats, picnic areas and swimming beaches. The lakes are also ringed by hiking trails and linked via a pleasant wooded ramble that passes the spectacular 100ft-high **Cascade Falls**.

Of the more than 30 miles of trails in Moran State Park, about half are open seasonally for mountain biking and one or two for horses. Get a trail map from the park headquarters at the southern end of Cascade Lake.

Orcas Island Historical Museum MUSEUM

(www.oracsmuseum.org; 181 North Beach Rd, Eastsound; admission $5; ⊙10am-4pm Tue-Sun late May-late Sep) Housed in a series of six original homesteader cabins dating from the 1880s, this island museum relates the pioneer and local history of Orcas and the San Juan Islands. Besides the usual collection of household goods, tools, weapons and photographs, there's a history of the lime-kiln industry and a focus on Orcas' first residents, the North Straits Salish.

FREE Rosario Mansion Museum MUSEUM

(Rosario Resort; ⊙9am-8pm) Set in the eponymous resort, these rooms tell the life and times of former Seattle mayor, shipbuilder and groundbreaking environmentalist Robert Moran, who lived here from 1906 until 1938. Look out for the ship memorabilia and the huge custom-made organ.

Turtleback Mountain Preserve

NATURE RESERVE

Saved from possible development when it was bought for $18.5 million as public land in 2007, Orcas' second mountain (rising to 1519ft) was in private hands for so long that most people had forgotten what was there. The answer: fragile wetlands, Garry Oak savannah, spectacular overlooks, wild orchids and acres of solitude. It now has trails open to hikers (daily) and bikers/horse-riders (alternate days). There are two trailheads; one on Crow Valley Rd, the other on Wild Rose Lane near Deer Harbor.

Horse-trail riding on the mountain is run out of nearby **Turtlehead Farm** (www.turtleheadfarm.com; 231 Lime Quarry Rd; 🏇) for $48 an hour. It also offers half-day horse-riding programs for kids ($60).

Boating & Whale-Watching WATER ACTIVITIES

Deer Harbor Charters (www.deer

harborcharters.com; Deer Harbor Resort) offers year-round whale-watching trips departing from either Deer Harbor or the Rosario resort. The boats run on biodiesel and sightings of orca and minke whales are common. Prices are $52/69 low/high season for a half-day cruise.

Orcas Boat Rentals (☎360-376-7616; www.orcasboats.com) at Deer Harbor Marina has powerboats and sailboats from $250 per half-day.

🛏 Sleeping

Fear not. An Orcas 'resort' is a quiet, modest place; nothing like the beachside all-inclusives of Cancun or Puerto Vallarta. There are also numerous private rentals available – see www.orcasislandchamber.com for details. Book well ahead in July and August when the island is insanely popular.

Rosario Resort & Spa RESORT $$

(☎360-376-2222; www.rosario-resort.com; Rosario Way; d/ste from $129/229; ❄️🛜♨️🏊) This magnificent seafront mansion built by former shipbuilding magnate Robert Moran in 1904 is now the centerpiece of an upscale resort, though the setting has lost none of its F Scott Fitzgerald–style romance. While the old mansion remains the resort's centerpiece, the 180 modern rooms sprawled across the surrounding grounds retain deft design touches and the complex includes tennis courts, a swimming pool, a marina and elaborately tiled spa facilities.

Outlook Inn HOTEL $$$

(☎360-376-2200; www.outlookinn.com; Main St, Eastsound; r with shared bathroom $99, motel r $199, ste $329) Eastsound's oldest and most eye-catching building, the Outlook Inn (1888) is an island institution that has kept up with the times by expanding into a small bayside complex. The cheapest rooms have shared bathrooms, while all rooms in the motel-style east building have ensuites. The positively luxurious bay-view suites boast Jacuzzi tubs. Also onsite is the rather fancy New Leaf Cafe.

Doe Bay Village Resort & Retreat

CABIN RESORT $

(☎360-376-2291; www.doebay.com; hostel dm $55, cabin d from $90, yurts from $120; 🛜) There are resorts, and then there's Doe Bay, 18 miles east of Eastsound on the island's easternmost shore – as lovely a spot as any on Orcas. By far the least expensive resort in the San Juans, Doe Bay has the atmosphere of an artists' commune cum hippie retreat cum New Age center. Accommodations include campsites, a small hostel with dormitory and private rooms, and various cabins and yurts, most with views of the water. There's also a natural-foods store, a café, yoga classes ($10), an organic garden and special discounts for guests who arrive by bike. The sauna and clothing-optional hot tub are set apart on one side of a creek.

Deer Harbor Resort & Marina RESORT $$$

(☎888-376-4480; www.deerharbor.org; cottages $189-259, ste $209-399) Nearly every building in this little hamlet, set alongside one of the island's loveliest harbors, is for rent, ranging from motel-style bungalows to quaint old-fashioned cottages, all featuring deck-top hot tubs. Boat and bike rentals, tennis courts and a small restaurant and market are all on the premises.

Orcas Hotel
HOTEL **$**

(☎360-376-4300; www.orcashotel.com; Orcas Landing; r with shared/private bathoom $89/134) One of the island's oldest structures, the Orcas hotel was built in 1904, ancient history by island standards. Refurbished in the 1990s, the rather pokey interior is like something from the pages of a stiff Jane Austin novel, with narrow corridors, patterned wallpaper and a carefully manicured garden. Perched on a bluff above the ferry terminal, there are a dozen smallish rooms here, along with a restaurant and a small coffee/sandwich bar. While not in the luxury bracket it has a certain Old World vitality.

Orcas Suites at Rosario
APARTMENTS **$$**

(☎360-376-6262; www.orcassuites.com; r/ste $129/279; ❀☀) Routinely overlooked, these plush suites on a bluff above the Rosario are pitched at decidedly unplush prices. Fabulous one-bedroom apartments come with full kitchens and extra Murphy beds and hide-a-beds.

West Beach Resort
CABIN RESORT **$$**

(☎1-877-937-8224; www.westbeachresort.com; cottages from $189) Welcome to another rustic cabin-resort with its own shop, café and marina on Orcas' shimmering waterfront. This one is on the west shore facing Waldron Island and crimson Canadian sunsets.

Moran State Park
CAMPGROUND **$**

(☎360-376-2326; hiker/cyclist sites $14, camp-sites $21) The largest camping area in the San Juans has more than 150 campsites (no hookups) at four lakeside locations: one at Mountain Lake and three at Cascade Lake. Reservations are a must in summer.

Smuggler's Villa Resort
RESORT **$$**

(☎360-376-2297; www.smuggler.com; N Beach Rd; 6-person townhouses $299; ☀☀) A little windswept and on the north shore, this small complex comprises 20 reasonably sized holiday houses right on the beach. Family-orientated facilities include an outdoor pool and tennis court.

✖ Eating

You'll find a surprising variety of good eating places in the small settlement of East-sound. Elsewhere there are restaurants and cafés in Doe Bay, Olga, Rosario, Deer Harbor and Orcas Village.

TOP CHOICE Bilbo's Festivo
MEXICAN **$$**

(310 A St, Eastsound; mains from $14; ☺4-9pm) Even if Mexican isn't your *fuerte,* it's difficult to go wrong in this funky outdoor-indoor restaurant with its rustic Mexican furnishings and fairy-lit garden slap bang in the middle of Eastsound. Try the generous dinner platters that come with refried beans, homemade guacamole, warm tortillas and some of the best enchiladas you'll taste this side of – oh – Seattle. Beware, there's a wide selection of margaritas.

✎ Inn at Ship Bay
SEAFOOD **$$$**

(☎360-376-5886; www.innatshipbay.com; 326 Olga Rd; mains $17-22; ☺5:30-11pm Tue-Sat) It ain't cheap but the locals reserve big kudos for this upmarket place that quite possibly offers some of the best fare on the island. Seafood is the specialty and it's served in an attractive 1860s orchard house a couple of miles south of Eastsound. There's also an on-site 11-room hotel (doubles $175 to $195).

New Leaf Cafe
MODERN **$$$**

(☎360-376-2200; Main St, Eastsound; mains $24-32; ☺5:30-11pm Thu-Mon) Two words: crab cakes. Throw in some ginger-pear butter and a bit of habanero cream and you might want to think about canceling your ferry till next week. The New Leaf is the island's most successful attempt at fine dining. It's a little tough on the wallet but compliment those crab cakes with fondue and a formidable lamb shank and it might actually be worth the financial investment.

Enzo's Italian Caffè
CAFÉ **$**

(365 North Beach Rd, Eastsound; sandwiches $6-8; @❀) Enzo's allegedly does the best joe in town and accompanies it with a fine line in carrot cake and an even better one in gelati. If you're just off the ferry, you can remind yourself that you're still not too far from 'civilization' with a creamy crepe or a filling panini while tweeting all and sundry on your laptop (yes, the wi-fi's gratis).

Cafe Olga
CAFÉ **$$**

(Olga Rd, Olga; mains $9-11; ☺Mar-Dec) The definitive Orcas hangout is a quiet and isolated café-art gallery in the three-building settlement of Olga, on the island's secluded eastern saddlebag. Living up to the hype, the scones, cinnamon buns and pies here are stupendous and if you've just busted a gut cycling up and down Mt Constitution you'll probably want to invest in the calorific overload.

Passionate for Pies   PIES **$**
(460 Main St, Eastsound; ⊘9am-6pm Wed-Mon, 11am-6pm Sun) You *will* be after visiting this new Eastsound nook offering savory (roasted organic chicken) and sweet (coconut cream) pies concocted on the premises.

Sunflower Café   CAFÉ, SANDWICHES **$$**
(www.thesunflowercafe.com; cnr Main St & North Beach Rd, Eastsound; lunch $9-12; ⊘7:30am-3:30pm) Amid stiff competition, the Sunflower nails first prize in the best-baked-goods-on-the-island category, thanks primarily to its crispy bagels.

Mamie's Restaurant   DINER **$$**
(⊘7:30am-7:30pm) There are worse places to watch the boats come in than clapboard Mamie's, perched above the ferry dock in Orcas Landing with a menu anchored by burgers and fish 'n' chips.

Doe Bay Café   HOMESTYLE FOOD **$$**
(mains $14-26) Religiously sustainable, Doe Bay has its own organic garden and a tight network of trusted farm suppliers. Ever had pizza topped with locally 'foraged' mushrooms? Thought not.

🛍 Shopping

No malls, but some interesting local crafts might leave you departing with more than you arrived with.

Crow Valley Pottery & Gallery (www.crowvalley.com; Main St, Eastsound; ⊘10am-5pm) sells everything from jewelry to paintings, but its specialty is hand-painted pottery, all conceived and produced on the island. They also maintain a **cabin** (2274 Orcas Rd; ⊘10am-5pm May-Sep) exhibiting more pottery, glasswork and garden art.

ℹ Information

Orcas Island Chamber of Commerce (www.orcasisland.org; 120 North Beach Rd, Eastsound; ⊘10am-3pm Mon-Sat)

ℹ Getting Around

If you're not biking, the **Orcas Island Shuttle** (www.orcasislandshuttle.com) can meet most of your transport needs, arranging car rental (from $60), 24-hour taxis, and a May-to-September public bus (one way $6).

Lopez Island
POP 2590

While some of the smaller San Juans are known for their standoffish 'No Trespassing' signs, Lopez – or *Slow-pez* as it's sometimes known – is the ultimate friendly isle where local motorists give strangers the 'Lopezian wave' (two fingers raised from the steering wheel) and you can leave your bike outside the village store and it'll still have both wheels when you return several hours later.

Though less well set-up for tourism than its two more populous neighbors, Lopez's tight-knit community and well-organized infrastructure offer a surprisingly varied selection of campgrounds and B&Bs. Lopez village is the island's centerpiece, a pin-prick of a settlement that holds a weekly summer farmers market and boasts a couple of enterprising restaurants. Lopez Island Vineyards showcases the island's local wine production.

Every April Lopez stages the ironically named **Tour de Lopez**, a laid-back noncompetitive cycle race where winning is incidental. The balloons are out again on July 4, when the island temporarily breaks out of its sleepy stupor to host what is, allegedly, the state's most electrifying **firework display**.

◉ Sights

Lopez Island Historical Museum   MUSEUM
(www.lopezmuseum.org; Lopez Village; ⊘noon-4pm May-Sep) This tiny museum exhibits antiquated farm machinery, early pioneer photos and various rotating exhibitions. What it lacks in scale it makes up for in charm.

Spencer Spit State Park   STATE PARK
One of only four state parks on the San Juan archipelago. Two sand spits have formed a marshy lagoon that is a prime spot for various species of waterfowl. It's a good place to kayak, fish and beachcomb.

Lopez Island Vineyards   WINE TASTING
(www.lopezislandvineyards.com; 724 Fisherman Bay Rd; ⊘noon-5pm Fri & Sat May-Sep) It's been making wines from grapes grown organically on the island since 1987. Napa Valley it ain't, but you can drop by in the summer to sample its Madeleine Angevine and Siegerrebe varieties.

Port Stanley Schoolhouse   HISTORICAL BUILDING
The restored 1917 schoolhouse is run by the local historical society and offers a

THE OUTLYING ISLANDS

Stand on the clamorous ferry dock at Anacortes during the halcyon summer months and you'll quickly realize that you're not the only one with designs on the San Juans' beauty. But don't get dragged down by the crowds. Ninety-nine percent of these vociferous vacationers are heading to one of the big four – San Juan, Orcas, Lopez or Shaw. A quick bit of mental arithmetic will reveal that this leaves approximately 168 islands largely tourist-free. Granted, many of the lesser San Juans are privately owned and/or hard to reach, but with a bit of furtive planning, genuine Robinson Crusoe experiences are possible, especially in the spring and fall. Here's a quick rundown of the options.

Other Inhabited Islands

The fourth-largest San Juan, **Cypress Island** (pop 40) has a salmon hatchery, 25 miles of trails and is a popular kayaking destination, while **Waldron Island** (pop 104) – perhaps the quirkiest island of all – is inhabited by a feisty contingent of back-to-the-landers who live without electricity or landline phones and are well known for their self-sufficiency. Two of the more visited 'populated' islands are **Stuart Island** (pop 40) and **Sucia Island** (pop 4). Stuart, the last landfall before Canada, has a schoolhouse, a light station, 3.5 miles of trails, 18 campsites and an unmanned 'honesty store' where you can buy souvenir T-shirts. Sucia (whose name means 'dirty' in Spanish, though it's anything but) is easily accessed by a March-to-November private ferry from Orcas and has a large state park, 60 campsites, access to drinking water and 10 miles of hiking trails.

Uninhabited Islands & Marine State Parks

Remoter still are the uninhabited islands, many of which are designated state parks or earmarked as pit-stops on the Cascadia Marine Trail (see p98). Recommended are

» **Matia Island** (145 acres) – six campsites and a short loop trail that between 1892 and 1921 was home to US Civil War veteran, Elvin A Smith, aka the 'Hermit of Matia Island.'

» **Patos Island** (207 acres) Seven campsites and a light station.

» **Jones Island** (188 acres) Has 24 campsites and a herd of resident black-tail deer.

» **James Island** (113 acres) Has 13 campsites, great for crabbing.

» **Posey Island** (1 acre) Two campsites, renowned for its crimson sunsets and beautiful wildflowers.

Outlying Islands (www.outerislandx.com) on Orcas Island can organize various trips and boat transfers to the outlying San Juans. Phone ☎360-376-3711 or check out the website. Alternatively, you can visit with your own boat/kayak. Primitive campsites generally cost $19 per night.

good photo op. To get to the schoolhouse from Lopez Village, take the road east past Hummel Lake. Turn left at the T-junction and follow the road around.

Activities

Skippered day and overnight fishing trips are available from **Harmony Charters** (www.harmonycharters.com; 973 Shark Reef Rd) and **Kismet Sailing Charters** (☎360-468-2435), both of which operate out of Fisherman Bay. Visitors select from a number of organized packages, or they can schedule individualized tours or cruises. Harmony Charters does lunch cruises on a 63ft yacht or an overnight cruise with meals and chef (per person $325).

For cycling and kayaking opportunities, see the boxed text, p104.

Sleeping

MacKaye Harbor Inn B&B $$$
(☎360-468-2253; www.mackayeharborinn.com; 949 MacKaye Harbor Rd; r $175-235; ☎) Relatively isolated on Lopez's southern reaches, this 1927 farmhouse contains four

bedrooms and one harbor-view suite and regularly gets good press. The cheap kayak rental and complimentary mountain bikes make it one of the best deals on the island.

Lopez Islander Resort
RESORT $$
(☑800-736-3434; www.lopezfun.com; Fisherman Bay Rd; s/d/ste $90/129/249; ⊛ ⊛) Equipped with a full-service restaurant, swimming pool, Jacuzzi and gym, this bona fide 're-sort' sits alongside a 64-slip marina in Fisherman Bay, where sea planes soar and eagles glide. Rooms run the gamut of sin-gles, views, deluxe, suites and bungalows. What it lacks in intimacy it makes up for in amiability and good service. The resort offers free parking spots for guests at the Anacortes ferry terminal.

Odlin County Park Campground
CAMPGROUND $
(☑360-378-1842; 148 Odlin Rd; hiker/cyclist sites $20, campsites $22) Handily situated a mile south of the ferry landing and 3 miles north of Lopez Village, this pleasant waterfront campground features a picnic area, vault toilets and mooring buoys. There is an ad-jacent sandy beach, and hiking trails disap-pear off into the surrounding woods.

Edenwild Inn
B&B $$$
(☑360-468-3238; www.edenwildinn.com; Lopez Rd, Lopez Village; r $170-195) Eden is the word at this Victorian-style mansion in Lopez Village with its lovely formal gardens, wide porch and meticulous attention to detail. Encased in what must be the island's most sumptuous setting are eight individually crafted rooms, all with private bathrooms. All of the island's low-key facilities are with-in shouting distance.

✖ Eating
In keeping with their salutary 'waves,' Lo-pezians are congenial and hospitable peo-ple who are always happy to engage visitors in casual chit-chat. Hang around in one of the village's small cafés and you'll soon be on first-name terms with half the island. All of Lopez' eating places are located on the main drag in tiny Lopez Village.

Cafe La Boheme
CAFÉ $
(Lopez Rd; ☺7am-4pm) Puffed cushions and Middle Eastern–style sofas lure you into this tiny local caffeine station, where you can listen to a cacophony of local opinions – everything from 'No drama Obama' to the merits of biodiesel versus gas – over coffee and cookies.

Bay Cafe
SEAFOOD $$$
(☑360-468-3700; www.bay-café.com; 9 Old Post Rd; mains $17-23) Lopez's one and only attempt at fine dining offers romantic sun-set views right on the water, with classic fish dishes, including Dungeness crab and seafood tapas. You can even cobble together a true Lopez meal of island-raised beef and wine from the local vineyard.

Holly B's Bakery
CAFÉ, BAKERY $
(www.hollybsbakery.com; Lopez Rd; ☺Apr-Nov) With a welcome dearth of multinational coffee chains, Holly's heads the early-morning latte and pastry rush. Follow the smell of freshly baked bread.

Isabel's Espresso
CAFÉ $
(Lopez Rd) A retro wood-paneled coffee bar that offers a fine selection of java coffee, herbal teas and fruit shakes, and features colorful furnishings and a small book collection.

Vortex Juice Bar
SANDWICHES, JUICE $
(Lopez Rd S; lunch dishes $5-7) Fresh juices are Vortex's forte, made with whatever fruits and vegetables are on hand. Above-average salads and wraps are among its other healthy offerings.

❶ Information
Angie's Cab (☑360-468-2227) Taxi.

Lopez Island Chamber of Commerce (www. lopezisland.com; Lopez Rd, Lopez Village) For information about businesses and recreation.

Shaw Island
The quietest and smallest of the four main San Juan Islands, tranquil Shaw is famous for its restrictive property laws and hand-some Benedictine monastery. Here, envel-oped in a pristine, tree-carpeted time warp, Catholic nuns tend to llamas, wild deer for-age on deserted roadways and idyllic sandy beaches are sprinkled with rather forebod-ing 'no trespassing' signs.

Aware of rising property prices and the burgeoning resort development of their larger and swankier neighbors, Shaw is-landers have steadfastly resisted the lure of the tourist dollar and chosen to remain pri-vate. That's not to say that travelers aren't welcome. Plenty of ferries arrive daily on Shaw, but with only one campsite offering just 11 overnight berths, opportunities to linger are limited.

For purists, that is what the island is all about. Shaw is fondly redolent of Orcas 30 years ago (and the rest of America 60 years ago), a close-knit rural community where neighbor still helps out neighbor and kids play happily in the countryside free from the paranoia of modern living. Until the early 2000s, the ferry wharf and the island's only store were managed by three Franciscan nuns who collected tickets and directed traffic in bright-yellow safety vests worn over their dark-brown habits. But in 2004 the Franciscans moved on and today only the Benedictine and the Sisters of Mercy orders remain.

For the curious, Shaw is worth a slow spin on a mountain bike or an afternoon of quiet contemplation on a pebbly beach. History buffs can break the reverie at the **Shaw Island Historical Museum** (Blind Bay Rd), while perennial peace-seekers can find lazy solace on quiet South Beach in **Shaw Island County Park** (☑360-378-1842; Squaw Bay Rd; tent sites $14) with overnight room for 11.

Olympic Peninsula & Washington Coast

Best Places to Eat

» Bella Italia (p129)
» Waterfront Pizza (p127)
» Oyster House (p114)
» Dooger's Seafood & Grill (p137)

Best Places to Stay

» Lake Quinault Lodge (p123)
» Shelburne Country Inn (p137)
» Olympic Club Hotel (p117)
» Lake Crescent Lodge (p121)

Why Go?

It took a lucrative series of 'tweenage' vampire novels to put the Olympic Peninsula on most people's radar. But if you've come here purely in search of *Twilight* parapher-nalia, you're missing 99% of what this wild, storm-lashed, fog-shrouded landmass is all about. The Olympic Peninsula is an unblemished wilderness of the highest order with an interior redolent of Middle Earth and an end-of-the-con-tinent coastline that makes Big Sur look positively calm. Then there's the precipitation. While Seattleites whine about a little winter drizzle, the Hoh Rain Forest is drown-ing in up to 200in of rain a year. There's an upside to all this water, of course; it's green here, a thousand verdant shades of it if you stare hard enough. And it's virgin too. Untouched in over a millennium lie sapphire lakes, rarely climbed mountains, and ancient cedar and spruce trees older than most of Europe's medieval castles.

When to Go

Olympia

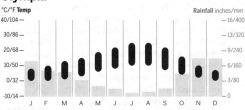

March Visit Port Townsend's unique Victorian Days festival

July & August Best hiking op-portunities and least likelihood of rain

August (third week) Long Beach's Inter-national Kite Festival

OLYMPIA

POP 43,330

Small in size but big in clout, state capital Olympia is a musical, political and outdoor powerhouse that punches well above its 43,000 population. Look no further than the streetside buskers on 4th Ave belting out acoustic grunge, the smartly-attired bureaucrats marching across the lawns of the resplendent state legislature, or the Gortex-clad outdoor fiends overnighting before rugged sorties into the Olympic Mountains. Truth is, despite its classical Greek-sounding name, creative, out-of-the-box Olympia is anything but ordinary. Progressive Evergreen college has long lent the place an artsy turn (creator of *The Simpsons,* Matt Groening, studied here) while the dive bars and secondhand guitar shops of downtown provided an original pulpit for riot grrrl music and grunge.

◉ Sights & Activities

FREE **Washington State Capitol**

NOTABLE BUILDING

(☉8am-4:30pm) Looking like a huge Grecian temple, the Capitol complex dominates the town. Its beautiful setting, in a 30-acre park overlooking Capitol Lake with the Olympic Mountains glistening in the background, is a visitor favorite. The campus' crowning glory is the magnificent **Legislative Building**. Completed in 1927, it's a dazzling display of craning columns and polished marble, topped by a 287ft dome that is only slightly smaller than its namesake in Washington, DC.

As well as the Legislative Building, visitors are welcome to peek inside both the Supreme Court or **Temple of Justice** flanked by sandstone colonnades and lined in the interior by yet more marble, and the **Capitol Conservatory**, which hosts a large collection of tropical and subtropical plants.

The oldest building on the campus is the **Governor's Mansion**, built in 1908. The home of the governor is open for tours only on Wednesday; call to reserve a space. Outdoor attractions include the Vietnam War Memorial, a sunken rose garden, a replica of the Roman-style fountain found in Tivoli Park, Copenhagen, plus a Story Pole carved by Chief William Shelton of the local Snohomish tribe in 1938. The manicured grounds are an attraction in themselves and a well-marked path zigzags down to Capitol Lake where it connects with more trails.

State Capital Museum

MUSEUM

(211 W 21st Ave; adult/child $2/1; ☉10am-4pm Tue-Fri, noon-4pm Sat & Sun) This premier museum is housed in the 1920s Lord Mansion, a few blocks south of the campus, and preserves the general history of Washington State from the Nisqually tribe to the present day.

Hands On Children's Museum KIDS ACTIVITIES

(106 11th Ave; admission $7.95, free 1st Fri of month 5-9pm; ☉10am-5pm Mon-Sat, noon-5pm Sun; ⍩) Resuscitate the kids next to the State Capitol with creative exhibits on human anatomy and nature including a simulated x-ray machine and a TV studio where children can create their own weather reports.

FREE **Old State Capitol** NOTABLE BUILDING

(600 S Washington St; ☉8am-noon, 1-5pm Mon-Fri) Eye-catching in Sylvester Park, this maverick building was constructed in 1892 in an unusual Romanesque-revival style and now acts as an office for the State Superintendent of Public Instruction. Its nine-story central tower was badly burned in 1928, and the building's 11 turrets fell off during a 1949 earthquake. Nonetheless, the old capitol, with its castle-like facade and fairytale flourishes, is still a head-turner. Pick up a brochure for a self-guided tour at the 2nd-floor reception area.

Percival Landing Park PARK

When Olympia was founded, its narrow harbor was a mudflat during low tides, but after years of dredging, a decent harbor was established. This park is essentially a boardwalk along the harbor that overlooks the assembled pleasure craft and provides informative display boards describing Olympia's past as a shipbuilding port and a center of the lumber and cannery trades.

Olympia Farmers Market MARKET

(700 Capitol Way N; ☉10am-3pm Thu-Sun Apr-Oct) Second only to Seattle's Pike Place in size and character, Olympia's local market is a great place to shop for organic herbs, vegetables, flowers, baked goods and the famous specialty oysters.

Batdorf & Bronson Tasting Room

COFFEE-TASTING

(www.dancinggoats.com; 200 Market St NE; ☉9am-4pm Wed-Sun) Located in the company's coffee-roasting house, this aromatic concern allows caffeine junkies to sample choice brands from Africa, Indonesia and Latin America. Knowledgeable staff provide the background facts.

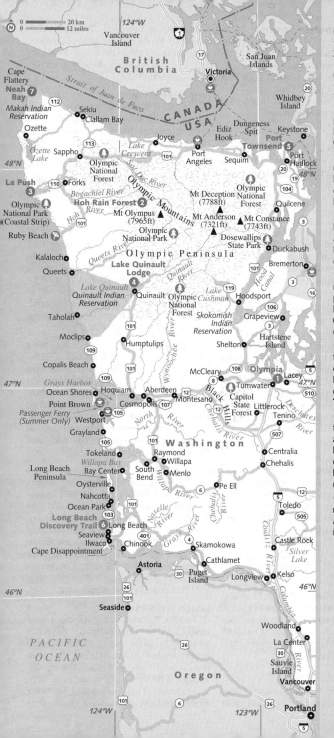

Olympic Peninsula & Washington Coast Highlights

1 Discover a precocious new band in a dive bar in **Olympia** (p115)

2 Think you've uncovered a real-life hobbit in the moss-covered **Hoh Rain Forest** (p122)

3 Find solitude, but no vampires, on a mist-enshrouded beach at **La Push** (p132)

4 Drive (or hike) miles to enjoy sweet-potato pancakes for breakfast in the **Lake Quinault Lodge** (p123)

5 Debate whether to don kayaking gear or a Victorian bowler hat in nostalgia-obsessed **Port Townsend** (p126)

6 Try to evoke the sense of accomplishment felt by Lewis and Clark on the **Long Beach Discovery Trail** (p138)

7 Visit one of the nation's best Native American museums in **Neah Bay** (p130)

FREE **Yashiro Japanese Garden** GARDEN
(900 Plum St; ⊙10am-10pm) Adjacent to the city hall, this small garden marks a collaboration between Olympia and its Japanese sister city, Yashiro. Highlights include a bamboo grove, a pagoda and a pond and waterfall; stone lanterns and other gifts from Yashiro adorn the grounds.

🛌 Sleeping

Phoenix Inn Suites HOTEL **$$**
(☎360-570-0555; www.phoenixinn.com; 415 Capitol Way N; s/d $99/109; ❉🐾🛜♨) The modern Phoenix is good value and dazzles guests with its sparkling modern interior and indoor pool and hot tub. What this small chain hotel lacks in character and charm, it makes up for in cleanliness, service and all-round comfort. The location, adjacent to Percival Landing, also puts you within baseball-pitching distance of one of Olympia's best oyster restaurants.

Swantown Inn B&B **$$**
(☎360-753-9123; www.swantowninn.com; 1431 11th Ave; r $119-179; 🛜) In the true tradition of Washington state B&Bs, the Swantown Inn features great personal service and meticulous attention to detail in a 1887 Queen Anne–style mansion that is listed on the state historical register. Within sight of the imposing capitol dome, there are four elegantly furnished rooms, plus wi-fi internet access and a formidable breakfast that features the local specialty, ginger pancakes.

Governor Hotel HOTEL **$$**
(☎360-352-7700; www.olywagov.com; 621 Capitol Way S; d $160; ❉🛜🐾♨) The Governor seems to have suffered a little since its Ramada Inn days with the question 'refurbishment?' hot on the lips of many recent guests. But with its downtown location overlooking serene Sylvester Park plus its outdoor pool, fitness center, restaurant and convention facilities, it's still Olympia's largest and most obvious central accommodation choice.

Olympia Inn MOTEL **$**
(☎360-352-8533; 909 Capitol Way S; r from $55; ❉) This rough-and-ready downtown motel is the city's most central cheap option. No-frills rooms are clean and kitted out with the standard refrigerator/microwave/cable TV motel triumvirate.

🍴 Eating

Few places in the Pacific Northwest have as many good vegetarian or veg-friendly restaurants as Olympia. The city is also renowned for its delicate Olympic oysters, home-roasted coffee (Batdorf & Bronson), myriad ethnic eateries and cheap brunches. Then there's the beer.

TOP CHOICE **Oyster House** SEAFOOD **$$**
(320 W 4th Ave; seafood dinners $15-20; ⊙11am-11pm, till midnight Fri & Sat) Olympia's most celebrated restaurant also specializes in its most celebrated cuisine, the delicate Olympia oyster, best served pan-fried and topped with a little cheese and spinach. Try them with the surprisingly delicious potato skins in a booth overlooking the placid harbor.

Basilico ITALIAN **$$**
(607 Capitol Way S; mains $15-19; ⊙5-9pm Mon-Sat) 'Come to Italy without leaving your hometown' boasts the blurb, and you might well believe it after tucking into the *vongole delle Cinque Terre* and the rack of lamb. In true Italian fashion the menu is presented as antipasto, primi and secondi. Pasta is handmade and the gelato is – well – you can guess. There's also an excellent wine selection.

Spar Cafe Bar PUB, DINER **$**
(114 4th Ave E; breakfast $4-6, lunch $6-9; ⊙7am-9pm) A legendary local café and eating joint now owned by Portland's McMenamin brothers, who have maintained its authentic wood-panel interior. You could spend all morning here eating brunch, shooting pool, admiring the cigar collections and discussing the latest music trends. Come back later for some of the real thing – live.

Darby's Café DINER **$**
(211 5th Ave SE; lunch $7; ⊙7am-9pm Wed-Fri, 8am-9pm Sat & Sun; 🍴) This glorified greasy-spoon on 5th isn't very greasy at all and pays equal respect to vegetarians and vegans. Unfussy food is served at a leisurely pace and without frills, but the breakfast scrambles, hash browns, and biscuits and gravy have garnered a loyal following. The decor is what polite people would call 'quirky' while the clientele is Olympia shabby-chic.

Lemon Grass Restaurant THAI **$**
(212 4th Ave W; mains $8-10; 🍴) Olympia is renowned for its ethnic eateries – the Asian variants in particular – meaning you'll sometimes have to line up to get into places like Lemon Grass. Once inside, few are disappointed by the quality or the price. This is everything Thai food should be: crisp, fresh and as spicy as you want (choose from

a one to four rating). There's also a wide selection of vegetarian options.

 Drinking

It's a toss-up which is better: Olympian beer or Olympian coffee. Cruise the bars and come to your own conclusions.

Batdorf & Bronson
CAFÉ

(513 Capitol Way S; ☺6am-7pm Mon-Fri, 7am-6pm Sat & Sun) Olympia's most famous coffee outlet is notably good, even in the caffeine-fuelled Pacific Northwest. If you like your morning brew fairtrade, shade-grown and certified organic, this is the place to come. For travelers with an insatiable caffeine addiction, head down to the company's new roasting house for expert banter.

Fish Tale Brew Pub
BREWPUB

(515 Jefferson St) Threatened with bankruptcy less than a decade ago, the Fishbowl has returned to brew with a vengeance, its classic selection of organic beers and India Pale Ales making it Washington's second-largest microbrewery. The company's cozy pub just across the road from its famous brewery is a must for all visiting beer aficionados and serves great oyster burgers.

☆ Entertainment

Olympia's music scene is cutting edge. Long before Nirvana played their formative gigs here, the place was a breeding ground for indie, lo-fi and anti-folk sounds spearheaded by musical pioneers such as Calvin Johnson, member of the band Beat Happening and founder of K Records. To see music at its roguish best, look out for buskers on 4th Ave and read homemade posters on lampposts.

Washington Center for the Performing Arts
THEATER

(☎360-753-8586; 512 Washington St) Comedy, art, ballet and plays – this is Olympia's primary venue for national touring shows and other cultural activities, and brings the city to center stage in Washington's surprisingly varied cultural life.

State Theater
THEATER

(☎360-786-0151; 202 4th Ave E) Harlequin Productions stages an eclectic lineup of contemporary plays and classics in this recently restored theater. Expect everything from Shakespeare to little-known musicals.

Capitol Theatre
THEATER

(☎360-754-6670; 206 E 5th Ave) Of 1924 vintage, the Beaux Arts–inspired Capitol Theater is the headquarters of the Olympia film society and puts on everything from Fellini movies to Rick Steves travel presentations. There is a film festival held every November and the occasional rock or rap concert.

DON'T MISS

OLYMPIA'S MUSIC SCENE

While Olympia's alternative music scene may have quieted down a little since the distorted days of grunge and riot grrrl in the early 1990s, innovative local artists are still very much in evidence in many of the city's bars, brewpubs and theaters, and seeking them out is a proverbial rite of passage. Dip into *Volcano,* the weekly South Puget Sound music paper, or start your search at one of the following places:

4th Ave Tavern (210 4th Ave E) This retrofitted bar, with pool tables, pinball machines and an excellent selection of microbrews, is one of the best places to catch local bands on Friday and Saturday nights.

Le Voyeur (404 4th Ave E) Monday is movie night, Wednesday is trivia night and the rest of the week is reserved for showcasing the latest names on the ever-innovative Olympia music scene.

Manium (421 4th Av) Home of Olympia's underground punk, metal and indie scenes, Manium bills itself as a 'collectively organized music and performance venue.' Shows here just sort of 'happen,' so be sure to keep your eye on the local posters and music press.

Brotherhood Lounge (119 Capitol Way N; ☺4pm-2am) Strange art, precariously hung Bollywood film banners and big, polite tattooed dudes working the bar await at this favored meeting place for Olympia's hip and arty crowd, which hosts regular music concerts with everything from punk to Black Sabbath impersonators, plus a Sunday-night DJ.

❶ Information

State Capitol Visitor Center (cnr 14th Ave & Capitol Way; ☺10am-2pm Oct-Apr, till 4pm May-Sep) Offers information on the capitol campus, the Olympia area and Washington state. Note the limited opening hours.

USFS office (1835 Black Lake Blvd) West of town; backcountry permits for wilderness camping in Olympic National Park can be obtained here.

❶ Getting There & Away

Bus

Five Greyhound buses a day link Olympia to Seattle ($11.50, 1½ hours) and other I-5-corridor cities from its **station** (107 7th Ave E). **Grays Harbor Transportation Authority** (www. ghtransit.com) offers a bus service to Aberdeen on the Pacific Coast ($2, 1½ hours).

Train

Amtrak (www.amtrak.com) *Cascade* and *Coast Starlight* trains stop at **Centennial Station** (6600 Yelm Hwy) in Lacey, the only volunteer-staffed train station in the world (apparently). Five trains a day link Olympia with Seattle ($18 to $24) and five with Portland ($26 to $30). Bus 64 goes between the station and downtown hourly 6:30am to 7:30pm, or it's a 3-mile walk.

❶ Getting Around

The **Capital Aeroporter** (www.capair.com) has frequent service to Sea-Tac, leaving from Phoenix Inn Suites, 415 Capitol Way N ($24, two hours). Reservations are suggested.

Olympia's free public bus system is **Intercity Transit** (www.intercitytransit.com). The downtown transit center is at State Ave and Washington St.

OLYMPIC PENINSULA

Cut off by water on three sides from the rest of the state, the remote Olympic Peninsula exhibits all the insular characteristics of a separate island. Dominated by the Olympic National Park, the region's main population centers are in the northeast and include Port Angeles, Port Townsend and the drier, balmier settlement of Sequim, now a budding retirement community. Protected climatically by the Olympic Mountains, outdoor activities abound here.

Exempt from strict wilderness regulations, the area outside of the Olympic National Park is largely given over to the lumber industry. Further west, clinging to the wild Pacific Coast, you'll find a couple of large Native American reservations.

History

Some of the peninsula's Native American history is well documented in the Ozette excavations that unearthed a 500-year-old Makah village in 1970. Other native groups included the Quileute and the Quinault.

European sailors were exploring the Northwest coast as early as 1592 but contact with the local people didn't occur until some two centuries later, when the land was claimed by the Spanish, who subsequently planted a colony at Neah Bay.

Port Townsend was established as the peninsula's premier settlement in 1851 and the first expanses of virgin forest began to fall to the lumberer's saws in the 1880s when the mill towns of Aberdeen and Hoquiam sprang up in the south.

Early attempts to explore the interior were limited until the 1930s, when US 101 pushed through the deep forests, linking longtime coastal communities by road for the first time. Finally, in 1938, following a 40-year struggle among conservationists, industrialists and logging companies, the Olympic National Park was established in the heart of the peninsula.

Olympic National Park

Declared a national monument in 1909 and a national park in 1938, the 1406-sq-mile Olympic National Park shelters a unique rain forest, copious glaciated mountain peaks and a 57-mile strip of Pacific coastal wilderness that was added in 1953. One of North America's last great wilderness areas, most of the park remains relatively untouched by human habitation, with 1000-year-old cedar trees juxtaposed with pristine alpine meadows, clear glacial lakes and a largely roadless interior.

Opportunities for independent exploration in this huge backcountry region abound, be it hiking, fishing, kayaking or skiing. The park's distinct and highly biodiverse ecosystem is rich in plant and animal life, much of it – such as the majestic Roosevelt elk – indigenous to the region. Boasting 17 large, car-accessible campgrounds and 95 backcountry campgrounds, overnight excursions in the park are both easy and rewarding.

SEX, LIES & CENTRALIA

Founded by an African American slave in 1852, Centralia entered historical folklore in 1919 when laborers from the Industrial Workers of the World labor union (the 'Wobblies') opened fire on members of the American Legion in what became known as the Centralia Massacre. These days it's better known for its cluttered antique shops and Amtrak train station.

But the overriding reason to make this rather mundane mining and lumber town a pit stop on the long drive (or train ride) north or south is to stay at a converted brothel. The accommodation in question is the **Olympic Club Hotel** (☑360-736-5164; 112 N Tower Ave; bunk/queen/king $40/60/70; 🛜🎦) a 'venue hotel' run by Portland's McMenamin brothers where you can eat, sleep, drink, shoot billiards, listen to music and go to the cinema, all in the same evening and – more to the point – all without having to leave the hotel. The Olympic Club dates from 1908 when it opened as a 'gentlemen's resort' designed to satisfy the various drinking, gambling and sexual vices of transient miners and loggers. In 1996 the turn-of-the-century building was taken over by the McMenamins, who restored the brothel to its former glory complete with creaking floorboards, Tiffany lamps and art-deco murals (but without the erstwhile nighttime shenanigans). Downstairs you'll still find a bar, billiard room, restaurant and small movie theater where, in true Portland fashion, friendly waitresses will bring in food orders during the movie as guests recline in sofas and armchairs. Upstairs, atmospheric bedrooms (all with shared bathrooms) sport arty graffiti chronicling the misdemeanors of past guests.

If you're overnighting you can enjoy a hearty brunch at the acclaimed **Berry Fields** (201 S Pearl St; mains $10), situated in Centralia's biggest antique mall, where the cinnamon buns are the size of soccer balls.

EASTERN ENTRANCES

The eastern entrances to Olympic National Park are less developed than the north and west, but are handy for visitors traveling over the Hood Canal from Seattle and the 'mainland.'

Dosewallips River Valley   WILDERNESS VALLEY
This narrow valley (doe-sey-wal-ups) is surrounded by some of the highest mountains in the Olympics, including Mt Anderson and Mt Deception. The gravel Dosewallips River Rd terminates at the ranger station 15 miles from US 101, where hiking trails begin.

Staircase   PARK ENTRANCE
Staircase is another favorite entrance for hikers, and is popular with families, anglers and boaters bound for nearby Lake Cushman State Park. The **Staircase Ranger Station** (☑360-877-5569) is just inside the park boundary, 16 miles from US 101 and the small town of Hoodsport.

The trail system here follows the drainage of the North Fork Skokomish River, which is flanked by some of the most rugged peaks in the Olympics. The principal long-distance trail is the **North Fork Skokomish Trail**, which leads up this heavily forested valley, eventually crossing into the Duckabush

River valley to intercept other trans-park trail systems. Ambitious day-hikers might consider following this trail 3.7 miles to the **Flapjack Lakes Trail**, an easy 4-mile climb up to several small lakes that shimmer beneath the crags of the Sawtooth peaks.

A popular short hike follows the south bank of the North Fork Skokomish River through lush old-growth forest along the **Staircase Rapids Loop Trail**. Continue up the trail a short distance to the Rapids Bridge, which crosses over to the North Fork Skokomish Trail and makes for a nice 2-mile loop.

🛏 Sleeping

Dosewallips State Park   CAMPGROUND $
(☑888-226-7688; tent/RV sites $21/28) Near Brinnon along US 101 is this 425-acre, year-round campground situated in an expanse of meadow, close to the mouth of the Dosewallips River and facing Hood Canal. There are 100 tent spaces, 40 utility spaces, a dump space and two showers.

Camp Cushman   CAMPGROUND $
(☑360-877-6770; 7211 N Lake Cushman Rd; tent/RV sites $22/28) Eight miles northwest of Hoodsport, this campground is centered on a large reservoir on the Skokomish River,

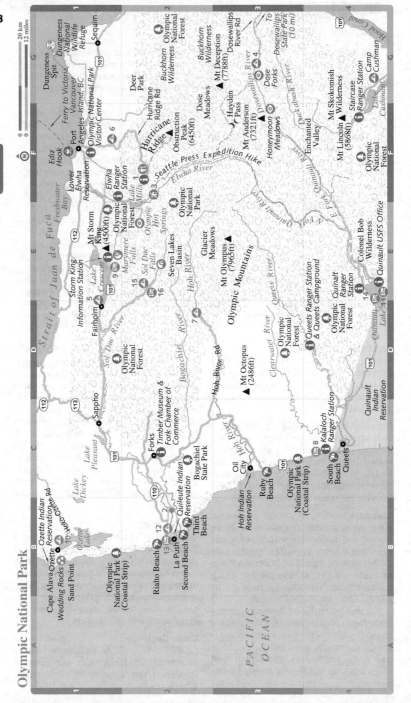

Olympic National Park

Activities, Courses & Tours

🛏 Sleeping

popular with anglers, water-skiers and campers. There are 82 campsites open from early Memorial Day (late May) to Labor Day (early September).

NORTHERN ENTRANCES

The most popular access to Olympic National Park is from the north. Port Angeles is the park's urban hub, and other good access points are Hurricane Ridge, the Elwha Valley and Lake Crescent, the park's largest lake.

Hurricane Ridge   VISITORS CENTER

South of Port Angeles the Olympic Mountains rise up to Hurricane Ridge, one of the park's most accessible viewing points and an active ski station in the winter. Starting in Race St, the 18-mile Hurricane Ridge Rd climbs up 5300ft toward extensive wildflower meadows and expansive mountain vistas often visible above the clouds.

The **Hurricane Ridge Visitor Center** (⊙9:30am-5pm daily summer, Fri-Sun winter) has a snack bar, gift shop, toilets and ski and snowshoe rentals, but no overnight accommodation or camping. The weather here can be fickle. Call ☑360-565-3131 for the latest conditions.

Hurricane Ridge is a good base for many activities including cross-country and downhill skiing, and snowboarding from mid-December to March, weekends only. The **ski area** (www.hurricaneridge.com; 🖶) has two rope tows and a lift, and is one of only two national park ski areas in the US.

Hurricane Ridge is also the takeoff point for a number of short hikes leading through meadows to vista points. **Hurricane Hill Trail**, which begins at the end of the road leading up, and the **Meadow Loop Trails** network, starting at the visitors center, are popular, moderately easy hikes. The first half-mile of these trails is wheelchair accessible.

From Hurricane Ridge, you can drive a rough, white-knuckle 8-mile road to **Obstruction Peak**, laid out by the Civilian Conservation Corps (CCC) in the 1930s. Here, hikers looking for long-distance treks can pick up either the **Grand Ridge Trail**, which leads 7.5 miles to Deer Park, much of the way above the timberline, or the **Wolf Creek Trail**, an 8-mile downhill jaunt to Whiskey Bend, where it picks up the Elwha Trail.

Elwha River Valley   WILDERNESS VALLEY

The Elwha, the largest river on the Olympic Peninsula, and Lake Mills (actually a reservoir) are popular **trout fishing** havens. Elwha River Rd turns south from US 101 about 8 miles west of Port Angeles. Follow it for 10 miles to the **Elwha Ranger Station** (480 Upper Elwha Rd). The road immediately forks. Turn west to reach the Olympic Hot Springs trailhead, or turn east toward Whiskey Bend to reach the Elwha River and other trailheads.

Commercially developed as a resort in the 1930s, the **Olympic Hot Springs** once featured cabins that have long since disappeared. In 1983, park supervisors closed the road out, and the area has largely returned to nature. The 2.2-mile hike along the old roadbed is well worth it – what's left of the old pools steam alongside the rushing Boulder Creek, all in a verdant deep-forest grove.

From Whiskey Bend, the **Elwha Trail** leads up the main branch of the Elwha River and is one of the primary cross-park long-distance hikes. Day-hikers may elect to follow the trail for 2 miles to Humes Ranch, the remains of a homestead-era ranch.

Lake Crescent   SCENIC LAKE

If you're heading anticlockwise on the Olympic loop from Port Angeles toward Forks, one of the first scenic surprises to leap out at you will be luminous Lake Crescent, a popular boating and fishing area and a departure point for a number of short national park hikes. The area is also the site of the Lake Crescent Lodge, the oldest of the park's trio of celebrated lodges (the others are the Quinault and the Kalaloch)

BACKCOUNTRY HIKES IN OLYMPIC NATIONAL PARK

Many skirt the park's well-trampled edges on easily accessible 'touch the wilderness' hikes. Far fewer plunge into the Olympic's mossy, foggy, roadless interior. Here are a few ways in.

Seattle Press Expedition Hike

One of the most popular cross-park treks follows the pioneering route taken by James H Christie, a former Arctic explorer who answered the call of the *Seattle Press* newspaper in 1889 to 'acquire fame by unveiling the mystery which wraps the land encircled by the snow-capped Olympic range.' Starting at the Whiskey Bend trailhead on the Elwha River, the route tracks south and then southwest through the Elwha and Quinault River valleys to Lake Quinault covering 44 moderately strenuous miles. Called the Seattle Press Expedition Hike, it commonly takes walkers five days to complete.

Pacific Coastal Hikes

There are two long-distance beach hikes along Washington's isolated coast. The most northerly is the 32.7-mile stretch between the Makah Shi Shi trailhead near Cape Flattery and Rialto Beach near La Push (a shorter 20.2-mile version runs from Ozette to Rialto Beach) which commonly makes up a moderate five-day, four-night trek. This hike stays faithfully close to the shoreline meaning a good understanding of tidal charts is imperative. There are 14 campgrounds en route, eight of which take reservations.

The more southerly hike runs from Third Beach just south of La Push to the Oil City trailhead at the mouth of the Hoh River. This 17.5-mile route is more precipitous and tougher than the northern route, with the trail ascending and descending over numerous headlands. As a consequence, fewer people do it. All seven campsites on this segment are first-come, first-served.

If you are contemplating a trek along the coast, request information from the **National Park Service** (www.nps.gov/olym), buy good maps, learn how to read tide tables and be prepared for bad weather year-round.

The Scenic Bits

Though the Seattle Press Expedition hike is the Olympics' Blue Riband trek, it isn't necessarily the park's most scenic. Purists rave about the **Enchanted Valley**, which you can reach by trekking 13 miles beyond the Graves Creek trailhead northeast of Lake Quinault. After the late-June snowmelt it is possible to lengthen this hike by continuing over 4464ft Anderson Pass and descending to the Dosewallips Trailhead on the park's eastern side. Another favorite is a circular hike from the Deer Park trailhead southeast of Port Angeles. After a 4.3 mile walk out to the Three Forks backcountry campground you can trek up over **Cameron Pass** and **Gray Wolf Pass** for fantastic views of McCartney Peak (6728ft) and Mt Deception (7788ft).

For all of the above, hikers should first take stock of local weather conditions (June to September is the recommended walking window), wise up on wilderness rules and regulations, and pack all necessary camping equipment and supplies. Hikers will also need to acquire a backcountry pass ($4.88) from the Wilderness Information Center (p124) in Port Angeles before commencing. For more information on this and other backcountry hikes check out the national park website at www.nps.gov/olym.

---

that first opened in 1916. The best stop-off point is in a parking lot to the right of SR 101 near the **Storm King Information Station** (☎360-928-3380), only open in the summer. A number of short hikes leave from here, including the **Marymere Falls trail**, a 2-mile round trip to a 90ft cascade that drops down over a basalt cliff. For a more energetic hike, climb up the side of **Mt Storm King**, the peak that rises to the east of Lake Crescent. The steep, 1.7-mile ascent splits off the Barnes Creek Trail.

Trout fishing is good here – the lake is deep with steep shorelines – though only artificial lures are allowed. Rowboat rentals ($9/25 per hour/half day) are available at Lake Crescent Lodge in the summer months.

Sol Duc River Valley
HOT SPRINGS

The 14-mile interior road that leads off US 101 into the heart of the national park along the headwaters of the Sol Duc River is worth a turn for some great day hikes, a dip in a natural spa and a vivid glimpse of the amazing Olympic rain forest. Note how the trees along the roadside become taller and more majestic almost immediately.

As Native American legend tells it, the geological phenomenon at Sol Duc is the legacy of a battle between two lightning fish. When neither fish won the contest, each crawled beneath the earth and shed bitter tears, forming the heated mineral springs here. These springs have been diverted into three large tiled pools for health and recreation at Sol Duc Hot Springs Resort. Entry costs $10/6.75 for an adult/child. There's also a standard swimming pool to cool off in, as well as a restaurant, snack bar, gift shop and overnight accommodations.

The road ends 1.5 miles past the resort, and this is where most of the trails start. The most popular hike is the 0.75-mile **Sol Duc Falls Trail**, where the river plummets 40ft into a narrow gorge. Other more strenuous hikes cross the bridge at the falls and climb the **Deer Lake Trail** along Canyon Creek. This sometimes-steep, 8-mile round-trip trail reaches the tree-rimmed lake then joins the **High Divide Trail** before tracking back via the Seven Lakes Basin, a popular overnight destination. Another good leg-stretcher is the 2.5-mile **Mink Lake Trail**, departing from the resort. The marshy lake is noted for its birdwatching and wildlife-viewing.

🛏 Sleeping

TOP CHOICE ➤ Lake Crescent Lodge
HISTORIC HOTEL $$

(☑360-928-3211; www.olympicnationalparks.com; 416 Lake Crescent Rd; lodge r with shared bathroom $68-85, cottages $132-211; ☺May-Oct; ❄🛜) Built in 1915 as a fishing resort, this venerable shake-sided building is the oldest of the Olympic National Park lodges and, along with the Lake Quinault Lodge, leads the way in style and coziness. To add star appeal, President FD Roosevelt stayed here in 1937 – a year before he made the Olympics a national park – and the lodge's fanciest rooms are still known as the 'Roosevelt cottages.' Located lakeside and endowed with an im-

pressive restaurant that serves up grilled duck breast and elk rib rack, the lodge is reasonably priced, fantastically placed and well known for its environmentally sustainable practices. Make reservations in advance, as it is only open May to October.

🚩 Sol Duc Hot Springs Resort
CABIN RESORT $$

(☑360-327-3583; www.olympicnationalparks.com; RV sites $23, r $115-169; ☺late Mar-Oct; ❄🛜) While Sol Duc lacks the classic touches of the more luxurious Lake Quinault and Kalaloch lodges, this well-known spa retreat packs a punch with its therapeutic spring waters and easy access to surrounding forest. Furthermore, while there are enough facilities onsite – mineral pools, small store and restaurant – to make the place feel self-contained, you still get the tangible sense of being in a remote wilderness area. Thirty-two modern but basic cabins offer private bathrooms and, in some cases, a kitchenette. Aside from the steaming waters there is also a massage service available. Day hikers and visitors can use the Spring Restaurant or poolside deli. There are 17 RV sites for hire, but no tent sites.

Sol Duc Campground
CAMPGROUND $

(☑360-327-3534; campsites $14) This 82-site facility is immediately upstream from the Sol Duc Hot Springs Resort and, with its tall fir and cedar trees and mossy undergrowth, offers a quintessential Olympic rain forest experience. It's also handy for both the local trails and the spa.

Fairholm Campground
CAMPGROUND $

(☑360-928-3380; campsites $12; ☺year-round) The only national park campground on Lake Crescent features 88 sites, a general store and boat rentals. It's on the lake's west end.

Heart o' the Hills Campground
CAMPGROUND $

(☑360-452-2713; 876 Hurricane Ridge Rd; campsites $12) Five miles south of Port Angeles, this is the closest campground to Hurricane Ridge, with 105 sites.

WESTERN ENTRANCES

The Pacific side of the Olympics is the most remote part of the park and home to the foggy, moss-draped temperate rain forests. It is also the wettest area, receiving 12ft of rain annually, and you can expect a soaking at any time.

CLIMBING MT OLYMPUS

Mt Olympus (7965ft) is the Olympic National Park's highest and most commonly climbed peak, though, due to extensive glaciers and fickle weather, ascents should not be undertaken lightly. Access is via the Hoh Trail, which extends for 17 miles from the Hoh Rain Forest Visitor Center to Glacier Meadows. The campground here is frequently used as a base camp for ascents of the mountain. Much of the remaining climb is on glaciers and along craggy escarpments. Most people make the ascent between June and early September, although some begin as early as April. Each year Mt Olympus causes injuries and claims lives, usually from falls into glacial crevasses or exposure during storms. Guided climbs are available through various agencies. Try **Mountain Madness** (206-937-8389; www.mountainmadness.com), which is based out of Seattle and offers guided five-day summit attempts starting from $875.

US 101 is the only road that accesses this vast, heavily wooded area. Paved roads penetrate the interior at the Hoh Rain Forest and Lake Quinault, but are sometimes washed out.

TOP CHOICE **Hoh Rain Forest**   RAIN FOREST

The most famous section of the Olympic rain forest, the Hoh River area offers a variety of hikes and an interpretive center. If you have room for only one stop on the western side, this should be it. The paved Upper Hoh Rd winds 19 miles from US 101 to the visitor center passing a **giant Sitka spruce tree** along the way. This lord of the forest is 270ft high and over 500 years old.

At the end of Hoh River Rd, the **Hoh Rain Forest Visitor Center** (360-374-6925; 9am-4:30pm Sep-Jun, 9am-6pm Jul & Aug) offers displays on the ecology of the rain forest and the plants and animals that inhabit it, as well as a bookstore. Rangers lead free guided walks twice a day during summer.

Leading out from the visitor center are several excellent day hikes into virgin rain forest. The most popular is the **Hall of Moss Trail**, an easy 0.75-mile loop through the kind of weird, ethereal scenery that even Tolkien couldn't have invented. Epiphytic club moss, ferns and lichens completely overwhelm the massive trunks of maples and Sitka spruces in this misty forest. The 1.25-mile **Spruce Nature Trail** is another short interpretive loop leading out from the visitor center. There is also a short wheelchair-accessible nature trail through a rain forest marsh.

The **Hoh River Trail** is the major entry trail into the wide, glacier-carved Hoh River Valley. It is also the principal access route to Mt Olympus. The trail follows an easy grade for 12 miles, and day-hikers can use it as a pleasant out-and-back excursion.

Queets River Valley   WILDERNESS VALLEY

The Queets Corridor was added to the park in 1953 in an attempt to preserve one of the peninsula's river valleys all the way from its glacial beginnings to the coast. It is one of the park's least accessible areas.

The unpaved Queets River Rd leaves US 101 and almost immediately drops into the national park. The road then follows the river for 13 miles before ending at **Queets Ranger Station** (360-962-2283). From here, there is one popular day hike – the gentle 3-mile **Queets Campground Loop Trail**.

Experienced or adventurous hikers can elect to ford the Queets River in late summer or fall and explore the **Queets Trail**, which leads up the river for 15 miles before petering out in heavy old-growth rain forest.

Lake Quinault   SCENIC LAKE

Situated in the extreme southwest of the Olympic Peninsula, the enchanting Quinault River Valley is one of the park's least crowded corners. Clustered around the deep-blue glacial waters of Lake Quinault lie forested peaks, a historic lodge and some of the oldest (and tallest) Sitka spruce, Douglas fir and western red cedar trees in the world.

The lake itself offers plenty of activities such as fishing, boating and swimming, while upstream both the north and south branches of the Quinault River harbor a couple of important trans-park trails.

The lake may be accessed from the north and the south. The south shore hosts the tiny village of Quinault, complete with the luscious Lake Quinault Lodge, a **USFS office** (360-288-2525; 353 S Shore Rd), restaurant, couple of stores, **post office** (S Shore Rd) and gas station. The North Shore Rd passes the **Quinault Ranger Station**

(📞360-288-2444) before climbing up to the North Fork Quinault trailhead.

Lake Quinault is part of the Quinault Indian Reservation, and fishing is regulated by the tribe; check locally for tribal licenses and regulations. Boat rentals are available from Lake Quinault Lodge.

A number of short hiking trails begin just below Lake Quinault Lodge; pick up a free map from the USFS office. The shortest of these is the **Quinault Rain Forest Nature Trail**, a half-mile walk through 500-year-old Douglas firs. This short trail adjoins the 3-mile **Quinault Loop Trail**, which meanders through the rain forests before circling back to the lake. The Quinault region is renowned for its huge trees. Close to the village is a 191ft Sitka spruce tree (purported to be up to 1000 years old), and nearby are the world's largest red cedar, Douglas fir and mountain hemlock trees.

Beyond the lake, both the north and south shore roads continue up the Quinault River Valley before merging at a bridge just past Bunch Falls. From here, more adventurous hikers can sally forth into backcountry. The area's sparkling highlight is the photogenic **Enchanted Valley Trail** which climbs up to a large meadow (a former glacial lake bed) traversed by streams and springs, and resplendent with wildflowers and thickets of alders. To the north rise sheer cliff faces and peaks craning 2000ft from the valley floor; during spring snowmelt, the 3-mile precipice is drizzled by thousands of small waterfalls.

The **Enchanted Valley hike** starts out from the Graves Creek Ranger Station at the end of the S Shore Rd, and is a 26-mile trip there and back. Long-distance hikers can continue up to Anderson Pass (19 miles from Graves Creek) and link up with the **West Fork Dosewallips Trail** to complete a popular trans-park trek.

The classic Seattle Press Expedition hike passes through the North Fork Quinault River valley to join the lengthy Elwha River trail system further north.

🛏 Sleeping

🔝 Lake Quinault Lodge

NATIONAL PARK LODGE **$$$**

(📞360-288-2900; www.olympicnationalparks.com; 345 S Shore Rd; cabin $125-243, lodge $134-167; ❄🏊) Everything you could want in a historic national park lodge and more, the 'Quinault' has a huge, roaring fireplace, peek-a-boo lake views, a manicured cricket-pitch-quality lawn, huge comfy leather sofas,

a regal reception area and – arguably – the finest eating experience on the whole peninsula. The latter is thanks to the memorable sweet potato pancakes with hazelnut butter that are served up in the beautiful lakeside restaurant for breakfast (and are worth trying even if you're not staying here). Built in 1926, the Quinault's warmth and character are no secret and advance reservations are recommended. Trails into primeval forest leave from just outside the door.

Quinault River Inn

MOTEL **$**

(📞360-288-2237; 8 River Dr, Amanda Park; r $115; ❄🛜) A sort of motel meets mountain lodge, the River Inn is handily positioned on US 101 next to the eating and gas facilities at Amanda Park. Its position right on the Quinault River makes it popular with fishermen who get up at the crack of dawn to hit the water. Rooms are warm and well maintained, with decent-sized beds and copious TV channels. Bonuses include a small gym, attractive cedar wood decor and extra-friendly service. There are also some RV sites ($27).

Queets Campground

CAMPGROUND **$**

(📞360-962-2283; campsites $10) Located at the end of Queets River Rd (not recommended for RVs), this small campground with 20 primitive sites is tucked amid temperate rain forest.

Hoh Campground

CAMPGROUND **$**

(📞360-374-6925; campsites $12) Adjacent to the Hoh Rain Forest Visitor Center, the campground features 88 sites, most alongside the Hoh River.

ℹ Information

Olympic National Park Visitor Center (www.nps.gov/olym; 3002 Mt Angeles Rd; ◷9am-4pm) is about a mile south of Port Angeles and is the park's most comprehensive information center. Aside from giving out excellent free maps and leaflets, the center offers children's exhibits plus a bookstore, a replica of a prehistoric Makah seal-hunting canoe and a 25-minute film entitled *Mosaic of Diversity* shown in a small auditorium. Pick up a detailed free park map along with an even more detailed 'Wilderness Trip Planner' with backcountry trails and campgrounds marked.

USFS headquarters (www.fs.fed.us/r6/olympic; 1835 Black Lake Blvd SW; ◷8am-4:30pm Mon-Fri) is outside Olympia and is the information font for everything on the Olympic National Forest, a 630,000-acre area that borders much of the park's perimeter. Alternatively, you can try the field offices in Hoodsport, Quilcene, Quinault and Forks. These offices distribute free backcountry permits for wilderness camping in the park as well as Northwest Forest Passes ($5), required for parking at trailheads in the forest.

Park admission fees are $15 per vehicle and $5 per pedestrian/cyclist, and are valid for seven days for park entry and re-entry. An annual 'passport' for one year's unlimited entry costs $30. Fees are collected year-round at the Hoh and Heart o' the Hills entry points, and from May to October at Elwha, Sol Duc and Staircase entrances. (Payment is not mandatory where there is no entrance station or when an entrance station isn't open.)

Backpackers must register for overnight stays in backcountry areas. There's a $5 permit fee for groups of up to 12, valid for two weeks from purchase, plus a $2-per-person nightly fee for anyone over 16 years old. You can get permits from the **Wilderness Information Center** (☑360-565-3100; www.nps.gov/olym/planyourvisit/wic.htm; 600 E Park Ave, Port Angeles; ☉8am-4:30pm Apr-Sep), behind the visitor center. You can also get them from the Hoh visitor center (p122) or from ranger stations throughout the park.

Olympic Coastal Strip

Coast lovers in the Pacific Northwest tend to head for Oregon where the beaches are famously wide, windswept and accessible. Further north in Washington the facilities gradually thin out until beyond Gray's Harbor you're confronted with one of the most undisturbed slices of coastal wilderness in the US. Here tiny Native American towns list populations in the hundreds rather than the thousands and, bar a 15-mile stretch of Hwy 101, there are few roads. Outside of small Native American reservations around Oil City, La Push and Ozette, 53 miles of this wild coast is protected as part of the Olympic National Park (added in 1953). Parts of it haven't changed since pre-colonial times.

OZETTE

Former home of the Makah tribe, whose ancient cliff-side village was destroyed in a mudslide in the early 18th century before being unearthed in the 1970s, Ozette is more than just a well-excavated archaeological pit. It is also one of the most accessible slices of isolated beach on the Olympic coastal strip.

The Hoko–Ozette road leaves Hwy 112 about 3 miles west of Sekiu and proceeds 21 miles to **Lake Ozette Ranger Station** (☉8am-4:30pm), on Ozette Lake. There is no village here but, from the ranger station, two boardwalk trails lead out to one of two

beaches at Cape Alava and Sand Point. The 3.3-mile **Cape Alava Trail** leads north to the westernmost point of land in the continental US and is the site of the ancient Makah village, where archaeologists unearthed 55,000 artifacts, many of which are on display at the Makah Museum in Neah Bay. The southern **Sand Point Trail** from Lake Ozette Ranger Station leads 3 miles to beaches below a low bluff; whale-watchers often come here in the migration season.

The two Ozette trails can easily be linked as a long day hike by walking the 3 miles between Cape Alava and Sand Point along the beach (beware of the tides) or overland (although the trail is brushy and primitive).

The high point of this hike is the **Wedding Rocks**, the most significant group of petroglyphs on the Olympic Peninsula. Approximately a mile south of Cape Alava, the small outcropping contains carvings of whales, a European square-rigger and fertility figures. The site was traditionally used for Makah weddings and is still considered sacred.

RUBY BEACH TO SOUTH BEACH

This southernmost portion of the Olympic coastal strip, between the Hoh and Quinault Indian Reservations, is abutted by US 101, making it more accessible than the beaches further north. Your first stop here should be **Ruby Beach**, where a short 0.2-mile path leads down to a large expanse of windswept beach embellished by polished black stones and wantonly strewn tree trunks. Heading south toward Kalaloch (*klay*-lock), other accessible beachfronts are unimaginatively named Beach One through to Beach Six, all of which are popular with beachcombers. At low tide, rangers give talks on tidal-pool life at Beach Four and on the ecosystems of the Olympic coastal strip. For information about this area, contact the **Kalaloch Ranger Station** (☑360-962-2283; ☉9am-5pm May-Oct).

🛌 Sleeping

Between May and September, advance reservations are required to stay at the designated campsites along the beach at Cape Alava and Sand Point. To make a reservation contact the Wilderness Information Center (p124) or reserve online. In addition, campers must obtain a wilderness permit.

Kalaloch Lodge HISTORIC HOTEL **$$$**
(☑360-962-2271; www.olympicnational parks.com; 157151 US 101; lodge $134-285, cabins $143-289; ✳) A little less grand than the

Lake Quinault and Lake Crescent lodges, the Kalaloch (built in 1953) nonetheless enjoys an equally spectacular setting perched on a bluff overlooking the crashing Pacific. In addition to rooms in the old lodge, there are log cabins and motel-style units, and a family-friendly restaurant and store that offer incomparable ocean views. Various trails lead down to the nearby beaches.

Lake Ozette Campground　　CAMPGROUND $
(☑360-963-2725; campsites $12) The 15 sites fill every day before noon at this small camp on Lake Ozette, a popular playground for boats and kayaks.

Mora Campground　　CAMPGROUND $
(☑360-374-5460; campsites $12) Along the Quillayute River, 2 miles east of Rialto Beach, Mora offers 95 regular sites. Guided nature walks take off from here in the summer.

Northeastern Olympic Peninsula

Hugging the protected coast of the Strait of Juan de Fuca, the northeast corner of the Olympic Peninsula is the region's most populated enclave and provides a popular gateway to the national park. It's famous for its dry climate (courtesy of the Olympic rain shadow), and outdoor activities such as sea kayaking and whale-watching abound, while a rare historical treat awaits travelers in time-warped Port Townsend. Thanks to numerous ferry connections (Port Angeles to Victoria/Canada, Port Townsend to Whidbey Island and Seattle to Bainbridge Island), the area is easily accessible from the population centers of Puget Sound.

PORT TOWNSEND
POP 8925

Back in the 1880s a number of nascent settlements were vying to become Washington's preeminent city (Walla Walla, Ellensburg and eventual winner Seattle to name but three). An early casualty in the battle for urban supremacy was Port Townsend, a speculation-fuelled boomtown at the nautical entrance to busy Puget Sound that went bust in the great 'Panic of 1893.' Port Townsend's loss was a catastrophe for the local businessmen of the day, but the cloud had a long-term silver lining. After years of dire poverty when there wasn't even enough money to demolish the old unused buildings, Port Townsend did a *volte-face* and experienced a flowery 1970s renaissance. The rebirth, based on urban rejuvenation and tourism, has endowed the northwest with one of only two historic seaports in the US – a frozen-in-time slice of red-bricked Victorian architecture caught at its 1890s high watermark. Throw in inventive eateries, elegant fin de siècle hotels and an unusual stash of year-round festivals and you've got a Pacific Northwest rarity – a weekend vacation that doesn't require hiking boots.

⊙ Sights

Port Townsend is one of the few places on the Olympic peninsula where you can change your naturalist's hat for a historical one. The town has a large and valuable stash of handsome Victorian buildings dating from the 1860s to about 1893 (when the economy collapsed). Styles run the gamut of Italian Renaissance, Queen Anne, Greek revival and Gothic. The Victorian shop fronts of Water St were mostly built in a manic five-year building boom between 1886 and 1891.

Art galleries are another of the town's fortes and you can pick up a map of 12 of the best, all clustered within four blocks of the ferry dock, at the visitors center. Higher up on the bluff, be sure to stop and admire the 100ft clock tower of the **Jefferson County Courthouse** (1892) and also **Manresa Castle** (now a hotel).

Jefferson County Historical Society Museum　　MUSEUM
(210 Madison St; adult/child $4/1; ⊙11am-4pm Mar-Dec) The local historic society runs this well-maintained exhibition area that includes mock-ups of an old courtroom and jail cell, along with the full lowdown on the rise, fall and second coming of this captivating port town. The society also runs the **Rothschild House** (cnr Jefferson & Taylor Sts; admission $4; ⊙11am-4pm May-Oct) up on the bluff, with an atmospheric interior furnished in period fashion.

Fort Worden State Park　　STATE PARK $
(www.parks.wa.gov/fortworden; 200 Battery Way; ⊙6:30am-dusk Apr-Oct, 8am-dusk Nov-Mar) This attractive park located within Port Townsend's city limits is the remains of a large fortification system constructed in the 1890s to protect the strategically important Puget Sound area from outside attack – supposedly from the Spanish during the 1898 war. The extensive grounds and historic buildings have been refurbished in recent years into a lodging, and nature and history

park; sharp-eyed film buffs will recognize the setting as the backdrop for the movie *An Officer and a Gentleman*. The **Commanding Officer's Quarters** (admission $4; ☉10am-5pm daily Jun-Aug, 1-4pm Sat & Sun Mar-May & Sep-Oct), a 12-bedroom mansion, is open for tours, and part of one of the barracks is now the **Puget Sound Coast Artillery Museum** (admission $2; ☉11am-4pm Tue-Sun), which tells the story of early Pacific coastal fortifications.

Fort Worden offers a number of camping and lodging possibilities. Hikes lead along the headland to **Point Wilson Lighthouse Station** and some wonderful windswept beaches. On the park's fishing pier is the **Port Townsend Marine Science Center** (532 Battery Way; adult/child $5/3; ☉noon-6pm Tue-Sun summer) featuring four touch tanks and daily interpretive programs.

🏃 Activities

It's not all history. Port Townsend is the center for sea kayaking on Puget Sound and Fort Worden is a stop on the Cascadia Marine Trail. **PT Outdoors** (1017B Water St) rents single kayaks from $25 an hour and offers guided tours from $60/45 per adult/child for two to three hours. **Puget Sound Express** (www.pugetsoundexpress.com; 431 Water St) offers four-hour whale-watching tours from May to October for $85/65 per adult/child, or an eight-hour excursion that includes a stopover in Friday harbor on San Juan Island.

PT Cyclery (252 Tyler St; rentals per hr/day $7/28), on a back lot on Tyler St, has mountain bikes and tandems for rent. They also provide local trail maps.

☞ Tours

The historical society organizes guided **Walking Tours** (adult/child $10/5) around town from June through September. Enquire at the museum. **Art Walks** leave on the first Saturday evening of every month. Ask at the visitors center for details.

✿ Festivals & Events

Port Townsend has a busy calendar of annual events. These are two highlights.

Centrum   MUSIC

(www.centrum.org) A nonprofit arts foundation based at Fort Worden State Park, Centrum sponsors an endless stream of arts and music festivals and seminars, many held at the fort. Among the most popular are the Festival of American Fiddle Tunes and Jazz Port Townsend, both in July. Contact Centrum for a schedule.

Victorian Days   HISTORIC

(www.victorianfestival.org) In late March this unique festival offers an array of exhibits, walking tours and craft workshops. Horses and carriages are dusted off, refined manners are polished and half the town dons asphyxiating corsets or austere waistcoats to relive the days when lamb-chop whiskers and handlebar mustaches were the height of fashion.

🛏 Sleeping

Waterstreet Hotel   HOTEL $

(☎360-385-5467; www.waterstreethotelporttownsend.com; 635 Water St; r $50-160; ⊛❋⊜) Of Port Townsend's old dockside hotels, the easy-on-the-wallet Waterstreet has to be the best bargain in town. There is a price for the giveaway room fees, however. The hotel is above a pub, hence late-night noise – though generally good-natured and exuberant – can infringe annoyingly on your pre-hiking beauty sleep. If it's peace and tranquility you're after, hit the uptown B&Bs. A multitude of rooms can accommodate between two and six people. Some have shared bathrooms.

Palace Hotel   HOTEL $

(☎360-385-0773; www.palacehotelpt.com; 1004 Water St; r $59-109;❋⊜) Built in 1889, this beautiful Victorian building is a former brothel that was once run by the locally notorious Madame Marie, who did her dodgy business out of the 2nd-floor corner suite. Each of the 15 rooms is named after the girl who used to occupy it. Reincarnated as an attractive period hotel with antique furnishings and old-fashioned claw-foot baths, the Palace's former seediness is now a thing of the past, as a quick glance inside the exquisite lobby will testify.

Old Consulate Inn B&B   B&B $$

(☎360-385-6753; www.oldconsulateinn.com; 313 Walker St; r $110-210) Another Queen Anne masterpiece, this former residence of the German consul is a splendid eight-room B&B adorned with the kind of authentic 19th-century decor that will leave you thinking you've wandered into the pages of a Henry James novel. The only trouble is, you'll want to linger here all day, sampling the breakfast, shooting balls in the pool room or relaxing in a hot tub set rather romantically in an outdoor gazebo.

Manresa Castle   HOTEL $$

(☎360-385-5750; www.manresacastle.com; cnr 7th & Sheridan Sts; d/ste $109/169) One of

Port Townsend's signature buildings has been turned into a historic hotel-restaurant that's light on fancy gimmicks but heavy on period authenticity. This 40-room mansion castle, built by the town's first mayor, sits high on a bluff above the port and is one of the first buildings to catch your eye as you arrive by ferry. The vintage rooms may be a little spartan for some visitors, but in a setting this grandiose it's the all-pervading sense of history that counts. The most expensive room is in a turret.

Olympic Hostel
HOSTEL $

(☑360-385-0655; 272 Battery Way; www.olympichostel.net; dm member/nonmember $26/29, d $68) A hostel with a bit of a difference, this 30-bed HI affiliate is situated in the historic barracks at Fort Worden with great views over the bay toward Mt Rainier. Private rooms are available, along with shared showers, a kitchen, common room and an all-you-can-eat pancake breakfast.

Fort Worden State Park
CAMPGROUND $

(☑360-344-4400; www.parks.wa.gov/fortworden; 200 Battery Way; campsites $34 plus $8 one-off reservation fee) A variety of 80 RV hookup sites, many of them beachfront, plus a handful of hiker/cyclist sites ($14). Amenities include kitchen shelters, flush toilets and hot showers.

Swan Hotel
HOTEL $

(☑360-385-6122; www.theswanhotel.com; cnr Monroe & Water St; r from $140; ☎) Stay in rooms in an eye-catching three-story mansion with impressive wrap-around porches, or in three well-decked-out one-story cabins close to the waterfront action. There's even a penthouse suite.

✗ Eating

TOP CHOICE Waterfront Pizza
PIZZA $

(951 Water St; large pizzas $11-19) Quite simply the best pizza in the state, this buy-by-the-slice outlet inspires huge local loyalty and will satisfy even the most querulous of Chicago-honed palates. The secret: crisp sourdough crusts, or creative but not over-stacked toppings? Who knows? Just don't leave town without trying it.

Silverwater Café
FUSION $$

(237 Taylor St; lunch $6-10, dinner $10-17; ⊙11:30am-10pm, till 11pm Sat & Sun) The Silverwater provides a romantic atmosphere in the not-too-fancy setting of a classic Port Townsend Victorian-era building. Renowned for its creatively prepared lo-cal dishes such as ahi tuna and artichoke parmesan pâté, the restaurant also rustles up more homely desserts such as the not-to-be-missed blackberry pie.

Salal Café
BRUNCH $

(634 Water St; breakfast $7-8, lunch $8-9; ⊙7am-2pm) Local consensus suggests that this is Port Townsend's best breakfast/brunch spot and there are numerous culinary awards to back up the claim. The Salal specializes in eggs. Scrambled, poached, frittatas, stuffed into a burrito or served up as an omelet, you can ponder all varieties here during a laid-back breakfast or a zippy lunch.

Victorian Square Restaurant
SANDWICHES $$

(940 Water Street; lunch $7-10; ✓) An interesting nook below street level (entered via a stairway) that was a rum-smuggling haven back in Port Townsend's bad old days, Vic Square's 21st-century reincarnation is as an easygoing lunch stop/candy bar – though the rich desserts at the front counter are equally 'sinful.' Offbeat hot sandwiches include a crab and artichoke melt and a black bean garden burger and you can stave off any long waits with a game of cards (a deck is provided at each table).

Belmont Restaurant & Saloon
SEAFOOD $$

(925 Water St; mains $7-12) Dine on seafood in a lace-shaded booth or on a dais overlooking the water in a one-time dockside saloon that once heaved with crowds of brokers, hustlers and merchant seamen.

El Sarape
MEXICAN $$

(628 Water St; mains $6-13; ✓) Decked out in traditional red, white and green, El Sarape is proudly Mexican, with plenty of seafood and vegetarian options for those who just can't face another chicken burrito.

Nifty Fiftys Soda Fountain
DINER $

(817 Water St) Step out of the 1890s and into the 1950s in this lurid diner for clam strips, root-beer floats and Elvis on the jukebox – if your heart will take it.

⬤ Drinking & Entertainment

Rose Theatre
THEATER

(235 Taylor St) A Northwest diamond and an architectural emblem for the city, this gorgeously renovated movie theater lay woefully abandoned for 37 years before being brought back to life in the 1990s as an art cinema, replete with bohemian café and buttered popcorn. If only there were more like it.

Water Street Brewing & Ale House

BREWPUB

(639 Water St) Shoot pool, play darts, eat seafood, swig beer, chat up the locals, swig more beer... the Water Street heaves beneath the eponymous hotel in a Victorian building that once witnessed far more outlandish behavior.

🔒 Shopping

Downtown Water St has all kinds of independent shops housed in handsome Victorian buildings. Look out for Native American crafts, art galleries, antiques, books, gifts and outdoor apparel.

ℹ️ Information

Port Townsend Visitor Center (www.ptchamber.org; 440 12th St; ⊙9am-5pm Mon-Fri, 10am-4pm Sat, 11am-4pm Sun) Pick up a useful walking-tour map and guide to the downtown historic district here.

ℹ️ Getting There & Around

BOAT **Washington State Ferries** (⌨206-464-6400) operates 15 trips every day to Keystone on Whidbey Island from the terminal in downtown (car and driver/passenger $11.45/2.65, 30 minutes).

Puget Sound Express (www.pugetsoundexpress.com; 431 Water St) boats depart to San Juan Island at 9am between March and October (one way/round trip adult $52/78, child $42/53, bicycles and kayaks round trip $12.50, 2½ hours).

BUS **Jefferson Transit** (www.jeffersontransit.com; 1615 W Sims Way) serves Port Townsend and outlying areas in Jefferson County. Buses travel as far west as Sequim, where connections can be made to Port Angeles and points west on Clallam County's intercity transit system. To the south you can connect with Mason County transit in Brinnon. The basic fare is $1.50.

To reach Port Townsend from Seattle on weekdays, take the ferry from downtown Seattle to Bainbridge Island (35 minutes). At the ferry dock catch Kitsap Transit bus 90 to Poulsbo (20 minutes), and transfer to the Jefferson Transit bus 7 to Port Townsend (one hour).

For a more direct journey, **Olympic Bus Lines** (www.olympicbuslines.com) offers connections to and from its Port Angeles–Seattle run, by reservation. Shuttles arrive and depart from the Haines Place Park and Ride on E Sims Way. Fares are $39/49 to downtown Seattle/Sea-Tac airport.

PORT ANGELES

POP 18,397

Despite the name, there's nothing Spanish or particularly angelic about Port Angeles. Propped up by the lumber industry and backed by the steep-sided Olympic Mountains, people come here to catch a ferry for Victoria, Canada, or plot an outdoor excursion into the nearby Olympic National Park rather than for the town per se.

Named Puerto de Nuestra Señora de los Angeles by Spanish explorer Francisco Eliza in 1791 (the name was later anglicized), Port Angeles entered history in 1862 when president Abraham Lincoln created a navy and military reserve around the natural harbor and made it only the second planned city in the US (after Washington, DC). Though the fishing industry has declined in recent years, Port Angeles has added dynamism to its cultural life with a fine arts center and numerous public sculptures.

👁 Sights & Activities

🚩 Olympic Discovery Trail

INTRA-URBAN TRAIL

(www.olympicdiscoverytrail.com) The trail is an ongoing project that ultimately aims to link Port Townsend and Forks by an off-road hiking-biking trail. About 30 miles of the trail is already complete between Port Angeles and Sequim, starting at the end of **Ediz Hook**, the sand spit that loops around the bay before cutting east along the waterfront. You can pick up the trail at the base of the City Pier, site of the **Feiro Marine Life Center** (adult/child $2.50/1; ⊙10am-6pm Tue-Sun Jun-Sep, noon-4pm Sat & Sun Oct-May; 👶) where hands-on touch tanks are inhabited by the aquatic denizens of the strait.

Bikes for the Olympic Discovery Trail can be rented at **Sound Bikes & Kayaks** (www.soundbikekayaks.com; 120 Front St; bike rental per hr/day $9/30).

FREE **Clallam County Museum** MUSEUM (cnr 1st & Oak Sts; ⊙8:30am-4pm Mon-Fri, closed holidays) Housed in the 1927 Federal Building, the museum retells the story of the community's growth. Two-hour **Heritage Tours** (www.portangelesheritagetours.com; adult/child $12/6) run twice daily Monday to Saturday at 10am and 2.30pm (10.30am and 2pm in the winter). The tour includes the town's 'lost' underground, buried when the downtown area was raised in the early 1900s.

FREE **Port Angeles Fine Arts Center** ART GALLERY (1203 E Lauridsen St; ⊙11am-5pm Tue-Sun) Here you'll find the work of many of the professional artists who live on the peninsula. The gallery is high above the city amid a 5-acre sculpture garden with views over the strait.

Sleeping

Olympic Lodge
HOTEL $$

(☑360-452-2993; www.olympiclodge.com; 140 Del Guzzi Drive; r from $119; ❄@🖵🏊) There are plenty of reasons to make this your Olympic National Park HQ, including a swimming pool, on-site bistro, so-clean-they-seem-new rooms and complementary cookies and milk. It's the most comfortable place in town – no contest.

Downtown Hotel
HOTEL $

(☑360-565-1125; www.portangelesdowntownho tel.com; 101 E Front St; d with shared/private bath-room $45/65; ❄🖵) Nothing special on the outside but surprisingly elegant within, this family-run place down by the ferry launch is Port Angeles' secret bargain. Bright rooms are decked out in wicker and wood, while showers and communal hallways are kept surgically clean. The Corner House diner downstairs is an ideal place for breakfast.

Tudor Inn
B&B $$

(☑360-452-3138; www.tudorinn.com; 1108 S Oak St; r $135-160) With its black-and-white wood beam exterior, this inn manages to look authentically Tudor, although it was built a good 400 years after Henry VIII chopped off Ann Boleyn's head. Constructed by – guess who? – an Englishman in 1910, this refurbished home juxtaposes modern bathroom amenities with fine antiques and an alluring library. Five guestrooms retain their own individual quirks and surprises, and a full English breakfast fortifies hikers striking out for the Olympics.

Port Angeles Inn
MOTEL $$

(☑360-452-9285; www.portangelesinn.com; 111 E 2nd St; r $89-110; ❄🖵) A better-than-average family-run motel perched on the bluff above downtown, with views over the harbor, this inn offers a complimentary breakfast.

Eating

TOP CHOICE **Bella Italia**
ITALIAN $$

(118 E 1st St; mains $12-20; ⊙from 4pm) Bella Italia has been around a lot longer than Bella, the heroine of the *Twilight* saga, but its mention in the book as the place where Bella and Edward Cullen go for their first date has turned what was already a popular restaurant into an icon. In the book Bella has mushroom ravioli and a coke (now one of the most ordered menu items), but more discerning gastronomes might want to opt for the clam linguine, chicken marsala or smoked duck breast washed down with an outstanding wine from a list featuring 500 selections.

Crab House
SEAFOOD $$$

(221 N Lincoln St; mains $15-30; ⊙5:30-11pm) Dungeness crabs are the featured item on the menu at the Crab House and in the light of your location – a few miles from the region's eponymous spit – they don't come much fresher than this. The restaurant is in the waterfront Red Lion Hotel and has striking views across the water. Halibut, salmon and an array of steaks are also served here.

Corner House
DINER $

(101 E Front St; mains $6-8) Head to this traditional diner tucked beneath Downtown Hotel for hot sandwiches and burger-and-fries inspired comfort food with no frills attached. With a 6am opening it's a good place to catch an early breakfast before the morning ferry sailing to Victoria.

Thai Peppers
THAI $

(222 N Lincoln St; mains $8-10) There aren't many ethnic eateries in this neck of the woods, so stock up on your green curry and pad thai noodles at this friendly establishment where the congenial waitresses will offer you spicy sauces, sharp service and plenty of tasty food.

ℹ Information

Adjacent to the ferry terminal you'll find the **Port Angeles Visitor Center** (www.portangeles.org; 121 E Railroad Ave; ⊙8am-8pm May 15-Oct 15, 10am-4pm Oct 16-May14). Olympic National Park visitor center (p123) is 1 mile south of town, off Race St.

ℹ Getting There & Around

AIR **Horizon Air** (www.horizonair.com) has six direct flights daily from Seattle to Fairchild International Airport, just west of Port Angeles. There are other Horizon flights that link Port Angeles to interstate Portland.

BOAT Black Ball Transport's **MV Coho ferry** (www.cohoferry.com) provides passenger and automobile service to Victoria (adult/child/car and driver $11.50/5.75/44 one way, 1½ hours), with three crossings a day from May to September. There are two crossings a day the rest of the year, although service is briefly halted during January for maintenance. The passenger-only **Victoria Express** (☑360-452-8088) runs three or four times a day from late May through September (adult/child $12.50/7, one hour); there's a $2 fee to transport a bicycle.

BUS **Olympic Bus Lines** (www.olympicbuslines. com) runs two buses a day to and from Sequim (adult/child $8/4, 30 minutes), the Seattle

Greyhound terminal (adult/child $39/20, 2½ hours) and Sea-Tac Airport (adult/child $32/16, 3½ hours). Buses arrive and depart from the transit terminal at Front and Oak Sts.

Clallam County's **The Bus** (www.clallamtransit.com) travels as far west as Neah Bay and La Push and as far east as Diamond Point. In Port Angeles, the main transfer center is at Oak and Front Sts, conveniently near the ferry dock and visitors center.

Northwestern Olympic Peninsula

Despite not falling within the boundaries of the Olympic National Park, the northwest section of the Olympic Peninsula remains sparsely populated and remote. Logging is a primary industry here and, in the cultural sphere, four different Native American reservations offer plenty of local legends and history.

Forks is the area's only major settlement, though the fishing town of Neah Bay is reachable by public bus and boasts one of the finest museums of Native American history in the US. The beautiful coastline around La Push in the west provides another worthwhile diversion.

NEAH BAY
POP 794

Isolated Neah Bay is a rather lackluster settlement that sits amid breathtaking coastal scenery at the end of Hwy 112 in North America's extreme northwestern corner. Hit hard by the decline in the salmon fishing industry, this small fishing town, characterized by its weather-beaten boats and craning totem poles, is home of the Makah Indian Reservation.

⊙ Sights & Activities

Makah Museum   MUSEUM
(TOP CHOICE) (www.makah.com; 1880 Bayview Ave; admission $5; ⊙10am-5pm, closed Mon & Tue Sep-May) Hosted by the Makah Reservation, this museum displays artifacts from one of North America's most significant archaeological finds and is reason enough to visit the town. Exposed by tidal erosion in 1970, the 500-year-old Makah village of Ozette proved to be a treasure trove of native history, containing a huge range of materials including whaling weapons, canoes, spears and combs. The museum's centerpiece is a mock-up of an old Ozette longhouse.

Cape Flattery   VIEWPOINT

The end of the road (in the literal sense) is at a parking lot at the end of a 4-mile gravel track west of the Makah Tribal Center. From here a 0.75-mile boardwalk leads out to a dramatic promontory known as Cape Flattery, the most northwesterly point in the lower 48 states. From the four observation decks atop this wild, wind-buffeted point, cliffs fall 60ft to the raging Pacific. Just offshore is Tatoosh Island, with a lighthouse and Coast Guard station. The cape is frequented by 250 species of bird and is a good place to watch for whales during migration season.

Users of the trail are required to purchase a permit ($10) issued by the Makah Cultural Center (inside the Makah Museum) or at the marina.

🛏 Sleeping & Eating

Cape Motel   MOTEL $
(☎360-645-2250; Neah Bay; r $45-75; ❇) Like most accommodations in Neah Bay, this place doesn't aspire to much beyond the regular fishing crowd, but having reached the end of the road in mainland America, what more could you want than four walls, a roof and a small kitchenette? There's also an RV park and tent spaces available.

Makah Maiden Café   SEAFOOD $$
(1471 Bayview Ave; mains $5-17; ⊙4am-11pm) A great waterfront vista, cozy booths and a pre-dawn opening time make this a favorite hangout for local fishers. But, as well as providing your essential early-morning caffeine jolt, the 'Maiden' is also a good bet for seafood, and is renowned for its summer salmon bakes on the beach. Don't miss 'em!

FORKS

Forks, a small lumber town on Hwy 101, was little more than a speck on the Washington state map when publishing phenomenon Stephenie Meyer set her now famous vampire novel *Twilight* here in 2003. Ironically, Meyer – America's answer to JK Rowling – had never been to Forks when she resurrected the ghoulish legacy of Bela Lugosi et al with the first of what has become a series of insanely popular 'tweenage' books. Not that this has stopped the town from cashing in on its newfound literary fame. Forks has apparently seen a 600% rise in tourism over the last five years, the bulk of the visitors being of gawky, wide-eyed under-15-year-old girls who are more than a little surprised to find Forks for what it really is – chillingly ordinary (and wet). For those who haven't got a clue about what *Twilight* is (where have you been for the last five years?), Forks makes a serviceable overnight stop on the Olympic perimeter road or a lunch break before a last push west to La Push.

◉ Sights & Activities

Aside from the *Twilight* kitsch, Forks is pretty sleepy.

Timber Museum MUSEUM
(Hwy 101; admission $3; ☺10am-4pm mid-Apr–Oct) Next door to the chamber of commerce, the Timber Museum commemorates the early settlers and loggers of the region. Included in the museum's collection is a steam donkey (used to transport logs), pioneer farming implements and a fire lookout tower.

Fishing Tours FISHING
You can organize fishing trips for steelhead and coho salmon from $250/320 for one/

two people per day on the local rivers at the **Three Rivers Resort** (☏360-374-5300; 7764 La Push Rd), 8 miles west of Forks on Hwy 110. The lodge also rents surf and boogie boards for Pacific Coast adventurers.

🛏 Sleeping

Forks Motel MOTEL $
(☏360-374-6243; 432 S Forks Ave; s/d $65/70; ❄🐾📶) Forks' archetypal motel is glued to the side of US 101, tempting tired drivers to call it a day and put their feet up. Above average in the standard motel stakes, this place has 73 straightforward units including two kitchen suites and a Jacuzzi suite. There's a small pool, plenty of local fishing information and – above all – a very friendly welcome.

Pacific Inn Motel MOTEL $
(☏360-374-9400; 352 S Forks Ave; r from $89; ❄📶) Opposite the Forks Motel, the Pacific Inn offers similar standard rooms, plus a handful that have adopted a

---

THE TWILIGHT ZONE

It would have been impossible to envisage a decade ago: diminutive Forks, a depressed lumber town full of hard-nosed loggers, reborn as a pilgrimage site for 'tweenage' girls following in the ghostly footsteps of two fictional sweethearts named Bella and Edward. The reason for this weird metamorphosis is the *Twilight* saga, a four-part book series by US author Stephenie Meyer about love and vampires on the foggy Olympic Peninsula that in seven short years has shifted nigh on 100 million books and spawned three Hollywood movies. With Forks acting as the book's main setting, the town has catapulted to international stardom and thrown up one of Washington's strangest ironies – Bud-slugging lumberjacks in dive bars juxtaposed with romance-hungry 15-year-olds shopping for kitschy vampire paraphernalia (of which there is plenty). Economic reasons have so far ensured that relations between the two camps have remained cordial. Forks' tourist numbers have gone through the stratosphere since the 2008 release of the first *Twilight* movie and the financial rewards in this isolated, boom-bust town have been felt by everyone.

Ironically, not much was actually filmed in Forks. Many film locations were in Oregon, including some Forks High School scenes shot in Portland. You'll have better luck in nearby Port Angeles, where key scenes were shot (check out www.portangelesdowntown.com for specifics).

Dazzled by Twilight (www.dazzledbytwilight.com; 11 N Forks Ave; ☺10am-6pm; 🚻) runs two *Twilight* merchandise shops in Forks (and another in Port Angeles) as well as the Forks **Twilight Lounge** (81 N Forks Ave). The lounge hosts a downstairs restaurant along with an upstairs music venue that showcases regular live bands and a bloodcurdling 5pm to 8pm Saturday-night tween karaoke. The company also runs four daily **Twilight Tours** (adult/child $39/25; ☺departing 8am, 11.30am, 3pm & 6pm) visiting most of the places mentioned in Meyer's books. Highlights include the Forks High School, the Treaty Line at the nearby Rivers Resort, and a sortie out to the tiny coastal community of La Push.

In La Push itself, *Twilight* boat tours operated by the **Quileute Nation** (www.quileute nation.org) sail out to Bella and Jacob's cliff (from which Bella jumps in *New Moon*). You'll probably see plenty of seabirds but no Robert Pattinson.

Twilight theme (lots of reds and blacks and some film posters).

Bogachiel State Park
CAMPGROUND $

(☎360-374-6356; Hwy 101; tent/RV sites $17/24) The most convenient campground is 6 miles south of Forks, right on the Bogachiel River, with 37 sites, piped water and flush toilets.

✖ Eating

The In Place
DINER $$

(320 S Forks Ave; sandwiches $4-7, mains $9-17) Forks is no culinary Rome meaning you'll probably have to settle for this mediocre home-style cooking place on US 101 opposite the Forks Motel. Burgers, serve-yourself salads and soups are offered in well-worn booths. Save the best till last – a slice of bumbleberry pie.

ℹ Information

Get orientated at the **Forks Chamber of Commerce** (www.forkswa.com) which shares digs with the Olympic National Park and the **USFS Recreation Information Station** (551 S Forks Ave) along the southern approach to Forks. The rec station is staffed by knowledgeable rangers, and is the place to get backcountry permits, maps, tide charts and animal-resistant containers for coastal camping.

LA PUSH

La Push, 12 miles west of Forks on Hwy 110, is a small fishing village at the mouth of the Quillayute River and home of the Quileute Indian tribe, some of the peninsula's oldest inhabitants.

Known for its raw, untamed beaches, La Push is popular with surfers and sea kayakers who love to ride the dramatic Pacific waves, especially in January. Outside of this, the settlement is revered primarily for its remoteness and isolation (despite a recent influx of *Twilight* hunters). Tracking north along the Mora road will bring you to **Rialto Beach** and the start of a 24-mile coastal hike north to Cape Alava. Just outside of La Push are the trailheads to rugged Third and Second Beaches (1.4 miles and 0.8 miles respectively). Third Beach is the starting point for a popular three-day beach hike (p120) to Oil City, 17 miles south, at the edge of the Hoh Indian Reservation.

🛏 Sleeping & Eating

Quileute Oceanside Resort
RESORT $-$$

(☎360-374-5267; www.quileutenation.org; tent/RV sites $15/25, motel r $55-78, cabins $80-160, town house $120-160) Sitting above one of Washington's most beautiful beaches, the tribe-owned-and-operated resort has accommodations ranging from basic A-frame cabins with sleeping-bag loft and toilet (no shower) to deluxe oceanfront cottages with stone fireplaces and whirlpool tubs. Somewhere in the middle are standard motel rooms in two buildings with balconies. No reservations are accepted for camping or RVs.

River's Edge Restaurant
SEAFOOD $$

(☎360-374-5777; 41 Main St; mains $8-25) One of the few restaurants on this stretch of coast. Stick to the freshly caught seafood options and look out for outdoor barbecues in the summer when salmon is baked in the Quileute tradition. Located in an old boathouse, the restaurant is famous for its free ornithological shows courtesy of the resident eagles and pelicans.

ℹ Getting There & Away

Clallam Transit (www.clallamtransit.com) offers three daily buses between Forks and Neah Bay (11/four hours), and three between Forks and La Push (55 minutes). The Forks–Port Angeles bus (No 14) runs eight times daily (four on Saturday) and takes one hour 20 minutes. Buses south from Forks to Lake Quinault (11/ two hours) are operated by **Jefferson Transit** (www.jeffersontransit.com) and run three to four times daily. Note: no buses operate on Sundays.

WASHINGTON COAST

The stretch of Washington coast from Ocean Shores down to Cape Disappointment at the mouth of the Columbia River, with its expansive beaches and locally run oyster farms, is the state's maritime playground. Free of the wild coves and stormy sea stacks common further north, this is where the whole of Washington (and beyond) comes to sail, fish, fly kites and hang out.

None of the various resorts that scatter the coast in this region are particularly large – or legendary. But, though pockets of modern commercialism may have diluted the quaintness of places such as Long Beach and Ocean Shores, there are still enough state parks, wildlife refuges and lonesome stretches of sand to hide an abundance of unheralded local secrets.

Further east the I-5 corridor cuts from Olympia down to Portland whizzing past Centralia, Castle Rock (with access to Mt St

Helens) and the US (and first) incarnation of Vancouver.

Grays Harbor Area

Once home to the Chehalis tribe, Grays Harbor was first charted by non-native explorers in 1792, when American Robert Gray arrived in the bay, which acts as an estuary for the Chehalis River. Farming, fishing and fur trading were the staple of the settlers in the 1840s and '50s, though this was quickly replaced by lumber in the 1880s. With most of the mills now closed, Grays Harbor has become a sleepy backwater, although the area is doing its best to lure in tourism with a variety of charter fishing and beachcombing activities.

ⓘ Getting There & Away

BOAT A passenger ferry crosses from Westport to Ocean Shores six times daily mid-June to Labor Day, and on weekends only May to mid-June and September ($6/10 one way/round trip). Purchase tickets at Float 10. Call **Westport/Ocean Shores Ferry** (☏360-268-0047) for information.

BUS Grays Harbor Transit (www.ghtransit.com) runs weekday buses from Aberdeen to Olympia (two hours, six daily), Lake Quinault (one hour, four daily), Ocean Shores (11/two hours, 10 daily), Westport (30 minutes, seven daily) and Centralia Amtrak station (11/two hours, one daily). There are connections to the Long Beach Peninsula with **Pacific Transit System** (www.pacifictransit.org). The downtown Aberdeen bus station is on Wishkah and G Sts, in Hoquiam at 7th and J Sts.

OCEAN SHORES

Washington State's most popular coastal resort is a manufactured beach haven known as Ocean Shores that was constructed in the 1960s on a scenic stretch of shoreline some distance south of the Quinault Indian Reservation. While the settlement boasts its fair share of clichéd resort activities including golf, dune buggy-riding and gambling at the Quinault Beach Resort and Casino, the area is far from spoiled with kite-flying, canoeing (there are over 20 miles of interconnecting canals) and razor clamming (digging in the sand for razor clams) also enduringly popular.

✦ Activities

You can rent boats to ply the region's ubiquitous canals at **Runabout Cart & Pedal Boat Rental** (598 Point Brown Ave SE). Beach horseback riding can be arranged through **Nan-Sea Stables** (255 State Route 115). If the weath-

er turns ugly (and it often does), check out the local history, wildlife and geology at **Ocean Shores Interpretive Center** (1013 Catala Ave SE; admission free; ◷10am-4pm Apr-Sep).

For further information, you can contact **Ocean Shores Chamber of Commerce** (www.oceanshores.org; Catala Mall, 899 Point Brown Ave).

🛏 Sleeping & Eating

Ocean Crest Resort   HOTEL **$$**
(☏360-276-4465; Hwy 109, Sunset Beach; studio $52-159, ste $112-177; ☒) Just south of Moclips, this is a stellar self-contained resort and hotel overlooking the Pacific with a good selection of room prices and a decent, if exceedingly expensive, restaurant. Bonuses include a heated indoor pool, sauna and upstairs lounge where you can snuggle down and keep your eye out for passing whales. Private beach access is down a winding, wooded path.

Galway Bay Irish Pub   PUB **$$**
(880 Point Brown Ave) It's a long way from the Emerald Isle, but if you're missing your Guinness, Harps or Paddy Burke's white Irish stew, pack your fiddle and roll up here for fine music, loquacious locals and plenty of humorous hospitality.

ABERDEEN & HOQUIAM

The tourist blurb likes to talk them up but, in reality, Olympic twins Aberdeen and Hoquiam comprise one pretty gritty city. Nonetheless, there's a rousing history hidden behind the boarded-up shops and general air of decay. Much of it can be told through the life stories of the famous locals. Despite (or perhaps *because of*) the apparent decrepitude, the cities have churned out enough noted citizens to fill a Hollywood Boulevard–style 'Walk of Fame'. Kurt Cobain of Nirvana was born in Aberdeen, Denver Broncos quarterback John Elway spent his childhood in Hoquiam, and aviation pioneer William Boeing made his first inroad into big business by buying up extensive tracts of timberlands around Grays Harbor.

Aberdeen developed around a salmon-packing plant in the 1870s and Hoquiam's first lumber mill opened in 1882. By 1910 there were over 30 lumber mills ringing the harbor and the burgeoning twin towns had earned a reputation as the roughest places in the nation, replete with whorehouses, gambling dens and a sky-high murder rate. Following the Great Depression, when the lumber mills were reduced to less than a dozen, Grays Harbor hit a long decline exacerbated by an equally catastrophic fall in Pacific salmon stocks. When a planned nuclear facility went bust in 1982 the unemployment rate doubled and the gritty rough-around-the-edges feel can still be sensed today.

The twin towns' **Grays Harbor Chamber of Commerce** (www.graysharbor.org; 506 Duffy St; ⊙9am-5pm Mon-Fri) affords visitors a warm welcome. Pop by for free maps and plenty of informative leaflets.

⊙ Sights & Activities

First impressions deceive. There's actually more to Aberdeen and Hoquiam than meets the eye.

Lady Washington   HISTORIC SHIP

For some interesting local history, check out this full-scale replica of one of the ships piloted by Captain Robert Gray when he first sailed into Grays Harbor. The ship is open for tours when moored at **Grays Harbor Historical Seaport** (www.ladywashington. org; 813 E Heron St, Aberdeen; adult/child $3/1; ⊙10am-5pm). It's still used as a working boat.

Arnold Polson Museum   MUSEUM

(1611 Riverside Ave, Hoquiam; adult/child $2/50¢; ⊙11am-4pm Wed-Sun Jun-Sep, noon-4pm Sat & Sun Oct-May) Built in 1924 by one of the timber barons of Hoquiam, this 26-room edifice is filled with period furniture, clothing, a doll collection and logging implements.

Aberdeen Museum of History   MUSEUM

(111 E Third St, Aberdeen; admission by donation; ⊙10am-5pm Tue-Sun) Aberdeen's archive plots the history of this tough mill town from its earliest days, with a strong focus on the lumber industry. You can also ask here about the self-guided **Kurt Cobain Tour** around some of the former houses and hangouts of the late Nirvana star. Cobain and other local luminaries are honored in a Hollywood-style **Walk of Fame** that exhibits star-shaped plaques to former famous residents (and there are many) along Heron and Wishkah Sts.

🛏 Sleeping

Hoquiam's Castle   B&B **$$$**

(☎360-533-2005; www.hoquiamcastle.com; 515 Chenault Ave, Hoquiam; r $145-195; 🐾) Part museum (adult/child $4/1), part B&B, part local landmark, this ornate Victorian mansion was built in 1897 on a hill above Hoquiam by Robert Lytle, a wealthy lumber tycoon. The lavish furnishings and meticulous period details are some of the most authentic you'll see in the state and include lots of dark wood, delicate antiques and even a fully working Victorian bathroom. The four rooms are labeled king's, queen's, princess' and knight's, and there's an opulent lobby where traditional afternoon tea can be taken. Nonguests are welcome to view the house most afternoons.

A Harbor View Inn   B&B **$$**

(☎360-533-7996; www.aharborview.com; 111 W 11th St, Aberdeen; d/ste $139/225) Aberdeen's answer to Hoquiam Castle is another Victorian masterpiece; its five clean, quirky rooms blow everything else in town out of the water.

Olympic Inn   MOTEL **$**

(☎360-532-8161; www.aberdeenolympicinn. com; 616 W Heron St, Aberdeen; r from $67; ✳@🛜) Beware; the twin towns' motels can be gritty. The Olympic's standout features are that it's clean, recently upgraded and has Belgian waffles for breakfast. Not so gritty after all.

🍴 Eating

Billy's Bar & Grill   PUB, STEAKHOUSE **$$**

(E Heron St, Aberdeen; mains from $10) If you're passing through on your way to the national park, this place makes a worthwhile pit stop. In the rootin' tootin' days of yore, the bars in Aberdeen were haunted by Billy Gohl (better known as Billy Ghoul), a murderous fellow who robbed and killed drunken sailors and loggers. Billy and the era are both commemorated at this handsome old bar and restaurant with good sandwiches, full dinners and regional microbrews. The place has a split entry, meaning children and non-drinkers can use the dining area.

Back Stage Espresso   CAFÉ **$**

(1234 Main St, Aberdeen; ⊙9am-9pm Mon-Thu, 9am-8pm Fri & Sat, 9am-7pm Sun) In the shuttered-up, darkly depressed streets of downtown Aberdeen, this cozy coffee bar confecting Olympia's aromatic Batdorf & Bronson's brew provides a welcome pick-me-up from the chill outside. Even better, it's next door to the recently remodeled D & R Theater and an equally tempting ice-cream bar called **Scoops**.

WESTPORT

Guarding the entrance to Gray's Harbor, stormy Westport is famous for its deep-sea fishing, rugged surfing and isolated beachcombing possibilities. Once the largest whaling port on the west coast and the largest charter fishing center in the Northwest, the town has suffered since restrictions were placed on salmon fishing in the last couple of decades. In a bid to reinvent itself as Washington's most happening coastal destination, Westport has invested heavily in a chain of restaurants, condos and golf courses. Still on offer are the ever-popular chartered fishing trips and whale-watching expeditions, though the backbone of the fishing industry disappeared years ago.

For more information, contact the **Westport-Grayland Chamber of Commerce & Visitors Center** (www.westportcam.com; 2985 S Montesano St; ☉9am-5pm Mon-Fri, 10am-3pm Sat & Sun), located at the turnoff from Hwy 105.

⊙ Sights

Westport Maritime Museum   MUSEUM
(2201 Westhaven Dr; adult/child $3/1; ☉10am-4pm Memorial Day-Labor Day, noon-4pm Thu-Mon Sep-May) This former Coast Guard station was built in 1939 and boasts some great period photos and artifacts of seafaring days gone by. A separate building houses the sixton, 18ft-high **Fresnel lens**, manufactured in France in 1888, that beamed for over 70 years from the lighthouse of Destruction Island, 50 miles north of Westport.

Grays Harbor Lighthouse   LANDMARK
(1020 West Ocean Ave; admission $3; ☉10am-4pm May-Sep, noon-3pm Oct-Apr) Westport's own beacon also used a Fresnel lens until recently, when it was replaced by a simpler electronic device. To reach the lighthouse – the tallest in the state at 107ft – return to uptown Westport and head west on Ocean Ave. You can also bike or hike there along the **Westport Maritime History Trail**, a 6.5-mile pedestrian pathway that passes the marina and treks along a dune trail into Westhaven State Park. Tours of the lighthouse are available through the maritime museum. Just beyond the lighthouse, **Westport Light State Park** has wind-screened picnic sites and access to a stretch of beach that's closed to motor vehicles in summer.

🏃 Activities

Charter fishing is still a hot drawcard in Westport. The best fishing season runs from April through October (depending on the fish). Regular trips target black rockfish, Ling cod, salmon, halibut and tuna, using live bait and conforming to set fishing limits. One-day licenses can be purchased with the excursion. Deckhands can fillet your fish for an extra fee and even arrange to have it vacuum-packed, smoked or stored. Prices tend to start at around $115 per person per day for salmon fishing and up to about $230 for halibut, but shop around.

Most of these charter companies also run whale-watching excursions in the spring. Stroll along the marina and check the offerings. An hour-long excursion will generally cost around $30/20 per adult/child.

For more about charter fishing contact **Deep Sea Charters** (www.deepseacharters.net; 2319 Westhaven Dr, Westport), or procure a full list of operators at the visitors center.

🛏 Sleeping & Eating

Glenacres Inn B&B   B&B $
(☑360-268-0958; 222 N Montesano St, Westport; d $50-82, cottage $160; 🛜) Westport's contribution to the vintage B&B scene is this large house on the hill where – legend has it – Bobby Kennedy once stayed the night (albeit 45 years ago). Having changed ownership in the last couple of years, the inn has undergone some renovations though it still earns an affordable midrange pricetag. Bathrooms are small, but there's wi-fi, morning coffee and deer on the lawn. There's also a small cottage in the grounds for families or larger groups.

One-Eyed Crab   SEAFOOD $$$
(2309 Westhaven Dr; mains $20-30) A new-ish small, family-run place operated by people who know their crab. Aside from the obvious (Dungeness, of course), there's a decent seafood chowder, clams, prawns, scallops and crab legs – wait for it – deep fried. Service can be a little tardy but, hey, this is low-key Westport, not Seattle.

Long Beach Peninsula

The name's hardly original, but of the half a dozen or so Long Beaches in the US, the Washington version – a 28-mile-long sand spit that lies directly to the north of the Columbia River estuary – is unequivocally the longest (less proven is its claim to be the *world's* longest beach). The adjoining 28 miles of seaside development aren't quite as unique. There's nothing particularly eye-catching about the amusement arcades, cheap motels and trinket shops that characterize Hwy 103, though none of the half-dozen or so settlements are large or high-rise. Much of the beach itself is overrun with pickup trucks in peak season (as Washington state beaches are considered highways). Purists might prefer the Willapa Bay side of the peninsula, with its old towns, oyster beds and wildlife viewing. The main settlements on the peninsula, running north to south, are Oysterville, Nahcotta, Ocean Park, Klipsan Beach, Long Beach, Seaview and Ilwaco.

OYSTERVILLE & NAHCOTTA

The charm of these old communities – the only ones on the bay side of the Long Beach Peninsula – derives not just from their history but also from the absence of the beachfront towns' carnival atmosphere. Here, wildlife viewing, oyster harvesting and gracious dining occupy residents and visitors alike. Oysterville stands largely unchanged since its heyday in the 1870s, when the oyster boom was at its peak.

◉ Sights & Activities

Oysterville TOWN

Oysterville is filled with well-preserved Victorian homes including the 1863 **Red Cottage** (Territory Rd) near Clay St, which served as the first Pacific County courthouse, and the **Big Red House** (cnr Division St & Territory Rd), the original home of Oysterville cofounder RH Espy, built in 1871. Other historic buildings include a one-room schoolhouse and the 1892 **Oysterville Church** (cnr Clay St & Territory Rd); pick up a walking-tour brochure here.

Leadbetter Point State Park Natural Area STATE PARK

(Stackpole Rd) The 807-acre Leadbetter Point State Park Natural Area, 3 miles north of Oysterville, is a kind of buffer between the straggling developments of Long Beach Peninsula and a section of the Willapa National Wildlife Refuge, a narrowing band of dunes increasingly breached by Pacific waves. Though most people just meander down to the reedy shores of Willapa Bay, two hiking trails lead through forest and marshes to reach these lowering dunes, as good a place as any in the Northwest to watch for shorebirds.

⊨ Sleeping & Eating

Moby Dick Hotel & Oyster Farm
HOTEL $$

(☎360-665-4543; www.mobydickhotel.com; 25814 Sandridge Rd, Nahcotta; d incl breakfast $90-150) You can take yoga classes in a yurt or get intimate with the whale vertebrae that furnish the patio in this 1929 structure that once served as a Coast Guard barracks. Other features include a sauna, three communal lounge rooms and a celebrated restaurant that serves up delicious oysters picked from its very own oyster beds. Bold colors and eclectic themes characterize the 10 well-appointed rooms (two of which have private bathroom) and a substantial three-course breakfast should keep you going all day.

Bailey's Bakery & Café BAKERY, CAFÉ $

(www.baileysbakerycafe.com; 26910 Sandridge Rd, Nahcotta; snacks from $3; ☺8am-3pm Thu-Sat & Mon, from 9am Sun) Sharing digs with Nahcotta post office, this small nook serves locally roasted Long Beach coffee and the lauded 'thunder buns': currants, pecans, honey butter glaze and a whole lot of bun.

LONG BEACH & SEAVIEW

Long Beach (population 1283) and Seaview (population 516) comprise the major population center on the peninsula. Both towns began as beach resorts in the late 1880s. A few old inns from this era have been beautifully restored, though the modern strip on Hwy 103 (aka Pacific Way) is lined with T-shirt shops, middlebrow boutiques and bumper-car arenas. To the west, the beach is separated from the town by a wide swathe of dunes and dwarf pines and remains pretty wild, especially along the 8.2-mile Discovery Trail.

◉ Sights & Activities

Beaches BEACHES

Primary **beach access** points in Long Beach are off 10th St SW and Bolstad Ave; a 0.25-mile boardwalk links the two entryways. In Seaview, take 38th Place, just south of Hwy 101. Cars and trucks aren't allowed on these busy beaches in summer, but the beach north of Bolstad Ave to Ocean Park is open to vehicles year-round.

Note that surf swimming here is dangerous due to strong waves and quickly changing tides. Instead of plunging into the water, you might hit the saddle and ride on horseback along the endless dunes. Several Long Beach outfitters offer horseback-riding tours (solo riding is discouraged); try **Back Country Wilderness Outfitters** (www.longbeach horserides.com; 409 SW Sid Snyder Dr). Biking along the boardwalk is another fun activity. **OWW** (cnr 10th St & Ocean Beach Blvd) rents out bicycles ($5 per hour) and mopeds ($18).

Kite-Flying KITES

Thousands of people descend on Long Beach during the third week of August for the **Washington State International Kite Festival**, billed as the largest such event in the western hemisphere. Festival-goers seek to gain new world records: the greatest number of kites in flight at one time, the largest kite flown, the longest time aloft and so on.

With some 150,000 people attending the festival annually, it was just a matter of time before someone opened the **World Kite Museum & Hall of Fame** (303 Sid Snyder Dr; adult/child $5/3; ⊙11am-5pm daily Jun-Aug, Fri-Mon Sep-May; 🏛). If you think a museum devoted to the history and artistry of kites might be a bore, think again. Kites have been used for scientific research, aerial photography, mail delivery and reconnaissance – as well as for amusement – for centuries. The whole story's here, along with the largest, smallest and wackiest kites.

🛏 Sleeping

Shelburne Country Inn & Restaurant
HOTEL **$$$**
(☑360-642-4142; 4415 Pacific Way; r $139-199; mains $22-28; ⊙from 5:30pm; 🛜) Many consider the restaurant at the Shelburne Country Inn one of the showplaces of Northwest cuisine. The dining room, dominated by arched stained-glass windows salvaged from an English church, is certainly one of the most charming you'll find. Local seafood, fish, poultry and lamb are served with a consistently inventive flair. An English-style pub on the premises serves lighter fare. The inn itself is a Washington classic with 17 elegant guestrooms at giveaway prices when you factor in the complementary cookies, wi-fi, fresh flowers and gourmet breakfast.

Our Place at the Beach MOTEL **$**
(☑800-538-5107; www.ourplacelongbeach.weebly.com; 1309 Ocean Beach Blvd, Long Beach; r $62; 🛜🐾) Nothing fancy, but under new ownership and keen to please, this smallish motel offers good beach access (5 minutes' walk through the dunes), a small gym, two hot tubs and comfortable if slightly dated rooms. It's an easy walk to all of Long Beach's downtown facilities.

🍴 Eating

TOP CHOICE **Dooger's Seafood & Grill** SEAFOOD **$$**
(900 Pacific Way S; mains $12-20) Sit down at simple diner-style tables for a huge array of fresh seafood, most of it nabbed from local waters. The delicious 'combination plate' showcases the works: calamari, salmon, halibut, prawns and – best of all – oysters, all of them sautéed to perfection and served with a complementary salad. Dishes can be taken as full plates or smaller 'lite bites.'

Cottage Bakery & Deli BAKERY, CAFÉ **$**
(118 Pacific Way S; cakes from $0.85) Opens at 4am and, with cakes and pastries this good, you might want to consider queuing outside waiting for the sun to rise and the oven timer to zing 'baked to perfection.' Less stalwart hunger-mongers roll in for breakfast around 8am: a healthy bowl of porridge followed by a slightly less healthy glazed old-fashioned doughnut. Old signs on the walls advertise war bonds, but the quality of the cakes never changes.

❶ Information
For an excellent information portal on the whole peninsula see www.funbeach.com.
Long Beach Peninsula Visitors Bureau (www.funbeach.com; cnr Hwy 101 & Pacific Hwy, Seaview; ⊙9am-5pm Mon-Sat, 10am-4pm Sun) Can help you get reservations for the area's motels and lodgings.

❶ Getting There & Around
Pacific Transit System (www.pacifictransit.org) runs buses throughout Pacific County, from Aberdeen to towns along the Long Beach Peninsula via South Bend and Raymond, and as far south as Astoria, Oregon. Bus 20 runs approximately once an hour between Ilwaco and Oysterville from around 6am to 7pm weekdays ($0.50, 40 minutes), less often on Saturday and not at all on Sunday. Bus 24 connects Ilwaco with Astoria (30 minutes, Monday to Friday only). There are no connections east toward Longview and Kelso.

ILWACO
POP 950

More salt-of-the-sea than salt-of-the-earth, blink-and-you'll-miss-it Ilwaco is the Washington coast's main fishing port. What passes for downtown is a collection of wooden cabin-style homes overlooking a boat-filled harbor. The early growth of the salmon-canning industry here was aided by the development of salmon traps, a method of catching the fish that was made illegal in the 1930s.

Unlike the rest of the Long Beach Peninsula, Ilwaco is hemmed in by rocky hills. West of town, on a rugged promontory above the mouth of the Columbia River in Cape Disappointment State Park, are the remains of Fort Canby, a Civil War–era bulwark designed to protect river shipping from Confederate interference. The newly opened hiking/biking Discovery Trail terminates here.

◉ Sights

Columbia Pacific Heritage Museum
MUSEUM

(115 SE Lake St; adult/child $5/3, free Thu; ◎10am-4pm Tue-Sat, noon-4pm Sun) Investigating ancient Chinook culture, along with the exploration and trade of successive Spanish, Russian, British and American explorers, is this fine museum. It also features the *Old Ilwaco,* a restored narrow gauge passenger train also known as the *Nahcotta,* that ran along the peninsula railway.

TOP CHOICE Cape Disappointment State Park
STATE PARK

(Hwy 100; ◎dawn-dusk) Although little remains of the original Fort Canby that once stood in what is now 2 miles southwest of Ilwaco, the location is of considerable interest because of its interpretive center, wild beach area and hiking trails (8 miles in total) to its two dramatic lighthouses.

Established in 1852, Fort Canby was heavily armed during the Civil War to prevent Confederate gunboats from entering the Columbia River. Upgraded dramatically during WWII, the fort stood as the principal defender of the river. Although no shots were fired from Fort Canby, a Japanese submarine did manage to penetrate close enough to the Oregon side to fire on Fort Stephens in 1942.

Lewis and Clark camped near here in November 1805 and visited the cape while searching for a winter camp. Their whole cross-continental journey is faithfully recounted at the sequentially laid-out **Lewis & Clark Interpretive Center** (Hwy 100; adult/child $5/2.50; ◎10am-5pm) on a high bluff inside the state park overlooking the point where the Columbia River meets the Pacific. There's a succinct 20-minute film recounting their journey.

From the interpretive center, a hiking trail leads half a mile to **Cape Disappointment Lighthouse**. Built in 1856, it's the oldest such structure still in use on the West Coast. On the other side of the park (accessible via a trail), the **North Head Lighthouse**, built in 1896, offers tours from $2.50. Call the park for more details.

🏃 Activities

Unsurprisingly, Ilwaco has plenty of charter fishing options, with expeditions sallying forth in search of salmon, sturgeon, halibut or bottom fish, depending on the season. Charters start at $85 per person and set sail at the crack of dawn. Try **Sea Breeze Charters** (www.seabreezecharters.net) for some of the best organized trips. The office is right on the harbor front.

🛏 Sleeping & Eating

Cape Disappointment State Park Campground
CAMPGROUND $

(☑360-642-3078; Hwy 100; tent/RV sites $21/28, yurts & cabins $40) There are nearly 250 sites in two zones: by the beach and around a lake near the park entrance. Coin-operated hot showers and flush toilets are within easy reach. Yurts, cabins and three former lightkeeper's residences provide further unique accommodation options.

'OCEAN IN VIEW! O, THE JOY'

For American history buffs, Long Beach and the adjacent hulk of Cape Disappointment are hallowed ground. In November 1805, William Clark of the Discovery Corps arrived here looking for his first close-up glimpse of the Pacific Ocean. One year after leaving St Louis, Missouri on a journey to map and explore the barely known continent, Clark, along with fellow explorer Meriwether Lewis and three dozen others, had finally staggered into a sheltered cove on the Columbia River 2 miles west of the present-day Astoria Bridge and christened it 'Station Camp.' Adamant to find a better winter bivouac, Clark and several companions continued the hike west to the Long Beach peninsula, coming to a halt near present-day 26th St where Clark dipped his toe in the Pacific and carved his name on a cedar tree for posterity. The route of this historic three-day trudge has been recreated in the **Long Beach Discovery Trail**, which runs from the small town of Ilwaco near the mouth of the Columbia River to Clark's 26th St turnaround. Officially inaugurated in September 2009, the trail has incorporated some dramatic life-sized sculptures along its 8.2-mile length. One depicts a giant grey whale skeleton, another recalls Clark's recorded sighting of a washed-up sea sturgeon, while a third recreates in bronze the original cedar tree (long since uprooted by a Pacific storm).

Inn at Harbor Village   HOTEL $$

(☑360-642-0087; www.innatharborvillage. com; 120 Williams Ave NE; r $115-185; ☎) One of Washington's most improbable and creative accommodations is this recently refurbished 1928 Presbyterian church, with its sloped ceilings and nine exquisite guestrooms. The parlor has an old grandfather clock, plus you can enjoy the delights of a complimentary breakfast and wine. The inn is set in woodland, an easy walk from Ilwaco port.

Don's Portside Café/Pizzeria   DINER $

(303 Main St; breakfast from $4, lunch $7-9; ◷4am-3pm) Don's is the sort of greasy-spoon diner where only three letters on the neon CAFÉ sign work and half of the weatherbeaten locals look as if they've just staggered in off the (original) Lewis and Clark Trail. No matter, this place is all about good old Ilwaco-ian atmosphere, which means great pies and chirpy service – even at 4am!

Vancouver

POP 143,560

There was a T-shirt doing the rounds of Vancouver not so long ago emblazoned with the words 'Vancouver *not* BC, Washington *not* DC, Clark County *not* Kansas, near Portland *not* Maine.' The said garment probably revealed as much about Vancouver's sense of humor than it did about the city itself. Though a good 60 years older than its Olympic-hosting namesake to the north, Vancouver, WA has long suffered from a case of mistaken identity (yes, the occasional BC-bound traveler still rolls in here assuming they've reached Canada), plus the notion that, despite a population of 143,000 (making it the fourth largest metropolis in Washington), it's usually viewed as little more than a glorified suburb of Portland. Recent efforts to rename it have been met with both enthusiasm and mirth (Fort Vancouver was the most popular choice), but the gutsy citizens have put on a brave face. Aside from a talent for self-depreciation, Vancouver WA offers pioneer history, a decent weekend farmers market, and the oldest surviving fort in the Pacific Northwest. Go on, give it a whirl.

◉ Sights & Activities

TOP
CHOICE **Vancouver National Historic Reserve**   HISTORIC RESERVE

(www.fortvan.org) Situated within easy walking distance of the city center is Vancouver's –

and one of Washington's – most important historical monuments. Comprising an archaeological site, the region's first military post, a waterfront trail and one of the nation's oldest operating airfields, the complex's highlight is the reconstructed **Fort Vancouver Historic Site** (www.nps.gov/fova; adult/family $3/5; ◷9am-5pm). Here resident rangers and actors in period costume skillfully summon up the era from 1825 to 1845, when the fort was under the sole administration of the British Hudson Bay Company (the so-called Oregon Country was run jointly by the British and the Americans until 1846). Within the stockaded grounds, you can learn how the fort was once a center for the burgeoning Northwest fur trade and a bulwark in a shaky 40-year alliance between the Americans and the British. As historical presentations go, it's one of the most entertaining and educational walkabouts in the state. Tours generally leave on the hour.

Travelers should also pop into the **visitors center** (612 E Reserve St; admission free; ◷9am-5pm), which boasts a small museum and a fascinating video on the Lewis and Clark expedition that wound up near here in November 1805.

Along the north side of E Evergreen Blvd are the historic homes of **Officers Row**. Built between 1850 and 1906 for US Army officers and their families, they are currently rented out as offices and apartments. Three of the homes are open for self-guided tours. **Grant House** (1101 Officers Row; admission free; ◷11am-9pm), built in 1850 from logs and later covered with clapboard, now houses a restaurant. **Marshall House** (◷9am-5pm), home to General George Marshall in the 1930s, is a grand Queen Anne–style mansion. The **OO Howard House** built in 1879 was a non-commissioned officer's club during WWII and was restored to its former elegance in 1998. It now houses a small gift shop. Ask at the visitors center about guided walks. Elsewhere, the lovely open spaces of the historic reserve are great places to enjoy a picnic, fly a kite or take a stroll. At the time of writing, a land bridge was being built to connect the reserve with the Columbia River waterfront.

Pearson Air Museum   MUSEUM

(☑360-694-7026; 1115 E 5th St; adult/child $7/5; ◷10am-5pm Wed-Sat) Just east of Fort Vancouver, this museum is devoted to the colorful history of Northwest aviation. A number of historic planes are on display in the main hangar, surrounded by exhibits on the golden age of flight.

🛏 Sleeping

Heathman Hotel
HOTEL **$$**

(☏360-254-3100; www.heathmanlodge.com; 7801 NE Greenwood Dr; r from $139; ✲🛜🏊) Er...are you still in Portland? Defying Vancouver's image as a ho-hum 'suburb,' the Heathman is the city's best hotel by several miles. Calling yourself a mountain lodge when you're slap-bang in the middle of a metro area might seem cheeky to some, but this place more than carries the moniker with an eye-catching lobby, beyond-the-call-of-duty service, sleep-invoking bed mattresses and several notebooks worth of thoughtful extras.

Briar Rose Inn
B&B **$**

(☏360-694-5710; www.briarroseinn.com; 310 W 11th St; r with shared bathroom from $85; ✲🛜) A 1908 Craftsman-style home turned B&B with antique-laden rooms, the Briar Rose is one of the few accommodations in the vicinity of downtown Vancouver. Venture further out and you're in big chain hotel/motel land and a substantial hike from the downtown core.

🍴 Eating

Beaches
STEAKHOUSE, SEAFOOD **$$**

(www.beaches.simplehelix.com; 1919 SE Columbia River Dr; mains from $15; 🍴) An ebullient place right on the river, Beaches gets points for its atmosphere, happy hour and cheery service. The food is basic American fare (pizzas, steak, fish 'n chips) with some nice surprises (steamed clams). Add it all up and it's worth a detour.

Farmers Market
MARKET **$**

(W 8th St, cnr Columbia St; ⊘10am-6pm) One of the best and cheapest places to eat in Vancouver is at this daily indoor/outdoor farmers market in Esther Short Park. Inside you'll find German deli sandwiches, tasty pastries and excellent pad thai noodles for as little as $5.

Grant House Restaurant
FUSION **$$**

(☏360-696-1727; 1101 Officers Row; mains from $15; ⊘lunch Mon-Fri, dinner Tue-Sat, brunch Sun) A more refined experience can be found at the Vancouver National Historic Reserve in this original restaurant. There's wine tasting on Tuesday evenings 5pm to 7pm.

ℹ Information

Southwest Washington Visitors & Convention Bureau (☏360-750-1553; 101 E 8th St, Ste 240)

ℹ Getting There & Away

Bus

Three Greyhound buses a day stop in Vancouver on their way between Portland and Seattle.

Train

Amtrak (www.amtrak.com) runs a coastal service to Seattle in the north and Portland in the south.

The *Empire Builder* stops in Vancouver before heading west to Pasco, Spokane and, ultimately, Chicago. **Tri-Met Transit** (www.trimet.org) offers frequent service between downtown Portland and Vancouver's 7th St transit center.

Washington Cascades

Why Go?

Grafted onto one of the more temperamental segments of the Pacific Ring of Fire, the Washington Cascades are a rugged, spectacular mountain range capped by five potentially lethal volcanoes: Mt Baker, Glacier Peak, Mt Rainier, Mt Adams and – fieriest of all – Mt St Helens.

Renowned for their world record–breaking precipitation and copious crevasse-covered glaciers, the highest Cascade peaks are vast stand-alone mountains that dominate almost every vista in the western state and create dry, scrubby, almost desert-like conditions further east.

Protected within a string of overlapping wilderness areas and national parks, the mountains offer some of the most awe-inspiring backcountry adventures in the US, if you don't mind bedding down in a tent and swapping your expensive Ralph Lauren scent for slightly less fragrant bug repellent. For the less outdoor-attuned, rarified Cascadian beauty can be glimpsed through the windows of cars, buses and trains, or enjoyed in a handful of classic 'parkitecture' lodges.

Best Places to Eat

- » Copper Creek Inn (p163)
- » Duck Brand Cantina (p153)
- » Stehekin Pastry Company (p156)
- » Twisp River Pub (p155)

Best Places to Stay

- » Sun Mountain Lodge (p153)
- » Ross Lake Resort (p150)
- » Paradise Inn (p162)
- » Buffalo Run Inn (p146)

When to Go
Mt Rainier National Park

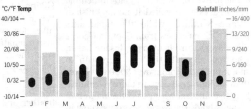

December–January Cascade ski areas get big dumpings of snow

February The 'Legendary Mt Baker Banked Slalom' snowboarding extravaganza

July–early October Higher elevations are snow-free from early July for a short, intense hiking season.

NORTH CASCADES

Dominated by Mt Baker and – to a lesser extent – the more remote Glacier Peak, the North Cascades is made up of a huge swathe of protected forests, parks and wilderness areas that dwarf even the expansive Rainier and St Helens parks to the south. The crème de la crème is the North Cascades National Park, a primeval stash of old-growth rain forest, groaning glaciers and untainted ecosystems whose savage beauty is curiously missed by all but 2500 or so annual visitors who penetrate its rainy interior.

Geologically different to the South Cascades, these wild northern giants are peppered with sharp, jagged peaks, copious glaciers and a preponderance of complex metamorphic rock. This gives them their distinctive alpine feel and has helped create the kind of irregular, glacier-sculpted characteristics that have more in common with the mountains of Alaska than the 'rounder' ranges further south. Thanks to their virtual impregnability, the North Cascades were a mystery to humans until relatively recently. Steep peaks such as Liberty Bell weren't climbed until the late 1940s, the first road was built across the region in 1972 and, even today, it remains one of the Northwest's most isolated outposts.

Mt Baker Area

Of all Washington's snow-capped volcanoes, Baker is possibly the most majestic, a massive icy dome that towers over the US–Canadian border and is clearly visible everywhere from Vancouver, BC, to Seattle. Legendary among snowboarders and hikers, Baker has been revered by the indigenous natives of Puget Sound for millennia. The Coast Salish called it Koma Kulshan (White Sentinel), while the mountain's modern name comes from Captain George Vancouver's third lieutenant, Joseph Baker, who was allegedly the first European to spot it in 1792. Though over 3000 feet lower than Mt Rainier, Baker is a more volcanically active and snowier peak; the mountain actually holds the world record for snow in a single season (1140 inches in 1998-9).

Baker was first ascended by an Englishman, Edmund Coleman, in 1868. The modern route, though more straightforward than Rainier, requires travel across one of the mountain's 10 permanent glaciers.

◎ Sights

Mt Baker Scenic Byway   SCENIC HIGHWAY
The 57-mile drive east along Hwy 542 from metropolitan Bellingham to the otherworldly **Artist Point** through moss-draped forests and past melodious creeks is one of the Northwest's most magic-invoking drives. Glacier, 33 miles in, is the last main settlement on the route. Seven miles further on, turn right on Wells Creek Rd and after half a mile you'll encounter **Nooksack Falls**, which drop 175ft into a deep gorge. This was the site of one of America's oldest hydropower facilities, built in 1906 and abandoned in 1997. Back on Hwy 542 the road begins to climb in earnest until you reach **Heather Meadows** at mile post 56. The Mt Baker Ski Area is here, and just up the road is **Austin Pass**, a picnic area and the starting point of several hiking trails.

☆ Activities

Climbing

The two principal routes up Mt Baker ascend **Coleman Glacier**, on the northwest side of the mountain, and **Easton Glacier**, on the south side. Both require two to three days, with a night spent camping at the base of the glacier. Technical equipment is highly recommended. The northern ascent begins at the Heliotrope Ridge trailhead and continues across Coleman and Roosevelt Glaciers for a final steep and icy climb up the North Ridge to the summit. Novice climbers should consider classes and guided climbs. Contact the **American Alpine Institute** (www.aai.cc; 1515 12th St, Bellingham, WA 98225) in Bellingham, which offers general training programs, along with guided climbs up Mt Baker for $590 (three days).

Hiking

While Mt Baker offers plenty of advanced hikes for experienced walkers, there are also a handful of easier options that leave from the Artist Point parking lot and are manageable for families. Most are snow-free by mid-July. The interpretive **Artist Ridge Trail** is an easy 1-mile loop through heather and berry fields with the craggy peaks of Mts Baker and Shuksan scowling in the background. Another option is the 0.5-mile **Fire & Ice Trail**, adjacent to the Heather Meadows Visitors Center, which explores a valley punctuated by undersized mountain hemlock. The 7.5-mile **Chain Lakes Loop** tat starts at the Artist Point

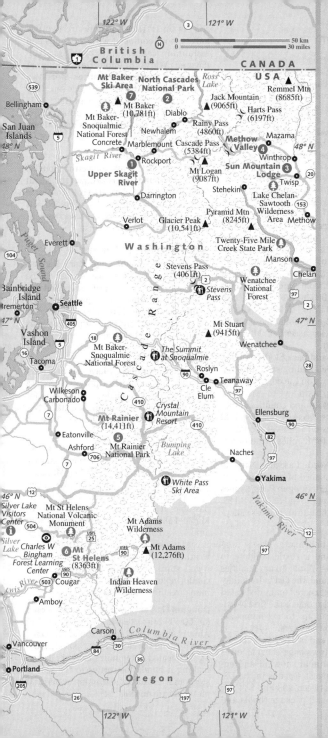

Washington Cascades Highlights

1 Watch bald eagles soar above the **Upper Skagit River** (p146) during a frigid January float trip

2 Hike cross-country through the **North Cascades National Park** (p147) to the hidden village of Stehekin.

3 Sit in an alfresco hot tub outside the **Sun Mountain Lodge** (p153) trying to remember if you've ever enjoyed a more tranquil view

4 Break trail with a pair of cross-country skis in the sunny **Methow Valley** (p154)

5 Be one of the lucky few to reach the top of **Mt Rainier** (p159) when the clouds clear

6 Watch new life tentatively re-emerge on **Mt St Helens** (p166)

7 Follow in the tracks of snowboarding legends at the **Mt Baker Ski Area** (p144)

Hwy 20, the only road across the North Cascades, closes yearly between Marblemount and Mazama due to heavy winter snowfalls. As a rule, the road is blocked from late November to early/mid April, though unseasonal snow has sometimes kept it closed until June. Call ☎888-766-4636 for road conditions.

parking lot before dropping down to pass a half-dozen icy lakes surrounded by huckleberry meadows.

Many of Mt Baker's best trails start lower down on Hwy 542 from a series of unpaved forest roads. The 7.4-mile out-and-back **Heliotrope Ridge Trail** begins 8 miles down unpaved USFS Rd 39, 1 mile east of Glacier and takes hikers from thick old-growth forest to flower-filled meadows and, ultimately, a breathtaking Coleman Glacier overlook. At the 2-mile point the path for the Coleman Glacier ascent of Mt Baker branches to the left.

The 11-mile out-and-back **Skyline Divide Trail** is another spellbinding stroll through forests and meadows on the edge of the Mt Baker Wilderness, with eye-to-eye views of the main mountain and countless other more distant peaks. Access is via USFS Rd 37, which branches off USFS 39 soon after Hwy 542 and runs for 12 miles to the 4400ft trailhead.

Access to the North Cascades National Park and an abundance of multiday backcountry hikes is via **Hannegan Pass**, 5 miles from the trailhead at the end of USFS Rd 32. Walk in through a beautiful roadless valley.

Skiing

Baker prides itself in being the classic 'non-resort' ski area and a rustic antidote to Whistler in Canada. While luxury facilities are thin on the ground, the fast, adrenaline-fueled terrain has garnered many dedicated admirers. It was also one of the first North American ski locations to accommodate and encourage snowboarders.

Situated at the end of Hwy 542, the **Mt Baker Ski Area** (www.mtbaker.us) receives record-breaking annual snowfall and enjoys one of the longest seasons in the US. Lift tickets cost between $38 and $44 per day. A basic ski rental package (boots and skis) is an extra $35. There are two day lodges, both equipped with ski shops and restaurants/cafeterias: the new Cascadian-flavored **White Salmon Day Lodge** at milepost 52 and the **Heather Meadows Day Lodge** four miles higher up. The nearest overnight lodging is in Glacier, 25 miles away. Decent cross-country skiing is possible on the forest roads lower down Hwy 542.

White-Water Rafting

Rafters can put in just above the Douglas Fir Campground and ride down the North Fork Nooksack, a class III river, to Maple Falls, a total of 10 miles. For a guided raft trip, contact **River Riders** (www.riverrider.com); trips run June to August.

🎿 Festivals & Events

The iconic **Mt Baker Legendary Banked Slalom** (www.lbs.mtbaker.us) is one of the world's premier snowboard events and has been won by the biggest names in the sport. Inaugurated inauspiciously in 1985, it takes place in a natural river gully doubling up as a half-pipe in early February.

🛏 Sleeping

The Baker area doesn't have many private lodges or motels/hotels. However, there are plenty of cottages, chalets and cabins for short-term rent (minimum is usually two nights). For more information see www.mtbakerlodging.com.

Inn at Mt Baker   B&B **$$**
(☎360-599-1359; www.theinnatmtbaker.com; 8174 Mt Baker Hwy; r $155-165) When Mt Baker breaks through the clouds, the views from this attractive, well-run B&B are unsurpassable. It's situated seven miles east of Maple Falls, and uncluttered rooms and ample skylights give it a light, airy feel. Breakfast is taken on a spectacular deck – weather permitting – in the summer. When it gets stormy you can enjoy heated floors, comfortable rocking chairs and a cozy communal reading room. No kids.

Douglas Fir Campground   CAMPGROUND **$**
(☎360-599-2714; Mt Baker Hwy; campsites $16) An attractive USFS campground on scenic Hwy 542 and the North Fork Nooksack River. It's located three miles east of Glacier, making it handy for sorties to the village store and restaurant. Drinking water and pit toilets are on site.

Silver Fir Campground
CAMPGROUND $

(☎360-599-2714; Mt Baker Hwy; campsites $16)
Ten miles up from the Douglas Fir on Hwy
542, the Silver Fir is equally scenic though
a little more remote from Glacier. There are
pit toilets and drinking water.

✖ Eating

Milano's Restaurant & Deli
ITALIAN $$

(9990 Mt Baker Hwy; dinner $16-20) In common
with much of the Mt Baker area, Milano's
doesn't win any 'wows' for its fancy interior
decor. But when the pasta's al dente, the
bread's oven-fresh and you've got an appe-
tite that's been turned ravenous by succes-
sive bouts of white-knuckle snowboarding,
who's complaining?

Graham's
DINER, PUB $$

(9989 Mt Baker Hwy; dinner $15-19) Across the
road from Milano's, Graham's is your second and last eating option in Glacier. Food
is billed as international (try the meatloaf or
fish tacos) and decent microbrews are served
from an antique wooden bar. There's live
music at weekends and an adjacent grocery
store that sells good smoothies and cookies.

❶ Information

Jointly run by the national forest and park ser-
vices, ✐**Glacier Public Service Center** (1094
Mt Baker Hwy; ⊙8am-4:30pm Memorial Day-
Oct, 9am-3pm Sat & Sun Oct-Mar) is just east of
Glacier. At this handsome stone lodge built by the
Civilian Conservation Corps is a small bookstore,
interpretive displays on the park and a ranger
to answer questions. In summer, there's also
a staffed visitors center at **Heather Meadows**
(Mile 56 Mt Baker Hwy; ⊙8am-4:30pm Jun-Sep).

For more information about the wilderness
area, contact the people at **Mt Baker Ranger
Station**, located at the junction of Hwy 9 and
Hwy 20 in Sedro-Woolley.

❶ Getting There & Away

Mt Baker is accessed by Hwy 542 (Mt Baker
Scenic Byway), from Bellingham via Kendall or the
Baker Lake Rd, off Hwy 20 west of Concrete, which
dead-ends at the northern end of Baker Lake.

Public transportation is scant and many boarders hitchhike (usual risks apply). From Christmas
to February, shuttles sometimes run from Bellingham. Check at the visitors center in Bellingham.

Upper Skagit River Valley

Tracking up through the foothills of the
North Cascades, the youthful Skagit River

becomes increasingly narrow and fast-
flowing. Settlement here is spread out and
thin on the ground. Blink and you'll miss
the small roadside towns of Concrete (population 790), Rockport (population 102) and
Marblemount (population 251) and, aside
from a sprinkling of campgrounds and a
couple of inns, your next decent accommodation will be in Mazama on the other side
of the mountains. Due to snow blocks, the
stretch of Hwy 20 between Marblemount
and Mazama is closed to traffic between
mid-November and early April.

⊙ Sights

Baker Lake & Lake Shannon
SCENIC LAKES

Just north of Concrete are two reservoirs
formed by a pair of dams on the Baker
River. Washington's largest colony of nesting osprey is found at Lake Shannon. Baker
Lake is a popular place to launch a boat and
go fishing for kokanee salmon or rainbow
trout. There are also several hiking trails.

Baker Lake Rd runs along the west side of
the lake, passing several campgrounds and
the **Shadow of the Sentinels**, a wheelchair-
accessible trail through old-growth Douglas
firs. Beyond the end of the road, the relatively flat **Baker River Trail** makes a good
family hike, running 2.6 miles up the jade
river past huge old cedars and beaver ponds.

To reach the lakes, turn north off Hwy 20
onto Baker Lake Rd, which is 6 miles west
of Concrete.

TOP⃝ CHOICE Upper Skagit Bald Eagle Area
WILDLIFE CENTER

The Bald Eagle area is essentially the 10-
mile stretch of the Skagit River between
Rockport and Marblemount. After salmon
spawn, their spent carcasses become meals
for the more than 600 eagles that winter
here. January is the best time to view the
eagles, which are present from November
through early March.

Those who want to learn more about
these illustrious raptors should visit the
✐**Bald Eagle Interpretive Center** (www.
skagiteagle.org; Alfred St, Rockport; ⊙10am-4pm
Sat, Sun & holidays mid-Dec–mid-Feb). Guided
walks around the eagle sanctuary leave
from here, one block south of Hwy 20, at
1:30pm weekends and holidays.

🏃 Activities

Climbing

Since the washing out of the White
Chuck River trail in 2003, **Glacier Peak**,

Washington's oft-forgotten wilderness volcano, is usually tackled from the **North Fork Sauk River Trail** which begins at a trailhead off the Mountain Loop Hwy. The push to the top takes you across the Sitkum Glacier, a relatively nontechnical but steep route to the 10,541ft summit. The 2003 storm also damaged this route. Check ahead. Seattle-based **Mountain Madness** (www.mountainmadness.com) offers this as a guided four-day trip from $800, depending on group size.

Rafting

One of the preferred ways of seeing the Skagit's abundant eagle population is on a winter float trip. To combat the cold, the boats provided by **Skagit River Guide Service** (www.ackerlunds.com; Mount Vernon) use propane heat and are equipped with comfy cushioned seats. They also serve hot cocoa, coffee and spicy cider. Trips run early November to mid-February and cost $65 for three hours.

Sleeping

Buffalo Run Inn TOP CHOICE MOTEL $$
(✆360-873-2103; www.buffaloruninn.com; 58179 Hwy 20, Marblemount; s/d/tr $49/69/89) Situated on a sharp bend on Hwy 20, the Buffalo doesn't look much from the outside. But within its wooden walls is a clean, scrubbed mix of modern motel (kitchenettes, TVs and comfy beds) and backcountry cabin (kitschy bear and buffalo paraphernalia). Five of the 15 rooms share baths and a sitting area upstairs. There's a hearty serve-yourself breakfast and communal eating area.

Hi-Lo Country Hotel HOTEL $$
(✆360-853-7946; www.hilo-country.com; 45951 Main St, Concrete; ste from $160) A wooden structure in Concrete might sound like an oxymoron, but this place injects some brand-new style into a somewhat neglected Cascades town. Just opened at the time of research, the Hi-Lo offers a bakery, café and a handful of stylish suite rooms in a handy cusp-of-the-mountains setting.

Ovenell's Heritage Inn B&B $$
(✆360-853-8494; 46276 Concrete Sauk Valley Rd; r with shared bathroom $90, cabins $135; @☎) The B&B tag doesn't really do Ovenell's justice. In reality, it's a 500-acre working cattle ranch abutting the Skagit River with various accommodations, namely four inn rooms (one of which has a private bathroom), five rustic wooden cabins (sleeping up to four) and an eight-person 'guesthouse.' Breakfast is available for the inn guests, and the stunning rural setting with views of ospreys, eagles and Mt Baker is complimentary for everyone. The ranch is a couple of miles south of Concrete.

Eating

Cascadian Farms JUICE BAR $
(Hwy 20 milepost 100; milkshakes $5; ☺9am-7pm May-Oct) The first of half a dozen organic snack huts on the Cascades Loop, this place, 3 miles east of Rockport, offers fresh injections of organic blueberry fruit shakes, ice cream or coffee. It's housed in an Indonesian-style Batak hut, and you can sup from your cup at an outdoor picnic table before taking a self-guided tour around the adjacent organic farm.

Marblemount Diner DINER $$
(60147 Hwy 20, Marblemount; lunch $7-9, mains $13-18; ☺11am-8pm Mon, Thu & Fri, 8am-8pm Sat & Sun) A filling as-much-as-you-can-eat breakfast buffet (served 8am to 11am) at weekends is the highlight of this friendly diner with booths, tables and seating at the bar. Obey 'rule one' of all buffets: arrive early before all the food is taken and/or dried out.

Buffalo Run Restaurant DINER $$
(60084 Hwy 20, Marblemount; lunch $7-9, mains $15-20; ☺lunch & dinner Thu-Tue ✗♥) The first and last decent restaurant for miles is (fortuitously) friendly and tasty as long as you don't mind being greeted by the sight of several decoratively draped animal skins and a huge buffalo head mounted on the wall. Among the buffalo stroganoff and buffalo burgers there are also, quite surprisingly, a few good vegetarian options.

North Cascades National Park

Ordained in 1968, the North Cascades National Park is Alaska transplanted in the lower 48, one thousand square miles of dramatic, daunting wild country strafed with mountains, lakes, glaciers (over 300 of them) and wildlife, and with almost no trace of civilization. Schizophrenic weather, massive precipitation, thick rain forest and vertiginous cliffs have long ensured the remoteness of the park's mountains; steep, alpine behemoths furnished with names like Mt Terror, Mt Fury, Mt Despair and Forbidden Peak. Aspiring bushwhackers and free-climbers

To Native Americans, Stehekin at the head of Lake Chelan was 'the way through,' a vital trade route that linked the rainy coast with the dry interior. For adventurous modern hikers nothing much has changed. Eschewing the motor car and most other 21st-century 'comforts,' Stehekin is reachable only by boat or foot. For hikers, there are three main entry points – all from the north.

The quickest and most popular is via spectacular 5392ft **Cascade Pass**, reached via a steep 3.7-mile path that starts at the parking lot at the end of the Cascade River Rd, 23 miles southeast of Marblemount. After ascending to the pass, the trail continues down the other side into the Stehekin River Valley, where it joins briefly with the Pacific Crest Trail before homing in on High Bridge. From here it's 11 miles along the Stehekin Rd to the ferry landing, or you can opt to catch the four-times-daily Stehekin shuttle (summer only). The total hiking distance is 32 miles (or 21 miles if you catch the bus).

Route two starts at Colonial Creek campground at Mile 130 on Hwy 20. Follow the wondrous **Thunder Creek Trail** through old-growth forest and past vertiginous glaciers up to Park Creek Pass (6059ft) before descending on the **Park Creek Trail**, 8 miles to the junction with the Stehekin Rd. From here follow the Stehekin River down to High Bridge where, once again, you can either walk or catch the shuttle to Stehekin (45 miles in total, or 34 if you use the bus).

The easiest route starts at Rainy Pass at Mile 157 on Hwy 20 and follows the well-marked and flat-ish **Pacific Crest Trail** along Bridge Creek into the Stehekin River Valley. The trail, once more, comes out at High Bridge: total distance 19 miles to High Bridge, or 30 to Stehekin.

All of the above trips are multiday hikes that take between two and four days depending on your speed. Numerous backcountry campsites are available en route. For greater comfort (and a lighter pack) you can take advantage of a tent-to-tent hiking service offered by the **Stehekin Adventure Company** (☎509-682-4494; www.stehekin outfitters.com). The company maintains large outfitter tents at the Cottonwood and Bridge Creek campsites, equipped with stove, cots, kitchen utensils and food. The cost is $95 for two people and an extra $25 per person thereafter. Phone ahead to reserve.

love the unique challenges offered by this eerie wilderness (most of the peaks weren't climbed until the 1930s). The less adrenalin-hungry stick close to arterial Hwy 20 and prepare for the drive of a lifetime.

For administrative reasons, the park is split into two sections – north and south – separated in the middle by the Ross Lake National Recreation Area, which encases a spectacular 20-mile section of the North Cascades Highway (US 20). Bordering the park's southern border around Stehekin lies a third region, the Lake Chelan National Recreation Area, a 62,000-acre protected park that surrounds the fjord-like Lake Chelan. To avoid confusion, the three zones are managed as one contiguous area and overlaid by the Stephen Mather Wilderness, created in 1988.

While it is possible to get a basic overview of this vast alpine wilderness by motoring through in a car on US 20 making use of the numerous pullouts and short interpretive hikes that litter the route, to

taste the park's real gritty essence you'll need a tent, a decent rucksack and a gung-ho sense of adventure. Call in at the visitor center in tiny Newhalem and let the glimmering peaks seduce you.

⊙ Sights

Ross Lake   SCENIC LAKE
Ross Lake stretches north for 23 miles, all the way across the Canadian border but – in keeping with the wild Cascades terrain – is accessible only by trail or water. Incorporated into the Ross Lake National Recreation Area, the lake was formed by the building between 1937 and 1949 of the **Ross Dam**, an ambitious hydroelectric project that was designed to generate much-needed electricity for the fast-growing Seattle area. You can hike down to the Ross Dam from a trailhead on Hwy 20 (milepost 134). The trail descends for 1 mile and crosses over the dam. For an extra leg-stretch you can follow the west bank of Ross Lake another mile to Ross Lake Resort.

WASHINGTON CASCADES NORTH CASCADES NATIONAL PARK

North Cascades National Park

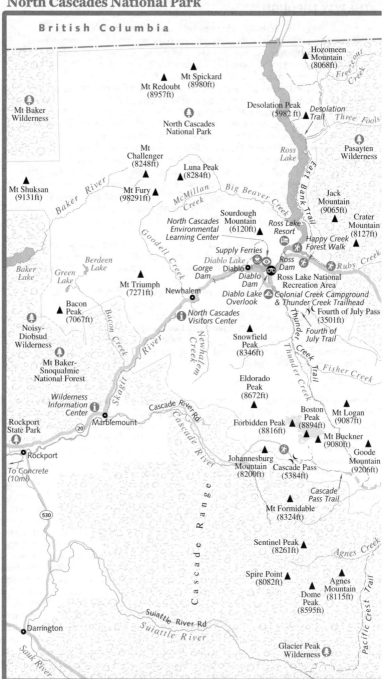

British Columbia

Hozomeen Mountain (8068ft)

Free our Creek

Mt Spickard (8980ft)

Mt Redoubt (8957ft)

Mt Baker Wilderness

North Cascades National Park

Desolation Peak (5982 ft) Desolation Trail

Three Fools

Ross Lake

Pasayten Wilderness

East Bank Trail

Mt Challenger (8248ft)

Luna Peak (8284ft)

Big Beaver Creek

Jack Mountain (9065ft)

Baker River

McMillan Creek

Mt Shuksan (9131ft)

Mt Fury (98291ft)

Crater Mountain (8127ft)

Sourdough Mountain (6120ft)

North Cascades Environmental Learning Center

Ross Lake Resort

Happy Creek Forest Walk

Goodell Creek

Berdeen Lake

Supply Ferries

Diablo Lake

Gorge Dam

Diablo

Ross Dam

Ruby Creek

Baker Lake

Green Lake

Mt Triumph (7271ft)

Newhalem

Diablo Dam

Ross Lake National Recreation Area

Bacon Peak (7067ft)

Diablo Lake Overlook

Colonial Creek Campground & Thunder Creek Trailhead

North Cascades Visitors Center

Fourth of July Pass (3501ft)

Noisy-Diobsud Wilderness

Bacon Creek

Newhalem Creek

Snowfield Peak (8346ft)

Thunder Creek

Fourth of July Trail

Mt Baker-Snoqualmie National Forest

River

Eldorado Peak (8672ft)

Fisher Creek

Thunder Creek Trail

Wilderness Information Center

Skagit River

Cascade River Rd

Boston Peak (8894ft)

Mt Logan (9087ft)

Rockport State Park

Marblemount

Forbidden Peak (8816ft)

Mt Buckner (9080ft)

Goode Mountain (9206ft)

Rockport

Cascade River

Johannesburg Mountain (8200ft)

Cascade Pass (5384ft)

To Concrete (10mi)

Cascade Range

Cascade Pass Trail

Mt Formidable (8324ft)

Sentinel Peak (8261ft)

Agnes Creek

Spire Point (8082ft)

Agnes Mountain (8115ft)

Dome Peak (8595ft)

Pacific Crest Trail

Darrington

Suiattle River Rd

Suiattle River

Glacier Peak Wilderness

Sauk River

Diablo Lake   SCENIC LAKE

Just below Ross Lake, Diablo Lake is held back by the similarly huge 389ft **Diablo Dam**. A pullout off Hwy 20 known as the **Diablo Dam Overlook** provides incredible views of the turquoise-green lake framed by glacier-capped peaks. Diablo was the world's highest arch-type dam at the time of its completion in 1930, and building it in such a hostile region with no road access was one of the greatest engineering feats of the inter-war age. Diablo Lake is popular with kayakers and canoeists (there's a launch site at Colonial Creek campground). The water's turquoise hue is a result of powered rock ground down by glaciers.

☛**North Cascades Environmental Learning Center** (www.ncascades.org), on the north banks of Diablo Lake, is operated by the North Cascades Institute in partnership with the National Park Service. The center offers free, first-come-first-served day hikes and activities every Saturday in the summer (from 8.30am) and a variety of weekend retreats from $245, including on-site food and accommodation. See the website for more details.

Seattle City Light runs twice-daily **supply ferries** (adult/child one way $10/5) from the ferry dock situated on the right just after you cross the Diablo Dam. The first ferry leaves at 8.30am and turns round at the Ross Powerhouse dock at 9am. The second leaves Diablo at 3pm and turns round at 3.30pm. Visitors can take the ferry one way and hike back to the Diablo Dam on the moderate 3.8-mile **Diablo Lake Trail**.

🏃 Activities

Hiking

Free permits are required for backcountry camping in the park and must be obtained in person from the Marblemount Wilderness Information Center (p150) or at a park ranger station.

One of the park's most challenging but rewarding day hikes is the strenuous **Sourdough Mountain Trail** which gains a mile in height for the 5.5 miles (one way) traveled on the ground. Most concede the effort is worth it; the views of Cascadian peaks and turquoise Diablo Lake 5000-plus feet below are some of the best in the park.

The 3.7-mile hike to 5384ft **Cascade Pass** is the best loved in these mountains, and gets you very quickly up into a flower-carpeted,

WASHINGTON CASCADES NORTH CASCADES NATIONAL PARK

glacier-surrounded paradise that will leave you struggling for superlatives (see p147).

From the south end of the Colonial Creek Campground (Mile 130, Hwy 20), the long **Thunder Creek Trail** leads along a powerful glacier-fed river through old-growth forest and clumps of wildflowers flourishing in the dank forest. After 2.5 miles the **Fourth of July Trail** branches left to a pass of the same name and makes a good early-season hike (10 miles round trip from the campground). Alternatively you can continue along Thunder Creek to Park Creek Pass and, ultimately, Stehekin.

Just past the Ross Dam trailhead at Mile 134.5, the easy and wheelchair-accessible **Happy Creek Forest Walk** (0.5 miles) gets you an up-close look at the forest on a raised boardwalk.

At Rainy Pass, the **Pacific Crest Trail** (PCT) crosses Hwy 20. To sample the trail, strike out north from here for 6800ft **Cutthroat Pass** (4 miles). Heading in the other direction down the PCT will bring you to Bridge Creek Campground, 12 miles away, where you can pick up the road to Stehekin. Several more leisurely hikes also start from Rainy Pass. Try the easy 4-mile out-and-back walk to cirque-cradled **Lake Ann**.

Just to the west of Washington Pass, between Miles 161 and 162, the **Blue Lake Trail** is an ambling 2.2-mile climb through sub-alpine meadows to Blue Lake, at 6250ft.

Rafting

Although it doesn't offer the heart-in-the-mouth white-water runs of less tamed waterways, the dam-controlled Upper Skagit makes for a good class II or III family trip through old-growth forest, offering plenty of opportunities for wildlife-watching. A number of companies offer excursions here including **Alpine Adventures** (www.alpineadventures.com). Prices start at $74/59 per adult/child.

Sleeping & Eating

TOP CHOICE **Ross Lake Resort** FLOATING CABINS $$
(206-386-4437; www.rosslakeresort.com; d cabin $112-136, q cabin $239; mid-Jun–Oct) The floating cabins at this secluded resort, on the lake's west side just north of Ross Dam, were built in the 1930s for loggers working in the valley soon to be flooded by Ross Dam. There's no road in – guests can either hike the 2-mile trail from Hwy 20 or take the resort's tugboat-taxi-and-truck shuttle from the parking area near Diablo Dam. Cabins vary in size and facilities, but all feature electricity, plumbing and kitchenettes. Bunkhouse cabins accommodate 10 people ($130 for up to six, plus $8 per each additional person). Bedding and kitchen supplies are provided, but guests should bring food. The resort rents canoes ($22 per day), kayaks ($30) and motorboats ($67), and operates a water-taxi service for hikers destined for trailheads around the lake. If you need to pick up some food, stop by the Skagit General Store in Newhalem, which has sandwiches, fudge and hot coffee.

Newhalem Creek Campground

CAMPGROUND $
(877-444-6777; Hwy 20 Mile 120; campsites $12, reserve sites $21) Handily situated near the North Cascades Visitors Center and surrounded by short interpretive trails, this 111-capacity campsite can accommodate large RVs. It's open year-round. If it's full try the smaller Goodall Creek campground one mile to the west on Hwy 20.

Colonial Creek Campground CAMPGROUND $
(206-386-4495; Hwy 20 Mile 130; campsites $12) These 142 campsites skirt the Thunder Arm of Diablo Lake on either side of the highway. On the south side, several walk-in campsites among dense woods offer a chance to get away from the cars. There are toilets and water, but no showers or hookups. In summer, naturalist programs are given nightly in the amphitheater. Open year-round.

❶ Information

North Cascades Visitors Center (502 Newhalem St; 9am-5pm May 1-Oct 31) In Newhalem; an essential orientation point for visitors, even for those just sticking to Hwy 20 and not strictly entering the park itself. A walk-through exhibit mixes informative placards about the park's different ecosystems with nature videos. Expert rangers will enlighten you on everything from melting glaciers to the fickleness of the weather. Various short trails track the Skagit River and Newhalem Creek, the longest of which is the 1.8-mile River Loop Trail. Park rangers give interpretive talks in the vicinity in the summer.

Wilderness Information Center (7280 Ranger Station Rd, Marblemount; 7am-6pm Sun-Thu & 7am-8pm Fri & Sat May-Oct) Pick up backcountry permits here.

'Hozomeen, Hozomeen; most beautiful mountain I've ever seen'

Traveling in Washington without a car might seem a bit onerous; but, a little over 50 years ago, Jack Kerouac, beatnik writer and author of the seminal travel novel *On the Road*, traversed the lower 48's most northwesterly state with no more than an overnight bag and an upturned thumb. Unbeknownst to many, Kerouac never owned a car and only learned to drive – somewhat reluctantly – at the age of 34. His first adventurous foray into the Pacific Northwest, documented in the later chapters of the book *The Dharma Bums*, came about when he hitched from California up to the North Cascade Mountains to work as a fire lookout on isolated Desolation Peak in the summer of 1956.

Kerouac spent 63 solitary days atop Desolation Peak, passing his hours in a small hut with panoramic views of the surrounding wilderness. With so much time on his hands, he had plenty of opportunity to contemplate life, the universe and his ever-evolving Buddhist philosophy, as he gazed out over Ross Lake and the twin-peaked majesty of looming Hozomeen (8066ft), a mountain he referred to rather chillingly as 'the Void.'

It is undocumented how many fire alarms Kerouac raised during his time in the Cascades, though he did famously use his collected scribblings in *Desolation Angels*, published in 1965, a novel that provides a fascinating insight into both the mountain scenery and the writer's ongoing battle with his inner demons.

It is still possible to hike the **Desolation Trail** up to Desolation Peak (6102ft) and ponder the fire lookout – built in 1933 – where Kerouac passed so many hours. The hike is 6.8 miles one way and is pretty strenuous, although you'll be richly rewarded with the same stunning vistas that inspired Kerouac. To complete the hike in a day you'll need to catch a water taxi from Ross Lake Resort to the trailhead on the upper east side of Ross Lake. Alternatively the hike can be incorporated into a longer backcountry adventure.

Methow Valley

After the white-knuckle drive across the North Cascades, the mellower Methow Valley, situated immediately to the east, offers a more tranquil and less terrifying antidote. Bucolic, surprisingly sunny and pleasantly isolated in winter when Hwy 20 shuts down due to snow blockage, this is where the sporty and the savvy come to hot air balloon, horseback ride and mountain bike. Winter is, arguably, an even better time to visit. Resisting the economic lure of big-name ski resorts, the local nonprofit Methow Valley Sport Trails Association has pieced together the second-largest network of cross-country skiing trails in North America.

MAZAMA

The first settlement to the east of the North Cascades wilderness is little more than a pin-prick on the map – albeit a very pleasant one – with broad mountain-backed vistas and a couple of excellent places to stay. Tiny Mazama (the name means 'mountain goat' in Spanish) marks the gateway to the Methow Valley (heading east) and the North Cascades (heading west).

⊙ Sights

Harts Pass SCENIC ROAD

If you prefer white-knuckle car rides to white-water rafting trips, consider taking the single lane gravel track up to Hart's Pass (6197ft), Washington's highest drivable road, and also its most vertigo-inducing. If the narrow, winding route and scary unguarded drop-offs don't knock the wind out of you, the panoramic views certainly will. To get to Harts Pass head northwest on Lost River Rd (also known as Mazama Rd), past the Mazama Country Inn to USFS Rd 5400. The road is paved for the first 12 miles and the last dozen are gravel. At Harts Pass, there's still more of a climb for the intrepid driver; head another 3 miles up to **Slate Peak** (7450ft), where – after a short hike from the road's end – the view from an abandoned fire lookout is....well, go and see. Slate Peak is also the site of the northernmost road access to the Pacific Crest Trail in the USA.

⚡ Activities

Mazama marks the western extent of the Methow Community Trail and has plenty of cross-country skiing trails (see p154). In summer, the same trails become routes for hikers, mountain bikers and horseback riders.

Bikes can be rented at the Freestone Inn for $35 a day. For horseback riding, cattle drives, and fishing and hunting trips contact **Early Winters Outfitting** (www.earlywintersoutfitting.com; HCR 74 Box B6, Mazama, WA 98833) in Mazama.

Most of the best trails start on Harts Pass Rd (USFS Rd 5400).

🛏 Sleeping & Eating

Both of the following places have excellent in-house restaurants.

Freestone Inn   HOTEL **$$$**
(☑509-996-3906; www.freestoneinn.com; 17798 Hwy 20; r/ste from $175/225, 1-bed cabin from $179; 🖥📶) Freestone Inn is a more luxurious version of the Mazama Country Inn with similar facilities encased in a more expensive wrapping. The on-site Jack's Hut adventure center can put you in touch with at least a dozen outdoor adventures, everything from snowmobiles to balloon tours. The Kids Venture program is great for children.

Mazama Country Inn   HOTEL **$$**
(☑509-996-2681; www.mazamacountryinn.com; 42 Lost River Rd, Mazama; lodge r $95-145, cabin $150-300; 🖥📶) The word 'inn' doesn't really do justice to this comprehensive place, a self-contained rustic oasis situated on the edge of the Pasayten Wilderness, close to Mazama. Aside from 18 simple but comfortable rooms, the inn lies at the nexus of countless outdoor activities in the area with numerous ski and bike trails starting from just outside the front door (rentals are available). Other facilities include a pool, gym, squash and tennis courts, sauna and the best restaurant for miles. The inn also rents a number of self-contained cabins around Mazama.

ℹ Information

The US Forest Service maintains the **Methow Valley Visitors Center** (24 West Chewuch Rd; ◷8am-5pm May-Oct) on Hwy 20 at the western end of Winthrop.

WINTHROP & AROUND

Winthrop (population 349) is – along with Leavenworth – one of two themed towns on the popular Cascade Loop. Once a struggling mining community, it avoided 'ghost town' status in the 1960s when it was made-over to look like a cowboy settlement out of the Wild West. Though, on paper, it sounds more Hollywood back-lot than *Gunfight at the OK Corral*, the Gary Cooper touches are surprisingly authentic. Winthrop's *High Noon* shopfronts hide a genuine frontier spirit (the road ends in winter not far beyond here), and hide some fantastic eating places and accommodation.

The area's first European settler was Harvard-educated Guy Waring, who in 1891 built a trading post at the confluence of the Chewuch (*chee*-wok) and Methow Rivers. When the mining business dried up after 1915, Winthrop teetered catastrophically on the brink of extinction, until Robert Jorgenson, the architect who had redesigned Leavenworth, stepped forward with his false-fronted shops and assorted cowboy memorabilia.

Winthrop's renaissance coincided with the opening in 1972 of the North Cascades Hwy, which brought in a flood of new visitors. When the highway closes in the winter, Winthrop becomes the Methow's main cross-country skiing HQ.

◉ Sights

Winthrop's photogenic core is compact and cheery with plenty of gift shops, coffee bars and a decent bookstore.

Shafer Museum   MUSEUM
(www.shafermuseum.com; 285 Castle Ave; admission by donation; ◷10am-5pm Memorial Day–Labor Day) It's hard to differentiate the reconstructed buildings in the museum from the rest of Winthrop, such is the town's eerie authenticity. However, the museum does retain one original construction – a log cabin known as 'the Castle,' built by Winthrop founder Guy Waring in 1896 as a present to his wife.

FREE **North Cascade Smokejumper Base**   MUSEUM
(23 Intercity Airport Rd; admission free; ◷8am-5pm Jun-Oct) Few Washington outsiders will know the first thing about smoke-jumping – a method of fire-fighting that involves parachuting out of a plane into a rural area to tackle a forest fire before it gets out of control. It's hard to avoid feeling humbled by the heroic exploits of the people who have been trained to do it. The Methow Valley is often seen as the birthplace of modern smoke-jumping (which was first pioneered in the 1930s); learn all about it by stopping here, halfway between Winthrop and Twisp.

🏃 Activities

The Winthrop area is famous for its cross-country ski trails (see p154), with the best network of trails congregated around Sun Mountain Lodge 10 miles to the west.

During the summer months the trails are given over to hiking, mountain biking and horseback riding. They range from the 2.5-mile **Sunnyside Loop**, with jaw-dropping vistas of the North Cascades, to the more adventurous **Pete's Dragon** with its white-knuckle twists and turns. Horseback riding around Beaver Pond and Patterson Lake is another popular summertime option. You can rent bikes (per two hours/four hours/day $15/25/35) from Sun Mountain Lodge; helmets are included. Guided horseback treks go from adult/child $35/30 for 1½ hours, or $110/90 for a half-day.

Fishing for steelhead trout and chinook salmon is popular in the Methow River, but anglers are required to use catch-and-release techniques for these endangered species. **Moccasin Lake**, a mile-long hike from Patterson Lake Rd, has very good fly-fishing, with rainbow trout averaging 3lb to 5lb.

Another unique Methow experience is hot-air ballooning. **Morning Glory Balloon Tours** (509-997-1700; www.balloonwinthrop.com; 960 Hwy 20, Winthrop) operates serene early-morning balloon flights over the valley between March and November. Flights cost $195/150 per adult/child and last one hour.

Sleeping

TOP CHOICE **Sun Mountain Lodge** HOTEL $$$
(509-996-2211; www.sunmountainlodge.com; Box 1000, Winthrop, WA 98862; lodge r $160-346, cabin $160-620; ⊛⊜⊛⊛) Without a doubt one of the best places to stay in Washington, the Sun Mountain Lodge benefits from its incomparable natural setting, perched like an eagle's nest high above the Methow Valley. The 360-degree views from its highly lauded restaurant are awe-inspiring and people travel from miles around just to enjoy breakfast here. Inside, the lodge and its assorted cabins manage to provide luxury without pretension, while the outdoor attractions that are based around its extensive network of lakes and trails could keep a hyperactive hiker, cyclist or skier occupied for weeks. Not surprisingly, the Sun Mountain is pricey, but if you have just one splurge in the Washington wilderness east of Seattle, this should be the place.

Hotel Rio Vista HOTEL $$
(509-996-3535; www.methow.com/~riovista; 285 Riverside Ave; d $110-145; ⊛⊜) A woody, Wild West–themed central option, the Rio Vista lives up to its Spanish name with fine views over the fast-flowing Methow River,

which races within pebble-skimming distance of its rear deck. Rooms are laid out motel-style, but are given extra shine with a riverside hot tub and individual room balconies offering magnificent Methow sunsets.

Wolf Ridge Resort B&B $$
(509-996-2828; www.wolfridgeresort.com; 412b Wolf Creek Rd; d/ste $93/165; ⊛⊜⊛) It's hard to decide when Wolf Ridge is better; in winter when it's bisected by the Methow Community Trail cross-country skiing commute, or in the summer when the rustling larches and gurgling Methow River lend it a splendid bucolic flavor. The place is a mix of hotel-style rooms and one- and two-room cabins with a preponderance of wood and plenty of extra-curricular activities – factor in pool, hot tub, volleyball and a ski-warming hut.

Duck Brand Hotel HOTEL $
(509-996-2192; www.methownet.com/duck; 248 Riverside Ave; s/d $69/79; ⊛) An apparition from *The Good, the Bad and the Ugly,* the Duck Brand is never short of character and bills itself, quite proudly, as an 'alternative to the ordinary.' Perched above a popular cantina slap bang in the middle of the town are six small but cozy rooms, all with private bath tubs and air-con.

Eating

TOP CHOICE **Duck Brand Cantina**
MEXICAN, BRUNCH $$
(www.methownet.com/duck; 248 Riverside Ave; mains $7-15; ⊙breakfast, lunch & dinner) No standard Mexican restaurant, the 'Duck' nonetheless serves quesadillas, enchiladas and tacos that could roast the socks off any authentic Monterey diner. The Wild West saloon-style cantina also churns out a mean American breakfast. In the winter the hearty porridge will keep you skiing all day.

Arrowleaf Bistro FUSION $$$
(509-996-3920; www.arrowleafbistro.com; 253 Riverside Ave; mains $15-27; ⊙lunch & dinner) Winthrop's poshest restaurant, with its starched white tablecloths and polished wine glasses, is a notable departure from the saloon-bar staples elsewhere. But the Arrowleaf works hard to justify its price tag with knowledgeable waiting staff, an excellent riverside setting, and a menu that contains such un-cowboy–like treats as pistachio-crusted halibut and maple brined pork chops.

Old Schoolhouse Brewing BREWPUB $
(www.oldschoolhousebrewery.com; 155 Riverside Ave; mains $9-14) Carb-load on beer in this

CROSS-COUNTRY SKIING IN THE METHOW

Broad, beautiful and littered with trails, the Methow is to cross-country skiing what Aspen is to downhill, but with only a fraction of the fame. To devotees of the more environmentally congruous free-heel method this is the primary draw: no crowds, no Gortex fashion parade, and no beer-fuelled après-ski – just you, miles of sugary powder and the Cascades.

With 200km of groomed trails, the valley comprises the second-largest cross-country skiing area in the US (after California's Royal Gorge). But, unlike other ski areas, there's no resort pampering here. A bucolic mix of farmland, aspen groves, rivers and old barns, the Methow is a real-life rural community whose far-sighted residents have created a nonprofit organization, the ☑**Methow Valley Sport Trails Association** (MVSTA; www.mvsta.com). When it's not fighting off profit-hungry ski-resort developers, the MVSTA promotes and protects a well-maintained trail system that enables skiers to meander at will between a handful of huts, cabins, lodges and small settlements.

The network's 'aorta' is the 20 mile **Methow Community Trail** (MCT), a flat, central valley route groomed for classic and skate skiing that plies its way between strategically placed warming huts (with water and toilets), linking Winthrop with the even tinier settlement of Mazama. Higher up but equally comprehensive are the interconnecting Rendezvous and Sun Mountain Lodge trail systems.

Between early December and late March you can ski door-to-door between various accommodation options including the Sun Mountain Lodge, Freestone Inn, Wolf Ridge Resort and Mazama Country Inn. For information on the Rendezvous huts check www.rendezvoushuts.com. Ski rental ($19 first day, $13 a day thereafter) and MVSTA trails passes (one/three days $20/51) are available at outlets in the Sun Mountain Lodge, **Methow Cycle & Sport** (www.methowcyclesport.com; ⊗9:30am-6pm Mon-Sat, 10am-5pm Sun) in Winthrop, and Mazama Junction in Mazama.

The Methow Valley Ski School is based at the Sun Mountain Lodge. Group lessons cost $22. One lesson is usually sufficient to get started.

The valley's trails are all clearly marked on a free local map: green for easy, blue for intermediate, black for challenging. Distance markers follow the Nordic metric system (ie kilometers, not miles).

unusual pub that occupies a former little red schoolhouse on the main street where you can choose from an impressive range of homebrew ales; aficionados opt for the light-bodied Black Canyon Porter or the heavier, darker Grampa Clem's Brown Ale. Classic pub grub highlights outlaw chili, and fish 'n chips with a Japanese twist. There's live music and an open mic on Friday.

Sheri's　　　　　　　　　　CAFÉ **$**
(201 Riverside Av) This delightful alfresco café and ice-cream parlor adjacent to Sheri's Sweet Shoppe is the best place to snatch an espresso and hot, sticky cinnamon bun (the buns are placed tantalizing on a counter on the sidewalk as soon as they leave the oven). In keeping with the surroundings, the bar stools are made out of horse saddles and behind the coffee cabin you can enjoy a quick round of crazy golf while they blast steam into your grande cappuccino.

ℹ **Information**

Winthrop Chamber of Commerce (www. winthropwashington.com; 202 Riverside Ave) At the corner where Hwy 20 enters downtown.

TWISP
POP 938

The largest of the Methow Valley's three tiny settlements, Twisp is a stomping ground for fishermen, bird-watchers (this is prime bald eagle country) and appreciators of fine ale – it's the site of a rip-roaringly good brew-pub. Contrary to its one-horse-town image, Twisp is also the crucible of a budding artist's community, though outdoor activities have long been its raison d'être.

◉ **Sights & Activities**

Diminutive Twisp supports a small art gallery in the shape of the **Confluence Gallery & Art Center** (☎509-997-2787; www.confluencegallery.com; 104 Glover St; admission free; ⊗10am-3pm Wed-Sat) but, outside of this, the main attractions are outdoors related. Hikes in the area are popular, with a number of them fanning off the Twisp River Rd that proceeds west of town along the banks of the Twisp River. Try the 7-mile **Eagle Creek Trail** that starts from the trailhead on W Buttermilk Creek Rd (11 miles west of Twisp) or strike out further into the **Lake Chelan-Sawtooth Wilderness Area**.

If you don't mind a few snowmobiles, **cross-country skiing** is easy along the flat Twisp River Rd. Nearer to downtown, trails start at the Idle-a-While Motel and meander around Twisp and along the Methow River.

🛏 Sleeping & Eating

Idle-a-While Motel   MOTEL **$**
(☑509-997-3222; www.idle-a-while-motel.com; 505 N Hwy 20; r $70-100, cottage $90-125; ❄️🛜) You could quite easily idle here for a night or two, as you sally forth in a clockwise direction on the Cascade Loop. Situated on Hwy 20 with basic but perfectly comfortable rooms, it might not be the Sun Mountain Lodge, though it does have a hot tub, plus a number of winter skiing trails starting directly outside its door.

[TOP CHOICE] **Twisp River Pub**   BREWPUB **$**
(www.methowbrewing.com; 201 Hwy 20; ⊙11:30am-11pm Wed-Sun; 🛜) Twisp might look like the back of beyond, but inside the walls of this beer-fuelled establishment there are enough food, music and ale variations to keep the most fidgety of travelers happy. Encircling the culinary world from Africa to Asia, the menu includes bratwurst, Thai peanut stir-fry, Greek salad and the good old steak sandwich. Made-from-scratch beers are brewed on the premises and music rocks the rafters at least twice a week.

ℹ Information

Twisp Ranger Station (502 Glover St; ⊙7:45am-4:30pm Mon-Fri) On Twisp's main street; has information on trails and campgrounds in the Okanogan National Forest.

Twisp Visitor Information Center (www.twispinfo.com; 201 S Methow Way) Operates out of the Methow Valley Community Center.

Stehekin

What, no road access? Cut off from the rest of Washington's highway network by craggy mountains, Stehekin is that rarest of modern American settlements – one that is unreachable by car. Visitors get here either by boat/seaplane across Lake Chelan, or by a trio of long-distance hikes (see p147) through the wilderness-flecked North Cascades National Park to the north.

Such purposeful inaccessibility has worked wonders for the settlement's special beauty. Untouched by the foibles of 21st-century culture, Stehekin (population 76) has become a byword for solitude, and a magnificent obsession for backcountry adventure enthusiasts keen to break away from the pleasure cruisers and water-skiers who ply Lake Chelan further south.

Though Stehekin does have *one* road and a handful of cars (all of which have been ferried here from Chelan or elsewhere), its isolation is both unusual and refreshing. The vast majority of visitors arrive in the settlement as part of a 90-minute stopover on a day trip from Chelan on one of two different passenger boats. Stick around after they've gone home and you'll feel more like Robinson Crusoe.

◉ Sights

If you're not staying overnight, it's hard to wander far with only a few hours. **Buckner Orchard**, near Rainbow Falls, is one of the Stehekin area's oldest settlements and makes for a refreshing walk. Once there, you'll find a homestead cabin built in 1889, plenty of old farm equipment and trees that keep on bearing apples. Head 3.4 miles up Stehekin Valley Rd, turn left at the far end of the Rainbow Creek bridge and look for a sign about 20 yards off the road, marking the **Buckner Orchard Walk**, an easy 1-mile round trip to the apple orchards. Park rangers offer guided walks here at 2.15pm at weekends in the summer. From just past the bridge, there's also a short path leading to the 312ft **Rainbow Falls**.

🏃 Activities

Boating
The **Stehekin Adventure Company** (www.stehekinoutfitters.com; day trips adult/child $50/40) offers raft trips on the Stehekin River in the spring and summer, as well as two-hour kayak trips on Lake Chelan (adult/child $35/20).

Cycling
You can rent bikes from **Discovery Bikes** (www.stehekindiscoverybikes.com; per hr/day $4/20), five minutes from the boat dock. Prices include helmets, racks and maps. Discovery Bikes can also shuttle cyclists

and their bikes up the road to the Stehekin Valley Ranch, which is just far enough to bike back down the valley in time to catch the 2pm boat back to Chelan.

Fishing

The lower Stehekin River is open for seasonal catch-and-release fishing, with cutthroat and rainbow trout living in the upper river. **Stehekin Fishing Adventures** (www.stehekinfishingadventures.com) offers all number of guided fishing trips (from $210 per day) on Lake Chelan. Cabin rental is also available.

Hiking

Backpackers planning an overnight stay will need a backcountry camping permit, which can be obtained at Golden West information Center or from the Chelan Ranger Station.

The easy **Lakeshore Trail** starts at the Golden West Information Center and heads south near Lake Chelan's shore. It's 6 miles to views of the lake and valley at Hunts Bluff. It's also possible to make this into a backpacking trip; Moore Point is 7 miles from the trailhead, while Prince Creek, the trail's endpoint, is 17 miles (the *Lady of the Lake* ferry picks up twice daily here). Watch out for rattlesnakes along the way.

Other treks include the 5-mile **Rainbow Loop Trail**, with great lake and valley views; and the **Purple Creek Trail** toward 6884ft Purple Pass, 7.5 miles away.

For longer backcountry excursions see the boxed text p147.

Horse-Riding

From the Stehekin Valley Ranch **Cascade Corrals** leads three-hour horseback rides to Coon Lake ($50 per person), as well as guided hikes into the mountains with gear carried on horseback. Make bookings for all these activities at the **Courtney Log Office** (☑509-682-4677; www.courtneycountry.com), 200 yards from the boat dock.

🛏 Sleeping

There are various cabins for rent in the river valley. Check the www.stehekin.com for links and more information.

Stehekin Landing Resort   HOTEL $$
(☑509-682-4494; www.stehekinlanding.com; PO Box 457, Chelan, WA 98816; r $112-175, kitchen units $165-185; @🛜) Being Stehekin, this isn't really a standard American resort, which is rather fortuitous given the surroundings. Conveniently located next to the ferry landing, its 28 varied rooms have lake

views and a good level of comfort. There's also a recreation room (with TV), open-all-day restaurant, hot tub and the village's only grocery store (albeit a tiny one). Sit back, switch your brain off and stick your e-mail on automated response.

Stehekin Valley Ranch   CABINS $$$
(☑509-682-4677; www.stehekinvalleyranch.com; tent cabin per person $95, ranch cabin per person $115) All number of activities go on at this well-organized place 9 miles upriver from the boat landing, including cycling, horseback riding, kayaking and hiking. Even better, the price for lodging in the ranch's rustic cabins includes all meals at one of Stehekin's few proper dining establishments, along with a bus to get there. Tent cabins are simple, canvas-topped affairs, with screened windows and showers in a nearby building. Ranch cabins have private bathrooms.

Golden West Information Center
    CAMPGROUND $
(☑360-856-5700, ext 340, then ext 14) Provides information and backcountry camping permits for the 11 NPS-maintained primitive campsites along the road up the valley. All camps have pit toilets, but only the Purple Point Campground provides potable water.

🍴 Eating

There are only three places to eat in Stehekin – the two listed here as well as the restaurant in the Stehekin Landing Resort.

TOP
CHOICE **Stehekin Pastry Company**
    CAFÉ, BAKERY $
(www.stehekinpastry.com; Stehekin Valley Rd; pastries $2-6) In a large city this improbable coffee and pastry shop would do a roaring trade. Out in the middle of a wilderness area it appears like a mirage and is guaranteed to give fresh ardor to even the most challenging of hikes. Two miles up the valley from the boat landing, this is where to come for espresso, cinnamon buns, pies and baked-from-scratch pastries. You can take the 'bakery special' shuttle service to get there.

Stehekin Valley Ranch   TRADITIONAL $$
(☑509-682-4677; www.stehekinvalleyranch.com; breakfast & lunch $5-8, dinner $13-18; ⊙breakfast, lunch & dinner; 🅿) Reservations are required here for the daily set dinner menu (there's a $3 shuttle service from the dock to the lodge at 5:30pm). Grill items like burgers (beef and veggie) and fish are also available.

ℹ️ Information

🏷️Golden West Information Center (PO Box 7, Stehekin, WA 98852; ⏱️8:30am-5pm May-Oct, 12:30am-2pm Oct-May) A short walk up the hill from the boat landing. Here you'll find rangers, wilderness permits, summer naturalist programs, kids activities, a 10-minute video on the surrounding area and the Golden West Art Gallery.

ℹ️ Getting There & Away

Chelan Airways (www.chelanairways.com; 1328 W Woodin Av, Chelan) Provides seaplane service between Stehekin and Chelan for $79/158 one way/round trip.

Lake Chelan Boat Company (www.ladyof thelake.com; PO Box 186, Chelan, WA 98816) Operates the 285 passenger *Lady of the Lake II* ferry (no cars) leaving from Chelan boat dock daily at 8:30am and arriving at Stehekin at 12:30pm. It makes a 90-minute stopover before returning at 2pm (arriving back in Chelan at 6pm). The round-trip cost is $39. Alternatively, you can travel on the faster *Lady Express,* which cuts the four-hour boat trip in half (leave Chelan 8:30am, arrive Stehekin 10:45am). The *Lady Express* lays over in Stehekin for one hour before heading back at 11:45am (arriving back in Chelan at 2:20pm). The round-trip cost is $59. Both boats stop on the way at Lucerne.

ℹ️ Getting Around

Although there are roads and cars *in* Stehekin, there are no roads *to* Stehekin. Courtesy transportation to and from the boat landing is included in most lodging prices.

Bicycles are the easiest way to get around. See p155 for rental options. If you'd prefer to bring your own, the Lake Chelan Boat Company charges $24 round trip for bike transportation.

From late May to early October, the NPS runs the **Stehekin Shuttle Bus** (📞360-856-5700) up and down Stehekin Valley Rd four times a day. The 11 miles from the boat landing to High Bridge where the drivable road ends costs $5/2.50/5 per adult/child/bike.

Chelan & Around

POP 3522

Chelan is an elongated natural lake (as opposed to a reservoir) that once provided a prime fishing ground for Native Americans. Today it is an outstanding recreation spot for anyone with a penchant for water sports. Surrounded by wineries, apple orchards, hotels and a slightly incongruous water park, the lake's southern shore is taken up by its eponymous town, while 55 miles to the north lies a get-away-from-it-all antidote, isolated Stehekin. Yin and yang – take your pick.

🏃 Activities

Water Recreation

Lake Chelan shelters some of the nation's cleanest water and has consequently become one of Washington's premier water recreation areas. Not surprisingly, the place is cheek to jowl in summer, with all number of speedboats, jet-skis and power-craft battling it out for their own private slice of water. To avoid any high-speed collisions, try renting a kayak from **Lake Rider Sports** (www.lakeridersports.com; 510 E Woodin Ave; day s/d $50/70) and paddling up the lake to see some undiluted Cascadian nature first hand.

There are public beaches at **Lakeside Park**, near the west side of town, and at **Lake Chelan State Park**, 9 miles west on S Lakeshore Rd. On the north shore, **Don Morse Memorial Park** is an in-town water funland, with a beach, boat launch, bumper boats and go-carts.

If you have kids, don't even think they'll let you sneak past **Slidewaters Water Park** (www.slidewaters.com; 102 Waterslide Dr; day pass adult/child $17/14; ⏱️10am-7pm May-Sep; 🅿️) off W Woodin Ave. It's on a hill above the *Lady of the Lake* boat dock.

Fishing is popular in Lake Chelan with lake trout, kokanee salmon, ling cod and smallmouth bass relatively abundant. For guided fishing excursions, try **Darrell & Dad's Family Guide Service** (www.darrell anddads.com; 231 Division, Manson; per person half/full day from $130/176).

Manson is a small lakeside community eight miles northwest of Chelan and the swimming area at **Manson Bay Park** features several floating docks.

Other Activities

Mountain bikers should stop by the ranger station and pick up a map of USFS roads open to **cycling**. One popular trail follows the north fork of Twenty-Five Mile Creek, climbing steeply for 3 miles before leveling out through pine forest and eventually meeting the **Devil's Backbone** trailhead.

At **Echo Ridge** near Manson, there are 35 miles of traffic-free trails ideal for **mountain biking**. In winter these are utilized for **cross-country skiing**.

WASHINGTON CASCADES CHELAN & AROUND

CHELAN WINE COUNTRY

In May 2009 Lake Chelan became Washington's 11th certified AVA (American Viticultural Area). There are currently 15 wineries in a region stretching from Chelan up lake to just beyond Manson.

A mild lake effect adds distinctive features to the wine here. You can test the water (and wine) in **Vin du Lac** (www.vindulac.com; 105 Hwy 150; ⊘11am-7pm) tasting room situated on a hilltop above Chelan, where an old orchard now knocks out decent syrah and chardonnay. There's also an on-site bistro.

Uncle Tim's Toys (www.uncletimstoys.com; Lakeshore Marina & Park) in Chelan rents out bikes and ski equipment.

🛌 Sleeping

Midtowner Motel   MOTEL $
(☑509-682-4051; www.midtowner.com; 721 E Woodin Ave; r $65-99; ✱@🛜⊠) This bargain is a healthy five blocks from the town center and lake, a small price to pay considering the reasonable fee and the above-average motel facilities. These include free internet in the reception, coffee on tap, a Jacuzzi and an indoor/outdoor swimming pool. Rooms have the cleanliness one would expect in a five-star hotel.

Campbell's Resort   HOTEL $$$
(☑509-682-2561; www.campbellsresort.com; 104 W Woodin Ave; r/ste from $155/225; ✱🛜⊠) The plushiest place in town, Campbell's hogs the waterfront along Manson Hwy with its 170 guest rooms, marina, two swimming pools, restaurant, pub and 1200ft stretch of sandy beach. Modern rooms are spotless and have balconies, but the privilege of staying here doesn't come cheap – especially in the summer when rates triple.

Best Western Lakeside Lodge   HOTEL $$$
(☑509-682-4396; www.lakesidelodge.net; 2312 W Woodin Ave; d $199-259; ✱🛜⊠) This trusty chain has nabbed the best location in town aside grassy Lakeside Park, which boasts Chelan's most idyllic municipal setting along with the town's best stretch of sand-and-shingle beach. There's a lovely pool, complimentary breakfast, top lake views, and suitably well-furnished rooms, though

you may spend a lot of time dodging the plethora of passing convention delegates.

Lake Chelan State Park   CAMPGROUND $
(☑509-687-3710; S Lakeshore Rd; campsites/RV sites $21/28) A guarded swimming beach, picnic areas and a boat launch make this a busy summertime destination. Of the nearly 150 sites, there are some nice lakeside spots and 35 RV hookups. Reservations are necessary in summer.

✗ Eating

TOP⟩ **Vogue**   CAFÉ, WINE $
CHOICE (www.thevoguelounge.com; 117 E Woodin Ave; 🛜) On the surface, Vogue seems like a fresh, new Seattle-style coffee bar. But there's a lot more to this place than meets the eye. Putting aside the ubiquitous chai lattes and blueberry muffins, this venerable and popular 'café' showcases everything from live music (at weekends) and local art to a selection of its own jams and vinaigrettes. It also acts as a popular tasting room for aspiring wine connoisseurs. There's alfresco seating out front and wi-fi access inside to boot.

Campbell House Restaurant & Second Floor Pub   FUSION $$
(☑509-682-4250; 104 W Woodin Ave; mains $14-20; ☑) Chelan's fanciest dining spot, Campbell House rises above the burger banality with the dizzying delights of scallop vol-au-vent, Northwest mixed grill (duck, salmon and beef), stuffed Portobello and coconut prawns. A decent batch of non-meat alternatives (including eggplant parmesan) should surprise the salad-weary vegetarian. The upstairs pub serves pricey snacks and fancy vodka cocktails.

BC MacDonald's   BURGERS, PUB $$
(☑509-682-1334; 104 E Woodin Ave; mains $8-16; ☑) Don't be fooled by the name – you won't find any Big Macs or Chicken McNuggets at this kid-friendly pub-restaurant which possesses what must be one of the longest bars in the Pacific Northwest. The burgers are good, the calamari makes a stalwart appetizer and the beer is possibly the best in town. It ain't fancy, but it works. And no clowns.

ℹ Information

Chelan USFS/NPS Ranger Station (428 W Woodin Ave; ⊘7:30am-4:30pm Mon-Fri) For a wealth of information on Wenatchee National Forest and other protected areas.

Lake Chelan Visitors Center (www.lakechelan.com; 102 E Johnson Ave) Tourist information.

ⓘ Getting There & Around

Chelan Airways operates a daily seaplane service to Stehekin from the airfield, 1 mile west of town on Alt US 97 (see p157 for details).

The *Lady of the Lake II* and the *Lady Express* board at least one boat daily for trips across Lake Chelan to Lucerne and Stehekin. The **dock** (www.ladyofthelake.com) is located on the south shore, just a mile west of downtown on Alt US 97.

Wenatchee-based **Link Transit** (www.linktran sit.com) provides bus services between Manson and Wenatchee (1½ hours) via Chelan (15 minutes) on route 21. For those traveling to/from Chelan, buses stop on the south side of Johnson Ave, right next to the local visitors center.

SOUTH CASCADES

More rounded and less hemmed in than their saw-toothed cousins to the north, the South Cascades are nonetheless higher. Their pinnacle in more ways than one is 14,411ft Mt Rainier, the fifth highest mountain in the lower 48 and arguably one of the most dramatic stand-alone mountains in the world. Further south, fiery Mt St Helen's needs zero introduction while unsung Adams glowers way off to the east like a sulking middle child.

Most of the South Cascades are protected by an interconnecting patchwork of national parks, forests and wilderness areas. The largest and most emblematic of these is Mt Rainier National Park, inaugurated in 1899, while the most unusual is the Mt St Helens National Volcano Monument, formed in 1982, two years after the mountain's eruption.

While development inside the parks is refreshingly light, keen downhill skiers can find solace at Crystal Mountain just outside the limits of Mt Rainier National Park which, while no Whistler, is the largest ski resort in Washington state.

Mt Rainier National Park Area

Emblazoned on every Washington license plate and visible throughout much of the western state, Mount Rainier is the contiguous USA's fifth-highest peak and, in the eyes of many, its most awe-inspiring.

Close to Puget Sound's urban areas and unobstructed by any other peaks, the mountain's overwhelming presence, set off by its 26 glaciers, has long enraptured the millions of inhabitants who live in its shadow. Though it's an iconic peak to bag, climbing Rainier is no picnic; old hands liken it to running a marathon in thin air with crampons stuck to your shoes. Approximately 10,000 people attempt it annually.

Beneath Rainier's volatile exterior, even darker forces fester. As an active stratovolcano that recorded its last eruptive activity as recently as 1854, Rainier harnesses untold destructive powers that, if provoked, could threaten downtown Seattle with mudslides and cause tsunamis in Puget Sound. Not surprisingly, the mountain has long been imbued with myth. The Native Americans called it Tahoma or Tacoma, meaning the 'mother of waters,' George Vancouver named it Rainier in honor of his colleague and friend Rear Admiral Peter Rainier, while most Seattleites refer to it reverently as 'the Mountain' and forecast the weather by its visibility.

Encased in a 368-sq-mile national park (the US' fifth national park when it was inaugurated in 1899), the mountain's forest-covered foothills harbor numerous hiking trails and huge swathes of flower-carpeted meadows. When the clouds magically disappear during long, clear days in July and August, it becomes one of Washington's most paradisiacal playgrounds

NISQUALLY ENTRANCE

This southwestern corner of Mt Rainier National Park is its most developed (and hence most visited) corner. Here you'll find the park's only lodging, the only year-round road and the strung-out gateway settlement of Ashford that offers plenty of useful park-related facilities.

Hwy 706 enters the park about an hour and a half's drive southeast of Seattle, just past Ashford and adjacent to the Nisqually River. After the entry tollbooth, a well-paved road continues east offering the first good views of Mt Rainier – weather permitting – a few miles further on at Kautz Creek.

At the 7-mile mark you'll pass Longmire, the park's main orientation point, replete with lodging, food and hiking trailheads. From here the road climbs steeply for 12 miles, passing numerous hairpin turns and viewpoints until it emerges at the elevated alpine meadows of Paradise.

◉ Sights

Longmire   VISITOR CENTER

Worth a stop to stretch your legs or gain an early glimpse of Rainier's mossy old-growth

WASHINGTON'S SKI AREAS

Despite taunts from Rocky Mountain purists who compare Washington's snow to 'wet concrete,' the state maintains a dozen excellent downhill ski areas. Those with an aversion to crowds will be doubly impressed. Only one of the centers (Crystal Mountain) is classed as a resort, and it's tiny compared to Aspen or Whistler. Here's a quick precis of what's on offer.

» **Crystal Mountain** The largest ski area in Washington and the state's only destination 'resort' tops out at 7000ft. A huge variety of terrain and small ski village are complemented by killer Mt Rainier views.

» **Summit at Snolquamie** The closest ski area to Seattle (read: busy) also boasts the largest floodlit ski network in the US.

» **49 Degrees North** Recent expansion has made this 2350-acre ski area in northeast Washington the state's second largest – yet it's still quiet. The accessible terrain gets big votes from families.

» **Mt Baker** Rugged, undone and legendary among snowboarders, Baker gets twice as much annual snow (650 inches) than other resorts. Its advanced terrain offers some white-knuckle backcountry options.

» **Mission Ridge** Situated 12 miles south of Wenatchee, Mission is celebrated for its light, fluffy powder and 300-plus days of annual sunshine.

» **Stevens Pass** Established in 1937, Stevens is a day ski area popular with Seattleites. Uniquely, its facilities are powered entirely by wind.

» **Loup Loup** Just east of Winthrop, this small 550-acre ski bowl is economical, safe and has almost no lines. Great for first-timers.

» **Hurricane Ridge** This tiny ski center (only three lifts) just inside the Olympic National Park is the westernmost in the lower 48.

» **Bluewood** Adrift from the Cascades in the southeast of the state, modern Bluewood runs on diesel generators and is lauded for its good tree-skiing and dry snow.

» **White Pass** A laidback, less frenetic alternative to nearby Crystal Mountain that spawned the legendary Mahre brothers (gold and silver slalom medalists in the 1984 Winter Olympics).

» **Mt Spokane** Only 28 miles east of Spokane, this is the nearest ski area to a large population center. Learning to ski? Look no further.

» **Leavenworth Ski Hill** A tiny facility with two tow ropes that is renowned for its ski-jumping opportunities.

forest, Longmire was the brainchild of a certain James Longmire who first came here in 1883 during a climbing trip when he noticed the hot mineral springs that bubbled up in a lovely meadow opposite the present-day National Park Inn. He and his family returned the following year and established Longmire's Medicinal Springs, and in 1890 he built the Longmire Springs Hotel. Since 1917 the National Park Inn has stood on this site – built in classic 'parkitecture' style – and is complemented by a small store, some park offices, the tiny **Longmire Museum** (☑360-569-2211, ext 3314; admission free; ☺9am-6pm Jun-Sep, 9am-5pm Oct-May) and a number of important trailheads.

Paradise   VISITOR CENTER

'Oh, what a paradise!' exclaimed the daughter of park pioneer James Longmire on visiting this spot for the first time in the 1880s. Suddenly, the high mountain nirvana had a name, and a very apt one at that. One of the snowiest places on earth, 5400ft-high Paradise remains the park's most popular draw with its famous flower meadows backed by dramatic Rainier views on the days (a clear minority annually) when the mountain decides to take its cloudy hat off. Aside from hiding numerous trailheads and being the starting point for most summit hikes, Paradise guards the iconic Paradise Inn (built in 1916 and refurbished in 2008) and the informative **Henry M Jackson Visitor**

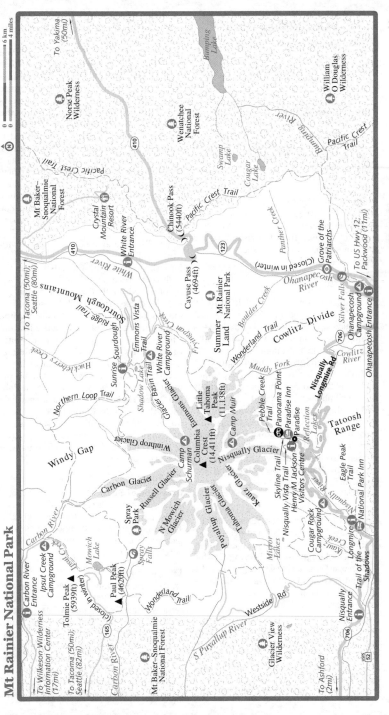

Mt Rainier National Park

ℹ PARK INFORMATION

For information on the park check out the National Park Service website at www.nps.gov/mora, which includes downloadable maps and descriptions of 50 park trails.

Park entrance fees are $15 per car and $5 for pedestrians and cyclists (those under 17 admitted free), and are valid for seven days from purchase. A $30 annual pass admits the pass-holder and accompanying passengers for 12 months from date of purchase.

Center (◷10am-7pm daily Jun-Oct, 10am-5pm Sat & Sun Oct-Dec), completely rebuilt and re-opened in 2008. Park naturalists lead free interpretive hikes from the visitors center daily in summer, and snowshoe walks on winter weekends.

🏃 Activities

CLIMBING

Mt Rainier was first climbed in 1870 by Hazard Stevens and PB Van Trump, and these days approximately 10,000 climbers attempt the summit annually with a 60% success rate. The most popular route starts at Paradise and involves a brief night's rest at Camp Muir before rising between midnight and 2am to don crampons and ropes for the climb over Disappointment Cleaver and the Ingraham Glacier to the summit. All climbers going higher than Camp Muir must register at the **Paradise Ranger Station** next to the Henry M Jackson Visitors Center. Excellent four-day guided ascents are led by **Rainier Mountaineering Inc** (☏360-569-2227; www.rmiguides.com; per person $926).

CROSS-COUNTRY SKIING

During the winter the road is generally plowed as far as Paradise, and people take to the trails on cross-country skis and snowshoes. The **Longmire Ski Touring Center** (◷8am-6pm Sat & Sun Thanksgiving-Apr), in the Longmire General Store, has trail information, lessons and cross-country ski and snowshoe rentals.

HIKING

Rainier's textbook long-distance hike is the 93-mile **Wonderland Trail** that completely circumnavigates the mountain with a cumulative elevation gain of 21,400 feet. Longmire is its most popular starting point, with the majority of hikers tackling the route over 10 to 12 days in a clockwise direction in July or August. There are 18 backcountry campsites en route.

For a shorter hike from Longmire you can test your mettle on the precipitous **Eagle Peak Trail**, a steep 7.2-mile out-and-back hike. A more laid-back look at some old-growth forest and pastoral meadows is available on the signposted **Trail of the Shadows** loop, a 0.8-mile trail that begins across the road from the museum and is wheelchair accessible for the first 0.4 miles.

Paradise, situated at 5400ft, has a much shorter hiking season than Longmire (snow can persist into late June), but its wildflower pastiche, which includes avalanche lilies, western anemones, lupine, mountain bog gentian and paintbrush, make the experience spectacular.

The Paradise area is criss-crossed with trails, of all types and standards, some good for a short stroll (with the kids), others the realm of more serious hikers. To get a close-up of the Nisqually Glacier follow the 1.2-mile **Nisqually Vista Trail**. For something more substantial hike the 5-mile **Skyline Trail**, starting behind the Paradise Inn and climbing approximately 1600ft to **Panorama Point**, with good views of Mt Rainier and the neighboring Tatoosh Range.

Intrepid day-hikers can continue up the mountain from Panorama Point via the **Pebble Creek Trail** to the permanent snowfield track that leads to **Camp Muir**, the main overnight bivouac spot for climbing parties. At 10,000ft, this hike is not to be taken lightly. Take sufficient clothing and load up with a good supply of food and water.

👉 Tours

Gray Line of Seattle   BUS TOURS
(www.graylineofseattle.com) Runs bus tours of the park mid-June to late September. The 10-hour tour (adult/child $59/29.50) picks up from most downtown Seattle hotels starting at 7.30am.

🛏 Sleeping

TOP CHOICE **Paradise Inn**   HISTORIC LODGE $$$
(☏360-569-2413; www.mtrainierguestservices.com; r with shared/private bathroom $104/154; ◷mid-May–Sep) A historic 'parkitecture' inn constructed in 1916, the Paradise has long been part of the national park's fabric. Designed to blend in with the environment and constructed almost entirely of local materials, including exposed cedar logs in the Great Room, the hotel was

an early blueprint for National Park Rustic architecture countrywide. Reopening in 2008 after a two-year, $30 million, earthquake-withstanding revamp, the small-ish rooms (some with shared bath) retain their close-to-the-wilderness essence, while the communal areas are nothing short of regal.

National Park Inn HISTORIC LODGE **$$**
(☑360-569-2411; www.mtrainierguestservices. com; r with shared/private bathroom $110/148; ☀) The pride of Longmire, parts of which date from 1917, goes out of its way to be rustic with no TVs or telephones in the rooms and small yet cozy facilities. But who needs HBO and the Discovery Channel when you've got fine service, fantastic surroundings and delectable complimentary afternoon tea and scones served in the comfortable dining room? Book ahead in the summer.

Whittaker's Motel & Bunkhouse HOSTEL **$**
(☑360-569-2439; www.whittakersbunkhouse. com; 30205 SR 706 E; dm/d $35/85) Part of Rainier's 'furniture,' Whittaker's is the home base of legendary Northwestern climber Lou Whittaker, who first summited the mountain at the age of 19 and has guided countless adventurers to the top in the years since. Down-to-earth and comfortable, this place has a good old-fashioned youth-hostel feel with cheap sleeps available in six-bed dorms. The alluring onsite **Whittaker's Café & Espresso** (☉7am-9pm) is a fine place to hunker down for breakfast – none of those saran-wrapped day-old muffins here. It's open weekends only in winter.

Nisqually Lodge MOTEL **$$**
(☑360-569-8804; www.escapetothemountains. com; 31609 SR 706 E; r $95-125; ☀☎) With an expansive lobby complete with crackling fireplace and huge well-stocked rooms, this lodge is far plusher than an average motel. The outdoor Jacuzzi, simple help-yourself breakfast and easy access to the park pretty much seal the deal in this price bracket.

Cougar Rock Campground CAMPGROUND **$**
(☑360-569-2211; campsites late Jun–Labor Day $15, rest of season $12; ☉late May–mid-Oct) Cougar Rock, 2.3 miles north of Longmire on the way to Paradise, has 173 individual campsites and flush toilets. Rangers lead campfire talks on summer evenings.

✕ Eating

Aside from the two historic inns, the only eating in the park is in the cafeteria of the Henry M Jackson Visitor Center. Ashford,

just outside the Nisqually entrance, has half a dozen options, spearheaded by the Copper Creek Inn.

163

TOP CHOICE **Copper Creek Inn** BRUNCH **$**
(www.coppercreekinn.com; 35707 SR 706 E, Ashford; breakfast $6-9; ☉7am-9pm) Forget the historic inns. This is one of the state's great rural restaurants, and breakfast is an absolute must if you're heading off for a lengthy hike inside the park. Situated just outside the Nisqually entrance, the Copper Creek has been knocking out pancakes, wild blackberry pie and their own home-roasted coffee successfully for over 50 years. Stop by to taste the food and you'll soon understand why.

National Park Inn HOMESTYLE **$$**
(mains $16-19; ☉lunch & dinner) Hearty hiking fare is served at this homely inn-restaurant and – in the absence of any real competition – it's surprisingly good. Try the pot roast or the chicken with honey glaze, and make sure not to miss the huge blackberry cobbler with ice cream that will require a good 2-mile hike along the Wonderland Trail (which starts just outside the door) to work off.

Paradise Inn HOMESTYLE **$$$**
(☉lunch & dinner Jun-Sep) The huge stone fireplace is the highlight of this dining room and it easily overshadows the food, which doesn't yet live up to the 2008 refurbishment. Buffalo meatloaf and crab mac and cheese are the most enticing options.

❶ Information

In Longmire, the museum can field basic questions.

Ashford Visitors Center (30027 SR 706; ☉9am-5pm Nov-Apr, till 8pm May-Oct) The best source of information outside the park; located 6 miles before the Nisqually entrance. Has a shop, maps, leaflets and helpful staff.

❶ Getting There & Around

Between June and September the **Paradise Shuttle** runs between Longmire and Paradise Friday to Sunday. There's an onward link to Ashford outside the park gates on Saturday and Sunday only. The shuttle runs every 45 minutes on Friday and every 20 minutes on Saturday and Sunday.

OHANAPECOSH ENTRANCE

Ohanapecosh (o-*ha*-nuh-peh-*kosh*) in the park's southeastern corner is accessed by the small settlement of Packwood, 12 miles to the southwest on US 12. Packwood harbors a small number of eating and sleeping options. Shoehorned between Mt Rainier and its two southern neighbors, Mt St Helens and Mt Adams, this is a good base for travelers wanting to visit two or more of the mountains. Linked to Paradise by Hwy 706, Ohanapecosh's roads are generally closed in the winter months due to adverse weather conditions, making it less accessible than Nisqually.

Activities
HIKING

Starting just north of the Ohanapecosh Visitors Center, the 1.5-mile **Grove of the Patriarchs Trail** is one of the park's most popular short hikes and explores a small island (the grove) in the Ohanapecosh River replete with craning Douglas fir, cedar and hemlock trees, some of which are over 1000 years old.

Sleeping & Eating

Cowlitz River Lodge MOTEL **$$**
(☎360-494-4444; www.escapetothemountains.com; Hwy 12 at Skate Creek Rd; r incl breakfast $80-95; ❈❖) Probably the most convenient accommodation for both Mts Rainier and St Helens, the Cowlitz is the sister motel to Ashford's Nisqually Lodge (p163) and offers 32 above-average motel rooms along with the obligatory outdoor Jacuzzi.

Hotel Packwood HOTEL **$**
(☎360-494-5431; 104 Main St; tw/d with shared bathroom $29/39, d $49; ❖) A frontier-style hotel with a wraparound verandah, the Packwood ain't fancy but it's authentic – and at this price, who can argue? There are nine varied rooms in the renovated 1912 establishment, two of which can accommodate four people. Chuck in free wi-fi, free coffee and the odd elk roaming in the grounds and you're laughing – hysterically!

Peters Inn STEAKHOUSE **$$**
(☎360-494-4000; www.peters-inn.com; Hwy 12 near Skate Creek Rd; lunch specials $8, mains $11-15) This local steak house features a lunch counter and a cozy dining area, but is best known for its breakfasts which include endless coffee refills, pancakes, eggs and homemade country fries on the side. There's also a lounge and three rooms available for overnight stays.

Ohanapecosh Campground CAMPGROUND **$**
(☎360-494-2229; Hwy 123; campsites May-Jun & Sep-Oct $12, late Jun-Labor Day $15) Near the visitors center, this NPS facility has 188 campsites and flush toilets. Rangers lead campfire talks on summer evenings.

❶ Information

Destination Packwood (www.destinationpackwood.com; 12990 US Hwy 12; ⊙8.30am-5pm Mon-Fri) A good source of information for the White Pass area.

Ohanapecosh Visitors Center (⊙9am-5pm May–mid-Oct) At the park's southeastern corner on Hwy 123. The displays here focus on tree identification and the local old-growth forest. Rangers also offer information on hiking trails.

WHITE RIVER ENTRANCE

Rainier's main eastern entrance is the gateway to Sunrise, which at 6400ft marks the park's highest road. Thanks to the superior elevation here, the summer season is particularly short and snow can linger well into July. It is also noticeably drier than Paradise, resulting in an interesting variety of sub-alpine vegetation, including masses of wildflowers.

The views from Sunrise are famously spectacular and – aside from stunning closeups of Mt Rainier itself – you can also, quite literally, watch the weather roll in over the distant peaks of Mts Baker and Adams. Similarly impressive is the glistening Emmons Glacier which, at 4 sq miles in size, is the largest glacier in the contiguous USA.

Activities
HIKING

Day hikes from Sunrise offer dramatic scenery and rewarding mountain vistas, and while the crowds here can be thick in the summer, the lack of tour buses makes it substantially quieter than Paradise.

A trailhead directly across the parking lot from the Sunrise Lodge Cafeteria provides access to the **Emmons Vista**, with good views of Mt Rainier, Little Tahoma and the Emmons Glacier, the largest glacier in the lower 48 states. Nearby, the 1-mile **Sourdough Ridge Trail** takes you out into pristine sub-alpine meadows for stunning views over the Washington giants of Mt Rainier, Mt Baker, Glacier Peak and Mt Adams.

To get to **Emmons Glacier**, you'll need to set off from the White River Campground, 13 miles by road from Sunrise. Look out for both mountain goats and mountain climbers ascending the Inter Glacier as you track west along the **Glacier Basin Trail**. The official overlook is about 1 mile from the campground along a spur path to the left.

Sleeping & Eating

White River Campground CAMPGROUND **$**
(☎360-663-2273; campsites $12; ⊙late Jun–mid Sep) This 112-site campground is 10 road

miles or 3.5 steep trail miles downhill from Sunrise. Facilities include flush toilets, drinking water and crowded, though not unpleasant, camping spaces.

Sunrise Lodge Cafeteria   CAFETERIA $
(☑360-569-2425; snacks $5-7; ☺10am-7pm Jun 30-Sep 16) As the only eating joint in a 30-mile radius, Sunrise's post-hike chili can look deceptively appetizing. There's not a lot else here apart from the ubiquitous hot dogs and hamburgers, and there's no overnight accommodation.

❶ Information
Sunrise Visitors Center (☺10am-6pm early Jul-early Sep)

Wilderness Information Center (☺7.30am-4.30pm) At the White River entrance; dispenses backcountry permits and hiking information.

CARBON RIVER ENTRANCE
The park's northwest entrance is its most isolated and undeveloped corner, with two unpaved (and unconnected) roads and little in the way of facilities, save a lone ranger station and the very basic Ipsut Creek Campground. But while the tourist traffic might be thin on the ground, the landscape lacks nothing in magnificence or serendipity.

Named for its coal deposits, Carbon River is the park's wettest region and protects one of the few remaining examples of inland temperate rain forest in the contiguous USA. Dense, green and cloaked in moss, this verdant wilderness can be penetrated by a handful of interpretive trails that fan off the Carbon River Rd.

For close-up mountain views head for Mowich Lake on a separate road which branches off a few miles outside the park entrance. This is Rainier's largest and deepest lake and a starting point for various wilderness hikes. In close proximity to Mowich is the Carbon Glacier, the nation's lowest glacier; its snout touches an elevation of 3520ft.

⚡ Activities
HIKING
To experience the rare thrill of walking inside a thick canopied temperate rain forest, venture out on the 0.3-mile **Rainforest Trail**, just inside the park entrance. The trail loops via a raised boardwalk past huge-leafed ferns and giant dripping trees.

The 3520ft snout of the **Carbon Glacier** can be accessed via a trail from the Ipsut Creek Campground, which proceeds southeast for 3.5 miles to a constructed overlook.

Hikers are warned not to approach the glacier, as rockfall from its surface is unpredictable and dangerous. This hike is technically part of the longer Wonderland Trail.

From Mowich Lake, one extremely popular trail heads south and passes **Spray Falls** on its way to **Spray Park**, flush with wildflowers late in the summer. It's almost three miles to Spray Park, but with numerous steep switchbacks above the falls the trail is far from easy.

🛏 Sleeping
Ipsut Creek Campground   CAMPGROUND $
(☑360-829-5127; campsites free with wilderness camping permit; ☺year-round, weather permitting) This free campground is at the end of the Carbon River Rd and has 12 campsites and one group site. There are pit toilets but no drinking water. Ipsut currently has no road access; walk-ins only.

❶ Information
Wilkeson Wilderness Information Center (☺8:30am-4pm May-Nov, 7:30am-7:30pm Jun-Aug) Come here to pick up permits for backcountry camping and for north side climbs; located 21 miles from the Carbon River entrance.

Crystal Mountain
Just outside the northeast corner of Mount Rainier National park lies **Crystal Mountain Resort** (www.skicrystal.com;), Washington's largest ski area, 39 miles east of Enumclaw off Hwy 410. This is the state's only ski 'resort' with various overnight accommodations at the base. However, in reality, Crystal still functions primarily as a day-use area due to its relative proximity to Seattle and Tacoma. The mountain's 2600 acres, first opened in 1962, have an incredible array of terrain including some wonderful backcountry. In winter 2010 it opened the state's first gondola. Daily lift passes are $73/65 per adult/child (with gondola).

🛏 Sleeping & Eating
A variety of condos are available at the mountain base from **Crystal Mountain Lodging** (www.crystalmountainlodging.com). Aside from the resort eating options, there are a couple of restaurants on the mountain itself.

Alpine Inn   HOTEL $$
(☑360-663-2262; www.crystalhotels.com; r from $95; ☎) Run by Crystal Mountain Hotels, this Bavarian-style inn looks as if it's been

dragged across from kitschy Leavenworth on the other side of the Wenatchee National Forest. Cozy, comfortable and playing deftly on its European image, the inn boasts a restaurant, rathskeller, deli and ski/snowboard shop. Watch out for the Wiener schnitzel in the restaurant.

Alta Crystal Resort   SUITES $$$
(☎360-663-2500; www.altacrystalresort.com; 2-6 person ste from $199; 🛜🏊) This resort is popular year-round thanks to its proximity to the Crystal Mountain ski resort (winter) and the Sunrise Lodge Cafeteria and trailheads (summer). It's one of the area's plushest accommodations (though it's technically outside the park). Encased in 22 wooded acres and bisected by bubbling Deep Creek, it consists of 24 suites housed in three chalets surrounding a pool and Jacuzzi. One-bedroom suites sleep up to four and loft suites accommodate up to six. All have kitchenettes and wood stoves or fireplaces.

ℹ Getting There & Away

On weekends and holidays from December to March a **shuttle bus** (☎206-626-5200; adult/child $35/25) transports skiers to/from Seattle.

Mt St Helens

Thanks to a 1980 eruption that set off an explosion bigger than the combined power of 1500 atomic bombs, Washington's 87th tallest mountain needs little introduction. What it lacks in height Mt St Helens makes up for in fiery infamy; 57 people perished on the mountain on that fateful day in May 1980 when an earthquake of 5.1 on the Richter scale sparked the biggest landslide in recorded history and buried 230 sq miles of forest under millions of tonnes of volcanic rock and ash.

When the smoke finally lifted, Mt St Helens sported a new mile-wide crater on its north side and had lost 1300ft in height. Resolving to leave nature to its own devices, the Reagan Administration created the 172-sq-mile Mt St Helens National Volcanic Monument in 1982. A visit here today will demonstrate how, over three decades on, nature has restored much life to the mountain, although the devastation wreaked by the explosion is still hauntingly evident.

◉ Sights

The plethora of Mount St Helen's visitor centers can be a little confusing. Consult the information below for the highlights of each. The entrance fee for the **Mt St Helens National Volcanic Monument** is $8.

TOP CHOICE ➤ **Johnston Ridge Observatory**
INTERPRETIVE CENTER
(☉10am-6pm May-Oct) Situated at the end of Hwy 504 and looking directly into the mouth of the crater, the observatory has exhibits that take a more scientific angle than the Silver Lake center, depicting the geologic events surrounding the 1980 blast and how they advanced the science of volcano forecasting and monitoring. The paved one-mile round trip **Eruption Trail** offers once-in-a-lifetime views over toward the crater.

Mt St Helens Silver Lake Visitor Center
INTERPRETIVE CENTER
(3029 Spirit Lake Hwy; admission $3; ☉9am-5pm May 1-Sep 30; 👶) Situated five miles east of Castle Rock on Hwy 504, the Silver Lake is the best introduction to the monument. There's a classic film and various exhibits including a mock-up of the volcano where you can duck beneath the cone for displays on the subterranean workings of the mountain. Outside is the one-mile **Silver Lake Wetlands Trail**.

FREE **Hoffstadt Bluffs Visitors Center**
INTERPRETIVE CENTER
(www.hoffstadtbluffs.com; 15000 Spirit Lake Hwy; ☉9am-6pm) At Mile 27, this impressive post-and-beam structure has a good restaurant – the Fire Mountain Grill – and panoramic views of the Toutle River Valley. Exhibits focus on St Helens' ecology pre-blast. This is where you can organize helicopter tours (per person $149) over the crater.

FREE **Charles W Bingham Forest Learning Center**   INTERPRETIVE CENTER
(17000 Spirit Lake Memorial Hwy; ☉10am-4pm Fri-Sun mid-May–Oct) Situated at Mile 33 on Hwy 504, the learning center is basically a showcase for the lumber industry, though it does run another interesting film about the eruption. There are restrooms and a gift shop on site.

Coldwater Lake   NATURAL SITE
Coldwater Lake, 43 miles east of Castle Rock, was created in 1980 when water backed up behind a dam caused by debris was brought down by the eruption. The recreation area here (restrooms, phone, boat launch) is the starting point of the 0.6-mile **Birth of a Lake Trail**, a paved interpretive

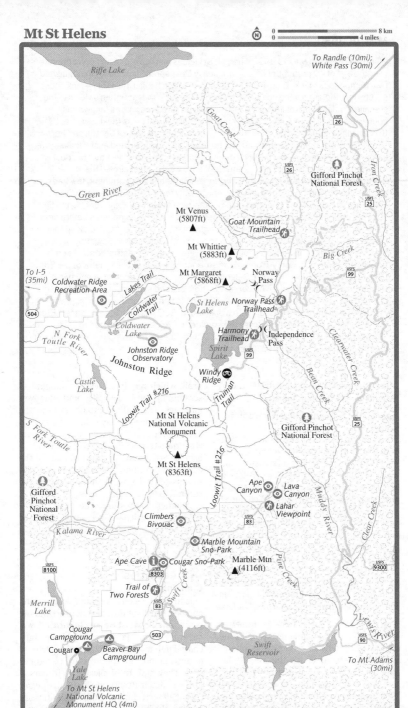

Riffe Lake

To Randle (10mi);
White Pass (30mi)

USFS 26

Gifford Pinchot
National Forest

USFS 26

USFS 25

Goat Creek

Green River

Iron Creek

Mt Venus
(5807ft) ▲

Goat Mountain
Trailhead

Big Creek

Mt Whittier
(5883ft) ▲

To I-5
(35mi)

Coldwater Ridge
Recreation Area

Mt Margaret
(5868ft) ▲

Norway
Pass

USFS 99

Lakes Trail

St Helens
Lake

Norway Pass
Trailhead

504

Coldwater
Trail

Coldwater
Lake

Harmony
Trailhead

Independence
Pass

N Fork
Toutle River

Spirit
Lake

Clearwater Creek

Johnston Ridge
Observatory

Johnston Ridge

USFS 99

Castle
Lake

Windy
Ridge

Bean Creek

Loowit Trail #216

Truman
Trail

S Fork Toutle
River

Mt St Helens
National Volcanic
Monument

Gifford Pinchot
National Forest

USFS 25

Gifford
Pinchot
National
Forest

Mt St Helens
(8363ft) ▲

Loowit Trail #216

Ape
Canyon

Lava
Canyon

Muddy's River

Lahar
Viewpoint

Kalama River

Climbers
Bivouac

USFS 83

Clear Creek

Marble Mountain
Sno-Park

USFS 8100

Ape Cave

Cougar Sno-Park

USFS 8303

Marble Mtn
(4116ft) ▲

Pine Creek

USFS 9300

Merrill
Lake

Trail of
Two Forests

USFS 83

Swift Creek

Lewis River

Cougar
Campground

503

Cougar ●

Beaver Bay
Campground

Swift
Reservoir

USFS 90

Yale
Lake

To Mt Adams
(30mi)

To Mt St Helens
National Volcanic
Monument HQ (4mi)

0 ____ 8 km
0 ____ 4 miles

MAY 18, 1980

Where were you on May 18, 1980 when Mt St Helens blew its top? Pacific Northwesters over the age of 40 remember it as an unusually clear spring day quickly extinguished by a humungous black cloud. But first there was a loud bang. One of St Helens' most perplexing riddles was the noise – or lack of it. People in the mountain's vicinity (the so-called 'quiet zone') claim they heard nothing, whereas people as far away as Vancouver, Canada jumped out of their seats. Another curiosity was the dust fall-out. Due to prevailing winds from the west, the major population centers of Seattle and Portland avoided any choking smog. Instead, the huge volcanic cloud drifted east, cloaking Yakima in 5 inches of dust and bringing darkness at noon to Spokane. Later on, dust was reported as far away as Minnesota and within two weeks it had circled the globe.

Though scientists had known an eruption on St Helens was imminent, few had predicted its magnitude. The loss of comparatively few lives (57) was partly down to luck. First, the eruption happened on a Sunday when the mountain's logging parties were on weekend vacation. Second, it happened at 8:32am, 90 minutes before an army of homeowners was due to be let into the restricted 'red zone' to pick up their possessions (the area had been evacuated two weeks earlier in anticipation of an imminent eruption). In fact, only four people were inside the restricted zone at the time of the explosion: Harry Truman, the stubborn 83-year-old proprietor of the Spirit Lake Lodge;, David Johnston, a US Geographical Survey volcanologist; and two further amateur volcanologists. All perished. The blast and subsequent landslide also claimed 7000 animals, 40,000 salmon, 47 bridges and over 185 miles of highway. The federal government was left with a bill for over $2.7 billion in today's prices. President Jimmy Carter, after flying over the smoldering volcano, is reported to have said: 'Someone said the area looked like a moonscape. But the moon looks more like a golf course compared to what's up here.'

WASHINGTON CASCADES SOUTH CASCADES

hike that seeks to demonstrate the regrowth of vegetation in the area.

Spirit Lake & Windy Ridge Viewpoint
NATURAL SITE

More remote but less crowded than Johnston Ridge is the harder-to-reach Windy Ridge viewpoint on the mountain's eastern side, accessed via USFS Rd 99. Here visitors get a palpable, if eerie, sense of the destruction that the blast wrought with felled forests, desolate mountain slopes and the rather surreal sight of lifeless Spirit Lake, once one of the premier resorts in the South Cascades. There are toilets and a snack bar at the viewpoint parking lot, which is often closed until June. Steps ascend the hillside for close-up views of the crater. A few miles down the road you can descend 600ft on the one mile-long **Harmony Trail** (hike 224) to Spirit Lake.

Ape Cave
NATURAL SITE

Ape Cave is a 2-mile-long lava tube formed 2000 years ago by a lava flow that followed a deep watercourse. It's the longest lava tube in the Western Hemisphere. Hikers can walk and scramble the length of Ape Cave on either the 0.8-mile **Lower Ape Cave Trail** or the 1.5-mile **Upper Ape Cave**

Trail, which requires a certain amount of scrambling over rock piles and narrower passages. The trail eventually exits at the upper entrance. You can bring your own light source or rent lanterns for $4 at **Apes' Headquarters** (8303 Forest Rd; ⊙10:30am-5pm Jun-Sep), located at the entrance to the caves, and tag onto free ranger-led explorations offered several times a day in the summer.

Another interesting side trail is the 0.6-mile wheelchair-accessible **Trail of Two Forests**, on a boardwalk across a 1900-year-old lava flow that once buried an ancient forest.

🏃 Activities
Climbing

Due to Mt St Helens' delicate volcanic state, climbers must obtain a permit to ascend the peak from the **Mt St Helens Institute** (www.mshinstitute.org). Permits should be purchased online and cost $22 April to October (a maximum of 100 permits are issued per day). They have to be picked up in person at the Lone Fir Resort on SR 503 in Cougar. Although no technical climbing abilities are needed, the hike is no walk in the park and many summit-seekers camp by the trailhead at Climber's Bivouac the night before climbing. The bivouac is situated 14 miles northeast of Cougar at the end of USFS Rd 830 (a narrow gravel road that spurs off USFS Rd 83 at Cougar Sno-Park). From here, the **Monitor Ridge Trail** (hike 216A) ascends 1100ft in 2.3 miles to reach the timberline, from where you must scramble 5 miles over lava chunks and loose pumice fields to reach the summit cliffs. Allow eight to 12 hours to make the round trip.

The Mt Helens Institute offers guided climbs in July and August for $150 per person.

Hiking

Aside from the short walks mentioned already, there are some longer hikes. You can circumnavigate Coldwater Lake on the 9-mile **Lakes Trail/Coldwater Trail** (hikes 211 and 230) through an area of forest blowdown and developing shrubs. With 2500ft of ascent, the trail is graded 'difficult.' Another popular volcanic ramble is the **Truman Trail** (hike 207), named after the unfortunate Harry Truman who perished in the eruption, that leads from the Windy Ridge Viewpoint through pumice fields and wildflower fields for 5.7 miles.

Mt St Helens' version of Rainier's Wonderland trail is the 30-mile **Loowit Trail** (hike 216) that circumnavigates the volcano, crossing numerous ecosystems. Since the destructive storms that wracked the whole Pacific Northwest area in November 2006 the trail quality has been patchy; enquire at the Silver Lake Visitor Center before setting out.

Skiing

Long considered the smaller, quieter sibling of Crystal Mountain, **White Pass** (www.skiwhitepass.com) ski area, 50 miles west of Yakima on US 12, was expanded in 2010, doubling in size to 1500 acres and incorporating a new mid-mountain lodge.

Tours

Eco Tours of Oregon   VOLCANO TOUR (www.ecotours-of-oregon.com; 3127 SE 23rd Ave, Portland, OR) Runs a Mt St Helens volcano tour from mid-June to late September. The eight-hour tour ($59.50 plus $8 park entry fee) leaves from Portland's hotels at 9am and visits the Silver Lake Visitor Center, Coldwater Recreation area and Johnston Ridge Observatory.

Sleeping & Eating

Good chow can be found at **Fire Mountain Grill** in the Hoffstadt Bluffs Visitor Center and the **Backwoods Café** at the Eco Park Resort.

White Pass Village Inn   CONDOS $$$ (☑509-672-3131; www.whitepassvilageinn.com; 38933 US 12; studio $130, 1-bed condo $176; 🐕🍴) Adjacent to the White Pass skiing area, this condo complex is open year-round meaning it's also good for Yakima wine tours and sorties into Mt Rainier National Park (12 miles away). Condo sizes range from studios to deluxe and all have kitchenettes and private bathrooms. The outdoor pool is heated to spa temperatures in the winter, and there is a store and laundry next door.

Eco Park Resort   CAMPGROUND, CABINS $ (☑360-274-6542; www.ecoparkresort.com; 14000 Spirit Lake Hwy; campsites & RV sites $17, yurts $60, cabins $80-90) The closest full-service accommodation to the blast zone offers campsites and RV hookups, basic cabins and rather incongruous Genghis Khan-style yurts. Shared bathrooms are known as 'wilderness comfort stations.' Owned by the family whose Spirit Lake Lodge was swept away by the 1980 eruption, the resort also features the Backwoods Café which serves anything as long as it's beef.

Blue Heron Inn   B&B $$ (☑360-274-9595; www.blueheroninn.com; Hwy 504; d/ste $159/205; 🐕) A welcome B&B in an accommodation-lite area, the Blue Heron offers seven rooms, including a Jacuzzi suite, in a large house almost opposite the Silver Lake Visitor Center on Hwy 504. Rooms are clean if unspectacular, but the views of Silver Lake and Mt St Helens are spellbinding – weather permitting.

Seaquest State Park   CAMPGROUND $ (☑206-274-8633; Hwy 504; campsites/RV sites $21/28; ⊙year-round) Directly across from the entrance to the Mt St Helens Visitors Center, Seaquest has 90 campsites, including a separate hiker/cyclist camp area, with flush toilets and showers.

Information

Gifford Pinchot National Forest official site (www.fs.fed.us/gpnf) The mountain's best online information portal.

Mt St Helens Volcanic Monument Headquarters (42218 NE Yale Bridge Rd, Amboy, WA; ⊙8am-5pm Mon-Fri Oct-May, 8am-5pm Mon-Sat

Jun-Sep) On Hwy 503, 16 miles southeast of Cougar on the mountain's south side.

❶ Getting There & Away

There's no public transport to Mount St Helens unless you join an organized tour. The easiest car access is along Hwy 504 which branches east from I-5 at Castle Rock.

South West Washington Charter Tours (www. swwashingtonchartertours.com) Runs a winter ski shuttle to White Pass from Olympia/Centralia for $25/20.

Mt Adams

Adams is the state's forgotten peak, the second tallest of Washington's Cascades but a mountain that has long been overshadowed by Rainier's height and St Helen's explosive power. Nonetheless Adams remains an impressive mountain; the lack of a major glacier on its south side allows for a comparatively easy, non-technical ascent for aspiring peak-baggers. On its lower slopes Adams is renowned for the juicy huckleberries and pretty wildflowers that fill its grassy alpine meadows during a short but intense summer season.

Protected in the 66-sq-mile Mt Adams Wilderness, Adams sports plenty of picturesque hikes including the much-loved **Bird Creek Meadow Trail**, a 3-mile loop that showcases the best of the mountain's meadows, wildflowers and waterfalls.

Mt Adams is one of the easiest Cascade peaks to climb, and is often used as a trial peak for beginners. While most climbs are nontechnical slogs up a glacier, even these require basic climbing gear. The easiest approach (grade II) is from the south, via Cold Springs Campground, and up the South Spur to the summit. The climb is best between May and August. Climbers should sign in and out at the USFS ranger station at either Trout Lake or Randle. For guided hikes contact Seattle-based **Mountain Madness** (www.mountainmadness.com).

🛏 Sleeping

Serenity's CABINS $$
(☎509-395-2500; www.serenitys.com; 2291 Hwy 141; cabin $89-259; 🛜) A mile south of Trout Lake on Hwy 141, Serenity's offers four beautifully presented cabins in the woods in the shadow of snow-sprinkled Mt Adams. Wonderfully landscaped and amply equipped with kitchens, bathrooms, wood stoves, Jacuzzis, welcome cookies (homemade) and a bottle of wine, this is true luxury in the wilderness. Dining is also available.

Takhlakh Lake Campground CAMPGROUND $
(☎509-395-3400; campsites $15) Fifty-four campsites with running water and pit toilets are situated here, 25 miles north of Trout Lake on USFS Rd 23.

❶ Information

Mt Adams Ranger District USFS Office (2455 Hwy 141; ⊙8am-4:30pm Mon-Sat Oct-May, daily Jun-Sep) For huckleberry permits and information on hiking and climbing; in Trout Lake village.

❶ Getting There & Away

The easiest access to Mt Adams is from the Columbia River Gorge near Hood River (Oregon). From here Hwy 141 proceeds north for 25 miles to the tiny community of Trout Lake. Access from the north is from Randle on US 12 and is only passable in the summer.

Central & Eastern Washington

Best Places to Eat

» Saffron Mediterranean Kitchen (p197)

» Birchfield Manor Restaurant (p183)

» München Haus (p175)

» Yellow Church Café (p181)

Best Places to Stay

» Enzian Inn (p174)

» Inn at Goose Creek (p181)

» Davenport Hotel (p189)

» Marcus Whitman Hotel (p197)

Why Go?

If states were delineated purely by geography, Washington east of the Cascade Mountains would be an entirely separate entity. While the west breeds evergreen trees, liberal cities, perennial rain and gourmet coffee, the east is the polar opposite; a land of sunbaked hills and big blue skies stuffed with private vineyards, rodeo towns and huge Native American reservations.

The east's geographic identity is intrinsically linked to the mighty Columbia River, which has transformed both the landscape and the economy. This once-parched rural region now features gargantuan dams and ambitious irrigation projects that have converted barren valleys and scrubby steppe into a veritable Garden of Eden. The metamorphosis has had a knock-on effect for tourism. Man-made lakes have provided a nexus of outdoor recreation, while the rich, irrigated soil has propelled the region into an enological rival to California, producing some of the nation's youngest, fruitiest and most promising new wines.

When to Go

Spokane

July & August	September	December
Wall-to-wall sunshine for wine-tasting trips in the Columbia River Valley.	Ellensburg's Labor Day Rodeo is Central Washington's biggest show.	Hit Bavarian Leavenworth for the picturesque Christmas Lights Festival.

CENTRAL WASHINGTON

Caught in the foothills of the grandiose Cascade Mountains, central Washington is a geographic crossroads where dramatic alpine peaks fold with eerie suddenness into a barren steppe-like desert broken only by the winding presence of the Columbia River and its irrigating manmade dams.

Wenatchee and Leavenworth are the most interesting urban centers here and both are popular stopping-off points on the scenic Cascade Loop drive. Aside from Leavenworth's Bavarian bonhomie, outdoor adventures are the main draw.

Leavenworth

POP 2074

Blink hard and rub your eyes. This isn't some strange Germanic hallucination. This is Leavenworth, a former lumber town that underwent a Bavarian makeover back in the 1960s after the rerouting of the cross-continental railway threatened to put it permanently out of business. Swapping wood for tourists, Leavenworth has successfully reinvented itself as a traditional *Romantische Strasse* village, right down to the beer and sausages, and the lederhosen-loving locals (25% of whom are German). The classic *Sound of Music* setting helps; as does the fact that Leavenworth serves as the main activity center for sorties into the nearby Alpine Lakes Wilderness and Wenatchee National Forest.

⊙ Sights

Leavenworth's small Bavarian hub is centered on Front St, where gabled alpine houses nestle in the shadow of the craggy peaks of the North Cascade Mountains in scenes reminiscent of Bavaria. A leisurely stroll through this diminutive, if distinctly surreal, alpine community, with its European cheese-mongers, dirndl-wearing waitresses, wandering accordionists and neatly stacked log piles, is one of Washington state's oddest, but at the same time most endearing, experiences.

Nutcracker Museum   MUSEUM
(www.nutcrackermuseum.com; 735 Front St; admission $2.50; ⊙2-5pm; ⊕) If you have a penchant for obscure, highly specialized museums, stop by the Nutcracker on Leavenworth's main drag, which specializes in nutcracker dolls. Ebony, metal, boxwood,

ivory and porcelain, there are numerous varieties here; 5000 of them in fact, along with a shop downstairs where you buy your very own nut-cracking souvenirs.

Waterfront Park   PARK
Tucked out of view but surprisingly close, this green area provides Leavenworth with access to the Wenatchee River. Wander down 9th St and follow the leafy domain over a footbridge and onto Blackbird Island, where you can catch a glimpse of Sleeping Lady Mountain ringed by a border of green foliage. Interpretive signs furnish the route and help explain the local plant and animal life.

Leavenworth National Fish Hatchery   HATCHERY
(12790 Fish Hatchery Rd; admission by donation; ⊙8am-4pm) Of three thriving fish hatcheries on the Columbia River, this is the largest and, quite possibly, the most interesting. Created to provide a spawning ground for salmon that had been blocked from migrating upriver by the construction of the Grand Coulee Dam in the 1930s, the ongoing fish-rearing project produces some 1.6 million Chinook salmon a year. The young smolt are released into Icicle Creek each spring from where they migrate to the Pacific.

From the hatchery, you can hike the mile-long **Icicle Creek Interpretive Trail** and learn about the local ecology and history.

🏃 Activities

Hiking

Leavenworth offers ample opportunities for hiking. The most diverse selection of trails can be found in the nearby Alpine Lakes Wilderness and vary from an easy 3.5-mile river loop to a challenging two- to three-day backcountry slog. Pick up a trail map at the chamber of commerce.

Skiing

The area around Leavenworth has some diverse skiing opportunities, including downhill skiing, cross-country skiing, tubing, snowshoeing and even ski jumping. A number of hotels rent skis and equipment, or you can enquire at **Der Sportsman** (837 Front St). The **Leavenworth Winter Sports Club** (www.skileavenworth.com) is a local umbrella organization, and its website contains a wealth of local ski information. The club helps maintain 26km of mostly level trails at Icicle River, Waterfront Park and **Leavenworth Ski Hill** (day pass adult/child $15/12; ⊙3-7pm Wed & Fri & 9.30am-7pm Sat & Sun late Dec-Feb). The Hill

Central & Eastern Washington Highlights

1 Listen to the alpenhorn over a German-style breakfast in Leavenworth's **Enzian Inn** (p174)

2 Watch the sunset over the Cascades from the dining car of Amtrak's **Empire Builder** (p186)

3 Mingle with students and sup good coffee at the **Ellensburg Rodeo** (p181)

4 Recline regally in the grandiose lobby of Spokane's **Davenport Hotel** (p190)

5 Admire the after-dark laser show at the **Grand Coulee Dam** (p192)

6 Pair home-grown food with ever-improving wines in quality restaurants at **Walla Walla** (p198)

7 Go on a rock-climbing sortie in the **Alpine Lakes Wilderness** (p176)

has 5km of trails lit for night skiing, a tubing park and a rather famous ski jump.

Rafting

The 18.5-mile stretch of the Wenatchee River from Leavenworth to Monitor promises some of the biggest rapids in the state (class III and IV) and one of the best ways to catch them is to join an organized rafting trip. Locally run **Osprey Rafting Co** (☑509-548-6800; www.ospreyrafting.com; 4342 Icicle Rd) offers everything from high-adventure white-knuckle rides on class III and IV rapids ($90, 4½ hours) to contemplative downstream floats on rented inner tubes (day-long floats $15). The May and June snowmelt season sees the river at its wildest.

Climbing

A well-known nexus for Washington's climbing community, Leavenworth's classic climb is **Castle Rock** in Tumwater Canyon, about 3 miles northwest of town off US 2. A newer focal point for climbers is Icicle Creek Canyon in the Alpine Lakes Wilderness, where challenging rock climbing requires a USFS permit. **Snow Creek Wall** is an old stalwart in this area, but there are several hundred other climbs here, most of which have been developed in the last 15 years. **Leavenworth Mountain Sports** (www.leavenworthmtnsports.com; 220 US 2; ⊙10am-6pm Mon-Fri, 9am-6pm Sat & Sun) rents rock shoes, harnesses and other climbing gear.

Cycling

The **Devil's Gulch trail** (25 miles, four to six hours) and **Mission Ridge trail** (26 miles, four to seven hours) are two of the most popular off-road bike trails in the state. **Freund Canyon** is an intermediate 8.3-mile loop and is classed as the best single-track bike trail in the Leavenworth area. It is also home to the annual Bavarian Bike and Brews Race. Der Sportsman rents bikes from $25 a day.

Horseback & Sleigh Riding

For the archetypal Leavenworth wintertime experience, contact **Eagle Creek Ranch** (www.eaglecreek.ws; 7951 Eagle Creek Rd), which offers *Jingle Bells*-evoking sleigh rides from $15 per person. When the snow clears you can try your hand at **horseback riding** on one- to two-hour trail rides ($26 to $45).

★ Festivals & Events

Book well ahead for accommodation during the following festivals.

Oktoberfest BEER
(www.leavenworthoktoberfest.com) This popular annual beer festival makes a good family outing – believe it or not – with a special *kinderplatz* (kids zone) set up in town. Festivities include German food, beer, arts and crafts, live music and a special Bavarian 'beer-tapping' ceremony. The festival usually runs over three weekends in October. Free shuttles are laid on.

TOP CHOICE Christmas Lights CHRISTMAS
Leavenworth's alpine houses look like a Christmas card at the best of times, and no more so than in the first three weeks of December when the locals relight the town three times on the first three Saturdays of the month. There's live music, carol singing and, of course, an appearance by Father Christmas.

🛏 Sleeping

Leavenworth has possibly the best selection of accommodations in the state outside Seattle.

TOP CHOICE Enzian Inn HOTEL $$
(☑509-548-5269; www.enzianinn.com; 590 Hwy 2; d/ste $155/255; ⚫⚫) Most hotels get by on one quirk, but the Enzian broadcasts at least a half-dozen, the most obscure of which is the sight of long-term owner, Bob Johnson, giving a morning blast on his famous alpenhorn before breakfast. If this doesn't send you running enthusiastically for your lederhosen, cast an eye over the free putting green (with resident grass-trimming goats), the gorgeous classical (indoor and outdoor) swimming pools, the panoramic upstairs restaurant (where you can partake in a German breakfast buffet), or the nightly pianist who'll pound out your musical requests in the Bavarian lobby.

Run of the River Inn B&B $$$
(☑509-548-7171; www.runoftheriver.com; 9308 E Leavenworth Rd; ste from $240; ⚫) A real romantic dream, the Run of the River is a stress-free, kid-free, smoke-free B&B where all the rooms are suites and breakfast will be the tastiest, most creative and largest meal of the week,month or year. The suites are pure luxury, with deluxe Jacuzzis, fluffy bathrobes, fireplaces, hiking gear, binoculars (the inn is next to a bird refuge) and an old-fashioned typewriter just in case guests get poetically inspired. Very, very special.

Hotel Pension Anna
HOTEL $$
(☏509-548-6273; www.pensionanna.com; 926 Commercial St; r $149-230, chapel ste $239-330) Service, authenticity and attention to detail; this meticulously furnished old-world hotel adheres to all three, from the imported Austrian-style furniture, to the warm genuine greetings to the hearty European-inspired breakfast. There is even a spacious suite housed in the adjacent St Joseph's chapel that the owners rescued and moved here in 1992.

Bavarian Lodge
HOTEL $$$
(☏509-548-7878; www.bavarianlodge.com; 810 Hwy 2; d/ste $149/249; ❂☎☲) This lodge takes the Bavarian theme to luxury levels in a plush, clutter-free establishment with modern – but definably German – rooms complete with gas fires, king-size beds, funky furnishings and a serve-yourself buffet breakfast. Outside there's a heated pool and hot tub, while the suite rooms upstairs have huge Jacuzzi baths wedged into a cozy Bavarian turret.

Linderhof Inn
MOTEL $$
(☏800-828-5680; www.linderhof.com; 690 Hwy 2; r $89-160; ☎☲) Take a basic motel concept and give it a cheery German makeover with tumbling flower baskets, gabled roofs, a substantial breakfast, a heated spa pool, and an unbeatable alpine backdrop. The result is the Linderhof; nothing fancy, but a million metaphoric miles from your typical grungy motor inn.

Bavarian Ritz
HOTEL $$
(☏509-548-5455; 633 Front St; d/ste $89/149; ❂☎☲) Wedged into Bavarian-style Front St, the Ritz is a vintage 1903 inn that was reincarnated in Leavenworth's 1960s German makeover. Promoting a wide selection of room types and a couple of decent downstairs restaurants, the facilities fall short of full-blown luxury status, though the vista-studded sundeck and the extravagant four-poster beds in the Royal King suites should keep visiting Europhiles happy.

Leavenworth Village Inn
HOTEL $$
(☏509-548-6620; www.leavenworthvilageinn.com; 1016 Commercial St; d/ste from $79/159; ☎) Huge rooms at economical prices. Recent remodeling has ensured this place is both modern and bereft of the frilly German touches ubiquitous elsewhere in town.

Eightmile Campground
CAMPGROUND $
(☏800-274-6104; 4905 Icicle Rd; campsites $16) The closest campground to Leavenworth on Icicle Rd on the way to the Alpine Lakes Wilderness; there are 45 campsites here and access to the Enchantment Lakes area.

✗ Eating

⬆TOP CHOICE München Haus
GERMAN $
(www.munchenhaus.com; 709 Front St; sausages $5; ☷) The Haus is 100% alfresco, meaning the hot German sausages and pretzels served up here are essential stomach-warmers in the winter, while the Bavarian brews do a good job of cooling you down in the summer. The casual beer-garden atmosphere is complemented by vibrant flower baskets, laidback staff and a stash of top-quality relishes including cider kraut and mustard to spice up your bratwurst. There are even vegan varieties.

Café Christa
GERMAN $$
(www.cafechrista.com; upstairs 801 Front St; mains $14-18; ☉lunch & dinner) If you came to Leavenworth to sample authentic German cooking, you won't be disappointed by what's on offer here. Christa's features quaint European decor, discreet yet polite service and a menu that rustles up a plethora of old-world classics such as Bratwurst, Wiener schnitzel and Jäger schnitzel served with sauce, red cabbage and spätzle. Even better, you can wash it all down with an accompanying stein of Hofbräuhaus Munich lager.

South
MEXICAN $$
(www.southleavenworth.com; 913 Front St; mains $15-21; ☉lunch & dinner) Leavenworth is as much about irony as kitsch and South – a Mexican restaurant in a proudly German town – is the living embodiment of it. If you get sick of sausages and sauerkraut (most people crumble after three days), divert here. Opened in 2007, the Mexican menu with Cuban and Peruvian inflections is cool and creative but always true to its Hispanic roots. Highlights of a made-from-scratch roll-call are the tangy guacamole, the self-proclaimed 'to-die-for' Oaxaca *mole*, the melt-in-your-mouth nachos and 30-odd types of tequila. Just in case your confidence deserts you, it also offers – irony of ironies – good old German sausage.

Andreas Keller
GERMAN $$
(www.andreaskellerrestaurant.com; 829 Front St; mains from $15; ☉lunch & dinner) The definitive Leavenworth experience lurks in this cavernous basement or *rathskeller,* with a genuine Oktoberfest atmosphere inspired by lederhosen-clad accordionists crooning

Bavarian drinking songs. To add to the authenticity, the head chef is German and prepares wonderful Wiener schnitzels, potato salad, sauerkraut, red cabbage and rye bread.

Renaissance Café
GERMAN **$$**
(www.therenaissancecafe.com; 217 8th St; breakfast & lunch $5-7, dinner $12-14; ⊘breakfast, lunch & dinner) You can get all kinds of food specialties at this subterranean restaurant, including the ubiquitous German sausage platter. Hearty breakfasts include a design-it-yourself omelet with a choice of 21 ingredients intended to satisfy hungry hikers; or you can carbo-load on granola, pancakes, oatmeal or pastries. The Renaissance also packages 'lunch to go' for hikers, kayakers, skiers or horseback riders.

Visconti's
ITALIAN **$$**
(www.viscontis.com; 636 Front St; ⊘lunch & dinner) If you get bored of Bavaria, head south (figuratively speaking) to Visconti's, where you may think you've reached Italy, so good is the ravioli – and the wines.

Gustav's Grill & Sports Pub
PUB **$**
(www.gustavsleavenworth.com; 617 US 2; sausages & sandwiches $6-7) In an onion-domed building on Hwy 2, Gustav's boasts a rooftop beer garden and lots of good Northwest brews on tap to complement its less remarkable sausages and deli sandwiches.

☆ Entertainment

Leavenworth Summer Theater THEATER
(☑box office 509-548-2000; Hwy 2 & Icicle Rd; tickets $12-20; ⊘shows Jul & Aug) Leavenworth's flirtation with kitsch doesn't just end in the Bavarian village. If a Julie Andrews sound-alike singing *Do-Re-Mi* doesn't send you rushing back to Seattle for a distorted grunge fix, proceed to the Ski Hill Amphitheater during the summer months for a full-length production of Roger's and Hammerstein's *The Sound of Music,* performed against an authentic alpine backdrop.

ℹ Information

Leavenworth Chamber of Commerce & Visitor Center (www.leavenworth.org; 940 US 2; ⊘8am-5pm Mon-Thu, 8am-6pm Fri & Sat, 10am-4pm Sun) If you're not immediately sold on the town's rather unusual German makeover, come here and they'll attempt to convince you otherwise.

Leavenworth Ranger Station (600 Sherbourne; ⊘7:30am-4:30pm) Off US 2 at the east end of town; provides information on recreational opportunities and issues various types of permits.

ℹ Getting There & Around

Bus

Northwestern Trailways (☑800-366-3830; www.northwesterntrailways.com) buses stop in Leavenworth twice daily on their way between Seattle ($28, three hours) and Wenatchee ($8, 40 minutes). The bus stop is on Hwy 2 by the post office.

Link Transit (www.linktransit.com) bus 22 passes up US 2 between Leavenworth and Wenatchee ($1, 50 minutes), via Peshastin and Cashmere, 20 times daily Monday to Friday (no weekend service).

Train

In 2009 **Amtrak** (www.amtrak.com) inaugurated the newest station on its country-wide passenger network in Leavenworth. The legendary *Empire Builder* now stops in the attractive Bavarian village twice daily at the town's Icicle Station on its route between Seattle and Chicago. Connections to Portland, Oregon and Vancouver, BC run through Seattle.

Around Leavenworth

ALPINE LAKES WILDERNESS

The Alpine Lakes Wilderness is a 614-sq-mile protected area of rough crenellated mountains, glacier-gouged valleys, and – as the name implies – gorgeous sapphire lakes (more than 700 of them, in fact). Crisscrossed by trails and popularly accessed from the Icicle Canyon Rd west of Leavenworth, the wilderness offers a handful of easy day hikes along with plenty of more substantial backcountry jaunts that require good fitness, shrewd forward planning and a decent pair of walking boots.

The area's close proximity to Seattle makes this former logging and mining region popular with hikers; the Enchantment Lakes area requires a $3 permit in the summer (enquire at Leavenworth Ranger Station). Good entry points are from the Icicle Rd (USFS Rd 7600) off Hwy 2 and on a dirt road just north of Tumwater campground on US 2.

The **Icicle Gorge Trail** is the most accessible hike here, an easy 3.6-mile river loop that gives you an enticing taste of what this pristine wilderness is all about. Other trailheads dot Icicle Rd and lead off into a network of popular trails. Pick up a leaflet at Leavenworth Chamber of Commerce & Visitor Center.

LAKE WENATCHEE

Swimming, boating and fishing entertain summertime visitors to Lake Wenatchee, 23 miles north of the city of Wenatchee (and actually much closer to Leavenworth). You can hike the 4.5-mile trail up Dirtyface Peak, cycle around the lake, or sign on with one of the rafting companies on Hwy 207 for a float trip.

Once there's snow on the ground, Lake Wenatchee becomes a great cross-country ski area, with 20 miles of marked and groomed trails, though skiers may have to dodge weekend snowmobilers. More trails criss-cross the Lower Chiwawa River area off the Chumstick Hwy, including a 5-mile scenic loop trail (closed to snowmobiles) that follows the Wenatchee River. Alternatively, you can head further west into the **Henry M Jackson Wilderness** on USFS Rd 6500 (off Hwy 207) at Little Wenatchee Ford campground, where a number of trails hook up with the **Pacific Crest Trail**.

To reach the lake, head north on Chumstick Hwy, or take US 2 west of town, then turn north onto Hwy 207. **Link Transit** (www.linktransit.com) runs a bus up here six times daily (35 minutes). For further area details contact the **Lake Wenatchee Ranger Station** (22976 Hwy 207; ⊙8am-4:30pm Mon-Fri, plus Sat Mar-Sep).

Wenatchee

POP 27,856

In the age of micro-blogging and lightning-fast text messages, the definition of Wenatchee can be condensed into six familiar letters: 'APPLES.' Pink Lady, Gala, Braeburn, Golden Delicious; the varieties are endless in a city that not inaccurately describes itself as the 'Apple Capital of the World' (the region produces more than half of the total US crop). Lying on the banks of the Columbia River, Wenatchee's position is eye-catching even if its mall/fast food/cheap motel-infested suburbs aren't. The town itself isn't exactly teeming with pulsating distractions, but there are plenty of outdoor adventures nearby and with its handy transport connections, Wenatchee is an OK place to crack open your suitcase for the night and sample a slice of apple pie.

◎ Sights

Wenatchee Valley Museum & Cultural Center   MUSEUM

(www.wenatcheevalleymuseum.com; 127 S Mission St; adult/child $5/2; ⊙10am-4pm Tue-Sat) Welcome to another good municipal museum, which places its main focus on – surprise, surprise – apples. Exhibits include a re-creation of a 1920s apple-packing shed and a farm shop from the 1890s. Look out for memorabilia on local hero Clyde Pangborn, the first man to fly nonstop across the Pacific in 1931.

FREE **Washington Apple Commission Visitors Center**   VISITOR CENTER

(www.bestapples.com; 2900 Euclid Ave; ⊙8am-5pm Mon-Fri, 9am-5pm Sat, 10am-4pm Sun May-Dec) Washington's, America's and – quite possibly – the world's self-styled apple capital is also home to the this little-visited yet surprisingly interesting exposé on Gala, Fuji, Golden Delicious et al. Find out how apples are grown, harvested, transported and sold in a number of interpretive displays and an enlightening 20-minute video.

Ohme Gardens   GARDENS

(www.ohmegardens.com; 3327 Ohme Rd; adult/child $7/3.50; ⊙9am-6pm Apr-Oct) Three miles north of town on Alt US 97, the Ohme showcases the mighty Columbia River at its best, with 9 acres of terraced alpine gardens emerging like an oasis from the barren rock.

Apple Capital Recreation Loop Trail   PARK

Wenatchee's inter-urban trail is a 10-mile walk- and cycle-way that starts and finishes in **Riverfront Park** and stretches along both sides of the Columbia River adjacent to downtown. Locals and visitors alike come here to stroll, cycle or rollerblade along this rather industrial stretch of the river. Access to the park can be gained at the end of 5th St or by crossing a railway footbridge at the end of 1st St. Once on the trail, head north to **Wenatchee Confluence State Park**, or south to reach a footbridge across to East Wenatchee, where the trail continues along the Columbia's somewhat more pastoral east bank – and passes through some orchards!

☆ Activities

You can rent bikes (per day $35) or in-line skates for the Apple Capital Recreation Loop Trail at **Arlberg Sports** (25 N Wenatchee Ave; ⊙10am-6pm Mon-Sat, noon-5pm Sun), next to the Convention Center.

ROADSIDE FRUIT STANDS

Remember fresh produce? Just when you thought the world was ripe for junk food domination, in step Washington's mouthwatering fruit stands to reignite your diet with something crisp, colorful and healthy. Standing out amid the ubiquitous malls, fast-food franchises and drive-through restaurants of North Central Washington, these impromptu seasonal fruit outlets are run by enterprising local farmers who haul their freshly plucked produce from the nearby fields and orchards to sell roadside from semipermanent stores, carts, or just plain old boxes. Apples are the most ubiquitous crop, but you can also find apricots, pears and countless others when the season's in full swing. One of the best tracts of road to 'shop' is the stretch of Hwy 2/97 going north between Wenatchee and Chelan on the east side of the Columbia River. Look out in particular for **Lone Pine Fruit & Espresso** (23041 Hwy 97), housed in a century-old apple packing shed near Orondo, and **B&B Fruit Stand**, which has been in operation since the early 1960s, 2.5 miles north of the Odabashion Bridge.

If you feel like ice skating, go to the **Riverfront Park Ice Arena** (2 5th St; admission $4; ☉Oct-Mar).

Downhill skiers covet the dry powder covering the slopes of **Mission Ridge** (www.missionridge.com; full-day lift tickets adult/child $50/32; ☉9am-4pm Thu-Mon late Nov-early Apr), located 12 miles southwest of Wenatchee. The resort features a vertical drop of 2200ft and 35 runs with four lifts and two rope-tows.

🛏 Sleeping

If you don't go in for chain hotels, it will be a struggle to find an independent lodging in franchise-filled Wenatchee, where the arterial N Wenatchee Ave is studded with all number of Travelodges, Super 8s and Econo Lodges.

WestCoast Wenatchee Center Hotel
HOTEL $$

(☏509-662-1234; www.coasthotels.com; 201 N Wenatchee Ave; r $100; ❋🛜🛍) Best of the boring bunch of chain hotels is this large central franchise that is handily connected to the convention center by a sky-bridge and draws a regular business crowd. Rooms are well furnished, if a little characterless, and there's an above-average rooftop restaurant (the Wenatchee Roaster and Ale House) and a fitness center.

Wenatchee Confluence State Park
CAMPGROUND $

(☏509-664-6373; 333 Olds Station Rd; tent/RV sites $21/28) The campground, with 51 hookups and eight tent spaces, is on the north bank of the Wenatchee River. It's an ideal spot for active travelers: besides a swimming beach, there are athletic fields, tennis and basketball courts and 4.5 miles of trails.

Warm Springs Inn
B&B $$

(☏509-662-8365; www.warmspringsinn.com; 1611 Love Lane; r $115-140; ❋🛜) Situated on 10 acres by the Wenatchee River, this 1917 mansion turned B&B has six individually crafted rooms, river views, and a manicured English garden with a shaded gazebo.

Inn at the River
MOTEL $$

(☏509-888-7378; www.innatriverher.com; 580 Valley Mall Parkway; s/d $115/140; 🛜🛍) You're in East Wenatchee's strip-mall land, but at least you're near the river. A notch above standard motel facilities, this inn has a heated pool and super-clean rooms.

🍴 Eating

Tastebuds Coffee & Wine
CAFÉ, WINE BAR $

(www.tastebudscoffeewine.com; 212 5th St; 🛜) In a leading wine region in a famously coffee-obsessed state, Tastebuds' concept makes absolute sense. So why have so few people thought of it to date? The idea goes something like this: take an aromatic European-style coffee bar, chuck in a few cool Northwest furnishings (fireplace, accented browns, and plenty of bottles on shelves) and, as the day wears on, let it metamorphose into a wine bar. There's food too, of course; more like appetizers than main meals (try the cheeses and rich tortes), though all of it is delicious and just waiting to be paired with some nicely matured Columbia Valley grapes.

Windmill
STEAKHOUSE $$$

(☏509-665-9529; www.thewindmillrestaurant.com; 1501 N Wenatchee Ave; mains $23; ⏰5-9pm) Sitting pretty amid North Wenatchee's northern mall strip is this eye-catching Dutch-style windmill, in business since 1931 and still knocking out a fine selection of steaks, scintillating seafood and home-made desserts. If in doubt, try the New York whiskey pepper steak with a baked potato. Not surprisingly, the Windmill's reputation precedes it and you may have to arrive early in order to reserve some elbow room ahead of the adoring locals.

Cellar Café
CAFÉ $

(www.cellarcafe.org; 249 N Mission; ⏰9am-3pm Mon-Fri; ▨) Putting up a brave rearguard action in Wenatchee's strip-mall zone, the Cellar is encased in a traditional craftsman house complete with outdoor seating and a koi pond. Made-from-scratch lunches include excellent wraps, quiches and a formidable apple crisp (this is 'apple town,' after all).

Inna's
UKRAINIAN $$

(www.innascuisine.com; 26 N Wenatchee Ave; mains $15-20; ⏰lunch & dinner Tue-Sat) Central and eastern Washington is not renowned for its ethnic eateries (Leavenworth aside), but if you're craving borscht, piroshki or good old-fashioned Ukrainian dumplings, the search ends here. Run by a Ukrainian couple from Odessa, Inna's has added an Eastern European flavor to Wenatchee's clutch of above-average eateries. The menu even dares to venture a few time-zones to the west with a Paris salad, Greek gyros and Italian meatballs.

Owl Soda Fountain
SODA FOUNTAIN $

(25 N Wenatchee Ave; ⏰until 5pm) A classic old-fashioned soda fountain of 1950s vintage, with lurid color schemes, peanut-butter-and-jelly sandwiches, and humongous milkshakes plunked down on the bar in front of you. All that's missing is an Elvis impersonator with stick-on sideburns.

ⓘ Information

Wenatchee National Forest Headquarters
(215 Melody Lane) North of town at the junction of Hwy 285 and US 2.

Wenatchee Valley Convention & Visitors Bureau (www.wenatcheevalley.org; Ste 100, 5 S Wenatchee Ave) For information and walking-tour maps.

ⓘ Getting There & Around

Air

Horizon Air services the **Pangborn Memorial Airport** (www.pangbornairport.com) in East Wenatchee, with four or five flights daily to and from Seattle (from $125 one way).

Bus

All bus and rail transit services are centralized at **Columbia Station** (300 S Columbia Ave), at the foot of Kittitas St. **Northwestern Trailways** (www.northwesterntrailways.com) runs daily buses to Seattle (direct), Spokane via Moses Lake, and Pasco via Yakima.

Apple Line (www.appleline.us) runs a handy once-a-day service running north (departing 2.30pm) to Chelan Falls ($16), Pateros ($18) and Omak ($22) and south (departing 9.10am) to Ellensburg ($20).

You can get to the nearby towns of Leavenworth via Cashmere (bus 22, $2, 50 minutes) and Chelan via Entiat (bus 21, $2, one hour) on frequent **Link Transit buses** (www.linktransit.com). Buses run until 5pm or 6pm Monday to Friday and are equipped with bike racks.

Train

The **Amtrak** (www.amtrak.com) *Empire Builder* stops daily in Wenatchee on its way between Seattle and Chicago, heading westbound at 5:38am and eastbound at 8:42pm.

Yakima Valley

With its scorched hills interspersed with geometrically laid-out vine plantations and apple orchards, the Yakima River Valley glimmers like a verdant oasis in an otherwise dry and barren desert. Arising from the snowy slopes of Snoqualmie Pass and flowing deceptively southeast (and away from the Pacific) until it joins courses with the mighty Columbia, the fast-flowing Yakima River supports a lucrative agricultural industry that churns out copious amounts of cherries, vegetables and peaches, along with three-quarters of the US hop output and the world's largest yield of apples.

Markedly drier and hotter than Washington's wet west coast, much of the valley survives on as little as 8in of rain a year (Seattle gets 37in) and temperatures can rise to over 100°F in the summer.

A huge demand for agricultural labor to work in the fields and orchards during the fruit-picking season has brought a large Mexican population to the valley and, with 40% of Yakima county's population now registered as Hispanic, you'll hear as many 'buenos dias' as 'good mornings.' The vast Yakama Native American Reservation to the southwest adds a strong Native American element to the population mix.

ELLENSBURG
POP 17,141

Take an archetypal American small town; give it a stately college, a smattering of historic buildings, and more coffee bars per head than anywhere else in the US (allegedly); then throw in the largest and most lauded rodeo in the Pacific Northwest. Welcome to Ellensburg, town of improbable juxtapositions, where erudite college undergraduates rub shoulders with weekend cowboys in a small yet salubrious collegiate town where two-thirds of the 16,000 population are registered students. Like most Washington towns, Ellensburg has its fair share of peripheral motel/mall infestations, but body-swerve the familiar big boxes and you'll uncover a compact but select cluster of venerable red-brick buildings born out of the 'City Beautiful' movement in the early 1890s.

Ellensburg's location on the cusp of the Eastern Cascades and the flat, fertile Columbia River basin throws up two radically different types of adventure opportunities (rugged to the east, refined to the west). Seattleites regularly cross Snoqualmie Pass to sup local wine and enjoy seemingly endless summer sunshine. Easterners stop by on their way to the snowier mountains.

Once touted as the 'Pittsburg of the West' for its plentiful coal and iron-ore deposits, Ellensburg suffered the fate of many western towns in 1889 when a fire tore the heart out of nine blocks of its central business district. The present-day historical core, though small in size, is the result of an industrious post-fire rebuilding process.

◉ Sights

Downtown Historic District   HISTORIC SITE
Beautified by a compact yet charismatic grid of Victorian buildings, central Ellensburg deserves an unhurried morning or afternoon's exploration. Kick off at the friendly chamber of commerce, where you can get informative maps of the downtown historic district, roughly contained between Main St, 6th and 3rd Aves. Sprinkled with antique shops, galleries and cafés, the quarter is dominated by the **Davidson Building**, Ellensburg's signature postcard sight built in 1889 by local attorney, John B Davidson. Also worth checking out is the **Kittitas**

County Historical Museum (www.kchm.org; 114 E 3rd Ave; donations accepted; ⊙10am-4pm Mon-Sat Jun-Sep, noon-4pm Tue-Sat Oct-May), housed in the 1889 Cadwell Building, known mostly for its petrified-wood and gemstone collections but also boasting a cleverly laid-out history section documenting the backgrounds of Croatian, Arabic and Welsh immigrants. Equally intriguing are the paintings of native son John Clymer at the **Clymer Museum** (www.clymermuseum. com; 416 N Pearl St; admission free; ⊙10am-5pm Mon-Fri, 10am-4pm Sat, noon-4pm Sun), whose all-American subjects graced *Saturday Evening Post* covers in the 1950s and '60s.

For kids try the **Children's Activity Museum** (www.childrensactivitymuseum.org; 118 E 4th Ave; admission $4.25; ⊙10am-5pm Wed-Sat; ♿), which has a miniature cowboy ranch, science lab and other engaging hands-on exhibits.

Olmstead Place State Park Heritage Area   HISTORICAL PARK
FREE (921 N Ferguson Rd; ⊙8am-5pm) Four-and-a-half miles southeast of Ellensburg off the I-90, the historical theme continues with log cabins, pioneer barns and other farm buildings dating from 1875 to 1890. They depict early homestead life in the Kittitas Valley.

Thorp Grist Mill   HISTORIC SITE
FREE (www.thorp.org; ⊙11am-3pm Thu-Sat, noon-4pm Sun Jun-Sep) Another view of frontier agriculture is on display in the small town of Thorp, 8 miles northwest of Ellensburg at what was once a de facto meeting place for local farmers. The mill, now a rural museum, dates from 1873.

Chimpanzee & Human Communication Institute   WORKSHOPS
(☎509-963-2244; www.cwu.edu/~cwuchci; cnr Nicholson Blvd & D St; adult/student $11/8.50; ⊙9:15am & 10.45am Sat, 12:30pm & 2pm Sun Mar-Nov) As well as having a rather picturesque campus, Central Washington University has gained some renown for its studies of communication between humans and chimpanzees. Several of its chimps have learned to communicate using American Sign Language. On weekends the institute presents an informative, hour-long 'Chimposium' workshop that includes an audience with the chimps. The discussions on linguistics and primate behavior are interesting; reservations are recommended.

🏃 Activities

South of Ellensburg, Hwy 821 through the Yakima Canyon offers a scenic alternative to the busy I-82. Rafting on the Yakima River is a popular activity here, with **Rill Adventures** (www.rillsonline.com; Thorp Hwy) offering raft and kayak hire. Catch-and-release fishing is another drawcard.

🎉 Festivals & Events

Ellensburg Rodeo
RODEO

TOP CHOICE (www.ellensburgrodeo.com) Ellensburg's ultimate festival takes place on Labor Day weekend in tandem with the Kittitas County Fair. It's ranked among the top 10 rodeos in the nation and is one of central Washington's biggest events. Come prepared to see some hard riding and roping – participants take this rodeo very seriously, as there is big money at stake.

🛏 Sleeping

Inn at Goose Creek
HOTEL $$

TOP CHOICE (☎509-962-8030; www.innatgoosecreek.com; 1720 Canyon Rd; r from $99; 🛜) Surely one of the most imaginative motels around, this establishment off the I-90 is not your standard fancily restored period piece – even if it looks like it from the outside. Inside is a different story, however, and the Victorian Honeymoon Suite is just one of 10 eclectic room choices, a list that also includes the Ellensburg Rodeo Room (complete with cowboy memorabilia) and the I Love Christmas Room (with its red-and-green Santa carpet).

Wrens Nest B&B
B&B $$

(☎509-925-9061; www.wrensnest.com; 300 E Manitoba Ave; r $90-110) This is a typical small-town B&B encased in a 1912 Craftsman-style home. Experienced B&Bers will appreciate the familiar touches: welcome tea and cookies, beyond-the-call-of-duty service, individually furnished rooms, relaxed guest-to-guest interaction and substantial (and creative) breakfasts.

Guesthouse Ellensburg
B&B $$

(☎509-962-3706; www.guesthouseellensburg.com; 606 Main St; r $135) This unique guesthouse, handily located opposite the chamber of commerce on Main St, doubles as a wine shop and tasting room and the proprietors certainly know their enology. Two restored Victorian rooms are furnished with English antiques, four-poster beds and flat-screen TVs, while downstairs in the tasting room you can discuss viticulture until the grapes ripen with free tasting sessions and generous discounts for guests.

🍴 Eating

Yellow Church Café
FUSION $$

TOP CHOICE (www.yellowchurchcafe.com; 111 S Pearl St; brunch $8-10, dinner $13-23; ⊙breakfast, lunch & dinner) Top in the Ellensburg 'quirky' stakes is this bright-yellow former church built by the German Lutherans in 1923 and now converted into an unconventional restaurant that serves spiritually enlightening food. The breakfast – including the aptly named St Benedict's eggs – has won widespread recommendations, while the elegant dinner options have been well matched with local wines from the expert owners, who also run the nearby Guesthouse Ellensburg.

D&M Coffee
CAFÉ $

(www.dmcoffee.com; 301 N Pine St; coffee $2-3) With allegedly more coffee bars per head than anywhere else in the US, you're certainly spoiled for choice when it comes to satisfying your morning caffeine habit in Ellensburg. D&M is the local roasting company and the best of its quintet of local outlets is situated opposite the Kittitas County Museum. Funky stools and an academic atmosphere make it an ideal place to linger.

Sazón
FUSION $$$

(www.sazonellensburg.com; 412 N Main St; mains from $20; ⊙4-9pm, till 10pm Fri & Sat; 👶) Sazón is a culinary hybrid, equally comfortable with date-night fine-dining and kid-friendly brunch (weekends only, from 9am to 2pm). The menu is similarly eclectic: BC salmon served with gnocchi, or chili garlic shrimp with pad thai. There's also a succinct but tasty tapas menu, plus those weekend brunches with more than a dozen specialist egg concoctions.

Valley Café
FUSION $$

(www.valleycafeellensburg.com; 105 W 3rd Ave; dinner mains $9-25) This diminutive art-deco construction, in business since 1938, has a restaurant and café, along with an excellent selection of Washington wines, nicely paired with the accompanying food. Check out the cioppino, the rack of lamb or the ahi tuna. The interior is furnished with unpretentious booths and there's also a takeout section.

ℹ Information

Ellensburg Chamber of Commerce (www.ellensburg-chamber.com; 609 N Main St; ⊙8am-5pm Mon-Fri, 10am-2pm Sat) For maps and information; the building is shared by

THE GORGE AMPHITHEATER

Gorge-ous and 100% natural, 'The Gorge' is a stunning alfresco music venue perched on the banks of the Columbia River, 40 miles east of Ellensburg. Regularly touted as the most spectacular rock venue in North America, the steeply banked natural amphitheater with space for 25,000 on an expansive terraced lawn leaves most concert-goers at a loss for words. The performers are less laconic. Numerous international stars have stepped up to the microphone here including the Who, the Police, David Bowie and Van Morrison, and many of the sets have entered rock legend. Pearl Jam made their 2005-06 album 'Live at the Gorge' into a box set, while the Dave Matthews Band has serenaded the impossibly crimson Columbia River sunsets more than 30 times.

Though the dry East Washington weather minimizes show cancellations, visitors should be prepared for hot afternoon temperatures (bring plenty of water and sunscreen) and cool evenings (pack a sweater). The Gorge is best accessed off I-90 (exits 143 or 149). The site has a general store, an ATM and overnight camping with showers, drinking water and portaloos. For more information on summer concerts and tickets see www.gorgeconcerts.com.

the US Forest Service and Ellensburg Rodeo offices.

❶ Getting There & Around

Although Ellensburg is a busy crossroads for regional buses, there's no real bus station.

Greyhound (www.greyhound.com) buses stop at the Pilot gas station at I-90 exit 106, 2 miles from the town center. The ticket window is in the Subway sandwich shop. Buses here leave for Seattle ($22.50, two hours, five daily), Spokane via Moses Lake ($32, four hours, three daily) and Yakima ($11, 45 minutes, three daily). Some Yakima buses continue on to the Tri-Cities and beyond.

Apple Line (www.appleline.us) runs one bus daily to Wenatchee, Chelan Falls, Pateros and Omak. It leaves Ellensburg at 1pm.

Bellair Shuttle (www.airporter.com) runs five daily buses to Sea-Tac Airport and Seattle to the east and Yakima to the west. It stops next to Starbucks on the Central Washington University campus.

From the Greyhound stop, **Rodeo Town Taxi** (☏509-929-4222) can get you downtown for $5.

YAKIMA
POP 84,074

Not long after the Northwest's weighty clouds have dumped most of their precipitation on Seattle and the Cascade Mountains they arrive in the parched east, lighter, whiter, or – if you're lucky – vanquished altogether. All the more reason to pull into balmy Yakima, the so-called 'Palm Springs of Washington,' not the state's prettiest or most interesting city, but certainly one of its sunniest. If you can see past the limitations of Yakima's rather dull downtown, the settlement's rural periphery beckons like an enologist's wet dream, a kind of Washingtonian Dordogne without the historic villages but with enough reputed vineyards to keep any French wine snob happy for, well, at least an afternoon.

Founded on its present site in 1884, Yakima takes its name from the Yakama Native American people, who inhabited this valley for centuries before an 1855 treaty created the Yakama Native American Reservation.

One third of the city of Yakima's population is Hispanic.

❂ Sights

TOP⟩ **Yakima Valley Museum** MUSEUM
CHOICE⟩ (www.yakimavalleymuseum.org; 2105 Tieton Dr; adult/senior $5/3; ⊙10am-5pm Mon-Sat, closed Mon Nov-Mar; ⊕) This highly educational and entertaining museum is one of the state's best. It tells the story of the region from a geographic and historic viewpoint, with a strong emphasis on agriculture and the Yakama Native American heritage. Prize exhibits include a number of horse-drawn conveyances and some early motor vehicles, plus a full working mockup of a 1930s Depression-era soda fountain. In yet another section, the **Children's Underground** (⊙1-5pm Tue-Fri, 10am-5pm Sat) does a good job of incorporating Yakima's human and natural history into a number of hands-on exhibits for kids.

Adjacent to the museum is **Franklin Park**, a broad lawn planted with evergreens that features a playground, picnic tables, and – an important feature in sunbaked Yakima – a swimming pool.

Yakima Historic District
HISTORIC SITE

Yakima's rather modern downtown is punctuated by a handful of interesting structures. Art-deco aficionados will appreciate the craning **Larson Building** on East Yakima Ave, with its ornate – some would say ostentatious – lobby, while thespians will find solace in the grand Italianate **Capitol Theater**, which hosts everything from live music concerts to public speaking events. 'Historic' Front St consists of one square block downtown – half of which is given over to a parking lot – and is noteworthy for its old station depot and the bizarre **Track 29**, a collection of antique railcars now converted into a row of eye-catching knick-knack shops.

Yakima Greenway
PARK

(www.yakimagreenway.org) A pleasant oasis in an otherwise unremarkable city, the Greenway is best accessed via Sarg Hubbard Park at I-82 exit 33. It's a 10-mile path for walkers and cyclists that tracks the fast-flowing Yakima River through a string of parks and recreation areas. One good stop-off point is the **Yakima Area Arboretum** (www.ahtrees.org) just east of exit 34, where a collection of more than 2000 species of trees and shrubs spreads out over 46 acres of landscaped gardens. You can procure a free walking-tour brochure at the **Jewett Interpretive Center** (1401 Arboretum Dr; admission free; ⊙9am-4pm Tue-Sat).

🛏 Sleeping

TOP CHOICE Ledgestone Hotel
HOTEL $$

(☎509-453-3151; www.ledgestonehotel.com; 107 North Fair Ave; ste from $109; ✳@🛜) Hallelujah – a new hotel in Yakima that isn't one of the usual suspects. Opened in 2008, the Ledgestone is modern, funky and a little bit different. All its rooms are one-bedroom suites with mini-kitchens, lounge areas, bathrooms and separate bedrooms (with their own flat-screen TVs). There's even a little office nook. Fortuitously, the suites are sold at standard room prices and there's a fitness room, laundry services and a few air miles thrown in for free.

Hilton Garden Inn
HOTEL $$

(☎509-454-1111; www.hiltongardeninn1.hilton.com; 607 E Yakima Ave; r from $139; ✳🛜🏊) This new-ish city-center facility adds a touch of much-needed elegance to the usual downtown business-style stopovers. Aside from spotlessly presented rooms, the hotel offers a decent-sized gym, an indoor pool, a

lounge and an American grill, along with highly professional service.

Birchfield Manor
B&B $$

(☎509-452-1960; www.birchfieldmanor.com; 2018 Birchfield Rd; manor r $119-159, cottage r $139-219; 🛜) Renowned for its flavorful food and well-stocked Washington wine cellar, the Birchfield offers unusual antique-filled rooms in a pleasant park-like setting 2 miles east of Yakima off Hwy 24. Five manor rooms are complemented by six guest cottages, some with double Jacuzzi. The manor, which makes a great alternative to the standard Yakima hotel chains, also serves as a first-class restaurant.

🍴 Eating

For a wine region, Yakima is disappointing for food, though a strong Hispanic community provides a good excuse to go Mexican. Look out for semipermanent taco trailers for the true taste of Guadalajara – or should that be 21st-century Yakima?

TOP CHOICE Birchfield Manor Restaurant
FUSION $$$

(☎509-452-1960; www.birchfieldmanor.com; 2018 Birchfield Rd; mains from $20; ⊙dinner) Revered by locals and an increasing number of in-the-know Seattleites, the Birchfield is a sublime dining experience offered in an intimate 1910 B&B. While the accommodation here is considered top-end, the food is even better. The booking system is unusual: reservations must be made in advance and seating is at set times, but everything from the bread to the after-dinner chocolates to the knowledgeable service is impeccable. The highlights are the mains: salmon in puff pastry with chardonnay sauce, Steak Diane in a brandy cream sauce, all expertly paired with local wines (the place has its own cellar). Exquisite!

The Greystone
FUSION $$$

(☎509-248-9801; www.greystonedining.com; 5 N Front St; mains $22-39; ⊙from 6pm Mon-Sat) This long-time Yakima staple, housed in one of the city's original saloons at the base of the century-old Lund Building, is considered to be the city's premier Northwest cuisine venue. A substantial if pricey menu lists many adventurous options, from crab legs to duck breast. Local wines are de rigueur.

Yakima Sports Center Restaurant
BURGERS $$

(☎509-453-4647; 214 E Yakima Ave; mains $10-18) There are no pretensions at this young happening place bang in the city center, which presents live bands every Friday and Saturday. Dive in to sample from an extremely varied menu with stalwart treats such as fish 'n chips, gnocchi, and blue cheese–crusted tenderloin. The beer menu is equally voluminous.

Tequila's Family Mexican Restaurant
MEXICAN $

(Track 29, 1 W Yakima Ave; mains $9) With a large Hispanic population, Yakima is the crucible of Washington-Mexican food, and a good place to sample the *real* stuff is at this offbeat place that occupies three vintage railcars at the rear end of the Track 29 shopping mall. Emphasizing seafood, the atmosphere attempts to replicate the Jalisco coast with Corona umbrellas shading the boardwalk deck. A *torta* (overstuffed sandwich with refried bean spread) makes a hearty lunch.

☕ Drinking

Gilbert Cellars
CAFÉ $

(www.gilbertcellars.com; 5 N Front St; ☺noon-9pm Mon-Thu, till 11pm Fri & Sat, till 5pm Sun) This refined downtown tasting room ($5 for five tastings) has the air of a classy wine bar. Service is knowledgeable and unpretentious and there are some excellent cheese-based snacks.

Northtown Coffee
CAFÉ $

(www.northtowncoffee.com; 28 N 1st St; ☺6am-midnight Mon-Fri, 7am-midnight Sat & Sun) A bit of Portland repositioned to Central Washington (which is no bad thing), Northtown sells PDX's famous Stumptown coffee in cozy nooks. Get comfortable – it's open till midnight daily.

🛍 Shopping

Known as **Track 29** (1 W Yakima Ave), Yakima's old train platform has been given over to a string of false-fronted eateries and quirky boutiques, some housed in old railroad cars, that makes for a pleasant boardwalk stroll. You'll find a smattering of antiques and collectibles, gemstones, essential oils and herbs. Rumors were mounting at time of writing that the whole complex was going to be moved across the road to make it more visible to passing trade on Yakima Ave.

ℹ Information

Yakima Valley Visitors & Convention Bureau
(www.visityakima.com; 10 N 8th St)

ℹ Getting There & Around

The **Greyhound bus station** (602 E Yakima Ave) is located at the corner of 6th St. There are two departures daily to and from Seattle via Ellensburg ($40, three hours) and two to Spokane via Ellensburg or Pasco ($51, four hours plus). Other buses continue on to Portland, the Tri-Cities and beyond.

More comfortable is the **Bellair Shuttle** (www.airporter.com) with five daily buses to Seattle ($41) via Ellensburg ($10) and Sea-Tac ($36). The bus picks up in Yakima from the Howard Johnson hotel at 9 N 9th St.

Yakima Transit (www.ci.yakima.wa.us/services/transit) runs a local service Monday to Saturday, from 6:30am until around 6:30pm. The transit center is on the corner of S 4th St and E Chestnut Ave. Adult fare is $0.75.

YAKIMA VALLEY WINE COUNTRY

Created in 1983, the Yakima Valley is Washington's oldest American Viticultural Area (AVA) and is sprinkled with more than 50 wineries, most of them small, family-run affairs. While it's not quite the Napa Valley in terms of dining potential, a drive or cycle through these dry yet deceptively fertile fields, breezing past vineyards, orchards, hop pastures and roadside vegetable stalls, gives a good insight into local wine culture; 40% of Washington's wine grapes are grown here.

Decent stopovers between Yakima and the Tri-Cities include the communities of Zillah, Sunnyside and Prosser, while the Yakima Valley Hwy (old US 12), or 'Wine Country Rd,' which parallels the busy I-82, makes for a pleasant pastoral alternative drive.

There are literally dozens of wineries that offer tasting and scenic picnic opportunities in this area. See www.wineyakimavalley.org for an up-to-date list. Prosser-based **Chinook Wines** (www.chinookwines.com; Wine Country Rd, Prosser; ☺tastings noon-5pm Sat & Sun May-Oct), in operation since 1983, is known for its classy whites, particularly its chardonnay and sauvignon blanc. For some good reds, head to **Severino Cellars** (www.severinocellars.com; 1717 1st Ave, Zillah; ☺10am-6pm Mon-Sun Mar-Nov, 11am-5pm Sat & Sun Dec-Feb) in Zillah for fruit-forward syrahs and merlots.

An excellent source of information for the entire valley can be found online at www.yakimavalleywine.com.

TOPPENISH
POP 8946

If you make one stop in the Yakima Valley you would do well to check out off-the-wall Toppenish, a living art festival that has become locally famous for its 60 or more historic **murals** adorned Banksy-style on most of the downtown buildings. Chronicling the events from Yakama and Northwestern history, the first mural was painted back in 1989. Later additions include evocative tableaus of the valley's more recent Mexican immigrants employed in the agricultural sector.

Further information and mural guides can be procured from the **Toppenish Chamber of Commerce** (www.toppenish.net; 504 S Elm St; ☺11am-4pm Mon-Sat).

Another rather unique Toppenish institution is the **American Hop Museum** (www.americanhopmuseum.org; 22 S B St; admission $3; ☺10am-4pm May-Sep), a temptation for all beer-lovers, that chronicles the history of the American hop-growing industry from its humble beginnings in New England in the early 1600s.

The history of the Yakama Native Americans is well documented at the **Yakama Indian Nation Cultural Center** (www.yakamamuseum.com; 280 Buster Rd; adult/child $6/4; ☺8am-5pm Mon-Fri, 9am-5pm Sat & Sun), which exhibits costumes, baskets, beads and audiovisual displays, and includes a gift shop, library, restaurant and heritage theater (with occasional tribal dances).

An interesting historical curiosity is contained in an old fort complex preserved in the 200-acre **Fort Simcoe State Park** (5150 Fort Simcoe Rd; ☺interpretive center 9am-4:30pm Wed-Sun Apr-Oct), an oasis of green in the midst of scorched desert hills. It was built in 1855, but served as a fort for only three years until the creation of the Yakama Reservation in 1859. Listed on the National Register of Historical Places, the park now acts as an interpretive center with a handful of original buildings still intact.

Bordered by Canada to the north and Idaho to the east, northeastern Washington is dominated by the understated yet populous city of Spokane, and is internationally famous for producing one of the 20th century's greatest engineering marvels, the gargantuan Grand Coulee Dam. However, the region is little visited and only a few small towns scatter the protected hills and boreal pine forests of the Okanogan and Colville National Forests. Climatically, the northeast is a transition zone, with a dry belt running immediately east of the Cascade Mountains, while wetter, more humid air seeps into the verdant Kettle River and Selkirk Mountain ranges closer to Idaho. This precipitous region marks Washington's only real incursion into the Rocky Mountains.

Spokane

POP 202,319

Washington's second-biggest population center (edging out Tacoma by about 5000 people) is one of the state's latent surprises and a welcome break after the treeless monotony of the eastern Scablands. Situated at the nexus of the Pacific Northwest's so-called 'Inland Empire,' this understated yet confident city sits clustered on the banks of the Spokane River close to where British fur traders founded a short-lived trading post in 1810. American settlers set up Spokane proper in the 1870s and, despite a destructive fire in 1889, the city has prospered in

THE EMPIRE BUILDER ACROSS THE CASCADES

Across the world railways have long acted as society's great melting pots, where people from all walks of life can mix, converse and cross-fertilize. Cars tend to insulate you from your fellow travelers, airplanes have a habit of making everyone impossibly irritable, while trains with their ample space and continually changing cargo of people actively encourage interaction and allow valuable glimpses into the myriad towns and cultures along the way.

With its two-level superliner carriages and grand imperial name, Amtrak's Seattle-to-Chicago *Empire Builder* runs along the former Great Northern Railroad on a route that is a proverbial A to Z of the American West. Yet, unlike other more tourist-oriented trains, it's not prohibitively expensive: a standard 'coachliner' seat can cost as little as US$150, while roomettes with private bathrooms go from US$420. Throw in forests, prairies, ghost mining towns and snow-capped mountains and you're onto one of the biggest bargains in the US, a magnificent journey significant not just for its amazing scenery but for the fascinating insights into American life that you see on board.

For reservations and further details see www.amtrak.com

the years since. Though rarely touted in national tourist blurbs, Spokane hosts the world's largest mass participation running event (May's annual Bloomsday), a stunning gilded age hotel (the Davenport) and a spectacular waterfall throwing up angry white spray in the middle of its downtown core. It was also the childhood home of that famous old crooner Bing Crosby, and remains the smallest city to have ever hosted an Expo (the 1974 World's Fair). Prepare yourself for some interesting revelations; there's more to this modest metropolis than meets the eye.

◉ Sights

Riverfront Park
PARK

(www.spokaneriverfrontpark.com) The former site of Spokane's 1974 World's Fair and Exposition, this park provides a welcome slice of urban greenery in the middle of downtown. It has been redeveloped in recent years with a 17-point **sculpture walk**, along with plenty of bridges and trails to satisfy the city's abundance of amateur runners.

The park's centerpiece is **Spokane Falls**, a gushing combination of scenic waterfalls and foaming rapids that can get pretty tempestuous after heavy rain. There are vari-

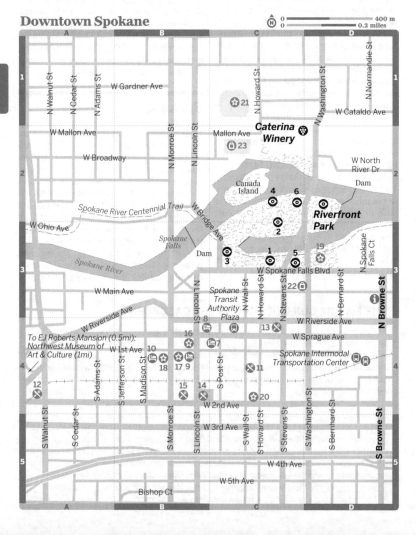

Downtown Spokane

ous viewing points over the river, including a short **gondola ride** (adult/child $7.25/4; ☺11am-6pm Sun-Thu, till 10pm Fri & Sat Apr-Sep) which takes you directly above the falls, or the cheaper and equally spectacular **Monroe St Bridge**, built in 1911 and still the largest concrete arch in the USA.

In the center of the park, the 151ft **clocktower** has become the city's signature sight and was originally part of a railway depot built in 1902. The kitschy **Pavilion** is a small amusement park in the summer and an **ice rink** (☺noon-8pm Mon-Thu, noon-5pm & 7-10pm Fri & Sat, noon-5pm Sun Nov-Mar; 🎫) in the winter. The adjacent **Imax Theater** (adult/child $8.25/5.75; ☺noon-7pm daily Mar-Oct, Fri-Sun & holidays Oct-Mar) seats 385 people and boasts a 53ft-high screen. Films screen hourly.

Like some relic from an old-fashioned fairground, the 1909 hand-carved **carousel** (adult/child $2/1.50; ☺noon-5pm weekends & holidays; 🎫) is a kid's classic and, along with the larger-than-life **Radio Flyer Wagon** sculpture, should keep families occupied for a couple of hours. A miniature tour train ($4.75) can cart you from A to B in the park, or you can join the walkers and joggers on the **Spokane River Centennial Trail** (www.spokanecentennialtrail.org), which extends for 37 miles to the Idaho border and beyond.

Riverside State Park   PARK

(www.riversidestatepark.org) Track the Centennial Trail 3 miles to the west and you'll end up here in 10,000 acres of protected forest and trails where you can run, walk or cycle to your heart's content. Among the park's natural highlights is the **Bowl & Pitcher**, a deep gorge with huge boulders at a bend in the river 2 miles north of the southern entrance. A swinging suspension bridge, built in the 1930s by the Civilian Conservation Corps, crosses the river here.

History also has its place here. Fur trader David Thompson of the North West Company built a trading post in 1810 just north of Nine Mile Falls, beyond the Centennial Trail's northern endpoint. The site is commemorated by the **Spokane House Interpretive Center** (admission free; ☺10am-6pm Thu-Mon Jun-Aug), where several modest exhibits tell the story with photos and dioramas.

Nearby, you can explore one of Thompson's trapping routes, much as it may have looked in his time, at the **Little Spokane River Natural Area**. A 3.6-mile hiking and cross-country skiing trail through the protected wetland begins about half a mile beyond Spokane House along Hwy 291. Great blue herons nest in the cottonwoods and Native American **pictographs** can be found at Indian Painted Rocks. The area is perhaps best appreciated in a kayak.

Downtown Spokane

Gonzaga University MUSEUMS

(www.gonzaga.edu) Founded in 1887 by the Jesuit Order, Gonzaga University is famous for its college basketball team, and one particularly celebrated former student, the incomparable Harry Lillis 'Bing' Crosby, who came here to study in 1920. The immortal Bing donated a comprehensive collection of his recordings and paraphernalia to the college in later life, and these are displayed in the **Bing Crosby Memorabilia Room** (502 E Boone Ave; ☺8am-midnight daily during school year; hours vary Jun-Sep), at the Crosby Student Center. A bronze statue of the crooner – who moved to Spokane at the age of three in 1906 – stands out front, with his prized golf clubs in tow.

In the university art center at the end of Pearl St is the **Jundt Art Museum** (202 E Cataldo Ave; ☺10am-4pm Mon-Thu, 10am-9pm Fri, noon-4pm Sat, hours vary Jun-Sep), housing a good collection of classical sculpture and painting, as well as an 18ft chandelier by glass artist Dale Chihuly.

Northwest Museum of Arts & Culture

MUSEUM

(www.northwestmuseum.org; 2316 W 1st Ave; adult/concession $7/5; ☺10am-5pm Wed-Sat) Encased in a striking state-of-the-art building in the historic Browne's Addition neighborhood, this museum has – arguably – one of the finest collections of indigenous artifacts in the Northwest. Leading off a plush glass foyer overlooking the Spokane River are four galleries showcasing Spokane's history, as well as a number of roving exhibitions that change every three to four months. Your ticket also earns you the right to visit the adjacent English Tudor revival **Campbell House**.

Wineries TASTING ROOMS

While Walla Walla and the Yakima Valley are the most obvious stops on the Washington wine-tasting circuit, Spokane has also developed a decent clutch of wineries and tasting rooms with knowledgeable staff on hand to help decipher the flavors. For wholesome reds, including some widely lauded cabernet sauvignons, try the kid-friendly **Caterina Winery** (www.caterinawinery.com; 905 N Washington; ☺noon-6pm Wed-Sun) on the northern outskirts of Riverfront Park. If white's more your tipple, try the riesling and chardonnays at the **Latah Creek Wine Cellars** (www.latahcreek.com; 13030 E Indiana Ave; ☺9am-5pm), east of the city off I-90 exit 289.

🏃 Activities

Running aside, Spokane's outdoor activities center around golf and skiing. A refreshingly unhyped ski resort can be found at the **Mt Spokane Ski & Snowboard Park** (www.mtspokane.com; [🚠]), located 31 miles northeast of Spokane at the end of Hwy 206. It features a 2100ft vertical drop. There are several trails for cross-country in, and just past, nearby Mt Spokane State Park.

✦ Festivals & Events

Bloomsday Run RUNNING

(www.bloomsdayrun.org) The world's biggest timed road race attracts up to 60,000 runners, walkers and wheelchair racers every year on the first Sunday in May. The 7.5-mile (12km) course bisects

---

BLOOMSDAY

It is said that Spokane breeds two sorts of citizens: those who run Bloomsday and those who watch. Born out of the 1970s running craze, the 12km Bloomsday Run professes to be the largest timed road race in the world. There's merit in the claim. Outstripping the longer and more arduous New York Marathon, Spokane's annual May dash regularly garners a minimum 50,000 participants and reached a peak of 61,298 runners in 1996.

Bloomsday was the brainchild of local runner and schoolteacher Don Kardong, a US representative in the 1976 Olympic marathon (where he finished a respectable fourth in two hours, 11 minutes), who suggested putting good use to Spokane's fine riverside trails in the wake of the 1974 World's Fair. An impressive 1000 runners turned out for the first race in 1977, which was won by the gazelle-like Frank Shorter. The event mushroomed the following year when the presence of US marathon legend Bill Rodgers cemented its lofty reputation. Good organization, an attractive course and high-class opposition have since made Bloomsday one of the highlights of the US running calendar, with its manageable 12km (7.5-mile) course attracting many runners for whom a marathon is a step too far. There's even a 'Fit for Bloomsday' campaign targeted primarily at kids.

For entry details check the official race website at www.bloomsdayrun.org.

downtown and garners plenty of local enthusiasm.

Hoopfest
BASKETBALL

(www.spokanehoopfest.net) An enormous outdoor basketball tournament held at Riverfront Park and in the downtown streets in late June.

🛏 Sleeping

Goodbye, boring franchise accommodation; hello, classy independent hotels. Spokane has some of the best. Read on....

Montvale Hotel
BOUTIQUE HOTEL **$$**

(☑509-747-1919; www.montvalehotel.com; 1005 W 1st Ave; r from $109; ❇🛜) One of a trio of independent downtown hotels, the Montvale is situated in a former brothel, though you'd have to be Sherlock Holmes to work it out. Don't be fooled by the small, rather plain lobby either. Upstairs, a refined inner quadrangle has a distinctly European capital city feel. Rooms continue the continental theme, mixing plush old-world furnishings with plenty of up-to-date technological gadgets. Down in the basement you'll find **Catacombs**, a medieval-themed restaurant.

Hotel Lusso
BOUTIQUE HOTEL **$$**

(☑509-747-9750; www.hotellusso.com; 808 W Sprague Ave; d/ste $129/299; ❇🛜) A classy accommodation option worthy of any city, the Lusso is forced to play second fiddle to the delectable Davenport in the hotel heaven of Spokane. Offering gorgeously plush rooms that are on a par with its illustrious neighbor, its luxurious lobby boasting Italian-style fountains and the exquisite Cavallino lounge, while upstairs the surprises continue with glittering marble bathrooms and solid wooden furnishings. Service is equally spiffy.

EJ Roberts Mansion B&B
B&B **$$$**

(☑509-456-8839; www.ejrobertsmansion.com; 1923 W 1st Ave; ste $140-200; 🛜) You haven't really absorbed Spokane until you've sniffed around the upper-crust Browne's Addition and its 'stately' homes. After nearly 25 years of renovation, this historic 1889 Queen Anne mansion that once belonged to a local railroad tycoon is back in business as a plush five-suite B&B. Retaining its 'Victorian' essence without being too frilly, its exquisite breakfasts (salmon quiche anyone?) are accompanied by equally exquisite service.

Hotel Ruby
BOUTIQUE MOTEL **$**

(☑509-747-1041; www.hotelrubyspokane.com; 901 W 1st Ave; d from $69; ❇🛜🖥) This

DAVENPORT HOTEL

As much historic monument as luxury sleepover, the **Davenport** (☑509-455-8888; 10 S Post St; r standard/deluxe $219/239; ❇🛜🖥) is quite simply one of the most memorable hotels in the Pacific Northwest. The winner of copious awards, this AAA four-diamond beauty was constructed in 1914 on the designs of talented architect Kirtland Cutter. The ostentatious lobby extracts a sharp intake of breath from most visitors; everything from the huge fireside vases to the garbage buckets in the restrooms exhibit an incredible attention to detail. Even if you're not staying here, be sure to check out the ornate Marie Antoinette Ballroom, and the truly lavish guest rooms with their beautifully hand-carved custom-made beds. The newer, funkier Davenport Tower wing showcases an improbable safari theme (think stuffed animals and zebra-striped chairs) yet still somehow manages to look sophisticated.

new boutique motel has replaced an old Rodeway inn. Furnished with modern gadgets and funky color accents, it has an unbeatable downtown location opposite the Davenport.

Riverside State Park
CAMPGROUND **$**

(☑888-226-7688; 4427 N Aubrey L White Parkway; tent/RV sites $21/28) Located at the Bowl and Pitcher area on a bend in the Spokane River, this pleasant campground 5 miles northwest of downtown has 32 sites, showers, restrooms and a store.

🍴 Eating

Europa Pizzaria Restaurant
ITALIAN **$$**

(www.europapizzaria.com; 125 S Wall St; mains $12-17; ⏱lunch & dinner) Forget the pizza moniker; Europa is far more than just a cheese-and-tomatoes joint. Hidden in the bowels of the Great Northern Railway, the interior decor is both shabby and chic, with gilded-age sofas pushed next to garishly patterned bar stools. Then there's the food: pizzas yes, but also calzones and *rotolos* (a kind of pizza-pastry crossover). The pasta's from the top drawer – all the Italian classics in either half or full portions. And save space for the desserts – we're talking triple layer chocolate mousse and mud pie.

Frank's Diner   BREAKFAST $

(www.franksdiners.com; 516 W 2nd Ave; breakfast $5-9; ☺breakfast & lunch) A little west of downtown but worth the walk is this enchantingly restored vintage railway car that knocks out a classic breakfast including extraordinarily good eggs and no-frills biscuits and gravy. Frank's operated as a Seattle diner from 1931 until it was moved to Spokane in 1991. Arrive early to beat the queues.

Rock City Grill   AMERICAN-ITALIAN $$

(www.rockcitygrill.com; 505 W Riverside Ave; mains $12-19; ☺lunch & dinner) A new-wave American-Italian *cucina* glows translucent blue in this atmospherically lit shopping-mall favorite. The menu offers foods to go, an expansive wine list and items such as one-person artichoke heart and Thai pizza for as little as $13.

Elk Public House   PUB $

(1931 W Pacific Ave; lunch $8-10) Situated on a leafy street corner in the salubrious Browne's Addition, the Elk is a favorite neighborhood pub that turns out a kicking soup and sandwich lunch menu best enjoyed alfresco on the street. Also featured is a menu of Northwest beers plus live music at weekends.

Steam Plant Grill   FUSION $$

(www.steamplantgrill.com; 159 S Lincoln; mains $15-23; ☺lunch & dinner) It's amazing how attractive a rusty old coal elevator and a hulk of obsolete steam and electrical equipment can be made to look. Set in the neoindustrial confines of Kirtland Cutter's once-legendary old steam plant, this unfussy, eye-catching restaurant serves everything from a Thai chicken wrap to a plate of New Zealand lamb chops. Beers are brewed onsite courtesy of Coeur d'Alene Brewing Company.

Clinkerdagger   FUSION $$

(☎509-328-5965; www.clinkerdagger.com; 621 W Mallon Ave; mains $20; ☺lunch & dinner) If you want good food and a classic Spokane Falls view, this is the place for you. Wedged into the old-fashioned Flour Mill, the Clinkerdagger has wraparound windows and a dining deck jutting out over the river. The food is as elegant as the setting and includes grilled king salmon and rock-salt roasted prime ribs.

Mary Lou's Milk Bottle   DINER $

(802 W Garland Ave; burgers $5-8; ☺11am-8pm) Only in America! A tiny diner shaped like a milk bottle (honest!) that does phenomenal made-from-scratch cheeseburgers and milkshakes that come in the jug they were mixed in.

Wild Sage American Bistro   FRENCH $$$

(www.wildsagebistro.com; 916 W 2nd Ave; mains $18-28) Relatively informal fine-dining served in a small-ish bistro on 2nd. A fairly standard menu hides some pleasant surprises such as goat-cheese stuffed free-range chicken breast.

☻ Drinking & Entertainment

From opera to billiards, Spokane has the best nighttime entertainment scene east of the Cascades.

Northern Lights Brewing Company

BREWPUB

(www.northernlightsbrewing.com; 1003 E Trent Ave) A student hangout situated near the Gonzaga University, Spokane's best microbrewery serves all kinds of weird and wonderful flavors, including an enticing blueberry crème ale and an eye-watering chocolate *dunkel* (dark German beer), all of which are brewed right on the premises. Food-wise, check out the cod and chips cooked in batter made with the brewery's own pale ale.

Far West Billiards   POOL HALL

(www.farwestbilliards.com; 1001 W 1st Ave) An unintimidating pool hall and gallery space next to the Montvale Hotel that serves about two dozen beers to accompany your game. If you need a snack, there's falafel and fajitas.

Opera House   MUSIC VENUE

(www.spokanecenter.com; 334 W Spokane Falls Blvd) Part of the Spokane Convention Center at Riverfront Park, the Opera House hosts touring companies and the Spokane Symphony.

Bing Crosby Theater   THEATER

(www.mettheater.com; 901 W Sprague Ave) The former Met, now named after local hero Bing, presents concerts, plays, film festivals and the Spokane Opera in a fairly intimate setting.

Dempsey's Brass Rail   NIGHTCLUB

(www.dempseysbrassrail.net; 909 W 1st Ave) Dempsey's offers alternative entertainment with drag cabaret shows and a dancefloor, all against a crimson background. It's definitely gay-friendly, but plenty of straights venture in as well.

Spokane Interplayers Ensemble THEATER (www.interplayers.com; 174 S Howard St) Spokane's local theater offers Broadway-style entertainment from September to June.

Spokane Veterans Memorial Arena

MUSIC, SPORT

(www.spokanearena.com; 720 W Mallon Ave) Catch major touring acts at this 12,500-seat hall opposite the Flour Mill.

Shopping

The signature twin smokestacks visible all over Spokane comprise **Steam Plant Square** (www.steamplantsquare.com; 159 S Lincoln St), an upgrade of a 1915 power facility where shops, cafés and restaurants now mingle with the factory's former boilers and pipes. Another historic building-cum-mall is the **Flour Mill** (www.flourmillspokane.com; 621 W Mallon Ave), built in 1890 as the region's major wheat-grinding facility. Remodeled for the 1974 Expo, the mill now houses restaurants, pricey boutiques and galleries.

Auntie's Bookstore (www.auntiesbooks.com; 402 W Main Ave) is a fantastic indie bookshop with an excellent travel section, plenty of erudite book readings and the fine onsite **Liberty Café** with salads, sandwiches and coffee.

Information

Spokane Area Visitor Information Center (www.visitspokane.com; 201 W Main Ave at Browne St)

Getting There & Away

Air

From **Spokane International Airport** (www.spokaneairports.net), 8 miles southwest of downtown off US 2, Alaska, Horizon, Southwest and United airlines all offer daily services to and from Seattle, Portland, Denver, Chicago and Phoenix.

Bus

All buses arrive at and depart from the **Spokane Intermodal Transportation Center** (221 W 1st Ave), a combination bus-and-train station. **Greyhound** (www.greyhound.com) buses head off daily to Seattle ($39, six hours, three daily) and Pasco ($45, 2½ hours), the former via Moses Lake and Wenatchee.

Train

The **Amtrak** (www.amtrak.com) Chicago–Seattle *Empire Builder* divides in Spokane with trains heading to both Portland via Pasco and Seattle via Wenatchee once a day in either direction. Fares are Chicago $263, Portland $62 and Seattle $62.

 Getting Around

Spokane Transit (www.spokanetransit.com) buses depart from streets bordering the Plaza, a huge indoor transit station at Sprague Ave and Wall St. Bus fare is $1.25. Bus 64 runs hourly on weekdays between the Plaza and Spokane International Airport, from 6:20am to 5:50pm.

Grand Coulee Dam Area

Utilizing the raw power of the mighty Columbia River was always going to be logistically difficult. The problem was solved in the 1930s by the building of the gargantuan Grand Coulee dam, still the largest concrete structure in the US. Aside from providing enough hydroelectric power to fuel multiple cities, the dam irrigates more than half a million acres of central Washington and provides year-round recreation (and tourist dollars) for millions of people. All said, its economic importance dwarfs its significant physical presence.

GRAND COULEE DAM

The **Grand Coulee Visitor Arrival Center** (📞509-633-9265; ☉9am-5pm, till dusk May-Sep) details the history of the dam and surrounding area with movies, photos and interactive exhibits, while free guided **tours** of the facility run on the hour from 10am until 5pm (May to September) and involve taking a glass-walled elevator 465ft down an incline into the Third Power Plant, where you can view the tops of the generators from an observation deck.

Similarly spectacular is the nightly **laser show** (☉May-Sep after dark) – purportedly the world's largest – which illustrates the history of the Columbia River and its various dams against a gloriously vivid backdrop.

Accommodations in Grand Coulee itself can be found in a number of places, none better than the **Columbia River Inn** (📞509-633-2100; www.columbiariverinn.com; 10 Lincoln St, Coulee Dam; r/ste $105/205; 🐾) opposite the visitor arrival center. It offers a swimming pool, gym/sauna and rooms with dam-view balconies. For no-nonsense café grub, try the **Melody Restaurant** (📞509-633-1151; 512 River Dr; mains $6-10), which has a well-placed exterior deck for laser-show viewing.

CENTRAL & EASTERN WASHINGTON GRAND COULEE DAM AREA

LAKE ROOSEVELT NATIONAL RECREATION AREA

A 150-mile-long reservoir held back by the Grand Coulee Dam, Lake Roosevelt is a major recreation area that is popular with anglers, boaters, canoeists and water-skiers.

Dry, sunny weather prevails here, drawing people to camp and play on the lake's southern white-sand beaches. As the lake inches its way north to Canada, the desert cliffs and high coulee walls give way to rolling hills and orchards, becoming dense forests of ponderosa pine around Kettle Falls.

As recreation areas go, Lake Roosevelt remains refreshingly undeveloped, and few roads penetrate its isolated shoreline. To explore the area in any great length you'll need a boat. The lake offers a plethora of boat launches, with fees starting at $6 for seven days and $40 for a year. One of the best places to organize other water-based activities – such as fishing, canoeing and water skiing – is at the **Keller Ferry Campground** (☑509-633-9188; campsites May-Sep $10, Oct-Apr $5), located 14 miles north of the town of Wilbur. The free **Keller Ferry** (⊙6am-11pm) crosses Lake Roosevelt near the campground, linking Hwy 21 and providing access to the Sanpoil River and the town of Republic to the north.

To uncover the history of the area visit **Fort Spokane Museum & Visitor Center** (admission free; ⊙10am-5pm May 26-Oct 10) off Hwy 25, 23 miles north of Davenport, where original fort buildings from 1880 tell the story of how white settlers attempted to quell the region's Native American tribes.

Your best bet for general information about the area is the **Lake Roosevelt National Recreation Area Headquarters** (www.nps.gov/laro; 1008 Crest Dr; ⊙8am-4pm), in Coulee Dam. Park admission is free.

Okanogan River Valley

A geographical extension of British Columbia's Okanagan region, the Okanogan (note the subtle change of spelling) forms Washington's biggest yet most sparsely populated county and remains one of the lesser-known parts of the state. With much of the land given over to the Colville Indian Reservation there are not a lot of obvious attractions here, though if you wander under the radar you'll uncover eerie ghost towns and lonely mountain ranges.

Okanogan – which derives from the native Salish word for 'rendezvous' – is also the name of the diminutive county capital (population 2484) that lies 29 miles to the east of Twisp at the nexus of US 20 and US 97. In recent decades Okanogan has effectively merged with the nearby town of Omak (population 4721), though neither settlement is a budding tourist center.

Omak is famous for its annual **Omak Stampede** (held in August), a well-known local spectacle that includes the notorious 'Suicide Race,' a 210ft plunge down a 60-degree slope on horseback followed by the fording of the 50yd-wide Okanogan River. Not surprisingly, the event has raised the ire of numerous animal rights groups. Regional tourist information is available from the **Omak Visitor Information Office** (www.omakchamber.com; 401 Omak Ave) just east of downtown.

◉ Sights

Fort Okanogan State Park   STATE PARK
To get acquainted with local history call in at the interpretive center at **Fort Okanogan State Park** (junction of US 97 & Hwy 17; admission free; ⊙9am-5pm Wed-Sun May-Sep), 4 miles northeast of the town of Brewster. It tells the story of the valley's original Native American inhabitants and relates how three different fur-trading companies successively occupied the site of the old fort in the early 19th century.

Okanogan County Historical Museum
                                       MUSEUM
(www.okanoganhistory.org; 1410 N 2nd St, Okanogan; admission $2; ⊙10am-4pm Memorial Day-Labor Day) You can also make a quick but interesting pit stop at this museum to admire the pictures of frontier photographer Frank Matsura, who first visited this lonely region in 1890.

🏃 Activities

The varied landscape around Okanogan and Omak offers plenty of outdoor possibilities, including a small winter ski center at the **Loup Loup Ski Bowl** (www.skitheloup.com; day pass adult/child $38/24; ⊙Dec-Mar; 🚡), just off US 20, 18 miles west of Okanogan. Hiking and biking are also popular here in the summer.

The **Bike Shop** (www.theokbikeshop.com; 137 S 2nd Ave) in Okanogan rents bikes, skis and snowshoes from $15 a day.

🛏 Sleeping & Eating

Omak Inn MOTEL **$**
(☎509-826-3822; www.omakinnwa.com; 912 Koala Dr; r $80; 🌐🏊) If you're staying the night, try this inn, with gym, indoor pool and hot tub. The 20 rooms in the new wing added in 2004 are the best bet.

Breadline Café CAFÉ **$**
(www.breadlinecafe.com; 102 S Ash St; mains $10-17; ⏰11am-9pm Tue-Fri, 9am-9pm Sat & Sun) The most colorful eating joint by far, this place is a bit of the Omak furniture located in an old bottling plant; it acts like a local community center.

❶ Getting There & Away

The **Apple Line** (www.appleline.us) runs a daily bus to and from Omak through Okanogan, Chelan Falls, Wenatchee (for Amtrak connections) and Ellensburg (for Greyhound bus connections).

Colville National Forest

Wedged into Washington's northeast corner abutting the borders of Idaho and Canada lies the 1.1 million-acre Colville National Forest, a vast and relatively remote corner of the state that spans the Kettle River and Selkirk Mountain ranges and is bisected in the west by the Columbia River and Lake Roosevelt. Lying in the foothills of the Rocky Mountains, this wild region is home to grizzly bears, cougars and the last remaining herd of caribou in the lower 48 states. Some of the loveliest scenery can be found in the isolated Salmo-Priest Wilderness Area, which is criss-crossed by hiking trails. Colville makes a good base for exploring the Selkirks and the Pend Oreille River area.

COLVILLE

The area's main settlement is a small town embellished with parks and some gracious older buildings. It acts as a good base camp for exploring Lake Roosevelt and the surrounding national forest.

◉ Sights & Activities

Keller Heritage Center Museum & Park
HISTORIC SITE
(www.stevenscountyhistoricalsociety.org; 700 N Wynne St; adult/child $5/2; ⏰10am-4pm Mon-Sat, 1-4pm Sun May-Sep) Colville town's most notable attraction has as its centerpiece Keller House, a large bungalow with attractive Craftsman details, built in 1910. Dispersed around the house are reconstructed versions of a pioneer blacksmith's shop, schoolhouse, trapper's cabin, sawmill and a fire lookout tower.

Little Pend Oreille National Wildlife Refuge WILDLIFE REFUGE
(www.fsw.gov/littlependoreille) Bird-watchers should swing down to this 41,573-acre refuge where McDowell Lake attracts waterfowl. To reach the **refuge headquarters** (1310 Bear Creek Rd; ⏰7:30am-4pm), take US 20 for about 8 miles east of Colville, then

---

GHOST TOWNS

Northeast Washington may lack the coffee flavors of Seattle and the alternative music of Olympia, but it does harbor some classic American ghost towns.

The eeriest of the stash is **Molson**, 4 miles south of the Canadian border near Oroville. It's a former mining town that suffered the misfortune of going bust not once but twice in the early years of the 20th century. Molson mark 1 was founded in 1900 by John W Molson of beer-brewing fame, and within a year it had morphed into a viable settlement of 300 fuelled by mining speculation. But the speculators had over-predicted. The still nascent town's fortunes nosedived the following year as the mines dried up and the population fell to almost single figures. The rebirth came in 1905 with the arrival of the Great Northern Railroad, which led to the development of a new town sited half a mile to the north. New Molson thrived until the late 1920s when the Great Depression put a brake on its delicate economy. The final curtain fell in 1935 with the cessation of railroad operations.

Today, ghostly remnants of Old Molson make up a rather spooky indoor and outdoor museum complete with bank, law office, store and various outbuildings. It's run by the Molson Historical Society; entrance to these dusty relics is by donation and you can grab a cup of coffee in the old red-brick schoolhouse afterwards.

After exhuming the ghosts of Molson, you can head to two more skeletal settlements, **Nighthawk**, a railroad/mining nexus founded in 1903, and **Bodie**, founded in 1896 by over-optimistic gold prospectors.

turn south on Narcisse Creek Rd. The Mill Butte Trail starts from the refuge headquarters, gaining 600ft in 3 miles. Free camping is available on six designated sites within the refuge from April to December. There's no drinking water available.

49 Degrees North
SKI AREA

(www.ski49n.com; 3311 Flowery Trail Rd, Chewelah; ⊙closed Wed & Thu except holidays; ⛷) Despite having little star appeal, 49 Degrees is actually the state's second-largest ski area behind Crystal Mountain. Hidden in the Selkirk Mountains 42 miles due north of Spokane on US 395, there are an incredible 75 runs here served by five chairlifts, along with a good 25ft dumping of winter snow. The beginner's runs are particularly good, and the area is often sold as a family resort. Expect ski clubs and childcare but no overnight facilities. A Nordic center with 16km of trail was added in 2006. If you're approaching from Colville, 49 Degrees is located 30 miles to the southeast near the town of Chewelah, about 25 miles south of the true 49th parallel (the US-Canadian border).

🛏 Sleeping & Eating

Cheap accommodation around Colville is plentiful in motels and campgrounds.

FREE Douglas Falls Grange Park
Campground
CAMPING $

(☑509-684-7474; Douglas Falls Rd; ⊙May-Sep) Alongside Mill Creek 7 miles north of town.

Selkirk Motel
MOTEL $

(☑509-684-2565; 369 S Main St; r from $60; ❄) Fulfills the three Cs: comfortable, convenient and clean.

For catfish, Cajun chicken, steak or an Asian stir-fry, head to **Stephani's Oak Street Grill** (157 N Oak St; mains $14-21; ⊙11am-9pm Tue-Sat).

❶ Information

Colville Chamber of Commerce (www.colville.com; 121 E Astor St) For local information.

Colville National Forest Ranger Station (765 S Main St) Has the lowdown on hiking and camping.

KETTLE FALLS

The question that tickles most people to Kettle Falls is: where are the falls? The answer is: they've disappeared. The original Kettle Falls, a series of cascades and rapids that was once a favored fishing spot for Native Americans, was inundated in the late 1930s by water that backed up behind the new Grand Coulee Dam (ultimately forming present-day Lake Roosevelt). The spectacular natural sight wasn't the only casualty. A town that had been founded 3 miles south of the falls in the 1880s had to be uprooted piece by piece and moved a few miles east to be rebuilt alongside the existing settlement of Meyers Falls (bisected by a much smaller waterfall). The two towns amalgamated in the 1940s to form 'new' Kettle Falls. These days it is largely a blue-collar lumber settlement set in an attractive valley that – somewhat ironically – acts as a base for water activities on the lake that once drowned it.

To get a glimpse of the town before its relocation, drop by the **Kettle Falls Interpretive Center** (⊙11am-5pm Wed-Sat May-Sep), just north of US 395, to see a giant photo mural showing the pre-dam Columbia as it crashed through Kettle Falls.

SOUTHEASTERN WASHINGTON

Parched, remote, and barely served by public transportation, southeastern Washington is the state's loneliest corner and is characterized by the dry volcanic plateaus and denuded lava flows of the inhospitable 'Scablands' region, exposed by the Missoula floods at the end of the last ice age. Tourism – and its attendant attractions – was on a backburner here until the early 1990s when wine growers in and around Walla Walla began to realize the town's potential as a new Sonoma, and wine connoisseurs started arriving from around the globe.

For many it was as if the region's fortunes had turned full circle. Established as one of Washington's first permanent settlements in 1836 when Marcus Whitman rolled off the Oregon Trail and founded a mission in the foothills of the Blue Mountains, the southeast was once a hive of commercial activity that sat on the cusp of Washington's burgeoning frontier. But as the settlers pushed west in the late 19th century, the Columbia River Basin slipped into a self-imposed coma, made all the more terminal when the US government opened up the Hanford nuclear complex near Richland in 1942. Not surprisingly, the stigma of secret bomb-making factories and contaminated waste sites has been hard to dislodge.

SCENIC DRIVE – SHERMAN PASS

The 35 miles of Hwy 20 between Kettle Falls and the town of Republic has been designated the **Sherman Pass Scenic Byway** and interpretive sites along the route have been beefed up in recent years. Eleven miles west of Kettle Falls on Hwy 20 (at Canyon Creek, Mile 335) you'll find the **Log Flume Heritage Site** in the middle of a ponderosa pine forest. The site provides a snapshot of logging history, with several interpretive displays along a mile-long, winding, wheelchair-accessible trail. Further on is the **Growden Heritage Site**, which relates stories of the Civilian Conservation Corps in the 1930s and '40s; while closer to Republic, near the crest of the 5575ft pass, is the **White Mountain Interpretive Center**, with stunning views toward British Columbia, Canada.

A new mock train depot in Kettle Falls acts as an excellent information portal for the drive. It's situated on the corner of US 395 and Juniper St and is open daily year-round.

Tri-Cities

POP 235,841

Three cities (Pasco, Kennewick and Richland) situated at the confluence of three rivers (the Snake, Columbia and Yakima) sounds like a promising proposition, but while the Tri-Cities can offer plenty in the way of wine-quaffing and water sports they rarely feature in the front line of Washington's tourist push. Part of the reason is that, historically, the Tri-Cities have been closely associated with the notorious Hanford site, the top-secret plutonium-processing plant that manufactured 'fat boy,' the atomic bomb dropped on Nagasaki in 1945, and subsequently stayed in operation throughout the Cold War. Although largely decommissioned since the early 1990s, recent studies have revealed that Hanford's operations have leaked a significant amount of radioactive waste into the Columbia River.

Eschewing their nuclear image, the Tri-Cities have grown and prospered in recent years through wine production, agriculture and – ironically – a massive (and still ongoing) Hanford clean-up campaign (which still employs thousands).

◎ Sights & Activities

Riverside Greenway　　　MONUMENT, TRAIL

To see the Tri-Cities in their best light, stay close to the broad Columbia River, which reveals its only stretch of free-flowing water at the **Hanford Reach National Monument**.

Kennewick's **Columbia Park** is a vast greenway complete with a golf course, playing fields, campground and boat moorage, while the 23-mile paved **Sacagawea Heritage Trail** acts as a connecting hiking and biking artery between the three cities using the river as its marker.

Museums　　　MUSEUMS

Museum-wise Richland has the comprehensive **Columbia River Exhibition of History, Science & Technology** (CREHST; www.crehst. com; 95 Lee Blvd; adult/child $4/3; ◎10am-5pm Mon-Sat, noon-5pm Sun), which documents Columbia River history, the journey of Lewis and Clark (who passed though here in 1805) and the inevitable chronicling of the Hanford project. Meanwhile, over in Kennewick, the **East Benton County Historical Museum** (www.ebchs.com; 205 Keewayden Dr; admission $4; ◎noon-4pm Tue-Sat) tracks local history and has some exhibits on 'Kennewick Man,' a 9300-year-old skeleton of a Caucasian male found on the banks of the Columbia in 1996, that blew the anthropological history of North America wide open.

⊨ Sleeping & Eating

Clover Island Inn　　　HOTEL $$

(☑509-586-0541; www.hotelkennewick.com; 435 Clover Island Dr, Kennewick; r from $89; ❋@⊛❋) You won't have trouble finding an economical motel in the Tri-Cities but, if you want something a little plusher, hit the locally owned Clover Island Inn, which is situated on its own island in the Columbia River. This unique establishment boasts 152 rooms, its own boat dock and panoramic views from the top-floor Crow's Nest Restaurant. You can borrow bikes to use on the abundant paths for free.

Atomic Ale Brewpub & Eatery　　BREWPUB $

(www.atomicalebrewpub.com; 1015 Lee Blvd; pizzas $9-12, sandwiches $6; ◎closed Sun) A perceptible Hanford-inspired 'gallows humor' pervades this cheery microbrewery and eatery, well known for its wood-fired specialty pizzas and top-notch soups (try the red potato). But first blast off with a locally crafted Half-Life Hefeweizen, Plutonium Porter or Atomic Amber. Real intellectuals grab an Oppenheimer Oatmeal Stout.

ℹ️ Getting There & Around

Greyhound (www.greyhound.com) and **Amtrak** (www.amtrak.com) share a new terminal at 535 N 1st Ave in Pasco. Greyhound buses go to Spokane ($45, 2½ hours), Portland ($59, four hours) and Seattle ($59, 4½ hours) via Yakima and Ellensburg. Amtrak's *Empire Builder* stops here en route to Portland at 5:35am ($65, 4½ hours); eastbound, it passes through at 8:57pm on the way to Spokane ($27, 3½ hours) and Chicago.

Walla Walla

POP 31,350

'Walla Walla, so good they named it twice,' or so the understandably biased locals would have you believe. The stanza probably seemed like a bad joke a couple of decades ago when Walla Walla's most well-known landmark was the state's largest penitentiary. These days the naysayers are laughing on the other side of their faces. The reason: wine. Walla Walla and its surrounding vineyards now concoct some of the best vintages in the US, challenging California in the same way the 'Sunshine State' once took on the French. Furthermore, Walla Walla, more than any Washington town, has fermented the ingredients to support a burgeoning wine culture including a historic Main Street, a handsome college, a warm summer climate and a growing clutch of fine restaurants where pairing wine and food is as common as pairing couples on a blind date.

Located in a rich agricultural area, Walla Walla supplements its much-sought-after vineyards with pea and asparagus production, apple orchards and its famous sweet onions. Equally distinctive in the undulating countryside are 454 wind turbines belonging to the massive Stateline Wind Energy Center, a groundbreaking environmental project that is a vital source of Washington's renewable energy.

🅞 Sights

Historic Downtown   HISTORIC SITE
You don't need to be sloshed on wine to appreciate Walla Walla's historical and cultural heritage. Its **Main Street** has won countless historical awards, and to bring the settlement to life the local chamber of commerce has concocted some interesting walking tours, with leaflet including maps and numbered icons.

The 1.5-mile 'Downtown Walk' starts at the 1928 **Marcus Whitman Hotel** and proceeds in a loop around the historic buildings of Main and Colville Sts. A couple of other walks showcase the historic homes that dot the suburbs with Queen Anne, neoclassical and Gothic Carpenter-style architecture. Also be sure not to miss the gorgeous **Whitman College** campus and the lush confines of **Pioneer Park** nearby.

Fort Walla Walla Park   HISTORIC SITE
This fine historic site showcases the original buildings from a US army installation that existed here from its inception in 1858 until 1910 – everything from the officer's quarters to the quartermaster's stable. The grounds now house the Department of Veteran's Affairs Medical Center. Slightly west of here is the **Fort Walla Walla Museum** (755 Myra Rd; adult/child $7/3; ⊙10am-5pm Apr-Oct; ⊕), a pioneer village of 17 historic buildings, including a blacksmith shop, an 1867 schoolhouse, log cabins and a railway depot, arranged around a central meadow. On a hill above the village, the fort's old cavalry stables house the museum proper, with collections of farm implements, ranching tools and what could be the world's largest plastic replica of a mule team.

Whitman Mission   HISTORIC SITE
(www.nps.gov/whmi; Swegle Rd; adult/child $3/free; ⊙8am-6pm) An erstwhile stop on the Oregon Trail and infamous site of the 1847 Whitman 'massacre,' when white missionary Marcus Whitman and a dozen others were murdered by Cayuse Indians, this potent historic site 7 miles west of Walla Walla contains a museum and marked sites and monuments indicating where the mission once stood.

Wineries

With its laidback, small-town feel, excellent syrahs and plethora of unpretentious local wineries, Walla Walla is the best place in the state to indulge in a bit of wine touring.

Woodward Canyon Winery (11920 US 12; ⊙10am-5pm), in a restored 1870s farmhouse, is a standout among the best of the local wineries that are found around Lowden, roughly 12 miles west of Walla Walla on US 12. It has been in operation since 1981. Try the cab sav or chardonnay.

Back in town you can stop by at an ever-expanding number of tasting rooms:

Canoe Ridge TASTING ROOM
(www.canoeridgevineyard.com; 1102 W Cherry St; ☺11am-4pm Oct-Apr, till 5pm May-Sep) Has a tasting room in an old 1905 streetcar engine house. Try the Merlot Reserve and the Gewürztraminer.

Forgeron Cellars TASTING ROOM
(www.forgeroncellars.com; 33 W Birch St; ☺11am-4pm) Established in 2001; headed up by a Parisian who studied viticulture at Dijon University before heading west. Check out the smooth, balanced cabernet sauvignons and full-bodied syrahs.

Walla Walla Wineworks TASTING ROOM
(www.waterbrook.com; 31 E Main St; ☺11am-6pm Mon-Thu, till 9pm Fri & Sat) A tasting room for the Waterbrook Winery; also offers cheese and ham plus live music on Wednesday nights, which you can enjoy while sipping its signature chardonnay.

🏃 Activities

Aside from halcyon bike rides between wineries, Walla Walla's best outdoor opportunities are in **Umatilla National Forest** (www.fs.fed.us/r6/uma), a protected area in the Blue Mountains three-quarters of which lies across the state border in Oregon. The Washington section contains plenty of hiking trails. Consult the **Ranger Station** (1415 W Rose St) in Walla Walla. Also here is **Ski Bluewood** (www.bluewood.com; day pass adult/child $42/33; 🚠), 52 miles northeast of Walla Walla near the town of Dayton. Bluewood is something of a revelation to most visitors who (wrongly) assume that southeast Washington is flat and not particularly snowy. The ski area is small, with 20 runs, but has a high base elevation of 4545ft.

🎉 Festivals & Events

The **Walla Walla Sweet Onion Blues Fest** (☎509-525-1031), held in mid-July at Fort Walla Walla, celebrates the valley's renowned crop (now upstaged by the region's wine). There are food booths and recipe contests, as well as live music provided by touring blues acts.

The mid-May **Balloon Stampede** sees competitors launch dozens of hot-air-filled craft into the air at 6am.

🛏 Sleeping

Marcus Whitman Hotel HOTEL **$$**
(☎509-525-2200; www.marcuswhitmanhotel.com; 6 W Rose St; r/ste $139/$279; ❄📶) Walla Walla's best known landmark is also the town's only tall building, impossible to miss with its distinctive rooftop turret visible from all around. In keeping with the settlement's well-preserved image, the red-brick 1928 beauty has been elegantly renovated with ample rooms kitted out in rusts and browns, and embellished with Italian-crafted furniture, huge beds and killer views over the nearby Blue Mountains. The onsite **Marc** restaurant is one of the town's fanciest eating joints.

Green Gables Inn B&B **$$**
(☎509-525-5501; www.greengablesinn.com; 922 Bonsella St; r $140-175; ❄) While it's a long way from Prince Edward Island – the setting for the novel *Anne of Green Gables* – this comfortable inn in a 1909 Craftsman-style home plays heavily on the classic book's literary themes, featuring five rooms named after instances in Lucy Maud Montgomery's famous novel. Come here to enjoy candlelit breakfasts, a shady wraparound porch, and rooms replete with bathrobes, fresh flowers and cable TV.

Inn at Abeja SUITES **$$$**
(☎509-522-1234; www.abeja.net; 2014 Mill Creek Rd; r $245-295; 📶) Ever wanted to stay at a full working winery? Well, if you've got your own transportation and approximately $250 in spare change you can spend a night at this historic farmstead set in the foothills of the glowering Blue Mountains 4 miles east of Walla Walla. Luxury accommodation is provided in five self-contained converted buildings (the largest of which is over 800 sq ft). It's the perfect base for a wine tour.

Colonial Motel MOTEL **$**
(☎509-529-1220; www.colonial-motel.com; 2279 Isaacs Ave; r from $70; ❄📶) A simple family-run motel halfway to the airport, the Colonial is welcoming and bike-friendly with safe bike storage and plenty of local maps.

🍴 Eating

Walla Walla is defined by its wine and food, and its restaurants are befitting of a far larger city. Most are scattered around the small downtown core.

TOP CHOICE **Saffron Mediterranean Kitchen** MEDITERRANEAN **$$$**
(☎509-525-2112; www.saffronmediterraneankitchen.com; 125 W Alder St; mains $15-27; ☺2-10pm, till 9pm winter) This place isn't about cooking, it's about alchemy; Saffron takes seasonal, local ingredients and turns them into – well – pure gold. The Med-inspired

menu lists dishes such as pheasant, ricotta gnocchi, amazing flatbreads and weird yogurt/cucumber combo soups that could stand up against anything in Seattle. Then there are the intelligently paired wines – and beers. Not surprisingly, Saffron is insanely popular (and small); reserve ahead.

T-Maccarones
MEDITERRANEAN $$$

(☎509-522-4776; www.tmaccarones.com; 4 N Colville St; ⊘dinner, breakfast Sun) Another good reason to come to Walla Walla is T-Maccarones, a contemporary restaurant with Italian inflections that's guaranteed to reignite your tired palate after a tough day in the wine-tasting rooms. Big hitters include pear salad, beef tenderloin, prawn polenta and a house fontina mac and cheese. It's food as art, so book ahead.

Brasserie 4
FRENCH $$$

(☎509-529-2011; 4 E Main St; mains $15-25; ⊘closed Mon, lunch Tue & dinner Sun) Sharing a latitude with Bordeaux and a French passion for growing grapes, it was only a matter of time before Walla Walla came over all *français*. Cool, minimalist Brasserie 4 is one of its best manifestations, where the wait staff knows their wines and the Gallic-inspired food is more than just a few pretentious names on the menu. Try the *moules frites* (mussels and fries), cheese plate or excellent steaks.

Whitehouse-Crawford Restaurant
FUSION $$

(☎509-525-2222; www.whitehousecrawford.com; 55 W Cherry St; mains from $20; ⊘5-10pm Wed-Mon) If you're feeling flush, bypass the town's ample cafés and make a beeline for this fine-dining establishment housed in an impressively renovated 1905 woodworking mill. Great local seafood and produce highlight the seasonally (and daily) varying menu.

The Marc
FRENCH $$$

(☎509-525-2200; www.marcuswhitmanhotel. com; 6 W Rose St; mains from $20) Widely lauded fine-dining in the Marcus Whitman hotel; try to bag the private chef's table in the kitchen where you'll get a special meal prepared for you as you watch.

Olive Marketplace & Café
CAFÉ $

(21 E Main St; breakfast & sandwiches $7-12; ⊘breakfast, lunch) Run by T Maccerones in the historic 1885 Barrett Building, this breezy café/market serving breakfast and lunch is a good place to line your stomach for the impending wine-tasting.

🍷 Drinking

Mill Creek Brewpub
BREWPUB

(www.millcreek-brewpub.com; 11 S Palouse St) Walla Walla's only brewpub is an accommodating place, with outdoor seating and decent snacks such as mushroom burgers and fish 'n chips. Situated at the top end of Main St and close to Whitman College, it welcomes minors and sells small 6oz taster glasses of the local microbrews, including the smooth Walla Walla Wheat and the ever-popular English-style IPAs.

Coffee Perk
CAFÉ

(4 1st St; sandwiches $6; 🛜) A student hangout notable for its giant old-fashioned bookcase stocked with everything from Dickens to Mark Twain's *Innocents Abroad*. If the literature doesn't perk you up, the coffee will.

☆ Entertainment

Walla Walla Symphony
MUSIC VENUE

(www.wwsymphony.com) Yes, the supposed rural backwater of Walla Walla has had a symphony orchestra since 1907 and the group is currently led by musical director Yaacov Bergman. Tackling everything from Holst to Gershwin, it runs an annual six-concert series in the Cordiner Hall at Whitman College.

Harper Joy Theatre
THEATER

(N Park St & Boyer Ave; adult/senior $10/7) Walla Walla's culture vultures wander over to Whitman College's theater department for renditions of Shakespeare, Rodgers and Hammerstein, and plenty of local fare.

ℹ Information

Walla Walla Valley Chamber of Commerce
(www.wallawalla.org; 29 E Sumach St; ⊘8:30am-5pm Mon-Fri, 9am-3pm Sat & Sun) Provides four excellent walking-tour maps of the town plus plenty of information on wine tours.

ℹ Getting There & Around

Air

Horizon Air (www.alaskaair.com) has daily flights to Sea-Tac (from $170 return) from the **Walla Walla Regional Airport** (www.wallawallaairport. com), which is northeast of town off US 12.

The local bus service is operated 6:30am to 5:30pm weekdays by **Valley Transit** (www.valley transit.com).

Bus

Greyhound (www.greyhound.com) buses run once daily to Seattle ($67, seven hours) via Pasco, Yakima and Ellensburg; change buses in Pasco for Spokane. Comfortable **Grape Line**

(www.grapeline.us) buses run thrice daily to Pasco ($7)

Pullman & The Palouse Region

Another of Washington's liberal university towns, Pullman (population 24,675) lies in the midst of the golden Palouse region, a fertile pastiche of rolling hills and well-tilled agricultural fields replete with wheat, lentils, barley and peas that is excellent for cycling.

◎ Sights & Activities

Washington State University UNIVERSITY
(WSU; www.wsu.edu) Situated 7 miles west of the Idaho state line, most of Pullman's sights are related directly to expansive WSU, which accommodates more than 22,000 students and one of Washington's leading agricultural schools. Worth seeking out in this small 'city within a city' is the WSU's **Museum of Art** (admission free; ⊙10am-4pm Mon-Wed & Fri, 1-5pm Sat & Sun, 10am-10pm Tue), in the Fine Arts Center at Stadium Way and Wilson Rd, which mounts some lively, well-curated shows featuring Northwestern artists.

Other WSU museums include the **Jacklin Collection** (admission free; ⊙8am-5pm Mon-Fri), in room 124 of the Webster Physical Sciences Building. It showcases more than 2000 specimens of petrified wood.

The **Museum of Anthropology** (110 College Hall; admission free; ⊙9am-4pm Mon-Fri) documents fossils relating to human evolution.

🛏 Sleeping & Eating

Hilltop Inn & Restaurant INN $$
(⌨509-332-0928; 928 NW Olsen St; s/d $105/110; ✴🌐🐾) A worthwhile stopover a mile outside town, with views toward the university.

Ferdinand's EATERY $
(⌨509-335-2141; 101 Food Quality Bldg at the WSU Creamery; milkshakes $3; ⊙9:30am-4:30pm Mon-Fri) Possibly one of Pullman's most famous eateries; sells the locally concocted Cougar Gold cheese (white sharp cheddar, sold by the can) along with milkshakes, ice cream and a decent espresso.

❶ Information

Pullman Chamber of Commerce (www.pullman-wa.com; 415 N Grand Ave) For a full lowdown on the area and its facilities.

❶ Getting There & Away

Northwestern Trailways (www.northwesterntrailways.com) links Pullman to other cities via Spokane ($22, 1½ hours), and Moscow ($5, 15 minutes) and Lewiston ($12, 45 minutes) in Idaho from the **bus station** (NW 1002 Nye St) behind the Dissmore supermarket. There are also connections to Boise, Idaho ($49, 6½ hours).

Portland

Why Go?

Dynamic yet laid back, Portland is a superstar city. It's Oregon's largest metropolis, with a bustling, vibrant downtown across the Willamette River from charming neighborhoods full of friendly (and often zany) people. It hums with a youthful vitality, and is home to a landslide of liberal idealists – but located in a state where backroads brim with Republican red. It's a place where Gore-Tex rain jackets in fine restaurants are as common as sideburns on a hipster. It's a haven for eco-activists, cyclists, grungsters, outdoor nuts, vegans, gardeners and dog-lovers, all supporting countless brewpubs, coffeehouses, knitting circles, lesbian potlucks and book clubs. It's a livable metropolis with pretty neighborhoods and a friendly, small-town atmosphere – an up-and-coming destination that has finally found itself, but keeps redefining its ethos with every controversy. Portland is racially progressive, culturally diverse and politically charged, and – as many folks from out of state have discovered – an awesome spot to plant roots, settle in and chill out for while.

Best Places to Eat

» Paley's Place (p219)

» Higgins (p217)

» Laurelhurst Market (p219)

» Pok Pok (p221)

» Bamboo Sushi (p219)

Best Places to Stay

» Ace Hotel (p214)

» Nines (p214)

» Hawthorne Portland Hostel (p217)

» Kennedy School (p216)

» Jupiter Hotel (p216)

When to Go
Portland

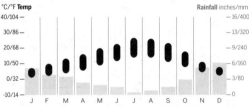

April–May
Long-awaited springtime flowers start blooming

June–September
Festivals galore, including the Oregon Brewer's Festival and the Bite of Oregon

November–March Rainy season: visit museums, galleries, coffee shops, brewpubs...

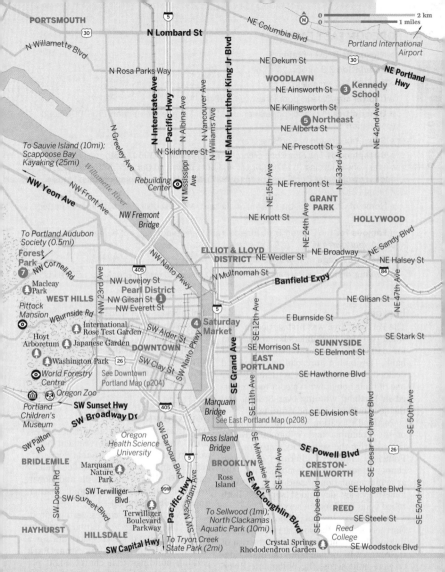

Portland Highlights

1 Explore the many restaurants and art galleries in Portland's chic **Pearl District** (p207)

2 Sample a wide variety of microbrews in Portland, which boasts around 30 breweries and **brewpubs** (p223)

3 Visit eclectic **Kennedy School** (p216) and watch a movie, drink a beer, soak in the hot tub or spend the night

4 Wander through crafts stalls at the **Saturday Market** (p205), grab a bite to eat and take in street performers' antics

5 Party with the hip (or just obnoxious) 'Last Thursday' crowds on NE Alberta in the **Northeast** (p208), where artists, musicians and buskers compete for attention

6 Catch a flick at one of Portland's many pizza-and-beer **movie houses** (p225), offering second-run screenings for $3

7 Take a walk in **Forest Park** (p210), the country's largest urban park, with more than 70 miles of woodsy trails

OREGON FAST FACTS

» **Nickname** Beaver State

» **Population** 3.8 million

» **Area** 95,997 sq miles

» **Capital city** Salem (population 154,000)

» **Other cities** Portland (population 582,000), Eugene (population 150,000), Bend (population 82,000)

» **Sales tax** Oregon has no sales tax

» **Birthplace of** *The Simpsons* creator Matt Groening (b 1954), notorious figure skater Tonya Harding (b 1970), writer and poet Raymond Carver (1938–88), pop and jazz trumpeter Doc Severinsen (b 1927), Nobel prize–winning chemist Linus Pauling (1901–94)

» **Home of** Crater Lake, the Oregon Shakespeare Festival, Nike, McMenamins, spotted owls

» **Famous for** the Oregon Trail, forests, rain, beer, pinot noir, not being able to pump your own gas

» **State beverage** milk (dairy's big here)

» **Driving distances** Portland to Eugene 110 miles, Astoria to Brookings 350 miles

History

The Portland area was first settled in 1844 when two New Englanders bought a claim for 640 acres on the Willamette's west bank. They built a store, plotted streets and decided to name the new settlement after one of their hometowns: a coin toss resulted in Portland winning over Boston, and the new town was up and running.

Portland's location near the confluence of the Columbia and Willamette Rivers helped drive the young city's growth. San Francisco and the Californian gold rush clamored for Oregon lumber, while the growing population of settlers in the Willamette Valley demanded supplies. Both relied upon Portland for services.

The city's status got a boost when the Northern Pacific Railroad arrived in 1883, linking the Pacific Northwest to the rest of the country. In the late 1880s the first bridges were built across the Willamette River, and the city spread eastward. Portland kept growing steadily, also benefiting from the WWII shipbuilding boom.

Today over half a million people live in the Greater Portland area. Shipping operations have since moved north of downtown, the Old Town has been revitalized and the once-industrial Pearl District now brims with expensive lofts and sophisticated boutiques. Big sports and outdoor-clothing manufacturers like Nike, Adidas and Co-

lumbia Sportswear help drive the economy, along with high-tech companies like Intel and Tektronix.

Despite its economic ups and downs, Portland continues to attract new settlers, each with their own hopes and dreams for a new life.

◉ Sights

DOWNTOWN

Downtown Portland is an urban success story. An activist city government began work in the 1970s to ensure that Portland's business and nightlife did not flee the city center. They were successful, and downtown Portland remains a vibrant destination both day and night.

But with success comes certain problems – like parking. You can get lucky by finding a metered street space, but for a similar price there are six **SmartPark** parking buildings that charge $1.50 per hour. Check www.portlandonline.com/smartpark for their locations and hours.

Pioneer Courthouse Square   SQUARE
(Map p204) The heart of downtown Portland, this brick plaza is nicknamed 'Portland's living room' and is the most visited public space in the city. When it isn't full of hackysack players, sunbathers or office workers lunching, the square hosts concerts, festivals, rallies, farmers markets – and even summer Friday-night movies (aka

'Flicks on the Bricks'; details at www.pioneercourthousesquare.org/calendar).

One of Portland's grandest Victorian hotels once stood here, but it fell into disrepair and was torn down in 1951. Later the city decided to build Pioneer Courthouse Square, and grassroots support resulted in a program that encouraged citizens to buy and personalize the bricks that eventually built the square. Names include John F Kennedy, Bruce Springsteen and Frodo Baggins.

Across 6th Ave is the **Pioneer Courthouse** (Map p204). Built in 1875, this was the legal center of 19th-century Portland.

South Park Blocks   PARK

Two important museums flank the South Park Blocks, the 12-block–long greenway that runs through much of downtown. The blocks themselves are a fine leafy refuge from downtown's bustle, and host a farmers market and occasional art shows.

The **Oregon Historical Society** (Map p204; ☑503-222-1741; www.ohs.org; 1200 SW Park Ave; adult/child $11/5; ☺10am-5pm Tue-Sat, noon-5pm Sun) is the state's largest historical museum, and includes a research library (with limited hours).

Across the park, the excellent **Portland Art Museum** (Map p204; ☑503-226-2811; www.portlandartmuseum.org; 1219 SW Park Ave; adult/child $12/9; ☺10am-5pm Tue, Wed & Sat, to 8pm Thu & Fri, noon-5pm Sun) has an especially good collection of Asian and Native American art. Upstairs galleries contain a small international collection, and blockbuster exhibits are mounted regularly.

At the southern end of the South Park Blocks is **Portland State University** (Map p204), the city's largest university.

Portland Building   BUILDING

(Map p204; cnr SW 5th Ave & SW Main St) This notoriously controversial 15-story building was designed by Michael Graves and catapulted the postmodern architect to celebrity status. People working inside the blocky, pastel-colored edifice, however, have had to deal with tiny windows, cramped spaces and a general user-unfriendliness. The Portland Building suffered from major design flaws that later proved very costly to fix. Not a great start for what was considered to be the world's first major postmodern structure; at least it's been made somewhat green with an eco roof installed in 2006.

Towering above the main doors of the Portland Building is **Portlandia**, an immense statue of the Goddess of Commerce, Portland's supposed patroness. This crouching figure is, at 36ft, the second largest hammered-copper statue in the world (after the Statue of Liberty).

Tom McCall Waterfront Park PARK & FOUNTAIN
(Map p204) This popular riverside park, which lines the west bank of the Willamette River, was finished in 1978 after four years of construction. It replaced an old freeway with 2 miles of paved sidewalks and grassy spaces, attracting heaps of joggers, in-line skaters, strollers and cyclists. During the summer, the park is perfect for hosting outdoor events like the Oregon Brewers Festival (p214). Walk over the Steel and Hawthorne bridges to the **Eastbank Esplanade** (Map p204), making a 3-mile loop.

Salmon Street Springs Fountain (Map p204), on Salmon St near the river, cycles through computer-generated patterns. On hot days, kids (and adults) take turns plunging through the jets. North of the Burnside Bridge is the **Japanese-American Historical Plaza**, a memorial to Japanese Americans who were interned by the US government during WWII.

Old Town & Chinatown   NEIGHBORHOOD
The core of rambunctious 1890s Portland, the once-seedy Old Town used to be the lurking grounds of unsavory characters, but today disco queens outnumber drug dealers. It's one of the livelier places in town after dark, when nightclubs and bars open their doors and the hipsters start showing up.

Running beneath Old Town's streets are the **shanghai tunnels**, a series of underground corridors through which unscrupulous people would kidnap or 'shanghai' drunken men and sell them to sea captains looking for indentured workers. Call the **Cascade Geographic Society** (☑503-622-4798; tours by appointment; adult/child $12/7) for tours.

The ornate **Chinatown Gates** (Map p204; cnr NW 4th Ave & W Burnside St) define the southern edge of Portland's so-called Chinatown – you'll be lucky to find any Chinese people here at all (most are on 82nd Ave over to the east). There are a few token Chinese restaurants, but the main attraction is the **Classical Chinese Gardens** (Map p204; ☑503-228-8131; www.portlandchinesegarden.org; NW 3rd Ave & Everett St; adult/child $8.50/6.50; ☺10am-6pm). It's a one-block haven of tranquility, reflecting ponds and manicured greenery. Free tours available with admission.

PORTLAND

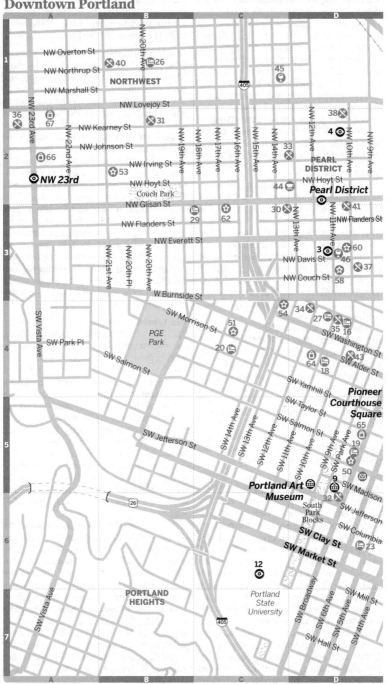

NW Overton St
NW Northrup St
NORTHWEST
NW Marshall St

NW Lovejoy St

NW 23rd Ave
NW 22nd Ave
NW 21st Ave
NW 20th Ave
NW 20th Pl
NW 19th Ave
NW 18th Ave
NW 17th Ave
NW 16th Ave
NW 15th Ave
NW 14th Ave
NW 13th Ave
NW 12th Ave
NW 11th Ave
NW 10th Ave
NW 9th Ave

NW 20th Ave

405

36
67
66

⊙ **NW 23rd**

NW Kearney St
NW Johnson St
NW Irving St
53
NW Hoyt St
Couch Park
NW Glisan St
NW Flanders St

NW Everett St

W Burnside St

NORTHWEST

40
26

45

38
4 ⊙

**PEARL
DISTRICT**

NW Hoyt St
44
Pearl District ⊙

30
41
NW Flanders St

3 ⊙
46
60
NW Davis St
58
NW Couch St
37

54
34
27
35 16
SW Washington St

51
SW Morrison St

**PGE
Park**

SW Vista Ave
SW Park Pl
SW Salmon St

20

64
18
SW Alder St
43

SW Yamhill St
SW Taylor St
SW Salmon St

**Pioneer
Courthouse
Square**

SW Jefferson St

SW 14th Ave
SW 13th Ave
SW 12th Ave
SW 11th Ave
SW 10th Ave
SW 9th Ave
SW Park Ave

65
19
50
9 SW Madison
32
SW Jefferson

Portland Art
Museum

South
Park
Blocks

SW Clay St
SW Market St

SW Columbia
23

26

12 ⊙

**PORTLAND
HEIGHTS**

SW Vista Ave

405

Portland
State
University

SW Broadway
SW 6th Ave
SW 5th Ave
SW 4th Ave
SW Mill St

SW Hall St

31

33
62
29

Saturday Market & Skidmore Fountain

MARKET, FOUNTAIN

(Map p204; ☑503-222-6072; www.portlandsatur
daymarket.com; SW Ankeny St & Naito Pkwy;
⊙10am-5pm Sat & 11am-4:30pm Sun Mar-Dec)
Victorian-era architecture and the lovely
Skidmore Fountain (Map p204) give the
area beneath the Burnside Bridge some
flair. Hit it on a weekend to catch the **Saturday Market** (⊙10am-5pm Sat, 11am-4.30pm
Sun Mar-Dec), a fun outdoor crafts fair with
street entertainers and food carts.

Beside the fountain is the **New Market
Theater** (Map p204), built in 1871 as Port-
land's first theater for stage productions.
It's now home to shops and restaurants.

WEST HILLS

This area is known for its exclusive homes,
windy streets and Forest Park (see p210).

Pittock Mansion

HISTORIC HOUSE

(Mapp201; ☑503-823-3623; www.pittockmansion
.org; 3229 NW Pittock Dr; adult/child $8/5;
⊙11am-4pm, closed Jan) This grand and beautiful 1914 mansion was built by pioneer/
entrepreneur Henry Pittock, who revitalized the *Oregonian* newspaper. Guided
tours are available, but it's worth visiting
the (free) grounds simply to have a picnic
while taking in the spectacular views.

International Rose Test Garden

GARDENS

(Map p201; ☑503-823-3636; www.rosegarden
store.org; 400 SW Kingston Ave; ⊙7am-9pm)
These gardens practically gave Portland its
'Rose City' nickname. They sprawl across
five acres of manicured lawns, fountains and
flowerbeds, and on a clear day you can catch
peeks of downtown and Mt Hood. Over 500
rose varieties grow in the permanent gardens, including many old and rare varieties.
From April through September the scent and
colors are intoxicating. Call ahead for tours.

Japanese Garden

GARDENS

(Map p201; ☑503-223-1321; www.japanesegarden.
com; 611 SW Kingston Ave; adult/child $9.50/6.75;
⊙noon-7pm Mon, 10am-7pm Tue-Sun) Just uphill from the roses lies this tranquil, formal
garden. The grounds encompass 5.5 acres of
tumbling water, koi ponds, ornamental cherry trees, a ceremonial teahouse (no drinks
served!) and a sand garden. Tours are available, and hours are limited in winter.

Oregon Zoo

ZOO

(Map p201; ☑503-226-1561; www.oregon
zoo.org; 4001 SW Canyon Rd; adult/child
$10.50/7.50; ⊙8am-6pm May 15-Sep 15; 🐾) In

Downtown Portland

Top Sights

NW 23rd A2
Pearl District D2
Pioneer Courthouse Square E5
Portland Art Museum D5
Saturday Market F4

Sights

1 Chinatown Gates F3
2 Classical Chinese Garden F3
3 In Good Taste D3
4 Jamison Square Fountain D2
5 Japanese-American Historical Plaza F3
6 Mill Ends Park F5
7 Museum of Contemporary Craft E3
8 New Market Theater F4
9 Oregeon Historical Society D5
10 Pioneer Courthouse E5
11 Portland Building E5
12 Portland State University C6
13 Salmon Street Springs Fountain F6
14 Skidmore Fountain F4
15 Tom McCall Waterfront Park F5

Sleeping

16 Ace Hotel D4
17 Benson Hotel E4
18 Governor Hotel D4
19 Heathman Hotel D5
20 Hotel deLuxe C4
21 Hotel Fifty F5
22 Hotel Lucia E4
23 Hotel Modera D6
24 Hotel Monaco E4
25 Hotel Vintage Plaza E4
26 Inn at Northrup Station B1
27 Mark Spencer Hotel D4
28 Nines E5
29 Northwest Portland Hostel C3

Eating

30 Andina C3
31 Café Nell B2
Clyde Common .... (see 16)
32 Higgins D6
33 Irving Street Kitchen D2
34 Jake's Famous Crawfish D4
35 Kenny & Zuke's Delicatessen D4
36 Laurelwood Public House & Brewery A2
37 Little Big Burger D3
38 Lovejoy Bakers D2
39 Mother's Bistro F4
Nong's Khao Man Gai .... (see 43)
40 Paley's Place B1
41 Silk D3
42 Voodoo Donuts F4
43 Ziba's Pitas D4

Drinking

44 Barista D2
45 BridgePort Brewpub C1
Departure Restaurant & Lounge .... (see 28)
46 Deschutes Brewery D3
47 Gilt Club E3
48 Saucebox E4
49 Thirst Wine Bar F7

Entertainment

50 Arlene Schnitzer Concert Hall D5
51 Artists Repertory Theatre C4
52 Berbati's Pan F4
53 Cinema 21 .... B2
54 Crystal Ballroom C4
55 Dante's F4
56 Darcelle XV F3
57 Embers E3
58 Gerding Theater D3
59 Hobo's F3
60 Jimmy Mak's D3
61 Keller Auditorium E6
62 Mission Theater C3
63 Silverado F4

Shopping

64 Canoe D4
65 Columbia Sportswear D5
66 Gilt Jewelry A2
67 Seaplane A2

summer, ride the Zoo Train from the rose gardens to this excellent zoo. There's a primate house, a 'penguinarium' and plenty of specialty exhibits. Enclosures are spacious and semi-natural, and big-name music concerts take place on the zoo's lawns in summer.

Portland Audubon Society
BIRD REHABILITATION CENTER
(503-292-6855; www.audubonportland.org; 5151 NW Cornell Rd; store 10am-6pm Mon-Sat, 10am-5pm Sun, trails open dawn-dusk) Nestled in a gulch beside Forest Park. Visit the bookstore and wildlife rehabilitation cen-

ter, then walk along 4 miles of forested trails in the nature sanctuary.

Washington Park PARK
(Map p201) This enormous park complex, which includes the city's zoo, rose gardens and an arboretum, is perched on the slopes of the West Hills.

FREE **Hoyt Arboretum** GARDEN
(Map p201; ☑503-865-8733; www. hoytarboretum.org; 4000 SW Fairview Blvd; ☺visitor center 9am-4pm Mon-Fri & 9am-3pm Sat, park 6am-10pm) Twelve miles of trails wind through this 187-acre ridgetop garden above the zoo. It's home to over 1000 species of both native and exotic trees, and offers easy walks any time of year.

Portland Children's Museum MUSEUM
(Map p201; ☑503-223-6500; www.portlandcm. org; 4015 SW Canyon Rd; admission $8; ☺9am-5pm; ⊞) A great place to entertain the kids.

World Forestry Center
FORESTRY INTERPRETATION CENTER
(Map p201; ☑503-228-1367; www.worldforestry. org; 4033 SW Canyon Rd; adult/child $8/5; ☺10am-5pm; ⊞) Informs the public about the importance of the world's forests.

NORTHWEST
When Portlanders talk about the Northwest, they are referring to the attractive neighborhood surrounding NW 21st and 23rd Aves, north of W Burnside St. The residential heart of late-19th-century Portland, this area hums with street life.

Fashionable NW 23rd Ave brims with clothing boutiques, home decor shops and cafés. Restaurants – including some of Portland's finest – lie mostly along NW 21st Ave. This is a great neighborhood for strolling, window-shopping and people-watching. Parking is tough but not impossible.

Just east of Northwest, the **Pearl District** (Map p204) is an old industrial precinct that has transformed itself into Portland's swankiest neighborhood. Warehouses have been converted to fancy lofts commanding some of the highest real estate prices in Oregon. It's a great place to walk around, checking out upscale boutiques, trendy restaurants and Portland's highest concentration of art galleries. Every first Thursday of each month, many galleries extend their evening hours and show off new exhibits.

Be sure to visit the **Museum of Contemporary Craft** (Map p204; ☑503-223-2654; www.museumofcontemporarycraft.org; 724 NW Davis St; adult/senior $3/2; ☺11am-6pm Tue-Sat, to 8pm 1st Thu of every month) with a fine, growing collection of excellent regionally made crafts – especially ceramics.

The Pearl is bordered by NW 9th Ave, NW 14th Ave, W Burnside St and NW

PORTLAND: A BRIEF ORIENTATION

Portland is not a difficult place to get around, but there are a few things you should know.

Portland lies just a few miles south of the Washington border; it's about 15 minutes from the border metropolis of Vancouver Washington (note: This is a very different city from Vancouver BC, in Canada). It's also way inland, about a 1½-hour drive from the Pacific Coast.

The Willamette River flows through the center of town, dividing the city into east and west. Burnside St divides north from south, organizing the city into four quadrants: Northwest, Southwest, Northeast and Southeast. Make sure you understand this, as the same address could exist on both NE Davis St and NW Davis St, which are on opposite sides of the river!

(There's also North Portland, which oddly enough is more to the west of NE Portland, but many tourists don't make it this far.)

Northwest and Southwest Portland include downtown, historic Old Town, the chic postindustrial Pearl District and exclusive West Hills. Close to downtown but across the river is the Lloyd District, an extension of downtown that's anchored by a glass-towered convention center and a big shopping mall.

Northeast and Southeast Portland are mostly tree-lined, late-19th-century residential neighborhoods, each with its own trendy cluster of shops and restaurants. Popular commercial streets include N Mississippi Ave, NE Alberta St, SE Hawthorne Blvd and SE Division St. Sellwood is furthest south and is a pretty neighborhood with antique stores and yuppies.

Lovejoy St, though it's creeping northward toward the river.

NORTHEAST

Most of Portland's east side is residential, but just across the Willamette River the modern Lloyd District is like an extension of downtown. Here lies the nation's first full-blown shopping mall, **Lloyd Center** (Map p208; ☎503-282-2511; 2201 Lloyd Center), along with the twin-glass-tower **Oregon Convention Center** (Map p208; ☎503-235-7575; www.oregoncc.org; 777 NE MLK Jr Blvd) and the **Rose Garden Arena** (Map p208;

East Portland

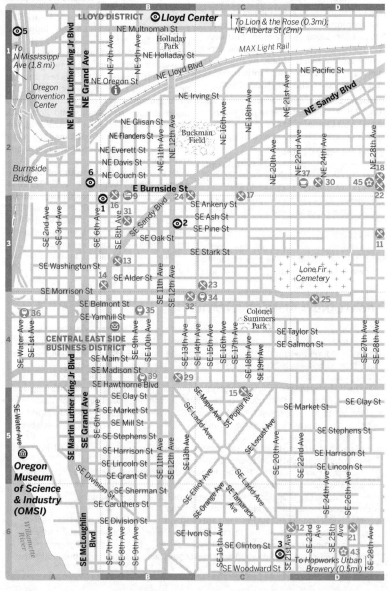

503-235-8771; www.rosequarter.com; 1 Center Crt), home of the Trail Blazers (p226).

Further up the Willamette, N Mississippi Ave has experienced an amazing revival in the past few years. Run-down buildings have been transformed into trendy shops, cafés and restaurants – with the main an-

chor being the **ReBuilding Center** (Map p201; 503-331-1877; 3625 N Mississippi Ave; www.rebuildingcenter.org; 9am-6pm Mon-Fri, 10am-5pm Sun), a cool recycling warehouse full of donated housing materials where you can find nearly anything building-related. Amnesia Brewing (p223), which makes excellent beer, is also based here.

Northeast of Mississippi, creatively spunky NE Alberta St (Map p201) is another success story. The stretch between NE 15th and NE 33rd Aves has revamped itself from a ribbon of vacant buildings, dubious bars and drug dealing into one of Portland's hippest streets. Despite the gentrification, it's still ethnically diverse and home to small art galleries, boutiques, studios, bars and cafés. Don't miss the summertime art walk/street party that takes place every last Thursday of the month – it's a hoot.

SOUTHEAST

Southeast is laced through with several trendy streets and good walking parks. The corner of E Burnside and 28th Ave boasts a few blocks' worth of wine bars, fine restaurants and cafés. Nearby is pretty **Laurelhurst Park** (Map p208), with towering conifers and a lake. To the south is SE Belmont St (between 28th and 35th Sts), with its own stretch of casual eateries, bars and shops.

For a dose of hippie-hipster culture, visit the bohemian SE Hawthorne Blvd (between 30th and 50th Aves). It's a dynamic string of bookstores, cutesy shops, vintage clothing stores, brewpubs and cafés. You're almost guaranteed to be accosted by panhandlers or political activists; to escape them, head east to **Mt Tabor Park**, a small extinct volcano that has great walking trails and good city views. Nearby is also Division St, another stretch of popular restaurants and shops surrounded by residential neighborhoods.

Finally, way to the south lies Sellwood, an old working-class neighborhood known for its antique stores.

Oregon Museum of Science & Industry
MUSEUM

(OMSI; Map p208; 503-797-4000; www.omsi.edu; 1945 SE Water St; adult/child $12/9; 9:30am-7pm mid-Jun–Aug, varied otherwise;) This excellent museum offers hands-on science exhibits for kids, along with other temporary exhibits. There's also an Omnimax theater, planetarium shows and a submarine tour (all separate charge). Parking is $2.

Crystal Springs Rhododendron Garden
GARDENS
(Map p201; ☑503-823-3640; 6015 SE 28th Ave; Tue & Wed admission free, Thu-Mon $3; ⊙dawn-dusk) To the south is the 9.5-acre garden near Reed College. Its large, beautiful grounds are covered with more than 2000 full-grown rhododendrons and azaleas and a large lagoon; peak bloom is late April.

Oaks Bottom Wildlife Refuge
WILDLIFE REFUGE
Located in Sellwood, this large wetland has a nearby bike path and good bird-watching.

FREE **Oaks Amusement Park**
AMUSEMENT PARK
(☑503-233-5777; www.oakspark.com; 7805 SE Oaks Park Way; ride bracelets $11.75-14.75; 🚼)
Sellwood attraction popular with families.

🏃 Activities

Hiking

Forest Park
PARK
(Map p201) With over 5000 acres under its belt, this is the USA's largest park within city limits. There are more than 70 miles of trails for hikers, runners and dog-walkers, and some excellent fire roads for cyclists. The **Wildwood Trail** starts at the Hoyt Arboretum and winds through 30 miles of forest, with many spur trails allowing for loop hikes. Some other trailheads into For-

est Park begin at the western ends of NW Thurman and NW Upshur Sts.

Tryon Creek State Park
STATE PARK

(☑503-636-9886; 11321 SW Terwilliger Blvd) Out past Lewis & Clark College, in Southwest Portland. This verdant 670-acre forest offers a nature center, streamside wildlife and 8 miles of trails, including a 3-mile paved bike path. Late March brings wondrous displays of trillium, a wild marsh lily.

Cycling

Portland has been voted the USA's top bike-friendly city, and also boasts the highest percentage of bicycle commuters. For you, this means that great trails for both road and mountain bikes exist, including the fine **Springwater Corridor**. It heads from near the Oregon Museum of Science & Industry (p209) all the way to the suburb of Boring – over 21 miles long, though until a connector is finished you'll have to pedal a few blocks of Sellwood's pleasant residential streets.

Mountain bikers shouldn't miss **Leif Erikson Dr**, a great old dirt logging road leading 11 miles into Forest Park and offering occasional peeks over the city. Most hiking trails are off-limits to bikes, so please don't ride them.

For scenic farm country, head to **Sauvie Island** (p213), 10 miles northwest of downtown Portland. This island, the largest in the Columbia River, is prime cycling land – it's flat, has relatively little traffic and much of it is a wildlife refuge.

Try to snag a free *Portland by Bicycle* or *Bike There!* map from a visitor center or a bike shop; both detail friendly bike streets and trails.

For bicycle rentals, see p228. If you're a visiting cyclist and want to meet like-minded folk, check out Friendly Bike Guesthouse (p216). And for local bike news, see www.bikeportland.org.

Cycling events worth taking part in:

Bridge Pedal
CYCLING EVENT

(www.bridgepedal.com) Where thousands of Portlanders bike over bridges closed or partially closed to vehicular traffic; held in August.

Pedalpalooza
CYCLING FESTIVAL

(www.bikeportland.org) Two-week celebration in mid-June of the city's uniquely creative bike culture, including a naked ride.

Sunday Parkways
CYCLING EVENT

(www.portlandsundayparkways.org) A few times a year, Portland closes off certain streets to motor vehicles so families can ride safely together and everyone enjoys entertainment that gets set up.

On the Water

Summer in Portland means finding cool things to do on hot days, and fortunately there's a few.

On hot days, visit the **Salmon Street Springs Fountain** (see p203) or the **Jamison Square Fountain** (Map p204; NW Johnson & 10th), both of which attract splashing kids as the mercury rises.

Matt Dishman Community Center
SWIMMING POOL

(☑503-823-3673; 77 NE Knott St; admission $2.50-4, depending on age) Swimmers should grab their suits and beeline to the indoor pool here. Call for hours. It's just north of the Lloyd District.

US Grant Park
SWIMMING POOL

(☑503-823-3674; cnr NE 33rd Ave & US Grant St; admission $2.50-4) For an outdoor experience, try the pool here. Call for hours.

North Clackamas Aquatic Park
AQUATIC PARK

(☑503-557-7873; www.co.clackamas.or.us/ncprd/aquatic; 7300 SE Harmony Rd, Milwaukie; adult $10, child $5-7) About 10 miles south of downtown Portland are these water slides and indoor wave pool. There's also an outdoor volleyball court and climbing wall, along with adults-only hot tub. Hours vary widely, so call ahead.

Portland Kayak Company
KAYAK TOURS

(☑503-459-4050; www.portlandrivercompany.com) Kayak tours around Ross Island in the Willamette River. Rentals too.

Scappoose Bay Kayaking
KAYAK TOURS, RENTALS

(☑503-397-2161, 877-272-3353; www.scappoosebaykayaking.com; 57420 Old Portland Rd) To get away from the city, head to serene Scappoose Bay, 25 miles northwest of downtown Portland. Tours and rentals.

Spa Services & Massage

These are only a few spas in town; those listed below all offer massage services. For treatment-oriented 'yoga massage' bodywork, check out www.elleesyoga.com.

Dragontree Spa
SPA

(☑503-221-4123; www.thedragontree.com; 2768 NW Thurman St, Northwest District) Hedonism on earth, with a full range of spa services in gorgeous surroundings.

PINCH THOSE PENNIES – PORTLAND FOR FREE

Dead broke, or just don't feel like spending a fortune?

Click on **Around the Sun** (www.aroundthesunblog.com) for free things going on around Portland. Plenty of events in the city don't require admission; check www.travelportland.com/event_calendar for more.

Here are some things to do around Portland for free (or cheap):

» **International Rose Test Garden** (p205)

» **Hoyt Arboretum** (p207)

» **Forest Park** (p210)

» **Crystal Springs Rhododendron Garden** (p210) Tuesday and Wednesday free, otherwise $3.

» **Saturday Market** (p205)

» **Powell's City of Books** (p227)

» **Portland Audubon Society** (p206)

» **Portland Art Museum** (p203) Free admission from 5pm to 8pm on the last Friday of each month.

» **Portland Children's Museum** (p207) Free admission from 4pm to 8pm on the first Friday of each month.

» **Oregon Zoo** (p205) Admission only $4 on the second Tuesday of each month.

» **Oregon Museum of Science & Industry** (OMSI; p209) Admission only $2 on the first Sunday of each month.

» **World Forestry Center** (p207) Admission only $2 on the first Wednesday of each month.

» **Free Rail Zone** (aka Fareless Square; p228)

Loyly SPA
(Map p208; ☑503-236-6850; www.loyly.net; 2713 SE 21st Ave) Scandinavian-style steam and sauna facilities, plus Swedish massage.

Common Ground SPA
(☑503-238-1065; www.cgwc.org; 5010 NE 33rd) Best for its large, outdoor soaking pool in a Zen-like patio.

≈ Courses

If you're in the area for while and want to take a specific class, consider **Portland Community College** (www.pcc.edu), which offers courses on nearly anything you can think of.

In Good Taste COOKING
(Map p204; ☑503-248-2015; www.ingoodtastestore.com; 231 NW 11th Ave) Want to cook better? Then point your spatula here for cheese making, knife-wielding and wild mushroom cooking courses (among many others).

Caprial & John's Kitchen COOKING
(Map p208; ☑503-239-8771; www.caprialandjohnskitchen.com; 609 SE Ankeny) Run by a couple who have their own PBS cooking show.

Elements Glass GLASS BLOWING
(☑503-228-0575; www.elementsglass.com; 1979 NW Vaughn St) Glass-artist wannabes can take a beginners course at Portland's largest glassblowing shop, just north of the Pearl District.

Mazamas ADVENTURE CLUB
(☑503-227-2345; www.mazamas.org; 527 SE 43rd Ave) Plug into the outdoor-adventure community with courses on mountaineering, rock climbing and Nordic skiing, among others, run by this educational organization.

FH Steinbart Co BREWING
(Map p208; ☑503-232-8793; www.fhsteinbart.com; 234 SE 12th Ave) A store which offers seasonal classes, along with a great selection of home-brewing equipment.

820 Lounge BAR
(☑503-284-5518; www.mintand820.com; 816 N Russell St, Elliot District) Learn to make avocado daiquiris with Lucy Brennan, voted one of America's top 10 bartenders by www.playboy.com. Classes cost $75 per person and take place monthly.

Offbeat Portland

Portland is certainly eccentric – 'Keep Portland Weird' is the city's unofficial motto. For more oddball museums than those listed below, check www.hiddenportland.com.

Vaux Swifts BIRDWATCHING
(http://audubonportland.org/local-birding/swift watch) Every September, tens of thousands of these little birdies roost in Chapman Elementary School's old brick chimney. Seeing them spiral down in their multitudes, right at sunset, is an unforgettable sight.

Pdx Adult Soapbox Derby SOAPBOX DERBY
(www.soapboxracer.com; ☉mid-late August) Great spectator fun, where homemade, non-motorized vehicles (from Mr Potato Head models to aerodynamic speedsters) swoosh down Mt Tabor's sinewy road, driven by costumed contestants.

Trek in the Park THEATER PERFORMANCE
(www.atomic-arts.org; Woodlawn Park at cnr Claremont & Oneonta; ☉Sat & Sun Jul) Are you a Star Trek fan visiting Portland on a weekend in July? Then you *must not* miss Trek in the Park, which features a local theater company putting on a famous Star Trek episode from the original series. It's well-done and hilarious; go early to score a good seat.

Voodoo Doughnut DOUGHNUT SHOP
(Map p204; ☑503-241-4704; www.voodoodoughnut.com; 22 SW 3rd Ave; ☉24hr) There's nothing quite like this standing-room-only, downtown hole-in-the-wall (pun intended).

It bakes up creative, sickly sweet treats – go for the surprisingly good bacon maple bar or the 'voodoo doll' (shaped like a...well, yes). Also at 1501 NE Davis.

Mill Ends Park MINIATURE PARK
(Map p204) Having the largest park (Forest Park) within city limits perhaps isn't an oddity, but having the smallest one might be. Mills End Park – located on the median strip at SW Naito Parkway and Taylor St – is a circle of green 24in in diameter (it's the reputed home to leprechauns).

FREE **Stark's Vacuum Museum** MUSEUM
(Map p208; ☑503-232-4101; www.starks.com/about_us/vacuum; 107 NE Grand Ave; ☉8am-7pm Mon-Fri, 9am-4pm Sat) Located in a vacuum cleaner store (no surprise there). It'll really suck you in.

☞ Tours

For kayak tours, see p211.

EverGreen Escapes ECO TOURS
(☑503-252-1931, 866-203-7603; www.evergreenescapes.com) Half- and full-day tours and 'experiences' of Portland and its surrounding regions, using biodiesel vehicles.

Portland Spirit CRUISES
(☑503-224-3900, 800-224-3901; www.portlandspirit.com) Tour Portland from the water; cruises offer sightseeing, historical narratives and/or meal combinations.

Portland Walking Tours WALKING TOURS
(☑503-774-4522; www.portlandwalkingtours.com) Food, chocolate, underground and even ghost-oriented tours.

OFF THE BEATEN PATH: SAUVIE ISLAND

About a 20-minute drive from downtown is Sauvie Island (www.sauvieisland.org), an agricultural oasis providing an excellent break from Portland's bustle. Its flat, 12-mile country-road loop also makes it a popular place for weekend cyclists.

The 12,000-acre **Sauvie Island Wildlife Area** includes a wetland sanctuary for thousands of migratory ducks, geese, tundra swans, bald eagles and Sandhill cranes. Permanent residents include peregrine falcons, great blue herons, foxes and beavers. The refuge is closed from October to mid-April and requires a $7 parking permit; get one from the **Fish & Wildlife Office** (☑503-621-3488; 18330 NW Sauvie Island Rd) or an island store.

During summer, don't miss the opportunity to pick strawberries, peaches, corn and flowers – try **Kruger's** or **Sauvie Island Farms**, both on NW Sauvie Island Rd. Plant lovers can head to the excellent, 2-acre **Cistus Nursery** (22711 NW Gillihan Rd), which specializes in Mediterranean and Southern Hemisphere plants.

Beach-heads should visit **Walton Beach**, a decent stretch of sand on the island's eastern side. Leashed dogs are allowed, but fires and camping are not. The pricey $7 parking permit applies here too. Nudies can head towards **Collins Beach** at the northern end, past the pavement.

Pdx Run Tours RUNNING TOURS
(☑845-206-8227; www.pdxruntours.com)
A great use of time: get exercise and a
guided tour of Portland at the same time.

Portland Bicycle Tours BICYCLE TOURS
(☑503-360-6815; www.portlandbicycletours.
com) See the City of Roses (and its surrounding areas) on two wheels.

Forktown FOOD TOURS
(☑503-701-7249; www.forktown.com) Experience Stumptown from your taste buds'
point of views.

⭐ Festivals & Events

There's some sort of festival in Portland
nearly every summer weekend; even each
neighborhood seems to have its own. See the
visitor center for a complete list of events.

Portland International Film Festival
FILM FESTIVAL
(☑503-221-1156; www.nwfilm.org) Oregon's
biggest film event highlights almost 100
films from over 30 countries, screened in
several movie houses downtown. It's held
mid to late February.

Portland Rose Festival ROSE FESTIVAL
(☑503-227-2681; www.rosefestival.org) Late
May to early June. Rose-covered floats,
dragon-boat races, a riverfront carnival,
fireworks, roaming packs of sailors and
the crowning of a Rose Queen all make
this Portland's biggest celebration.

Queer Pride Celebration GAY CELEBRATION
(☑503-295-9788; www.pridenw.org) Keep
Portland queer: enjoy a kick-off party,
take a cruise or join the parade along
with Dykes on Bikes. Held in mid-June.

Waterfront Blues Festival BLUES FESTIVAL
(www.waterfrontbluesfest.com) Enjoy top
blues acts, music and partying at Waterfront Park in early July; proceeds go to
the Oregon Food Bank.

Oregon Brewers Festival BEER FESTIVAL
(☑503-778-5917; www.oregonbrewfest.com) In
the last full weekend in July you can quaff
microbrews from near and far in Waterfront Park – everyone's happy and even
nondrinkers have fun. Plenty of food stalls.

Bite of Oregon FOOD FESTIVAL
(www.biteoforegon.com) All the food you
could think of eating, much of it from
great local restaurants – and some of it
from Portland's now-famous food carts.
Good microbrews too. Held early August,
it benefits Special Olympics Oregon.

Art in the Pearl ART FESTIVAL
(☑503-722-9017; www.artinthepearl.com) On
Labor Day weekend some 130 carefully
selected artists come together to show
and sell their fine works. Plenty of food
and live music, plus kids' activities.

Holiday Ale Festival BEER FESTIVAL
(☑503-252-9899; www.holidayale.com) Takes
place under covered tents in Pioneer
Square in early December, but you have
to be 21 and over. Seasonal beers are a
highlight, and there's mead too.

🛏 Sleeping

Tariffs listed are for the summer season,
when reservations are a good idea. Prices at
top-end hotels depend on occupancy, so are
variable. Ask about discounts; AAA membership often gets you 10% off.

Portland has plenty of chain hotels and
budget motels, though their locations won't
all be downtown. And if you're a McMenamins fan, keep your eye out in 2011 for the
upcoming Crystal Hotel, at 303 SW 12th St.

Parking costs listed are per day.

DOWNTOWN & NORTHWEST

TOP CHOICE **Ace Hotel** BOUTIQUE HOTEL $$
(Map p204; ☑503-228-2277; www.ace
hotel.com; 1022 SW Stark St; d with shared/
private bathroom from $95/140; ❁❋@) Cur-
rently Portland's trendiest place to sleep
is this unique hotel fusing classic, indus-
trial, minimalist and retro styles together.
From the photo booth and sofa lounge in its
lobby to the recycled fabrics and furniture
in its rooms, the Ace makes the warehouse
feel work. A Stumptown coffee shop on the
premises adds even more comfort. Parking
costs $20.

Nines BOUTIQUE HOTEL $$$
(Map p204; ☑877-229-9995; www.thenines.com;
525 SW Morrison St; r from $209; ❁❋@🛜) For
the ultimate in uber-fancy celebrity-like
luxury, there's the Nines. Take the elevator to reception on the 8th floor, where the
huge lobby rises six stories and is flooded in
light from the glass roof. And don't miss the
Departure Lounge, on the 15th floor, a restaurant that features an outdoor patio with
outstanding city and river views. Rooms are
equivalently nice, of course; parking costs
$32. Toto, we're not in Portland anymore.

📝 **Hotel Vintage Plaza** HOTEL $$
(Map p204; ☑503-228-1212, 800-263-2305;
www.vintageplaza.com; 422 SW Broadway; r from

Portland is a great place both to raise children and visit with them, and sunny week-ends mean the city's lush parks, shopping streets and farmers markets are filled with parents pushing baby strollers and dragging toddlers. So if you're looking to entertain kids here, there are some excellent options to consider.

The **Oregon Zoo** (p205) is a perennially popular destination; don't miss 'zoolights' during the holiday season, when the zoo becomes a winter wonderland filled with lit-up trees and animal figures. Parents also love the nearby **Portland Children's Museum** (p207), a great place to keep the kids busy with hands-on learning activities and exhibits. Next door, **World Forestry Center** (p207) offers similar experiences but with a woodsy twist.

Another big family spot is the **Oregon Museum of Science & Industry** (p209), which combines fun with learning and has grown-up attractions as well. For outdoor laughs, head south to the riverside **Oaks Amusement Park** (p210). There are dizzying rides, go-karts and a skating rink. Hours vary widely, so call or check the website.

Hot day? Get ideas from the On the Water section on p211.

Really great kid-friendly eateries include **Old Wives' Tales** (Map p208; 503-238-0470; 1300 E Burnside St; 8am-8pm Sun-Thu, till 9pm Fri & Sat), **Laurelwood Public House & Brewery** Sandy Branch (Map p204; 503-282-0622; 5115 NE Sandy Blvd); Kearney Branch (503-228-5553; 2327 NW Kearney St) and **Urban Grind Coffeehouse** (Map p208; 503-546-0649; 2214 NE Oregon St).

$139; For muted luxury there's this historic and tasteful hotel with a winery theme. Rooms are large, stylish and lovely; the king suites are huge at 700 sq ft, and some have large soaking tubs. Good restaurant, daily wine reception and pet friendly. It's a Kimpton, which means they do their part for the environment by recycling, using eco-friendly products and conserving resources. Parking costs $33 (hybrids pay half).

Inn at Northrup Station   BOUTIQUE HOTEL $$
(Map p204; 503-224-0543, 800-224-1180; www.northrupstation.com; 2025 NW Northrup St; r from $144;) Almost over the top with its bright color scheme and funky decor, this super-trendy hotel boasts huge artsy suites, many with patio or balcony, and all with kitchenettes or full kitchens. There's a cool rooftop patio with plants, and complimentary streetcar tickets are included (the streetcar runs just outside).

Hotel Lucia   BOUTIQUE HOTEL $$
(Map p204; 503-225-1717, 877-225-1717; www.hotellucia.com; 400 SW Broadway; r from $169;) Those seeking luxurious tranquility in busy downtown Portland should head to this minimalist hotel with limited color scheme (black and white are big here) and cutting-edge artwork in the lobby. There are iPod docking stations and flat-screen TVs, and plush robes come standard. Parking costs $30.

Hotel Monaco   BOUTIQUE HOTEL $$
(Map p204; 503-222-0001, 888-207-2201; www.monaco-portland.com; 506 SW Washington St; r from $179;) The lavishly loud lobby is decorated with Asian wallpaper, sensual furniture, patterned carpeting and brightly painted walls. The spacious rooms are a bit less whimsical – though still somewhat extravagant in their decoration. Wine reception in the afternoons, and supremely pet friendly – a lab roams the premises and goldfish are available for company. Parking costs $33.

Governor Hotel   HOTEL $$$
(Map p204; 503-224-3400, 800-554-3456; www.governorhotel.com; 614 SW 11th Ave; r from $199;) Those not looking for newfangled frills will likely appreciate the Governor, an old-fashioned hotel with grand lobby and spacious, classy executive-style rooms. For even more hedonistic comfort, go for the penthouse suites with glamorous terrace overlooking the city ($349). Parking costs $27.

Mark Spencer Hotel   HOTEL $$
(Map p204; 503-224-3293, 800-548-3934; www.markspencer.com; 409 SW 11th Ave; d from $129;) A no-nonsense downtown option is this simple yet slightly refined choice, hosting spacious, good rooms, all with kitchens. There's complimentary tea with cookies in the afternoon, and evening

wine receptions. Don't be afraid of the alleyway-like entrance – they're friendly inside. Parking costs $16.

Northwest Portland Hostel
HOSTEL $

(Map p204; ☑503-241-2783; 425 NW 18th Ave; dm $22-25, d $54-74; ✆❄@◎⊚) Perfectly located between the Pearl District and NW 21st and 23rd Aves, this friendly and clean hostel takes up four old buildings and features plenty of common areas (including a small deck) and bike rentals. Dorms are spacious and private rooms can be as nice as in hotels, though all share outside bathrooms. Non-HI members pay $3 extra.

Hotel Modera
BOUTIQUE HOTEL $$

(Map p204; ☑503-484-1084, 877-484-1084; www.hotelmodera.com; 515 SW Clay; r from $149; ✆❄@◎⊚) New, slick and almost futuristic-looking hotel with attractive front courtyard boasting a living wall of native plants. Hip rooms with huge glass walls. Parking costs $27.

Hotel Fifty
HOTEL $$

(Map p204; ☑503-221-0711, 877-505-7220; www.hotelfifty.com; 50 SW Morrison St; r from $149; ✆❄@◎⊚) Large contemporary hotel near the river with sleek, modern rooms; splash out and get a river view for a few more bucks. Good services; parking costs $20.

Heathman Hotel
HOTEL $$

(Map p204; ☑503-241-4100, 800-551-0011; www.heathmanhotel.com; 1001 SW Broadway; r from $209; ❄@⊚) A Portland institution, the Heathman has top-notch services and one of the best restaurants in the city. Rooms are elegant, stylish and luxurious. Parking costs $29.

Hotel deLuxe
HOTEL $$

(Map p204; ☑503-219-2094, 866-895-2094; www.hoteldeluxeportland.com; 729 SW 15th Ave; r from $189; ✆❄◎⊚) Historic hotel with old Hollywood movie theme and tasteful, modernized rooms. Get a suite for more space and ask for an upper-floor exterior room if you want views. Parking costs $25.

Benson Hotel
HOTEL $$$

(Map p204; ☑503-228-2000, 800-663-1144; www.bensonhotel.com; 309 SW Broadway; r $190-850; ❄⊚) The lobby is at this decadent hotel is lined with walnut and filled with huge chandeliers, marble floors and an elegant bar-restaurant. Some rooms can be small. Parking costs $29.

NORTHEAST & SOUTHEAST

TOP CHOICE Kennedy School
HOTEL $$

(☑503-249-3983, 888-249-3983; www.mcmenamins.com; 5736 NE 33rd Ave; d $109-130; ✆⊚) Portland's most unusual institution, this former elementary school is now home to a hotel (sleep in old classrooms!), restaurant with great garden courtyard, several bars, a microbrewery and movie theater. Guests can use the soaking pool for free, and the whole school is decorated in McMenamins' funky art style – mosaics, fantasy paintings and historical photographs. It's a unique stay and very Portland.

Jupiter Hotel
BOUTIQUE MOTEL $$

(Map p208; ☑503-230-9200, 877-800-0004; www.jupiterhotel.com; 800 E Burnside St; r $104-129 Sun-Thu, $124-159 Fri & Sat; ✆❄⊚) The hippest hotel in town, this slick, remodeled motel is within walking distance of downtown and right next to Doug Fir, a top-notch live music venue. Standard rooms are tiny – go for the Metropolitan instead, and ask for a pad away from the bamboo patio if you're more into sleeping than staying up late. Kitchenettes and bike rentals available; check in after midnight for a discount.

Clinton St Guesthouse
GUESTHOUSE $

(☑503-234-8752; www.clintonstreetguesthouse.com; 4220 SE Clinton St; d $70-105; ✆❄⊚) Four simple but beautiful rooms (two with shared bathroom) are on offer in this lovely Craftsman house in a residential neighborhood. Furnishings are elegant, the linens luxurious, and your hosts gracious. Located in a great residential neighborhood with many restaurants within walking distance. Breakfast is included.

Friendly Bike Guesthouse
GUESTHOUSE $

(☑503-799-2615; www.friendlybikeguesthouse.com; 4039 N Williams Ave; rooms $76; ✆⊚) Smack on N Williams, one of Portland's main cycling thoroughfares, is this unique bike-oriented guesthouse. Rooms all share bathrooms in this pretty house, and there are laundry facilities, secure lockups for your ride and even a basement workshop for tune-ups. Shared rooms available ($36 to $45 per bed/bunk). It's all so very Portland.

Bluebird Guesthouse
GUESTHOUSE $

(Map p208; ☑503-238-4333; www.bluebirdguesthouse.com; 3517 SE Division St; r $60-95; ✆❄@⊚) Nicely located on a lively section of SE Division, this pleasant guesthouse is in a beautiful old arts-and-crafts house with country kitchen and small grassy backyard.

A ROSE, BY ANY OTHER NAME...

Portland seems to have endless nicknames; here are a few:

» **City of Roses** Our lovely roses do well here.

» **PDX** Portland's airport code.

» **Stumptown** Many stumps were created to make this town.

» **Bridge City** We have 10 bridges over the Willamette!

» **River City** Referring to the Willamette, not the nearby Columbia.

» **Beervana** Local microbrews are the tops.

» **Rip City** Coined by a sportscaster during a Trailblazer game.

» **P-Town** It's shorter than Portland.

» **Puddletown** All that rain!

» **Little Beirut** Courtesy of George H W Bush, during his visit here.

There are seven tasteful rooms, two with private bathroom, and they're all different sizes. Plenty of good restaurants and shops are within walking distance.

Lion & the Rose   B&B **$$$**
(☑503-287-9245, 800-955-1647; www.lionrose. com; 1810 NE 15th Ave; d $199-219; ❤✳@☎) Located at the edge of upscale Irvington, this turreted Queen Anne mansion is almost over the top with its fine antiques and flowery decoration. All six rooms come with private bathroom, and the large basement apartment has a kitchenette. This gay-friendly place is close to shops, bars, cafés and the MAX. Weekday rates are $20 cheaper, and rates are discounted November through April.

White Eagle   HOTEL **$**
(☑503-282-6810; www.mcmenamins.com; 836 N Russell St, Elliot District; dm $45-50, d $50-65; ❤☎) In a small but hip industrial part of town is this old renovated hotel, another in the McMenamins empire. Nightly live rock-and-roll music creeps up from the downstairs saloon – where you check in – so it's easy to rock into the night. Then just stumble upstairs into one of the 11 spartan but lovely rooms (all with sinks-in-room and shared bathrooms down the hall) and relish in your great-value deal.

Hawthorne Portland Hostel HOSTEL **$**
(Map p208; ☑503-236-3380, 866-447-3031; www.portlandhostel.org; 3031 SE Hawthorne Blvd; dm member/nonmember $24/27, d $55/61; ❤@☎) This eco-friendly hostel has good vibes and a great Hawthorne location. The private rooms are good and dorms spacious; all share outside bathrooms. There

are summertime open-mic nights in the grassy backyard, and bike rentals available. Very environmentally conscious; composts and recycles, uses rainwater to flush toilets, and has a nice eco-roof. Discounts to those bike touring.

✖ Eating

Portland has become nationally recognized for its food scene, with dozens of young, top-notch chefs pushing the boundaries of ethnic and regional cuisines. Casual clothes are acceptable even at higher-end places, where reservations are a good idea. Fast-food lovers should consider looking up the various branches of **Burgerville** (local, seasonal ingredients; www.burgerville.com) and **Laughing Planet** (vegetarian-friendly burritos; www.laughingplanetcafe.com), but the city's best fast food is dished up at the more than 500 food carts.

DOWNTOWN & NORTHWEST
Office workers and students flock to pods of food carts in the area: SW 5th Ave and SW Stark; SW Alder between 10th and 11th Aves; SW 3rd between Washington and Stark; and SW 4th between Hall and College.

Ⓣ○ₚ‖ **Higgins** FRENCH-INFLUENCED **$$$**
꜀ₕₒᵢ꜀ₑ (Map p204; ☑503-222-9070; www.higgins .ypguides.net; 1239 SW Broadway; mains $20-30; ◷11:30am-midnight Mon-Fri, 4pm-midnight Sat & Sun) In 1994, chef/owner Greg Higgins opened the doors to one of Portland's groundbreaking restaurants. These days, Higgins feels more classically elegant than cutting edge, but still features French-inspired dishes using seasonal Northwest

TOP PORTLAND FOOD CARTS

Stumptown is famous – *really* famous – for its food carts (see p434). For a good guide see www.foodcartsportland.com; for some of the best, just read on.

Garden State (4237 N Mississippi St; www.gardenstatecart.com) Luscious meatball heroes; also at 7907 SE 13th.

Sugar Cube (4237 N Mississippi St; www.thesugarcubepdx.com) Insanely creative cupcakes, desserts, milkshakes...

Ziba's Pitas (Map p204; SW 9th Ave & SW Alder St; www.zibaspitas.com) Delicate, paper-thin, stuffed Bosnian pitas.

Nong's Khao Man Gai (Map p204; SW 10th & SW Alder St; www.khaomangai.com) Tender poached chicken with rice. That's it – and enough.

Grilled Cheese Grill (1027 NE Alberta Ave; www.grilledcheesegrill.com) Grilled cheese sandwiches served in an old school bus.

Koi Fusion (☑503-789-0848; www.koifusionpdx.com) Creative Asian fusion; call for the changing daily location.

Sip (3029 SE 21st; www.sipjuicecart.com) Fresh, organic and vegan juices, smoothies and even milkshakes.

Potato Champion (Map p208; SE 12th Ave & Hawthorne; www.potatochampion.com) Twice-fried fries and exotic dipping sauces

Whiffies (Map p208; SE 12th Ave & Hawthorne; www.whiffies.com) Sweet and savory, deep-fried pies.

ingredients. The beer list is the best in town; ask for pairing suggestions for any course.

Clyde Common   EUROPEAN **$$**
(Map p204; ☑503-228-3333; www.clydecommon.com; 1014 SW Stark; mains $10-23; ◷11:30am-midnight Mon-Thu, to 2am Fri & Sat, 5-10pm Sun) Attached to the hip Ace Hotel, this spot is Euro-bistro-meets-cool-Scandinavian-chic. Be ready for communal tables, where you'll dig into pork liver terrine, whole grilled dorade or tagliatelle with veggies. Great wines by the glass and unique cocktails, which are churned out from the bar by expert hands.

Lovejoy Bakers   BAKERY **$**
(Map p204; www.lovejoybakers.com; 939 NW 10th Ave; mains $8-11; ◷6am-6pm Mon-Wed, 6am-8pm Thu-Sun) An open, airy space fills with the sweet smells of fine baked goods. Fresh breads become memorable sandwiches, served alongside crisp salads and warming soups. An affordable dinner menu means mussels, cheese plates, fish, burgers and wines by the glass, or simply stop by for a croissant and coffee to start the day.

Kenny & Zuke's Delicatessen   JEWISH DELI **$**
(Map p204; www.kennyandzukes.com; 1038 SW Stark; mains $8-12; ◷8am-8pm Mon-Thu, 8am-9pm Fri-Sun) The only place in the city for real Jewish deli food: bagels, pickled her-ring, homemade pickles and latkes. But the real draw here is the house pastrami, which is cut to order and gently sandwiched in one of the best Reubens you'll ever eat. Bustles at breakfast.

Andina   PERUVIAN **$$**
(Map p204; ☑503-228-9535; www.andinarestaurant.com; 1314 NW Glisan; mains $19-33; ◷dinner Sun-Thu, to midnight Fri & Sat) A modern take on traditional Peruvian food produces delicious entrees like filet mignon topped with king oyster mushroom salsa and black beer sauce. Then there's the quinoa with beets, or mushrooms with truffle oil. If you're looking for lighter fare, hit the bar for tapas, great cocktails and live music.

Café Nell   AMERICAN **$$**
(Map p204; ☑503-295-6487; www.cafenell.com; 1987 NW Kearney; mains $9-21; ◷11am-10pm Mon-Fri, 9am-10pm Sat, 9am-2pm Sun) This little bistro in Nob Hill is both cozy and sophisticated. Large portions of comfort food range from breakfast omelets and oysters on the half shell to pot roast and grilled trout, while happy hour means classic cocktails, frites, soup and a cheese plate.

Little Big Burger   BURGERS **$**
(Map p204; www.littlebigburger.com; 122 NW 10th Ave; mains $4-8; ◷lunch & dinner) A simple six-

item menu takes fast food to the next level with mini burgers made from prime ingredients. Try a beef or veggie burger topped with cheddar, Swiss, chevre or blue cheese, with a side of truffled fries – then wash it down with a can of craft beer or a root-beer float. Heaven on earth.

Silk
VIETNAMESE **$$**

(Map p204; 503-248-2172; www.phovanrestaurant.com/silk; 1012 NW Glisan; mains $9-12; lunch & dinner Mon-Sat) Vietnamese-food lovers are in for a treat at this gorgeous Pearl District restaurant. Everything is fresh and delicious, from the banana blossom salad to claypot catfish to the beef noodle soup. Try the mango daiquiri too. Also at 3404 SE Hawthorne and 1919 SE 82nd, both with the old name (Pho Van) and a slightly less fancy menu.

Irving Street Kitchen
SOUTHERN **$$**

(Map p204; 503-343-9440; www.irvingstreetkitchen.com; 701 NW 13th Ave; mains $17-26; brunch Sat & Sun, dinner daily) Southern food goes upscale at this Pearl District haunt, which specializes in super crispy fried chicken, ham served with buttermilk biscuits and red pepper jelly, grits and gumbo. The wine list is notable, and save room for the butterscotch pudding served in Mason jars.

St Honoré Boulangerie
BAKERY-CAFÉ **$**

(www.sainthonorebakery.com; 2335 NW Thurman; light meals $5-10; 7am-8pm) Popular for its luscious breads and pastries, this modern-rustic bakery in the Northwest District also serves tasty panini sandwiches, vegetarian soups, seasonal salads and oven-fired pizzas. Try your luck at snagging a sidewalk table on a warm sunny day.

Jake's Famous Crawfish
AMERICAN SEAFOOD **$$$**

(Map p204; 503-226-1419; www.mccormickandschmicks.com; 401 SW 12th Ave; mains $17-32; 11:30am-10pm Mon-Thu, to midnight Fri & Sat, 3-10pm Sun) Saunter into this classic joint, reservation in hand. You'll need it – some of Portland's best seafood can be found here within an elegant old-time atmosphere. The oysters are divine, the crab cakes a revelation and the horseradish salmon your ticket into heaven. Come at 3pm for (cheap) happy hour.

NORTHEAST & SOUTHEAST

TOP CHOICE **Laurelhurst Market**
AMERICAN **$$$**

(503-206-3097; www.laurelhurstmarket.com; 3155 E Burnside St; mains $18-22; dinner) Hugely vegetarian-unfriendly is this hip and meaty spot, where grass-fed steaks, pork

219

PALEY'S PLACE

Paley's Place (Map p204; 503-243-2403; www.paleysplace.net; 1204 NW 21st Ave; mains $20-34; dinner), established by Vitaly and Kimberly Paley, is one of Portland's premiere restaurants, offering a creative blend of French and Pacific Northwest cuisines. Whether it's the duck confit, Kobe burger or veal sweetbreads, you can count on fresh ingredients, excellent service and a memorable experience. Reservations required.

chops, briskets and mussels frites (!) dominate the menu. Or try the popular and excellent bacon cheeseburger with white cheddar and aioli – yum. Just be prepared to wait; no reservations for parties under six. There's also a small butcher counter selling quality meats and great lunchtime sandwiches.

Bunk Sandwiches
SANDWICHES **$**

(Map p208; www.bunksandwiches.com; 621 SE Morrison St; mains $4-9; breakfast & lunch Mon-Sat) Leaving this specialty sandwich shop feeling greasy is a mandatory part of the experience. Not for low-fat lovers, these sandwiches combine great bread with delicious meats and require multiple napkins. Try the meatball parmigiana, the roast beef or anything with pork belly.

Beaker & Flask
NORTHWESTERN **$$**

(Map p208; 503-235-8180; www.beakerandflask.com; 720 SE Sandy Blvd; mains $12-21; 5pm-midnight Mon-Wed, to 1am Thu-Sat) Sure the name sounds bar-ish and the space, too, feels more like a modern lounge than a restaurant. But it's the food here that shines, from grilled rabbit or seared salmon to expertly prepared small plates of fried softshell crab or sweetbread succotash. The inventive drinks (and their names) aren't bad either: try the Comb Over or Daddy Issues.

Bamboo Sushi
SUSHI **$$**

(Map p208; 503-232-5255; www.bamboosushipdx.com; 310 SE 28th Ave; mains $9-13; dinner) Bamboo claims to be the first 'certified sustainable' sushi restaurant in the world, and this being Portland – we believe them. Eco-friend twist aside, it's hard to find fish that tastes this good, anywhere. And don't forget the cooked dished either, like the Alaskan black cod with smoked soy and roasted garlic glaze. Eating green never felt so good.

Toro Bravo
SPANISH $$

(☏503-281-4464; www.torobravopdx.com; 120 NE Russell St; mains $7-16; ☺dinner) Sure, you could order the burger here and be happy, but it's the endless list of tapas that should guide your choices; you'll want to try the radicchio salad, salt cod fritters and paella. Be prepared for a wait – this place has an enduring reputation for deliciousness.

S¿Por Qúe No? Taquería
MEXICAN $

(www.porquenotacos.com; 3524 N Mississippi Ave; tacos $3-4, mains $6.50-11; ☺lunch & dinner) Pricey for a taquería, but the ingredients are good, and so is the vibe. Great tacos, or try the Bryan's Bowl – essentially a tortilla-less burrito in a bowl – and down it with a pomegranate margarita. It's a tiny place, and the line often goes out the door. Another branch at 4635 Hawthorne has a funky back patio.

DOC
ITALIAN $$$

(☏503-946-8592; www.docpdx.com; 5519 NE 30th Ave; mains $18-24; ☺dinner Tue-Sat) Enter this tiny Northeast establishment and find yourself in the middle of the kitchen, a purposeful way to introduce you to an intimate dining experience that marries Northwest ingredients with simple Italian cooking. Expect tender pastas, perfectly cooked meats and a memorable cheese course. Splurge for wine pairings and you won't be disappointed.

Castagna
EUROPEAN $$$

(Map p208; ☏503-231-7373; www.castagnarestaurant.com; 1752 SE Hawthorne Blvd; mains $14-31; ☺dinner Wed-Sat) There's nothing common about chef Matthew Lightner's menu. The young, rising star transforms seasonal ingredients into works of art with surprising textures and flavors (think frozen wasabi ice and birch wood syrup). More familiar dishes grace the menu at the attached café.

Nostrana
ITALIAN $$

(Map p208; ☏503-234-2427; www.nostrana.com; 1401 SE Morrison; mains $12-20; ☺lunch Mon-Fri, dinner daily) Wood-fired pizzas (served uncut for authenticity), pasta with lamb bacon and flat iron steak with arugula round out the classic Italian dishes at this very popular gem of a restaurant. Chef Cathy Whims makes meals feel special, and the three-course dinner for $25 is a steal. Reservations are a good idea.

Simpatica Dining Hall
AMERICAN $$

(Map p208; ☏503-235-1600; www.simpaticacatering.com; 838 SE Ash St; prix fixe $35-45; ☺prix fixe dinners 7pm Fri & 7:30pm Sat, brunch 9am-2pm Sun) One of Portland's most popular Sunday brunch spots (hello fried chicken and waffles!) also serves great prix fixe dinners. Make new friends at long communal tables, which hold braised meats, sweet soups and rustic pastries – all made with seasonally appropriate ingredients and served family-style.

Farm Café
AMERICAN/NORTHWEST $$

(Map p208; ☏503-736-3276; www.thefarmcafe.com; 10 SE 7th Ave; mains $15-22; ☺dinner; ☑) From outside it's just an old white house, and you'll wonder what all the fuss is about. This is it: well-priced, vegetarian food (plus a few good fish options) that's lovingly prepared and made using only local and organic ingredients. Add some good cocktails, a relaxing backyard patio, and you've got a memorable dining experience.

Biwa
JAPANESE $$

(Map p208; www.biwarestaurant.com; 215 SE 9th Ave; mains $7-12; ☺5pm-midnight) Based on a Japanese Izakaya, this tiny basement spot makes its own noodles for rich udon and ramen, and grills meats to accompany pickles and rice. Take note of the flights of quality sake and shochu, which are hard to find in Portland.

Navarre
EUROPEAN $$

(Map p208; ☏503-232-3555; www.navarreportland.blogspot.com; 10 NE 28th Street; small plates $4-8, large plates $10-18; ☺4:30-10:30pm Mon-Thu, 11am-11:30pm Fri, 9:30am-11:30pm Sat, 9:30am-10:30pm Sun) The kind of place that feels truly European: no frills, with a serious food focus. A paper-list menu lists various small plates (don't call them tapas), which rotate daily – though a few popular dishes are fixed commodities. Expect a simple and truly delicious approach to crab cakes, lamb and roasted veggies. Weekend brunch is just as good.

Pambiche
CUBAN $$

(Map p208; www.pambiche.com; 2811 NE Glisan St; mains $11-19; ☺11am-10pm Sun-Thu, 8am-midnight Fri & Sat) Portland's best Cuban food, with a trendy and riotously colorful atmosphere. All your regular favorites like *ropa vieja* are available, but leave room for dessert. Lunch is a good deal, but happy hour is even better (2pm to 6pm Monday to Friday,

10pm to midnight Friday and Saturday). Be prepared to wait for dinner.

Country Cat
SOUTHERN $$
(☎503-408-1414; www.thecountrycat.net; 7937 SE Stark St; mains $15-20; ⊗breakfast, lunch & dinner) Foodies flock to Portland's Montavilla neighborhood for this diner's skilled fried chicken, smoked duck leg and cobblers. Early birds will find hash, fluffy pancakes and whiskey custard French toast.

Bar Avignon
EUROPEAN $$
(Map p208; ☎503-517-0808; www.baravignon.com; 2138 SE Division St; mains $9-17; ⊗4pm-midnight) A romantic setting for snacky plates or real entrees, the kind of quiet café that makes you want to linger over a special bottle of wine at the bar or at sidewalk tables. Happy hour is a good way to get a taste for the place.

Lauro
MEDITERRANEAN $$
(Map p208; ☎503-239-7000; www.laurokitchen.com; 3377 SE Division St; mains $12-21; ⊗dinner) Renowned owner-chef David Machado opened his SE Division restaurant in 2003, beginning a neighborhood revitalization that continues today. Mediterranean-inspired dishes like chicken tagine and stuffed lamb shoulder grace the menu. Only the freshest, most local ingredients are used. Also recommended:

Otto's Sausage Kitchen
DELI $
(www.ottossausage.com; 4138 SE Woodstock Blvd; sausage sandwiches $3-4; ⊗9:30am-6pm Mon-Sat, 11am-5pm Sun) Awesome house wieners, chicken sausages and pork links grilled up outside a deli in the Woodstock neighborhood. Look for the smoke.

Ken's Artisan Pizza
PIZZA $$
(Map p208; ☎503-517-9951; www.kensartisan.com; 304 SE 28th Ave; small pizzas $11-14; ⊗dinner Tue-Sun) Glorious wood-fired, thin-crust pizzas – and a long wait to try them (no reservations). Super-trendy atmosphere, with huge sliding windows that open to the street on warm nights.

La Buca
ITALIAN $
(Map p208; ☎503-238-1058; www.labucaitaliancafe.com; 40 NE 28th Ave; mains $8-12; ⊗lunch Mon-Fri, dinner daily;) Basic Italian food at great prices, includes tasty dishes of pasta, paninis, salads and salmon. Don't forget to peek at the specials board.

Fire on the Mountain
BARBECUE $
(Map p208; ☎503-280-9464; www.portlandwings.com; 4225 N Interstate Ave; mains $8-10; ⊗lunch & dinner) Best known for their buf-

DON'T MISS

POK POK

Thai street food with a twist draws crowds of flavor seekers to **Pok Pok** (Map p208; ☎503-232-1387; www.pokpokpdx.com; 3226 SE Division St; mains $9-14; ⊗lunch & dinner). To endure the inevitable long wait, start with some Thai-inspired drinks and snacks across the street at the restaurant's bar, the **Whiskey Soda Lounge**. There you can dream about the upcoming fish sauce wings, coconut rice and green papaya salad. There'a a second location at 1469 NE Prescott St.

falo wings; plenty of creative sauce options. Salads and sandwiches too. There's another branch at 1708 E Burnside.

Pad Thai Kitchen
THAI $
(Map p208; ☎503-232-8766; 2309 SE Belmont St; mains $8-12; ⊗11am-3pm & 5-10pm Mon-Fri, noon-10pm Sat & Sun) Delicious Thai food served with a no-nonsense briskness. Order the drunken noodles, pumpkin curry or, of course, sweet and sticky pad thai.

Pine State Biscuits
SOUTHERN $
(Map p208; www.pinestatebiscuits.com; 3640 SE Belmont St; mains $4-8; ⊗7am-2pm) Heart-stopping fried chicken and biscuit sandwiches, with possible egg, cheese and gravy additions. Another location is at 2204 NE Alberta.

Little T American Baker
BAKERY $
(Map p208; www.littletbaker.com; 2600 SE Division St; mains $7-10; ⊗7am-5pm Mon-Sat, 8am-2pm Sun) Best baguette in town, as well as quiches, salads and pastries.

Drinking

Check out www.barflymag.com for opinionated, spot-on reviews. Oregon bars and pubs are all legally required to be nonsmoking.

Bars

Horse Brass Pub
BAR
(☎503-232-2202; www.horsebrass.com; 4534 SE Belmont St; ⊗11am-2:30am Mon-Fri, 9am-2.30am Sat & Sun) Portland's most authentic English pub, cherished for its dark-wood atmosphere, excellent fish 'n chips (or try the artery-clogging scotch egg) and 50 beers on tap (that's right). Play some darts, watch soccer on TV or just take it all in.

BRUNCH ANYONE?

Portlanders love brunch, and on weekends you'll see long lines at all the popular spots. Weekend hours are usually from 9am to 2pm; some places are only open Saturday and Sunday. Here are some of Portland's favorites:

Tasty n Sons (☑503-621-1400; 3808 N Williams Ave) Superb small plates in a high-ceilinged warehouse.

Screen Door (Map p208; ☑503-542-0880; 2337 E Burnside St) Southern specialties and exceptional French toast.

Bakery Bar (Map p208; ☑503-477-7779; 2935 NE Glisan St) Excellent breakfast sandwiches on homemade biscuits or English muffins.

Tin Shed (☑503-288-6966; 1438 NE Alberta St) Hot NE Alberta St spot with awesome outside patio.

Zell's Café (Map p208; ☑503-239-0196; 1300 SE Morrison St) Great scones, potatoes and salmon scramble.

Mother's Bistro (Map p204; ☑503-525-5877; 212 SW Stark St) Upscale downtown brunch spot offering a guaranteed wait.

Gravy (☑503-287-8800; 3957 N Mississippi Ave) Hip N Mississippi Ave joint serving up huge portions.

Crush
BAR

(Map p208; ☑503-235-8150; www.crushbar.com; 1400 SE Morrison St; ☺4:30pm-2am Tue-Fri & Sun, 6pm-2am Sat) Slip into this sexy lounge with all the pretty people, order one of the exotic cocktails and speak up – it gets loud, what with all the dancing and shows. The menu's vegetarian (try the brunch) and it's popular with both straight and lesbian women – which makes for a great girls' night out.

Laurelthirst Pub
BAR

(Map p208; ☑503-232-1504; http://mysite.ncnetwork.net/res8u18i/laurelthirstpublichouse; 2958 NE Glisan St; ☺11am-midnight Mon-Wed, 11am-1am Thu, 11am-2am Fri, 9am-2am Sat, 9am-midnight Sun) Great acoustic bands spill the crowds onto the sidewalk at this dark, funky neighborhood joint. The music – which plays nearly every night – is free until the evening, when you'll likely cough up just a $5 cover. Good beer and wine selection (but no liquor), along with fine breakfasts.

Departure Restaurant & Lounge
BAR

(Map p204; ☑503-802-5370; www.departure portland.com; 525 SW Morrison St; ☺4pm-midnight Tue-Thu, to 2am Fri & Sat) This rooftop restaurant-bar (atop the 15th floor of the Nines Hotel) fills a deep downtown void: a cool bar with unforgettable views of Pioneer Courthouse Sq and the Willamette River. The vibe is distinctly spaceship LA, with mod couches and sleek lighting. Hit

happy hour from 4pm to 6pm for select $5 drinks and $20 bottles of wine.

Saucebox
BAR

(Map p204; ☑503-241-3393; www.saucebox. com; 214 SW Broadway; ☺4:30pm-2am Mon-Fri, 5pm-2am Sat & Sun) Metro-sleek restaurant with pretty bar staff serving upscale Asian-fusion cuisine, but also very popular for its wide selection of drinks – including creative cocktails (try the chocolate-coffee Foxy Brown). DJs fire up at 10pm, with snappy tunes and dancing potential.

Also recommended:

Gilt Club
BAR

(Map p204; ☑503-222-4458; www.giltclub. com; 306 NW Broadway; ☺5pm-2am Mon-Sat) A grownup, elegant joint in Old Town. Upscale dinner menu and great cocktails.

Alibi
BAR

(☑503-287-5335; 4024 N Interstate; ☺11am-2:30am Mon-Sat, 11am-1am Sun) Tiki-bar heaven, with karaoke on weeknights, fun crowds and great Polynesian kitsch. Greasy-spoon grub.

Thirst Wine Bar
BAR

(Map p204; ☑503-295-2747; www.thirstbistro. com; 315 SW Montgomery St; ☺3-10pm Tue-Thu & Sun, to 11pm Fri & Sat) This bar's best on a warm summer day, when the sidewalk tables tempt passersby with a fine river view.

Back Stage Bar
BAR

(Map p208; ☏503-236-9234; www.mcmenamins
.com/603-back-stage-bar-home; 3702 SE
Hawthorne Blvd; ☺4pm-1am Mon-Fri, 2pm-1am
Sat, 2pm-midnight Sun) Hidden gem behind
the Bagdad Theater, with seven-story-
high space, pool tables galore and tons of
personality.

Brewpubs
It's crazy, but Portland has over 30 breweries within its borders – more than any other
city on earth. The choices are endless, but
below is a starting list.

For funky atmospheres (think renovated
funeral parlors and historic schools) there's
no beating **McMenamins** (www.mcmena
mins.com). The empire includes brewpubs
all over the Pacific Northwest, each offering
their own ales along with brews from other
producers. Thirsty parents should head to
family-friendly Laurelwood Public House
(p215), though many brewpubs welcome
kids until 9pm or so.

TOP CHOICE **Hair of the Dog Brewing** BREWPUB
(Map p208; ☏503-232-6585; www.hair
ofthedog.com; 61 SE Yamhill; ☺2-8pm Wed-Sun)
Beer geeks rejoiced when this brewery finally opened its first pub in 2010. The new digs
house brewing operations and a spacious
tasting room within sight of the downtown
skyline. HOTD brews special beers, some of
which are 'bottle-conditioned' (the brewing
cycle is finished inside the bottle), which
results in complex flavors and high alcohol
contents.

Deschutes Brewery
BREWPUB

(Map p204; ☏503-296-4906; www.deschutes
brewery.com; 210 NW 11th Ave; ☺11am-11pm Mon-
Thu, to midnight Fri & Sat) The Portland branch
of this Bend brewery offers the same great
beers, only on a larger scale. The stuff is
brewed here, too, which makes pints at the
bar extra fresh and tasty – or grab a table
under the carved-wood arches framing the
restaurant area.

Amnesia Brewing
BREWPUB

(☏503-281-7708; 832 N Beech St; ☺2-11pm Mon-
Thu, noon-midnight Fri-Sun) At the ReBuilding
Center, this is hip Mississippi St's brewery,
with a casual feel and picnic tables out front.
For excellent (and despite the name, memorable) beer, try the Desolation IPA. Other good
drops are Amnesia Brown or Wonka Porter.
An outdoor grill offers burgers and sausages,
and there's live music on weekends.

Widmer Gasthaus
BREWPUB

(☏503-281-3333; www.widmer.com; 955 N Russell St, Elliot District; ☺11am-10:30pm Sun-Thu, to
11:30pm Fri & Sat) In a trendy industrial area
in the north, this yuppified brewery-restau-
rant offers very tasty beers – some available
only here. Their Hefeweizen (unfiltered
wheat beer) is a good choice, and goes well
with the schnitzel. Widmer Gasthaus has
weekend tours, and sports on TV, and it's
close to live music at the White Eagle.

Lucky Labrador Brewing Company
BREWPUB

(Map p208; ☏503-236-3555; www.luckylab.com;
915 SE Hawthorne Blvd; ☺11am-midnight Mon-Sat,
noon-10pm Sun) This is a large, no-nonsense
beer hall (good for groups) with a wide selection of brews – though limited bar and food
menu. 'Miser Mondays' means pints under
$3, and the back patio is dog-friendly and
shows movies in summer. Other branches
at 1945 NW Quimby St and 1700 N Killingsworth St.

Also recommended:

Upright Brewing
BREWPUB

(☏503-735-5337; www.uprightbrewing.com;
240 N Broadway, Suite 2, Lloyd District; ☺4:30-
9pm Fri, 1-6pm Sat & Sun) Basement brewery
with intimate tasting room for sampling
farmhouse-inspired ales. Only open Friday to Sunday.

Belmont Station
BREWPUB

(☏503-232-8538; www.belmont-station.com;
4500 SE Stark St; ☺3-11pm Mon-Fri, noon-11pm
Sat, noon-9pm Sun) Excellent rotating taps
in a simple café. Attached to one of the
city's best bottle shops.

Hopworks Urban Brewery
BREWPUB

(☏503-232-4677; www.hopworksbeer.com;
2944 SE Powell Blvd; ☺11am-11pm Sun-Thu, to
midnight Fri & Sat) All organic beers served
in an eco-styled building with bicycle
frames above the bar.

Green Dragon
BREWPUB

(☏503-517-0660; www.pdxgreendragon.com;
928 SE 9th Ave; ☺11am-11pm Sun-Wed, to 1am
Thu-Sat) Owned by Rogue Breweries, but
serves 49 guest taps in an echoey eastside warehouse.

BridgePort Brewpub
BREWPUB

(Map p204; ☏503-241-7179; www.bridgeport
brew.com; 1313 NW Marshall St; ☺11:30am-11pm
Tue-Thu, to midnight Fri & Sat) Almost too-
fancy brewery with bakery, espresso bar,
atrium and rooftop bar. Also at 3632 SE
Hawthorne Blvd (Map p208).

Coffeehouses

Portland is full of good coffee shops, and everyone has their neighborhood favorite. Here are a few to try:

TOP CHOICE **Heart** COFFEEHOUSE
(Map p208; ☑503-206-6602; www. heartroasters.com; 2211 E. Burnside; ⊗7am-7pm) Feels like a modern science lab devoted to the art of roasting and tasting the perfect bean.

Barista COFFEEHOUSE
(Map p204; ☑503-274-1211; www.baristapdx. com; 539 NW 13th Ave; ⊗7:30am-6pm Mon-Sat) The famous barista Billy Wilson crafts coffee drinks made of beans from various specialty roasters.

Albina Press COFFEEHOUSE
(☑503-282-5214; 4637 N Albina Ave; ⊗6am-8pm) Pure nirvana for its delicious cups of coffee, artistically constructed by award-winning baristas.

Stumptown Coffee COFFEEHOUSE
(☑503-230-7797; www.stumptowncoffee.com; 4525 SE Division St; ⊗6am-7pm Mon-Fri, 7am-7pm Sat & Sun) The first micro-roaster to put Portland on the coffee map. Also at 3356 SE Belmont St.

Pied Cow Coffeehouse COFFEEHOUSE
(Map p208; ☑503-230-4866; 3244 SE Belmont St; ⊗4pm-midnight Mon-Thu, 4pm-1am Fri, noon-1am Sat, noon-12am Sun) Gorgeous, colorful and bohemian Victorian house with lots of atmosphere and a lovely garden patio. Hookahs available.

☆ Entertainment

The best guide to local entertainment is the free *Willamette Week* (www.wweek.com), which comes out on Wednesday and contains complete listings (and cover charges) of all theater, music, clubs, cinema and events in the metro area. Also, try the *Portland Mercury* (www.portlandmercury.com).

Live Music

See also Laurelthirst Pub (p221). For summer outdoor entertainment, check what's happening at the Oregon Zoo (www.ore gonzoo.org/Concerts).

Doug Fir ECLECTIC
(Map p208; ☑503-231-9663; www.dougfirlounge. com; 830 East Burnside St; ⊗7am-2:30am) Paul Bunyan meets the Jetsons at this ultra-trendy venue that has transformed the LoBu (lower Burnside) neighborhood from seedy to slick. Doug Fir books edgy, hard-to-get

talent, drawing crowds from tattooed youth to suburban yuppies. The restaurant (open 21 hours a day) is good; located next to their rock-star quality Jupiter Hotel (p216).

Dante's ROCK
(Map p204; ☑503-226-6630; www.danteslive. com; 350 W Burnside St; ⊗concerts almost daily) This steamy red bar books vaudeville shows along with national acts like the Dandy Warhols and Concrete Blonde. The stage is intimate and the lighting low – everybody looks good. Drop in on Monday night at 10pm for the ever-popular Karaoke from Hell.

Berbati's Pan ECLECTIC
(Map p204; ☑503-226-2122; www.berbati.com; 10 SW 3rd Ave) Popular and buzzing, this established music venue plus restaurant nabs some of the more interesting acts in town. Expect big band, swing, acid rock and R&B music, along with a crowd of all ages. Outdoor seating and pool tables are a plus.

Crystal Ballroom ECLECTIC
(Map p204; ☑503-225-0047; www.mcmenamins. com; 1332 W Burnside St) Major acts have played at this large and historic ballroom, including the Grateful Dead, James Brown and Jimi Hendrix. The 'floating' dance floor bounces at the slightest provocation, making for some pretty wild times while you're cutting up the rug.

Mississippi Studios ALTERNATIVE
(☑503-288-3895; www.mississippistudios.com; 3939 N Mississippi Ave) Recently expanded but still intimate venue; good for checking out budding acoustic talent, along with more established musical groups. Excellent sound system and outdoor patio concerts too. Located right on trendy N Mississippi Ave.

Jimmy Mak's JAZZ
(Map p204; ☑503-295-6542; www.jimmymaks. com; 221 NW 10th Ave; ⊗Mon-Sat) Stumptown's premier jazz venue, serving excellent Mediterranean food in their fancy dining room. There's a casual bar with pool tables and darts in the basement. Music starts at 8pm.

Hawthorne Theatre ECLECTIC
(Map p208; ☑503-233-7100; www.hawthornet heater.com; 1507 SE 39th Ave) All-ages music venue in the heart of hip Hawthorne Blvd, good for live rock, reggae, punk, pop, metal and country music. Intimate stage, high balcony and 21-and-over section for the legal boozehounds.

Cinemas

Portland has plenty of multiplex cinemas, but it's the great selection of old personality-filled theaters – often selling beer and pizza, along with cheap tickets – that makes going to the movies a joy here.

Cinema 21   ARTHOUSE CINEMA
(Map p204; ☑503-223-4515; www.cinema21. com; 616 NW 21st Ave) Portland's premiere art-house and foreign-film theater.

Kennedy School   CINEMA
McMenamins' premiere Portland venue. Watch movies in the old school gym. See p216 and check www.mcmenamins.com for current showings.

Bagdad Theater   CINEMA
(Map p208; ☑503-249-7474; www.mcmenamins. com; 3702 SE Hawthorne Blvd) Another awesome McMenamins venue with bargain flicks; on Tuesday they're only $2.

Mission Theater   CINEMA
(Map p204; ☑503-223-4527; www.mcme namins.com; 1624 NW Glisan St) Come early for a front-row balcony seat at this beautiful McMenamins theater.

Laurelhurst Theater   CINEMA
(Map p208; ☑503-232-5511; www.laurelhurst theater.com; 2735 E Burnside St) Great pizza-and-beer theater with nearby nightlife.

Clinton Street Theater   ALTERNATIVE CINEMA
(Map p208; ☑503-238-8899; www.clintonst theater.com; 2522 SE Clinton St) Old neighborhood theater screening independent and revival films.

Hollywood Theatre   ALTERNATIVE CINEMA
(☑503-281-4215; www.hollywoodtheatre.org; 4122 NE Sandy Blvd) Historic art-deco spot playing classic, foreign and quirky independent movies.

Theater & Performing Arts

Arlene Schnitzer Concert Hall   CONCERT HALL
(Map p204; ☑503-248-4335; www.pcpa. com/events/asch.php; 1037 SW Broadway) The Oregon Symphony performs in this beautiful, if not acoustically brilliant, downtown venue.

Artists Repertory Theatre   THEATER
(Map p204; ☑503-241-1278; www.artistsrep. org; 1515 SW Morrison St) Some of Portland's best plays, including regional premieres, are performed in two intimate theaters.

Keller Auditorium   THEATER
(Map p204; ☑503-248-4335; www.pcpa. com/events/keller.php; 222 SW Clay St) The Portland Opera, Oregon Ballet Theatre and Oregon Children's Theatre all stage performances here.

Gerding Theater   THEATER
(Map p204; ☑503-445-3700; www.pcs.org; 128 NW 11th Ave) The city's main theater company, Portland Center Stage, now performs here – a renovated Pearl District landmark boasting state-of-the-art features.

Gay & Lesbian Venues

For current listings see *Just Out* (www.just out.com), Portland's free gay bi-weekly. Or grab a *Gay and Lesbian Community Yellow Pages* (www.pdxgayyellowpages.com) for other services. For more information, check out www.travelportland.com/lgbt.

Start St, around NE 10th St, has several edgy gay bars. For an upscale, mixed-crowd bar, lesbians should head east to Crush (p221).

Darcelle XV   GAY CABARET SHOW
(Map p204; ☑503-222-5338; www.darcelleXV. com; 208 NW 3rd Ave; ☺Wed-Sat) Portland's Vegas-style cabaret show, featuring glitzy drag queens in big wigs, fake jewelry and over-stuffed bras. Musical performances are spiced with corny comedy while hapless audience members are picked out and teased. Male strippers perform at midnight on Friday and Saturday.

Embers   NIGHTCLUB
(Map p204; ☑503-222-3082; www.emberspdx. net; 110 NW Broadway) Regulars come to meet up for the music (from '80s tunes to techno to pop), amateur drag shows, fun dance floor and friendly camaraderie. There are different themes on different nights (Wednesday is Goth) and everyone is welcome, whether they be gay, lesbian, straight or undecided.

Hobo's   RESTAURANT/PIANO BAR
(Map p204; ☑503-224-3285; 120 NW 3rd Ave) Past the old historic storefront here is a classy restaurant–piano jazz bar popular with older gay men. It's a quiet, relaxed place and good for a romantic dinner or drink; for some activity, head to the pool tables in back. Live music starts at 8pm from Wednesday to Sunday.

Silverado   STRIP CLUB
(Map p208; ☑503-224-4493; www.silveradopdx. com; 318 SW 3rd Ave) Almost nightly stripper shows (Monday is karaoke) catering to men. Mixed crowd, communal bathrooms, cheap

drinks, potential groping and muscled dancers, so bring plenty of dollar bills and expect a wild time.

Spectator Sports

Trailblazers
(www.nba.com/blazers) The City of Roses' major league basketball team; they play at the Rose Garden Arena.

Winter Hawks
(www.winterhawks.com) Beervana's major-junior hockey team.

Timbers
(www.portlandtimbers.com) New franchise soccer team for PDX; will play in PGE Park.

Rose City Rollers
(www.rosecityrollers.com) Roller derby in Stumptown? You bet.

🔒 Shopping

Portland's downtown shopping district extends in a two-block radius from Pioneer Courthouse Square. **Pioneer Place** – an upscale mall – is between SW Morrison and SW Yamhill Sts, east of the square. The large shopping mall, **Lloyd Center**, is on the eastside.

The Pearl District is full of high-end galleries, boutiques and home-decor shops – and don't miss Powell's City of Books. On the first Friday of each month galleries stay open longer and people fill some of the Pearl's streets amid a party atmosphere. And on weekends there's the fun Saturday Market (p205).

Northwest's fanciest shopping street is **NW 23rd Ave**, nicknamed 'trendy-third.' This is where Portland's branches of Gap, Pottery Barn and Restoration Hardware live, among many other fancy stores and people.

Eastside has many trendy shopping streets that also host restaurants, cafés and bars. **SE Hawthorne Blvd** is the biggest of these, **N Mississippi Ave** is the most recent and **NE Alberta** is the most artsy and funky. On the last Thursday of each month, NE Alberta throws its own wild street party with budding artists, musicians and performers of all kinds.

If you're feeling up for the drive, find outlet malls at **Woodburn Company Stores** (in Woodburn, south of Portland about 30 miles) or **Columbia Gorge Premium Outlets** (in Troutdale, just east of Portland). And for some fun, off-the-beaten-path shops, visit www.portlandpicks.com.

TOP CHOICE | Music Millennium | MUSIC
(☑503-231-8926; 3158 E Burnside St; ⊙10am-10pm Mon-Sat, 11am-9pm Sun) In the age of dying record shops, this place is a revelation. Extensive collections of everything from classic rock to straight-up classical. Check the listings of live in-store performances and grab a 'Keep Portland Weird!' sticker while you're here.

Imelda's and Louie's | SHOES
(Map p208; ☑503-281-7708; 3426 SE Hawthorne Blvd; ⊙10am-7pm Mon-Fri, 10am-6pm Sat, 11am-6pm Sun) One of Portland's best shoe stores carries an array of kicks for men and women. Rows of stacked boxes can be tricky to navigate, but it's worth the trouble. Also has great bags, wallets, hats and jewelry. Second location at 935 NW Everett.

Flutter | GIFT
(☑503-288-1649; 3948 N Mississippi Ave; ⊙11am-6pm Mon-Sat, 11am-5pm Sun) One of N Mississippi Ave's most interesting shops, with reclaimed and refurbished items for the home, vintage jewelry, books and ephemera. Peruse the birdcages, gothic wedding gowns, ornate pillows and feathery hats.

Canoe | GIFT
(Map p204; ☑503-889-8545; 1136 SW Alder St; ⊙10am-6pm Tue-Sat, 11am-5pm Sun) If you're looking for a unique gift for a discerning person, especially those who like modern design, this is the place. Carefully crafted items from artisans around the globe include everything from wood-handled cheese tools to beautiful ceramics and delicate vases.

Seaplane | CLOTHES
(Map p204; ☑503-234-2409; 2226 NW Lovejoy St; ⊙11am-6pm) A serious boutique packed with one-of-a-kind items from local designers. Don't head here looking for sales or bargains; these pieces will take a chunk out of the bank account, but you won't see anyone else wearing what you've got on.

Frock Boutique | CLOTHES
(☑503-595-0379; 1439 NE Alberta St; ⊙10am-6pm Tue-Sat, 10am-4pm Sun & Mon) One of Alberta Street's most accessible clothing stores. Check out the array of screen-printed T-shirts, sundresses, wool hats, patterned socks, onesies for babies and more. Also recommended:

Land | GIFTS & ART GALLERY
(☑503-451-0689; 3925 N Mississippi Ave; ⊙10am-6pm Wed-Sat, 10am-5pm Sun) Unique,

fun and crafty gifts of all kinds, plus an art gallery upstairs.

Gilt Jewelry
JEWELRY
(Map p204; ☑503-226-0629; 720 NW 23rd Ave; ☺11:30am-6pm Tue-Sat, noon-5pm Sun) Fine vintage jewelry on the main floor and modern, locally made new pieces upstairs.

Queen Bee Creations
BAGS
(☑503-232-1755; 3961 N Williams Ave; ☺10am-7pm Mon-Sat, noon-5pm Sun) One-of-a-kind bags, wallets and bike panniers sewn on site.

Columbia Sportswear
SPORTSWEAR
(Map p204; ☑503-226-6800; 911 SW Broadway; ☺9:30am-7pm Mon-Sat, 11am-6pm Sun) Flagship store for local sportswear company; outlet at 1323 SE Tacoma St in Sellwood.

Bookstores
Broadway Books
(☑503-284-1726; www.broadwaybooks.net; 1714 NE Broadway) Good general, independent bookstore with especially strong literary fiction, biography and Judaica sections.

CounterMedia
(☑503-226-8141; 927 SW Oak St) Liberally minded books on fringe culture and vintage erotica.

In Other Words
(☑503-232-6003; www.inotherwords.org; 8 NE Killingsworth St) The US's last nonprofit feminist bookstore. Plenty of community events take place here, and it's a valuable resource center as well.

Powell's City of Books
(☑503-228-4651; www.powells.com; 1005 W Burnside St) The USA's largest independent bookstore, with a whole city block of new and used titles. Has other branches around town, including at 3723 and 3747 SE Hawthorne.

Reading Frenzy
(☑503-274-1449; www.readingfrenzy.com; 921 SW Oak St) Emporium of indie zines, comics and books that supports independent and alternative media.

ℹ️ Information
Emergency & Medical Services
Call ☑911 for medical, fire or crime emergencies.

Legacy Good Samaritan Hospital (☑503-413-7711; 1015 NW 22nd Ave) Convenient to downtown.

Police station (☑503-823-0000; 1111 SW 2nd Ave) Downtown.

Internet Access
Practically all coffee shops have wi-fi. All Multnomah County (Portland's county) libraries have free internet access and wi-fi.

Backspace (☑503-248-2900; www.back space.bz; 115 NW 5th Ave) This youth-oriented hangout has arcade games, Stumptown coffee, vegetarian snacks, live music, live hours and – of course – internet access.

Central Library (☑503-988-5123; www.mult colib.org; 801 SW 10th Ave) Downtown; for other branches check the website.

Urban Grind Coffeehouse (☑503-546-0649; www.urbangrindcoffee.com; 2214 NE Oregon St) Slick café with a few public computers, free wi-fi, a kids play area and great coffee roasted on premises.

Media
Just Out (www.justout.com) Free bi-weekly serving Portland's gay community.

KBOO 90.7 FM (www.kboo.fm) Progressive local radio station run by volunteers; alternative news and views.

Portland Independent Media Center (www. portland.indymedia.org) Open publishing source of community news and lefty activism.

Portland Mercury (www.portlandmercury. com) The local sibling of Seattle's *The Stranger;* this free weekly is published on Thursday.

Willamette Week (www.wweek.com) Free alt-weekly covering local news and culture, published on Wednesday.

Money
Portland is full of banks with exchange services and ATMs. At the Portland airport, in the main ticket lobby, is **Travelex** (☑503-281-3045; ☺5:30am-4:30pm).

Post
Post office Main branch (☑503-294-2399;620 SW Main St); 7th St branch (☑503-234-6182; 1020 SE 7th Ave).

Tourist Information
Nature of the Northwest Visitor Center (☑503-673-2331; www.naturenw.org; 800 NE Oregon St, Suite 965; ☺9am-12:30pm & 1-4pm Mon-Fri) Offers outdoor and geologic information; has books, brochures and all kinds of maps.

Visitor Information Center (☑503-275-8355, 877-678-5263; www.travelportland.com; 701 SW 6th Ave, in Pioneer Courthouse Sq; ☺8:30am-5:30pm Mon-Fri, 10am-4pm Sat, 10am-2pm Sun) Tri-Met offices are also here.

Websites
Around the Sun (www.aroundthesunblog.com) Free things going on around Portland.

FREE RAIL ZONE

One of downtown Portland's greatest features is this free transportation zone, the area bordered by the Willamette River, NW Irving St and I-405 (and extending across the river, all the way through to the Lloyd Center District). Whether it's the MAX or streetcar, all trips that start and end within these areas cost nothing; pay only if you wind up leaving this magical space.

City of Portland (www.portlandonline.com) Stumptown's official website.

Gay Oregon (www.gaypdx.com) A resource for Portland's gay and lesbian communities.

Portland Food and Drink (www.portland foodanddrink.com) Unbiased reviews of Portland's restaurants, along with specialty articles.

Portland Picks (www.portlandpicks.com) A gal's trendy list of restaurants, shops, services and events.

Travel Portland (www.travelportland.com) What to do, where to go, how to save...

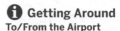 Getting There & Away
Air

Award-winning **Portland International Airport** (PDX; www.flypdx.com) provides service all over the country, as well as to several international destinations. Amenities include restaurants, moneychangers, bookstores (including three Powell's branches) and other services like free wi-fi. It's also well connected to downtown and other parts of Portland via light rail (see p228).

Bus

Greyhound buses leave from their **depot** (☑503-243-2357; www.greyhound.com; 550 NW 6th Ave) and connect Portland with cities along I-5 and I-84. Destinations include Chicago, Boise, Denver, San Francisco, Seattle and Vancouver, BC.

If you're traveling between Portland and Seattle and like comfort, try **Shuttle Express** (☑425-981-7000; www.shuttleexpress.com/seattle-to-portland), which provides service in large vans with wi-fi and coffee service.

Train

Amtrak (☑503-273-4866; www.amtrak.com; 800 NW 6th Ave), at Union Station, offers services up and down the West Coast. The *Empire Builder* travel to Chicago, the *Cascades* goes to Vancouver, BC, and the *Coast Starlight* runs from Seattle and LA.

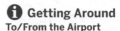 Getting Around
To/From the Airport

PDX is about 10 miles northeast of downtown, along the Columbia River. Tri-Met's light-rail MAX line takes about 40 minutes to get from downtown to the airport. If you prefer a bus, **Blue Star** (☑503-249-1837; www.bluestarbus.com) offers shuttle services between PDX and several downtown stops.

Taxis charge around $30 from the airport to downtown (not including tip).

Bicycle

It's easy to get around Portland on a bicycle (see p211).

Rental companies:

City Bikes Annex (☑503-239-6951; www.citybikes.coop; 734 SE Ankeny St)

Clever Cycles (☑503-334-1560; www.clevercycles.com; 908 SE Hawthorne Blvd)

Waterfront Bicycle Rentals (☑503-227-1719; www.waterfrontbikes.net; 10 SW Ash St)

Bus, Light Rail & Streetcar

Local buses and the MAX light-rail system are run by Tri-Met, which has an **information center** (☑503-238-7433; www.trimet.org; ⊙8:30am-5:30pm Mon-Fri) at Pioneer Courthouse Square (Map p204). A streetcar runs from the South Waterfront through Portland State University, downtown and the Pearl District to NW 23rd Ave. Within the downtown core, public transportation is free.

Tickets for MAX must be bought from ticket machines at MAX stations; there is no conductor or ticket-seller on board. Bus, light-rail and streetcar tickets are completely transferable within two hours of the time of purchase. If you're a night owl, be aware that a few buses and light-rail stop running at midnight, though some run later; check the website for details on a specific line.

Charter Service

For custom bus or van charters, try **EcoShuttle** (☑503-548-4480; www.ecoshuttle.net). Their vehicles run on 100% biodiesel.

Car

Most major car-rental agencies have outlets both downtown and at Portland's airport (PDX). Many of these agencies have added hybrid vehicles to their fleets. For an interesting car-sharing option, see www.zipcar.com.

Pedicab

For something different, contact **PDX Pedicab** (☑503-828-9888; www.pdxpedicab.com), which utilizes bicycle pedicabs with 'drivers' that pedal you around downtown. Unique and eco-friendly to boot.

Taxi

Cabs are available 24 hours by phone. Downtown, you can sometimes flag them down.

Broadway Cab (☑503-227-1234; www.broadwaycab.com)

Radio Cab (☑503-227-1212; www.radiocab.net)

Tram

Not particularly helpful to the tourist and many locals, Portland's controversial **aerial tram** (www.portlandtram.org; round-trip fare $4) connects the South Waterfront district to the Oregon Health & Science University hillside campus. It went over budget by tens of millions of dollars, but at least makes an interesting conversation piece as you drive under it on I-5.

The Willamette Valley & Wine Country

Includes »

Best Places to Eat

» Painted Lady (p234)

» Tina's (p234)

» Thistle (p235)

» Joel Palmer House (p235)

» Café Zenon (p245)

Best Places to Stay

» Abbey Road Farm B&B (p234)

» Allison Inn & Spa (p234)

» McMenamins Hotel Oregon (p235)

» Hanson Country Inn (p241)

» C'est La Vie Inn (p244)

Why Go?

Visiting the region's wineries is undoubtedly the major draw in the Willamette Valley, but it's not the only highlight. Visit humble Salem, Oregon's capital city, and its surrounding attractions (which include a waterfall-filled state park and a 2.5lb hairball – but not in the same place!). Pause and let your hair down in dynamic and liberal Eugene, full of energetic college students, pretty riverside parks and fine restaurants. And Oregon City, within Portland's southern suburbs, is the place to go for the history of the Pacific Northwest; this was the last pit stop for settlers on the Oregon Trail.

The Willamette Valley is well located: head east to the Columbia River Gorge, north to Washington and west to the coast. Everything is so close by you'll want to linger for longer than you planned, so stretch that schedule and put on your explorer's hat – you'll need it.

When to Go
Eugene

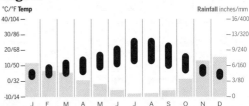

December– March Hot-spring heaven at Bagby, Beitenbush or Belknap Resort

June–September Wine tasting, river rafting, walking behind falls at Silver Falls State Park

September The Elizabethan Shrewbury Renaissance Fair and the artsy Fall Festival

Oregon City

POP 32,000

This nondescript little Portland suburb, nestled next to the Willamette River, was the final stop on the Oregon Trail and the first US city founded west of the Rockies. Despite its historic status and good location, Oregon City is visually plagued by an expanse of ugly paper-mill buildings and electric generators corseted around the 42ft Willamette Falls. The city features a bit of historic character downtown, a variety of old homes in surrounding neighborhoods and a free municipal elevator (between Railroad and 7th Sts) that offers good views of the area.

☉ Sights

FREE **McLoughlin House**   HISTORIC HOUSE
(☎503-656-5146; www.mcloughlinhouse.org; 713 Center St; ☉10am-4pm Wed-Sat, 1-4pm Sun) This 1845 house was built by John McLoughlin, who was called the 'father of Oregon' for his hand in helping found Oregon City – the West's first. At the time, most settlers lived in log cabins, and this two-story clapboard home (a National Historic Site) was then considered a mansion. Free tours are offered; check the website for free events that take place here.

Museum of the Oregon Territory   MUSEUM
(☎503-655-5574; 211 Tumwater Dr; ☉by appointment) History exhibits at this engaging museum offer a good interpretation of the local moonshine trade and of the **Willamette Meteorite**, the largest meteorite found in the US. Other displays include collections of intricately etched military mess kits and Native American basketry. Head up to the 3rd floor for a good view of the dam and falls. Open by appointment only.

Stevens-Crawford House Museum
MUSEUM
(☎503-655-2866; 603 6th St; ☉11am-3:30pm Thu-Sat) For a taste of the past, step into this 1907 museum. Owned by a pioneering family, the house still boasts most of its original furniture and hosts occasional exhibits, plant sales and a Christmas celebration.

❶ Information

State Welcome Center (☎503-657-9336; www.historicoregoncity.com; 1726 Washington St; ☉9:30am-5pm Mon-Sat, 10:30am-5pm Sun) A good place to go for information and a few pioneer exhibitions.

Champoeg State Heritage Area

One of the very first settlements in Oregon, Champoeg ('shampoo-e') was located on a flood plain along a bend in the Willamette River. After the historic 1843 vote, the town continued to grow as the era of riverboat travel brought increasing trade to the Willamette Valley. However, this bounty only lasted until December 1861, when an enormous flood swept through the Willamette drainage and the settlement, destroying most of it.

Now a state heritage area and popular family destination, **Champoeg State Heritage Area** (☎503-678-1251; www.oregonstateparks.org; 8239 Champoeg Rd NE; day use $5) is 25 miles southwest of Portland, off I-5 exit 278. There are 615 acres of old-growth woodland, grassy meadows, nature trails, historic sites and campgrounds. Films and displays at the **visitors center** (☉9am-5pm) explain the events that led up to the famous vote at Champoeg. There are also exhibits on the Calapooians and the flood patterns of the Willamette River. On summer weekends, various walks, tours and programs are offered.

The **Pioneer Mothers Memorial Cabin** (☎503-678-5537; adult/child $4/2; ☉1-5pm Fri-Sun Mar-Oct) is a reconstructed log cabin built by the local Daughters of the American Revolution. It's filled with objects brought across the Oregon Trail and other articles of frontier life. The 1852 **Robert Newell House** (☎503-678-5537; www.newellhouse.com; adult/child $4/2; ☉1-5pm Fri-Sun Mar-Oct) houses Native American artifacts and inaugural gowns worn by the wives of Oregon governors.

Be sure to reserve in summer for the pleasant sites, yurts and cabins at the **Champoeg Campground** (☎800-452-5687; tent sites/RV sites/yurts/cabins $19/24/36/39).

Newberg & Dundee

The gateways to wine country, these small cities were originally founded as Quaker settlements. Little of those original quiet ways remain however, and now strip malls and modern services are much of what you'll see. At least there's fine dining in the area, along with upscale countryside places to sleep. Dundee is 2 miles west of Newberg, on Hwy 99W.

The Willamette Valley & Wine Country Highlights

1 Go **wine tasting** (p237) in Newberg, McMinnville and around Salem

2 Sample gourmet restaurants from **Dundee** (p234) to **McMinnville** (p235) to **Eugene** (p245)

3 Explore the **Mackenzie River region** (p246) and go rafting, hiking and fishing

4 Do the sublime **Trail of Ten Falls Loop** (p240) – and walk behind waterfalls

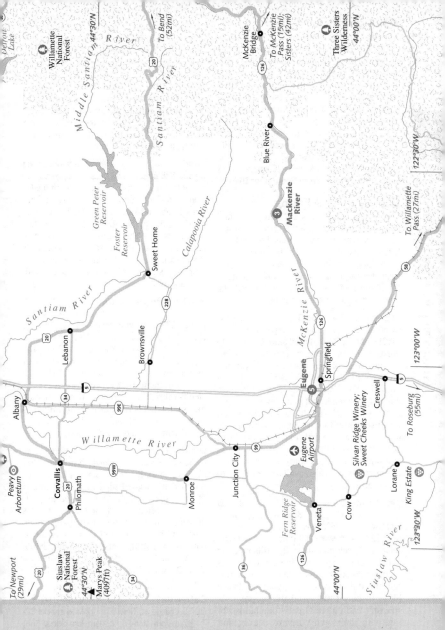

5 Experience **Eugene's** (p242) hippie counterculture during July's Oregon Country Fair

6 Visit Salem's **Willamette Heritage Center** (p237), with its pioneer buildings and water-run mill

7 Soak your tired muscles in the healing waters of **Bagby** or **Breitenbush Hot Springs** (p246)

◉ Sights & Activities

Hoover-Minthorn House MUSEUM

(☑503-538-6629; 115 S River St, Newberg; adult/child $3/0.50; ⊙1-4pm Wed-Sun Mar-Nov, 1-4pm Sat & Sun Dec & Feb) This house is where Herbert Hoover (the 31st president of the USA) grew up. Built in 1881, the restored home is now a museum of period furnishings and early Oregon history.

For pamphlets and information there's the **Chamber of Commerce** (☑503-538-2014; www.chelamvalley.org; 415 E Sheridan St, Newberg; ⊙9am-5pm Mon-Fri, 10am-3pm Sat & Sun); limited hours from September to May.

🛏 Sleeping & Eating

The closest camping is at Champoeg State Heritage Area (p231), about 7 miles southeast of Newberg. Chain hotels like the Shilo Inn and Best Western exist in Newberg.

Dundee has the area's best restaurants. Expect local, mostly organic ingredients at all of the region's top-drawer restaurants, along with exceptional wine lists.

Abbey Road Farm B&B B&B $$$

(☑503-852-6278, www.abbeyroadfarm.com; 10501 NE Abbey Rd, Carlton; d $210-250; ⊖※☎) For the ultimate country experience, head 8 miles west of Newberg to this working farm with lush vegetable garden and farm animals. Your hosts John and Judy have created a serene spot with modern comforts – you'll sleep in unique silos converted into five contemporary rooms with simple luxuries like Jacuzzis and memory-foam beds. You can milk goats in the morning and sample the cheese Judy makes. A three-bedroom house is also available ($375, two-night minimum).

⚡Allison Inn & Spa RESORT $$$

(☑503-554-2525, 877-294-2525; www.theallison.com; 2525 Allison Lane, Newberg; d from $295; ⊖※☎☒) If luxury is what you seek, then seek no longer: the Allison is the place. From its spacious, plush rooms to its relaxing soaking tubs to its excellent restaurant and great services, your needs are likely to be all met. And the on-premises spa isn't bad either. Great stone landscaping, with their own vineyard nearby, and it's eco-friendly to boot – solar panels grace most roofs, while hybrid/electric cars have their own parking spots.

TOP⧹ Painted Lady NORTHWESTERN $$$
CHOICE (☑503-538-3850; www.thepaintedlady restaurant.com; 201 S College St, Newberg; prix fixe $60-100; ⊙dinner Wed-Sun) Accomplished chefs Allen Routt and Jessica Bagley-Routt have used their wide travel and culinary experiences to open up this renowned restaurant in a renovated 1890s Victorian house. The four-course menu includes an appetizer, seafood course, main dish and dessert (vegetarian choices available), with the option for a wine pairing ($40 extra). Local, organic and seasonal ingredients are emphasized.

Tina's NORTHWESTERN-FRENCH $$$

(☑503-538-8880; www.tinasdundee.com; 760 Hwy 99W, Dundee; mains $27-35; ⊙lunch Tue-Fri, dinner Tue-Sun) Renowned restaurant that does lamb and duck to perfection though all the meat dishes are amazing (vegetarians beware – there are only a couple of choices for you). Try the salmon spring rolls if you can. The wine list and service are exemplary as well, and the best local ingredients are used.

Red Hills Provincial Dining

NORTHWESTERN $$$

(☑503-538-8224; www.redhills-dining.com; 276 Hwy 99W, Dundee; mains $24-32; ⊙lunch & dinner Tue-Sat, dinner Sun) Overlooking the highway is this unassuming yet excellent and award-winning restaurant. It offers a changing menu that reflects the area's agricultural riches, along with regional meats and seafood. There's a European influence in the dishes – all enhanced by an exceptional wine list and great desserts.

Dundee Bistro NORTHWESTERN $$

(☑503-554-1650; www.dundeebistro.com; 100 SW Seventh St, Dundee; mains $14-22; ⊙lunch & dinner) It's a good idea to reserve ahead at this popular restaurant – especially after 7pm, when the wine-tasting hordes descend. Tasty dishes like pappardelle pasta with shiitake mushrooms or Muscovy duck confit grace the menu, while the gourmet pizza offers a more casual option. On warm days go for the great back patio.

Coffee Cat COFFEEHOUSE $

(107 S College St, Newberg; drinks & snacks $2-7; ⊙7am-7pm Mon-Fri, 7:30am-7pm Sat & Sun) Trendy Newberg café with an artsy-vintage vibe and good drinks – for something different, try the white cloud mocha. Sandwiches, bagels and salads are available for the peckish, and there's an excellent coffee cake for dessert.

McMinnville

POP 32,500

At the heart of the region's wine industry lies busy and modern McMinnville, mostly charmless except for its historic, red-brick downtown district. Here you'll find older buildings, art galleries, boutiques and fine restaurants, along with a small-town feel as kids play on sidewalks and tourists stroll up and down the main artery of 3rd St. The main regional attractions are the area's fine wineries, of course.

◉ Sights

Evergreen Aviation Museum   MUSEUM
(☑503-434-4180; www.evergreenmuseum.org; 500 NE Captain Michael King Smith Way; adult/child $20/18; ☺9am-5pm) A mile east of McMinnville, this museum showcases Howard Hughes' *Spruce Goose,* the world's largest wood-framed airplane. In 1947, with Hughes at the wheel, the airplane flew for just under a mile – and never took off again. The museum also has an IMAX theater (admission separate), along with cafés and a wine-tasting room.

☆ Festivals & Events

Turkey Rama   FOOD
Held in July; anchored by 'the world's largest' turkey barbecue.

UFO Festival   UFOS
(www.ufofest.com) Held in May.

⌂ Sleeping

There are several chain hotels and motels in McMinnville, such as Motel 6 and Best Western. Surrounding town are a few countryside B&Bs; the chamber of commerce has details.

TOP CHOICE **McMenamins Hotel Oregon** HOTEL $
(☑503-472-8427, 888-472-8427; www.mcmenamins.com; 310 NE Evans St; d $50-110; ❂❀⏏) For a budget stay with personality there's this awesome downtown hotel. Expect the typical McMenamins eccentricities like eclectic artwork on all the walls; there's also an unbeatable rooftop restaurant-pub, mandatory for drinks on warm summer nights. Most of the classic old rooms share bathrooms, which are kept in good order.

Steiger Haus B&B   B&B $$
(☑503-472-0821; www.steigerhaus.com; 360 Wilson St; d $95-150; ❂) This friendly, casual home offers a little paradise right in downtown McMinnville. It's on a half-acre and features a hilly, woodsy backyard with good bird-watching. Five comfortable bedrooms are available, each with its own bathroom and some with a deck just outside.

Joseph Mattey House B&B   B&B $$
(☑503-434-5058; www.josephmatteyhouse.com; 10221 NE Mattey Lane; d $150-175; ❂❀⏏) About 3 miles northeast of town is this 1892 Queen Anne Victorian farmhouse featuring country-style atmosphere, charming old details and four comfortable rooms with quilts and lace. There's a great wraparound porch, plus a vineyard right past the lawn, and it's run by English owners.

Youngberg Hill Vineyard & Inn   INN $$$
(☑888-657-8668; www.youngberghill.com; 10660 SW Youngberg Hill Rd; d $200-350; ❂❀@⏏) There's no doubt about it – you're on this 700ft hill for the spectacular panoramic views. The eight rooms and suites at this large inn are luxurious, but you'll need to reserve ahead of time – especially for summer weekends, which are popular for weddings on the premises.

✗ Eating

There's good eating in McMinnville. For average pub fare with above-average views, head to the Hotel Oregon's rooftop resto-pub.

TOP CHOICE **Joel Palmer House** NORTHWESTERN $$$
(☑503-864-2995; www.joelpalmerhouse.com; 600 Ferry St, Dayton; mains $29-38; ☺dinner Tue-Sat) Renowned especially for its dishes laced with wild mushrooms (and hand-picked by the chefs – the Czarnecki family), this highly lauded restaurant is located just a few miles northwest of McMinnville. It's one of Oregon's finest eateries, turning local ingredients into unforgettable fine cuisine.

Thistle   NORTHWESTERN $$
(☑503-472-9623; www.thistlerestaurant.com; 228 NE Evans St; mains $18-20; ☺dinner Tue-Sat) Small but top-drawer restaurant run by Eric Bechard, an award-winning chef who fiercely believes in using local, organic ingredients whenever possible. The menu changes daily and is posted on a chalkboard, and while portions are small they are well created and truly delicious.

Bistro Maison   FRENCH $$$
(☑503-474-1888; www.bistromaison.com; 729 NE 3rd St; mains $20-29; ☺11:30am-2pm & 5-8pm Wed-Thu, 11:30am-2pm & 5-9pm Fri, 5-9pm Sat,

OREGON'S WINE BOUNTY

Oregon's first wineries started up in the 1850s, but it wasn't until the late 1960s and early 1970s, when a few Californians moved to Oregon and planted the first pinot noir grapes, that the region's modern winemaking potential started to fruit. David Lett, Charles Coury, David Adelsheim and Dick Erath are credited with the first pinot plantings; they saw potential in the northern Willamette Valley's mild climate and long, relatively mild summers, which not only foster the delicate pinot noir grape, but pinot gris, chardonnay and riesling as well.

Most vineyards are family owned and operated and welcome visitors to their tasting rooms, which range from grand edifices to homey affairs tucked into the corner of fermentation rooms. Get a winery map at McMinnville's chamber of commerce (p239), or check www.willamettewines.com, which will help you get a feel for the region's seven American Viticultural Areas (AVAs) and the more than 200 wineries and tasting rooms in the valley. While you'll find all manner of wineries in each zone, you'll start to taste similarities that stem from soil and weather in each AVA.

Visiting the Wineries

Before heading out, call or check wineries' websites for tasting-room hours and tasting fees (usually $5 to $10). On Thanksgiving weekend and Memorial Day weekend, many of the smaller wineries in the Valley, which don't usually open their doors to visitors, welcome guests. It's a great chance to meet winemakers and try new wines, but know you'll be joined by the masses, and traffic and parking can be a hassle.

Amity Vineyards (888-264-8966; 18150 Amity Vineyards Rd SE, Amity) Near the Eola Hills area around Amity; low-key and informal; produces a variety of good wine.

Archery Summit (503-864-4300; www.archerysummit.com; 18599 NE Archery Summit Rd, Dayton) Makes some of Oregon's very best pinot noirs (aged in caves).

Argyle Winery (888-427-4953; www.argylewinery.com; 691 Hwy 99W, Dundee) Makes impressive sparkling wines.

Domaine Drouhin (503-864-2700; www.domainedrouhin.com; 6750 Breymen Orchards Rd, Dayton) For grand atmosphere and panoramic views.

Elk Cove Vineyards (877-355-2683; www.elkcove.com; 27751 NW Olson Rd, Gaston) Beautiful winery off Hwy 47 near Gaston; has a nice riesling.

noon-8pm Sun) This European eatery is one of McMinnville's best restaurants, serving up all the stereotypical but tasty French treats like escargots, confit de canard, coq au vin and steak tartare. The lovely garden patio is mandatory on warm summer nights.

Nick's Italian Cafe   ITALIAN **$$$**
(503-434-4471; www.nicksitaliancafe.com; 521 NE 3rd St; mains $21-26, prix fixe $65; 11:30am-2:30pm & 5-9pm Mon-Fri, 5-9pm Sat, noon-8pm Sun) Going strong for over 30 years, Nick's doesn't offer slick, contemporary decor – but it does have renowned Italian cuisine, including a five-course fixed-price dinner. Come for lunch for excellent wood-fired pizza and panini; it's located next to the Hotel Oregon.

La Rambla   SPANISH **$$**
(503-435-2126; www.laramblaonthird.com; 238 NE 3rd St; mains $16-27; lunch & din-

ner) Try as much as possible by ordering several tapas, or go for the gusto with a complex main dish.

Golden Valley Brewery   BREWPUB **$$**
(www.goldenvalleybrewery.com; 980 NE 4th St; mains $9-33; lunch & dinner) Trendy brewery offering salads, sandwiches, pastas, burgers and steaks.

Cornerstone Coffee Roasters
          COFFEEHOUSE **$**
(216 NE 3rd St; drinks & snacks $4-6.50; 7am-10pm Mon-Thu & Sat, till 10pm Fri, 11am-5pm Sun) Casual coffee shop with good java.

ⓘ Information

Chamber of Commerce (503-472-6196; www.mcminnville.org; 417 NW Adams St; 9am-5pm Mon-Fri) Pick up a pamphlet to historic downtown McMinnville.

Erath Winery (☑800-539-9463; www.erath.com; 9409 NE Worden Hill Rd, Dundee) In the Dundee Hills AVA, which boasts rich red soil and the first grapes in the region, is this topnotch winery with a good pinot noir.

Ponzi Vineyards (☑503-628-12227; www.ponziwines.com; 14665 SW Winery Lane, Beaverton) In Beaverton, closer to Portland; one of Oregon's pioneer vineyards. Also has a wine-tasting room in Dundee (100 SW 7th St).

Sokol Blosser Winery (☑800-582-6668; www.sokolblosser.com; 5000 Sokol Blosser Lane, Dayton) A view of Mt Hood goes nicely with the chardonnay here.

Torii Mor (☑503-538-2279; www.toriimorwinery.com; 18325 NE Fairview Dr, Dundee) Produces small batches of quality wines, and has a pretty Japanese garden.

Willakenzie Estate (☑503-662-3280; www.willakenzie.com; 19143 Laughlin Rd, Yamhill) Hwy 240 leads west from Newberg to Willakenzie Estate; tucked in the rolling Chehalem Hills near Yamhill.

Yamhill Valley Vineyards (☑800-825-4845; www.yamhill.com; 16250 NW Oldsville Rd, McMinnville) Try the pinot gris; located west of McMinnville.

You don't have to visit wineries to try Willamette Valley wines. Tasting rooms offering wines from multiple winemakers have been popping up in many towns in the region, including Dundee, McMinnville and Carlton (just one of the signs the region's becoming even more of a wine destination). Also, most restaurants and cafés in wine country offer flights and extensive regional wine lists, and servers are well informed about food pairings and local wine makers.

Wine Tours

If you'd rather just sit back, drink and be driven, wine tours are offered:

Ecotours of Oregon (☑503-245-1428).

Equestrian Wine Tours (☑503-864-5253; jakepricestables@gmail.com) Tour on horseback.

Grape Escape (☑503-283-3380; www.grapeescapetours.com)

Oregon Wine Tours (☑503-681-9463; www.orwinetours.com)

Vista Balloon Adventures (☑503-625-7385; www.vistaballoon.com) Hot-air balloon ride.

Salem

POP 154,000

Hardly the most exciting state capital in the country, Salem is a peaceful and homely university city that exudes a slightly conservative air and is a popular destination for conferences. It would make a good day trip from Portland as it's just an hour's drive south. Highlights include the state capitol itself and a few museums, along with a pleasant riverfront park complete with carousel. Outside the city limits are more interesting destinations like a spectacular state park, some wineries and a garden.

◎ Sights

Willamette Heritage Center MUSEUM
(☑503-585-7012; www.missionmill.org; 1313 Mill St SE; adult/child $6/3; ◎10am-5pm Mon-Sat)-

This 5-acre complex houses grassy gardens, two gift shops, a clutch of pioneer buildings and two museums.

Collectively called the **Mission Mill Museum**, the **Jason Lee House** (1841), the **John Boon House** (1847), the **Methodist Parsonage** (1841) and an **old Presbyterian church** (1858) all look pretty much as they did in the 1840s and '50s. The **Thomas Kay Woolen Mill** was built in 1889 and was powered by Mill Creek, a section of which still runs through the grounds and turns waterwheels in the powerhouse.

Also on the grounds is the **Marion County Historical Society Museum** (☑503-364-2128; www.marionhistory.org; ◎noon-4pm Tue-Fri), with exhibits highlighting historic sites in the region. The museum is open by appointment on Saturday.

Oregon State Capitol
BUILDING

(☑503-986-1388; www.leg.state.or.us; 900 Court St; ⊙8am-5pm Mon-Fri) The state's first capitol building burned down in 1855, and a domed neo-Greek edifice was built to replace it. Unfortunately, that building also burned down (in 1935), and the current capitol building was completed in 1938. Bauhaus and art-deco influences are apparent, especially in the strident bas-relief in the front statuary and the hatbox-like cupola. The building is faced with gray Vermont marble, and the interior is lined with rose travertine from Montana.

The most notable features of the capitol are four Works Progress Administration-era **murals** lining the interior of the rotunda. There's also a galleria with exhibits put on by the local historical society. Surmounting the capitol building's top is the gleaming **Oregon Pioneer**, a 23ft-high gilded statue depicting a stylized, early male settler.

Free tours run are offered daily; call ahead to check schedules.

Willamette University
UNIVERSITY

(☑503-370-6267; www.willamette.edu; 900 State St) Just south of the capitol, Willamette University was the first university in the western USA and is well respected for its liberal-arts undergraduate program and law school. The visitor center has a walking tour leaflet of the university.

The oldest remaining building on the campus is **Waller Hall**, built between 1864 and 1867. The **Hallie Ford Museum of Art** (☑503-370-6855; 700 State St; adult/child $3/ free, admission free on Tue; ⊙10am-5pm Tue-Sat, 1-5pm Sun) houses works from Europe, the Middle East, Africa and Asia, along with the Pacific Northwest.

Bush's Pasture Park
PARK

One of Oregon's leading citizens of the late 19th century was Asahel Bush, a newspaperman and a highly successful banker who began building his rambling Italianate residence in 1877. Designed to be a self-sufficient farm, the grounds are now preserved as Bush's Pasture Park and include a large rose garden, a playground, picnic areas and walking trails.

The **Bush House Museum** (☑503-363-4714; www.salemart.org; 600 Mission St SE; adult/ child $4/2; ⊙noon-5pm Tue-Sun May-Sep, 2-5pm Oct-Apr) is open as a showplace of Victorian design. Note the marble fireplaces, 10 in all. Most of the wallpaper is from the original 1878 construction and was made in France.

The house is open for guided tours only; limited winter hours.

The reconstructed stable is now the **Bush Barn Art Center** (☑503-581-2228; www.salemart.org; ⊙10am-5pm Tue-Fri, noon-5pm Sat & Sun), which features three galleries. The main floor is given over to the work of local and regional artists and craftspeople – all art is for sale.

Deepwood Estate
HISTORIC HOUSE

(☑503-363-1825; www.historicdeepwoodestate.org; 1116 Mission St SE; adult/child $4/2; ⊙tours noon-5pm Sun-Fri) Not far from the Bush House, this 1894 Queen Anne mansion is topped by turrets and bejeweled with decorative moldings and beautiful stained-glass windows. There's free access to the grounds, which contain a nature trail and a formal English tea garden. The mansion is only open for guided tours, and Saturday is reserved for weddings. Limited winter hours.

AC Gilbert's Discovery Village
CHILDREN'S MUSEUM

(☑503-371-3631; www.acgilbert.org; 116 Marion St NE; 1-2yr $3, 3-59yr $6, over 60yr $4.50; ⊙10am-5pm Mon-Sat, noon-5pm Sun) Built to honor Salem native AC Gilbert, who invented the Erector Set, this hands-on children's museum is half technology-and-science workshops and half playroom. There's a wide range of fun activities, from a bubble room to a frozen shadows room to an outdoor tower maze and mammoth dig. Toddlers have their own section too.

Elsinore Theatre
THEATER

(☑503-375-3574; www.elsinoretheatre.com; 170 High St) A dazzling Tudor-Gothic landmark, opened in 1926 and once a silent-movie theater, is now a venue for theater and live music. Silent movies are shown monthly from October to May, with live accompaniment on a 1778-pipe Wurlitzer organ – one of the finest in the country. Tours by appointment.

Saturday Market
MARKET

(☑503-585-8264; www.salemsaturdaymarket.com; cnr Marion St NE & Summer St NE; ⊙9am-3pm Sat Apr-Oct) If you're around on a Saturday in summer, check out this crafts and farmers market that offers a taste of Salem's local culture.

☆ Festivals & Events

Oregon State Fair
FAIR

Salem's biggest party of the year; held at the fairgrounds and Expo Center for the 10 days prior to Labor Day.

Salem Art Fair & Festival   ART
Over 200 artists from around the country bring their work to the state's largest juried art show, held the third weekend of July at Bush Pasture Park.

🛏 Sleeping & Eating
Salem offers all the usual chain motels and hotels.

Betty's B&B   B&B $$
(✆503-399-7848; www.salemoregonbedand breakfast.com; 965 D Street; d $110; ❷✳🐾) Just two rooms – each with their own bathroom and decorated with antiques – are available at this small B&B run by your hospitable and knowledgeable host, Betty DeHamer. Breakfast is a gourmet affair, often made with produce from the garden, and the house is a restored Craftsman bungalow. If it's full, try the **Bookmark B&B** (✆503-399-2013), right next door.

Grand Hotel   HOTEL $$
(✆503-540-7800, 877-540-7800; www.phoenix grandhotel.com; 201 Liberty St SE; d from $129; ✳@🐾🏊) Salem's best lodgings are at this downtown hotel next to the city's conference center. Even standard rooms have sitting areas, and all are stylish, modern and elegant. It's geared towards business travelers, with amenities like indoor pool, spa, gym, restaurant and lounge; a breakfast buffet is also included.

Salem Campground & RVs   CAMPSITE $
(✆503-581-6736, 800-826-9605; www.salemrv.com; 3700 Hagers Grove Rd SE; tent/RV sites $20/29) Located behind Home Depot, Salem's closest campground features nearly 200 jam-packed campsites not far from a noisy highway. There are showers, a market and playground, but for a bit more nature head to Silver Falls State Park (p240).

Word of Mouth Bistro   AMERICAN $
(✆503-930-4285; www.wordofsalem.com; 140 17th St NE; mains $8-11; ⊙breakfast & lunch) If créme brulee French toast sounds good, then this small but excellent bistro should be on your food agenda. Other tasty (and unusual) treats include the blueberry pancakes, asparagus and brie omelet and prime rib benedict. Sandwiches and burgers rule the lunch menu.

Wild Pear   AMERICAN $
(www.wildpearcatering.com; 372 State St; mains $7-12; ⊙10am-5pm Mon-Sat) Popular modern deli serving up tasty soups, sandwiches

and salads, along with fancier options like a lobster and seafood melt. There are also fish tacos, Greek wraps, pizzas, homemade pastries and even *pho* (Vietnamese noodle soup) – they're really out to please all, and remain popular for it.

Best Little Roadhouse   AMERICAN $$
(www.bestlittleroadhouse.com; 1145 Commercial St SE; mains $9-22; ⊙11am-11pm Sun-Thu, till midnight Fri & Sat) This unique family-friendly dining spot has a comfortable modern atmosphere with separate bar area and sports on TV. Out back is a mini-golf course sporting waterfalls and fake-rock features, as well as a great shady patio for warm weather. The menu is lined with your typical meat-and-salad items, and there are local microbrews on tap.

Coffee House Café   COFFEEHOUSE $
(135 Liberty St NE; drinks under $4; ⊙breakfast, lunch & dinner;🐾) Fine hang-out spot with classic touches, open feel and free wi-fi. Sandwiches and wraps are available, the atmosphere is awesome and there's live music on Friday and Saturday nights. Attracts hippies.

ⓘ Information
Visitors Information Center (✆503-581-4325, 800-874-7012; www.travelsalem.com; 181 NE High St; ⊙8:30am-5pm Mon-Fri, 10am-4pm Sat)

ⓘ Getting There & Around
The Salem Airport is about 4 miles west of downtown. The **Hut Airport Shuttle** (✆503-364-4444; www.portlandairportshuttle.com) provides frequent service between Salem and Portland International Airport.

For long-distance bus services there's **Greyhound** (✆503-362-2428; 450 Church St NE). Trains stop at the **Amtrak Station** (✆503-588-1551; 500 13th St SE). **Cherriots** (✆503-588-2877; www.cherriots.org; 220 High St NE) buses serve the city; there's no weekend or holiday service.

Around Salem

Enchanted Forest   THEME PARK
(✆503-371-4242; www.enchantedforest.com; 8462 Enchanted Way SE, Turner; adult/child $10/9) Located 7 miles south of Salem, this children's theme park is a fun fantasyland offering rides (extra charge), a haunted house, European village, Western town and storybook themes, among other things. There are water light shows and a comedy theater in summer. Picnic grounds, gift

shops and food services are also available. Opening hours vary widely so check the website for details.

Oregon Garden & Gordon House

GARDEN & HISTORIC HOUSE

(☎877-647-2733; www.oregongarden.org; 879 W Main St; adult/student $10/8; ⊙9am-6pm) Plant-lovers shouldn't miss this garden, located 15 miles east of Salem outside Silverton. Over 20 specialty gardens are showcased on 80 acres, including a Northwest plant collection, miniature conifer section, children's garden and even a pet-friendly garden. There's a large hotel resort on the premises, along with wedding and conference facilities and outdoor pool and spa. Plenty of events take place here, including classes, lectures and outdoor summer concerts. Opening hours and admission prices vary year-round.

Next to the Oregon Garden is **Gordon House** (☎503-874-6066; www.thegordonhouse.org; 869 W Main St; tours $10), a home designed by Frank Lloyd Wright. It was built in 1964 and moved to its present location in 2002. It's best to reserve ahead for tours.

Mount Angel

TOWN & ABBEY

The little town of Mount Angel, with its Bavarian-style storefronts and lovely Benedictine abbey, is like an old-world holdover in the Oregon countryside. Visit in mid to late September, during **Oktoberfest** (☎503-845-9440; www.oktoberfest.org), for maximum effect. It is one of the state's largest harvest festivals, and thousands show up for brass bands, beer and dancers. Gothic-like **St Mary Catholic Church** (1910) is worth a visit for its mural-covered walls.

Open to everyone, the **Mount Angel Abbey** (☎503-845-3030; www.mountangelabbey.org; 1 Abbey Dve) is a delightful Benedictine monastery on grassy grounds set atop a hill that overlooks town. There's a modernist library designed by Finnish architect Alvar Aalto, plus a quirky museum featuring a 2.5lb pig hairball and deformed calves. There's also a **Russian Museum** on the premises; pick up a self-guided walking-tour map at the bookshop. Lodging is available to those seeking a spiritual retreat.

Mount Angel is 18 miles northeast of Salem on Hwy 214.

TOP CHOICE Silver Falls State Park

STATE PARK

(☎503-873-8681; day use $5) Oregon's largest state park, Silver Falls, 26 miles east of Salem on Hwy 214, is an easy day trip from Portland, Salem and Eugene. It offers camping, swimming, picnicking and horseback riding. Best of all are the hikes, the most famous being the **Trail of Ten Falls Loop**, a relatively easy 8-mile loop that winds up a basalt canyon through thick forests filled with ferns, moss and wildflowers. Featured on this hike are 10 waterfalls, several of which you can walk behind. A few roadside trailheads access this hike, but the most services are at the South Falls day-use area, the park's main entrance. This includes the **campground** (tent sites/RV sites/cabins $19/24/39).

Corvallis

POP 58,000

Proud to be home of Oregon State University (OSU), Corvallis is a bustling, youthful city at the base of the Oregon Coast Range. It lies on the edge of the Willamette River and is surrounded by miles of farms, orchards and vineyards. Downtown storefronts are filled with bakeries, bookstores and cafés, while the upscale riverfront area offers pleasant walking along with stylish restaurants and pubs. The university campus, where nearly half of the city's population studies or works, dominates just a few blocks to the west.

Corvallis is an easy place to spend a day just hanging out in bookstores or cafés, and it's also a good base from which to explore the surrounding region.

◎ Sights

Peavy Arboretum & McDonald Forest

FOREST

Both areas are administered by OSU and are popular with dog walkers. Peavy Arboretum has several interpretive trails that wind through 40 acres of forest. You can continue into McDonald State Forest, a research forest with several miles of hiking and mountain-bike trails. From Corvallis, take Hwy

---

WINERIES AROUND SALEM

One of Oregon's most-respected wine-growers is **Willamette Valley Vineyards** (☎800-344-9463; www.willamettevalleyvineyards.com; 8800 Enchanted Way, Turner), on an imposing hilltop south of town.

Stangeland Winery (☎503-581-0355; www.stangelandwinery.com; 8500 Hopewell Rd NW), north of Salem in the Eola Hills, is a smaller winery with good pinot noir.

and top Northwest artists showcase their work.

CELEBRATING WINE

Held at Linfield College in McMinnville in late July, the **International Pinot Noir Celebration** (☎800-775-4762; www.ipnc.org) is an important testing ground for pinot noir wines from all over the world. The three-day festival is immensely popular despite costing $975 per person (including some meals); there's a public tasting ($125) on Sunday.

A more egalitarian event, the **McMinnville Wine & Food Classic** (☎503-472-4033; www.macwfc.com) is held at the aviation museum in March.

99W north for about 5 miles, then turn left at Arboretum Rd and go almost a mile.

Marys Peak
FOREST

At 4097ft, Marys Peak, in the **Siuslaw National Forest**, is the highest peak in the Coast Range. Several hikes are strewn around the summit, and on a clear day there are views across the valley from the Pacific Ocean to the glacier-strewn Central Oregon Cascades.

To reach the summit, drive on Hwy 20 – past the nearby town of Philomath – and then take Hwy 34 for 8.5 miles. Turn right on Marys Peak Rd and go 9.5 miles to the Summit Trailhead; from the summit it's a half-mile walk. A Northwest Forest Pass (available at Peak Sports) or $5 day-use fee (payable on the spot) is required; there's also a campground nearby. Marys Peak Rd is closed above Mile 5.5 from about December to April.

★☆ Festivals & Events

da Vinci Days
ART/SCIENCE

(www.davincidays.org) Kinetic sculpture and home-built electric-car races are highlights of this funky arts-and-science celebration; held the third weekend in July.

Shrewsbury Renaissance Faire
FESTIVAL

(www.shrewfaire.com) Costumed players roam an Elizabethan marketplace, engaging visitors in late-16th-century small talk; held the second weekend in September in nearby Kings Valley.

Fall Festival
FESTIVAL

(www.corvallisfallfestival.org) Corvallis' premier festival takes place the last weekend in September. Live music fills the streets

🛏 Sleeping

Expect prices to skyrocket during key football games, graduation and other key university or city-wide festivals and events.

Hanson Country Inn
B&B $$

(☎541-752-2919; www.hcinn.com; 795 SW Hanson St; d $125-175; ☻✳🏠) Run for 24 years by Patricia Covey, this wonderful Dutch-colonial farmhouse – set in the countryside just minutes from downtown – once hosted travel writer Bill Bryson. The four rooms are comfortable and spacious, and two boast private decks. Two-bedroom cottage available; cats and a dog live on the premises. Popular with summer weddings.

Harrison House B&B
B&B $$

(☎541-752-6248, 800-233-6248; www.corvallis-lodging.com; 2310 NW Harrison Blvd; d $129-149; ☻✳@🏠) Dutch colonial B&B near the campus offering five tasteful and comfortable rooms, each with private bathroom (one is a cottage suite). The friendly hosts have plenty of information on the area, there are cozy common areas in which to socialize, and complimentary drinks – including wine – are offered.

Super 8 Motel
MOTEL $

(☎541-758-8088; www.super8.com; 407 NW 2nd St; d from $65; ☻✳@🏠🐾) Good budget motel with basic rooms and a pleasant location right next to the river and its walking trail. Larger rooms with two beds face the river.

Corvallis/Albany KOA
CAMPSITE $

(☎541-967-8521, 800-562-8526; www.koa.com; 33775 Oakville Rd; campsites/cabins $24/44, RV sites $32-35;🐾) Pleasant RV-oriented campground with small pool, mini-golf course and playground. Located 5 miles east of Corvallis just off Hwy 34. There's also camping at Marys Peak.

🍴 Eating

Bombs Away Café
MEXICAN FUSION $

(www.bombsawaycafe.com; 2527 NW Monroe Ave; mains $8-10; ⊙11am-midnight Mon-Fri, 5pm-midnight Sat) Long-running and popular eatery serving up Southwestern fare with a Northwest twist. Go for the basics like tacos, burritos or enchiladas, or try exotics like the cilantro-jalapeno tempeh burger or spicy African peanut soup. Local, sustainably-minded ingredients used.

McMenamins
AMERICAN $

(2001 NW Monroe Ave; mains $7-10; ⊙11am-10pm Mon-Wed, till midnight Thu-Sat, noon-10pm Sun) You can't go wrong with any McMenamins venue, where comfort foods like cheeseburgers and pepperoni pizzas (along with their own microbrews) are served up in creative interiors – check out the amazing copper trellis with painted ceramic sinks here. There is another branch at 420 NW 3rd St.

Beanery
COFFEEHOUSE $

(500 SW 2nd St; drinks $2.50-4, snacks $3-7; ⊙breakfast, lunch & dinner) Popular corner coffee shop grinding up local beans and offering fine snacks like sandwiches, quiches and pastries. Milkshakes, smoothies and floats too. Live music on weekends, and another smaller branch at 2541 NW Monroe Ave.

First Alternative
NATURAL GROCERY

(☑541-452-3115; 2855 NW Grant Ave; ⊙7am-9pm) For organic and local foods, go to this natural foods co-op with salad bar; it has another branch at 1007 SE 3rd St.

❶ Information

Corvallis Convention & Visitors Bureau (☑541-757-1544, 800-334-8118; www.visitcorvallis.com; 553 NW Harrison Blvd; ⊙9am-5pm Mon-Fri) Also open 10am to 3pm on Saturday July 4 to Labor Day.

❶ Getting There & Around

The nearest airport is in Eugene; **Omnishuttle** (☑800-741-5097; www.omnishuttle.com) has a shuttle to Corvallis. **Greyhound** (☑541-757-1797; www.greyhound.com; 153 NW 4th St) provides the city's long-distance bus services.

Local bus service is provided by **Corvallis Transit System** (CTS; ☑541-766-6998; www.corvallistransit.com). For an eco-transportation choice around town, contact **Corvallis Pedicab** (☑541-609-8949; www.corvallispedicab.com) or rent a bike at **Peak Sports** (☑541-754-6444; 135 NW 2nd St).

Eugene

POP 150,000

Full of youthful energy, liberal politics, alternative lifestylers and with a fun-loving atmosphere, eclectic Eugene is a vibrant stop along your I-5 travels. Also known as 'Tracktown,' the city is famous for its track-and-field champions – Nike was born here, after all. And while Eugene maintains a working-class base in timber and manufacturing, some of the state's most unconventional citizens live here as well – from ex-hippie activists to eco-green anarchists to upscale entrepreneurs to high-tech heads.

Eugene offers a great art scene, exceptionally fine restaurants, boisterous festivals, miles of riverside paths and several lovely parks. Its location at the confluence of the Willamette and McKenzie rivers, just west of the Cascades, means plenty of outdoor recreation in the area – especially around the McKenzie River region, Three Sisters Wilderness and Willamette Pass.

Sixty miles to the west is the Oregon coast, easily accessible via pretty Hwy 126. The city is also at the south end of the Willamette Valley, which boasts several world-class wineries. Eugene is an awesome place, for both energetic visitors and those lucky enough to settle here.

◉ Sights

Markets
MARKET

At E 5th Ave and Pearl St is the **5th St Public Market** (www.5stmarket.com; ⊙10am-7pm Mon-Sat, 11am-5pm Sun), an old mill that now anchors several dozen restaurants, cafés and boutique stores around a pretty central courtyard. Musicians and other performers occasionally entertain here.

For great fun and a quintessential introduction to Eugene's peculiar vitality, don't miss the **Saturday Market** (☑541-686-8885; www.eugenesaturdaymarket.org), held each Saturday from April through mid-November at E 8th Ave and Oak St. Between Thanksgiving and Christmas it's renamed the **Holiday Market** (www.holidaymarket.org) and moves indoors to the Lane Events Center at 13th Ave and Jefferson St.

University of Oregon
UNIVERSITY

(☑541-346-1000; www.uoregon.edu) Established in 1872, the University of Oregon is the state's foremost institution of higher learning, with a focus on the arts, sciences and law. The campus is filled with historic ivy-covered buildings and includes a **Pioneer Cemetery**, with tombstones that give vivid insight into life and death in the early settlement. Campus tours are held in the summer.

Museum of Natural and Cultural History
MUSEUM

(☑541-346-3024; http://natural-history.uoregon.edu; 1680 E 15th Ave; adult/child $3/2, free Wed; ⊙11am-5pm Wed-Sun) Housed in a replica of a Native American longhouse, this museum contains good displays on Native American artifacts and fossils – there's even a fun kids' 'laboratory' section.

Jordan Schnitzer Museum of Art   MUSEUM
(☑541-346-3027; http://jsma.uoregon.edu; adult/senior $5/3; 1430 Johnson Lane; ☺11am-8pm Wed, till 5pm Thu-Sat) This renowned museum offers a 13,000-piece rotating permanent collection of world-class art, with an Asian art specialty. Highlights include a 10-panel Korean folding screen and a standing Thai Buddha in gold leaf. Free admission on the first Friday of each month. Marché restaurant has an excellent café here.

Lane County Historical Museum   MUSEUM
(☑541-682-4242; 740 W 13th Ave; adult/child $3/0.75; ☺10am-4pm Tue-Sat) Old logging tools are prominent among the collection of historic artifacts preserved at this local museum. There's also a transportation collection that includes Oregon's oldest, best-preserved running gear (undercarriage) for a covered wagon.

Skinner Butte   VIEWPOINT
A hike up wooded Skinner Butte, directly north of downtown, provides a good orientation and a little exercise (drive up if you're feeling lazy). Eugene Skinner established the city's first business on the narrow strip of land along the Willamette River below, which is now **Skinner Butte Park**; there's a great playground for kids. And if you're a rock climber, don't miss the columnar basalt formations along the butte's lower western side.

Follow the path around the north side of Skinner Butte to the **Owens Memorial Rose Garden**, a lovely park with picnic benches and rose bushes (best June to August), along with the country's oldest Black Tartarian cherry tree, planted around 1847.

Alton Baker Park   PARK
Heaven for cyclists and joggers is this popular, 400-acre riverside park, which provides access to the **Ruth Bascom Riverbank Trail System**, a 12-mile bikeway that flanks both sides of the Willamette. There's good downtown access via the DeFazio Bike Bridge. See Paul's (p246) for bike rentals.

Hendricks Park Rhododendron Garden   GARDENS
Thousands of rhododendrons and azaleas erupt into bloom here in the spring, along with dogwoods and daffodils, peaking in May. The garden is part of a larger park that features native trees and shrubs, and during the rest of the year it's a quiet retreat with occasional lovely views worthy of a picnic. To get there head south on Agate St, turn left on 21st and left again on Fairmont, then right on Summit.

Science Factory   CHILDREN'S MUSEUM
(☑541-682-7888; www.sciencefactory.org; 2300 Leo Harris Pkwy; adult/senior $4/3; ☺noon-4pm Wed-Sun) Families with young kids can visit this children's museum, located in Alton Baker Park. Hands-on exhibits and a live iguana are among the highlights; weekend planetarium shows cost extra. Expansive lawns outside.

🏃 Activities

Pacific Tree Climbing Institute   TREE CLIMBING
(☑866-653-8733; www.pacifictreeclimbing.com; 605 Howard Ave; climbs from $200) Release your inner child and learn how to climb trees with this Eugene-based organization. Both day trips and overnight expeditions (that include spending the night up in a tree!) are available, and you won't need any climbing experience to partake – though being in good shape helps.

🎉 Festivals & Events

Oregon Bach Festival   MUSIC
(☑800-457-1486; www.oregonbachfestival. com) The great composer takes center stage, but other classical heavyweights like Beethoven, Brahms and Dvorak get a look-in as well. Held late June to mid-July.

WINERIES AROUND EUGENE

Nestled in the hills at the southern end of the Willamette Valley are some exceptional wineries. These include lovely **Silvan Ridge** (☑866-574-5826; www.silvanridge.com; 27012 Briggs Hill Rd; ☺noon-5pm), 11 miles southwest of Eugene. Nearby is **Sweet Cheeks** (☑541-349-9463; www.sweetcheekswinery.com; 27007 Briggs Hill Rd; ☺noon-6pm), with its beautiful tasting room. And **King Estate** (☑541-942-9874; www.kingestate.com; 80854 Territorial Rd; ☺11am-9pm) is a huge producer with outdoor marketplace and fine restaurant.

Oregon Country Fair
FAIR

(☎541-343-4298; www.oregoncountryfair.com)
This is a riotous celebration of Eugene's folksy, hippie past and present; held mid-July.

Oregon Festival of American Music
MUSIC

(OFAM; ☎541-434-7000; www.ofam.org)
American music is celebrated early August with a week-long concert series of jazz and contemporary show tunes.

Eugene Celebration
FESTIVAL

(☎541-681-4108; www.eugenecelebration.com)
Takes over downtown with parades, art shows and a lively street fair; late August.

🛏 Sleeping

Prices can rise sharply during key football games and graduation.

TOP CHOICE C'est La Vie Inn
B&B $$

(☎541-302-3014; www.cestlavieinn.com; 1006 Taylor St; d $125-140; 🐾❄@🛜) This gorgeous, restored Victorian house, run by a friendly French woman, is a neighborhood show-stopper and full of lovely details. Beautiful antique furniture fills the living and dining rooms, while the three tastefully appointed rooms offer comfort and luxury. Also available is an amazing suite with kitchenette ($225).

Excelsior Inn
INN $$

(☎541-342-6963, 800-321-6963; www.excelsior inn.com; 754 E 13th Ave; d $99-270; 🐾❄🛜) A stately, elegant and very comfortable inn with 14 rooms, each named after a famous composer. Reproduction antiques and wood floors blend with modern amenities for a luxurious experience, and one of Eugene's finest restaurants is on the premises. Breakfast is included.

Oval Door B&B
B&B $$

(☎541-683-3160, 800-882-3160; www.ovaldoor. com; 988 Lawrence St; d $85-185; 🐾❄@🛜) This friendly and laid back B&B has six homey rooms, all with private bath and individual decor. It has a great location near the center, yet is in a residential neighborhood. Gourmet breakfast is served, and the interior is shoes-off during rains.

Campbell House
INN $$

(☎541-343-1119, 800-264-2519; www.campbell house.com; 252 Pearl St; d $129-199; 🐾❄@🛜) A large inn with 18 rooms and lovely common spaces, Campbell House's lush garden is popular for weddings. Choose from small, cozy rooms, spacious suites with Jacuzzi and fireplace, or a two-bedroom suite ($349). Well located on a hill in an upscale neighborhood; breakfast buffet included.

Eugene Whiteaker Hostel
HOSTEL $

(☎541-343-3335; www.eugenewhiteakerhostel .com; 970 W 3rd Ave; dm $22-27, d $40-70; 🐾@🛜) This casual hostel is in an old rambling house. There's a kitchen for cooking, an artsy vibe, nice front and back patios to hang out in, and a free simple breakfast. Campsites are available ($10 per person), and there's an annex down the street.

Eugene Kamping World
CAMPSITE $

(☎541-343-4832, 800-343-3008; www.eugene kampingworld.com; 90932 S Stuart Way; tent/ RV sites $20/35) This large, tidy campground 6 miles north of Eugene (I-5 exit 199) has amenities like basketball and horseshoe courts, a laundry and a small store.

River Walk Inn
B&B $$

(☎541-344-6506, 800-621-2904; www.ariver walkinn.com; 250 N Adams St; d $100-120; 🐾🛜) Dutch colonial B&B with four simple, pretty rooms and casual, homey atmosphere. Close to the river; free bike rentals.

Secret Garden
INN $$

(☎541-484-6755, 888-484-6755; www.secret gardenbbinn.com; 1910 University St; d $125-245; 🐾❄🛜) Beautiful three-story house with 10 rooms, antique furniture and comfortable surroundings. Lush gardens.

Campus Inn
MOTEL $

(☎541-343-3376, 877-313-4137; www. campus-inn.com; 390 E Broadway; d from $70; 🐾❄@🛜) Pleasant motel near the university with spacious business-style rooms, small gym and communal Jacuzzi.

Timbers Motel
MOTEL $

(☎541-343-3345, 800-643-4167; www.timbers motel.net; 1015 Pearl St; d $69-109; ❄🛜) Tidy, centrally located motel with spacious rooms, some nicer than others (the cheapest are in the basement but can't be reserved).

✗ Eating

Two exceptional natural-food grocery stores are **Kiva** (☎541-342-8666; 125 W 11th St; ⊙9am-8pm Mon-Sat, 10am-6pm Sun) and **Sundance** (☎541-343-9142; 748 E 24th Ave; ⊙7am-11pm).

TOP CHOICE Beppe & Gianni's Trattoria
ITALIAN $$

(☎541-683-6661; www.beppeandgiannis. net; 1646 E 19th Ave; mains $16-20; ⊙dinner) One of Eugene's most beloved restaurants and certainly its favorite Italian food. Homemade pastas are the real deal here, and the desserts are excellent. Reservations only for groups of eight or more; otherwise, expect a wait.

Café Zenon
AMERICAN $$
(☑541-684-4000; www.zenoncafe.com; 898 Pearl St; mains $16-22; ☉11am-10pm Mon-Sat, 9:30am-2pm & 5-10pm Sun) Going strong for nearly 30 years, this downtown restaurant serves fine European-inspired main dishes – but it's the salads, appetizers and especially desserts that have folks coming back for more. Good service, wine list and brunches too.

Papa's Soul Food Kitchen
SOUTHERN $
(☑541-342-7500; 400 Blair Blvd; mains $6-10; ☉noon-2pm & 5-10pm Tue-Fri, 2-10pm Sat) Line up with the locals at this outrageously popular Southern-food spot, which grills up awesome jerk chicken, pulled-pork sandwiches, crawfish jambalaya and fried okra. Don't miss the Big Ass piece o' cake. The best part is the live blues music, which keeps the joint open late on weekends.

Red Agave
LATIN $$$
(☑541-683-2206; 454 Willamette St; mains $18-29; ☉5:30-11pm Mon-Thu, to midnight Fri & Sat) Caribbean and Latin American cuisine is featured here; consider the Chinook salmon with quinoa, poblano chile relleno or green molé enchiladas. Four kinds of margaritas, along with exotic cocktails, help it all go down easy.

McMenamins North Bank
AMERICAN $$
(22 Club Rd; mains $8-17; ☉11am-11pm Sun-Thu, to midnight Fri & Sat) Gloriously located on the banks of the mighty Willamette, this relatively modest (for a McMenamins) pub-restaurant boasts some of the best views in Eugene. Grab a riverside patio table on a warm, sunny day and order a burger with the Hammerhead ale – you can't get more stylin'.

Newman's Fish 'n Chips
AMERICAN $
(1545 Willamette St; mains $6-9; ☉10am-8pm Mon-Sat, 11am-7pm Sun) Fish market offering Eugene's best fish 'n chips. Some covered outdoor seating.

Sweet Life Patisserie
BAKERY $
(755 Monroe St; pastries $2.50-5; ☉breakfast, lunch & dinner) Eugene's best dessert shop; also serves organic coffee.

Keystone Café
CAFÉ $
(www.keystonecafe.net; 395 W 5th Ave; mains $7-9; ☉breakfast & lunch; ☑) The best breakfast in town, serving up organic omelets, vegan pancakes and tempeh scrambles. Nitrate-free bacon.

🍷 Drinking & Entertainment

Wandering Goat
COFFEEHOUSE
(268 Madison St; ☉7am-11pm Mon-Wed, 7am-midnight Thu & Fri, 8am-midnight Sat, 8am-10pm Sun) For quirky vibe and artsy atmosphere, hunt out this small coffee shop next to the railroad tracks. It roasts its own sustainably harvested beans, and the bagel with gravy is unique – and good. There's live music on weekends.

Sam Bond's
MUSIC VENUE
(☑541-431-6603; 407 Blair Blvd) Eugene's favorite live-music venue, located in an old garage. Nightly entertainment from 9pm on, with good organic pizza, happy-hour pints for $3, free bluegrass jams on Tuesday and nice outdoor patio for those sweltering summer nights.

Steelhead Brewing Co
BREWPUB
(199 E 5th Ave; ☉11:30am-11:30pm Sun-Thu, to 1am Fri & Sat) Classic, award-winning brewpub with all the usual suspects on the menu, plus around a dozen homemade brews including seasonal and dark beers, plus a raspberry ale. Bottoms up.

Beanery
COFFEEHOUSE
(152 W 5th Ave; ☉6am-11pm Mon-Sat, 7am-11pm Sun) Warm, casual space with vaulted ceilings and hosting a great organic coffeehouse. Enter through the alley in back.

Ninkasi Brewing Company
BREWERY
(272 Van Buren St; ☉10am-6pm Tue-Fri, 9am-4:30pm Sat) Head to the tasting room to sample some of Oregon's best microbrew.

🛈 Information

Visitors Association (☑541-484-5307, 800-547-5445; www.travellanecounty.org; 754 Olive St; ☉8am-5pm Mon-Fri, 10am-4pm Sat & Sun)

🛈 Getting There & Around

The **Eugene Airport** (☑541-682-5430; www.flyeug.com) is about 7 miles northwest of center. **Greyhound** (☑541-344-6265; www.greyhound.com) is at 987 Pearl St. Trains leave from the **Amtrak station** (☑541-687-1383; www.amtrak.com; 433 Willamette St).

Local bus service is provided by **Lane Transit District** (LTD; ☑541-687-5555; www.ltd.org). To get around on your own pedal power, head to **Center for Appropriate Transport** (☑541-344-1197; www.catoregon.org; 455 W 1st St) or **Paul's** (☑541-344-4150; 152 W 5th St) for bike rentals.

IN HOT WATER

A couple hours' drive east of Salem is one of Oregon's best free soaks – **Bagby Hot Springs** (www.bagbyhotsprings.org). You'll need to hike 1.5 miles through lush forest to reach these springs, but then you'll be rewarded with rustic private bathhouses and hollowed-log tubs. Be prepared to wait your turn on weekends. A $5 Northwest Forest Pass is required at the parking lot, where you shouldn't leave any valuables.

From Estacada, head 26 miles south on Hwy 224. This road turns into Forest Rd 46; keep going straight for 3.5 more miles, then turn right onto Forest Rd 63 and go 3.6 miles to USFS Rd 70. Turn right again and go about 6 miles to the parking area.

For a more developed soaking experience there's **Breitenbush Hot Springs** (☎503-854-3320; www.breitenbush.com), located east of Salem off Hwy 46, just past the town of Detroit. This peaceful retreat offers beautiful hot springs, along with massages, yoga, vegetarian food and simple lodgings. Day-use fees range from $14 to $26 per adult and require reservations. Call or check the website for directions.

McKenzie Region

The single name 'McKenzie' identifies a beautiful and mysterious river, a mountain pass, a spectacular historic highway and one of Oregon's most extraordinary and wondrous natural areas. Premiere recreational opportunities abound, from fantastic fishing to exceptional hiking to racy rafting trips.

The little community of McKenzie Bridge, 50 miles east of Eugene on Hwy 126, offers a few cabins and a market. Four miles east from here the highway splits and continues east as Hwy 242 (the Old McKenzie Hwy) over the Cascades toward McKenzie Pass on its way to Sisters, 34 miles distant (the pass is closed November to June). Hwy 126 continues north along the McKenzie River to US 20, which crosses the Cascades at Santiam Pass (4817ft, open year-round).

🏃 Activities

Hiking

One of Oregon's showcase 'Wild & Scenic Rivers,' the McKenzie is graced with the 26-mile **McKenzie River National Recreation Trail**, which follows the here-again, gone-again cascading river from its inception near the town of McKenzie Bridge. There are entry trailheads at several places along Hwy 126.

A good day hike is the 5-mile **Clear Lake Loop**, accessible via either Clear Lake Resort or Coldwater Cove Campground. It circles Clear Lake while passing a large spring, several groves of old-growth forest and an extensive lava flow.

Another series of easy hikes begins at the **Sahalie Falls**, where a footbridge crosses the upper falls viewpoint to join the Mc-Kenzie River Trail for a 2-mile stroll to Carmen Reservoir past **Koosah Falls**. On the highway side of the river is the more developed and shorter **Waterfall Trail**, which links Sahalie with Koosah Falls. Parts of this trail are wheelchair accessible.

Day hikes also reach the calm, emerald-colored **Tamolitch Pool** (aka Blue Pool) from the south. To reach the trailhead, turn off Hwy 126 at Trail Bridge Reservoir, following the gravel road to the right. The 2-mile trail passes through a mossy lava flow before coming upon the mighty McKenzie River surging up in a cliff-lined bowl of rock.

Fishing

The McKenzie River is one of the best fishing streams in Oregon, and the slower water and deep pools west of Blue River also offer good fishing. Check regulations with the **Fish & Wildlife Office** (☎541-726-3515) in Springfield. For fishing guides and equipment rental, check www.mckenzieguides.com.

Rafting

White-water rafting trips are popular on the McKenzie River's class I to III rapids from April to October. **High Country Expeditions** (☎888-461-7238; www.hcexpeditions.com) and **Oregon Whitewater Adventures** (☎800-820-7238; www.oregonwhitewater.com) operate on the McKenzie.

🛏 Sleeping

There are many lovely summer **campgrounds** (☎877-444-6777; campsites $10-18) in the area, which include **Paradise** (old-growth grove near white water), **McKenzie Bridge** (Douglas fir and cedar trees), **Delta** (scenic and enchanting) and **Ice Cap Creek** (a cliff-top location near a reservoir and waterfalls). Limited reservations are possible. Contact the ranger station for more information.

Reserve rooms in summer.

Belknap Hot Springs Lodge RESORT **$$**

(☎541-822-3512; www.belknaphotsprings.com; 59296 Belknap Springs Rd; tent/RV sites $25/35, d $100-185, cabins $65-400; ✿✳✖) This large mountain resort has something for everyone – camping, RV sites, rustic cabins, modern lodge rooms and even fancy houses. The reason to visit or stay here, however, are the spring-fed pools (non-guest fee $7 to $12).

Clear Lake Resort CABINS **$**

(☎541-967-3917; www.campingfriend.com/clear lakeresort; 13000 Hwy 20; tent & RV sites $18, cabins $64-117; ✿) These rustic lakeside cabins, 4 miles south of Hwy 20, are great – except for the diesel generators. More modern cabins are available; older ones share outside bathrooms. Rowboat rentals available. Bring bedding and cooking gear.

Harbick's Country Inn MOTEL **$**

(☎541-822-3805; www.harbicks-country-inn. com; 54791 McKenzie Hwy; d $70-110; ✿✳✖✿) Friendly and attractive motel with both older rooms and gorgeous remodeled ones (some with flat-screen TVs, kitchenette and jetted tubs). Eventually all will be converted, but this might take years. Nice grassy view out back. There's also a large apartment available ($110).

Horse Creek Lodge CABINS **$$**

(☎541-822-3243; www.hclodge.com; 56228 Delta Dr; cabins $108-115, house $390; ✿) Three one- and two-bedroom cabins with fireplace and kitchens are available at this lovely, secluded spot with artsy feel. The Delta House has four bedrooms and is great for large groups; it's a quarter-mile walk to the river. Two-night minimum during busy seasons; limited wi-fi.

Caddisfly Resort COTTAGES **$$**

(☎541-822-3556; www.caddisflyresort.com; 56404 McKenzie Hwy; cabins $99; ✿✿) Friendly, family-run place with just three rustic

'cottages' (two share a wall). All have a fully stocked kitchen, fireplace and deck near the river; two have separate bedroom plus sleeping loft, while the last is a one-bedroom cabin with sleeper sofa. Good for groups of four to seven people; a great deal.

Eagle Rock Lodge B&B **$$**

(☎541-822-3630; www.eaglerocklodge.com; 49198 McKenzie Hwy; d $130-225; ✿✳✿) This gorgeous B&B has eight rooms (some with fireplace and Jacuzzi) and over 4 acres of lovely lawns and gardens. Located right next to the river, with a great deck nearby.

McKenzie River Inn B&B **$$**

(☎541-822-6260; www.mckenzieriverinn.com; 49164 McKenzie Hwy; d $98-185; ✿✿) Another B&B with rooms and cabins.

✗ Eating

TOP CHOICE **Holiday Farm Resort** NORTHWESTERN **$$**

(☎541-822-3725; www.holidayfarmresort. com; 54455 McKenzie River Dr; mains $16-24; ⏲dinner) This elegant restaurant almost seems out of place in this 'rustic' region. Enjoy upscale dishes like hazelnut salmon, smoked bourbon baby back ribs and portabella mushroom ravioli. There's a lounge for hanging out, and riverside cottages are available (from $175). Reserve Friday and Saturday.

Rustic Skillet AMERICAN **$**

(54771 McKenzie Hwy; mains $6-16; ⏲6:30am-2pm Mon-Wed, to 8pm Thu-Sun) Go back in time at this very casual diner, which offers up pancakes and three-egg omelets for breakfast, a variety of sandwiches and burgers for lunch, and steaks and seafood for dinner. Homemade pies and a nice patio are highlights.

❶ Information

McKenzie Ranger Station (☎541-822-3381; www.fs.fed.us/r6/willamette; 57600 McKenzie Hwy; ⏲8am-4:30pm) Can help with trails and campgrounds, and sells permits.

Getting There & Away

Lane Transit District (☎541-687-5555; www. ltd.org) Bus 91 from Eugene provides services along Hwy 126 to the McKenzie Ranger Station.

Columbia River Gorge

Best Places to Eat

» Stonehedge Gardens &
Bistro (p255)

» Celilo Restaurant & Bar
(p255)

» Double Mountain Brewery (p255)

Best Places to Stay

» McMenamins Edgefield
(p249)

» Skamania Lodge (p252)

» Celilo Inn (p258)

Why Go?

Cleanly dividing Oregon and Washington is the spectacular Columbia River Gorge, which was carved some 15,000 years ago by cataclysmic glaciers and floods. Driving east on I-84 (or on the scenic Historic Columbia River Hwy) has you passing high waterfalls and nearly vertical mountain walls, all the while paralleling the mighty Columbia.

Hikers have plenty to keep them busy in the gorge, which features many steep, lovely trails that lead through canyons lined with ferns and gushing rivers, and across wildflower fields to grand vistas. Summer wind sports are legendary – the gorge channels westerlies inland against the current, creating world-class windsurfing and kiteboarding conditions. There are also mountain-biking and rafting possibilities, especially around Hood River.

Not into strenuous activity? The gorge offers highlights such as lovely waterfalls, agricultural bounties (don't miss the cherries in July!) and fine wine tasting. This is a special place, so take time to enjoy it.

When to Go
Hood River

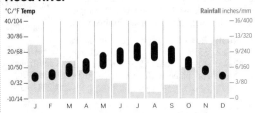

February–May	June–August	September–October
Waterfalls are at their gushing best, thanks to incessant winter and spring rains	Ripe cherries, great hiking weather and hot westerlies for kiteboarding	Luscious apples and pears, plus Hood River's Harvest Festival

The Western Gorge & Columbia River Highway

Finished in 1915, the Historic Columbia River Hwy winds its scenic way between Troutdale and the Dalles. Also known as US 30, this thoroughfare was the first paved road in the Northwest and America's first scenic highway; it was also the last leg of Lewis and Clark's Corps of Discovery expedition and the hellish finale for Oregon Trail pioneers.

The Columbia River Hwy offers access to gushing waterfalls in spring, wildflower displays in summer and awe-inspiring views all year round. Hikers have plenty of trailheads to choose from, and cyclists can cruise two stretches of the old highway renovated for non-vehicular use. It's slow going on busy weekends, however, and windy enough that trailers are not recommended.

For great views, head to **Portland Women's Forum Park** – it's just a parking lot but one of the best viewpoints into the gorge. Another great must-see panoramic spot is nearby **Crown Point**, which marks the western edge of the gorge. Here, the 1916 **Vista House**, an art nouveau–style rotunda, houses an **information center** (☑503-695-2230; ⊙9am-6pm), gift shop and snack stand. And everyone stops at **Multnomah Falls**, Oregon's tallest waterfall at 642ft, with a one-hour hike to the top. There's a **US Forest Service visitors center** (☑503-695-2372; ⊙9am-5pm) and refreshment stand at the base of the falls. Finally, hikers will love the very popular **Eagle Creek Trail** (see p252), the gorge's premier tromp; just be prepared for high trails with steep drop-offs.

There's camping at **Ainsworth State Park** (☑503-695-2301, 800-551-6949; www.oregonstateparks.org; tent/RV sites $17/20) though it caters more to RVs with crowded campsites and highway noise. For unique atmosphere, stay at the unforgettable **McMenamins Edgefield** (☑503-669-8610; 800-669-8610; www.mcmenamins.com; 2126 SW Halsey St, Troutdale; dm $30, d $70-119; ⊖❉☎) in Troutdale, worth a visit for its bars and restaurants alone. The **Multnomah Falls Lodge** (☑503-695-2376; www.multnomahfallslodge.com; ⊙8am-9pm) offers several dining options, from casual snacks to weekend summer barbecues to fine Northwest-style dinners; you can stay here too.

To reach the historic highway, take exit 17 or 35 off I-84.

Cascade Locks & Around

An early transportation center, Cascade Locks (at exit 44 off I-84) derives its name from the navigational locks, completed in 1896, that cut through the treacherous rapids here. The town flourished throughout the 1930s, when the area was home to thousands of Bonneville Dam construction workers. Bonneville Lake flooded the rapids in 1938 and they remain submerged.

◉ Sights & Activities

FREE **Cascade Locks Historical Museum** MUSEUM
(☑541-374-8535; Port Marina Park; ⊙noon-5pm Sun-Thu, 10am-5pm Fri & Sat; ⊙May-Sep) Housed in an old lockmaster's residence, this museum features Native American artifacts, a fish wheel and a basement taxidermy collection – including a very surprised bobcat.

Columbia Gorge Sternwheeler BOAT TRIP
(☑800-224-3901; www.portlandspirit.com; adult/child $28/18) Sightsee the Columbia River. Embark from the eastern end of Marine Park, where there are picnic tables, a café and gift shop. There are also jet boat rides and other types of cruises.

⌂ Sleeping & Eating

A couple of campgrounds, a few motels and some diners offer the basics. Most travelers stay in Hood River (p253), 14 miles to the east, or across the river at elegant Skamania Lodge (p254).

Bonneville Dam

This **dam** (☑541-374-8820; admission free; ⊙9am-5pm) was one of the largest New Deal projects of the Depression era. Completed in 1937, it was the first major dam on the Columbia River. Dam construction brought thousands of jobs, and the cheap electricity produced by the dam promised future industrial employment. Bonneville's two hydroelectric powerhouses back up the Columbia River for 15 miles and together produce over 1 million kilowatts of power.

The **visitors center** has good exhibitions and theaters showing videos of the dam's history. Downstairs, underwater windows allow visitors to watch salmon (and lampreys!) swim by. From the roof you can clearly see the **fish ladders**, which allow migrating fish to negotiate around the dams. There's

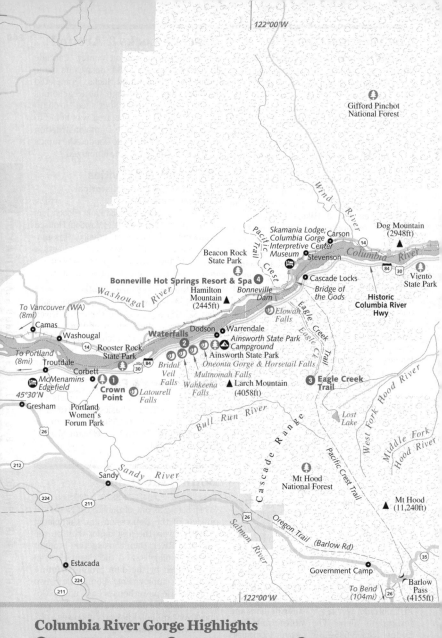

Columbia River Gorge Highlights

❶ Enjoy incredible panoramic views from Crown Point's **Vista House** (p249)

❷ Count dozens of gushing **waterfalls** (p256) up and down the gorge

❸ Hike up the premiere **Eagle Creek Trail** (p252) to heart-skipping heights

❹ Soak away your aches at **Bonneville Hot Springs Resort & Spa** (p252)

❺ Learn to catch the wind while **windsurfing** or **kiteboarding** (p254) around Hood River

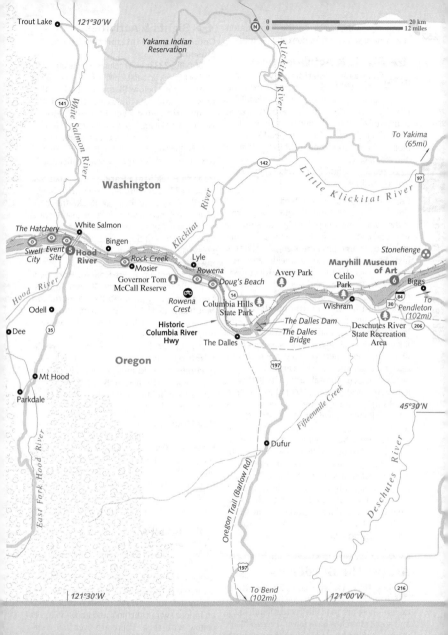

6 Explore the impressive
Maryhill Museum of Art
(p259), on Washington's side

7 Taste the gorge's spring
and summer's **fruit bounties**
(p253), or go **wine tasting**

another visitors center on the Washington side, where you can take powerhouse tours.

◉ Sights & Activities

FREE **Bonneville Fish Hatchery** HATCHERY
(☏541-374-8393; ☉7am-dusk) Next door, located on pretty grounds with picnic tables, is a visitor-friendly facility. There are several ponds full of rainbow trout and massive sturgeon – including a 10-footer named Herman – along with an educational exhibit, gift shop and small café.

To reach the dam and fish hatchery, take exit 40 off I-84.

Eagle Creek Recreation Area PARK

The beautiful, 13.2-mile **Eagle Creek Trail** is the gorge's most popular hike; on summer weekends, get here early to snag a parking spot. Early gorge promoters engineered this historic trail in 1910 to coincide with the opening of the Historic Columbia River Hwy.

The trail passes a dozen waterfalls as it meanders up wooded slopes and sheer rock walls through a narrow basalt canyon. Parts of the trail are perilously high and lack guard rails, making them dangerous for children and dogs. These sections have metal aid ropes, but even so those with vertigo issues should be extra careful.

It's 6 miles to **Tunnel Falls**, which crosses a dizzying bridge over a 150ft chasm before reaching a tunnel carved behind a waterfall. Backpack overnight at 7.5 Mile Camp to turn a tiring day hike into an easy two-day trip. **Punchbowl Falls** (4.2 miles round trip) and **High Bridge** (6.5 miles round trip) are turning points for shorter hikes.

The trail continues past Tunnel Falls for longer backcountry loops to viewpoints at Wahtum Lake and Benson Plateau, accessible via connections with the Pacific Crest Trail, Wy'East Trail No 434 and Ruckel Creek Trail No 405.

Across the Border

Driving Hwy 14 on the Columbia River Gorge on the Washington side has its advantages – there are roadside recreational lakes, and some stretches have fewer trees to block views. As a two-lane highway, however, it's slower and also much curvier than Oregon's I-84. You can reach Hwy 14 via a few key bridges including I-205 (between Portland and Vancouver, WA), Cascade Lock's Bridge of the Gods ($1 toll) and the Hood River Bridge (75 cent toll) at Hood River.

◉ Sights & Activities

Columbia Gorge Interpretive Center Museum MUSEUM

(☏800-991-2338; www.columbiagorge.org; 900 SW Rock Creek Dr; adult/child $7/6; ☉10am-5pm) Located just below Skamania Lodge, this museum attempts to weave together the many threads that form the area's history – Native Americans, early explorers, pioneer settlers, logging, fishing, shipping, power generation and recreation. It also claims to have the 'world's largest rosary collection.'

Beacon Rock State Park STATE PARK

(☏509-427-8265; www.parks.wa.gov; Hwy 14 Mile 35) Washington's Beacon Rock, the core of an ancient volcano, is a pleasant state park about 7 miles west of the Bridge of the Gods. It offers hiking, mountain biking and horseback riding trails, picnicking, camping (sites $21) and river access.

The ascent up 848ft **Beacon Rock** is a 0.75-mile trail with around 50 switchbacks. For a longer hike, climb 2445ft **Hamilton Mountain** (8 miles round trip, about 4½ hours); going just 1.25 miles leads to Hardy and Rodney Falls.

Beacon Rock is one of the few **rock-climbing** sites in the gorge. The majority of climbs are trad and multi-pitch, and for experienced climbers only. To protect raptor nests, climbing is not allowed from February to mid-July.

Dog Mountain HIKING

It's a steep 4 miles up the popular **Dog Mountain Trail**, but this is the best place in the gorge for late-spring wildflowers. Once on top, the views of the Columbia River and nearby Cascade volcanoes are spectacular. Allow approximately five hours round-trip and take a jacket – it's windy up there.

🛏 Sleeping

TOP CHOICE **Skamania Lodge** HOTEL $$$
(☏509-427-7700, 800-221-7117; www.skamania.com; 1131 SW Skamania Lodge Way; d from $200; ✆❋☀☎) Up the hill from the bridge is the gorge's biggest and cushiest resort. Facilities include hiking trails, tennis courts, a spa, an indoor swimming pool and an 18-hole golf course with shop. There are over 250 comfortable lodge rooms and suites with either forest or river views, plus three restaurants.

Bonneville Hot Springs Resort & Spa
HOTEL $$$
(☏866-459-1678; www.bonnevilleresort.com; 1252 E Cascade Dr; d from $200, pool day use

Mon-Thu $15, Fri-Sun $25; ⊖⊠❄@⊚) For a luxurious experience, head to this fancy resort and spa. With a grand, five-star lobby and stylish rooms (some with private hot tubs), this resort offers fine dining and full spa services. There's an elegant, 25m indoor pool filled with mineral water, plus indoor and outdoor Jacuzzis. The resort is about 3 miles east of the Bridge of the Gods; look for the entrance road ('Hot Springs Way') across from the Bonneville Dam visitor center road.

❶ Information
US Forest Service visitors center (☑509-427-2528; ⊙9am-5pm) In Skamania Lodge.

Hood River

One of the best windsurfing and kiteboarding destinations in the world is the dynamic town of Hood River. Strong river currents, prevailing westerly winds and a vast body of water provide the perfect conditions for these wind sports, attracting sometimes hundreds of photogenic enthusiasts who zip back and forth across the wide Columbia River.

But Hood River offers more than awesome winds. South of town, the Hood River drains a wide fertile valley planted with orchards. During spring, the area fills with the scent and color of pink and white blossoms, and roadside fruit stands peddle apples, pears, cherries, berries and vegetables. Premier wineries have also taken hold in the region, providing good wine-tasting opportunities. Hwy 35, which traverses the valley, continues south 40 miles to Mt Hood, Oregon's best-known mountain and a mecca for more great outdoor activities.

❂ Sights
Hood River County Historical Museum
MUSEUM
(☑541-386-6772; 300 E Port Marina Dr; donation $3; ⊙10am-4pm Mon-Sat, noon-4pm Sun Apr-Oct) The displays here include Native American artifacts (including intricate baskets) and antique everyday memorabilia from 1850 to 1950. Open April to October only; limited hours in fall.

Mt Hood Railroad
TRAIN RIDE
(☑541-386-3556, 800-872-4661; www.mthood rr.com; 110 Railroad Ave; adult/child from $25/15) Built in 1906, the railroad once transported fruit and lumber from the upper Hood

WORTH A TRIP

THE FRUIT LOOP

You'll come across promotional literature and maps on the Hood River County Fruit Loop at all Columbia River Gorge information offices. Covering 35 miles along scenic fertile lands, this driving loop takes you by family fruit stands, U-pick orchards, lavender fields, alpaca farms and winery tasting rooms. There are blossoms in spring, berries in summer, and apples and pears in fall – with plenty of festivals and celebrations also throughout the seasons (except for winter). It's a good way to sample the area's agricultural bounties while appreciating the local scenery too. Jump on the agritourism wagon; for more information and a list of events, check www.hoodriverfruitloop.com.

River Valley to the main railhead in Hood River. The vintage trains now transport tourists beneath Mt Hood's snowy peak and past fragrant orchards. Reserve in advance.

Lost Lake
LAKE
Take your own postcard photo of Mt Hood from Lost Lake, which frames the white peak rising from a deep-blue lake amid thick green forest. This inland side trip offers relief when the gorge gets too hot. To reach Lost Lake, which is 25 miles south of Hood River, take Hwy 281 from Hood River to Dee and follow the signs. Canoe and paddle boat rentals are available at the resort (www.lostlakeresort.com) here.

Saturday Market
MARKET
(⊙May-Sep) If you happen to be around town from May to September, check out the Saturday market at 5th and Columbia Sts for crafts, live music and a farmers market.

❁ Activities
Lovers of the grape can visit over a dozen wineries in the region for **wine-tasting** adventures. Stop by the chamber of commerce for a 'Columbia Gorge Wine Map,' which outlines all of them; you can also check www.columbiagorgewine.com.

Head south of town for great **mountain biking**. Most of the area's trails are off Hwy

SLICING UP THE COLUMBIA

On hot summer days, the inland desert climate of Eastern Oregon attracts cool air from the Pacific Coast, creating fierce winds that shoot westwards 80 miles through the narrow walls of the Columbia River Gorge. These westerlies, which directly oppose the river's flow, create some of the world's most optimal conditions for **windsurfing**, popular around Hood River since the 1980s. **Kiteboarding**, a relative newcomer on the block, also offers exciting speeds and airy acrobatics. On a good day you can witness hundreds of colorful sails cutting through the water at breathtaking speeds, a daring display of athleticism and beauty.

Good put-in spots in Washington include **Swell City**, **the Hatchery** and **Doug's Beach**. In Oregon, Hood River's **Event Site** is a major put-in location; other good ones include **Rock Creek** and **Rowena**. Wind conditions change frequently, making some locations better than others on any given day; for current conditions check www.iwindsurf.com.

For beginners, taking a lesson will make a world of difference. **Big Winds** (✆888-509-4210; www.bigwinds.com; 207 Front St, Hood River) is the biggest operator in the area and right downtown. **Brian's Windsurfing** (✆541-386-1423; www.brianswindsurfing.com; 100 Marina Way, Hood River) is another good option.

35 and Forest Rd 44 (which branches off Hwy 35 about 20 miles south of Hood River). Good local rides include Post Canyon, Surveyor's Ridge and Nestor Peak.

For **white-water rafting**, head to the White Salmon, Hood or Klickitat Rivers.

Cyclists, walkers, runners and skaters share the pavement on the refurbished stretch of the Historic Columbia River Hwy between Hood River and Mosier. No cars are permitted on the 4.5-mile road, which passes through two old highway tunnels and is popular with families. To reach the trailhead, head east out of downtown, cross Hwy 35, and continue up the hill to the parking area ($5 parking fee).

Discover Bicycles   CYCLING
(✆541-386-4820; 210 State St; ☉10am-6pm Mon-Sat, till 5pm Sun) rents mountain bikes and can give advice.

Kayak Shed   WATER SPORTS
(✆541-386-4286; 6 Oak St; ☉9am-5pm) Rents kayaks for $45 per day; in Hood River.

Wet Planet   WATER SPORTS
(✆877-390-9445; www.wetplanetwhitewater.com; 860 Hwy 141) White-water rafting tours; located nearby in Husum, WA.

★ Festivals & Events

The Hood River Valley springs to life the third weekend of April with the **Blossom Festival**. Local orchard tours are the highlight, along with food, music and crafts in town. Its fall version is the **Harvest Festival** in October.

🛏 Sleeping

Hood River is a popular place; you'll need reservations in summer. Listed here are summer weekend rates; during the off season and on weekdays prices tend to drop. There are around 20 B&Bs in town.

Columbia Gorge Hotel   HOTEL $$$
(✆541-386-5566, 800-345-1921; www.columbiagorgehotel.com; 4000 Westcliff Dr; d $209-289; ➋❋@🛜) Hood River's most famous stay is this historic Spanish-style hotel, set high on a cliff above the Columbia. Service is good, the atmosphere classy and the grounds lovely, and there's a fine restaurant on the premises. River view rooms cost more, but are worth it.

Lakecliff B&B   B&B $$
(✆541-386-7000; www.lakecliffbnb.com; 3820 Westcliff Dr; d $175; ➋❋🛜) Sitting on a cliff overlooking the Columbia River, this artsy B&B offers four simple but spacious rooms – most with gas fireplaces and amazing views. The 3 acres of lawns are popular for weddings in summer, and you can enjoy breakfast on the back deck while watching the windsurfers.

Hood River B&B   B&B $$
(✆541-387-2997; www.hoodriverbnb.com; 918 Oak St; d $85-140; ➋❋@🛜) Friendly owners Jane and Jim Nichols have made their casual B&B into a homey and comfortable place to stay. Choose from one of four rooms, two with private bathrooms. There are partial

river views from the breakfast room, and it's very close to downtown.

Inn of the White Salmon
INN $

(☎509-493-2335; www.innofthewhitesalmon. com; 172 West Jewett Blvd; dm $25, d $90-135; ⊜❄🖤) Over the bridge in White Salmon is this pleasant and contemporary 16-room inn with comfortable guest rooms in different styles. Interestingly enough, there's also a very nice eight-bed dorm room available.

Gorge View B&B
B&B $

(☎541-386-5770; www.gorgeview.com; 1009 Columbia St; dm $39, d from $95; ⊜❄@🖤) Catering to outdoor sports enthusiasts is this tasteful yet casual B&B. There's a four-bunk room for single travelers, along with peeks at the river views from the living room. Most rooms share a common bathroom; there's a two-bedroom apartment available. Open May to September only.

Hood River Hotel
HOTEL $$

(☎541-386-1900, 800-386-1859; www.hoodriver hotel.com; 102 Oak St; d $99-169; ⊜❄🖤) Located right in the heart of downtown, this fine 1913 hotel offers comfortable old-fashioned rooms with four-post or sleigh beds, some with tiny baths. The suites have the best amenities and views. Kitchenettes are also available, and there's a restaurant, sauna and Jacuzzi on the premises.

Vagabond Lodge
MOTEL $

(☎541-386-2992; www.vagabondlodge.com; 4070 Westcliff Dr; d $70-95; ❄🖤) Some rooms at this basic but friendly motel have river views, and suites come with amenities like fireplace, kitchenette and Jacuzzi. It's next to the highway but near woodsy areas and next door to the Columbia Gorge Hotel (and its pleasant gardens).

Viento State Park
CAMPGROUND $

(☎541-374-8811, www.oregonstateparks.org; exit 56 from I-84; tent/RV sites $17/20) Located 8 miles west of Hood River is this campground with showers near the highway and river; there's river access and walking trails.

Columbia River Gorge Hostel
HOSTEL $

(☎509-493-3363; www.bingenschool.com; cnr Cedar & Humboldt Sts; dm $19, d $49) Located in Bingen, WA, is this quirky and spartan hostel is located in an old, historic school two blocks up from the main highway. Lodgings are in the old basic classrooms (dorms have many beds) and facilities include a kitchen and old gym. Run by an eccentric hippie owner.

 Eating

 Stonehedge Gardens & Bistro
EUROPEAN-AMERICAN $$$

(☎541-386-3940; www.stonehedgegardens.com; 3405 Cascade Ave; mains $22-28; ☺dinner) Located at the end of a 0.3-mile gravel road, at the top of a hill, is this fine restaurant in a 1898 restored house. On a warm night, snag a table on the huge stone patio and order the seafood linguini, seared ahi or gorgonzola sirloin. Reservations for six or more only.

Celilo Restaurant & Bar
NORTHWESTERN $$

(☎541-386-5710; www.celilorestaurant.com; 16 Oak St; mains $16-21; ☺lunch & dinner) For upscale dining there's slick Celilo, a modern and beautiful restaurant with walls that open to the sidewalk on warm afternoons. Main dishes include the house-made tagliatelle pasta and pork shoulder glazed with quince purée; come for lunch for a more affordable and casual menu. Celilo utilizes quality, sustainable ingredients and practices.

Brian's Pourhouse
AMERICAN ECLECTIC $$

(☎541-387-4344; www.brianspourhouse.com; 606 Oak St; mains $12-27; ☺5-10pm Sun-Thu, to 11pm Fri & Sat) For great food and semi-upscale atmosphere there's this worthy eatery right on the main drag. The eclectic menu ranges from butternut squash gnocchi and goat-cheese pizza to fish tacos and rib-eye steak. There's outdoor seating for warm nights, when a few of the tasty, exotic cocktails would go down well indeed.

Double Mountain Brewery
BREWPUB $

(www.doublemountainbrewery.com; 8 4th St; sandwiches $6.50-9, pizzas $14-20; ☺11:30am-11pm Sun-Thu, to midnight Fri & Sat) For a casual bite, step into this small brewpub for a tasty sandwich or excellent brick-oven pizza. The menu is limited, but the food is great and the beer even better – especially if you like the hoppy stuff.

Full Sail Brewpub
BREWPUB $$

(☎541-386-2247; www.fullsailbrewing.com; 506 Columbia St; mains $10-13; ☺11:30am-9:30pm) Hood River's main brewpub offers salads, sandwiches and other pub grub, along with great river views and decent beer. An outdoor patio is a plus on sunny days, and there are free 30-minute tours in the afternoon.

 Information

Chamber of Commerce (☎541-386-2000, 800-366-3530; www.hoodriver.org; 720 E Port

COLUMBIA RIVER GORGE HOOD RIVER

TOP SEVEN WATERFALLS

Waterfalls are at their gushiest in spring. The following are all off US 30, listed from west to east.

» **Latourell Falls** (249ft) The first major waterfall as you come east on US 30. Hike 10 minutes to reach it, or go a mile to the top.

» **Bridal Veil Falls** (140ft) Two-tiered falls reached via an easy half-mile walk. A separate wheelchair-accessible trail passes through a meadow.

» **Wahkeena Falls** (242ft) Hike up the Wahkeena Trail, join Trail No 441 and head down to Multnomah Falls. Return via the road for the 5-mile loop.

» **Multnomah Falls** (642ft) The gorge's top attraction. Trail No 411 leads to the top (1 mile). Continue up foresty Multnomah Creek and the top of Larch Mountain (another 7 miles).

» **Oneonta Falls** (75ft) Located within the lovely, half-mile Oneonta Gorge. Carefully scamper over log jams and wade in water up to waist-high. Fun and worth it!

» **Horsetail Falls** (176ft) Just east of Oneonta Gorge. A 4.5-mile loop begins here, passing through Ponytail Falls and Triple Falls. Walk a half-mile east on US 30 (passing the Oneonta Gorge) to return.

» **Elowah Falls** (289ft) More isolated but pretty falls located about a mile off the highway. Hike to the top, then take a 0.7-mile side trail to McCord Creek Falls (2.5 miles round trip).

Marina Dr; ⊙9am-5pm Mon-Fri year-round, plus 10am-5pm Sat & Sun Apr-Nov) For tourist information.

US Forest Service office (☑541-308-1700; www.fs.fed.us/r6/columbia; 902 Wasco St; ⊙8am-4:30pm Mon-Fri) For hiking and camping information.

❶ Getting There & Away

Columbia Area Transit offers **Greyhound** (☑541-386-4202; www.greyhound.com; 720 E Port Marina Dr) buses that stop right at the chamber of commerce. Amtrak's *Empire Builder* stops daily at Bingen, on the Washington side of the gorge, along its Portland–Spokane leg.

The Dalles & Around

Located about 85 miles east of Portland, the Dalles features a decidedly different climate – much drier and sunnier. Though steadfastly unglamorous and down to earth, the city offers good outdoor recreation; there's decent camping and hiking, and fierce winds excellent for windsurfing and kiteboarding. The region hosts several good wineries and is also the nation's largest producer of sweet cherries. The Dalles has gone high-tech – Google has built a large server facility here to utilize the area's cheap hydroelectric power.

◉ Sights

TOP CHOICE **Columbia Gorge Discovery Center** MUSEUM

(☑541-296-8600; www.gorgediscovery.org; 5000 Discovery Dr; adult/child $8/4; ⊙9am-5pm) This museum covers the history of the gorge, from its creation by cataclysmic floods to the hardships pioneers had traversing it, to early settlements and transport in the area to the construction – and consequences – of its dams. The Lewis and Clark wing has an exhibit on animals the corps had to kill (including 190 dogs and a ferret); there's also a bird of prey educational program at 11am and 2pm Monday to Friday, where live raptors are featured.

Other amenities include a large theater, plenty of video narratives and a nice café with an outside deck. The discovery center is a couple miles west of the city.

Fort Dalles Museum MUSEUM

(☑541-296-4547; www.fortdallesmuseum.org; 500 W 15th St; adult/child $5/1; ⊙10am-4pm) This museum was once part of an 1856 fort and is Oregon's oldest history museum. It's a fascinating place full of historical items; highlights include an albatross-feather muff, human hair wreaths, a child's casket with window face hole and a bonnet worn at Ford Theatre the night Abraham Lincoln was assassinated. There are several antique

COLUMBIA RIVER GORGE

cars, stagecoaches and even a horse-drawn hearse. Across the street is a rare example of the area's Swedish architecture.

The Dalles Dam & Lock
DAM

The Dalles Dam, built in 1957, produces enough electricity to power a city of a million inhabitants. Access to this power came at a price, however. The dam's reservoir, Lake Celilo, flooded the culturally rich area around Celilo Falls, which was for thousands of years a Native American meeting place and fishery.

In Seufert Park, east on the frontage road from I-84 exit 87, is the **Dalles Dam Visitors Center** (✆541-296-9778; Clodfelter Way; ☺9am-5pm Jun-Sep). This information center contains the usual homage to hydroelectricity, along with exhibits on local history and a fish cam to view migratory salmon.

Columbia Hills State Park
STATE PARK

(✆509-767-1159; Hwy 14 Mile 85) Some of the most famous remaining **pictographs** (painted figures) along the Columbia River are at this Washington state park. The pictograph area can be visited only on a free guided tour at 10am on Friday and Saturday from April to October; reservations are required. The park's **petroglyphs** (carved figures) can be seen any time from April to October without a tour.

Rock climbers practice their moves on the basalt walls of **Horsethief Butte**, just east of the park entrance, and this section of the Columbia River is a good place for beginning windsurfers to catch some wind without strong river currents. The park also offers fishing and swimming in Horsethief Lake, as well as camping and hiking.

Rowena Crest
VIEWPOINT

On top of Rowena Crest are spectacular views and vast meadows now preserved as a wildflower sanctuary. **Governor Tom McCall Reserve**, on Rowena Plateau, is one of the best places to see native plants. Springtime wildflowers include balsamroot, wild parsley, penstemon and wild lilies. A two-mile hike climbs 1000ft and ends at **McCall Point**, which offers even better views.

To reach this section of the Historic Columbia River Hwy from the Dalles, follow W 6th St westward out of town until it becomes US 30. From the west, take I-84 exit 69 at Mosier, and travel east on US 30.

🏃 Activities

Hood River (p253) may be the gorge's **windsurfing** capital, but the wind blows hard at the Dalles too. Right in town, **Riverfront Park** (exit 85) is a good spot for beginners. **Avery Park**, 8 miles from town, offers access to the river from the Washington side. A favorite entry point with strong west winds is **Celilo Park**, about 10 miles east of town.

🎉 Festivals & Events

One of the Dalles' biggest summer events is **Fort Dalles Day**, held in July. There's music, dances, a parade and a popular rodeo.

THE FALL OF CELILO

On March 10, 1957, the newly constructed gates of the Dalles Dam closed for the first time, nearly halting the mighty Columbia. Eight miles upstream, it took only a few hours for Celilo Falls – an important Native American fishing ground – to be forever buried under the rising floodwaters. It was the end of a Native American identity, tradition and livelihood that dated back 10,000 years.

Over millennia, thousands of native peoples from as far away as the Great Plains and Alaska would gather at Celilo Falls – also known as *Wyam* ('the echo of falling water') – to fish for salmon, trade goods and socialize. Lewis and Clark stopped by in 1805 and were amazed by the variety and numbers of people they encountered here.

Celilo Falls' tallest drop only stood at 22ft – but in volume, the falls were the sixth largest in the world. Native Americans would risk their lives on rickety wooden platforms over the rushing currents while using dip nets to catch their 60lb quarry. It was a dangerous occupation – if they fell, survival was unlikely – but a good day could yield tons of fish.

Native American tribes were financially compensated for the submergence of the falls, but their cultural loss is priceless. Today, over 50 years later, Celilo Falls is still mourned by those who remember its glory – and recall the impact the area had on their ancestors' lives.

🛏 Sleeping

The Dalles has a decided lack of good bed and breakfasts, though there are a couple of interesting motels.

TOP CHOICE **Celilo Inn** BOUTIQUE MOTEL **$$**
(☎541-769-0001; www.celiloinn.com; 3550 East 2nd St; d $109-240; ❄@❂❅❋) The beautifully remodeled Celilo Inn was once an old motel, but is now a slick and trendy stay with gorgeous contemporary rooms, many offering views of the Dalles' bridge and dam. Luxurious touches include flat-screen TVs, 24-hour espresso and a cool pool for those guaranteed hot summer days.

Lyle Hotel HOTEL **$**
(☎509-365-5953, 800-447-6310; www.lylehotel.com; 100 7th St, Lyle, WA; d $75-85; ❄❂❋) Cross the river and head 8 miles west on Hwy 14 to tiny Lyle, where this old hotel has 10 nicely restored warm rooms. This isn't a luxurious place – shared bathrooms are down the hall and there are no TVs – but it's charming and relaxed. The restaurant serves good dinners (Wednesday to Sunday, $12 to $20) to both hotel and outside guests.

Cousins' Country Inn BOUTIQUE MOTEL **$$**
(☎541-298-5161; www.cousinscountryinn.com; 2114 West 6th St; d $80-159; ❄❂❅❋) Despite the name, this pleasant place offers beautiful modern rooms, the fanciest with gas fireplace, outdoor deck or patio and huge shower stalls with triple heads. Even regular rooms have flat-screen TVs, and some come with kitchenette. The swimming pool is a plus, and the restaurant (with 'saloon' is just across the parking lot.

Oregon Motor Motel MOTEL **$**
(☎541-296-9111; 200 W 2nd St; d $55-59; ❄❋) This basic motel offers mostly nothing-special rooms, though some are nicer than others. All have microwave, fridge and a good downtown location.

🍴 Eating

Cousins' Restaurant & Saloon AMERICAN **$$**
(www.cousinsthedalles.com; 2116 West 6th St; mains $8-13; ⊗breakfast, lunch & dinner) 'Hello cousin!' will be the first thing you hear after coming through the mooing and baaing sounds the front doors make. Specializing in home-style comfort food like meat loaf, pot roast and turkey with dressing, this old-fashioned place offers good food, large portions and friendly service. Great for breakfast.

Anzac Tea Parlour TEA PARLOUR **$**
(☎541-296-5877; www.anzactea.com; 218 W 4th St; drinks & snacks $2-9; ⊗11am-4pm Tue-Sat) Australian-style high tea is served in this romantic old house, an unlikely (though welcome) addition to the Dalles' food scene. Choose from dozens of exotic teas, and nibble on savory meat pies, quiches, crumpets and – of course – vegemite sandwiches. It's small and hours limited, so reserve ahead to guarantee a table.

Baldwin Saloon AMERICAN **$$**
(www.baldwinsaloon.com; 205 Court St; mains $9-15; ⊗lunch & dinner Mon-Sat) It doesn't look like much from the outside, but this 1876 building holds a colorful past – it's been a bar, a brothel and a coffin storage warehouse. Today it's a casual restaurant with interesting brick interior full of large oil paintings. The food isn't exceptional – but it's decent enough, with tasty natural beef burgers and good desserts. There's a historic bar, plus live piano music on Friday and Saturday from 7pm to 9pm.

Holstein's Coffee Co COFFEE SHOP **$**
(811 E 3rd St; drinks & snacks $1.50-4; ⊗5:30am or 6am-6pm, till 7pm Fri & Sat) There are a dozen kinds of fancy java drinks here (think raspberry mochas), along with even more smoothies and exotic 'coffee alternatives' like chai, yerba mate and Italian sodas. Enjoy pastries, breakfast sandwiches and a nice patio too.

ℹ Information

Chamber of Commerce (☎541-296-2231, 800-255-3385; www.thedalleschamber.com; 404 W 2nd St; ⊗8:30am-5:30pm Mon-Fri year-round, 10am-4pm Sat & Sun Memorial Day–Labor Day) Pick up brochures of the city's historic buildings and murals.

ℹ Getting There & Away

There are bus services at **Greyhound** (☎541-296-7595; 201 1st St). Amtrak stops at Wishram, on the Washington side of the Columbia River.

Eastern Gorge

East of the Dalles there are more towns than cities and the sights get fewer, but there are a couple of worthy places to check out.

DON'T MISS

MARYHILL MUSEUM OF ART

Eccentric Sam Hill is responsible for some of the most famous building projects in the gorge, including this impressive and worthwhile **museum** (☑509-773-3733; www.mary hillmuseum.org; 35 Maryhill Museum Dr, WA; adult/child $7/2; ☺9am-5pm Mar 15-Nov 15).

Spectacularly located on a bluff above the Columbia, this old mansion boasts an outstanding collection of Native American baskets and other artifacts, including a seal intestine parka and carved walrus tusks. Other notable exhibits include a large and amazing collection of chess sets, a variety of French fashion dolls, and drawings by Auguste Rodin. Outside are garden sculptures, picnic tables with fine views and roaming peacocks. There's also a café on premises.

In 2011 the Maryhill will break ground on a new wing, adding more collections rooms, educational and research spaces and outdoor interpretive areas with expansive views of the gorge.

The museum is in Washington, just across the Columbia; cross the Dalles bridge and head west for 3 miles.

◉ Sights

Stonehenge
MONUMENT

Not one for small gestures, Sam Hill built a full-scale replica of Salisbury Plain's Stonehenge on the cliffs above the Columbia River, about a mile east of the Dalles bridge in Washington. Dedicated as a memorial to Klickitat County's soldiers killed in WWI, his Stonehenge was built of poured concrete and represents an intact site (unlike its tumbled-down English cousin).

Hill planned that his Stonehenge would line up for celestial events such as equinoxes. It's a popular place for odd rites and ceremonies, and offers great views of the gorge.

Deschutes River State Recreation Area
STATE PARK

(☑541-739-2322, 800-452-5687; www.oregon stateparks.org; tent/RV sites $9/20) The Deschutes River, Oregon's second largest, cuts through Central Oregon and meets the Columbia at this fine state park. There are beautiful riverside campsites here; reserve in summer.

From the south end of the park, riverside **hiking trails** pass old homesteads, springs and groves of willow and locust trees. Keep an eye out for raptors and migrating songbirds. There is also a **mountain-biking trail** (originally a rail bed) that runs about 17 miles upriver from here.

Central Oregon & the Oregon Cascades

Best Places to Eat

» Blacksmith (p272)
» Ariana (p272)
» Jen's Garden (p268)
» Rendezvous Grill & Tap Room (p264)
» Kokanee Cafe (p267)

Best Places to Stay

» Timberline Lodge (p263)
» McMenamins Old St Francis School (p272)
» Oxford Hotel (p271)
» Five Pine Lodge (p268)

Why Go?

Love mountain tops? Well, that's what Central Oregon and its Cascades are all about. You can practically skip your way from peak to snowy peak here, from Mt Hood, to Jefferson, to Bachelor, to Three-Fingered Jack and the lovely Sisters volcanoes. As you can imagine, there's plenty of awesome skiing and mountaineering, along with stellar hiking and camping. And it's not just mountain-lovers who come – world-class biking, golfing, rafting, kayaking, fishing and rock climbing are also on offer. Did we mention there's also nearly 300 days of sunshine every year?

As much as the outdoors may beckon, the lively city of Bend provides plenty of good food and accommodations. Or head nearby to the sweet little town of Sisters for a more quaint and personal atmosphere. Add a must-stop visit to Mt Hood's historic Timberline Lodge, or a getaway stop in the region's many peaceful lakeside resorts, and you'll find that Central Oregon's many attractions are hard to beat.

When to Go

Bend

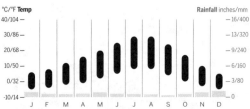

July & August	December–April	April–June
Summer weather; hike and camp around Mt Hood, or raft the Deschutes	Awesome skiing at Mt Bachelor, Willamette Pass and around Mt Hood	Prime time for rock climbing at Smith Rock or summiting Mt Hood

Mt Hood

The state's highest peak, Mt Hood (11,240ft), pops into view over much of northern Oregon whenever there's a sunny day, exerting an almost magnetic tug on skiers, hikers and sightseers. In summer, wildflowers bloom on the mountainsides and hidden ponds shimmer in blue, making for some unforgettable hikes; in winter, downhill and cross-country skiing dominates people's minds and bodies. Timberline Lodge, a handsome wood gem from the 1930s, offers glorious shelter and refreshments to both guests and nonguests all year round – and can't be missed.

Mt Hood rises above the Western Cascades, a ridge of older volcanoes stretching between Mt Rainier and Mt Shasta. These volcanoes erupted between 20 and 40 million years ago, and their peaks have long since eroded. Mt Hood began to burp toward the end of the last ice age, and geologists reckon that the mountain's last major eruption was about 1000 years ago.

Mt Hood is accessible year-round on US 26 from Portland (56 miles), and from Hood River (44 miles) on Hwy 35. Together with the Columbia River Hwy, these routes comprise the Mt Hood Loop, a popular scenic drive. Government Camp is at the pass over Mt Hood, and is the center of business on the mountain.

☀ Activities

If you park at designated winter recreational areas on Mt Hood (ie for cross-country skiing or snowshoeing), you'll need a Sno-Park permit (daily pass $4, three-day pass $7, season pass $20). These are available at gas stations, some Government Camp businesses and at Timberline Lodge.

During the rest of the year, a Northwest Forest Pass (daily $5, annual $30) is required to park at most hiking trailheads; buy them at ranger stations and from some Government Camp businesses.

Downhill Skiing

Mt Hood Meadows   DOWNHILL SKIING
(☎503-337-2222, snow report 503-227-7669; www.skihood.com; lift tickets adult/child $69/39) The largest ski area on Mt Hood; often has the best conditions. Facilities include two day-lodges with nine snack bars and restaurants.

Timberline Lodge   DOWNHILL SKIING
(☎503-272-3158, snow report 503-222-2211; www.timberlinelodge.com; lift tickets adult/child $56/36) Boasts the longest ski season in North America; its legendary lodge is a must-visit for bar drinks, fireplace sit-downs and upscale dinners.

Mt Hood Skibowl   DOWNHILL SKIING
(☎503-272-3206; www.skibowl.com; lift tickets adult/child $44/24) The USA's largest night-ski area and the closest skiing to Portland, making it popular with people who buzz out from the big city for an evening of skiing. Overall, it's smaller than Meadows or Timberline. Lift tickets are cheaper during the week.

Cooper Spur Ski Area   DOWNHILL SKIING
(☎503-352-7803; www.cooperspur.com; lift tickets adult/child $25/20) On the northeast slopes of Mt Hood; caters to beginners and families with mostly beginner/intermediate runs and a tubing area. A special pass ($35) includes equipment rentals and tubing.

Cross-Country Skiing

Trillium Lake, near the campground of the same name, is a very popular cross-country ski loop. **White River Canyon** is another good trail, and starts at a sno-park on Hwy 35 (about 4 miles north of Hwy 26).

Mt Hood Meadows Nordic Center (☎503-337-2222; www.skihood.com/The-Mountain/Nordic-Center; day pass $10) offers around 10 miles of groomed wooded trails. Several other free (ungroomed) trails start from the same parking area, including an easy mile-long trail to Sahalie Falls and a longer, more challenging one to Elk Meadows.

Teacup Lake (www.teacupnordic.org; trail fee $8) has 12 miles of groomed trails and a variety of terrain.

Hiking

An outstanding guide that includes Mt Hood hikes is William L Sullivan's *100 Hikes in Northwest Oregon*. It's also worth visiting a ranger station for maps and information on the many hikes in the area. A Northwest Forest Pass ($5) is required at most trailheads.

A popular trail loops for 7 miles via lovely **Ramona Falls**, which tumbles 120ft down a face of mossy columnar basalt. To reach the trailhead from Zigzag, turn north onto Lolo Pass Rd for 4 miles, then turn right on USFS Rd 1825 for 3 miles.

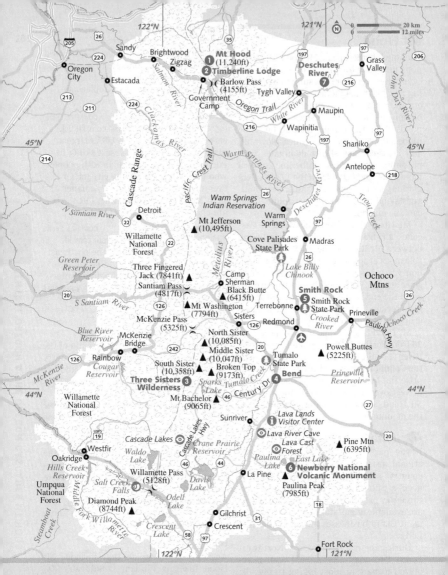

Central Oregon & the Oregon Cascades Highlights

1 Hike and camp in the wonderfully forested foothills around **Mt Hood** (p261)

2 Carve powder in winter (and summer!) above **Timberline Lodge** (p263)

3 Photograph summer wildflowers in the **Three Sisters Wilderness** (p269)

4 Sample **Bend's** finest cuisine, after golfing, rafting, skiing or hiking nearby (p269)

5 Set up a multipitch climb at spectacular **Smith Rock** (p271)

6 Peek through a lava tube at **Newberry National Volcanic Monument** (p274)

7 Go white-water rafting or fly-fish on the famous **Deschutes River** (p267)

Mt Hood is the second-most-climbed peak over 10,000ft in the world, after Japan's Mt Fuji. This isn't to say Mt Hood does not require both climbing skills and stamina; nearly every year, a few people die making the ascent. Climbing is best between May and mid-July, and a typical climb from Timberline Lodge (where registration is mandatory) on the south side takes 10 to 12 hours round trip. Experienced climbers who wish to organize their own expedition can check www.fs.fed.us/r6/mthood/recreation/climbing for details. Otherwise, be safe and go with a guide service:

Northwest School of Survival (☎503-668-8264; www.nwsos.com)

Timberline Mountain Guides (☎541-312-9242; www.timberlinemtguides.com)

Portland's **Mazamas** (☎503-227-2345; www.mazamas.org) is a mountaineering and hiking club (not a guide service) that sponsors climbs of many Northwest peaks, including Mt Hood. Membership isn't necessary, though mountaineering experience might be. And for climbing Mt Hood, experience certainly won't hurt.

Hike 1.5 miles up from US 26 to **Mirror Lake**, which reflects Mt Hood beautifully. You can hike a half-mile around the lake, then 2 miles beyond the lake to a ridge top. The trail begins between Miles 51 and 52 on US 26, a mile west of Government Camp.

Walk 2.6 miles on the mostly gentle **Old Salmon River Trail**, through riverside old-growth forests to the Salmon River Bridge. You can car-shuttle back or return the same way. To reach the trailhead, turn south from Zigzag on Salmon River Rd and drive 2.7 miles. The walk follows the road, but this doesn't detract from the hike. Check with a ranger station about this hike, as its course might change.

The mother of all trails is the 40.7-mile **Timberline Trail**, which circumnavigates Mt Hood along a scenic wilderness of waterfalls, quiet reflecting lakes, wildflower meadows and mountain vistas. You don't have to do it all at once, however. Noteworthy portions of the trail include the hike to McNeil Point and the short climb to Bald Mountain, both offering breathtaking scenery. From Timberline Lodge, Zigzag Canyon Overlook is a 4.5-mile round-trip through meadows of wildflowers to a canyon vista. Some trails can be snowbound until late July, so ask before you go.

Mountain Biking

When the snow is gone, **Mt Hood Skibowl** (☎503-272-3206; www.skibowl.com) is transformed into a mountain-bike downhill arena; bike rentals are available. If you're more the cross-country type, however, cross US 26 to the free Government Camp recreation trail network. The Crosstown Trail is a fair-

ly easy 3-mile single track between Glacier View and the Summit Ski Area. More challenging trails sprout from it.

Most of the cross-country ski trails in the area are good for summertime mountain biking. Trails shoot uphill from several points around the easy Trillium Lake loop.

🛌 Sleeping

Most area campsites cost $12 to $18 and have drinking water and vault toilets. Reserve ahead on busy weekends (☎877-444-6777; www.reserveusa.com), though some walk-in sites are usually set aside. For more information contact a nearby ranger station.

Tollgate and Camp Creek Campgrounds are further down US 26 with some nice streamside sites. Still Creek Campground is near Government Camp. Large and popular Trillium Lake Campground has great views of Mt Hood. Frog Lake Campground lies on the shores of tiny Frog Lake. Off the beaten track is Cloud Cap Campground, with easy access to the Timberline Trail. Robin Hood and Sherwood Campgrounds are toward the east, on Hwy 35.

TOP CHOICE **Timberline Lodge** LODGE $$
(☎503-272-3311, 800-547-1406; www.timberlinelodge.com; d $110-290; ❃🛜🏊) More a community treasure than a hotel, this gorgeous historic lodge offers a variety of rooms, from bunk rooms that sleep up to 10 to luxury suites. Huge wooden beams tower over multiple fireplaces, there's a year-round heated outdoor pool, and the ski lifts are close by. Enjoy awesome views of Mt Hood, nearby hiking trails, two bars and a good dining room.

TIMBERLINE LODGE

The building of Timberline Lodge in 1936 and 1937 was a huge project for the Works Progress Administration (WPA), which employed up to 500 workers to hand-construct the 43,700-sq-ft log-and-stone lodge.

To emphasize the natural beauty of the area, architects quarried local stone and cut local timber, also designing the six-sided central tower to echo the faceted peak of Mt Hood. The steeply slanted wings leading away from the common rooms are meant to shed the heavy snowfalls and resemble mountain ridges.

The interior of the lodge is where the workmanship is most evident. The central fireplace rises 92ft through three floors of open lobby. All the furniture was made by hand in WPA carpentry halls, and murals and paintings of stocky, stylized workers – in the style of Socialist Realist art – adorn the walls.

Timberline Lodge is a hotel, ski resort, restaurant and National Historic Landmark Anyone can stop by for a refreshment and look around – this building belongs to the wider community more than anything. And yes, some exterior shots of *The Shining* really were filmed here.

Huckleberry Inn
LODGE $$

(☑503-272-3325; www.huckleberry-inn.com; 88611 E Government Camp Loop; d $85-180; ☻�) Simple and comfortably rustic rooms are available here, and there's a 'bunk' room that sleeps up to 14. It's in a great central location in Government Camp, and has a casual restaurant (which doubles as the hotel's reception). Holiday rates go up 20%.

Doublegate Inn
B&B $$

(☑503-622-0629; www.doublegateinn.com; 26711 E Welches Rd; d $159-179; ☻☎) Lovely B&B boasting three very comfortable and beautiful rooms of all sizes, each with private bathroom. There's a second-story deck with peeks at the nearby Salmon River. Two dogs on premises; reservations necessary (no drop-ins).

Mt Hood Inn
HOTEL $$

(☑503-272-3205, 800-443-7777; www.mthood inn.com; 87450 E Government Camp Loop; d $159-179; ☻☎) Pleasant hotel-like rooms are on tap here, some with kitchenette and Jacuzzi. Located at the entrance to Government Camp, close to Mt Hood Skibowl and within stumbling distance of the Ice Axe Grill and its microbrewery.

Summit Meadow Cabins
CABINS $$

(☑503-272-3494; www.summitmeadow.com; cabins $180-250; ☻) These five rustic but comfortable cabins, each with different amenities (but all with kitchen), lie just south of Government Camp in the Trillium Lake basin. They make great bases for nature getaways. Trails surround the cabins; during winter, it's a 1.5-mile cross-country

ski in. Two-night minimum; rates higher on weekends. Reservations required.

Lost Lake Resort & Campground
LODGE, CAMPGROUND $

(☑541-386-6366; www.lostlakeresort.org; USFS Rd 1340; tent/RV sites $25/30, d $85-125, cabins $70-140) Six lodge rooms with kitchenettes, 120 campsites and seven very rustic cabins (bathroom outside, showers $4) are nestled on Mt Hood's northern flank. Bring bedding and towels. There's a small store and motorless boat rentals; fishing is possible.

Mt Hood Village RV Resort
CAMPING $

(☑503-622-4011, 800-255-3069; www.mt hoodvillage.com; 65000 E US 26; tent sites $20, RV sites $38-47, yurts $40-60, cabins $52-184; ☒) The area's only RV hookups; also has tent sites, yurts and cabins. Amenities include showers, indoor swimming pool, fitness center, store and a variety of sporting options.

✗ Eating

The Huckleberry Inn serves a decent family diner.

TOP CHOICE / Rendezvous Grill & Tap Room
NORTHWESTERN $$$

(☑503-622-6837; www.rendezvousgrill.net; 67149 E US 26; mains $19-26; ☉11:30am-9pm) In a league of its own is this excellent restaurant with outstanding dishes, such as herb-rubbed New York steak and sake-glazed wild salmon. Lunch means gourmet sandwiches, burgers and salads on the outdoor patio.

Cascade Dining Room   NORTHWESTERN $$$

(☏503-272-3104; www.timberlinelodge.com/cascade-dining-room; Timberline Lodge; mains $22-34; ⊘breakfast, lunch & dinner) Chef Jason Stoller Smith Fine prepares fine cuisine with a Northwestern emphasis at Timberline Lodge's elegant restaurant. The wine cellar is award-winning (boasting more than 300 Oregon pinots) and the staff is knowledgeable; this is the place for that special meal with great views and atmosphere. Reserve for dinner; breakfast and lunch are more casual.

Ram's Head Bar   AMERICAN $$

(www.timberlinelodge.com/rams-head-bar; Timberline Lodge; mains $12-14; ⊘11am-11pm) Located on the open 2nd floor of Timberline Lodge is this casual bar-eatery with great views of Mt Hood. It's a great place to hang out and nibble on buffalo wings, Caesar salad or a Reuben panini. In winter, snag a window seat and order a hot buttered brandy, spiced cider or microbrew – and you'll be in heaven.

Ice Axe Grill   BREWPUB $$

(www.iceaxegrill.com; 87304 E Government Camp Loop; mains $12-18; ⊘11:30am-9pm Sun-Thu, till 10pm Fri & Sat) Government Camp's only brewery-restaurant, the Ice Axe offers a friendly, family-style atmosphere and pub fare including good pizzas, shepherd's pie and gorgonzola-and-pepper bacon burgers. Veggie chili and lentil burgers too.

Barlow Trail Roadhouse   AMERICAN $

(69580 E US 26; mains $7-9; ⊘8am-9pm Tue-Thu, 7am-9pm Fri & Sat, 7am-8pm Sun) Old-fashioned eatery serving sandwiches, salads, steaks and nearly 20 kinds of burgers. Daily comfort-food specials such as chicken dumplings (Wednesday) and prime rib (Friday); good breakfasts too.

❶ Information

For maps, permits and information contact regional ranger stations, which include:

Hood River (☏541-352-6002; 6780 Hwy 35, Parkdale; ⊘8am-4:30pm Mon-Sat)

Mt Hood National Forest Headquarters (☏503-668-1700; www.fs.fed.us/r6/mthood; 16400 Champion Way, Sandy; ⊘7:30-11:30am & 12:30-4:30pm Mon-Fri)

ZigZag (☏503-622-3191; 70220 E Hwy 26, Zigzag; ⊘7:45am-4:30pm)

❶ Getting There & Away

Bus

There are several public transport options from Portland to the Mt Hood area. **Park & Ride bus**

(☏503-287-5438; www.skihood.com/Plan-Your-Trip/Transportation-Options/Park-and-Ride) transports skiers from three Tri-Met stops in Portland to Mt Hood Meadows on winter weekends and holidays; the cost is $79 for combination round-trip transportation and lift ticket.

Central Oregon Breeze (☏800-847-0157; www.cobreeze.com) provides transport from Bend to Portland, with possible stops in Government Camp. **Mt Hood Airporter** (☏800-831-7433) provides winter transport (weekends only, $5) from Government Camp to Timberline Lodge. It also has airport shuttles and private charter services.

Car

For road conditions, dial the **24hr information line** (☏503-588-2941, 800-977-6368). State law requires traction devices to be carried in vehicles during winter, and trailers are sometimes banned.

Lower Deschutes River

The Lower Deschutes River boasts some of the Northwest's most renowned whitewater rafting. For a dramatic peek at white water without getting wet, head to **Sherars Falls**, about 10 miles north of Maupin. You might see Native Americans dip-net fishing on wooden platforms right above the water (only tribal members from the Warm Springs Indian Reservation are allowed to fish here). Maupin provides most of the area's services.

⚓ Activities

Rafting

The Lower Deschutes River is ideal for rafting, with 97 miles of mostly class III rapids flowing though stark canyon landscapes and basalt cliffs before mingling with the Columbia to the north. Most expeditions are one-day adventures that leave from Harpham Flat, about 5 miles upstream from Maupin (the nearest town), and end about 15 miles down the river at Sandy Beach. Longer two- and three-day excursions are also available.

Maupin's outfitters include:

All Star Rafting (☏800-909-7238; www.asrk.com; 405 Deschutes Ave)

Deschutes River Adventures (☏800-723-8464; www.800-rafting.com; 602 Deschutes Ave)

Imperial River Company (☏800-395-3903; www.deschutesriver.com; 304 Bakeoven Rd).

You can also rent equipment yourself, but be sure to wear a safety vest.

A boater pass is required for all floaters (per person per day $2 weekdays, $6 to $8 weekends). It's available online at www.boaterpass.com, which also has details on this local system.

Fly-Fishing

Rafting isn't the only highlight in the area. Fly-fishing on the Deschutes River is challenging and world renowned – the remoteness of desert canyons makes this an unforgettable experience. In May and June, the stonefly hatch drives Redside trout (and anglers) into a frenzy, while fall means steelhead trout are in the crosshairs.

The **Deschutes Canyon Fly Shop** (☑541-395-2565; www.flyfishingdeschutes.com; 599 S US 197) and the **Deschutes Angler** (☑541-395-0995; www.deschutesangler.com; 504 Deschutes Ave), both in Maupin, are great places to buy gear and get advice. Call the **Fish & Wildlife Bureau** (☑541-296-4628; www.dfw.state.or.us/fish/The%5FDalles; 3701 W 13th St), in the Dalles, for current regulations.

🛏 Sleeping & Eating

Near Maupin are Bureau of Land Management (BLM) campgrounds with minimal facilities (sites $8 to $12, no reservations, bring water or a filter). Contact the **BLM Visitor Center** (☑541-395-2778; 7 N Hwy 197; ⊙10am-5pm Thu-Sun), just west of the Deschutes River Bridge, for details. Both the Oasis and the Imperial River Company have restaurants.

Imperial River Company MOTEL $$
(☑800-395-3903; www.deschutesriver.com; 304 Bakeoven Rd; d $89-129; ❋❖❂) Maupin's best stay is this modern riverside lodge, featuring a good variety of rooms that range from small and subdued to huge and magnificent. The imperial suite comes with private deck and jets in the tub ($229), while the restaurant boasts an awesome patio with log furniture and river views.

Oasis CABINS, CAMPGROUND $
(☑541-395-2611; www.deschutesriveroasis.com; 609 US 97 S; tent sites $20, cabins $40-85; ❖❋) These 11 tiny but cute cabins are a marvel of efficient design, and while they're not luxurious they are well-equipped (most have kitchenettes). There's a small restaurant on the premises, and raft shuttle services are offered. Campsites are at a different location nearby, closer to the river.

Maupin City Park CAMPGROUND $
(☑541-395-2252; 206 Bakeoven Rd; tent/RV sites $24/32) Next to the Imperial River Company, this camping ground has running water, showers and RV hookups – along with a boat ramp (day use $3 to $4).

Warm Springs Indian Reservation

Home to three native groups – the Wasco, the Warm Springs and the Paiute – Warm Springs Indian Reservation stretches from the peaks of the Cascades in the west to the banks of the Deschutes River to the east. The Wasco and Warm Springs tribes were confined here after a treaty with the US government in 1855; the Paiute were moved here after the Bannock Indian War of 1878.

The **Pi Ume Sha Treaty Days Celebration** is held on the third weekend of June at Warm Springs, with competitive dancing, horse races and a rodeo. For details contact the **Confederated Tribes of Warm Springs** (☑541-553-1161; www.warmsprings.com; 1233 Veterans St, Warm Springs).

Don't miss the excellent **Warm Springs Museum** (☑541-553-3331; www.museumatwarmsprings.org; 2189 US 26, Warm Springs; adult/child $7/3.50; ⊙9am-5pm), a wonderful evocation of traditional Native American life and culture, with artifacts, audiovisual presentations and re-created villages.

The tribe-owned **Kah-Nee-Ta Resort** (☑800-554-4786; www.kahneeta.com; RV sites $54, teepees $76, d from $155) is popular with families, especially sun-starved Portlanders. Facilities include a casino, golf, tennis, fishing and a double-Olympic-size spring-fed pool; $5 day-use parking fee.

Mt Jefferson & the Metolius River

The Metolius River bursts in all its glory from a ferny hillside, flowing north through a beautiful pine-filled valley as it passes beneath rugged Mt Jefferson, Oregon's second-highest peak (10,495ft). This gorgeous, peaceful region offers fine recreational opportunities that include great hiking and biking, world-class trout fishing, riverside campgrounds and comfortable lodges. Summer is fabulous and popular, but consider coming in fall when the crowds disperse and temperatures remain mild. In winter there's good cross-country skiing.

To find the head of the Metolius, turn north from US 20 onto Camp Sherman Rd (USFS Rd 14), then turn right at the marked

CENTRAL OREGON & THE OREGON CASCADES

sign and continue 1.4 miles. A short path leads through a forest of ponderosa pines to remarkable **Metolius Springs**, where the river flows out of a hillside.

✦ Activities

Hiking

Trails lead from the Metolius Valley up into the **Mt Jefferson Wilderness Area**. For a serious but fabulous day hike, head up to Canyon Creek Meadows, where summer produces a vibrant wildflower display and great views onto the rugged 7841ft **Three Fingered Jack** (4.5 miles round trip, Northwest Forest Pass required to park). To reach the trailhead from Sisters, drive 13 miles northwest on US 20. Just south of Suttle Lake, turn north on Jack Lake Rd, USFS Rd 12. It's about 8 miles to the trailhead, at USFS's Jack Lake Campground.

From the same access road, there is a shorter hike that leads to three mountain lakes. One mile from the turnoff of US 20, take a west-turning fork (USFS Rd 1210) toward **Round Lake**. From here an easy 2-mile trail leads past tiny Long Lake to **Square Lake**, the highest of the trio. Note that this area is still recovering from a large 2003 fire.

For less strenuous yet still excellent walking, follow the trails on either side of the Metolius River, accessed from Camp Sherman or any campground.

� Sleeping & Eating

The tiny community of Camp Sherman (14 miles from Sisters) provides a few lodges, two seasonal restaurants, a store (with gas pump) and not much else.

Area campsites include **Camp Sherman** (Forest Rd 1419; tent/RV sites $16) and **Riverside** (Forest Rd 14; walk-in tent sites $12), north and south of Camp Sherman, respectively. Both have water and vault toilets, and are by the river. For more information about area campgrounds, visit the **Sisters Ranger Station** (☑541-549-7700; www.fs.fed.us/r6/centraloregon; 207 N Pine St; ⊙8am-4pm).

Metolius River Lodges   CABINS **$$**
(☑800-595-6290; www.metoliusriverlodges.com; cabins $120-209; ⊖🐾) Just across the bridge from Metolius River Resort is this casual place with 13 cozy, rustic and comfy cabins – both attached and stand-alone – right next to the river. Many have kitchens and fireplaces, and some boast decks over the water (the 'salmonfly' cabin has the best view).

Metolius River Resort   CABINS **$$$**
(☑800-818-7688; www.metoliusriverresort.com; 25551 SW Forest Service Rd 1419; cabins $235; ⊖🐾) More like small houses than cabins, the 11 lovely cabins at this pleasant spot all have two bedrooms and well-equipped kitchens. They sleep two to six people and are all decorated differently (as they're owned by different people). The river is nearby.

Kokanee Cafe   NORTHWESTERN **$$$**
(☑541-595-6420; www.kokaneecafe.com; mains $18-24; ⊙5-9pm May-Oct) Located at the Metolius River Resort, this log-cabin restaurant offers fine Northwestern cuisine that includes the use of game, organic meats and wild fish. Great food; reserve ahead.

Hoodoo Mountain Resort

Oregon's oldest downhill **ski area** (☑541-822-3799; www.hoodoo.com; lift tickets adult/child $42/29) is 25 miles northwest of Sisters at the crest of the Cascades. Though it's small, Hoodoo has variety in its terrain, with good snow and some surprisingly challenging skiing. For conditions call ☑541-822-3337.

There's night skiing Friday and Saturday. Hoodoo also has groomed cross-country ski trails (Nordic pass $12) though many free, ungroomed trails start at the Sno-Parks near Santiam Pass.

Sisters

POP 1700

Straddling the Cascades and high desert, where mountain pine forests mingle with desert sage and juniper, lies the darling town of Sisters. Once a stagecoach stop and trade town for loggers and ranchers, Sisters is today a bustling tourist destination whose main street is lined with boutiques, art galleries and eateries housed in Western-facade buildings. Visitors come for the mountain scenery, spectacular hiking, fine cultural events and awesome climate – there's plenty of sun and little precipitation here. And while the town's atmosphere is a bit upscale, people are still friendly and the back streets still undeveloped enough that deer are often seen nibbling in neighbors' garden plots.

The town shows its cowboy spirit during the second weekend of June at the **Sisters**

Rodeo (☎800-827-7522; www.sistersrodeo.com), complete with parade, toe-tappin' music and rodeo queens. A month later, in mid-July, is the wildly popular **Outdoor Quilt Show** (☎541-549-6061; www.sistersout doorquiltshow.org). Over a thousand quilts are on display throughout the packed-out town, including many hung up outside buildings.

The Valley Retriever bus service connects Sisters with Eugene, Newport and Salem; it stops at the corner of Cascade and Spruce Sts.

🛏 Sleeping

Unless you camp, sleeping in Sisters is expensive; head to Bend (19 miles southeast) for budget motels. Nonreservable campsites (without showers) are available at the pleasant **city park** (tent sites $12, RV sites $15-38), at the southern end of Sisters. Reserve accommodation in summer – but especially during festivals, when prices go up.

Five Pine Lodge HOTEL $$$
(☎866-974-5900; www.fivepinelodge.com; 1021 Desperado Trail; d $189-219, cottages $199-219; ☺※🐾🏊) Five Pine is a superb Craftsman-style lodge with gorgeous, luxurious rooms, most of which have two floors, fireplace and deck or patio, plus bathtubs that open to the sitting area and fill from a ceiling spigot (really). Cabins are also available, and use of the gym next door is included.

Sisters Motor Lodge MOTEL $$
(☎541-549-2551; www.sistersmotorlodge.com; 511 W Cascade St; d from $89; ☺※🐾) Eleven cozy, clean and spacious rooms, each one unique, at this older but excellent motel. Expect homey decor and quilts on the beds, and modern comforts such as DVD player. Kitchenettes and two-bedroom suites available.

Blue Spruce B&B B&B $$
(☎541-549-9644, 888-328-9644; www.blue-spruce.biz; 444 S Spruce St; d $169-189; ☺※🐾) This fine B&B offers four spacious, themed rooms, all with fireplace, king bed, TV and private bathroom sporting jetted tub. There's a large grassy backyard and a great deck, and free bicycle rental is included.

Sisters Inn & Suites MOTEL $$
(☎541-549-7829; www.sistersinnandsuites.com; 540 US 20 W; d $99-120; ☺※🐾) At the edge of town is this motel with wonderful, spacious, remodelled rooms, all boasting slick contemporary decor, fridge, microwave and either patio or balcony. Kitchenettes available.

Sisters/Bend KOA CAMPGROUND $
(☎541-549-3021, 800-562-0363; www.koa.com; 67667 US 20 W; tent & RV sites $48-58, cabins $58-78; 🐾🏊) Comfortable sites about 3.5 miles southeast of Sisters and 15 miles northwest of Bend. Fun activities include mini-golf, a fishing pond and swimming pool with hot tub; there's also a store.

🍴 Eating

TOP CHOICE **Jen's Garden** FRENCH $$$
(☎541-549-2699; www.intimatecottage cuisine.com; 403 E Hood; mains $26; ☺5-9pm) One of Central Oregon's finest restaurants is this intimate spot with a limited but quality menu; expect dishes such as yogurt-marinated grilled lamb and duck breast over fois gras ravioli. A five-course menu runs $52, or choose the three-course menu for $39. Reserve ahead.

Bronco Billy's Ranch Grill & Saloon AMERICAN $$
(www.broncobillysranchgrill.com; 190 E Cascade Ave; mains $10-26; ☺11:30am-9pm) Right on the main drag and located in the historic Hotel Sisters is this old-time family joint. Meats are the highlight of the menu (think steaks, ribs, hot links and hamburgers), but for less carnage there are salads, sandwiches and a couple of Mexican specialty dishes.

Seasons Café & Wine Shop SANDWICHES $
(411 E Hood St; sandwiches $7; ☺lunch Mon-Sat) Line up with the locals at this popular sandwich shop and order the turkey with cranberry sauce, pastrami with sauerkraut or roast beef with blue cheese dressing. There are also salads, quiche and lots of wine. Lunch only.

Sisters Coffee Company COFFEEHOUSE $
(www.sisterscoffee.com; 273 W Hood Ave; ☺6am-6pm Mon-Sat, 6am-5pm Sun) Local, upscale bean roaster with high ceilings, stone fireplace, wonderfully comfortable furniture and lots of antlers on the walls. The coffee and pastries are good; head upstairs for seating with a view.

ℹ Information

Chamber of Commerce (☎541-549-0251; www.sisterschamber.com; 291 Main St; ☺10am-4pm Mon-Sat)

Sisters Ranger Station (☎541-549-7700; www.fs.fed.us/r6/centraloregon; 207 N Pine St; ☺8am-4:30pm) For camping and hiking information.

McKenzie Pass Area

From the lava fields of 5325ft McKenzie Pass you'll find stunning views of the Cascade Range and one of the youngest and largest lava flows in the continental USA. Intriguing hikes are scattered in the area.

Perched on a swell of frozen rock at McKenzie Pass, **Dee Wright Observatory** is a small fortress that was built out of lava in 1935 by the Civilian Conservation Corps. It surveys a desolate volcanic landscape, but on a clear day you can witness a dozen volcanic cones and mountain peaks from its arched windows. Nearby, a half-mile interpretive trail winds through the lava.

Two free primitive campgrounds (no water) in the area are **Scott Lake** and **Lava Camp Lake Campground**, both with lakeside campsites. The campsites can't be reserved.

A Northwest Forest Pass ($5, available at ranger stations) is required for the following activities. The **Upper & Lower Proxy Falls** tumble over glacier-carved walls to disappear into lava flows. A 1.2-mile loop trail begins directly east of Mile 64, about 12 miles east of McKenzie Bridge.

The **Pacific Crest Trail** crosses McKenzie Pass a half-mile west of the Dee Wright Observatory. It's 2.5 miles across barren lava flows to a spectacular viewpoint atop **Little Belknap Crater**. Bring water and sun protection.

The **Obsidian Trail** is a very popular access point into the Three Sisters Wilderness, but requires a free limited-entry permit (available through the McKenzie ranger station; see p247). The full loop to Obsidian Cliffs and back is 13 miles, but for a shorter hike go just 2.5 forested miles to a 50ft-high lava flow with exhilarating views of the Three Sisters.

Three Sisters Wilderness

This beautiful 283,400-acre region spans the Cascade Range and is highlighted by the glaciered Three Sisters, three recent volcanic peaks each topping 10,000ft. The west slope of the wilderness is known for dense old-growth forest laced with strong rivers and streams. The glorious **Pacific Crest Trail** traverses the area, easily accessed from Hwy 242 at McKenzie Pass.

USFS Rd 19, also known as the **Aufderheide National Scenic Byway**, edges the westernmost wilderness boundary as it makes the 65-mile connection between Rainbow on Hwy 126 and Westfir (near Oakridge on Hwy 58). From **French Pete Campground**, one popular trail along this route leads up **French Pete Creek** through old-growth forest for about 3 miles.

Another good hike is to **Green Lake Basin**, on a high plateau between 9173ft Broken Top and 10,358ft South Sister. These celadon-green lakes are the centerpiece of a tremendous wildflower display in July and August, when the area throngs with crowds – especially on weekends. Park at the Green Lakes Trailhead along Hwy 46, above Sparks Lake, and hike north. The 4.4-mile trail is fairly steep but passes some great waterfalls.

Strong hikers should consider climbing **South Sister**. It's Oregon's third-highest peak, but during summer the southern approach doesn't demand any technical equipment. The steep 5.6-mile trail begins near Devils Lake (just off the Cascade Lakes Hwy) and is passable only in late summer.

For more information contact the Bend-Fort Rock Ranger District. Note that a Northwest Forest Pass is required to park at the Green Lake Basin and South Sister trailheads.

Bend

POP 82,000

Bend is an outdoor lover's paradise. This is an energetic city where you can ski fine powder in the morning, paddle a kayak in the afternoon and take in a game of golf into the evening. Or would you rather go mountain biking, hiking, mountaineering, stand-up paddleboarding, fly-fishing or rock climbing? It's all close by, and top-drawer. Plus, you'll probably be enjoying it all in great weather, as the area gets more than 250 days of sunshine each year.

With the lovely Deschutes River carving its way through the heart of the city, Bend also offers a vibrant and attractive downtown area full of boutiques, galleries and upscale dining. Perhaps the best sign of the renewal in the city is just south where the Old Mill District has been renovated into a large shopping area full of brand-name stores, fancy eateries and modern movie theaters. Anchoring the area is the old paper mill building, dominated by three landmark smokestacks and home to outdoorgear giant REI.

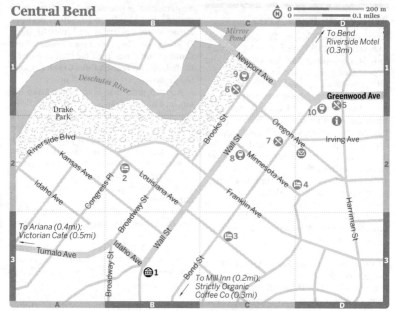

Not all of Bend is pretty, though – US 97 (3rd St) is a long commercial strip of cheap motels, fast-food restaurants and run-of-the-mill services. But something has had to support Bend's fast-growing population, which skyrocketed 50% in the last decade. While the economic slowdown has definitely affected the city's booming growth in recent years, Bend is likely to remain a mecca for those who seek to integrate the outdoors into their active lifestyles.

If you happen to be in Bend the second weekend in July, check out the **Bend Summer Festival** (www.c3events.com/events/Bend-Summer-Festival), which features artists, street performers, live music, plenty of food and lots of fun.

⊙ Sights & Activities

TOP CHOICE **High Desert Museum**   MUSEUM
(☎541-382-4754; www.highdesertmuseum.org; 59800 S US 97; adult/child $15/9; ⊙9am-5pm; 🖶) Don't miss this excellent museum 6 miles south of Bend on US 97. It charts the exploration and settlement of the West, using re-enactments of a Native American camp, a hard rock mine and an old Western town. The region's natural history is also explored; kids love the live snake, tortoise and trout exhibits, and watching the birds of prey and otters is always fun.

Central Bend   NEIGHBORHOOD
Beautiful **Drake Park**, right downtown, is a good place to start exploring Bend's many miles of riverfront walking trails.

SMITH ROCK, COVE PALISADES & MILL CREEK

Best known for its glorious rock climbing, **Smith Rock State Park** (☑541-548-7501; www.oregonstateparks.org; 9241 NE Crooked River Dr; day use $5) boasts rust-colored 800ft cliffs that tower over the pretty Crooked River. Nonclimbers have several miles of fine hiking trails, some of which involve a little simple rock scrambling. Nearby Terrebonne has a climbing store, along with some restaurants and grocery stores. There's **camping** (sites per person $4) right next to the park, or at Skull Hollow (aka 'The Grasslands,' no water; sites $5), 8 miles east. The nearest motels are a few miles south in Redmond.

Rent **boats** (☑541-546-3521) at the marina in spectacular Lake Billy Chinook, in **Cove Palisades State Park** (☑541-546-3412; www.oregonstateparks.org; day-use fee $5). Or hike the 7-mile **Tam-a-láu Trail** for spring wildflowers and great views. There's **camping** (tent/RV sites $20/26, cabins $80) near the lake, or motels 15 miles northeast in Madras.

The gently sloping Ochoco Mountains undulate across much of Central Oregon, offering good hikes near Prineville in the **Mill Creek Wilderness**. For a good one, follow US 26 east from town for 9 miles, and head north on USFS Rd 33 for about 10 miles to Wildcat Campground. From here a trail winds along the East Fork of Mill Creek through a lovely pine forest, eventually reaching **Twin Pillars**, a couple of spirelike volcanic crags (16.5 miles round trip). The **Prineville Ranger Station** (☑541-416-6500; www.fs.fed.us/r6/centraloregon; 3160 NE 3rd St; ☺7:45am-4:30pm Mon-Fri) has a list of nearby USFS campgrounds. There's plenty of accommodation in Prineville.

The **Deschutes Historical Center** (☑541-389-1813; 129 NW Idaho Ave; adult/child $5/2; ☺10am-4:30pm Tue-Sat) is in an old grade school and houses Native American and pioneer artifacts.

Mountain Biking

Bend is laced with bike trails. The 9-mile (one way) **Deschutes River Trail** runs from Lava Island Falls, just past the Inn of the Seventh Mountain, south to Dillon Falls. It's a lovely riverside route with separate paths for bikers, hikers and horses.

There's more mountain biking up Hwy 46 at **Swampy Lakes** and **Virginia Meissner Sno-Park** areas; Nordic ski routes become bike trails in summer.

Also fun are the mountain-bike routes up Skyliner Rd. Head west out of town on Galveston Ave and 9 miles up Skyliner Rd to the Skyliner's sno-play parking lot, the start of the 4.5-mile **Tumalo Falls Trail**; great views of rim rock and the 90ft-high Tumalo Falls await. And don't miss **Phil's Trailhead**, offering a variety of excellent forest trails just minutes from town.

Rent bikes at **Hutch's Bicycles** (☑541-382-9253; 725 NW Columbia St). It also offers (inexpensive) community rides and has another location at 820 NE 3rd St.

Water Sports

Rent kayaks, canoes and stand-up paddleboards from **Alder Creek Kayak & Canoe** (☑541-317-9407; www.aldercreek.com; 805 Industrial Way); classes and tours are also available. Raft the Deschutes (among other rivers) with **Ouzel Outfitters** (☑800-788-7238; www.oregonrafting.com); it also rents rafts and inflatable kayaks.

🛏 Sleeping

There's a countless supply of cheap motels, hotels and services on 3rd St (US 97). The Mill Inn has one dorm room for penny pinchers. During special festivals and events, Bend's lodging rates head north.

Oxford Hotel　　　　　　HOTEL $$$
(☑541-382-8436; www.oxfordhotelbend. com; 10 NW Minnesota Ave; d $199-259; ✷☺☎✷) Filling Bend's empty boutique-hotel niche is this gorgeous newcomer. The smallest rooms are huge (500 sq ft) and decked out in eco-features including soy-foam mattresses, cork flooring, 40% bamboo towels and dual-flush toilets. High-tech aficionados will love the iPod docks and smart-panel work desk (connecting your computer to the flat-screen TV). Suites with kitchen and steam shower available, and the basement restaurant is slick. Weekday rates slightly lower.

DON'T MISS

MCMENAMINS OLD ST FRANCIS SCHOOL

The McMenamin brothers do it again with this old schoolhouse remodeled into a classy 19-room **hotel** (☑541-382-5174; www.mcmenamins.com; 700 NW Bond St; d $120-175, cottages $210-370; ☺❋☎). The fabulously tiled salt-water Turkish bath is worth the stay alone, though nonguests can soak for $5. A restaurant-pub, three other bars, a movie theater and creative artwork completes the picture.

Pine Ridge Inn   INN $$

(☑541-389-6137, 800-600-4095; www.pineridgeinn.com; 1200 SW Century Dr; d $169-239; ☺❋☎) For modern luxury lodging there's this splendid place just outside the center of town. Many of the spacious suites have jetted tubs, romantic fireplaces and views of the Deschutes River and Old Mill District. There's a morning breakfast buffet and afternoon wine reception.

Lara House B&B   B&B $$$

(☑541-388-4064, 800-766-4064; www.larahouse.com; 640 NW Congress Pl; d $149-329; ☺❋☎) Lara House is a supremely elegant B&B with contemporary furniture, a sun room, small back deck and great location. All six beautiful rooms have thick carpeting, flat-screen TVs and private bathroom; honeymooners love the huge, romantic Summit suite.

Mill Inn   INN $$

(☑541-389-9198, 877-748-1200; www.millinn.com; 642 NW Colorado Ave; d $80-160; ☺☎) A 10-room boutique hotel with colorful, classy rooms decked out in velvet drapes and comforters. Full breakfast and hot tub use is included, and nice cabins are also an option (great for kids and pets). Another plus for budget travelers is the one dorm room available for $23 per bed.

Entrada Lodge   MOTEL $$

(☑541-382-4080; www.entradalodge.com; 19221 Century Dr; d from $89; ❋☎☒) Good, friendly and well-kept one-story motel about 2 miles south of town, on the road to Mt Bachelor. Clean, good-sized rooms, and the seasonal pool is a plus. Located in a woodsy area near hiking, biking and cross-country ski trails.

Bend Riverside Motel   MOTEL $$

(☑541-389-2363, 800-284-2363; www.bendriversidemotel.com; 1565 NW Hill St; d $78-159; ☺❋☎☒) Unmemorable rooms, but a wide range of them. Worth it if you get a riverside room; some have kitchen and fireplace. Indoor heated pool, sauna and Jacuzzi are pluses, as is the gated parking and nearby park.

Sonoma Lodge   MOTEL $

(☑541-382-4891; www.sonomalodge.com; 450 SE 3rd St; d $55; ❋☎) One of Bend's cheapest accommodations, with 17 good, spacious rooms – all with microwaves and refrigerators, and some with kitchenette. Located in a cluster of motels.

Tumalo State Park   CAMPGROUND $

(☑541-388-6055, 800-551-6949; www.oregonstateparks.org; 64120 OB Riley Rd; tent/RV sites $26/21, yurts $39) Riverside spots are best at this piney campground 5 miles northwest of Bend off US 20. Showers and flush toilets available.

✗ Eating

McMenamins Old St Francis School has a bar-restaurant with typical pub fare and long hours. The brewpubs listed under Drinking also serve decent food.

TOP CHOICE Blacksmith   STEAKHOUSE $$$

(☑541-318-0588; www.bendblacksmith.com; 211 NW Greenwood Ave; mains $16-27; ☺4:30-10pm) This renowned restaurant offers cowboy comfort food with a twist, such as gourmet meat loaf, grilled tenderloin with melted blue cheese and pan-fried trout in brown butter. A good-value, four-course meal is $24 (4:30pm to 5:30pm only), and the full bar puts out tasty, creative cocktails.

Ariana   MEDITERRANEAN $$$

(☑541-330-5539; www.arianarestaurantbend.com; 1304 NW Galveston Ave; mains $23-27; ☺5-9pm Tue-Sat) Cozy and intimate, Ariana is housed in an old bungalow and serves excellent Mediterranean-inspired cuisine. Start with the seared beef carpaccio before leading into organic spinach cannelloni or herbed rack of lamb. Reserve ahead – there are only 12 tables (sit outdoors in summer).

10 Below Restaurant & Lounge   NORTHWESTERN $$

(☑541-382-1010; www.oxfordhotelbend.com/the-kitchen.htm; 10 NW Minnesota Ave; mains $14-24; ☺6am-2pm & 5-10pm) Nestled in the basement of the Oxford Hotel is this upscale restaurant serving breakfast, lunch and dinner. Expect classy food, well-prepared and delicious. The $10 lunch special is quick and good value, while dinner means fancy dishes such as miso-glazed tuna loin or dijon-crusted rabbit.

Victorian Café   BREAKFAST **$$**
(1404 NW Galveston Ave; mains $8-14; ⊘breakfast & lunch) One of Bend's best breakfast spots, Victorian Café is especially awesome for its eggs Benedict (nine kinds). It's also good for sandwiches, burgers and salads. Be ready to wait for a table, especially on weekends.

⬛Pine Tavern   AMERICAN **$$**
(www.pinetavern.com; 967 NW Brooks St; mains $13-34; ⊘lunch & dinner Mon-Sat, lunch Sun) Long-running, popular and traditional family-friendly restaurant near the river. Everyone should find something to like here, from the great half-pound burger to smoked-salmon salad to house meat loaf to rib-eye steak. Awesome back patio.

Soba   ASIAN FUSION **$**
(www.eatsoba.com; 945 NW Bond St; mains $6.50-8; ⊘11am-9pm Mon-Thu, till 9:30pm Fri & Sat, noon-8pm Sun) Soba is a large and very casual eatery with great noodle dishes and rice bowls – the spicy shrimp soup is especially worth a shot. There are also a few appetizers and organic salads.

Strictly Organic Coffee Co   COFFEEHOUSE **$**
(www.strictlyorganic.com; 6 SW Bond St; ⊘6am-7pm Mon-Wed, till 8pm Thu, till 9pm Fri, till 6pm Sat, 7am-6pm Sun) Good coffee shop housed in an industrial space with outdoor front patio. The beans are roasted on the premises, and tasty light meals such as salads, sandwiches and wraps are available.

🍺 Drinking

McMenamins Old St Francis School has four bars and a gorgeous soaking pool.

Bend Brewing Co   BREWPUB
(www.bendbrewingco.com; 1019 NW Brooks St; ⊘11:30am-11pm Sun-Thu, till midnight Fri & Sat) This casual pub-restaurant has a good location near the river, with great patio for warm days. Order one of the award-winning brews, such as the hoppy Elk Lake India Pale Ale, or the robust Pinnacle Porter. Typical pub food (burgers and salads) also available.

Deschutes Brewery & Public House
                                    BREWPUB
(☑541-382-9242; www.deschutesbrewery.com; 1044 NW Bond St; ⊘11am-11pm Mon-Thu, till midnight Fri & Sat, till 10pm Sun) Bend's first microbrewery gregariously serves up plenty of food and handcrafted beers including Mirror Pond Pale Ale, Bachelor Bitter and Obsidian Stout. Free tours are given at their plant (☑541-385-8606; 901 SW Simpson Ave).

Astro Lounge   BAR
(www.astroloungebend.com; 147 NE Minnesota Ave; ⊘5pm-close Mon-Sat) This popular, trendy lounge is decked out in retro decor and singles looking for action. Upscale finger food and exotic cocktails (think key-lime pie martinis) are on offer, and cheap snacks are available during the 5pm to 7pm happy hour.

ℹ Information

Bend-Fort Rock Ranger District (☑541-383-4000; 1230 NE 3rd St; ⊘7:45am-4:30pm Mon-Fri) For area camping and hiking information.
Visitor & Convention Bureau (☑541-382-8048; www.visitbend.com; 917 NW Harriman St; ⊘9am-5pm Mon-Fri, 10am-4pm Sat & Sun)

ℹ Getting There & Around

The Redmond Municipal airport is located 18 miles north of Bend. **Central Oregon Breeze** (☑800-847-0157; www.cobreeze.com) provides an airport shuttle service, along with transport to Portland.

Amtrak Thruway buses link Bend with Chemult, where the nearest train station is located (65 miles south). Buses stop at Bend's **Lava Lanes Bowling Alley** (⊘541-382-2151; 1555 NE Forbes Rd).

Bend Area Transit (BAT; ☑541-322-5870; www.bendareatransit.com) is the local bus company in Bend. Green ways of getting around include **Green Energy Transportation & Tour** (☑541-610-6103; www.greenenergytransport.com), which provides area tours and shuttle services in a biodiesel van; and **Bend Cycle Cab** (☑541-408-6363; www.bendcyclecab.com), which uses bicycle pedicabs for downtown tours.

Mt Bachelor

Just 22 miles southwest of Bend is Oregon's best skiing – glorious Mt Bachelor (9065ft). Here, Central Oregon's cold, continental air meets up with the warm, wet Pacific air. The result is tons of fairly dry snow and plenty of sunshine – excellent conditions for skiing. With 370in of snow a year, the season begins in November and can last until May.

At **Mt Bachelor Ski Resort** (☑541-382-7888; www.mtbachelor.com; adult lift tickets from $50-70), rentals are available at the base of the lifts. Lift ticket prices depend on conditions. In Bend, you can stop for gear at **Powder House** (☑541-389-6234; 311 SW Century Dr). Shuttle buses (www.mtbachelor.com) run several times a day to Mt Bachelor from Bend.

Mt Bachelor grooms about 35 miles of cross-country trails, though the day pass (weekends and holidays $17, weekdays $14) may prompt skiers to check out the free trails at Dutchman Flat Sno-Park, just past the turnoff for Mt Bachelor on Hwy 46. This is as far as the snowplows maintain the highway during winter.

If there's adequate snow at lower elevations you can also cross-country ski from the Virginia Meissner or Swampy Lakes Sno-Parks, between Bend and Mt Bachelor on Hwy 46. To use all these Sno-Parks you'll need a Sno-Park permit, which is available from area businesses.

Newberry National Volcanic Monument

This relatively recent volcanic region (day use $5), highlighted by the Newberry Crater, showcases 500,000 years of volcanic activity. Start your visit at the **Lava Lands Visitor Center** (☑541-593-2421; www.fs.fed.us/r6/centraloregon/newberrynvm; ☺9am-5pm Jul 1-early Sep, days vary rest of year), about 13 miles south of Bend. The center is closed some days outside the peak season; check the website before you visit to make sure it will be open.

◉ Sights & Activities

Lava Formations   VOLCANIC FORMATIONS
For spectacular views, walk 1.5 miles up the nearby road to **Lava Butte**, a perfect cone rising 500ft above the surrounding lava flows; you can also drive here with a permit from the entrance gate.

Four miles west of the visitors center is **Benham Falls**, a good picnic spot on the Deschutes River. About 1 mile south of the visitors center, **Lava River Cave** (same hours as visitors center) is the only lava tube that's developed for visitors (bring a flashlight or rent one for $4).

About 6000 years ago, a wall of molten lava 20ft deep flowed down from Newberry Crater and engulfed a forest of mature

trees, resulting in the **Lava Cast Forest**. A mile-long interpretive trail is 9 miles east of US 97 on Lava Cast Forest Rd.

Newberry Crater   VOLCANIC CRATER
Newberry Crater was formed by the eruption of what was one of the largest and most active volcanoes in North America. Successive flows built a steep-sided mountain almost a mile above the surrounding plateau. As with Crater Lake, the summit of the volcano collapsed after a large eruption, creating a caldera.

Initially a single body of water, **Paulina Lake** and **East Lake** are now separated by a lava flow and a pumice cone. Due to the lakes' great depths and the constant flow of fresh mineral spring water, stocked trout thrive here. Looming above is 7985ft **Paulina Peak**.

A short trail halfway between the two lakes leads to the **Big Obsidian Flow**, an enormous deposit on the south flank of Newberry Crater. The **Newberry Crater Rim Loop Trail** encircles Paulina Lake and is a good place for hiking and mountain biking.

To get there from US 97, take Paulina East Lake Rd to Newberry Crater.

🛏 Sleeping

The monument's various campgrounds usually stay open from late May to October. Contact the Bend-Fort Rock Ranger District in Bend for more information.

There are a few cheap motels and restaurants in La Pine, about 30 miles south of Bend.

East Lake Resort   MOTEL, CABINS **$$**
(☑541-536-2230; www.eastlakeresort.com; 22430 E Lake Rd; d $75, cabins $99-169; ☎) This resort offers 12 rustic but comfortable cabins, most with kitchenettes and some with lake views. There are also four motel-type rooms with outside coin-op showers, a grocery store, tackle shop, café and boat rentals. Tent/RV sites are also available ($25).

Paulina Lake Lodge   CABINS **$$**
(☑541-536-2240; www.paulinalakelodge.com; cabins $110-213) A good place for outdoor enthusiasts, this lodge features a handful of charming log cabins (sleeping up to 10), a restaurant, general store, tackle shop and boat rentals.

LaPine State Park   CAMPGROUND **$**
(☑541-536-2071, 800-452-5687; www.oregon stateparks.org; 15800 State Recreation Rd; tent/RV sites $22, cabins $42-81) Just north

of La Pine on US 97, this scenic campground has sites near the Deschutes River, along with hot showers and flush toilets.

Cascade Lakes

Long ago, lava from the nearby volcanoes choked this broad basin beneath the rim of the Cascade Range. Lava flows dammed streams, forming lakes. In other areas, streams flowed underground through the porous lava fields to well up as lake-sized springs. Still other lakes formed in the mouths of small, extinct craters.

Hwy 46, also called the Cascade Lakes Hwy, loops roughly 100 miles between high mountain peaks, linking together this series of lovely alpine lakes (though many of them aren't visible from the road). Cyclists pedal the road in summer, while snowmobilers take over during winter. There are several trailheads in the area. Beyond Mt Bachelor, the road is closed from November to May.

Tiny **Todd Lake** offers views of Broken Top and relative seclusion, as getting here requires a quarter-mile hike. **Sparks Lake**, in a grassy meadow popular with birds, is in the process of transforming itself into a reedy marsh. **Hosmer Lake** is stocked with catch-and-release Atlantic salmon, making it popular with anglers (and osprey and beavers). **Little Lava Lake** is the source of the mighty Deschutes River.

The Deschutes is dammed at **Crane Prairie Reservoir**, where ospreys fish in the shallow lake water and use dead trees for nesting.

🛌 Sleeping

There are public campgrounds at each of the lakes along the route.

Some Cascade lakes have cabins on their shores, ranging from rustic to upscale. Restaurants, groceries and boat rentals are usually available. These resorts include:

Cultus Lake Resort (✆541-408-1560; www.cultuslakeresort.com)

Twin Lakes Resort (✆541-382-6432; www.twinlakesresortoregon.net)

Elk Lake Resort (✆541-480-7378; www.elklakeresort.net)

Crane Prairie Resort (✆541-383-3939; www.crane-prairie-resort-guides.com)

Not all are open all year; check details ahead of time.

Willamette Pass

Southeast from Eugene, the Willamette River leaves its wide valley and is immediately impounded into reservoirs. By Oakridge, the Willamette is restored to a rushing mountain river, and Hwy 58 climbs steadily up the Cascade Range's densely forested western slope.

At the Cascade crest, near Willamette Pass, are some beautiful lakes and wilderness areas, and Oregon's second-highest waterfall, 286ft **Salt Creek Falls**. There's good hiking here, and in winter the area is popular for downhill and cross-country skiing. Along the way, you can soak in warm waters at undeveloped **McCredie Hot Springs**; it's close to the road, popular with truckers, and clothing is optional. The unpaved turnout is just past Blue Pool Campground, about 50 miles east of Eugene.

The pass divides two national forests. For details on the Deschutes National Forest, contact the **Crescent Ranger District** (✆541-433-3200; 136471 Hwy 97 Nth, Crescent; ☉7:45am-4:30pm Mon-Fri). For information on the Willamette National Forest, including Waldo Lake, contact the **Middle Fork Ranger Station** (✆541-782-2283; www.fs.fed.us/r6/willamette; 46375 Hwy 58, Westfir; ☉8am-4:30pm Mon-Fri).

◉ Sights & Activities

Waldo Lake   LAKE

At an elevation of 5414ft on the very crest of the Cascades, Waldo Lake has no stream inlets – the only water that enters is snowmelt and rainfall. It is one of the purest bodies of water in the world and is the source of the Willamette River. The lake is amazingly transparent – objects 100ft below the surface are visible. Not only is it Oregon's second-deepest lake (420ft), it's also the state's second-largest lake (10 sq miles). No motorized boats are allowed, but afternoon winds make the lake popular for sailing. Three lovely USFS campgrounds flank the eastern half of the lake.

The west and north sides of the lake are contained in the **Waldo Lake Wilderness Area**, a 148-sq-mile area that abuts the Three Sisters Wilderness and is filled with tiny glacial lakes, meadows and hiking trails.

Odell & Crescent Lakes   LAKES

Immediately on the eastern slope of Willamette Pass is gorgeous Odell Lake, resting in a steep glacial basin. Hiking trails lead into relatively unexplored wilderness from lakeside campgrounds. In winter, the lake becomes a popular cross-country skiing destination.

A rustic lodge and popular campground ring Crescent Lake, which is popular for waterskiing, fishing and swimming. It's on Hwy 58 about 9 miles south of Willamette Pass, then 3 miles down National Forest Rd 60.

🏃 Activities

Hiking

A Northwest Forest Pass ($5) is required for the following hikes. Trails are snow-free from July to October.

The 22-mile **Waldo Lake Trail** encircles Waldo Lake. A less ambitious hike leads 3.4 miles from North Waldo Campground to rocky beaches at the outlet of the Willamette River; make it an 8-mile loop by returning via **Rigdon Lakes**, which lie at the base of a volcanic butte. Note that this hike is popular with mountain bikers, and goes through a 2006 fire area.

From the west end of Odell Lake, energetic hikers should consider the 5.3-mile one-way hike to **Yoran Lake** for a great view of 8744ft Diamond Peak. A popular hike from Odell Lake Lodge leads 3.8 miles to **Fawn Lake**, below two rugged peaks.

Skiing

The **Willamette Pass Resort** (☎541-345-7669; www.willamettepass.com; Hwy 58; lift tickets adult/child $45/27), 27 miles east of Oakridge, has steep slopes, great views and night skiing. Most of the 29 runs are rated intermediate to advanced, with a vertical drop of 1563ft. Eight-person gondolas run all year for both skiers and hikers/mountain bikers. The Pacific Crest Trail is less than a mile away (no bikes).

The resort also has 12 miles of groomed cross-country ski trails. **Odell Lake** is another popular spot for cross-country skiing.

🛏 Sleeping

Westfir Lodge   B&B $

(☎541-782-3103; www.westfirlodge.com; 47365 1st St, Westfir; d $80-95; ☺✳) A stone's throw from Oregon's longest covered bridge is this spacious B&B with eight homey guest rooms (some have bathroom down the hall) and a lovely flower garden. Check out the central vault, left over from the days when this building used to be a lumber company office.

Willamette Pass Inn   MOTEL $$

(☎541-433-2211;   www.willamettepassinn.com; Hwy 58; d $101-123, cabin $145; ☺⊛) This is the closest motel to the ski area, with very spacious and beautiful rooms, most boasting fireplaces and kitchenettes. Privately owned cabins are also available, and weekday rates are cheaper. It's 7 miles east of Willamette pass.

Odell Lake Resort   LODGE, CAMPGROUND $$

(☎541-434-2540; www.odelllakeresort.com; Hwy 58; campsites $14-17, d $70-85, cabins $100-200) This casual family resort has small lodge rooms, but you'll want to hang out in the fine living room downstairs anyway. Also available are about a dozen cabins, each with kitchen and fireplace, that sleep up to 16. There's a restaurant onsite, and boat rentals at the marina. Located 6 miles east of Willamette Pass, east of Odell Lake.

Crescent Lake Resort   LODGE $$

(☎541-433-2505; www.crescentlakeresort.com; National Forest Rd 60; cabins $95-215) A variety of cabins are on tap here, most with kitchen and some with fireplace; there's a three-night minimum from June to August and during holidays. Paddleboats, kayaks and mountain bikes are available for rent (snowmobiles in winter), and there's a restaurant with a nice patio too.

North Waldo Lake Campground

CAMPGROUND $

(off USFS Rd 5897; campsites $18) Campgrounds don't get much better than this lovely and rustic spot on Waldo Lake, but bring repellant. Located 11 miles off Hwy 58 near the end of USFS Rd 5898.

Oregon Coast

Why Go?

A drive along Oregon's coast is a must-do any time of year. Rocky headlands loom high above the ocean, providing astounding vistas, while craggy rocks lie scattered along the shoreline like oceanic sentinels. The Coast Range is deeply etched by great rivers and patched with forests, offering outdoor enthusiasts excellent boating, fishing and hiking. The Oregon Dunes – among the largest coastal dunes in the world – stretch for more than 50 miles and, just offshore, gray whales migrate from Alaska to Mexico and back.

Thanks to a far-sighted government in the 1910s, Oregon's 363-mile Pacific Coast was set aside as public land and strung with more than 70 state parks and protected areas. The northern Oregon coast has developed more quickly than the southern end, offering travelers a choice between bustling beach resorts and blissfully laid-back retreats. Everyone from campers to gourmet-lovers will find a plethora of ways to enjoy this exceptional region.

Best Places to Eat

- » Pacific Way Bakery & Cafe (p284)
- » Blackfish Café (p290)
- » Green Salmon Coffee House (p295)
- » Waterfront Depot (p297)

Best Places to Stay

- » Wildspring Guest Habitat (p304)
- » SeaQuest Inn B&B (p294)
- » Newport Belle (p291)
- » Heceta Head Lighthouse B&B (p295)
- » Commodore Hotel (p280)

When to Go
Newport

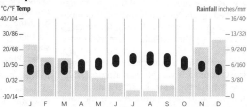

	July & August	November–June	December–March
	Hit the beach or go camping – but prepare for crowds and high prices	Gray whales migrate north (March–June) or south (November–February)	Storm-watchers' heaven – the crowds are gone and there's plenty of bargain lodging

NORTHERN OREGON COAST

Oregon's northern coast stretches from the mouth of the Columbia River south to Florence. Here lie the state's biggest and most touristy beach towns – Seaside, Cannon Beach and Lincoln City – while Depoe Bay is great for whale-watching and Newport is famous for its excellent aquarium.

Because of its popularity, the northern coast tends to get clogged with weekend visitors from Portland and the Willamette Valley. Since US 101 is mostly two-lane highway, traffic can slow to 20mph in sections – and there can be many RVs on the windy stretches. Also, expect to join the masses during summer months, when the beaches fill with crowds and lodging prices skyrocket (if you can even find a room). Weekdays are much less harried, but you might have to deal with a tad fewer services.

Astoria

POP 10,000

Named after America's first millionaire, John Jacob Astor, Astoria sits at the 5-mile-wide mouth of the Columbia River and was the first US settlement west of the Mississippi. The city has a long seafaring history and has seen its old harbor, once home to poor artists and writers, attract fancy hotels and restaurants in recent years. Cruise ships visit frequently, and inland are many historical houses, including lovingly restored Victorians – a few converted into romantic B&Bs.

Astoria has been the setting and shooting location for movies such as *The Goonies, Kindergarten Cop* and the *Free Willy* and *Ring* series; a new film museum has popped up recently to showcase them and other Oregon movies. Adding to the city's scenery is the 4.1-mile **Astoria-Megler Bridge**, the longest continuous truss bridge in North America, which crosses the Columbia River into Washington state. See it from the **Astoria Riverwalk**, which follows the trolley route between the west and east mooring basins, passing old canneries along the riverfront between 6th and 12th Sts.

There's also a weekly **Sunday Market** (cnr 12th & Commercial Sts; ⊙May-Oct), a combination farmers market and arts-and-crafts fair.

◉ Sights & Activities

Columbia River Maritime Museum MUSEUM
(⊘503-325-2323; www.crmm.org; 1792 Marine Dr; adult/child $10/5; ⊙9:30am-5pm) Astoria's seafaring heritage is well interpreted at this wave-shaped museum. It's hard to miss the Coast Guard boat, frozen in action, through a huge outside window. Other exhibits highlight the salmon-packing industry, local lighthouses and the river's commercial history; also check out the Columbia River Bar exhibit.

Flavel House HISTORIC BUILDING
(⊘503-325-2203; www.cumtux.org; 441 8th St; adult/child $5/2; ⊙10am-5pm) The extravagant Flavel House was built by Captain George Flavel, one of Astoria's leading citizens during the 1880s. This Queen Anne house has been repainted in its original colors and the grounds have been returned to Victorian-era landscaping; it has great views over the harbor too.

Oregon Film Museum MUSEUM
(⊘503-325-2203; 636 Duane St; adult/child $4/2; ⊙10am-5pm) Just below Flavel House is the small Oregon Film Museum, located in the old county jail. Two rooms and jail cells honor movies filmed in Oregon, especially Astoria's own *The Goonies*.

Heritage Museum MUSEUM
(⊘503-338-4849; www.cumtux.org; 1618 Exchange St; adult/child $4/2; ⊙10am-5pm) Housed in the former city hall, the Heritage Museum commemorates Astoria's various ethnic communities. Look for the Ku Klux Klan robes and the Klan letter supporting prohibition. There's also a room dedicated to the Clatsop tribe.

Liberty Theater HISTORIC BUILDING
(⊘503-325-5922; crn 12th & Commercial Sts) Downtown's Liberty Theater is a landmark boasting elaborate Italian Renaissance styling. It dates from 1925 and once hosted silent films and vaudeville performances; today, Pink Martini is a more likely act.

Astoria Column LANDMARK
($1 honor-system parking fee) Rising high on Coxcomb Hill, the Astoria Column (built in 1926) is a 125ft tower painted with scenes from the westward sweep of US exploration and settlement. The top of the column (you'll need to go up 164 steps) offers good views over the area, and the nearby 1.5-mile walking trail is another good leg-stretcher.

Oregon Coast Highlights

1 Nibble fish 'n chips, crab cakes or chowder in towns such as **Seaside** (p282)

2 Spot gray whales during their migrations at **Depoe Bay** (p290)

3 Hike the **Cape Falcon and Neahkahnie Mountain Trails** for awesome views (p286)

4 Check out the jellyfish, sea otters and sharks at Newport's **Oregon Coast Aquarium** (p291)

5 Stick to the coast for the stunning **Three Capes Drive** (p288)

6 Camp and hike among the towering sands of the **Oregon Dunes National Recreation Area** (p297)

7 Count lighthouses – like the super-photogenic one at **Heceta Head** (p294) – along the coast

Northern Oregon Coast

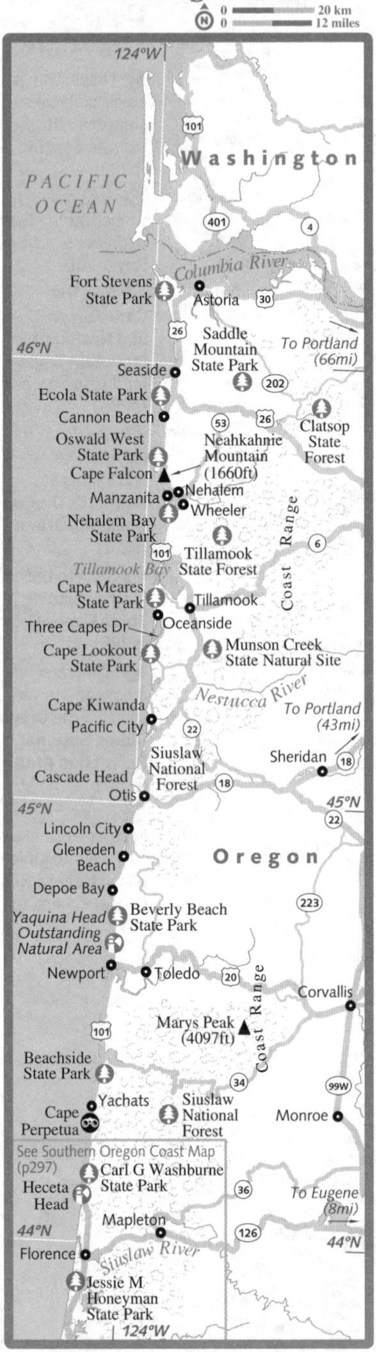

Lewis & Clark National Historical Park HISTORICAL PARK
(☎503-861-2471; www.nps.gov/lewi; adult/child $3/free; ⏱9am-6pm Jun-Aug, till 5pm Sep-May) Five miles south of Astoria, this historical park holds a reconstructed fort similar to the one the Corps of Discovery occupied during their miserable winter of 1805–06. There's expedition history and Clatsop artifacts at the visitor center, and costumed docents demonstrate common fort pastimes such as candle-making, leather-tanning and canoe-building.

Fort Stevens State Park STATE PARK
(☎503-861-1671; www.oregonstateparks.org/park_179.php) Ten miles west of Astoria, this park commemorates the historic military reservation that guarded the mouth of the Columbia River. Near the **Military Museum** (☎503-861-2000; day use $5; ⏱9am-6pm Jun-Sep, 10am-4pm Oct-May) are grim, warren-like garrisons dug into sand dunes – interesting remnants of the fort's mostly demolished military buildings. There's plenty of beach access and camping in the park, along with 9.5 miles of bike trails.

Boat Tours TOURS
Heading out to sea? Hook up with **Columbia River Eco Tours** (☎503-468-9197; www.columbiariverecotours.com) to check out Astoria from the water and spot some sea lions and ospreys. Or go fishing with **Tiki Charters** (☎503-325-7818; www.tikicharter.com), which provides all gear and sells licenses too.

Festivals & Events

Crab & Seafood Festival SEAFOOD FESTIVAL
Astoria's biggest annual event brings 200 wine and seafood vendors together the last weekend in April.

Fisher Poets Gathering FISHING
(www.clatsopcollege.com/fisherpoets) In late February this festival attracts creative folks from the fishing industry, who come together to share their songs, stories and poetry.

Sleeping

TOP CHOICE **Commodore Hotel** HOTEL $$
(☎503-325-4747; www.commodoreastoria.com; 258 14th St; d $69-129; ⊜📶) Hip travelers should beeline to this slick and trendy hotel, which offers small, chic, minimalist rooms. Choose either private bathrooms or go euro-style (sinks in rooms but baths down the hall). Great 'living room'-style

lobby with attached café. Room 309 has the best river view.

Cannery Pier Hotel
HOTEL $$$

(☑503-325-4996, 888-325-4996; www.cannery pierhotel.com; 10 Basin St; d $249-299; ❄🐾) Located on a pier at the west end of town, this luxurious hotel offers fine rooms right over the water, with bridge views, contemporary furnishings and open bathtubs. Perks include a Jacuzzi, afternoon wine socials, continental breakfast and free ride in a vintage car. Spa on premises.

Hotel Elliott
HOTEL $$

(☑503-325-2222, 877-378-1924; www.hotelel liott.com; 357 12th St; d $149-169; ❄✳🐾) Standard rooms have charming period elegance at this historic hotel. For more space, get a suite (the 'presidential' boasts two bedrooms, two baths, a grand piano and rooftop deck). There's also a rooftop terrace with great views, and a basement wine bar open Friday and Saturday nights.

Franklin Street Station B&B
B&B $$

(☑503-325-4314, 800-448-1098; www.astoria oregonbb.com; 1140 Franklin St; d $80-135; ❄🐾) Well-located B&B offering six classic rooms, each with private bath and some with balconies and river views. Good place to come if you want TV, fridge and microwave in your room (most have them), plus a full breakfast.

Rose River Inn B&B
B&B $$

(☑503-325-7175, 888-876-0028; www.roseriver inn.com; 1510 Franklin Ave; d $90-160; ❄🐾) This friendly, casual country-style B&B offers five pretty rooms, including a two-bedroom suite. The breakfast room offers river views; a chihuahua roams the premises. Kids over 12 only.

Norblad Hotel
HOTEL, HOSTEL $

(☑503-325-6989; www.norbladhotel.com; 443 14th St; dm $20, d $44-88; 🐾) Well located, this old hotel/hostel (ex-Hideaway Inn) has reasonable bunks, a range of simple, private rooms and a communal kitchen. Most rooms share outside bathrooms but some have flat-screen TVs and peeks of the river. Call ahead as there's no doorbell.

Grandview B&B
B&B $$

(☑800-488-3250; www.grandviewbedandbreak fast.com; 1574 Grand Ave; d $66-130; ❄🐾) This sprawling house features nine guest rooms, each with private bath and some with great views. Best if you're looking for privacy rather than meeting other guests, as common

spaces are limited and Charleen, the quirky owner, does ask that rules be followed (ie no alcohol on premises). Simple breakfast.

Crest Motel
MOTEL $

(☑503-325-3141, 800-421-3141; www.crestmotel astoria.com; 5366 Leif Ericson Dr; d $62-112; 🐾) Get a quieter room in the back, away from the road, at this decent motel on the eastern edge of town. 'View' rooms are best; they overlook the Columbia. It's located 4.5 miles from downtown Astoria.

Fort Stevens State Park
CAMPGROUND $

(☑503-861-1671; off US 101; tent sites/RV sites/ yurts $21/27/45) Nearly 500 sites (most RVs) are available at this campground 10 miles west of Astoria. Great for families; reserve ahead. There's an enormous and more expensive KOA campground across the highway.

🍴 Eating

Astoria is flush with good restaurants. Beer drinkers note: Rogue Brewery has a branch at 100 39th St.

Baked Alaska
NORTHWESTERN $$$

(☑503-325-7414; www.bakedak.com; 1 12th St; mains $18-24; ⊘lunch & dinner) One of Astoria's finest restaurants, Baked Alaska sits right atop a pier on the water – views are excellent. Lunch means 0.5lb gourmet burgers and blackened sirloin salad, while dinner mains range from grilled wild salmon to the 10oz rib-eye steak.

T Paul's Urban Café AMERICAN $$

(1119 Commercial St; mains $10-18; ⊙lunch & dinner Mon-Sat) With a slick yet funky atmosphere, this popular café serves up a large variety of gourmet quesadillas, sandwiches, salads and pastas. On Friday and Saturday, prime rib, lamb and pork dishes are added to the menu as well. Another branch is at 360 12th St.

Wet Dog Café BREWPUB $$

(www.wetdogcafe.com; 144 11th St; mains $9-21; ⊙lunch & dinner, till 2am Fri & Sat) For casual dining there's no beating this large, quirky pub, which brews its own beer with names such as Poop Deck Porter and Bitter Bitch IPA. The grub is typically publike, there are good water views and live music plays Thursday through Saturday. Partially solar-run.

Also recommended:

Blue Scorcher Bakery Café
COFFEEHOUSE $

(☑503-338-7473; www.bluescorcher.com; 1493 Duane St; mains $7-11; ⊙8am-5pm; 🖻) Very artsy, organic coffeehouse and bakery. Salads, sandwiches and a few savory plates. Doughnut-free.

Bridgewater Bistro NORTHWESTERN $$$

(☑503-325-6777; www.bridgewaterbistro.com; 20 Basin St; mains $16-25; ⊙lunch & dinner Mon-Sat, lunch Sun) Fine dining with great water views in a lofty space. The lunch and Sunday brunch menus are less expensive.

Drina Daisy BOSNIAN $$

(☑503-338-2912; www.drinadaisy.com; 915 Commercial St; mains $14-18; ⊙11am-9pm Wed-Sun) Excellent Bosnian food that includes rotisserie lamb, stuffed cabbage leaves and spinach pitas.

Astoria Coffeehouse & Bistro AMERICAN $

(☑503-325-1787; www.astoriacoffeehouse.com; 243 11th St; mains $8-17; ⊙7am-10pm) Small, hip café with attached bistro offering an eclectic menu.

❶ Information

Visitors center (☑503-325-6311; www.oldoregon.com; 111 W Marine Dr; ⊙9am-5pm)

❶ Getting There & Around

Astoria Transit Center (☑800-776-6406; 900 Marine Dr) Buses leave here to head down the coast or to Portland.

Pacific Transit (☑360-642-9418; www.pacifictransit.org) Buses go over the border to Washington.

Riverfront Trolley ($1) Astoria's trolley plies through the old cannery district, between the East and West Mooring Basins; daily in summer, weekends only in winter.

Seaside

POP 6300

Oregon's largest resort town is popular, gaudy and unpretentious Seaside, which attracts families and young folks looking for a fun and affordable beach getaway. On summer weekends and during holidays or festivals the town's central precinct – dominated by ice-cream shops, video-game arcades and gift stores – is thronged with tourists and takes on a carnival-like atmosphere. Bicycles and surreys have the run of Seaside's 2-mile boardwalk, called 'the Prom,' but at least most of the miles of sandy beach are relatively peaceful. During spring break, expect a wilder party atmosphere.

For more subtle attractions, visit the **Visitors Bureau** (☑503-738-3097; www.seasideor.com; 7 N Roosevelt Dr; ⊙8am-5pm Mon-Sat, 11am-5pm Sun). During the fourth weekend in August, the **Hood to Coast Relay Marathon** jams the main road between Portland and Seaside and packs out the town. The **Seaside Beach Volleyball Tourney** is held the second weekend in August.

Buses to Portland, Astoria and Cannon Beach stop daily at **Del's Service Station** (☑503-738-3651; www.oregon-point.com; cnr N Holladay Dr & US 101).

◉ Sights

Seaside Aquarium AQUARIUM

(☑503-738-6211; www.seasideaquarium.com; 200 N Promenade; adult/child $7.50/3.75; ⊙9am-7pm; 🖻) Families with kids will enjoy the aquarium, on the promenade. Don't expect anything like Newport's cutting-edge version, but rather a few fish tanks, a touch pool and a small indoor seal tank where you can feed the splashy critters.

Seaside Museum & Historical Society
MUSEUM

(☑503-738-7065; 570 Necanicum Dr; adult/senior $3/2; ⊙10am-4pm) Curious about Seaside's past? This museum displays old photos and relics; ask about Lewis and Clark's saltworks' history and summer re-enactments here.

⊙ Activities

Join the pedaling hordes on the promenade by renting bikes and four-wheel surreys at **Prom Bike & Hobby Shop** (⌨503-738-8251; 622 12th Ave). It also offers tandems, skates and strollers (and more). For surfing gear and advice on where to hit the waves, there's **Cleanline Surf Company** (⌨503-738-7888; 60 N Roosevelt Dr). It rents longboards for $15 to $20 per day, plus other gear.

Saddle Mountain State Natural Area
HIKING

(⌨503-861-1671) About 13 miles east of Seaside on US 26, Saddle Mountain State Natural Area features a popular 2.5-mile hiking trail that starts at 1650ft elevation and heads through alpine wildflower meadows to the top of Saddle Mountain (3283ft). Views of the Columbia River and the Pacific coastline are absolutely spectacular, but the trail is steep and grueling. Bring layers and be prepared for changeable weather.

🛏 Sleeping

Reserve in July and August, when two-night minimums might be required on weekends.

Sandy Cove Inn
BOUTIQUE MOTEL $$

(⌨503-738-7473; www.sandycoveinn.biz; 241 Ave U; d $99-199; ✆🖧🛜) A unique motel stay, this friendly, family-run place has 18 boutique rooms; all are different and tastefully decorated with fun themes and antiques. Jacuzzi suites and a house (four-night minimum) are also available. It's at the north end of town, three blocks from the beach.

Beachside Inn
UPSCALE MOTEL $$

(⌨503-738-5363; www.beachsideinn-seaside. com; 300 5th Ave; d $105-160; ✆🛜) Just a couple of blocks from the beach and close to downtown Seaside is this handful of cute rooms, all tastefully furnished with soft pastels and pleasant decor. Some have a kitchenette, while others just a microwave, coffeemaker and fridge – but all are very comfortable and clean. Reserve ahead; they're a good deal, and popular.

Hillcrest Inn
HOTEL $$

(⌨503-738-6273, 800-270-7659; www.seaside hillcrest.com; 118 N Columbia; d $89-165; ✆❄🛜) This Cape Cod–style inn offers a wide variety of simple but comfortable rooms and suites, some with kitchenette, jetted tubs and partial ocean views (rooms 123 and 129 are especially good). There's a nice grassy

common area, and the beach is a block away. It's great value; reserve way ahead for the really budget rooms ($40 and $65).

Inn of the Four Winds
INN $$

(⌨800-818-9524; www.innofthefourwinds.com; 820 N Promenade; d $149-249; ✆🛜) One of Seaside's most luxurious stays is this intimate inn with only 14 rooms. All are beautiful and most come with gas fireplace and an outside seating area boasting ocean views. Tempurpedic mattresses and flat-screen TVs are *de rigueur,* but best of all might be the complimentary cookies that greet you upon arrival.

Seaside Oceanfront Inn
HOTEL $$

(⌨503-738-6403,800-722-7766;www.theseaside inn.com; 581 S Promenade; d $159-309; ✆🛜) The front entry is strangely unwelcoming and reception is a restaurant counter, but it's the vistas out back that really matter. All 14 rooms have a light theme – such as 'Lewis and Clark' or 'Northwest Timber' (the fanciest one, with an ocean-view indoor Jacuzzi in the loft!) – and many boast ocean views. Breakfast is included at the good restaurant here.

Gilbert Inn
INN $$

(⌨503-738-9770; www.gilbertinn.com; 341 Beach Dr; d $119-159; ✆🛜) This 1892 Queen Anne house is located in a neighborhood of apartments, but it's just a block from the beach. Six guest rooms, all carpeted and decorated in traditional style; the attic room is huge. Children over 17 only; breakfast not available.

Seaside International Hostel
HOSTEL $

(⌨503-738-7911, 888-994-0001; www.seaside hostel.net; 930 N Holladay Dr; dm/d $26/59; ✆@🛜) For decent budget lodgings you can't beat this small hostel, offering good dorms and private rooms with bath – most opening to the parking area. There's a kitchen and TV room, but the highlight is the grassy backyard overlooking a river. Canoe and kayak rentals; HI members and cyclists get a $2 discount.

Bud's Campground & Grocery
CAMPGROUND $

(⌨503-738-6855; 4412 Hwy 101; tent/RV sites $22/35; 🛜) This pleasant campground has RV and tent sites with good facilities, plus full grocery store with crab pots and razor clam digging gear for rent. Located about 4 miles north of Seaside, just off the highway. For more tent camping try Astoria (15 miles north) or Cannon Beach (7 miles south).

DON'T MISS

PACIFIC WAY BAKERY & CAFE

Located in Gearheart, about 3 miles north of Seaside, this jewel of a **restaurant** (☎503-738-0245; www.pacificwaybakery-cafe.com; 601 Pacific Way; mains $14-29; ☺lunch & dinner Thu-Mon) is worth the trip. It serves excellent sandwiches and salads for lunch, while dinner means gourmet treats such as lavender-roasted duck – though gourmet pizza is also available. The bakery next door (open 7am to 3:30pm Thursday to Monday) has folks lining up outside.

✖ Eating

Lil' Bayou   SOUTHERN **$$**
(☎503-717-0624; www.lilbayou.net; 20 N Holladay Dr; mains $15-20; ☺4:30-10pm Wed-Mon) It's Mardi Gras every day at this colorful, Cajun-Creole restaurant, which offers some of the finest blackened catfish, seafood gumbo, crawfish pie and jambalaya this side of the Louisiana border. Generous portions, good service, tasty cocktails and occasional live music.

Norma's   SEAFOOD **$$**
(☎503-738-4331; www.normasoceandiner.com; 20 N Columbia; mains $13-22; ☺lunch & dinner) Look for the lighthouse shape atop this family-friendly restaurant, which serves up a medley of seafood dishes, from halibut steaks to Alaska king crab to four kinds of fish 'n chips. Steaks, pasta, salads and plenty of sandwiches also available.

McKeown's   AMERICAN **$$**
(☎503-738-5232;   www.mckeownsrestaurant.com; 1 N Holladay Dr; mains $10-21; ☺8am-10pm) Very family-friendly and popular, this large restaurant serves good breakfast, lunch and dinner, offering a full menu with something for everyone. Come during happy hour (3pm to 6pm) for $3 appetizers, and if you're super hungry on Sunday morning then the famous buffet is a must.

Seaside Coffee House   COFFEEHOUSE **$**
(5 N Holladay Dr; ☺7am-5pm) For good coffee in a casual atmosphere this comfortable and friendly coffee shop is located away from the beach madness. Order a banana fudge latte and lose yourself in a sofa. They roast the beans themselves and also sell in bulk.

Cannon Beach

POP 1700

Charming Cannon Beach is one of the most popular beach resorts on the Oregon coast. Several premier hotels here cater to a fancier clientele, as do the town's many boutiques and art galleries. In summer the streets are ablaze with flowers. Unlike Seaside's Coney Island–like atmosphere, Cannon Beach is toned down and much more refined. Lodging is expensive, and the streets are jammed: on a sunny Saturday, you'll spend a good chunk of time just finding a parking spot.

Just offshore is another reason for the town's popularity. Glorious Haystack Rock is a magnet for beachgoers – providing great photo opportunities and tide-pooling possibilities – and the wide sandy beach stretches for miles.

The **Chamber of Commerce** (☎503-436-2623; www.cannonbeach.org; 207 N Spruce St; ☺10am-5pm) has local information. Cannon Beach's largest festival, **Sandcastle Day** (held in June, dates depend on tides), has teams competing for originality and execution in sand sculpture.

◉ Sights & Activities

If you want to check out the local surfing, visit **Cannon Beach Surf** (☎503-436-0475; 1088 S Hemlock St) for board rentals and lessons. Landlubbers who like to pedal can rent three-wheeled sand bicycles at **Family Fun Cycle** (☎503-436-2247; 1160 S Hemlock St).

Beaches   BEACHES
The beaches here are some of the most beautiful in Oregon, with **Haystack Rock** and other outcroppings rising out of the surf. The best access is at the end of Gower St, a mile south. Busy **Tolovana Beach Wayside** is at the south end of town, along Hemlock St. Other beach points are accessible at the more remote **Hug Point State Park**, 3 miles south on US 101.

Ecola State Park   STATE PARK
(☎503-436-2844; day use $5) Located just north of town, Ecola State Park offers seclusion and great picnicking. Short paths at Ecola Point lead over the headland to dramatic views of Cannon Beach's sandy shore, sharply punctuated by stone monoliths and all hunkered beneath the Coast Range.

Leading north from here is an 8-mile stretch of the **Oregon Coast Trail**, which follows the same route traversed by the

Corps of Discovery in 1806. Highlights on this trail include a sandy cove at **Indian Beach** (which is popular with surfers, and even stood in for La Push beach in the original *Twilight* movie) and **Tillamook Head** (which offers a view of an inactive lighthouse).

🛏 Sleeping

Cannon Beach is pretty exclusive; for budget choices head 7 miles north to Seaside. Reserve ahead in July and August. For vacation rentals, check out www.visitcb.com.

Ocean Lodge   HOTEL $$$
(☎503-436-2241, 888-777-4047; www.theocean lodge.com; 2864 S Pacific St; d $269-389; ☺❄️🏐) This gorgeous place has some of Cannon Beach's most luxurious rooms, most with ocean view and all with fireplace and kitchenette. A complimentary continental breakfast, an 800-DVD library and pleasant sitting areas are available to guests.

Blue Gull Inn   UPSCALE MOTEL $$
(☎800-507-2714; www.haystacklodgings.com; 487 S Hemlock St; d $119-219; ☺🏐) These are some of the more affordable rooms in town, with comfortable atmosphere and toned-down decor, except for the colorful Mexican headboards and serapes on the beds. Kitchenettes available. Run by Haystack Lodgings, which also manages three other inns in town and does vacation rentals.

Argonauta Inn   INN $$
(☎800-822-2468; www.thewavesmotel.com; 188 W 2nd St; d $125-429; ☺🏐) This five-unit complex run by the Waves Motel features three suites, a two-bedroom townhouse and three-bedroom beach house that sleeps up to nine. All are simply decorated but casual and spacious; some have ocean views.

Waves Motel   UPSCALE MOTEL $$
(☎800-822-2468; www.thewavesmotel.com; 188 W 2nd St; d $125-429; ☺🏐) Disregard the word 'motel' here – this place is more like an upscale inn than a motor lodge. Furnishings are elegant and the rooms comfortable and bright, and some come with kitchens, two bedrooms and decks overlooking the beach.

Cannon Beach Hotel   HOTEL $$$
(☎503-436-1392, 800-238-4107; www.cannon beachhotel.com; 1116 S Hemlock St; d $140-240; ☺🏐) If you don't need much space, check out this classy, centrally located hotel. Standard rooms are lovely and tasteful but very small;

even the regular suites are tight. There's a good restaurant on the premises, however.

Sea Ranch RV Park   CAMPGROUND $
(☎503-436-2815; www.searanchrv.com; 415 Fir St; tent sites $33, RV sites $38-43, cabins $85-95) Pleasant Sea Ranch, on quiet Ecola Creek, is across from the turnoff to Ecola State Park and is popular with the local feral bunny population. Horseback riding is available. There are also primitive, 1.5-mile hike-in campsites ($10) at nearby Ecola State Park (bring water).

Wright's for Camping   CAMPGROUND $
(☎503-436-2347; www.wrightsforcamping.com; 334 Reservoir Rd; campsites $27) Family-run campground with clean bathhouse and pleasant, spacious sites in a woodsy forest. Plenty of tall trees – bring your hammock.

✕ Eating & Drinking

Newman's   EUROPEAN $$$
(☎503-436-1151; www.newmansat988.com; 988 S Hemlock St; mains $19-28; ☺dinner) Expect a fine dining experience at this small, quality restaurant on the main drag. Award-winning chef John Newman comes up with a fusion of French and Italian dishes such as duck breast with foie gras and lobster ravioli in marsala cream sauce. Desserts are sublime.

Lumberyard   AMERICAN $$
(☎503-436-0285; www.thelumberyardgrill.com; 264 3rd St; mains $11-25; ☺lunch & dinner Thu-Mon) This family-friendly eatery has something for everyone, including seven kinds of burgers (get one with four patties!), rotisserie specialties, pot pies, sandwiches, pizzas and steaks. There are booths for cozy dining, a front patio for warm days and a bar area for easy access to the hard stuff.

Cannon Beach Café & Deli   AMERICAN $$
(www.cannonbeachcafe.com; 1116 S Hemlock St; mains $14-18; ☺8am-9pm) Located in the Cannon Beach Hotel is this bright and contemporary corner bistro. The breakfast, lunch and dinner menus are all limited, but there are enough gourmet choices to satisfy most palates – and the takeaway service makes beachside picnics a snap.

Inspired! Café   AMERICAN $
(123 S Hemlock St; mains $6-14; ☺10am-6pm) Find this small café inside Dragonfly art gallery. Choose from several exotic appetizers, soups, hot wraps and small plates – you can't beat this spot for cheap, quick and artsy.

Sleepy Monk Coffee COFFEEHOUSE $
(www.sleepymonkcoffee.com; 1235 S Hemlock St; ⊙8am-4pm Fri-Sun) For organic, certified fairtrade coffee, try this little coffee shop on the main street. Sit on an Adirondack chair on the tiny front patio and enjoy the rich brews, all tasty and roasted on the premises. Good pastries too.

ⓘ Getting There & Around

Buses to Portland, Seaside and Astoria depart daily from **Family Market** (☑503-436-0515; 1170 S Hemlock St). The free hourly **Cannon Beach shuttle** (☑800-776-6406) runs the length of Hemlock St to the end of Tolovana Beach.

Manzanita

POP 750

One of the more laid-back beach resorts on Oregon's coast is the hamlet of Manzanita, boasting lovely white-sand beaches and a slightly upscale clientele. It's much smaller and far less hyped than Cannon Beach, and still retains a peaceful atmosphere. You can relax on the beach, take part in a few activities and perhaps hike on nearby Neahkahnie Mountain, where high cliffs rise dramatically above the Pacific's pounding waves.

Manzanita is located near the Nehalem River, which creates a wide estuarial valley and then a bay that is protected from the ocean by a 7-mile sand spit. Just to the south and right on the river, the historic fishing villages of Nehalem and Wheeler are becoming centers for antiques and river recreation.

Tillamook County Transportation (☑503-815-8283; www.tillamookbus.com) buses stop on 5th St near Laneda Ave, and connect to Tillamook, Cannon Beach and Portland.

🏃 Activities

Hiking

Nearby **Nehalem Bay State Park** (day use $5) has a good 2-mile walk (or sandy bike ride) on the Spit Trail, which finishes up at the end of a peaceful peninsula.

Five miles north is **Oswald West State Park** (☑503-368-3575), a beautiful preserve with dense coastal rain forest and two headlands. For a good hike, take the 2.4-mile trail to **Cape Falcon**, which offers expansive views and good bird-watching. For more exercise, climb 3.8 miles to the top of 1660ft **Neahkahnie Mountain**, which towers above Nehalem Bay and offers amazing views – on a clear day, you can see 50 miles out to sea.

Kayaking & Surfing

The quiet, bird-rich waters of Nehalem Bay are good for contemplative kayaking and bird watching; there's kayak rentals at **Wheeler on the Bay Lodge & Marina** (☑503-368-5780; 580 Marine Dr) in Wheeler, just 4 miles south of Manzanita.

Surfers and body boarders can head a quarter-mile from the highway parking lot to **Short Sand Beach**, which offers good waves. Rent bicycles and surfboards from **Manzanita Bikes & Boards** (☑503-368-3337; 170 Laneda Ave).

🛏 Sleeping

For vacation rentals, see www.oceanedge-vacation-rentals.com.

Coast Cabins CABINS $$$
(☑503-368-7113; www.coastcabins.com; 635 Laneda Ave; d $215-375; ◉🐾) Just five luxurious cabins are available at this lovely retreat near the entrance to town. All come with contemporary furnishings and kitchenette, but three are larger, two-story affairs. The simple, lovely gardens provide plenty of privacy.

Inn at Manzanita INN $$
(☑503-368-6754; www.innatmanzanita.com; 67 Laneda Ave; d $150-180; ◉🐾) This very pleasant inn is located right on the main street but within forested grounds. There are 14 cozy rooms, all with fireplace, balcony and jetted tub. The larger suites are best for families and come with kitchenette; there's also a three-bedroom penthouse ($385).

Old Wheeler Hotel HOTEL $$
(☑503-368-6000, 877-653-4683; www.oldwheelerhotel.com; 495 Hwy 101, Wheeler; d $99-160; ◉🐾) This lovely historic hotel, with views of Nehalem Bay, is located 4 miles south of Manzanita in Wheeler. The eight rooms are classically styled, decorated with antiques and some with Jacuzzi. There's a two-room suite, and continental breakfast is included.

Sea Haven Motel & Hostel MOTEL, HOSTEL $
(☑503-355-8101; www.seahavenmotel.net; 520 Hwy 101 N; r $59-89; ◉@🐾🐾) About 10 miles south in Rockaway beach on the highway is this unusual motel and hostel. Motel rooms are great (especially No 6), most sporting separate bedroom and kitchenette. The tidy hostel is next door and offers small dorms and private rooms, all with shared bath and kitchen use.

Nehalem Bay State Park CAMPGROUND $
(☑503-368-5154, 800-452-5687; campsites/
yurts $24/36) On the dunes of Nehalem
Spit, 3 miles south of Manzanita off US 101,
this big campground has showers, equestrian facilities, a boat ramp and even an
airstrip.

Also recommended:
Sunset Surf Motel MOTEL $
(☑503-368-5224; www.sunsetsurfocean.com;
248 Ocean Rd; d $89-159; 🛜🏊) Beachside
motel with wide range of rooms in three
buildings; ocean views.

Zen Garden B&B B&B $$
(☑503-368-6697; www.neahkahnie.net/zengar
den; 8910 Glenesslin Ln; d $130-160; 🛜🏊) B&B
offering two very private rooms. Peaceful
garden with soaking tub available ($20
extra).

Bunk House MOTEL $
(☑503-368-2865; 36315 N US 101; d $46-101)
Homely spot with seven good rooms (the
cheapest share a bathroom) and two
cabins.

✗ Eating

TOP CHOICE **Bread and Ocean** AMERICAN $$
(☑503-368-5823; www.breadandocean.
com; 154 Laneda Ave; panini sandwiches $8, din-
ner mains $15-23; ⊙breakfast & lunch Wed-Sun,
dinner Fri-Sun) You'll have to line up for exceptional panini, pasta salads and baked
goods at this small bakery-deli. Reserve for
dinner – there are only a handful of tables
inside, though the cute garden patio is the
place to be on warm days.

San Dune Pub AMERICAN $
(www.sandunepub.com; 127 Laneda Ave; mains
$8-10; ⊙11:30am-9pm) If you don't mind eat-
ing in a pub with sports on TV, step into
this joint. Burgers dominate the menu, but
they're special – try the blue-cheese bacon
or chipotle chicken. There are also a few
wraps and seafood choices, along with a
cozy back patio for sunny days.

Marzano's Pizza Pie PIZZA $$
(www.marzanospizza.com; 60 Laneda Ave; pizzas
$10-28; ⊙4-9pm) More than a dozen kinds
of top-quality pizzas are covered in choice
sauces and baked on a fire-heated stone.
Try the Italian sausage – it comes with
fresh mushrooms, roasted red onions and
homemade sausage. Calzones and salads
also available.

Manzanita News & Espresso COFFEEHOUSE $
(www.neahkahnie.net/newsespresso; 500 Lane-
da Ave; ⊙7:30am-5pm) This friendly, cozy café
has good coffee, pastries and sandwiches,
along with nice outdoor seating in front for
summer days. Specialty drinks won't faze
them – want a Cubano? Just ask.

Tillamook
POP 4800

Best known for its huge cheese industry, Til-
lamook is a nondescript town that's worth a
brief stop to down some dairy. Cheese pro-
duction began in Tillamook in the 1890s,
when an English cheesemaker brought his
cheddar-making techniques to the fledgling
dairies along Tillamook Bay. Thousands stop
here annually to visit the famed Tillamook
Cheese Visitors Center, which produces more
than 100 million pounds of the product ev-
ery year. The city's **chamber of commerce**
(☑503-842-7525; 3705 N US 101; ⊙10am-5pm
Mon-Fri, 10am-2pm Sat & Sun) is next door.

South of Tillamook, US 101 loses the
beaches and headlands and follows the
Nestucca River through pastureland and
logged-off mountains. The slower but pret-
tier Three Capes Drive begins in Tillamook
and follows the coast.

Tillamook County Transportation
(☑503-815-8283; www.tillamookbus.com) buses
depart from 2nd and Laurel Sts to Oceans-
ide and Netarts on the capes, as well as to
Manzanita and Portland.

⊙ Sights & Activities

Tillamook Cheese Visitors Centre
FOOD TASTING
(☑503-815-1300; www.tillamookcheese.com; 4175
N US 101; ⊙8am-8pm) Two miles north of town
is this tourist wonderland. Line up for free
cheese samples, lick down an ice-cream cone
or peek into the factory floor assembly line;
there's a café and gift shop too. There's less
hype at **Blue Heron French Cheese Com-
pany** (☑800-275-0639; www.blueheronoregon.
com; 2001 Blue Heron Dr; ⊙8am-8pm), just north
of town, which has cheese and jam tastings.
Its farm-animal petting pen and horse rides
make it more of a country experience.

Pioneer Museum MUSEUM
(☑503-842-4553; 2106 2nd St; adult/child $4/1;
⊙10am-4pm Tue-Sun) In town, this worth-
while museum has antique toys, a great taxi-
dermy room (check out the polar bear) and

THREE CAPES SCENIC DRIVE

Cape Meares, Cape Lookout and Cape Kiwanda are some of the coast's most stunning headlands, strung together on a slow, winding and sometimes bumpy 30-mile alternative to US 101. Head due west on 3rd St out of Tillamook instead of continuing south on US 101.

The forested headland at **Cape Meares** offers good views from its lighthouse, which is 38ft tall (Oregon's shortest). Short trails lead to Oregon's largest Sitka spruce and the 'Octopus Tree,' another Sitka shaped like a candelabra.

A panoramic vista atop sheer cliffs that rise 800ft above the Pacific makes **Cape Lookout State Park** a highlight. In winter, the end of the cape, which juts out nearly a mile, is thronged with whale-watchers. There are wide sandy beaches, hiking trails and a popular campground near the water.

Finally there's **Cape Kiwanda**, a sandstone bluff that rises just north of the little town of Pacific City. You can hike up tall dunes, or drive your truck onto the beach. It's the most developed of the three capes, with plenty of services nearby (don't miss Pelican Brewpub if you like beer). Watch the dory fleet launch their craft or, after a day's fishing, land as far up the beach as possible.

a basement full of pioneer artifacts. There are also curiously carved Neahkahnie stones meant to point to a legendary buried treasure near Manzanita.

Tillamook Naval Air Museum MUSEUM
(☎503-842-1130; www.tillamookair.com; 6030 Hangar Rd; adult/child $9/5; ⊙9am-5pm) Aircraft lovers shouldn't miss the large collection of fighter planes and the 7-acre blimp hangar. It's located 2 miles south of town.

Munson Creek Falls WATERFALL
At Munson Creek State Natural Site, 7 miles south off US 101, an easy quarter-mile hike through old-growth spruce reaches Munson Creek Falls, the highest waterfall in the Coast Range at 319ft (though some figures incorrectly claim it's 266ft).

Pacific Seafood FOOD TASTING
(☎503-377-2323; 5150 Oyster Dr; ⊙10am-8pm) To witness some of the fastest oyster shucking you'll ever see, head north about 6 miles to Pacific Seafood in Bay City. At the casual restaurant (mains $6 to $16) you can order simple seafood dishes, but be sure to head back to check out the assembly-line processing of oysters – it's quite a sight.

Lincoln City

POP 8000

More a sprawling modern beach resort than a serene seaside retreat, Lincoln City is a long series of commercial strips, motels, eateries and gift shops that front a fairly wide and lackluster stretch of sandy beach. As a local once put it, 'Lincoln City is five towns brought together in 1965 by the fact they needed a sewer system.' But the resort does serve as the region's principal commercial center, while boasting the Oregon coast's most affordable beachfront accommodations, and the surrounding area features some good hikes.

The self-proclaimed 'Kite Capital of the World,' Lincoln City hosts two **kite festivals**, held June and September. Enormous kites – some over 100ft in length – take off to twist and dive in the ocean breezes. There's also a big **sandcastle contest** in August.

Get more information at the **visitor center** (☎541-994-3302; www.oregoncoast.org; 540 NE US 101; ⊙10am-5pm). **Lincoln County Transit** (☎541-265-4900; www.lincoln.or.us/transit) buses connect to Newport and Yachats.

◉ Sights

Beaches BEACHES
Lincoln City's wide sandy beaches cater to holidaymakers, especially families. From mid-October to late May, brightly colored glass floats – hand blown by local artisans – are hidden weekly along beaches as part of an ongoing promotion. The main beach access points are at the D River Beach State Wayside, in the center of town; at Road's End State Wayside, off Logan Rd just north of town; and south along Siletz Bay at Taft City Park.

Jennifer Sears Glass Art Studio

GLASS BLOWING

(✆541-996-2569; www.jennifersearsglassart.
com; 4821 SW Hwy 101) Like glass-blowing?
Then don't miss the Jennifer Sears Glass
Art Studio where you can learn to blow
your own float – or just watch someone
else do it.

🕊 Activities

Hiking

At **Cascade Head**, two Nature Conservan-
cy trails access a 1200ft-high ocean vista.
The first is a mile-long upper trail from
Cascade Head Rd, 4 miles north of the Hwy
18 junction; the second is a 2.7-mile lower
trail that scales the headland from the end
of Three Rocks Rd, 1 mile north of town
along the Salmon River. At the end of USFS
Rd 1861 is the 2.6-mile trail down to **Harts
Cove**, a remote meadow along a cliff-lined
bay frequented by sea lions. USFS Rd 1861
and its trailheads are closed January to
mid-July in the interest of protecting wildlife. The lower Cascade Head trail stays
open year-round.

Other Activities

Canoeing and kayaking are possible on
Devil's Lake, east of town, and on Siletz Bay.
For local equipment rentals try:

Blue Heron Landing

WATER SPORTS

(✆541-994-4708; 4006 W Devil's Lake Rd) Has
various boats for hire.

Oregon Surf Shop

SURFING

(✆541-996-3957; www.oregonsurfshop.com;
3001 SW US 101) Surfing advice and rentals.

Bike Lincoln City

CYCLING

(✆541-996-2453; www.bikelincolncity.com; 923
SW 1st St) Bike hire.

FUN OREGON COAST FESTIVALS

» Newport's **Wine & Seafod Festival**
(p291; February)

» Astoria's **Crab & Seafood Festival**
(p280; April)

» Florence's **Rhododendron Festival**
(p295; May)

» Cannon Beach's **Sandcastle Day**
(p284; June)

» Lincoln City's **kite festivals** (p288;
June and September)

🛌 Sleeping

There are seemingly endless hotels and
motels on or near Lincoln City's main
drag.

Salishan Spa & Golf Resort

HOTEL $$$

(✆541-764-2371; www.salishan.com; 7760 N US
101, Gleneden Beach; d from $179; ☸@🛜🏊) If
you must have the very best, there's this
four-star luxury resort boasting a top-
notch 18-hole golf course, indoor (and out-
door) tennis courts and a gorgeous spa.
Rooms are tastefully done, very spacious
and sport gas fireplaces. Also onsite are
fancy shops, an indoor pool and fine din-
ing room.

Looking Glass Inn

INN $$

(✆541-996-3996, 800-843-4940; www.looking
glass-inn.com; 861 SW 51st; d $109-169; ☸🛜)
Simple but clean and comfortable rooms in
various sizes are featured here. Some have
kitchenette, fireplace and jetted tubs; the
two-bedroom suite is $249. There are far-
away views to the beach, which is across a
parking lot.

Brey House B&B

B&B $$

(✆541-994-7123, 877-994-7123; www.breyhouse.
com; 3725 NW Keel Ave; d $99-159; ☸🛜) For
a more personal experience, stay at this
homey, Cape Cod–style B&B just a block
from the beach. There are four comfortable
rooms with quilts on the beds, and a suite
with kitchen and fireplace is available. For
the best ocean view, snag the Admiral's
Room on the 3rd floor.

Devil's Lake State Park

CAMPGROUND $

(✆541-994-2002, 800-452-5687; www.oregon
stateparks.org; 1452 NE 6th Dr; tent sites/RV
sites/yurts $21/28/40) Located a short walk
to the beach, Devil's Lake includes showers,
flush toilets and fishing and boating on a
freshwater lake.

Also recommended:

Coast Inn B&B

B&B $$

(✆541-994-7932; www.oregoncoastinn.com;
4507 SW Coast Ave; d $109-198; ☸🛜) Casual
B&B offering three rooms (all with private bath), a great back deck with ocean
view and an artsy owner.

Ester Lee Motel

MOTEL $$

(✆541-996-3606, 888-996-3606; www.esterlee.
com; 3803 SW Hwy 101; d $91-161; 🛜) Good
range of rooms and cottages, many with
excellent ocean views. Located on a high,
tsunami-resistant bluff.

BLACKFISH CAFÉ

Blackfish (541-996-1007; www. blackfishcafe.com; 2733 NW US 101; mains $15-23; lunch & dinner Wed-Mon) is one of the coast's best restaurants, specializing in cutting-edge cuisine highlighting fresh seafood and seasonal vegetables. Chef Rob Pounding is an accomplished master at creating his simple but delicious Northwest-inspired dishes. Reserve ahead.

Sea Horse Oceanfront Lodgings MOTEL $$
(541-994-2101, 800-662-2101; www.seahorse motel.com; 1301 NW 21st St; d from $89;) Oceanfront motel with neat rooms. Kitchenettes, gas fireplaces and jetted tubs available.

Captain Cook Inn MOTEL $
(541-994-2522, 800-808-9409; www.captain cookinn.com; 2626 NE US 101; d from $69;) Good motel right on Hwy 101, with 17 well-maintained, pretty rooms. Kitchenettes available.

✕ Eating

The Salishan Spa & Golf Resport offers premier Northwestern cuisine and a legendary wine cellar.

Bay House NORTHWESTERN $$$
(541-996-3222; www.thebayhouse.org; 5911 SW US 101; mains $34-38; lunch Tue-Sat, dinner daily) Chef Sean McCart presides over the kitchen at this elegant establishment, creating a fine, periodically changing seafood and meat menu (posted daily on the website). Only the freshest top-quality ingredients are used, and the view is stunning. Small plates for lunch; live music on weekends.

Beach Dog Café BREAKFAS $
(www.thebeachdogcafe.com; 1266 SW 50th St; mains $7-10; 7am-3pm Tue-Sun) A great breakfast awaits you at this tiny café, completely decked out in dog-related decor and photos. Choose from a wide range of potato dishes, breakfast sandwiches, omelets and hot dogs. Just five tables, so a wait is guaranteed. No credit cards.

Kyllo's Seafood Grill AMERICAN $$
(541-994-3179; 1110 NW 1st Ct; mains $11-31; lunch & dinner) One of Lincoln City's few restaurants with an ocean view, popular and family-friendly Kyllo's offers good clam chowder, seafood, burgers and steaks. The deck is a must on hot days.

Depoe Bay

POP 1300

Located 10 miles south of Lincoln City, pleasant Depoe Bay is edged by modern timeshare condominiums but still retains some original coastal charm. It lays claim to having the 'world's smallest navigable harbor' and being the 'world's whale-watching capital' – pretty big talk for such a pint-sized town. Whale-watching and charter fishing are the main attractions in the area, though 5 miles south of town there is also the Devil's Punchbowl, an impressive collapsed sea cave that churns with waves and offers good tide pools nearby.

The **visitor center** (541-765-2889; www. depoebaychamber.org; 223 SW US 101, Suite B; 11am-3pm Sun-Wed, 9am-3pm Thu-Sat) is next to the Mazatlan restaurant. An impressive **Whale Watching Center** (541-765-3304; 119 SW US 101; 9am-5pm) has good exhibits and provides binoculars and views out to sea.

🛏 Sleeping & Eating

Trollers Lodge MOTEL $
(541-765-2287; www.trollerslodge.com; 355 SW US 101; d $65-102;) Come here for a dozen cute rooms and one- and two-bedroom suites (some with kitchenette), all decked out in casual country style. It's not on the water but you can hear the waves crashing.

Inn at Arch Rock INN $$
(541-765-2560; www.innatarchrock.com; 70 NW Sunset St; d $79-209;) This friendly, upscale inn has 13 very comfortable rooms and suites, most with sea view. They range widely in size and amenities; some have fireplace, kitchenette and sitting areas. Two bedroom suites available ($249 to $299).

Tidal Raves NORTHWESTERN $$
(541-765-2995; www.tidalraves.com; 279 US 101; mains $12-23; 11am-9pm) Both the food and the view are awesome at this popular restaurant overlooking the ocean. Seafood is a specialty, from Dungeness crab cakes to razor clam steaks to the coconut crusted shrimp. Good salads, soups and sandwiches also.

Newport

POP 10250

Oregon's second-largest commercial port, Newport is a lively tourist city with several fine beaches and a world-class aquarium – in 2011 it will become the homeport of NOAA, the National Oceanic and Atmospheric Administration. Good restaurants – along with some tacky attractions, gift shops and barking sea lions – abound in the historic bay-front area, while bohemian Nye Beach offers art galleries and a friendly village atmosphere. The area was first explored in the 1860s by fishing crews who found oyster beds at the upper end of Yaquina Bay.

One of the coast's premier events, the **Newport Seafood & Wine Festival** (www. newportchamber.org/seafood_wine.htm), occurs the last full weekend in February.

◉ Sights

TOP CHOICE **Yaquina Head Outstanding Natural Area** COASTAL PARK
(☑541-574-3100; 750 Lighthouse Dr; admission $7; ☺sunrise-sunset) Stretching a mile out to sea is the popular Yaquina Head, a grassy headland just north of Newport. Short trails lead to viewing areas for shorebirds, harbor seals and whales, and the tide pools are the best-managed on the coast. Visit the excellent **interpretive center** (☺9am-5pm) to explore different marine environments and the history of the coast's lighthouses. The coast's tallest, still-functioning **lighthouse** is at the tip of the headland and offers tours by docents in period costumes.

FREE **Hatfield Marine Science Center** SCIENCE CENTER
(☑541-867-0100; www.hmsc.oregonstate.edu; 2030 SE Marine Science Dr; ☺10am-5pm; ⊞) This excellent science center has more modest exhibits than its flashy aquarium neighbor and provides a more educational – and less bustling – alternative. It's free, but donate a few bucks to help run programs.

Yaquina Bay State Park STATE PARK
Situated on a bushy bluff above the north entrance of the bay, this (free) day-use park is popular for beach access and views over Yaquina Bay. Visit the **Yaquina Bay Lighthouse** (☺11am-5pm) – not to be confused with the Yaquina Head Lighthouse, 3 miles north – built in 1871 but decommissioned in 1874. The living quarters are preserved

DON'T MISS

OREGON COAST AQUARIUM

The region's top attraction, this cutting-edge **aquarium** (☑541-867-3474; www.aquarium.org; 2820 SE Ferry Slip Rd; adult/child $15.45/9.95; ☺9am-6pm; ⊞) is especially fun if you have kids along. Marine celebrities include seals, sea otters and a giant octopus, and there's an impressive deep-sea exhibit where you walk under Plexiglas tunnels and get an eyeful of sharks and rays swimming by. The jellyfish room is a surreal experience, while the touch tank appeals to everyone. There's also a good family-friendly café.

as an informal **museum** (☑541-265-5679; ☺11am-5pm).

FREE **Oregon Coast History Center** MUSEUM
(☑541-265-7509; www.oregoncoast.history.museum; 545 SW 9th St; ☺11am-4pm Tue-Sat) This two-building museum is located in both the 1895 Burrows House and a log cabin next door (open Thursday to Saturday only). On display are an impressive collection of Siletz artifacts, a rectangular grand piano and – most impressive of all – a large toothpick model of the Yaquina Bay Bridge. Check out the photos of wood-plank surfboards.

☆ Activities

Marine Discovery Tours WHALE-WATCHING
(☑800-903-2628; www.marinediscovery.com; 345 SW Bay Blvd; adult/child $36/18) This tour operator sets out on two-hour cruises to stalk whales and other marine life.

⮕ Sleeping

There are plenty of economy hotels on US 101.

TOP CHOICE **Newport Belle** B&B $$
(☑800-348-1922; www.newportbelle. com; South Bech Marina; d $145-165; ☺) For a unique stay there's no beating this stern-wheeler B&B – likely the only one of its kind. The five small but lovely and ship-shape rooms all have private baths and water views, while the common spaces are wonderful for relaxing. Best for couples; reservations required.

Sylvia Beach Hotel HOTEL $$
(☑541-265-5428; www.sylviabeachhotel.com; 267 NW Cliff St; d $100-193; ☺) This book-

themed hotel offers simple and classy rooms, each named after a famous author and decorated accordingly. The best are higher up, and the 3rd-floor common room has a wonderful ocean view. Breakfast is included; reservations mandatory. Rates Sunday to Thursday are lower.

Rogue Ales Public House   APARTMENTS **$$**
(541-961-0142; 740 SW Bay Blvd; apt $92-130) Just three one- or two-bedroom apartments huddle above this pub-restaurant – the original Rogue Ales brewery site – all with comfortable modern furnishings (including washer/dryer) and kitchenette. Rather than breakfast, two 22oz beers come with the package, making it a true 'Bed and Beer.'

Grand Victorian B&B   B&B **$$**
(541-265-4490, 800-784-9936; www.grandvic torianor.com; 105 NW Coast St; d $100-180;) Three rooms (two share one bathroom) are nestled in this green, three-story Victorian home. They're all beautiful and decorated with antiques; the suite is huge and awesome. A two-bedroom cottage next door is also available ($180).

Elizabeth Street Inn   HOTEL **$**
(541-265-9400, 877-265-9400; www.elizabeth streetinn.com; 232 SW Elizabeth St; d $169-209;) This lovely hotel has 68 elegantly furnished rooms, all with fireplace and balcony overlooking the ocean. Continental breakfast is included, and there's a common-use Jacuzzi and a small fitness room.

Beverly Beach State Park   CAMPGROUND **$**
(541-265-9278, 800-452-5687; www.oregon stateparks.org; tent sites/RV sites/yurts $21/27/46) This large campground, 7 miles north of town on US 101, has more than 250 sites, 21 yurts and hookups to cable TV. Also has showers and flush toilets.

South Beach State Park   CAMPGROUND **$**
(541-867-4715, 800-452-5687; www.oregon stateparks.org; tent & RV sites/yurts $27/40) Two miles south on US 101, this 227-site campground is especially good for large groups, and has showers, flush toilets and 27 yurts. Primitive sites are $10.

Also recommended:
Tyee Lodge B&B   B&B **$$**
(888-553-8933; www.tyeelodge.com; 4925 NW Woody Way; d from $185;) Five luxury rooms with fireplace and ocean peeks. Next door is the similar Ocean

House Inn, run by the same owner. Check the website for specials.

Waves Newport Motel   MOTEL **$$**
(541-265-4661, 800-282-6993; www.wavesof newport.com; 820 NW Coast St; d from $99;) Basic, good-sized rooms with fridge, coffeemaker, microwave – and some with sea views.

Newport City Center Motel   MOTEL **$**
(541-265-7381, 800-687-9099; www.newport citycentermotel.com; 538 SW Coast Hwy; d from $49;) Cheap, but smell your room first. Kitchenettes available.

Eating

Tables of Content in the Sylvia Beach Hotel is open to nonguests, but reservations are necessary (prix fixe dinners $23.50). Rogue Ales Public House serves typical pub grub such as pizza, burgers and seafood appetizers, plus plenty of beer (mains $9 to $16).

Saffron Salmon   NORTHWESTERN **$$$**
(541-265-8921; www.saffronsalmon.com; 859 SW Bay Blvd; mains $14-28; lunch & dinner Thu-Tue) Once you get past the stellar wall-to-wall view, dig into the lemon-brined chicken, spicy seafood stew or grilled lamb burger. Reserve for dinner.

Brewer's on the Bay   BREWPUB **$$**
(www.rogue.com; 2320 SW OSU Dr; mains $8-13; lunch & dinner) This casual eatery serves up buffalo wings, BLTs, clam chowder and Kobe burgers. The view of Yaquina Bay is a plus, and the bar's a great hangout. Walk through Rogues' giant fermentation tanks to get there.

Whale's Tale   AMERICAN **$$**
(452 SW Bay Blvd; mains $8-23; 9am-8pm Sun-Fri, till 8:30pm Sat) A local institution serving a good selection of sandwiches, soups and salads, along with fancier fare such as cioppino, oysters and seafood platters. Casually eclectic and full of marine-themed knick-knacks.

Also recommended:
Local Ocean Seafoods   SEAFOOD **$$**
(541-574-7959; www.localocean.net; 213 SE Bay Blvd; mains $10-21; lunch & dinner) Enjoy water views across the street while nibbling seafood dishes. Upscale but casual.

Canyon Way   NORTHWESTERN **$$**
(541-265-8319; www.canyonway.com; 1216 SW Canyon Way; mains $13-16; 3-9pm) Limited menu at this small restaurant located in

a famous local bookstore. Seafood and pastas; nice outdoor seating.

Panini Bakery BAKERY $
(232 NW Coast St; mains $5-8; ⊙7-11am Wed, 7am-7pm Thu-Mon) Lines form out the door at this tiny bakery-café. Exceptional pizza, bread and pastries.

❶ Information

Chamber of Commerce (☑541-265-8801, 800-262-7844; www.newportchamber.org; 555 SW Coast Hwy; ⊙8:30am-5pm Mon-Fri, 10am-2pm Sat)

❶ Getting There & Around

A free daily shuttle stops at key locations around town ($1 for nonhotel guests).

Bike Newport (☑541-265-9917; 150 NW 6th St) For bike rentals.

Lincoln County Transit (☑541-265-4900; www.co.lincoln.or.us/transit) Runs through Newport.

Valley Retriever Buslines (☑541-265-2253; 956 SW 10th St) Heads to Corvallis and other inland locations.

Yachats & Around

POP 675

One of the Oregon coast's best-kept secrets is the neat and friendly little town of Yachats (ya-*hots*). Lying at the base of massive Cape Perpetua, Yachats offers the memorable scenery of a rugged and windswept land. People come to small, remote inns and B&Bs just south of town to get away from the big cities, which isn't hard to do along this undeveloped coast.

Beginning at Cape Perpetua and continuing south about 20 miles is some spectacular shoreline. This entire area was once a series of volcanic intrusions which resisted the pummeling of the Pacific long enough to rise as oceanside peaks and promontories. Acres of tide pools are home to starfish, sea anemones and sea lions. Picturesque Heceta Lighthouse rises above the surf, while tiny beaches line the cliffs. There's plenty to see in the area, especially if you're a nature fan.

The **visitor center** (☑800-929-0477; www.yachats.org; US 101 & 3rd St; ⊙10am-4pm) is next to C&K Market. **Lincoln County Transit** (☑541-265-4900; www.co.lincoln.or.us/transit) runs through Yachats.

For an artsy souvenir to take back home, stop in at **Touchstone Gallery** (☑541-547-4121; www.touchstone-gallery.com; 2118 Hwy 101

N; ⊙10am-5pm), where more than two dozen Northwest artists are represented in colorful glass, whimsical pottery, unique jewelry and other creative mediums. Prices are surprisingly affordable; it's located across from Overleaf Lodge.

◉ Sights

TOP CHOICE **Cape Perpetua** SCENIC PARK
Located 3 miles south of Yachats, this volcanic remnant – one of the highest points on the Oregon coast – was sighted and named by England's Captain James Cook in 1778. Famous for its dramatic rock formations and crashing surf, the area contains numerous trails that explore ancient shell middens, tide pools and old-growth forests. Views from the cape are incredible, taking in coastal promontories from Cape Foulweather to Cape Arago. There's a day-use fee of $5.

The **visitors center** (☑541-547-3289; www.fs.fed.us/r6/siuslaw; ⊙10am-5:30pm daily Memorial Day-Labor Day, 10am-4pm Wed-Mon rest of year) details human and natural histories, and has displays on the Alsi tribe. There are also great viewing areas to watch whales. From the visitor center turnoff, head up Overlook Rd to the Cape Perpetua Viewpoint for a stunning ocean view.

Deep fractures in the old volcano allow waves to erode narrow channels into the headland, creating effects such as **Devil's Churn**, a mile north of the visitor center. Waves race up this chasm, shooting up the 30ft inlet to explode against the narrowing sides of the channel.

If you're looking for more than just a short stroll, start at the visitor center and climb 1.3 miles on the **St Perpetua Trail**, which passes through open meadows and Sitka spruces to one of the coast's best views. For an easier hike, the paved **Captain Cook Trail** (1.2 miles round trip) leads down to tide pools at Cooks Chasm, where the geyser-like spouting horn blasts water out of a sea cave.

The **Giant Spruce Trail** (2 miles round trip) leads up Cape Creek to a 500-year-old Sitka spruce with a 10ft diameter. The **Cook's Ridge-Gwynn Creek Loop Trail** (6.5 miles round trip) heads into deep old-growth forests along Gwynn Creek; follow the Oregon Coast Trail south and turn up the Gwynn Creek Trail, which returns via Cook's Ridge.

Beaches BEACHES
Beaches around here are small, secluded affairs that offer tide pools and rocky

promontories. At the mouth of Yachats River is **Yachats State Park**, which has a wheelchair-accessible trail along the surf, while 4 miles south of Yachats are **Strawberry Hill Wayside** and **Neptune State Park**, which offer intertidal rocks, sandy inlets and picnic tables; sea lions are common here.

Heceta Head Lighthouse   LIGHTHOUSE
(☑541-547-3416; day-use $5; ☺11am-3pm Mar-Apr & Oct, 11am-5pm Jun-Sep, varies rest of year) Built in 1894 and towering precipitously above the churning ocean, this lighthouse, 13 miles south of town on US 101, is supremely photogenic and still functions. Tours are available.

Sea Lion Caves   CAVES
(☑541-547-3111; www.sealioncaves.com; adult/child $12/8; ☺8:30am-6pm) A further 2 miles south on US 101 is an enormous sea grotto that's home to hundreds of groaning sea lions. An elevator descends 208ft to a dark interpretive area, and an observation window lets you watch Steller's sea lions jockeying for the best seat on the rocks. There are also outside observation areas, as occasionally there are no sea lions in the cave.

Little Log Church & Museum   MUSEUM
(☑541-547-3976; admission by donation; 328 W 3rd St; ☺noon-3pm Fri-Wed) In town, this museum displays historical items donated by local residents.

🛏 Sleeping

Overleaf Lodge   HOTEL $$
(☑541-547-4880, 800-338-0507; www.overleaf lodge.com; 280 Overleaf Lodge Lane; d from $185; ☺@⊛) Just north of center is this fancy resort-spa offering modest but spacious rooms, all with ocean views and some with balconies, fireplaces and Jacuzzis. Cottages are available, and continental breakfast is included. Next door is its sister property, the **Fireside Motel** (www.overleaflodge.com/fireside), with less expensive but still good rooms.

Yachats Inn   MOTEL, CONDO $$
(☑541-547-3456, 888-270-3456; www.yachat sinn.com; 331 S US 101; d $85-135; ☺⊛⊛) Just south of town are these simple and homely units (or more modern suites), some with kitchenette, fireplace and/or deck. Ocean views available to some, but the indoor pool and Jacuzzi are for all.

Ya'Tel Motel   MOTEL $
(☑541-547-3225; www.yatelmotel.com; cnr US 101 & 6th St; d $64-84; ☺⊛) This friendly, nine-room motel has large, clean rooms, some with kitchenette. It's a good deal and includes amenities such as fridges, microwave and coffeemaker; packets of hot chocolate and popcorn are thoughtful touches. A large room that sleeps six is available ($109).

Rock Park Cottages   COTTAGES $
(☑541-547-3214; www.trillian.com/rockpark/rock. htm; 431 W 2nd St; d $75-85; ⊛⊛) Five cute and comfy cottages with kitchenette are available here, some with peeks at the ocean. Room one comes with ocean glimpses. The large A-frame sleeps up to six and is great for families.

Beachside State Park   CAMPGROUND $
(☑541-563-3220, 800-452-5687; www.oregon stateparks.org; tent sites/RV sites/yurts $21/26/40) Five miles north of town on US 101, about 80 sites and two yurts are available at this beachside campground. Showers and flush toilets available.

Carl G Washburne State Park
                                            CAMPGROUND $
(☑541-547-3416, 800-452-5687; www.oregon stateparks.org; tent sites/RV sites/yurts $21/26/39) More than 60 woodsy sites and two yurts, along with showers and flush toilets. Located 12 miles south of town.

Cape Perpetua Campground CAMPGROUND $
(☑877-444-6777; www.recreation.gov; camp-sites $22; ☺mid-May–early Sep) This USFS campground, 2 miles south on US 101, has 38 beautiful sites.

SOUTH OF YACHATS

The following are ordered north to south.

See Vue   MOTEL $$
(☑541-547-3227, 866-547-3237; www.seevue.com; 95590 Hwy 101 S; d $95-120; ⊛⊛) This unique, lesbian-owned motel is set high above the surf, 6 miles south of Yachats on US 101. All 11 rooms come with a glorious ocean view, and each is decorated differently. Kitchenettes and fireplaces add convenience and coziness. Two-bedroom apartment available.

🔺TOP SeaQuest Inn B&B   B&B $$
🔺CHOICE (☑541-547-3782, 800-341-4878; www. seaquestinn.com; 95354 US 101 S; d $150-170; ☺@⊛) This gorgeous B&B, 7 miles south of Yachats, is located in a large wood-shingle, driftwood-decorated house that has stunning ocean views and down-to-earth artsy touches. Seven luxurious rooms (four with their own Jacuzzi) come with private deck and gourmet breakfast. The huge suite ($275) is heaven for romantic couples.

Ocean Haven
INN $$

(☑541-547-3583; www.oceanhaven.com; 94770 US 101; d $105-125; ☺☎) This casual five-room inn 8 miles south of Yachats is run by an eccentric couple who have banned Hummers from their parking lot. All rooms come with awesome ocean view, and the rustic cabin ($125) has hosted author Robert Bly. Whimsical details add personality to an already quirky place.

TOP CHOICE / Heceta Head Lighthouse B&B
B&B $$$

(☑866-547-3696; www.hecetalighthouse.com; 92072 Hwy 101 S; d $209-315; ☺☎) This 1894 Queen Anne B&B can't help but attract passersby. Located near the lighthouse trail, it's 13 miles south of town on US 101. Inside there are six pretty rooms, all simply furnished with period antiques, along with a classy, museum-like atmosphere. Breakfast is a gourmet sensation and reservations are definitely recommended.

✖ Eating

The Adobe Resort, right on Hwy 101 just north of the center, has a dining room (breakfast, lunch & dinner) with great ocean views.

TOP CHOICE / Green Salmon Coffee House
COFFEEHOUSE $

(www.thegreensalmon.com; 220 US 101; snacks under $7; ☺breakfast & lunch Tue-Sun; ☑) Organic and sustainable are big words at this eclectic wind-powered café, where tasty breakfast items (pastries, lox bagel, homemade oatmeal) are spectacular. Fairtrade coffee and creative drinks – think hibiscus coolers and seven kinds of hot chocolate – are also excellent.

Heidi's
ITALIAN $$

(☑541-547-4409; 84 Beach St; mains $8-13; ☺noon-8pm Wed-Sun) This friendly bistro offers some of the tastiest treats in town. Try the delicious shrimp melt or the oyster poor boy for lunch, or homemade pastas and pizzas for dinner. There are only eight tables, and a sea view to gaze over as you eat.

Drift Inn
AMERICAN $$

(☑541-547-4477; www.the-drift-inn.com; 124 N US 101; mains $9-15; ☺8am-10pm) Wood booths mean cozy dining at this popular restaurant. A decent range of creative dishes include the teriyaki rice bowl, southwest-style steak sandwich and crab and avocado pizza. Early birds can peck at the belgian waffle and spinach frittata.

Luna Sea Fish House
SEAFOOD $$

(www.lunaseafishhouse.com; 153 US 101; mains $8-14; ☺8am-9pm Mon-Thu, till 10pm Fri-Sun) Slightly more upscale than a portside shack, this very casual eatery serves up fresh fish and chips, clam chowder, fish tacos and steamed clams – among several seafood choices. Breakfast means salmon hash, or the seafood omelet or benedict.

SOUTHERN OREGON COAST

The flip side of its northern coastal counterpart, Oregon's southern coast is further from the major inland metropolises and consequently gets less attention, less traffic, less bustle and more solitude. Much of the coastline here is nearly pristine, with a wild and dramatic feel. Beautiful clean rivers gush from inland mountainsides down to the sea, offering exceptional salmon and steelhead fishing along with boating recreation. Life is laid-back and relatively subdued; if you find a sandy beach at the end of a hiking trail, chances are you'll have it to yourself.

But despite its remoteness, the southern coast is slowly attracting development and a finer class of tourism, and you won't have a hard time finding the occasional upscale resort, world-class golf course or amazing gourmet restaurant – if that's what you're looking for. Harboring a milder climate (and less precipitation) than the north has its advantages as well, and the scenic drives – especially from Port Orford to Brookings – boast some of the most memorable coastal views you'll ever set eyes on.

Florence

POP 8700

Much of Florence consists of a long, mind-numbing commercial strip that serves the needs of tourists and passing dune-buggy enthusiasts buzzing a path to the Oregon Dunes National Recreation Area just further south. Find your way to the Old Town neighborhood, however, and you'll see another, more charming side of the town: a quaint waterfront district nestled along the scenic Siuslaw River next to the Oregon coast's prettiest harbor.

A beauty pageant, parade and flower show are highlights of the **Rhododendron Festival**, which has been celebrated for more than

THE LONG WALK – THE OREGON COAST TRAIL

Following the Beaver state's coastline from Astoria to the California border is the Oregon Coast Trail (OCT), an adventurous 400-mile route that runs through sandy beaches, verdant forests and rocky headlands, as well as coastal towns and cities. This makes it a highly variable, 'noncontinuous' route, so expect about 300 miles on beaches and pavement – and the rest on actual dirt trails. Rivers require either fording or detouring to the closest bridge, and high tide may require inland jaunts at headlands (take a tide table). It's not necessarily a hard route, but there are few posted signs – so print out the state's downloadable maps (www.oregon.gov/OPRD/PARKS/OCT_main.shtml). Camping is free along beaches that aren't next to state parks or within view of residences, and many state parks have special hiker/cyclist sites ($5 to $6 per person).

Hiking the whole OCT takes a month or so, and is best done north to south due to prevailing winds and available literature. It will expose you to some of the Pacific Coast's most dramatic scenery, with stone monoliths rising straight out of the sea and beaches arcing for miles down the coast. It preserves public access lands and provides wonderful wildlife-viewing opportunities. Hike it all or just a few sections of it, and enjoy the spectacular views – there's one around every corner or two.

100 years to honor the ubiquitous shrubbery; it takes place the 3rd weekend in May. Ask about other local events at the **visitors center** (☑541-997-3128; www.florencechamber.com; 290 US 101; ◷9am-5pm Mon-Fri & 10am-2pm Sat, plus 11am-3pm Sun May-Oct). **Porter Stage Lines** (☑541-269-7183; www.kokkola-bus.com/PorterStageLines.html) provides long-distance bus services to Coos Bay and Eugene.

◉ Sights & Activities

Old Town   NEIGHBORHOOD

Boardwalks, fun shops, good restaurants and great views of the Siuslaw Bridge make Old Town a top place to explore. The **Siuslaw Pioneer Museum** (☑541-997-7884; cnr Maple & 2nd Sts; admission $3; ◷noon-4pm) is located in a 1905 schoolhouse and displays exceptional farming, fishing and logging artifacts, along with pioneer items and Native American artifacts.

Darlingtonia Wayside   BOG

Three miles north of downtown Florence on US 101 is Darlingtonia Wayside, where a short boardwalk overlooks a surreal bog of insect-eating pitcher plants (*Darlingtonia californica,* also known as cobra lilies).

C&M Stables   HORSEBACK RIDING

(☑541-997-7540; www.oregonhorsebackriding.com; 90241 N US 101) There's horseback riding on beaches and trails 8 miles north of Florence at these stables.

⌂ Sleeping

There are good accommodation choices to the north on US 101 towards Yachats. For

camping south of Florence, check out the Oregon Dunes National Recreation Area; 7 miles north of town is pleasant **Alder Dune Campground** (sites $20).

Blue Heron Inn B&B   B&B **$$**

(☑541-997-4091; www.blue-heroninn.com; 6563 Hwy 126; d $125-150; ⊜❀) Four beautiful rooms are available at this pleasant B&B, located 2.5 miles east of Florence right on Hwy 126. The owners are friendly and knowledgeable, there's a basement movie room and a great river view from the living room. Breakfast is gourmet.

Edwin K B&B   B&B **$$**

(☑541-997-8360; www.edwink.com; 1155 Bay St; d $150-175; ⊜❀) Sitting across the street from the Siuslaw River is the flowery Edwin K, which comes with six comfortable rooms. All are spacious, and two boast romantic open bathtubs. A five-course breakfast is served, and an apartment that sleeps four is also available.

Landmark Inn   UPSCALE MOTEL **$$**

(☑541-997-9030, 800-822-7811; www.landmarkmotel.com; 1551 4th St; d $65-145; ⊜❀) A fine deal, this pretty hilltop inn offers a dozen tasteful rooms and suites, some with kitchenette and two with Jacuzzi. A great choice for families; get room number 10 for the best view.

Lighthouse Inn   MOTEL **$$**

(☑866-997-3221; www.lighthouseinn-florence.com; 155 Hwy 101; d from $85; ⊜❀❀) Located right on Hwy 101 in town, this friendly motel is a bit fancier than most (some rooms

Southern Oregon Coast

face an interior hall). Rooms are homey and nice; the back ones are quieter and some come with kitchenettes. Some pet-friendly rooms have their own small patio.

Port of Siuslaw Campground CAMPGROUND $
(☑541-997-3040; www.portofsiuslaw.com; cnr 1st & Harbor Sts; tent & RV sites $22-30; ☎) RV-oriented, but tents accepted. Close to the old town, at the Marina (some sites with water views).

✖ Eating

Waterfront Depot NORTHWESTERN $$
[TOP CHOICE] (☑541-902-9100; www.thewaterfront depot.com; 1252 Bay St; mains $11-15; ☺4-10pm) This cozy, atmospheric joint is one of Florence's best restaurants. Come early to snag one of the few waterfront tables, then enjoy your Jambalaya pasta or crab-encrusted halibut. There are excellent small plates too if you want to try a bit of everything, and desserts are spectacular. Reserve ahead – it's well priced and very popular.

Feast NORTHWESTERN $$
(☑541-997-3284; www.eatafeast.com; 294 Laurel St; mains $16-25; ☺4-9pm Thu-Mon, 11am-3pm Sun) Run by a husband-and-wife chef team (Culinary Institute of America grads) is this fine, upscale restaurant. The menu is short and sweet, utilizing fresh ingredients, creative dishes and beautiful presentation – you're likely to leave wonderfully sated. Sunday brunch is gourmet.

International C-Food Market AMERICAN $$
(☑541-997-7978; www.icmrestaurant.com; 1498 Bay St; mains $8-20; ☺11am-9pm) A fabulous location right on the river makes for great views at this popular, lively eatery. Burgers, pasta, pizza and lots of seafood are on tap, and crab lovers should zero in on the all-you-can-eat Dungeness special ($45).

Oregon Dunes National Recreation Area

Stretching for 50 miles between Florence and Coos Bay, the Oregon Dunes form the largest expanse of oceanfront sand dunes in the USA. The dunes tower up to 500ft and undulate inland as far as 3 miles to meet coastal forests, harboring curious ecosystems that sustain an abundance of wildlife, especially birds. The area inspired Frank Herbert to pen his epic sci-fi *Dune* novels.

OREGON COAST OREGON DUNES NATIONAL RECREATION AREA

The southern half of the dunes is dominated by dune buggies and dirt bikes (off-highway vehicles, or OHVs); hiking is not recommended in these areas. It's possible to rent vehicles near Florence, Winchester Bay and Hauser from about $40 per hour. The northern half of the dunes is closed to OHVs, and instead preserved for wildlife and more peaceful human activities such as hiking and canoeing.

Get information at the **Oregon Dunes NRA Visitors Center** (☑541-271-6000; 855 Highway Ave; ⊙8am-4:30pm) in Reedsport; it's located next to the chamber of commerce.

🏃 Activities

Hiking

From the **Stagecoach Trailhead** (look for 'Siltcoos Recreation Area' sign 7 miles south of Florence), three short trails along a river and wetlands afford good wildlife viewing. One of these, the **Waxmyrtle Trail**, winds to the beach for 1.5 miles along the Siltcoos River, where herons, deer and waterfowl can be seen. Other trails lead to a freshwater lagoon or up to a forested vista point.

The wheelchair-accessible **Oregon Dunes Day Use Area** (Northwest Forest Pass required or $5 fee), 10 miles north of Reedsport, has good viewing platforms and also serves as a trailhead for a 2.5-mile round-trip hike to the beach. Two miles north is **Carter Lake Campground**, where the wheelchair-accessible **Taylor Dunes Trail** leads 0.5 miles to a viewing area. You can hike beyond here through dunes to meet the **Carter Dunes Trail** and head to the beach (3 miles round trip).

A challenging, 6.5-mile loop hike starts from Tahkenitch Campground, 8 miles north of Reedsport. Follow the **Tahkenitch Dunes Trail** west to reach the beach in about 2 miles, then walk south along the beach to directional posts for the **Threemile Lake Trail**, which returns hikers to the campground via a freshwater lake and deep forests.

For the area's biggest dunes (including the tallest at 500ft), take the **John Dellenbeck Trail** (10.5 miles south of Reedsport), which leads out across a wilderness of massive sand peaks before reaching the beach. The round-trip hike is 6 miles and involves some tough dune climbing, though it's only a half-mile on packed gravel if you want to just take a look.

🛏 Sleeping

There are cheap motels around Florence and Reedsport. Campgrounds (reserve in July and August) from north to south include (but are not limited to) the following:

Jessie M Honeyman State Park
CAMPGROUND $
(☑541-997-3641, 800-452-5687; www.oregon stateparks.org; tent sites/RV sites/yurts $21/26/39) Located 3 miles south of Florence on Cleawox Lake; massively popular for its easy access to the dunes. The lake is especially popular for swimming. Rent canoes, kayaks and pedal boats at the park concession; kayak tours also offered.

Tahkenitch Campground CAMPGROUND $
(☑877-444-6777; campsites $20) A good woodsy place to ditch those OHVs; also has trailheads. Located on US 101, 7 miles north of Reedsport.

Umpqua Lighthouse State Park
CAMPGROUND $
(☑541-271-4118, 800-452-5687; www.oregon stateparks.org; tent sites/RV sites/yurts/cabins $19/24/36/39) Pleasant, wooded campsites adjacent to tiny Lake Marie, which warms up nicely in summer. Six deluxe yurts (with TV, kitchen and bathroom) cost $76. Situated 6 miles south of Reedsport.

William M Tugman State Park
CAMPGROUND $
(☑541-759-3604, 800-452-5687; tent sites/yurts $20/39) On US 101, 8 miles south of Reedsport, this is a large campground with grassy open areas, 16 yurts and easy access to Eel Lake, popular for fishing and walking.

Eel Creek Campground CAMPGROUND $
(☑877-444-6777; campsites $20) The shrubby and very private sites here offer refuge from OHVs, along with a hiking trail to the dunes. Located on US 101, 10 miles south of Reedsport.

Primitive **sand camping** (www.fs.fed.us/r6/siuslaw/recreation/ohv/odnra/sandcamping; $10) is possible in the dunes at designated sites.

Reedsport

POP 4200

Five miles away from where the mighty Umpqua River joins the Pacific Ocean is Reedsport, the historic port that ushered out the immense bounty of logs cut in the wide Umpqua River drainage. Today Reedsport is a small town getting smaller, but it still boasts a few area attractions. Its location in the middle of the Oregon Dunes makes it an ideal base for exploring the region.

Take the kids to **Umpqua Discovery Center** (541-271-4816; www.umpquadiscovery center.com; 409 Riverfront Way; adult/child $8/4.50; 9am-5pm;) to explore the area's cultural and natural history through colorful murals and a few interactive displays. A free platform nearby offers good riverside views.

Umpqua Lighthouse State Park offers summer tours of a local 1894 **lighthouse** (541-271-4631; adult/child $3/2; 10am-4pm May-Oct,variesrestofyear);thelighthouse'smuseum is free. Opposite is a whale-watching platform, and a nearby nature trail rings freshwater Lake Marie, which is popular for swimming.

A herd of about 120 Roosevelt elk loiter at **Dean Creek Elk Viewing Area**, a roadside wildlife refuge 3 miles east on Hwy 38. These elk are Oregon's largest land mammal.

There are several inexpensive motels on Hwy 101, the main drag through town; for something a bit more special, head to Winchester Bay (just three miles south) and check into the **Salmon Harbor Landing Motel** (541-271-3742; www.salmonharborland ing.com; 265 8th St; d $54-64).

Need more? Contact the **Chamber of Commerce** (541-271-3495; www.reedsport cc.org; 855 Highway Ave; 8am-4:30pm Mon-Fri).

Coos Bay & North Bend

The no-nonsense city of Coos Bay (population 16,000) and its modest neighbor North Bend (population 10,000) make up the largest urban area on the Oregon coast. Coos Bay boasts the largest natural harbor between San Francisco and Seattle, and has long been a major shipping and manufacturing center for most of Southern Oregon. It was also once the largest timber port in the world. Today the logs are gone, but the tourists have taken their place.

Coos Bay's **Oregon Coast Music Festival** (www.oregoncoastmusic.com) takes place over two weeks in July.

◉ Sights & Activities

Coos Bay   NEIGHBORHOOD

The **Coos Art Museum** (541-267-3901; www.coosart.org; 235 Anderson Ave; 10am-4pm Tue-Fri, 1-4pm Sat), in a historic art-deco building, provides a hub for the region's art culture. Rotating exhibits from the museum's permanent collection are displayed, along with occasional shows of local artists' works. The old-style movie house **Egyptian Theatre** (541-269-8650; www. egyptian-theatre.com; 229 S Broadway) has fun Egyptian motifs and an original Wurlitzer organ.

Heaven for those with a sweet tooth, **Cranberry Sweets** (541-888-9824; www. cranberrysweets.com; 1005 Newmark Ave; 9:30am-5:30pm Mon-Sat, 11am-4pm Sun) has its factory here; watch candy being made (and sample it).

Coos Historical & Maritime Museum

MUSEUM

(541-756-6320; www.cooshistory.org; 1220 Sherman Ave; adult/senior $4/2; 10am-4pm Tue-Sat, noon-4pm Sun) In North Bend, just south of the McCullough Bridge, this museum displays exhibits from Native American culture to maritime shipwrecks.

🛏 Sleeping

Both towns have cheap motels along their main drags. There are campgrounds to the south, near Charleston, or north in the Oregon Dunes National Recreation Area.

Edgewater Inn   MOTEL **$$**

(541-267-0423, 800-233-0423; www.theedge waterinn.com; 275 E Johnson Ave, Coos Bay; d from $100; @) Tucked in behind Safeway and Fred Meyer's, this pleasant motel features clean, good-sized rooms (some with kitchenette and Jacuzzi). Get an upper room for views over the river; they're only $10 more. A business center, gym and indoor pool are fun diversions.

Old Tower House B&B   B&B **$$**

(541-888-6058; www.oldtowerhouse.com; 476 Newmark Ave, Coos Bay; d $85-150;) This pretty Victorian B&B (1872) offers two cozy rooms decorated with period antiques; each has its own bathroom (though they're not ensuite). A third room is available for groups who book all three rooms, with all rooms sharing the two bathrooms. There's a great sunroom for the continental breakfast (gourmet costs $9.50 extra), and a cottage is available for $135.

This Olde House B&B B&B $$
([✆]541-267-5224; www.thisoldehousebb.com; 202 Alder Ave, Coos Bay; d $95-165; [❄]) Not every B&B can claim to have hosted Robert Plant, even if they had no idea who he was at the time. There are five homey rooms at this casual B&B, all with private bath; the Redwood Room boasts the best amenities and view. Reservations are mandatory (even if you're a rock star).

Bay Bridge Motel MOTEL $
([✆]541-756-3151, 800-557-3156; 66304 US 101, North Bend; d from $70; [☎]) Run by the friendly and talkative 'Bay Bridge Betty,' this typical motel is located just north of the McCullough Bridge and has typical amenities, but some rooms boast very atypical bay views.

✖ Eating

TOP CHOICE **Porta** ITALIAN $$
([✆]541-756-4900; www.portarestaurant.com; 1802 Virginia Ave, North Bend; mains $20-26; [◷]dinner Thu-Mon) One of the best Italian restaurants in Oregon is this small eatery right here in North Bend. The dishes are creative, and the homemade pastas are exquisitely prepared, but this is 'slow food' – don't expect large portions. There are plenty of Italian wines; reservations are highly recommended.

Café Mediterranean MEDITERRANEAN $$
([✆]541-756-2299; www.cafemediterranean.net; 1860 Union St, North Bend; mains $8-19; [◷]lunch & dinner Mon-Sun, closes 7pm Sun) Walk past Café Mediterranean's unspectacular facade and settle into an appetizer of baba ghanoush or dolmas. Locals rave about the chicken shawarma, lamb kebabs and spanakopita, but falafels and hummus platters are also available. Friday and Saturday are hookah nights.

Blue Heron Bistro EUROPEAN $$
(www.blueheronbistro.com; 100 W Commercial Ave, Coos Bay; mains $10-16; [◷]lunch & dinner) Seafood and bistro fare with a European twist are served here, from pulled-pork sandwiches to Hungarian goulash to Weiner schnitzels and bratwurst. Wash it all down with a Belgian Chimay.

ℹ Information

Coos Bay Visitor Center ([✆]541-269-0215; www.oregonsbayareachamber.com; 50 Central Ave; [◷]9am-5pm Mon-Fri & 11am-3pm Sat, plus 11am-3pm Sun Jun-Sep)

North Bend Visitor Center ([✆]541-756-4613; www.northbendcity.org; 1380 Sherman Ave; [◷]10am-4pm)

ℹ Getting There & Around

Porter Stage Lines ([✆]541-269-7183; 275 Broadway), inside the old Tioga Hotel in Coos Bay, has long-distance services.

Charleston & Around

POP 3000

Charleston is a tiny bump of civilization on the Cape Arago Hwy, a commercial fishing port that sits just 8 miles southwest of bustling Coos Bay but feels worlds away. It makes a peaceful enough stopover and jumping-off point to a trio of splendid state parks on the Cape Arago headlands. South of Charleston is Seven Devils Rd, a winding shortcut between Charleston and Bandon that accesses a number of beaches south of Cape Arago, such as Whisky Run and Agate.

The **visitors center** ([✆]541-888-2311; www.charlestonoregon-merchants.com; 91143 Cape Arago Hwy; [◷]9am-5pm May-Sep) sits at the west end of the bridge.

◉ Sights & Activities

Sunset Bay State Park STATE PARK
([✆]541-888-4902; www.oregonstateparks.org) Three miles southwest of town on Cape Arago Hwy, this state park is nestled in a small, protected bay that once served as a safe harbor for fishing boats, and possibly pirates as well. Today it's popular with swimmers, hikers and tide-pool explorers. A 6-mile, cliff-edge stretch of the **Oregon Coast Trail** continues south from here to link all three state parks. Cape Arago Lighthouse sits just offshore on a rocky crag.

Shore Acres State Park STATE PARK
([✆]541-888-2472; www.shoreacres.net; day use $5) Beautiful rehabilitated gardens are the highlight of this unusual state park, 4 miles southwest of town on Cape Arago Hwy. Louis Simpson, an important shipping and lumber magnate, was exploring for new stands of lumber in 1905 when he discovered this wildly eroded headland. After buying up the 320 acres for $4000 he built a three-story mansion here, complete with formal gardens. It burned down in 1921. A trail leads to a glass-protected observation building on the cliffs where the mansion once stood, and then continues on to the beach.

Cape Arago State Park

STATE PARK

(www.oregonstateparks.org) A mile beyond Shore Acres is **Simpson Reef Viewpoint**, where you can spot shorebirds, migrating whales and several species of pinnipeds. Head another 0.5 miles to Cape Arago State Park and the terminus of Cape Arago Hwy, where grassy picnic grounds make for great perches over a pounding sea. Trails lead down to the beach and fine tide pools, while the **Oregon Coast Trail** heads back north to Shore Acres and Sunset Bay.

South Slough National Estuarine Research Reserve

INTERPRETIVE CENTER

(541-888-5558; www.southsloughestuary.org; 10am-4pm Tue-Sat) Charleston sits at the mouth of South Slough, a tidal river basin that turns into a vast, muddy estuary full of wildlife. Four miles south of Charleston on Seven Devils Rd is this excellent interpretive center, which has exhibits on estuarine ecology, also showcased in a 12-minute video. It runs events and programs all year long (check the website for details).

Several **walking trails**, ranging from 0.25 miles to 3 miles, offer glimpses of the local ecology. Canoeing is also possible in the area, but you'll need your own canoe.

Sleeping & Eating

Captain John's Motel

MOTEL $

(541-888-4041; www.captainjohnsmotel.com; 63360 Kingfisher Dr; d from $69; @) Popular with anglers, Captain John's keeps room smells down by providing an outside crab-cooking facility for guests. It's located right near the boat docks and offers well-kept motel rooms, some with kitchenette ($15 extra). Flower boxes add color.

Sunset Bay State Park

CAMPGROUND $

(541-888-4902, 800-452-5687; www.oregon stateparks.org; 89814 Cape Arago Hwy; tent sites/RV sites/yurts $19/24/36) Three miles southwest of town, this is a busy, sheltered beachside campground with 130 sites, eight yurts, a playground, showers and flush toilets.

Bastendorff Beach County Park

CAMPGROUND $

(541-396-3121, ext 354; www.co.coos.or.us/ ccpark/bastendorff/Bastendorff.html; Bastendorff Beach Rd; tent sites/RV sites/cabins $16/20/30) Two miles southwest of town, just off Cape Arago Hwy, this park has more than 90 pleasant wooded campsites in a developed campground near the beach. Reserve ahead.

Portside Restaurant

AMERICAN $$

(541-888-5544; www.portsidebythebay.com; 63383 Kingfisher Dr; mains $11-29; 11:30am-11pm) Seafood is comfort food at this excellent long-running restaurant, which offers a great bay view to boot. All the usual marine suspects dot the menu, along with terrestrial choices including chicken, beef and pasta. There's live music in the lounge on weekends. Reservations recommended.

Bandon

POP 3100

Optimistically touted as Bandon-by-the-Sea, this little town happily sits at the bay of the Coquille River. While Bandon as a whole may not yet be as captivating as some would like, the Old Town district has been gentrified into a picturesque harborside shopping location that offers pleasant strolling and window-shopping. The city's most noteworthy industry is cranberry farming, with neighboring bogs yielding a considerable percentage of the cranberry harvest in the US.

For information, harass the **Chamber of Commerce** (541-347-9616; www.bandon. com; cnr 2nd St & Chicago Ave; 10am-5:30pm). The **Cranberry Festival**, Bandon's largest civic event, is held the second weekend in September with a parade, craft fair and the glorious crowning of the Cranberry Queen.

Beachside Bike Rentals (541-329-0226; 175 2nd St) is the place to go for bikes.

Sights & Activities

Beaches

BEACHES

South of town, and not obvious from the highway, are miles of sandy beaches broken by outcroppings of towering rocks – home to a large number of chattering sea birds. Ledges of stone rise out of the surf to provide shelter for seals, sea lions and myriad forms of life in tide pools.

Head west to Beach Loop Dr for the best beach access points. There's good whale-watching here in the spring, and there's marine life to see all year round. At **Coquille Point**, at the end of SW 11th St, steps lead down to a beach interspersed with rocky crags and monoliths. Sea lions and shorebirds inhabit **Table Rock**, which lies just offshore and is protected as the Oregon Islands National Wildlife Refuge.

A path leads over the headland at Face Rock State Park Wayside to sandier beaches around **Face Rock**, a huge monolith with a human profile. Native American legends tell of a maiden and her pet kittens turned to stone by an evil sea god; they all now rise as sea stacks. A path winds along the headland and to the beach.

West of Old Town at the end of Jetty Rd, there's beach access near the **South Jetty**, with views of the Coquille Lighthouse.

Two miles north of Bandon, on the north shores of the Coquille River, are the windswept sands of **Bullards Beach State Park**. Visit the **Coquille Lighthouse** (☑541-347-2209; ☉10am-4pm daily May & Oct, 10am-4pm Mon & Tue & 10am-6pm Wed-Sun Jun-Sep), out of commission since 1939 and now a historic landmark.

Bandon Historical Society Museum
MUSEUM

(☑541-347-2164; 270 Fillmore Ave; admission $2; ☉10am-4pm Mon-Sat) This museum has exhibits on the area's historical industries and the Coquille Native Americans, along with memorable photos of Bandon's two devastating fires (1914 and 1936) and various shipwrecks.

Game Park Safari
ZOO

(☑541-347-3106; www.gameparksafari.com; adult/child $16/9; ☉9am-6pm Mar-Nov, 10am-4pm Sat & Sun Jan & Feb) For something different, visit Game Park Safari, 7 miles south on US 101, where you can meet lions and tigers and bears (oh my), among other wild (but hand-raised) animals.

Bandon Beach Riding Stables
HORSEBACK RIDING

(☑541-347-3423; 54629 Beach Loop Dr) Three miles south of downtown, offers horseback riding.

🛏 Sleeping

Lighthouse B&B
B&B $$

(☑541-347-9316; www.lighthouselodging.com; 650 SW Jetty Rd; d $140-245; ☻☎) With its location on the Coquille River, this five-room B&B provides great water and lighthouse views. All rooms are homey and pleasant, while the 3rd-floor Gray Whale Room boasts a Jacuzzi overlooking the water. The common area begs for extended lounging sessions and offers prime bird-watching.

Sea Star Guesthouse
GUESTHOUSE $

(☑541-347-9632; www.seastarbandon.com; 370 1st St; d $65-115; ☻☎) This harborside guesthouse offers six pleasant rooms, all comfortable and tastefully decorated, and each with its own amenities. The biggest suite

has a loft, kitchenette and water views, and sleeps up to six.

Sunset Oceanfront Lodging
MOTEL $

(☑541-347-2453, 800-842-2407; www.sunsetmotel.com; 1865 Beach Loop Rd; d $65-69; ☻☎☒) This large motel complex – across the road from the beach – offers a wide range of comfortable lodgings, from 'economy rooms' to suites to apartments and beach cottages. The 'Vern Brown' addition, plus some cottages, are just above the beach.

Windermere
UPSCALE MOTEL $$

(☑541-347-3710; www.windermerebythesea.com; 3250 Beach Loop Rd; d $129-198; ☻☎) Refurbished rooms range from simple motel-like rooms to a bit more upscale (and newer) suites with kitchenette, fireplace and private balcony or deck. All have stunning ocean views, however. Located about 2 miles southwest of the center.

Inn at Old Town
MOTEL $

(☑541-347-5900; www.innatoldtown.com; 370 Hwy 101; d $65-110; ☻☎) Right in the center of town is this friendly, family-run motel with just eight rooms. All are different – those downstairs are slightly bigger, but upstairs rooms have peeks at the river. King rooms in back are quieter.

Bullards Beach State Park
CAMPGROUND $

(☑541-347-2209, 800-452-5687; RV & tent sites/yurts $24/36) On US 101, 2 miles north of town, are 185 RV and tent sites, plus 13 yurts and easy beach access. Hot showers and flush toilets; reserve ahead.

🍴 Eating

Bandon Dunes Golf Resort, north of town, has good restaurants and a pub.

Wild Rose Bistro
NORTHWESTERN $$

(☑541-347-4428; 130 Chicago St; mains $22-30; ☉dinner) Some of the coast's tastiest food can be found at this cozy and popular bistro, which features a variety of dishes using the finest ingredients possible. Try seafood dishes such as pan-seared scallops or the wild sturgeon with pancetta. Homemade desserts seal the deal. Reservations recommended.

Alloro Wine Bar & Restaurant
ITALIAN $$

(☑541-347-1850; www.allorowinebar.com; 375 2nd St; mains $12-27; ☉4-9pm Sun-Thu, till 9:30pm Fri & Sat) This small and fancy restaurant boasts an Italian-influenced menu and a wide-ranging wine list. Order the handmade artichoke ravioli or risotto with lobster mushroom; there's also slow-

Unassuming **Langlois**, 14 miles south of Bandon, is the closest town to **Floras Lake**, a covert **windsurfing**, **kitesurfing** and **kayaking** destination. Only a thin sand spit separates this shallow springwater lake from the ocean. Summer is the peak season, though winter storms also attract adventurers. To reach the lake, head 1 mile south of Langlois on US 101, turn west onto Floras Lake Rd and follow the signs for 2.7 miles.

There are **campsites** (tent/RV sites $12/16) at the lake with showers available but no RV hookups. For more comfort, check into the lovely four-room **Floras Lake House B&B** (☑541-348-2573; www.floraslake.com; 92870 Boice Cope Rd; d $155-175; ☺🛜) nearby. There's a small market and café in Langlois, but bring groceries anyway.

Equipment rental and lessons are available at the lake from **Floras Lake Windsurfing** (☑541-348-9912; www.floraslake.com/flw2.html; Boice Cope Rd); take the short, unmarked path next to RV site 91, or ask at Floras Lake House for information.

roasted rabbit, Oregon lamb and Cacciucco, a Tuscan-style fish stew.

Lord Bennett's AMERICAN $$
(☑541-347-3663; www.lordbennett.com; 1695 Beach Loop Rd; mains $17-30; ☺lunch & dinner) A Bandon institution, this upscale restaurant has fine panoramic sea views and house specialties such as wild prawns, stuffed sole, and lamb chops – all served with the appropriate sides. There's a large selection of Oregon wines by the glass, and live music fills the lounge on weekends.

Bandon Coffee Café COFFEEHOUSE $
(www.bandoncoffee.com; 365 2nd St; snacks under $8; ☺6am-4pm Mon-Sat, till 3pm Sun) This modern, casual and popular coffee shop offers light meals such as sandwiches, burgers, pitas and bagels with lox, along with a warm atmosphere.

Cranberry Sweets CANDY STORE $
(www.cranberrysweets.com; cnr 1st St & Chicago Ave; ☺9am-5:30pm Mon-Sat, till 5pm Sun) Not an eatery per se, but rather an exceptional candy shop where you can fill up just on the multitude of luscious samples always on offer.

Port Orford

POP 1200

Perched on a grassy headland and wedged between two magnificent state parks, the hamlet of Port Orford is one of Oregon's true natural ocean harbors (most others are situated along river mouths). It's located in one of the most scenic stretches of coastal highway and there are stellar views even from the center of town. While Port Orford is still a small place, the outside world has discovered its charms: an upscale retreat is nestled a half-

mile from the center, and in 2010 renowned glass artist Chris Hawthorne opened a fancy gallery, along with the area's finest restaurant. The town has come a long way from its fishing and logging roots, and from when it was hit by the Japanese in WWII.

The **visitor center** (☑541-332-4106; www.discoverportorford.com; ☺9am-3pm Apr-Sep, hours vary rest of year) is at Battle Rock Wayfinding Point (in the center of town).

◉ Sights & Activities

Port Orford Heads State Park STATE PARK
A short drive along Coast Guard Rd leads to this state park, which has the best location in town. A couple of 20-minute loop trails offer fine panoramic views and a closer look at coastal flora. Deer and bunnies live on the grassy picnic grounds surrounding the **Lifeboat Station Museum** (☑541-332-0521; ☺10am-3:30pm Thu-Mon Apr-Oct), which was formerly a Coast Guard station. Check out the 36ft 'unsinkable' motor lifeboat on display.

Cape Blanco State Park STATE PARK
(☑541-332-6774) Four miles north of Port Orford, off US 101, this rugged promontory is the second most westerly point of the continental USA and host to a fine state park with hiking trails spreading out over the headland. Sighted in 1603 by Spanish explorer Martin d'Anguilar, Cape Blanco juts far out into the Pacific, withstanding lashing winds that can pass 100mph. Visitors can tour the **Cape Blanco Lighthouse** (☑541-332-2207; adult/child $2/free; ☺10am-3:30pm Tue-Sun Apr-Oct), built in 1870, the oldest and highest operational lighthouse in Oregon. A mile east and open the same hours is **Hughes House** (admission free), a restored Victorian home

built in 1898 by Patrick Hughes, an Irish dairy rancher and gold miner.

Humbug Mountain State Park STATE PARK

(☑541-332-6774) Six miles south of Port Orford, mountains edge down to the ocean, and heavily wooded Humbug Mountain rises 1750ft from the surf. When European settlers first came to the area in 1851, the Tututni Native Americans lived in a large village along the beach just north of here. At this state park, a 3-mile trail leads through the coast's largest remaining groves of Port Orford cedar to the top of the mountain for dramatic views of Cape Sebastian and the Pacific Ocean.

Prehistoric Gardens THEME PARK

(☑541-332-4463; 36848 US 101; adult/child $8/6; ⊙9am-6pm; ⊛) Twelve miles south of Port Orford, your kids will scream at the sight of a tyrannosaurus rex in front of this dinosaur park. Life-size replicas of the extinct beasties are set in a lush, first-growth temperate rain forest; the huge ferns and trees set the right mood for going back in time.

🛏 Sleeping

Redfish restaurant has a luxurious upstairs suite with ocean view ($375).

TOP CHOICE Wildspring Guest Habitat

LUXURY CABINS $$$

(☑866-333-9453; www.wildspring.com; 92978 Cemetery Loop; d $276-306; ⊖@🖙) A few acres of wooded serenity greet you at this quiet retreat, set in a sheltered grove a half-mile from town. Five luxury cabin suites, all filled with elegant furniture and modern amenities such as radiant-floor heating and slate showers, make for a very comfortable and romantic getaway. An outdoor Jacuzzi with spectacular views is included, as is breakfast.

Home by the Sea B&B B&B $$

(☑877-332-2855; www.homebythesea.com; 444 Jackson St; d $105-115; ⊖@🖙) If you want a friendly, casual and affordable stay, head to the house that Alan and Brenda built. This very homey place has just two bedrooms (one large and one small), plus awesome ocean views, and your hosts have some good stories.

Compass Rose B&B B&B $$

(☑541-322-7076; www.compassroseportorford.com; 42497 Gull Rd; d $135-160; ⊖🖙) This huge and gorgeous B&B is set on 12 acres of woodland with peeks at a nearby lake. It has four beautiful and contemporary rooms, all with private bathroom, and there are plenty of spacious common areas. You can walk along hiking trails and to the beach from here.

Castaway-by-the-Sea Motel MOTEL $

(☑541-332-4502; www.castawaybythesea.com; 545 W 5th St; d $75-135; ⊖@🖙🐾) Thirteen modern, pleasant and spacious ocean-view rooms are available here, some with kitchenette and loft, but all with great ocean views. Trivia: the Castaway claims to be the most westerly motel in the continental US.

Humbug Mountain State Park

CAMPGROUND $

(☑541-332-6774, 800-452-5687; www.oregon stateparks.org; tent/RV sites $17/20) About 100 comfortable, sheltered sites with access to showers and flush toilets available at this park, 6 miles south of Port Orford on US 101.

Cape Blanco State Park CAMPGROUND $

(☑541-332-6774, 800-452-5687; www.oregon stateparks.org; tent & RV sites/cabins $20/39) Located on US 101, 4 miles north of town on a high, sheltered rocky headland with beach access and great views of the lighthouse. Showers, flush toilets and boat ramp available.

🍴 Eating

For the freshest seafood offerings there's **Griffs**, a shack at the port.

🍴 Red Fish NORTHWESTERN $$

(☑541-336-2200; www.wix.com/lenabree/redfish; 517 Jefferson St; mains $12-21; ⊙7am-10pm Wed-Sun) Turning Port Orford on its sleepy head is this slick, seaview restaurant that at first glance would seem better located in Portland's Pearl District. Breakfast, lunch and dinner are all on offer here, and despite the fancy Northwest cuisine menu prices are reasonable. Reserve ahead.

🍴 Paula's Bistro FRENCH $$$

(☑541-322-9378; 236 6th St; mains $21-30; ⊙dinner Tue-Sat) The limited but quality menu at this French restaurant includes chicken gorgonzola pasta, rack of lamb Provencal and charbroiled pork chops. Paula, the owner-chef, decorates the bistro with her own spectacular art. Live music on weekends.

Crazy Norwegian AMERICAN $

(☑541-322-8601; 259 6th St; mains $8-12; ⊙lunch & dinner) A casual family spot famous for its excellent fish 'n chips. Soup, salad and sandwich fans won't be disappointed either, and there are homemade cakes and pies aplenty. Just be prepared to wait.

Gold Beach

POP 2200

At the mouth of the Rogue River, the ex-mining town of Gold Beach didn't amount to much until the early 20th century, when the salmon-rich waters caught the fancy of gentleman anglers such as Jack London and Zane Grey. Still a place for fishing vacations, this utilitarian town's other big attraction is jet-boat excursions up the Rogue River, one of Oregon's wildest and most remote. Wildlife-viewing is good, with deer, elk, otters, beavers, eagles and osprey.

◉ Sights & Activities

Cape Sebastian State Park   STATE PARK

The coast around Gold Beach is spectacular. Take a break at Cape Sebastian State Park, a rocky headland 7 miles south, for a panorama stretching from California to Cape Blanco. Flex your legs on a 1.5-mile walking trail to the cape; from December to April, keep your eyes peeled for whales.

Hikes   HIKING

The 40-mile **Rogue River Trail** ends (or begins) east of town at Illahe. Hike up the canyon 4.3 miles to the waterfall at Flora Dell Creek. For a shorter hike, drive 10 miles up USFS Rd 33 to the **Schrader Old Growth Trail**, which wanders for 1.5 miles through towering Douglas fir and Port Orford cedar.

Curry Historical Society Museum   MUSEUM

(☑541-247-9396; adult/child $2/0.50; 28419 Ellensburg Ave; ☻noon-4pm Tue-Sat, closed Jan) The Curry Historical Society Museum has displays on the area's mining, logging and Native American histories.

Jerry's Rogue Jets   JET-BOATING

(☑800-451-3645; www.roguejets.org) Ready for a jet-boat trip? Hold onto your hat and see Jerry's Rogue Jets, located at the south end of the Rogue River bridge.

⨶ Sleeping

There's great riverside camping up USFS Rd 33.

Tu Tu' Tun Lodge   LODGE $$$

(☑541-247-6664, 800-864-6357; www.tututun. com; 96550 N Bank Rogue Rd; d from $290; ☻@☎) One of Oregon's most exclusive hideaways is about 7 miles up the Rogue

River. Eighteen luxurious rooms and suites all come with river views, while a few boast fireplaces and private outdoor Jacuzzi. It's a romantic spot with a small golf course and an excellent dining room (open May to October). Two houses also available.

Ireland's Rustic Lodges   LODGE, CABINS $$

(☑541-247-7718; www.irelandsrusticlodges.com; 29346 Ellensburg Ave; d $99-220; ☎) A wide variety of accommodations awaits you at this woodsy place. There are regular suites with kitchenette, rustic one- and two-bedroom cabins, beach houses or even RV sites. A glorious garden sits in front while beach views are out back. Its sister lodging next door, the Gold Beach Inn, has even more options.

Endicott Gardens B&B   B&B $

(☑541-247-6513; www.endicottgardens.com; 95768 Jerry's Flat Rd; d $80-90; ☻☎) This countryside B&B has four modern, unpretentious rooms, two with private deck. Lovely lawns and gardens grow outside, and two studio apartments are available (rented weekly only from June to August). Located 3.5 miles east of town (on a blind curve); open May to mid-October.

Azalea Lodge   MOTEL $

(☑541-247-6635; www.azalealodge.biz; 29481 Ellensburg Ave; d from $79; ☻☎) This motel has good, clean, comfortable and unmemorable rooms featuring the typical amenities (fridge, microwave) in this price range. Back rooms are larger and quieter; continental breakfast included.

Secret Camp RV Park   CAMPGROUND $

(☑888-308-8338; www.secretcamprvpark.com; 95614 Jerry's Flat Rd; tent/RV sites $17/35; ☎) Three miles east of town, this nature-surrounded haven, complete with small creek, offers pretty sites for campers and full hookups for RV enthusiasts. Fire pits, horseshoes and volleyball are available. Free showers.

✖ Eating

The Cape Café   AMERICAN $$

(☑541-247-6114; 29251 Ellensburg Ave; mains $16-28; ☻dinner Wed-Sun) Upscale eatery offering sustainable, natural and local ingredients in their fine meals, from fresh fish to grass-fed beef to all-organic baking ingredients and vegetables. There are only a small handful of mains, with a 'lite fare' menu ($8 to $14) catering to small appetites and vegetarians.

Patti's Rollin 'n Dough Bistro

AMERICAN **$$**

(☎541-247-4438; 94257 N Bank Rogue Rd; mains $9-15; ☺breakfast & lunch Tue-Sun) This tiny bistro has a limited breakfast and lunch menu, but what's there really counts. Chef Patti Joyce has studied at the Culinary Institute of America, and it shows. Reservations recommended.

Spinners

AMERICAN **$$**

(☎541-247-5160; www.spinnersrestaurant.com; 29430 Ellensburg Ave; mains $9-27; ☺dinner) Tasty meats (whiskey strip steak, grilled duck, New Zealand lamb) and exceptional seafood (cedar-planked wild salmon, sea scallops scampi) are grilled up at this great local restaurant. Black Angus and bison burgers are also available, and the sea views aren't bad, either.

Also recommended:

Riverview

AMERICAN **$$**

(☎541-247-7321; 94749 Jerry's Flat Rd; mains $10-21; ☺dinner) Fine waterside restaurant up the river, offering exceptional pizza, seafood and meat dishes.

Porthole Café

AMERICAN **$$**

(☎541-247-7411; www.portholecafe.com; 29975 Harbor Way; mains $10-20; ☺lunch & dinner) Harborside restaurant with small but varied menu: Reuben sandwich, sesame chicken salad, blackened snapper, liver and onions. Good water views.

Biscuit Coffeehouse

COFFEEHOUSE **$**

(www.oregoncoastbooks.com/coffeehouse.htm; 29707 Ellensburg Ave; ☺7am-8pm Mon-Thu, till 9pm Fri & Sat, 8am-6pm Sun) Nestled in an excellent Gold Beach bookshop, this cheery café has homemade pastries and espresso.

❶ Information

Ranger Station (☎541-247-3600; 29279 Ellensburg Ave; ☺8:30am-12:30pm & 1:30-4:30pm Mon-Fri)

Visitors Center (☎800-525-2334; www.gold beach.org; 94080 Shirley Lane; ☺9am-5pm)

Brookings

POP 6500

Just 6 miles from the California border, Brookings is a balmy and bustling commercial town on the bay of the Chetco River. Tourists are drawn here more for the surrounding area than anything else: there's world-class

salmon and steelhead fishing upriver, and the coastline to the north is some of Oregon's most gorgeous. Winter temperatures hover around 60°F, making Brookings the state's 'banana belt' and a leader in Easter lily-bulb production; in July, fields south of town are filled with bright colors and a heavy scent.

Roads lead inland from Brookings up the Chetco River to the western edge of the Kalmiopsis Wilderness (p317). Oregon's only redwood forests are also found in this area.

❂ Sights & Activities

WWII Bomb Site

HISTORICAL SITE

Brookings was the site of one of the two mainland air attacks the US suffered during WWII. A seaplane launched from a Japanese submarine in September 1942 succeeded in bombing Mt Emily, behind the city (there were no casualties). The main goal of the attack was to burn the forests, but they failed to ignite. The Japanese pilot of that same seaplane returned to Brookings 20 years later and presented the city with his samurai sword, which was in his plane during the bombing; it's now displayed in Brookings' library.

Chetco Valley Historical Society Museum

MUSEUM

(☎541-469-5650; 15461 Museum Rd; admission by donation; ☺noon-4pm Sat & Sun) Once a stagecoach stop, the 1857 Blake House is now home to this museum. Stop in to see a quilt from 1844, an old Native American cedar canoe and an iron face supposedly cast resembling Queen Elizabeth I. Outside is the 'world's largest Monterey cypress.' Off-hours private tours are possible; call ahead.

Azalea Park

PARK

(Azalea Park Rd) This is a glorious, hilly park showcasing hundreds of azaleas, along with other pretty flora. Blooms are best in May and June. On Memorial Day weekend, the park becomes the focus of the annual **Azalea Festival**, with a floral parade and craft fair. There are Sunday concerts in July and August and a holiday light show in December.

Samuel H Boardman State Park

STATE PARK

Four miles north of Brookings, US 101 winds over 11 miles of headlands through Boardman State Park, which contains some of Oregon's most beautiful coastline. Along the highway are a number of roadside turnouts and picnic areas with short trails leading to secluded beaches and dramatic viewpoints. Marching far out to sea are tiny

OREGON COAST SOUTHERN OREGON COAST

island chains, home to shorebirds and braying sea lions.

Secluded **Lone Ranch Beach**, the southernmost turnoff, has picnic opportunities and tide pools in a sandy cove studded with triangular sea stacks. Half a mile north is the turnoff to **Cape Ferrelo**, a popular spot for spring whale-watching. A couple of miles north is **Whalehead Beach**, with glorious views.

North of the Thomas Creek Bridge (Oregon's highest at 345ft) is the turnoff for **Natural Bridge Viewpoint**, where you can see rock arches – the remnants of collapsed sea caves – just off the coast. At **Arch Rock Point**, 2 miles north, volcanic headlands have been eroded from an old lava tube.

Hikes
HIKING

There are short hiking trails 2 miles north of town at **Harris Beach State Park** (☑541-469-2021) on US 101. Enjoy views of Goat Island, Oregon's largest offshore island and a bird sanctuary, from the picnic area.

Nature trails at lush **Loeb State Park** (☑541-469-2021), 10 miles east of town on N Bank Chetco Rd, showcase two of Oregon's rarest and most cherished trees – redwood and myrtle. Check out the gorgeous 1.2-mile **Redwood Nature Trail** loop; the trailhead is on Chetco Rd, 0.25 miles past the park's entrance.

There's coastal access to the remote Kalmiopsis Wilderness (p317). For a fine 1.4-mile hike (but long drive), head 15 miles up N Bank Chetco River Rd, then right onto USFS Rd 1909 for another 15 miles to the Vulcan Lake trailhead. Get more detailed information at the ranger station.

Sleeping

South Coast Inn B&B
B&B $$

(☑541-469-5557, 800-525-9273; www.south coastinn.com; 516 Redwood St; d $119-149; ◎@☞) Bernard Maybeck designed this lovely Arts and Crafts–style house in 1917. It offers four rooms, one cottage ($129) and an apartment ($179). It's filled with antiques, and a gorgeous stone fireplace dominates the living room. The gardens are lovely.

Pacific Sunset Inn
MOTEL $

(☑541-469-2141; www.pacificsunsetinn.com; 1144 Chetco Ave; d from $60; ☞) Fine but slightly odd-looking budget motel with clean, good-sized rooms, possible vintage fixtures and basic amenities. Covered parking.

Alfred A Loeb State Park
CAMPGROUND $

(☑541-469-2021, 800-452-5687; www.oregon stateparks.org; campsites/cabins $20/39) There are almost 50 sites in a grove of myrtle trees, along with three riverside log cabins, showers and flush toilets. Located 10 miles east of Brookings on N Bank Chetco River Rd.

Harris Beach State Park
CAMPGROUND $

(☑541-469-2021, 800-452-5687; www.oregon stateparks.org; tent sites/RV sites/yurts $20/27/39) Two miles east of town on US 101, you can camp above the beach at one of 150 sites. Six yurts, showers, flush toilets and coin laundry are among the amenities.

Eating

The port has seafood and the excellent **Zola's Pizzeria**.

Art Alley Grille
AMERICAN $$

(☑541-469-0800; 515 Chetco Ave; mains $17-22; ◎lunch Tue-Sat, dinner Wed-Sat) Eat in an art gallery. Lunch (upstairs at 'The Snug') means $8 homemade salads and sandwiches, plus the opportunity to eat on a verandah in good weather. Dinner is downstairs and choices include great pasta, seafood and meat dishes.

Mattie's Pancake & Omelette
AMERICAN $

(15975 Hwy 101; mains $6.50-13; ◎breakfast & lunch Mon-Sat) This casual breakfast and lunch spot offers 20 kinds of omelets (crab and Swiss cheese) along with pancakes (chocolate chip!) and waffles – no surprise given its name. Sandwiches and salads for lunch.

Information

Chamber of Commerce (☑541-469-3181; www.brookingsor.com; 16330 Lower Harbor Rd; ◎9am-5pm Mon-Fri year-round, plus 11am-3pm Sat May-Sep)

Chetco Ranger Station (☑541-412-6000; www.fs.fed.us/r6/rogue-siskiyou; 14433 Hwy 101 S; ◎8:30am-4:30pm Mon-Fri) In the same building as the State Welcome Center.

State Welcome Center (☑541-469-4117; 14433 Hwy 101 S; ◎9am-5pm Mon-Sat, 11am-5pm Sun mid-May–Sep) Near the California border.

Ashland & Southern Oregon

Includes »

Best Places to Eat

» New Sammy's Cowboy Bistro (p312)

» Crater Lake Lodge Dining Room (p323)

» Summer Jo's (p316)

» Steamboat Inn (p320)

» Chateaulin (p312)

Best Places to Stay

» Crater Lake Lodge (p322)

» Wolf Creek Inn (p316)

» Country Willows (p309)

» Apothecary Inn (p314)

» Steamboat Inn (p320)

Why Go?

With a warm, sunny and dry climate that belongs in nearby California, Southern Oregon is the state's 'banana belt' and an exciting place to visit. Rugged and remote landscapes are entwined with a number of designated 'wild and scenic' rivers, which are famous for their challenging white-water rafting, world-class fly-fishing and excellent hiking. There's good birding in the area – especially for bald eagles – and exceptional lakes to visit, including spectacular Crater Lake. Campers will be in heaven.

Gold and timber originally brought pioneers to Southern Oregon cities, and today the migration continues with young families and California retirees seeking affordable housing. Downtowns have been revitalized, and there's plenty of culture in the area – Ashland is home to the renowned Oregon Shakespeare Festival, while nearby Jacksonville hosts the music lovers' Britt Festival. Centrally located between Seattle and San Francisco, Southern Oregon is certainly worth more than a short gas break if you're cruising the I-5.

When to Go
Ashland

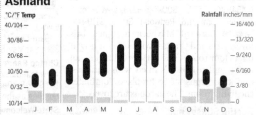

January Spot bald eagles (and other birds) at the Klamath Basin National Wildlife Refuges

July–September Crater Lake at her best, when you can drive all the way around the rim

June–September Prime summer months for the Oregon Shakespeare Festival and the Britt Festival

Ashland

POP 22,000

This pretty city is the cultural center of Southern Oregon thanks to its internationally renowned Oregon Shakespeare Festival (OSF), which runs for nine months of the year and attracts hundreds of thousands of theatergoers from all over the world. The festival is so popular that it's Ashland's main attraction, packing it out in summer and bringing in steady cash flows for the many fancy hotels, upscale B&Bs and fine restaurants in town.

Even without the OSF, however, Ashland is still a pleasant place where trendy downtown streets buzz with well-heeled shoppers and youthful bohemians. In late fall and early winter, those few months when the festival doesn't run, folks come to ski at nearby Mt Ashland. You can also ice-skate at lovely, 93-acre Lithia Park, which winds along Ashland Creek above the center of town (in summer it offers live concerts, duck ponds and picnic tables). And wine lovers take note – the area has several good wineries worth seeking out, exploring and tasting, of course.

Sights & Activities

Schneider Museum of Art   MUSEUM
(☑541-552-6245; www.sou.edu/sma; 1250 Siskiyou Blvd; suggested donation $3; ⊗10am-4pm Mon & Wed-Sat, 10am-8pm Tue, noon-4pm Sun) Ashland's culture extends beyond the OSF; if you like contemporary art, check out this Southern Oregon University museum. The university also puts on theater performances of its own, along with classical concerts and opera performances.

Jackson Wellsprings   HOT SPRING
(☑541-482-3776; www.jacksonwellsprings.com; 2253 Hwy 99) For a good soak check out this casual, New Age–style place, which boasts a mineral-fed swimming pool, private Jacuzzi tubs, saunas and steam rooms. It's one mile north of town.

ScienceWorks   MUSEUM
(☑541-482-6767; www.scienceworksmuseum. org; 1500 E Main St; adult/child $7.50/5; ⊗10am-5pm Wed-Sat, noon-5pm Sun; ⊕) Families with children shouldn't miss this hands-on interactive museum. It has plenty of fun science-oriented exhibits like a bubble room, hall of optical illusions and shadow wall that captures your silhouette.

Also try:

Adventure Center   RAFTING
(☑541-488-2819, 800-444-2819; www.rafting tours.com; 40 N Main St) Offers Rogue River rafting trips.

Kokopelli   RAFTING
(☑541-201-7694, 866-723-8874; www.kokopel liriverguides.com; 2475 Siskiyou Blvd) Rafting trips on the Rogue River.

Lithia Artisans Market   MARKET
If you're in town on a weekend between April and mid-November, catch this crafty market behind the plaza.

Mt Ashland Ski Resort   SKIING
(☑541-482-2897; www.mtashland.com) Powdery snow is abundant at this resort 16 miles southwest of town on 7533ft Mt Ashland.

Siskiyou Cyclery   BIKE HIRE
(☑541-482-1997; 1729 Siskiyou Blvd; ⊗10am-6pm Mon-Sat, 11am-4pm Sun) Pedal-pushers can rent a bike here to explore the countryside on Bear Creek Greenway.

🛏 Sleeping

In summer don't arrive without reservations – book a month ahead of time if possible. Rooms are cheaper in Medford, 12 miles north of Ashland. There's also camping, RV sites and teepees at Jackson Wellsprings (p309).

⭐TOP CHOICE Country Willows   B&B $$
(☑541-488-1590, 800-945-5697; www. countrywillowsinn.com; 1313 Clay St; d $140-260; ❋✳@🤖🏊) Only minutes from downtown is this luxurious B&B in the 'countryside,' complete with a few farm animals. The nine rooms, suites and a cottage sport a mix of antiques and contemporary furniture; some suites are as big as small apartments and have a kitchenette. The breakfast is gourmet, and hiking trails start from the premises.

Columbia Hotel   HOTEL $$
(☑541-482-3726, 800-718-2530; www.columbia hotel.com; 262-1/2 E Main St; d $89-149; ❋✳@🤖) The Columbia is an awesomely located 'European-style' hotel – which means most rooms share outside bathrooms. It's the best deal in downtown Ashland, with 24 quaint vintage rooms (no TVs), a nice lobby, and a thick historic feel. The rooms are on the 2nd floor and there's no elevator.

Ashland & Southern Oregon Highlights

1 Strut with the Bard at Ashland's **Oregon Shakespeare Festival** (p311)

2 Count bald eagles at **Klamath Basin National Wildlife Refuges** (p326)

3 Raft down the mighty **Rogue River** (p323), Oregon's premier white water

4 Spelunk the main grotto at **Oregon Caves National Monument** (p317)

5 Explore **Jacksonville's** (p314) historic downtown streets

6 Fly-fish the world-class waters of the North Umpqua River (p319)

7 Take a drive around gorgeous **Crater Lake** (p321)

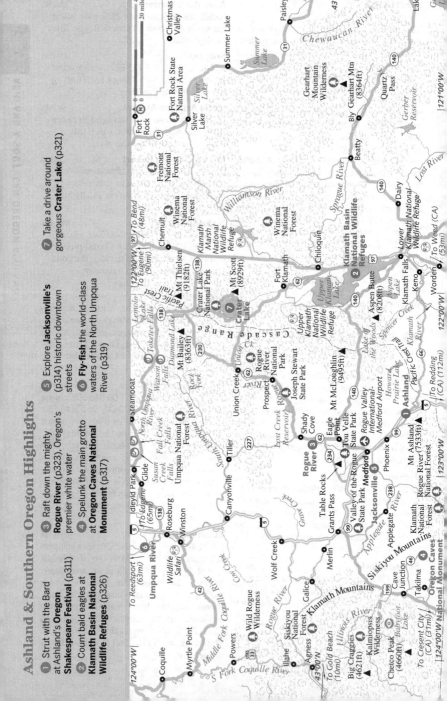

The Pacific Northwest is a hot spot for both traditional and innovative theater, and one top highlight is definitely Ashland's wildly popular Oregon Shakespeare Festival (OSF). Despite being deeply rooted in Shakespearean and Elizabethan drama, the festival also features revivals and contemporary theater from around the world.

As a young town, Ashland was included in the Methodist Church's cultural education program, called the Chautauqua Series. By the 1930s, one of the venues, Chautauqua Hall, had deteriorated to a dilapidated wooden shell. Angus Bowmer, a drama professor at the local college, noted the resemblance of the roofless structure to drawings of Shakespeare's Globe Theatre. He then convinced the town to sponsor two performances of Shakespeare's plays and a boxing match (the Bard would have approved) as part of its 1935 Fourth of July celebration. The plays proved a great success, and the OSF was off and running.

Eleven productions run from February to October in three theaters near Main and Pioneer Sts: the outdoor **Elizabethan Theatre** (open June to October), the **Angus Bowmer Theatre** and the intimate **New Theatre**. There are no Monday performances.

Performances sell out quickly; obtain tickets in advance at www.osfashland.org. You can also try the **box office** (541-482-4331; 15 S Pioneer St; tickets $20-96) for unclaimed tickets. Backstage **tours** (adult/child $12/8) also need to be booked well in advance.

Check the OSF Welcome Center (p313) for other events, which may include scholarly lectures, play readings, concerts and pre-show talks.

Palm
HOTEL $$

(541-482-2636, 877-482-2635; www.palm cottages.com; 1065 Siskiyou Blvd; d $95-205;) This is a fabulous example of a small motel remodeled into charming garden cottage rooms and suites (some with kitchens). It's an oasis of green on a busy avenue, complete with grassy lawns and a pool. A house next door is being remodeled into large suites ($249).

Ashland Creek Inn
HOTEL $$$

(541-482-3315; www.ashlandcreekinn.com; 70 Water St; d $230-350;) This gorgeous creekside inn offers 10 impeccable and eclectic suites, each with a nice living area. Most have a kitchenette and private deck over the water. There's a small but pretty garden and deck areas in which to relax, and a multicourse breakfast is included.

Arden Forest Inn
B&B $$$

(541-488-1496, 800-460-3912; www.afinn. com; 261 W Hersey St; d $140-290;) This is a lovely and comfortable B&B with five tastefully decorated rooms, a wonderful large garden and theater-loving hosts. It has a casual and liberal atmosphere, the gourmet breakfast is bountiful, and it's supremely gay-friendly.

Chanticleer Inn
B&B $$

(541-482-1919, 800-898-1950; www.ashlandbnb. com; 120 Gresham St; d $166-199;) This

lovely Craftsman B&B comes with six elegant rooms and your friendly host Ellen Campbell. The common areas are comfortable and tasteful, and the gardens are filled with lush plants. It's located in a peaceful residential neighborhood very close to the center.

Cowslip's Belle B&B
B&B $$

(541-488-2901, 800-888-6819; www.cowslip. com; 159 N Main St; d $165-245;) It's a short walk to the Plaza from this 1913 antique-filled bungalow with five good rooms or suites and a small grassy backyard with koi pond. The quietest rooms are in the back building and include two deluxe suites with Jacuzzi tubs and kitchens. For a less expensive route go for the 'vacation rental' option and cook your own breakfast.

Ashland Springs Hotel
HOTEL $$$

(541-488-1700, 888-795-4545; www.ashland springshotel.com; 212 E Main St; d $179-269;) This is a beautiful, renovated, historic landmark hotel with modest-sized but pleasant rooms and a noteworthy restaurant, Larks. Snag a corner room for great light and views. Great downtown location.

Ashland Hostel
HOSTEL $

(541-482-9217; www.theashlandhostel.com; 150 N Main St; dm $28, d $59-89;) There are separate men's and women's dorms at this central and somewhat upscale hostel. Most private rooms share bathrooms; some are connected to dorms (one cheap single is $40). Hang-out spaces include the cozy basement living room and sunny front porch.

Glenyan Campground
CAMPGROUND $

(☑541-488-1785, 877-453-6929; www.glenyanrv park.com; 5310 Hwy 66; tent/RV sites $22/32; ☎☀) This is a shady and pleasant 12-acre campground about 5 miles southeast of Ashland. Reserve a creekside spot, as they're the best. Playground, games room and store available.

Peerless Hotel
HOTEL $$$

(☑541-488-1082, 800-460-8758; www.peerless hotel.com; 243 4th St; d $160-269; ❂✻☎) European-style boutique hotel in a historic landmark building. Fine restaurant.

Iris Inn
B&B $$

(☑541-488-2286, 800-460-7650; www.irisinnbb. com; 59 Manzanita St; d $85-180; ❂✻☎) Well-located and long-running B&B with five lovely rooms and a garden deck/patio.

Ashland Motel
MOTEL $

(☑541-482-2561; www.ashlandmotel.com; 1145 Siskiyou Blvd; d $90-115; ✻☎☀) Newly remodeled rooms here are surprisingly hip and contemporary, and a great deal.

Manor Motel
MOTEL $

(☑541-482-2246, 866-261-9733; www.manor motel.net; 476 N Main St; d $69-125; ❂✻☎) Cute motel with pleasant rooms near downtown; kitchenettes available.

Cedarwood Inn
MOTEL $$

(☑541-488-2000, 800-547-4141; www.ashland cedarwoodinn.com; 1801 Siskiyou Blvd; d $92-148; ✻☎☀) Pleasant larger motel on a relatively quiet avenue. Indoor and outdoor pools. Ask for discounts.

Timbers Motel
MOTEL $

(☑541-482-4242, 866-550-4400; www. ashlandtimberslodging.com; 1450 Ashland St; d $89-125; ❂✻☎☀) Good, comfortable motel rooms, some with kitchenette.

✗ Eating & Drinking

There are plenty of great eating choices in Ashland, which levies a 5% restaurant tax. Make reservations during the Shakespeare festival.

TOP CHOICE New Sammy's Cowboy Bistro
AMERICAN $$$

(☑541-535-2779; 2210 S Pacific Hwy; mains $25-45; ☺lunch & dinner Wed-Sun) Some consider this funky spot, run by an eclectic couple, Oregon's best restaurant. There are only a handful of tables and the wine selections are spectacular (the dessert wine list alone is 16 pages long). Entrees are few but the flavor combinations can be incredible. Located in Talent, about 2 miles north of Ashland. Reserve weeks or months in advance; limited winter hours.

Chateaulin
FRENCH $$$

(☑541-482-2264; www.chateaulin.com; 50 E Main St; mains $17-34; ☺lunch & dinner) An upscale French restaurant serving renowned cuisine and excellent wines. Located just steps from the Shakespeare festival theaters, so it caters to the tourist crowds. Lunch means small plates, and prix-fixe dinners are available. Open late evening for after-theater drinks and desserts. The owners also run a wine shop next door.

Standing Stone Brewery
BREWERY-RESTAURANT $$

(www.standingstonebrewing.com; 101 Oak St; mains $9-16; ☺lunch & dinner) Popular, hip brewery-restaurant with burgers, salads and wood-fired pizzas. Fancier dinner choices include steaks, seafood and pasta, and there's also a half-dozen microbrews. Great back patio.

Morning Glory
CAFÉ $

(www.morninggloryrestaurant.com; 1149 Siskiyou Blvd; breakfast $9-12; ☺breakfast & lunch) This colorful, casual café is one of Ashland's best breakfast joints. Creative dishes include the Alaskan crab omelet, tandoori tofu scramble and shrimp cakes with poached eggs. For lunch there's soup, salad and sandwiches.

Thai Pepper
THAI $$

(84 N Main St; mains $15-18; ☺5:30-8.30pm) Small, contemporary Thai Pepper is known for its fiery Asian cooking. Choose the spicy lemongrass soup, green coconut chicken curry or sweet-and-soup shrimp. Creekside tables and exotic cocktails rein in the heat.

Greenleaf
AMERICAN $$

(☑541-482-2808; www.greenleafrestaurant .com; 49 N Main St; mains $9-13; ☺breakfast, lunch & dinner; ✐) This casual eatery offers a large variety of sandwiches, salads and pizzas, along with specials like spanako-pita, shepherd's pie and fish 'n chips. Good breakfasts, hormone-free meats and lots of vegetarian options too.

Rogue Valley Roasting Co
COFFEEHOUSE $

(www.roastingcoashland.com; 917 E Main St; drinks & snacks under $4; ☺6:45am-6pm Mon-Sat, 7am-3pm Sun) This quality coffeehouse serves up dark roasts and organic beans, along with gourmet teas and light snacks. The atmosphere is laid back and there's some outdoor seating, plus a computer and wi-fi.

Peerless on 4th
NORTHWEST $$$
(☏503-488-6067; www.peerlessrestaurant.com; 265 4th St; mains $15-34, small plates $11-16; ⊙dinner Tue-Sat) Best for tasting many 'small plates' rather than just one main (of which there are a few). Upscale restaurant with fresh ingredients and fine cuisine.

Amuse
FRENCH $$$
(☏541-488-9000; www.amuserestaurant.com; 15 N 1st St; mains $22-34; ⊙dinner Tue-Sun) Fine French bistro serving dishes like Parisienne gnocchi with oyster mushrooms and truffle-roasted game hen.

Dragonfly
LATIN, ASIAN FUSION $$
(☏541-488-4855; www.dragonflyashland.com; 241 Hargadine St; mains $9-14; ⊙breakfast, lunch & dinner) Great international creativity from chef Isabel Cruz: coconut French toast for breakfast, free-range chicken tamales for lunch and wok-fried rice bowls for dinner.

Loft
FRENCH-AMERICAN $$
(18 Calle Guanajuato; mains $15-23; ⊙lunch Tue-Sat, dinner Tue-Sun) What could be more Franco-American than white truffle-scented macaroni and cheese?

Noble Coffee
COFFEEHOUSE $
(www.noblecoffeeroasting.com; 281 4th St; drinks & snacks under $4; ⊙7am-4pm) Some of Ashland's best organic coffee, freshly roasted and pressed, siphoned or dripped to your specifications. Great atmosphere too.

Dagoba
CHOCOLATE
(☏541-482-2001; www.dagobachocolate.com; 1105 Benson Way) Chocolate lovers shouldn't miss a visit to the factory store and tasting room.

❶ Information

Ashland Chamber of Commerce (☏541-482-3486; www.ashlandchamber.com; 110 E Main St; ⊙9am-5pm Mon-Fri) An information booth at the Plaza is open summer weekends only.

OSF Welcome Center (76 N Main St; ⊙10am-6pm Tue-Sun) Can help with OSF-related questions.

❶ Getting There & Away

The nearest airport is 15 miles north in Medford. **Cascade Airport Shuttle** (☏541-488-1998) provides services from the airport to Ashland; reserve ahead. Local bus transportation is pro-

vided by **Rogue Valley Transportation District** (RVTD; ☏541-779-2877 www.rvtd.org).

Medford
POP 77,000

Southern Oregon's largest metropolis, Medford is well known for its fruit industry, especially pears and wine grapes. In the past decade the city has grown tremendously, drawing thousands of California retirees with its sunny warm weather. It's also well located, with plenty of affordable accommodation, and Ashland, Jacksonville, Crater Lake, Oregon Caves National Monument and the Rogue River valley are all a day trip away.

☉ Sights

Harry and David's Country Village
GOURMET FOOD STORE
(☏541-776-2277; 1314 Center Dr; ⊙9am-8pm Mon-Sat, 10am-6pm Sun) Medford's most famous tourist attraction is this outlet store of the giant mail-order fruit company. It offers nearby **plant tours** (☏877-322-8000; tours $5; ⊙Mon-Fri) with advance reservations.

Tou Velle State Park
STATE PARK
About 6 miles north of Medford on the Rogue River, this state park is popular for swimming and picnicking. About a mile beyond is **Table Rocks**, impressive 800ft mesas that speak of the area's volcanic past and are home to unique plant and animal species. Flowery spring is the best time for **hiking** to the flat tops, which were revered Native American sites. From downtown, follow Riverside Ave north and turn right on Table Rock Rd. After Tou Velle State Park, fork either left to reach the trailhead to Lower Table Rock (3.5-mile round-trip hike) or right for Upper Table Rock (2.5-mile round-trip hike). The **Bureau of Land Management** (BLM; ☏541-618-2200; www.or.blm.gov; 3040 Biddle Rd) has information and offers guided springtime hikes.

🛏 Sleeping & Eating

Medford's Riverside Ave has plenty of budget and midrange motels, but the cheapest can be a bit grungy and most are within earshot of the I-5.

Under the Greenwood Tree
B&B $$
(☏541-776-0000; www.greenwoodtree.com; 3045 Bellinger Lane; s/d $115/140; ❄✿🐾) Three miles from Medford, on the road to Jacksonville, this peaceful B&B is set on 10 acres of countryside. Four country-style rooms are decorated with antiques, and llamas and

chickens live out in the gardens and fields. The breakfast is a three-course affair.

Red Lion Hotel   HOTEL **$$**
(☑541-779-5811; www.redlion.com; 200 N Riverside Ave; d from $90; ☺❀☎⊛) Good midrange choice with spacious, very comfortable rooms – ask for a creekside room with balcony (if you don't mind the I-5 traffic). For a few bucks you can be right by one of the two outdoor pools. There's a restaurant, meeting rooms and fitness center on premises.

Medford Inn   MOTEL **$**
(☑541-773-8266, 877-473-7444; www.medford inn.com; 1015 S Riverside Ave; d $50-98; ☺❀ ☎⊛) This is a pleasant, typical motel with spacious, clean rooms and sheltered atmosphere. All rooms come with fridge and microwave, and there's a pool.

Cedar Lodge   MOTEL **$**
(☑541-773-7361, 800-282-3419; www.cedarlodge motorinn.com; 518 N Riverside Ave; d $48; ☺❀ ☎⊛) There are good standard rooms at Cedar Lodge, some with microwave and fridge. One of the better places on this drag, it boasts a heated outdoor swimming pool.

Porters   AMERICAN **$$**
(☑541-857-1910; www.porterstrainstation.com; 147 N Front St; mains $15-30; ☺dinner) This gorgeous, Craftsman-style restaurant is decked out in dark-wood booths and boasts an awesome patio next to the train tracks. Steak, seafood and pasta dishes dominate the menu. The attached bar stays open much later.

Organicos Natural Café   AMERICAN **$**
(☑541-245-9802; www.organicoscafe.com; 226 E Main St; mains under $10; ☺7am-7pm Mon-Sat; ⊗) Step up to the cafeteria here and order a panini-style sandwich or burger (choose from vegetarian/buffalo/organic beef). There's a salad bar, along with fresh juices and fruit smoothies. The theme – in case you haven't guessed yet – is all about local, organic, vegan and gluten-free.

ⓘ Information

Visitors Center (☑541-776-4021; www. visitmedford.org; 1314 Center Dr; ☺9am-6pm) Right next to Harry and David's.

ⓘ Getting There & Away

The **Rogue Valley International-Medford Airport** (☑541-776-7222) is 2.5 miles north of town, off Biddle Rd. **Greyhound** (☑541-779-2103; www.greyhound.com) is at the intersection of 9th and Front Sts, as is the **Rogue Valley**

Transit District (RVTD; ☑541-779-5821; www. rvtd.org).

Jacksonville

This former gold-prospecting town is the oldest settlement in southern Oregon and a National Historic Landmark. Small but endearing, the town's main drag – California St – is like a step back in time, lined with well-preserved brick-and-wood buildings dating from the 1880s. Today, folks come to stroll around downtown and enjoy the old-time atmosphere while exploring the many boutiques and galleries. Although summertime is great, Jacksonville has a certain magic touch in winter, when the crowds are lighter and magical holiday celebrations take hold.

Don't miss the Britt Festival, a world-class musical experience that runs all summer long. And in the surrounding Applegate Valley there are several wineries to visit, offering more varietals than just pinot noir; see www.applegatewinetrail.com for more.

⊙ Sights

Jacksonville Cemetery   CEMETERY
This 32-acre cemetery is worth a wander to explore historic pioneer grave sites chronicling wars, epidemics and other untimely deaths. The chamber of commerce has helpful literature with maps.

Trolley tours   TOURS
(adult/child $5/3) These narrated tours provide a good historical overview of the town; run daily.

⌂ Sleeping

Jacksonville has limited and mostly upscale accommodations (reserve ahead). There's more choice and less expensive accommodations 6 miles east in Medford (p313).

Apothecary Inn   B&B **$$**
(☑541-899-3998; www.apothecaryinn.com; 830 Upper Applegate Rd; d $105-125; ☺❀☎) There are just two rooms at this countryside B&B, cheerfully run by a young couple. On the grounds are miniature donkeys, llamas, chickens and Nigerian dwarf goats; two cats live in the house. There's also a vegetable garden, and there are plans for a fish-stocked pool and heirloom apple orchard. It's about 9 miles south of Jacksonville.

TouVelle House   B&B **$$$**
(☑541-899-8938, 800-846-8422; www.touvelle house.com; 455 N Oregon St; d $159-199; ☺❀☎@

THE BRITT FESTIVAL

In 1963, Portland conductor John Trudeau came to Jacksonville with a few friends, and they found themselves on the former hillside estate of Peter Britt (1819–1905), a Swiss photographer who made a name for himself after immigrating to Oregon. These musicians noticed the exceptional acoustics of the hillsides surrounding Britt's old home, and that same year built a plywood stage for a local orchestral performance. Thus was born the Pacific Northwest's first outdoor music festival.

In 1978 a pavilion was constructed and the festival continued to grow and attract top-notch artists. The nonprofit **Britt Festival** (☎541-773-6077; www.brittfest.org) is now a premier musical festival that also sponsors educational programs through the Britt Institute. For more information, head to the festival's website. And for more on Peter Britt and his many talents, go to www.peterbritt.org.

��) This gorgeous Craftsman house offers six elegant rooms, each with feather bed, down comforter and private bathroom. It's on spacious grounds with a pool, and just two blocks from downtown.

Jacksonville Inn　　HOTEL **$$$**
(☎541-899-1900, 800-321-9344; www.jacksonvilleinn.com; 175 E California St; d $159-199, cottages $270-465; ❀❄☎) This historic 1863 hotel is right downtown and has 12 beautiful, antique-filled rooms and cottages with flowery (but tasteful) decoration. There's an excellent upscale restaurant as well.

Magnolia Inn　　B&B **$$**
(☎541-899-0255, 866-899-0255; www.magnolia-inn.com; 245 N 5th St; d $139-169; ❀❄☎) The Magnolia is a pleasant, nine-room B&B boasting a guest kitchen (food warm-up only; no cooking) with a great covered verandah nearby. The rooms are all different and decorated with antiques, and breakfast is continental. It's across from the museum.

Stage Lodge　　HOTEL **$$**
(☎541-899-3953, 800-253-8254; www.stagelodge.com; 830 N 5th St; d $99-114; ❀❄☎) This modern hotel with 27 spacious and fine contemporary rooms is outside the heart of town.

Cantrall-Buckley Campground　　CAMPING **$**
(campsites $12) Located in Ruch, 10 miles west of Jacksonville on Hwy 238, this first-come, first-serve campground (showers available) is shaded by oak, fir and madrone trees. A pleasant river flows nearby.

✗ Eating

MacLevin's Deli　　DELI **$$**
(☎541-899-1251; 150 W California St; www.maclevinsonline.com; mains $7-18; ☉10am-4pm Mon & Thu, 8am-8pm Fri, 8am-6pm Sat, 8am-4pm

Sun) The Reubens are especially good at this Jewish deli – Jeff and Penelope, the owners, corn their own additive-free beef. And they can be quite the characters, a reason in itself to visit. Lots of tasty sandwiches, along with soups and salads.

Bella Union　　AMERICAN **$$**
(☎541-899-1770; www.bellau.com; 170 W California St; mains $11-25; ☉lunch & dinner) An old saloon from 1868, the Bella Union now serves up decent pizzas, pastas, salads, meat dishes and sandwiches; on a warm day, the back patio is heaven. The bar is open later.

GoodBean Coffee　　COFFEEHOUSE **$**
(www.goodbean.com; 165 S Oregon St; drinks & snacks under $4; ☉6am-6pm) This is a casual, trendy coffee shop with brick walls and sidewalk tables. Gourmet beans and bagel sandwiches are available.

ℹ Information

Chamber of Commerce (☎541-899-8118; www.jacksonvilleoregon.org; 185 N Oregon St; ☉10am-5pm Mon-Fri, 11am-4pm Sat & Sun)

ℹ Getting There & Away

RVTD bus 30 runs from Medford. For bike rentals, check with **Cycle Analysis** (☎541-899-9190; 535 N 5th St).

Grants Pass

POP 33,000

As a modern and not particularly scenic city Grants Pass isn't a huge tourist destination, but its location on the banks of the Rogue River makes it a portal to adventure. White-water rafting, fine fishing and jetboat excursions are the biggest attractions, and there's also good camping and hiking in the area. If you're here on a Saturday between mid-March and Thanksgiving be sure to check out the **Outdoors Growers' Market**, a farmers and craft market that draws the city together.

◉ Sights

Grants Pass is also the gateway to Oregon Caves National Monument (p317).

Wildlife Images   WILDLIFE REHABILITATION CENTER
(☑541-476-0222; www.wildlifeimages.org; 11845 Lower River Rd; adult/child $10/5; ☺tours 9am-5pm May-Sep, 9am-4pm Oct-Apr) Animal lovers shouldn't miss this nonprofit rehabilitation center for native creatures in trouble. It's located about 13 miles from Grants Pass, near Merlin; visits are by tour only.

⌂ Sleeping

There are plenty of economy motels lining 6th and 7th Sts.

Wolf Creek Inn   HOTEL $$
TOP CHOICE (☑541-866-2474; www.historicwolfcreek inn.com; 100 Front St; d $85-125; ❂✳?) Located 20 miles north of Grants Pass, this historic hotel and stagecoach stop once hosted celebrities like Jack London, Clark Gable and Mary Pickford. There are only nine period rooms available (No 9 is the biggest); breakfast included. Restaurant available.

Buona Sera Inn   MOTEL $
(☑541-476-4260; www.buonaserainn.com; 1001 NE 6th St; d $65-105; ❂?) An Argentine/French-Lebanese couple have lovingly renovated this old motel into a comfortable, and even slightly luxurious, place with 14 country-style rooms. All have quality linens and boast a fridge and microwave; some come with kitchenette.

Ivy House B&B   B&B $
(☑541-474-7363; 139 SW I St; s/d $65/75; ❂) A great deal, this lovely Arts and Crafts B&B is run by a gardening Englishwoman who uses composters and rain barrels to nourish her 100-year-old rosebushes. Five rooms decorated with antiques are available, one ensuite and four that share two bathrooms.

Redwood Motel   MOTEL $$
(☑541-476-0878, 888-535-8824; www.redwood motel.com; 815 NE 6th St; d $85-170; ❂?✖) Simple and spacious rooms with fridge and microwave are on offer at this central motel. Some have private Jacuzzi, but there's a communal hot tub (and pool) as well. Suites and kitchenettes available.

Weasku Inn Resort   INN $$$
(☑541-471-8000, 800-493-2758; www.weasku. com; 5560 Rogue River Hwy; d from $199, cabins from $225; ❂?) Situated about 5 miles east of town, this grand old lodge has hosted Clark Gable. Luxuriously rustic rooms and cabins are available (some with private Jacuzzi) and a continental breakfast, along with evening wine and cheese reception, is included.

Schroeder Park   CAMPGROUND $
(☑800-452-5687; 605 Schroeder Lane; tent sites/RV sites/yurts $19/22/30) This pleasant, riverside campground is 4 miles west of town, on the south side of the river. There are about 50 sites with showers and flush toilets, a dog park, playground and boat ramp.

Valley of the Rogue State Park
    CAMPGROUND $
(☑541-582-3128, 800-452-5687; www.oregon stateparks.org; 3792 N River Rd; tent sites/RV sites/yurts $19/24/36) Around 12 miles east of town, this riverside campground has 168 sites and six yurts. There are showers, flush toilets and a boat ramp.

✕ Eating

Summer Jo's   AMERICAN $$
(☑541-476-6882; www.summerjos.com; 2315 Upper River Rd Loop; mains $16-27; ☺breakfast, lunch & dinner Thu-Sun) This organic farm-restaurant utilizes veggies grown on the premises, along with sustainable seafood and quality meats. It offers exquisite dishes and is well worth the drive out: take G St southwest 1.4 miles, then turn left on Upper River Rd Loop. A great spot for lunch – sit outside on sunny days.

Aja   ASIAN $$
(☑541-471-1228; 118 NW E St; mains $9-18; ☺dinner Tue-Sat) It's just a small room with seven tables, but the food here is great. Try the Singapore-style noodles, Indonesian corn fritters or Mongolian baby back ribs. A couple runs the business here; she's the whiz in the kitchen and he's busy chatting and serving up front.

Laughing Clam   PUB RESTAURANT $$
(121 SW G St; mains $8-22; ☺lunch & dinner Mon-Sat) Exotic dishes like the cosmic Cajun catfish sandwich and magic mushroom burger are served up at this neon-lit, brick-walled eatery. More standard things like fish 'n chips, pasta and jambalaya are also available, along with a few rotating microbrews.

THE UNIQUE KALMIOPSIS WILDERNESS

One of Oregon's largest wilderness areas, the remote Kalmiopsis Wilderness is famous for its rare plant life and the state's oldest peaks – the Klamath Mountains. About 150 million years ago, offshore sedimentary beds buckled up into mountains separated from North America by a wide gulf. Vegetation evolved on its own, so by the time the mountains fused to the continent the plant life was very different from that of the mainland. The area also has the country's largest exposed serpentine rock formations.

Unusual and unique plant species are showcased on the steep, 0.75-mile hike to **Babyfoot Lake**. The pink-flowered *Kalmiopsis leachiana* and rare Port Orford cedar are found almost nowhere else on earth. Watch meadows for the carnivorous Darlingtonia (also called the pitcher plant or cobra lily) that traps insects for nourishment. To get to the trailhead, turn onto Eight Dollar Mountain Rd (USFS Rd 4201, 5 miles north of Cave Junction) and follow the signs for 17 winding miles. This road is impassable in winter.

Another section of the Kalmiopsis is accessible from the coastal town of Brookings (see p306). For more information and hiking trails, enquire at the ranger stations in Cave Junction and Brookings.

Taprock AMERICAN **$$**
(www.taprock.com; 971 SE 6th St; mains $10-21; ☺breakfast, lunch & dinner) Multimillion-dollar restaurant perched above the Rogue River; menu has something for everyone.

Rogue Coffee Roasters COFFEEHOUSE **$**
(roguecoffeeroasting.com; 237 SW G St; coffee & snacks under $6; ☺8am-5:30pm Mon-Fri, to 2pm Sat) Organic, exotic and fairtrade coffees, along with a few snacks.

Sunshine Natural Foods ORGANIC STORE **$**
(☑541-474-5044; www.sunshinefoodandvitamin. com; 128 SW H St; mains under $7; ☺9am-6pm Mon-Fri, to 5pm Sat; ☑) Organic groceries and natural foods, along with fruit smoothies and vegetable juices.

ⓘ Information

Chamber of Commerce (☑541-476-7717; www.visitgrantspass.org; 1995 NW Vine St; ☺8am-5pm Mon-Fri, 9am-4pm Sat, 10am-2pm Sun) Right off I-5 exit 58.

ⓘ Getting There & Away

Greyhound (☑541-476-4513; www.greyhound. com; 460 NE Agness Ave) Off I-5 near exit 55, about 2 miles from downtown.

Oregon Caves National Monument

This very popular tourist destination lies 19 miles east of Cave Junction on Hwy 46. The cave (there's only one) contains about 3 miles of passages, explored via 90-minute walking tours that expose visitors to dripping chambers and 520 rocky steps. The trail – which requires ducking at times – follows an underground waterway called the River Styx.

The Oregon Caves began as seafloor limestone deposits that were eventually hoisted into the Siskiyou Mountains. Molten rock forced its way up into rock faults to form marble, and acidified groundwater seeped through cracks to carve underground channels. Surface erosion eventually created an opening for air to enter, causing water to mineralize and create myriad formations, such as cave popcorn, pearls, moonmilk, classic pipe organs, columns and stalactites.

⊙ Sights & Activities

Cave Tours TOURS
(☑541-592-2100; www.nps.gov/orca; adult/child $8.50/6; ☺9am-6pm Jun-Sep, varies rest of year) Guided tours run at least hourly; they run half-hourly in July and August. Dress warmly, wear good shoes and be prepared to get dripped on. Due to safety, children less than 42in tall are not allowed on tours.

A handful of short nature trails surround the area, such as the 0.75-mile **Cliff Nature Trail** (offering good views) and the 3.3-mile **Big Tree Trail** (which loops through old-growth forest to a huge Douglas fir). You can stop for snacks or a meal at the Oregon Caves Chateau (p318), a beautiful old lodge. Also, some fine wineries are found en route to the caves.

Great Cats World Park ZOO
(☑541-592-2957; www.greatcatsworldpark.com; 27919 Redwood Hwy; adult/child $14/10) For something completely different, check out

this park 1.5 miles south of Cave Junction. This zoo/interactive big cat preserve proves cats *are* trainable – even if they're big enough to eat your head. Hours vary; call for info.

Sleeping & Eating

Kerby, just two miles north of Cave Junction, has the **Kerbyville Inn** (www.bridgeview wine.com/kerbyvilleinn/pnp) and **Holiday Motel** (☑541-592-3003). The Oregon Caves Chateau has a dining room and café.

TOP CHOICE **Out 'n' About Treesort** TREEHOUSE **$$** (☑541-592-2208; www.treehouses.com; 300 Page Creek Rd, Takilma; treehouse $110-280; ⊕) A must for families with inquisitive kids, this rustic but fun place offers 16 different kinds of treehouses, from small, round rooms 47ft up, to more terrestrial suites with kitchens. Not all have bathrooms, and some are only for those comfortable with heights. Ziplines and horseback riding available. It's in Takilma, 12 miles south of Cave Junction. Breakfast is included; reservations are crucial.

Oregon Caves Chateau HOTEL **$$** (☑541-592-3400, 877-245-9022; www.oregon caveschateau.com; d $90-165; ⊕May-Oct) Situated near the cave's entrance, this impressive six-story lodge has huge windows facing the forest, 23 simple, vintage rooms and a fine dining room overlooking a plunging ravine. Snacks and great milkshakes are served at the old-fashioned soda fountain.

Country Hills Resort CAMPGROUND, CABINS **$** (☑541-592-3406; www.countryhillsresort.com; 7901 Caves Hwy; tent/RV sites $16/22, d $65, cabins $75-95) A friendly, rustic place, this resort has five comfortable country-style rooms and six cabins that come with kitchenettes. It also offers creekside camping and full-hookup RV sites. It's on the way to Oregon caves; reserve in summer.

Junction Inn MOTEL **$** (☑541-592-3106; 406 Redwood Hwy; d from $70; ⊠) Cave Junction's largest motel, the Junction Inn has basic, no-nonsense rooms. A swimming pool cools things down in summer.

Cave Creek Campground CAMPGROUND **$** (☑541-592-4000; campsites $10) Fourteen miles up Hwy 46, this campground is 3.7 miles from the caves and has a 1.8-mile trail leading there. There are vault toilets, picnic tables and drinking water; no showers or hookups.

Wild River Brewing & Pizza Co PIZZA **$$** (www.wildriverbrewing.com; 249 Redwood Hwy; pizza $7-25; ⊕lunch & dinner) Another link of this small but good restaurant chain. There are large family tables inside, but if it's sunny, the back deck (overlooking a creek) is the place to be. Also offers great burgers and sandwiches.

❶ Information

Cave Junction, 28 miles south of Grants Pass on US 199 (Redwood Hwy), provides the region's services.

Illinois Valley Visitor Center (☑541-592-4076; 201 Caves Hwy; ⊕9am-4pm Mon-Fri, 10am-4:30pm Sat & Sun) Information on the area.

Wild Rivers Ranger District (☑541-592-4000; www.fs.fed.us/r6/rogue-siskiyou; 26568 Redwood Hwy; ⊕8am-4:30pm Mon-Fri).

Roseburg

POP 21,000

Sprawling Roseburg lies in a valley near the confluence of the South and North Umpqua Rivers. The city is mostly a cheap, modern sleepover for travelers headed elsewhere (such as Crater Lake), but it does contain a cute historic downtown area and is surrounded by award-winning wineries. Two exceptional area sights include a regional museum and drive-through safari park.

◉ Sights & Activities

Douglas County Museum MUSEUM (☑541-957-7007;www.co.douglas.or.us/museum; I-5 exit 123; adult/child $5/free; ⊕10am-5pm) Don't miss this excellent museum, which displays the area's cultural and natural histories. Especially interesting are the railroad derailment photos and history of wine exhibit. Kids have an interactive area and live snakes to look at.

Wildlife Safari ZOO (☑541-679-6761; www.wildlifesafari.net; I-5 exit 119; adult/child $18/12; ⊕9am-5pm; ⊕) Ten miles southwest near Winston is where you drive your car around a 600-acre park dotted with inquisitive ostriches, camels, giraffes, lions, tigers and bears – among other exotic animals. Includes a small zoo where 'encounters' are available.

Sleeping & Eating

Roseburg is host to plenty of budget and midrange hotel chains, most located just off I-5 on NW Garden Valley Blvd, or on NE Stephens St.

Hokanson's Guest House
B&B $

(☑541-672-2632; www.hokansonsguesthouse.com; 848 SE Jackson St; d $95-105; ☻) Just three charming rooms are available at this downtown B&B, each with a private bathroom. The 1882 Victorian is filled with antiques, and a Siamese cat roams the premises.

Rose City Motel
MOTEL $

(☑541-673-8209; 1142 NE Stephens St; d $46; ❋☎) A cheap motel on a busy avenue, but it's a great deal and the pride of place shows – there are plants here and there, and whimsical touches abound. Kitchenettes available.

McMenamins Roseburg Station Pub
AMERICAN $

(www.mcmenamins.com/286-roseburg-station-pub-brewery-home; 700 SE Sheridan St; mains $7-11; ☻lunch & dinner, till midnight Fri & Sat) This is a beautiful, cozy pub-restaurant in typical McMenamins style – old-fashioned and tasteful. Burgers, sandwiches and salads dominate the menu. It's in an old train depot; sit and order a microbrew on the sunny patio in summer.

Brix 527
CAFÉ $

(527 SE Jackson St; mains $8-13; ☻breakfast & lunch) A modern, hip café, Brix serves omelets, pancakes and French toast for breakfast, and burgers, gourmet sandwiches and salads for lunch.

ℹ Information

Fish & Wildlife Office (☑541-440-3353; 4192 N Umpqua Hwy; ☻8am-5pm Mon-Fri) For fishing the Umpqua.

Roseburg Visitor Center (☑541-672-9731, 800-444-9584; www.visitroseburg.com; 410 SE Spruce St; ☻9am-5pm Mon-Fri, 9am-4pm Sat, 10am-4pm Sun) Downtown.

ℹ Getting There & Away

Long-distance bus services are provided by **Greyhound** (☑541-673-3348; www.greyhound.com; 835 SE Stephens St).

North Umpqua River

From Roseburg, Hwy 138 winds east toward Crater Lake along the lovely North Umpqua, a designated 'wild and scenic' river, and one of the best-loved fly-fishing streams in Oregon. Deep forests crowd the river's boulder-strewn edge while volcanic crags rise above the trees. This corridor contains one of Oregon's greatest concentrations of waterfalls, and there are short hikes to most of them.

Between Idleyld Park and Diamond Lake are dozens of mostly USFS campgrounds, many right on the river. In summer, plan on pitching a tent unless you've reserved accommodation at one of the resorts.

ℹ Information

Colliding Rivers Information Center (☑541-496-0157; 18782 N Umpqua Hwy, Glide; ☻9am-5pm May-Sep) In Glide.

Diamond Lake Ranger District (☑541-498-2531; ☻8am-4:30pm Mon-Fri)

Diamond Lake Visitors Center (☑541-793-3379; ☻9am-5pm)

North Umpqua Ranger Station (☑541-496-3532; ☻8am-4:30pm Mon-Fri) Adjacent to the Colliding Rivers Information Center.

STEAMBOAT & AROUND

Fly-fishing is heaven here, offering steelhead, cutthroat trout, and Chinook and Coho salmon. Consult Roseburg's **Fish & Wildlife Office** (☑541-440-3353) for limits and restrictions.

Frothy rapids above Steamboat make this part of the river good for **rafting** and **kayaking**. Contact **North Umpqua Outfitters** (☑888-454-9696; www.nuorafting.com) for guided raft trips.

The 79-mile **North Umpqua Trail** begins near Idleyld Park and passes through Steamboat en route to the Pacific Crest Trail near Lemolo Lake. A worthwhile day hike to **Mott Bridge** travels 5.5 gentle miles upstream through old-growth forest; it starts from the Wright Creek Trailhead, a few miles west of Steamboat on USFS Rd 4711.

From the Susan Creek day-use area (just west of Susan Creek campground), the 1.2-mile **Indian Mounds Trail** passes **Susan Creek Falls** before climbing up to a vision-quest site. About 4 miles east is the 1-mile hike to the double-tier **Fall Creek Falls; Job's Garden Trail** is a 0.4-mile offshoot halfway up that leads to columnar basalt formations.

Turn up USFS Rd 38 at Steamboat to reach **Steamboat Falls**, where sea-run salmon and steelhead struggle to the top of the fast-moving falls from May to October. The best views are from the Steamboat Falls Campground, across the bridge.

Twenty-one miles east of Steamboat is the stunning, two-tiered **Toketee Falls**, flowing over columnar basalt. To reach it turn off on

USFS Rd 34; the hike there is just 0.4 miles. For a special treat, visit clothing-optional **Umpqua Hot Springs** (Northwest Forest Pass required, or pay $5 onsite); keep heading two miles up USFS Rd 34 past Toketee Falls, then turn right on Thorn Prairie Rd (USFS Rd 3401; possibly unsigned). After two more miles you'll reach the short trailhead.

Two miles past Toketee Junction on Hwy 138 is **Watson Falls**, which at 272ft is one of the highest waterfalls in Oregon. The 0.4-mile path begins at the picnic area on USFS Rd 37, but you can also see it from the parking lot.

🛏 Sleeping

TOP CHOICE **Steamboat Inn**   INN $$$
(☑541-498-2230, 800-840-8825; www.thesteamboatinn.com; 42705 N Umpqua Hwy; d $175-300; ☻❄🐾) The Steamboat offers lovely wood-paneled suites and cabins next to the river, along with larger modern cottages and houses nearby. All have comfortable amenities, and some come with a fireplace, kitchenette and soaking tubs. Its renowned restaurant is open to non-guests (prix-fixe dinner $50 to $85; reserve ahead). Located 38 miles east of Roseburg.

Dogwood Motel   MOTEL $
(☑541-496-3403; www.dogwoodmotel.com; 28866 N Umpqua Hwy; d $65-70; ☻❄🐾) At the Dogwood, actual log cabins house seven dark, rustic and tidy rooms, some with kitchenettes. A pretty garden out back offers a wood gazebo and koi pond, along with a picnic area. Located 11 miles east of Glide.

Umpqua's Last Resort   CAMPGROUND, CABINS $
(☑541-498-2500; www.golastresort.com; Hwy 138 at Dry Creek; tent & RV sites $18-26, cabins $49-69) It's hardly fancy – the small cabins just hold a bed (bring your own sleeping bag/linens). The larger ones are much more comfortable, with sofa, fridge and TV. All cabins share outside bathrooms. Located about 8.5 miles east of Steamboat.

Campgrounds on Hwy 38:

Susan Creek   CAMPGROUND
(campsites $14) A lovely place with showers 13 miles east of Glide.

Steamboat Falls   CAMPGROUND
(campsites $10) Isolated; up 5.6 miles on Steamboat Creek Rd (off Hwy 138), then across a bridge.

Boulder Flat   CAMPGROUND
(campsites $10) A primitive spot with no water, 36 miles east of Glide with views

of a spectacular (and phallic) lava formation down the river.

DIAMOND LAKE

This beautiful, deep-blue lake attracts motorboat and RV enthusiasts in summer, with activity centered on a bustling full-service resort. There's fishing, boating and swimming possibilities, along with a 12-mile paved bike path around the lake. Winter brings cross-country skiers.

Rising to the east of Diamond Lake is pointy **Mt Thielsen**, a 9182ft basalt spire. A 5-mile trail (10 miles round trip; Northwest Forest Pass required or pay $5 onsite) begins a mile north of the junction of Hwys 138 and 230 and stops 80ft short of the summit, which is attainable only with technical climbing skills.

Diamond Lake Campground (☑877-444-6777; USFS Rd 4795; campsites $16-22) has 238 sites and offers plenty of camping amenities at the north end of the lake. It's such a popular place that you should reserve ahead in summer.

Diamond Lake Resort (☑541-793-3333, 800-733-7593; www.diamondlake.net; 350 Resort Dr; d $79-249) offers motel-type rooms, studios, Jacuzzi suites and two-bedroom cabins with kitchens. Dining options include a café, a pizzeria and a fancier dining room. Boats, canoes, kayaks, bicycles, fishing gear and ski equipment are all available for rent.

LEMOLO LAKE

Ten miles north of Diamond Lake is Lemolo Lake, a much quieter, family-oriented resort with views across the reservoir to faraway Mt Thielsen.

The 1.7-mile hike to **Lemolo Falls** is worth the off-road drive. Turn off Hwy 138 onto USFS Rd 2610 (Lemolo Lake Rd) for 4.2 miles, then left onto USFS Rd 3401 (Thorn Prairie Rd) for half a mile. Then turn right onto USFS Rd 800 for 1.8 miles, and another right at USFS Rd 840 for 0.3 miles.

Poole Creek Campground (☑877-444-6777; USFS Rd 2610; campsites $15-20) is a popular USFS-maintained ground – the best sites are right near the lake. Only one group site is reservable.

Lemolo Lake Resort (☑541-643-0750; www.lemololakeresort.com; 2610 Birds Point Rd; hookups $28, cabins $85-250) is a casual and even funky place with a nondescript RV campsite, A-frame cabins, boat ramp, small store and a café-restaurant. Boat rentals are available, but you'll have to bring your

MT MAZAMA

The ancient mountain whose remains now form Crater Lake was Mt Mazama, a roughly 12,000ft volcanic peak that was heavily glaciered and inactive for many thousands of years until it came back to life 7700 years ago. A catastrophic explosion scattered ash for hundreds of miles as flows of superheated pumice flowed and solidified into massive banks. These eruptions emptied the magma chambers at the heart of the volcano, and the summit cone collapsed to form the caldera.

Only snowfall and rain contribute to the lake water. This purity and the lake's great depth give it that famous blue color. Sparse forests can be seen growing in pumice and ash in the Pumice Desert, just north of Crater Lake along N Entrance Rd.

own alcohol and TV. It's 5 miles off Hwy 138, up Lemolo/Birds Point Rd.

Crater Lake National Park

The gloriously still waters of Crater Lake reflect surrounding mountain peaks like a giant dark-blue mirror, making for spectacular photographs and breathtaking panoramas. **Crater Lake** (☑541-594-2211; www.nps.gov/crla; admission per vehicle $10, good for 7 days) is Oregon's only national park and also the USA's deepest lake at 1943ft deep.

You can hike and cross-country ski in the area, but most visitors just cruise the 33-mile loop **Rim Drive**, which is open from around June to mid-October and offers over 30 viewpoints as it winds around the edge of Crater Lake. A paved side road on the east side leads to amazing views from **Cloudcap Overlook**, almost 2000ft above the lake. Another nearby side road leads about 7 miles southeast to the **Pinnacles**, a valley of pumice and ash formations carved by erosion into 100ft spires called hoodoos.

The popular and steep mile-long **Cleetwood Cove Trail**, at the north end of the crater, provides the only water access at the cove. A two-hour **boat tour** (adult/child $28/18; ☺10am-3pm Jul–mid-Sep) is available, some include a brief layover at Wizard Island ($10 per person extra).

The park's popular south entrance is open year-round and provides access to Rim Village and Mazama Village, as well as the park headquarters at the Steel Visitors Center. In winter you can only go up to the lake's rim and back down the same way; no other roads are plowed. The north entrance is only open from early June to late October, depending on snowfall.

It's best to top up your gas tank before arriving at Crater Lake. There's reasonably priced gas at Mazama Village (summertime only); the closest pumps otherwise are in Prospect, Diamond Lake and Fort Klamath.

Summer is often cold and windy, so dress warmly.

Activities

For activities around Crater Lake, check out the good website www.thingstodonearcraterlake.com.

Hiking

Crater Lake has over 90 miles of hiking trails, though some higher ones aren't completely clear of snow until late July. From the east edge of the Rim Village parking lot, a 1.7-mile trail leads up 8054ft **Garfield Peak** to an expansive view of the lake; in July the slopes are covered with wildflowers. A strenuous 5-mile round-trip hike takes you to an even better lake vista atop 8929ft **Mt Scott**, the highest point in the park. For a steep but shorter hike, trek up 0.7 miles to the **Watchman**, an old lookout tower on the opposite side of the lake that boasts one of the park's best views. For flower enthusiasts, there is an easy 1-mile nature trail near the Steel Visitors Center that winds through the **Castle Crest Wildflower Garden Trail**.

Cross-Country Skiing

In winter, only the southern entrance road to Rim Village is kept plowed to provide access to several Nordic trails. Rentals are unavailable, so bring your own skis. Snowshoes are provided for free ranger-led **snowshoe walks**, which are held on weekends from Thanksgiving through March. Only experienced skiers should attempt the dangerous, avalanche-prone loop around Crater Lake, which takes three to five days and requires a backcountry permit from park headquarters.

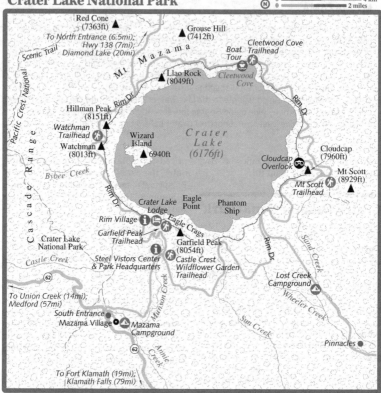

🛏 Sleeping & Eating

Other than Crater Lake Lodge (the only lodging at the lake itself) and Mazama Village (7 miles from the rim) – both of which are limited – the nearest noncamping accommodations are 20 to 40 miles away. Park lodging is closed from mid-October to late May, depending on snowfall.

Fort Klamath has several good lodgings. Union Creek and Prospect (see p324) and the Diamond Lake area (p320) all have nice, sometimes woodsy places. The drive-through towns of Chemult and Chiloquin have budget motels that are much less scenic. Finally, if you don't mind driving all day, there's lots of accommodations in Medford, Roseburg or Klamath Falls.

The park's eating facilities are limited as well, though you can always bring a picnic and find a fabulously scenic spot. Rim Village has a small café and there's an upscale dining room nearby at the lodge. Mazama Village has a small store and restaurant.

Crater Lake Lodge   LODGE $$
TOP CHOICE (📞541-594-2255, 888-774-2728; www.craterlakelodges.com; d $157-293; ☺) Open from late May to mid-October, this grand old lodge has 71 simple but comfortable rooms (no TV or telephones) – but it's the common areas that are most impressive. Large stone fireplaces, rustic leather sofas and a spectacular view of Crater Lake from the outside patio make this place special. There's a fine dining room too.

Cabins at Mazama Village   FOUR-PLEXES $$
(📞541-830-8700, 888-774-2728; www.craterlakelodges.com; d $129; ☺) These rooms are open late May to mid-October, with 40 pleasant rooms (no TV or telephones) in attractive four-plex buildings. They're 7 miles from Crater Lake, with a small grocery store and gas pump nearby.

Mazama Campground
CAMPGROUND **$**

(☑888-774-2728; www.craterlakelodges.com; Mazama Village; tent/RV sites $21/27) Located 7 miles from the lake and open approximately mid-June through September (depending on weather), this is the park's main campground. There are over 200 wooded sites, showers and a laundry; some sites are first-come, first-served.

Lost Creek Campground
CAMPGROUND **$**

(☑541-594-3100; campsites $10) Open mid-|July to mid-September, this campground is 3 miles southeast of the lake and offers just 16 tent sites. Water is available, but there are no showers. No reservations taken.

Crater Lake Lodge Dining Room
NORTHWESTERN **$$$**

(☑541-594-2255/3217; www.craterlakelodges. com/Crater-Lake-Dining-800.html; mains $27-36; ⊘7am-9pm) Crater Lake's finest dining is at the lodge, where you can feast on Northwest cuisine like blue cheese halibut and baked citrus duck. Try for a table with a lake view. Longer hours mid-June through September; dinner reservations recommended.

FORT KLAMATH & AROUND
Fort Klamath is 22 miles from Crater Lake.

Jo's Motel
MOTEL **$$**

(☑541-381-2234; www.josmotel.com; 52851 Hwy 62; tent sites/hookups $14/25, d $100-120; ⊜✳) Five well-kept and wood-paneled two-room suites with kitchens are available at this friendly motel. Bigger groups can go for the stand-alone cabins with a loft that sleep six. There are sites for campers and RV fans too, along with a tiny organic grocery store. Open February to October.

Crater Lake Resort
CABINS **$**

(☑541-381-2349; www.craterlakeresort.com; 50711 Hwy 62; d $65-100; ⊜☎) A great deal and awesome budget spot, this friendly place is just south of Fort Klamath and boasts excellent, well-maintained cabins with kitchens and decks (which overlook a creek). There are expansive grassy spots for the kids, a volleyball court and picnic tables. RV sites available ($25). Open May to October.

Crater Lake B&B
B&B **$$**

(☑866-517-9560; www.craterlakebandb.com; 52395 Weed Rd; d $129; ⊜☎) With great views of the surrounding area, this friendly B&B has three simple but comfortable rooms (each with a bathroom) that might remind

you of your parent's house. Open all year round.

Crystalwood Lodge
B&B **$$**

(☑541-381-2322, 866-381-2322; www.crystal woodlodge.com; 38625 Westside Rd; d $70-130; ⊜☎) Possibly the most dog-friendly B&B in Oregon; run by a woman who's done the Iditarod, and her sled dogs live on premises. Seven no-nonsense room and full kitchen available. Bats and swifts nest under the house eaves, making for great wildlife-watching right outside the door. It's on 130 acres; dog-washing facilities, fishing pond, hiking trails, birding and canoeing are all possible nearby. South of Fort Klamath, about 32 miles from Crater Lake.

❶ Information

Rim Visitor Center (☑541-594-3090; ⊘9:30am-4:30pm May-Sep) At Rim Village itself.

Steel Visitors Center (☑541-594-3100; ⊘9am-5pm May-Oct, 10am-4pm Nov-Apr) Three miles south of Rim Village; provides good information.

Rogue River

The Rogue is a legendary white-water river that flows from its headwaters at Crater Lake to its terminus at Gold Beach, on the Pacific Ocean – 215 miles total. A good stretch of it has been designated 'wild and scenic' (thus protected), and celebrities such as Zane Grey and Ginger Rogers have lived along its banks. The Rogue is prized for awesome steelhead and trout fishing, along with exceptional hiking, but it's also famous for world-class rafting.

For the serious adventurer, the Rogue offers everything from pulse-thumping class-IV rapids near the Wild Rogue Wilderness to more gentle waters upriver. A convenient base is the busy city of Grants Pass (p315). For those more into an afternoon float amid natural surroundings, there's the Shady Cove area (p324).

Some of the many outfitters that run the Rogue include:

High Country Expeditions (☑888-461-7238; www.hcexpeditions.com)

Orange Torpedo Trips (☑541-476-5061, 800-635-2925; www.orangetorpedo.com)

Rogue Wilderness, Inc (☑541-479-9554; 800-336-1647; www.wildrogue.com)

Sundance River Center (☑888-777-7557; www.sundanceriver.com)

WILD ROGUE WILDERNESS

Famous for its turbulent class-IV rapids, the Rogue River departs civilization at Grave Creek and winds for 40 untamed miles through a remote canyon preserved within rugged BLM land and the Wild Rogue Wilderness. This stretch is not for amateurs – a typical rafting trip here takes three to four days, and hiring an outfitter is mandatory for all but the most experienced.

Contact the BLM's **Smullin Visitors Center** (☎541-479-3735; www.blm.gov/or/resources/recreation/rogue; 14335 Galice Rd, Galice; ☺7am-3pm) for information. The center also issues rafting permits, which are required to float the Rogue without an outfitter (for details go to www.blm.gov/or/resources/recreation/rogue/about-permits.php).

The **Rogue River Trail** is a highlight of the region, and is at the west end of the Rogue River. This 40-mile track, best hiked in spring or fall, follows the rapids from Grave Creek to Illahe. Once used to transport mail and supplies from Gold Beach, the route follows a relatively easy grade through scrub oak and laurel past historic homesteads and cabins.

The full hike takes four to five days, but rustic lodges along the way can make your itinerary flexible. These include **Black Bar** (☎541-479-6507; www.blackbarlodge.net); **Marial** (☎541-474-2057); **Paradise** (☎888-667-6483; www.paradise-lodge.com); **Half Moon Bar** (☎888-291-8268; www.halfmoonbarlodge.com); and **Clay Hill** (☎503-859-3772; www.clayhilllodge.com). Rates run from $120 to $160 per person and typically include breakfast, dinner and a packed lunch; reserve ahead. Riverside camping is also a possibility; contact the Smullin Visitors Center.

A 7-mile round-trip hike to **Whiskey Creek Cabin** from Grave Creek makes a good day trip.

SHADY COVE

Although the real action is far downriver, most people find more peaceful adventures in the gentle waters north of scrappy Shady Cove – which has plenty of services. For general information visit the **McGregor Park Visitors Center** (☎541-878-3800; ☺10am-5pm Fri-Sun & holidays Memorial Day-Labor Day); it's located near the Cole M Rivers Fish Hatchery.

Raft rental options include **Raft The Rogue** (☎800-797-7238; www.rafttherogue.com; 21171 Hwy 62); **Raging Waters Raft Rental** (☎541-878-4000; www.upperrogue.org/ragingwaters; 21873 Hwy 62) and **Rogue Rafting Company** (☎888-236-3096; www.upperrogue.org/roguerafting; 7725 Rogue River Dr).

About 12 miles north of Shady Cove is **McGregor Park**, a popular raft put-in and picnic spot. Up by the dam is the large **Cole M Rivers Fish Hatchery**, where you can feed the fish for $0.25.

Area campgrounds include the expansive, well-serviced **Joseph Stewart State Park** (☎541-560-3334, 800-452-5687; www.oregonstateparks.org; tent/RV sites $17/20) and the more rustic **Rogue Elk Campground** (☎541-774-8183; campsites $18-22). For more comfort there's the decent **Royal Coachman Motel** (☎541-878-2481; www.royalcoachmanmotel.com; 21906 Hwy 62; d $53-78; ❀❋) and the much fancier **Edgewater Inn** (☎888-811-3171; www.edgewaterinns.com; 7800 Rogue River Dr; d from $105; ❋❀❂❐).

PROSPECT & UNION CREEK

Past Shady Cove, about 17 miles north, the valley walls close in, and the silvery river quickens and channels a gorge through thick lava flows. Dense forests robe the steep mountainsides, surrounding sparsely populated Prospect and Union Creek with uncrowded hiking trails, quiet camping and rustic lodging convenient to Crater Lake.

A mile south of Prospect on Mill Creek Dr is the 0.3-mile trail to **Mill Creek Falls** (173ft). A side shoot leads to the **Avenue of Giant Boulders**, where the Rogue River crashes through rocky boulders (scrambling required).

A good 4.6-mile hike (one way) starts from either the Woodruff Bridge picnic area or the River Bridge campground; you'll get views of the pretty **Takelma Gorge**. You can also hike 3.5 miles (one way) between **Natural Bridge**, where the Rogue River borrows a lava tube and goes underground for 200ft, and the magical **Rogue River Gorge**, where a narrow, turbulent section of river cuts a sheer-walled cleft into a lava flow.

Mill Creek, **River Bridge** and **Natural Bridge** campgrounds are primitive with no water (campsites $8 to $10; Natural Bridge is close to a lava tube). **Union Creek** (campsites $12) and **Farewell Bend** (campsites $16) campsites do have water. Make reservations at these two through www.roguerec.com.

For detailed camping and much more hiking information, contact the **High Cascades Ranger Station** (☎541-560-3400; www.fs.fed.us/r6/rogue-siskiyou; 47201 Hwy 62, Prospect; ☺8am-4:30pm Mon-Fri).

The grand old **Prospect Hotel** (☑541-560-3664, 800-944-6490; www.prospecthotel.com; 391 Mill Creek Dr; d $90-205; ☻❋☎) has small, charming B&B rooms (along with modern motel rooms), a wrap-around porch and a worthy dining room (open 5pm to 9pm summer only). The **Union Creek Resort** (☑866-560-3565; 56484 Hwy 62; d $59-64, cabins $90-255; ☻☎) is an old 1930s lodge with nine wood-paneled rooms (shared bathrooms outside) and a couple dozen rustic cabins that sleep two to 13 people; there's a restaurant nearby.

There are a few restaurants and other services in the town of Prospect; for a unique shopping experience check out the old gas station next to the Prospect Hotel, where local artists sell their wares (open 9am to 5pm in summer; ask at the hotel if it's closed).

Klamath Falls

POP 21,000

Sleepy is a good way to describe Klamath Falls. It has a lot of growth potential, boasting over 300 days of sunshine, affordable real estate, spectacular countryside and great recreational opportunities. But for now, it's still a small town with friendly people and an attractive downtown.

K Falls (as locals call it) is set on the shores of Lake Ewana, though the water is not visible from most of town. There are some key things to see, including the nearby Klamath Basin National Wildlife Refuge, which boasts a huge population of wintering bald eagles – along with over 350 other species of birds. Check out the surrounding high desert mountain terrain – amazing Crater Lake National Park is only 60 miles north, and there are lots of area lakes and fishing streams to explore. And for those into outdoor sports, you can boat, raft, fish and bike in summer and snowshoe or cross-country ski in winter – in other words, plenty to keep you active and busy.

☉ Sights & Activities

Downtown has quite a few old but noteworthy buildings – take a walk and discover them (the visitors center has a pamphlet). In winter there's **cross-country skiing** west on Hwy 140 at Lake of the Woods and north at Crater Lake.

Klamath County Museum   MUSEUM
(☑541-883-4208; 1451 Main St; admission $5; ☻9am-5pm Tue-Sat) Learn about the area's history at this quirky museum in the old armory. Along with natural-history dioramas and fine Native American basketry, look for the pelican figurine collection. The museum also maintains historic artifacts housed in the 1905 **Baldwin Hotel** (☑541-883-4207; 31 Main St; admission with tour $5; ☻10am-4pm Tue-Sat Jun-Aug).

Favell Museum of Western Art & Indian Artifacts   MUSEUM
(☑541-882-9996; www.favellmuseum.org; 125 W Main St; adult/child $6/3; ☻9:30am-5:30pm Mon-Sat) Here Native American tools, basketry and beadwork meet campy Western art. Over 60,000 arrowheads are on display, including one made of opal; also check out the miniature guns.

Hutch's   CYCLING
(☑541-850-2453; 808 Klamath Ave; ☻9am-6pm Mon-Sat, 11am-5pm Sun) Rents bikes and offers free bike rides in summer. Ask about the **OC&E Woods Line State Trail**, which follows a historical rail bed for 100 miles.

Adventure Center   RAFTING
(☑541-488-2819; www.raftingtours.com) Ashland-based; offers rafting trips on the Upper Klamath River.

🛏 Sleeping & Eating

Thompson's B&B   B&B $$
(☑541-882-7938; www.thompsonsbandb.com; 1420 Wild Plum Ct; d $115-125; ☻❋☎) Three miles west of center, in a residential neighborhood overlooking Upper Klamath Lake, is this comfortable B&B. The four rooms each have private bathrooms and two come with water views. It's like Grandma's house, but with great views.

Quality Inn   HOTEL $
(☑541-882-4666; www.choicehotels.com/hotel/or413; 100 Main St; d $78-98; ❋☎☒) There are fine, modern and spacious rooms at the Quality Inn that are a couple of steps up from basic budget motels. Amenities include a fitness center and heated outdoor pool. Nice, central location.

Maverick Motel   MOTEL $
(☑541-882-6688, 800-404-6690; www.maverickmotel.com; 1220 Main St; d $62-74; ❋@☎) Your typical motel. Get a room with two beds on the 2nd floor, overlooking the back street – these tend to be bigger, brighter and quieter than the ones in the front, and have peeks at faraway mountains. Ask for a discount.

Rocky Point Resort
RUSTIC RESORT $$

(☑541-356-2287; www.rockypointoregon.com; 28121 Rocky Point Rd; tent sites/hookups $22/28, d $85, cabins $140-160) Around 24 miles northwest of town is this rustic 'resort' on the shores of Upper Klamath Lake. The RV sites, rooms and cabins are in full view of each other and not the water. Still, the country-style accommodations are popular with boaters and anglers; there's a full-service marina, tackle shop, restaurant and canoes for rent. Open April through October.

Lake of the Woods Resort
RUSTIC RESORT $$

(☑541-949-8300, 866-201-4194; www.lakeofthewoodsresort.com; 950 Harriman Rte; RV sites $28-35, cabins $159-299; ☞) Located 32 miles west of Klamath Falls is this pleasant family resort with around 30 cabins. The marina rents boats; you can also rent mountain bikes in summer and snowshoes in winter. There's a restaurant, lounge and small store on premises. Two-night minimum; discount on weekdays.

Klamath Falls KOA
CAMPGROUND $

(☑541-884-4644, 800-562-9036; www.koa.com/where/or/37107; 3435 Shasta Way; tent sites $26-29, RV sites $35-42, cabins $53-57; ☞☒) This pleasant KOA is 3 miles southeast of the center. It has an outdoor pool and kids' playground. Prices are cheaper during the week.

Tobiko
JAPANESE $$

(☑541-884-7874; 618 Main St; sushi $4-13, small plates $8-14; ☺lunch & dinner Mon-Fri, dinner Sat & Sun) With a look that belongs more in a big city than small K Falls, upscale and stylish Tobiko serves up creative sushi rolls – along with chicken satay, seared ahi tuna and sake-steamed clams. Asian-influenced cocktails available.

Creamery
BREWPUB $$

(www.kbbrewing.com; 1320 Main St; mains $8-18; ☺lunch & dinner) The hippest place in town, the Creamery is a large brewpub-restaurant with all the usual favorites like burgers, pastas, salads, seafood and sandwiches. Microbrews include its decent Butt Crack Brown. There's a great back deck for sunny days.

Daily Bagel
CAFÉ $

(636 Main St; snacks under $7; ☺6am-5pm Mon-Fri, 7am-4pm Sat) This is a popular café toasting up great bagel sandwiches from Nova Scotia salmon lox to corned beef and sauerkraut to pizza toppings. Soups are also available.

ℹ Information

Discover Klamath Visitor Center (☑541-882-1501; www.discoverklamath.com; 205 Riverside Dr; ☺9am-5pm Mon-Fri, to 2pm Sat) Area information.

Klamath Falls Ranger District (☑541-883-6714; www.fs.fed.us/r6/frewin; 2819 Dahlia St; ☺8am-4:30pm Mon-Fri) For more on the local outdoors.

ℹ Getting There & Away

The **Klamath Falls airport** (☑541-883-5372) is 5 miles south of town. **BTS** (☑541-883-2877; www.basintransit.com; 1130 Adams St) provides regional bus services to surrounding cities from Monday to Saturday. **Amtrak** (☑541-884-2822; www.amtrak.com) is at Spring and Oak Sts.

Klamath Basin National Wildlife Refuges

The Klamath Basin is a broad, marshy floodplain extending from the southern base of Crater Lake into the northernmost part of California. The surrounding region

---

BALD EAGLE-WATCHING

Every November, hundreds of bald eagles travel from Canada and Alaska to winter in the Klamath Basin, feeding on the area's rich waterfowl populations. December through to February are prime viewing months, when you can spot dozens of these national symbols along the Lower Klamath Refuge and Tule Lake. To catch them flying out from their night roosts at first light, head to Bear Valley Refuge, an old-growth hillside located off Hwy 97 (turn west onto the Keno–Worden road just south of Worden, and after the railroad crossing go left onto a dirt road for half a mile; park on the shoulder).

In spring and summer you can also watch nesting bald eagles along the west side of Upper Klamath Lake and at Klamath Marsh National Wildlife Refuge. For more on bird life in the area, see www.klamathbirdingtrails.com.

offers some of the finest bird-watching in the West: six wildlife refuges, totaling more than 300 sq miles, support concentrations of over a million birds.

In the **Upper Klamath Refuge**, tule rushes fill the northwestern shore of shallow, marshy Upper Klamath Lake. Here there's shelter for colonies of cormorants, egrets, herons, cranes, pelicans and many varieties of ducks and geese. A 9.5-mile **canoe trail** starts at Rocky Point Resort (p326), 24 miles northwest of Klamath Falls off Hwy 140.

West of Worden, down near the border, **Bear Valley Refuge** is known mostly as a wintering area for bald eagles; 500 to 1000 gather here between December and March.

The **Lower Klamath Refuge** lies mostly in California. This mix of open water, shallow marsh, cropland and grassy upland offers the best year-round viewing and great access for motorists: a 10-mile **auto tour** begins off Hwy 161 (State Line Rd). Get information beforehand in Klamath Falls or at the **Refuge Headquarters** (☎530-667-2231; www.fws.gov/klamathbasinrefuges; 4009 Hill Rd) in Tulelake, California.

If you're in the area on President's Day weekend in mid-February, check out the four-day **Winter Wings Festival** (www.winterwingsfest.org), which draws together birdlovers of all kinds for lectures, workshops, field trips and wildlife art at the Oregon Institute of Technology in Klamath Falls.

Eastern Oregon

Why Go?

Eastern Oregon will amaze you. While much of it is extensive farmlands and desert plateaus, there are also stunners such as the gorgeous snowy peaks of the Wallowa Mountains. Or Hells Canyon, which dips deeper than even the Grand Canyon. Or the John Day Fossil Beds, with its eerily colorful hills and amazing rock formations. Or the truly incredible glacier-carved valleys of the Steens Mountain range.

This slice of Oregon was also the last arduous passage that the pioneers had to traverse on their journey west; in some places you can still see where their wagon ruts carved out the Oregon Trail. Gold was discovered in the region in the 1860s – making and breaking dozens of towns and cities – while there's also rich Native American history.

With a rodeo in every town and the Old West still palpable in spots, visiting Eastern Oregon is like going back in time – but forget the covered wagons and bring the digital camera instead.

Best Places to Eat

» Vali's Alpine Restaurant (p337)

» Terminal Gravity Brewing (p335)

» Meat Hook (p346)

» Snaffle Bit (p342)

» Nells-N-Out (p333)

Best Places to Stay

» Hot Lake Springs (p333)

» Geiser Grand Hotel (p341)

» Bronze Antler B&B (p336)

When to Go
Pendleton

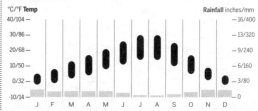

July–October	Spring or Fall	November–March
Drive the stunning Steens Mountain Loop or go hiking in the high Wallowas	Avoid the high-summer heat, and yell 'giddyup' at Pendleton's Round-Up	Colder weather makes hot springs that much more decadent

Pendleton

POP 17,500

Eastern Oregon's largest city, 'wild and woolly' Pendleton is a handsome old town famous for its wool shirts and big-name rodeo. It has managed to retain a glint of its old-time atmosphere and cow-poking past, and nestles between steep hills along the Umatilla River. All around are farms and ranchlands, though in the last few years at least one small boutique winery has popped up as a sign of the times, along with a million-dollar steakhouse complex. With its art galleries, antique shops and new businesses, Pendleton has become one of Eastern Oregon's most popular destinations.

Held in mid-September, the rowdy **Pendleton Round-Up** (☑800-457-6336; 1205 SW Court Ave), called 'the USA's best rodeo,' is an all-out Dionysian celebration featuring cowboy breakfasts, dances, bull riding and an Indian Pageant. There's also a big-name music concert. Reserve tickets and lodging way in advance.

◉ Sights & Activities

The paved River Parkway, located atop an old levee, follows the Umatilla for 2.5 miles and provides good recreational opportunities for residents and visitors alike.

Pendleton Woolen Mills   MILL
(☑541-276-6911; www.pendleton-usa.com; 1307 SE Court Pl; ☉8am-6pm Mon-Sat, 9am-5pm Sun) World-famous Pendleton Woolen Mills has been weaving blankets for more than 100 years, and is especially known for Native American designs. Free, short factory tours are given at 9am, 11am, 1:30pm and 3pm Monday to Friday year-round.

Pendleton Underground Tours   TOUR
(☑541-276-0730, 800-226-6398; www.pendletonundergroundtours.org; 37 SW Emigrant Ave; adult/senior $15/10) At the end of the 19th century, a shady network of businesses boomed beneath Pendleton's storefronts, driven underground by prohibition and social tensions. Saloons, Chinese laundries, opium dens, card rooms and other questionable businesses found cozy tunnels in which to operate. Pendleton Underground Tours lets you explore the town's infamous underground past, as well as an above-ground early-1900s brothel. Tours last 1½ hours; reserve ahead. Children under six are not allowed.

Museums

The worthwhile **Umatilla County Historical Museum** (☑541-276-0012; www.heritagestationmuseum.org; 108 SW Frazer Ave; adult/family $6/15; ☉10am-4pm Tue-Sat) is in Pendleton's old railroad station. There are pioneer exhibits and Native American artifacts; check out the caboose and one-room schoolhouse.

Witness Oregon's past from a Native American perspective at the spacious **Tamástslikt Cultural Institute** (☑541-996-9748; www.tamastslikt.org; 72789 Hwy 331; adult/child $8/6; ☉9am-5pm, closed Sun Nov-Mar), east of Pendleton off I-84 exit 216. State-of-the-art exhibits weave voices, memories and artifacts through an evolving history of the region.

If you miss the Pendleton Round-Up, visit the **Round-Up Hall of Fame** (☑541-278-0815; 1114 SW Court Ave; adult/child $5/4; ☉10am-4pm Mon-Sat). Here you can see the excitement of past round-ups via photographs and other memorabilia.

Children's Activities

Kids and their parents should make a beeline to the **Children's Museum of Eastern Oregon** (☑541-276-1066; www.cmeo.org; 400 S Main St; admission $3; ☉10am-5pm Tue-Sat; 🚼). It's more like a day center, boasting an art room, playground and classes. And if it's hot, head to the **Pendleton Family Aquatic Center** (☑541-276-0104; 1901 NW Carden Ave; adult/child $4/3; ☉noon-8pm early Jun-early Sep; 🚼), which features an Olympic-size pool and water slides.

🛏 Sleeping

There are several chain motels and hotels off I-84 and on Dorion Ave.

Rugged Country Lodge   MOTEL $
(☑541-966-6800, 877-778-4433; www.ruggedcountrylodge.com; 1807 SE Court Ave; d from $82; ☺❄🛜) Out-of-the-ordinary motel featuring tasteful, renovated rooms with personal touches such as down pillows and lavender sprigs on the bed. Surrounded by pretty planted strips. A good breakfast and homemade cookies are included.

Working Girls Old Hotel   HOTEL $
(☑541-276-0730; www.pendletonundergroundtours.org; 21 SW Emigrant Ave; d $75-95; ☺❄) Run by Pendleton Underground Tours, this one-time bordello offers four pretty, antique-filled rooms in Victorian style, along with one three-room suite. There's a kitchen

Eastern Oregon Highlights

1 Whoop it up at the **Pendleton Round-Up** (p329), an awesome rodeo

2 Find scenic heaven at **Hells Canyon** (p338), North America's deepest river gorge

3 Trek in the **Eagle Cap Wilderness** (p338), with or without a llama to help

4 Ooh and Ahh at the fantastic colors and rock formations of **John Day Fossil Beds** (p344)

5 Be amazed by the glacier-scoured valleys in the majestic **Steens Mountain region** (p349)

6 Cruise the amazing rock formations at **Succor Creek** and **Leslie Gulch** (p347)

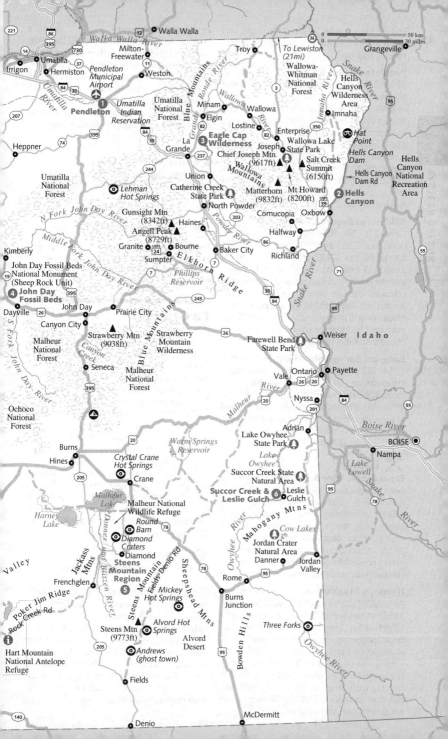

and dining room for all guests to share, and the downtown location is convenient. Reservations required.

Pendleton House B&B
B&B $$

(☑541-276-8581, 800-700-8581; www.pendleton housebnb.com; 311 N Main St; d $100-140; ☻❋☎) Near downtown is this pink 1917 Italian Renaissance mansion with its original furniture, wallpaper and even drapes. The home's details are amazing, and there's a relaxing front covered patio with wicker furniture. Be prepared to get to know your neighbors, however – the five beautiful rooms (two with half-baths) share just one full bathroom. A friendly dog lives here.

Wild Horse Resort & Casino
CAMPGROUND $

(☑541-278-2274, 800-654-9453; www.wildhorse resort.com; 72777 Hwy 331; tent sites/teepees $15/19, RV sites $24-32; ❋) There's plenty of grass and little shade, but this tidy campground is only 5 miles east of Pendleton and offers an outdoor heated pool and Jacuzzi. Even if you don't gamble, the free continental breakfast will draw you into the casino. Bring your own bedding for the teepees. Rates are cheaper Monday through Thursday.

Emigrant Springs State Park
CAMPGROUND $

(☑541-983-2277, 800-452-5687; www.oregon stateparks.org; I-84 exit 234; tent/RV sites $17/20, cabins $24-39) Located 26 miles east of Pendleton, this is a pleasant woodsy campground at some elevation, so it stays cool in summer. There's freeway noise, but quieter cabins are available (bring bedding).

✗ Eating

Great Pacific Wine & Coffee Co
AMERICAN $

(www.greatpacific.biz; 403 S Main St; drinks $1.50-4, mains $6-9; ☺10am-9pm Mon-Sat) This atmospheric coffee shop serves up hot and cold sandwiches, salads, baked stuffed croissants and gourmet Naples-style pizzas. There's plenty of java choices, wine by the glass and even microbrews on tap. Live bluegrass music livens the scene on Saturday nights.

Hamley's Steakhouse
AMERICAN $$

(☑541-278-1100; www.thehamleysteakhouse.com; 8 SE Court Ave; mains $10-34; ☺5-9pm Sun-Thu, till 10pm Fri & Sat) This 150-seat steakhouse has been gorgeously done up with wood floors, stone accents and tin ceilings. There's a bar with sports on TV (open later) and the men's bathroom has 'interesting' art work. Food is decent, with large portions. Hamley's empire also includes a first-rate Western shop, art gallery, café and wine cellar.

Prodigal Son Brewery
BREWPUB $

(www.prodigalsonbrewery.com; 230 SE Court Ave; mains $6-11; ☺11am-11pm Mon-Sat, noon-9pm Sun) Pendleton's newest and only brewery-pub is still wobbly on its feet, with a limited beer selection that includes a wheatstock Hefewiezen, a robust porter and two IPAs. A limited and average-quality pub menu offers appetizers, fish 'n chips, a couple of sandwiches and a burger.

❶ Information

Pendleton Chamber of Commerce (☑541-276-7411, 800-547-8911; www.pendleton chamber.com; 501 S Main St; ☺8:30am-5pm Mon-Thu, 10am-5pm Fri, 9:30am-3pm Sat)

❶ Getting There & Around

Pendleton Municipal Airport is 5 miles west of town on US 30. There are Greyhound bus services from the **Double J Drive Thru** (☑541-966-6675; 801 SE Court Ave).

La Grande

POP 13,000

Early French traders, upon seeing the broad, seemingly circular valley, declared it to be La Grande Ronde, or 'the Big Circle.' Indeed, from the historical marker on US 30 above town, it does seem as if the mountain peaks form a giant ring around the valley.

The Oregon Trail crossed this valley, and the pioneers rested here in preparation for traversing the challenging Blue Mountains. Some saw the valley's agricultural potential and its pretty Grande Ronde River, and decided to settle down instead. Today La Grande is home to Eastern Oregon University and provides services to the region; it also offers a surprising wealth of outdoor recreation, though the city itself isn't all that memorable.

◉ Sights

Oregon Trail Interpretive Center
OUTDOORS CENTER

(☑541-963-7186; I-84 exit 248; $5 Northwest Forest Pass required for parking; ☺8am-8pm Memorial Day-Labor Day) This center gives a visceral feeling of what travel was like for Oregon Trail pioneers crossing the Blue Mountains. Paths wind through the forest to ruts left by pioneer wagons – still visible after 150 years. The center is 13 miles west of La Grande and 3 miles on well-marked roads from the freeway exit.

🏃 Activities

Catherine Creek State Park HIKING
(☑800-551-6949; Hwy 203) There's good hiking at this park, about 23 miles southeast of La Grande. You can access the Eagle Cap Wilderness from a trail here, and there are mountaintop views from another hike nearby.

Fishing FISHING
Try fishing on the Grande Ronde for rainbow trout – test your luck near Starkey, off Forest Rd 51 about 20 miles from La Grande. Fly-fishing for steelhead is popular in spring and fall near the little community of Troy. Contact the **Fish & Wildlife Office** (☑541-963-2138; 107 20th St) in La Grande for current regulations and information.

TRT Raft & Rentals RAFTING
(☑541-437-9270; 1610 Alder St) Float beautiful, remote stretches of the Grande Ronde from Minam to Troy by renting rafts at this outfitters in Elgin; it also offers a shuttle service. Mountain biking is good in the area, though you'll have to bring your own bike.

Spout Springs Ski Resort SKIING
(☑541-566-0320; www.spoutspringsskiresort. com; 79327 Hwy 204; lift tickets $30) A small, low-key ski resort. There are several miles of groomed cross-country ski trails. For another nearby ski area, see Anthony Lakes (p341).

🛏 Sleeping

La Grande has a decided lack of interesting lodging in town, but there are a couple of places within a dozen miles that are atmospheric.

TOP CHOICE Hot Lake Springs HOTEL $$
(☑541-963-4685; www.hotlakesprings. com; 66172 Hwy 203; d $150-350; ❀❈☎) Eight miles southeast of La Grande is this grand new hotel, opened in 2010 after more than six years of restoration. It's in a historic old building that was once a hospital and is now not only a hotel, but a spa, restaurant, museum, art gallery and bronze foundry. There are 22 big, beautiful suites, each with its own theme, and breakfast is included. Foundry tours are available.

Union Hotel HOTEL $
(☑541-562-6135; www.theunionhotel.com; 326 N Main St; d $65-119; ❀❈) Eleven miles southeast of La Grande, in the town of Union, is this atmospheric, historic hotel. All 16 rooms are decorated individually and none have TVs or telephones, though three come

with kitchenette (there are common rooms with a TV and library, however). If you want to get away from it all, this is a good place to do it. One room with outside bath is $45.

Orchard Motel MOTEL $
(☑541-963-6160; www.orchard-motel.com; 2206 Adams Ave; d $39-49; ❀❈☎) Of the cluster of motels east of downtown, this is one of the nicer ones. Most of the 10 cozy, homey rooms come with microwave, coffeemaker and fridge.

Catherine Creek State Park CAMPGROUND $
(☑800-551-6949; Hwy 203; campsites $9) Some 23 miles southeast of La Grande, past the town of Union, this beautiful state-park campground has a clear fishing creek, though campsites are primitive.

Hilgard Junction State Park CAMPGROUND $
(☑800-551-6949; I-84 exit 252; campsites $9) Only 8 miles west of La Grande, this lovely riverside park is convenient but gets highway noise. Campsites are primitive; boat launch available.

🍴 Eating

Nells-N-Out AMERICAN $
(1704 Adams Ave; mains $3-8; ☺11am-11pm) Long-running drive-thru burger joint likely offering Eastern Oregon's best fast food (don't miss the curly fries). The milkshakes are legendary, and there are plenty of other fountain drinks to choose from. A few shady picnic tables are good for leg-stretching.

Ten Depot Street AMERICAN $$
(☑541-963-8766; www.tendepotstreet.com; 10 Depot St; mains $11-25; ☺5-10pm Mon-Sat) This longtime local favorite offers something for everyone, including a few surprises such as the Thai salad and emu burger. Classy old atmosphere, with a good selection of microbrews available. On Tuesday and Thursday there's live music.

Mt Emily Ale House BREWPUB $$
(www.mtemilyalehouse.com; 1202 Adams Ave; mains $8-15; ☺11:30am-close Tue-Fri, 4:30pm-close Sat) Attractive brewery-restaurant serving a decent variety of burgers, salads, gourmet pizzas and – of course – craft ales. Beer samplers (five tastes) are available if you can't decide; live music on Saturday.

Foley Station AMERICAN $$
(☑541-963-7473; www.foleystation.com; 1114 Adams Ave; mains $14-32; ☺11am-9pm Mon-Fri,

ALL ABOARD!

Railroad buffs and scenery lovers shouldn't miss the **Eagle Cap Excursion Train** (☏541-963-9000; www.eaglecaptrain.com), a slow-moving, nostalgic train ride that follows the Grande Rhone and Wallowa Rivers through rugged canyons and pleasant scenery. If you're lucky, you'll spot a Rocky Mountain elk or black bear, but you're much more likely to see bald eagles. And cows, of course – sometimes traipsing right on the tracks!

Connecting Elgin with Joseph, the Wallowa Union Railroad runs for 63 miles, mostly on Saturday from June to October. The 3½-hour trip runs $75 for adults, less for seniors and kids. And every once in a while, the train gets 'robbed' – with play money handed over – or a historian or wildlife biologist will make a special appearance. But even if you just experience the train ride by itself, it's sure to be memorable.

3-9pm Sat, 9am-9pm Sun) For brunch there's bacon waffles, for lunch get beer-battered cod or Cajun chicken linguini, and for dinner go for one of 10 kinds of steak. There are some creative, exotic touches to the menus here, along with classic old standbys. Lunch specials $6.

ℹ Information

Chamber of Commerce (☏541-963-8588, 800-848-9969; www.visitlagrande.com; 102 Elm St; ⏰9am-5pm Mon-Fri, till 3pm Sat)

ℹ Getting There & Away

Greyhound bus depot (☏541-963-5165; 2204 East Penn Ave) Bus services.

NEO Transit (☏541-426-3840; www.neotransit.org) Bus services between Joseph, Enterprise and La Grande.

Enterprise

POP 2000

Enterprise is a small, friendly place that's less expensive and pretentious than its nearby sister town of Joseph, just 6 miles away. However, it shares with Joseph an attraction for artists, as well as an exceptional location surrounded by grassy meadows, pine forests and the stunning Wallowa Mountains. Some of Enterprise's original buildings are still intact and there's a good selection of traveler's services, making it an ideal base for exploring northeastern Oregon – such as Hells Canyon and, of course, the Wallowas.

In September, Enterprise is host to **Hells Canyon Mule Days** (www.hellscanyonmuledays.com), a three-day event featuring a parade, quilt show, cowboy poetry and barrel racing.

🛏 Sleeping

Note that during certain events (especially Chief Joseph Days, held the last full weekend in July) prices tend to rise for area accommodations, which also become scarce.

Enterprise House B&B   B&B $$
(☏541-426-4238; www.enterprisehousebnb.com; 508 S 1st St; d $120-185; ⊖※📶) Enterprise's most majestic place to stay is this 1910 colonial revival mansion with wraparound porch and fancy wine cellar. The five antique-filled rooms are all lovely, and the common areas are elegant. Your hosts Jack and Judy are friendly and helpful too.

Barking Mad Farm   B&B $$
(☏541-215-2758; www.barkingmadfarm.com; 65156 Powers Rd; d $135-195) This countryside B&B has just three large, comfortable rooms, two with great mountain views and one with private deck. There's a wonderful front porch, plus shady backyard areas in which to hang out. Located a mile down Powers Rd, just before entering Enterprise from the west.

Ponderosa Motel   MOTEL $
(☏541-426-3186; www.ponderosamotel.hotels.officelive.com; 102 E Greenwood St; d $70-80; ⊖※📶) Right in downtown is this well-run motel with attractive wood-and-stone facade. The excellent rooms are clean and comfortable, and each has its own fridge, microwave and coffeemaker.

Wilderness Inn   MOTEL $
(☏541-426-4535; www.wildernessinn.hotels.officelive.com; 301 W North St; d $70-80; ※📶) A good budget choice, this basic motel has spacious rooms and a few amenities. Rooms out the back have two beds and offer more peace as well as mountain views

(from higher floors), though they'll cost a bit more. Sauna available.

Mountain View Motel & RV Park

MOTEL, CAMPGROUND **$**

(☑541-432-2982, 866-262-9891; www.rvmotel. com; 83450 Joseph Hwy; tent/RV sites $22/27, r $70-95; ❀❅❋) Located 3 miles from Enterprise on the way to Joseph is this fine spot with campsites, RV hookups and nice rooms (that sleep up to five) with kitchens. Political neutrality with the owner is best.

 Eating

TOP CHOICE **Terminal Gravity Brewing**

BREWPUB **$**

(www.terminalgravitybrewing.com; 803 School St; mains $7-11; ⊙11am-9pm Sun-Tue, till 10pm Wed-Sat) One of Oregon's best breweries is right here in town. There's limited inside seating, but on a warm summer evening you want to be outside on the front lawn with a tasty IPA and buffalo burger anyway. Pastas, salads and sandwiches dominate the menu.

El Bajio

MEXICAN **$**

(100 W North St; mains $8-12; ⊙11am-10pm) Some say El Bajio serves the tastiest and best-value Mexican food in town. Don't be put off by the building's facade, however; it's nicer inside, and friendly.

Cloud 9 Bakery & Café

CAFÉ **$**

(105 SE 1st St; mains $5-8; ⊙6:30am-4pm Mon-Fri) Popular for breakfast and lunch (they don't do dinner) is this downtown café serving bagels, salads, sandwiches and a few Mexican treats. They'll fix sandwiches to go for hikers.

ℹ️ **Information**

Chamber of Commerce (☑541-426-4622, 800-585-4121; www.wallowacountrychamber. com; 115 Tejaka Lane; ⊙8am-noon, 1-5pm Mon-Fri) Information; off Hwy 82. The forest service visitors center was temporarily located here in 2010, but will likely move to more permanent headquarters.

ℹ️ **Getting There & Around**

NEO Transit (☑541-426-3840; www.neotran sit.org) Buses between Joseph, Enterprise and La Grande.

Joseph

POP 1200

If ever there was a trendy Eastern Oregon town, it's Joseph. You can see its wealth right on the brick sidewalks, where well-groomed planter boxes and huge bronze statues sit proudly on every downtown corner. Many of the old storefronts are now glitzy boutiques, peddling everything from nature photos to huge, expensive bronzes. There seem to be more galleries than anything else, and Valley Bronze – one of the nation's largest foundries – anchors the artistic heart of this old frontier town.

Even while Joseph feels more like Santa Fe than your typical backcountry Western town, it has just enough boots-and-jeans street life to keep it from seeming completely fake. And simply heading a few blocks out of downtown brings you back into beautiful countryside – just a mile south is Wallowa Lake, a glacial basin flanked by gorgeous towering peaks. Joseph is also a good base for exploring the region's many other recreational highlights; there's even a tiny ski resort, Ferguson Ridge, about 8 miles away.

Chief Joseph Days (www.chiefjosephdays. com), held the last full weekend of July, features a rodeo, Native American dancing and cowboy breakfasts. And if you're here in mid-August, don't miss the **Bronze Blues & Brews Festival** (www.bronzeblues brews.com), which sees good jazz, microbrews and bronze sculptures on display.

NEO Transit (☑541-426-3840; www.neotran sit.org) has bus services between Joseph, Enterprise and La Grande.

◉ **Sights & Activities**

Joseph is most noted for its cast-bronze sculpture, thanks in part to **Valley Bronze** (☑541-432-7445; www.valleybronze.com; 18 S Main St). Foundry tours are $15 per person.

The **Wallowa County Museum** (☑541-432-6095; 110 S Main St; adult/child $2.50/free; ⊙10am-5pm Memorial Day-late Sep), housed in an 1888 bank building, is notable for its displays on local pioneer and Nez Perce histories; check out the 'ladies jail' out the back.

Out of town, the Wallowa-Whitman National Forest and the Hells Canyon National Recreation Area are laced with mountain biking trails, including the pretty, 10-mile Wagon Loop Rd. When snow falls, the area is good for cross-country skiing.

🛏️ **Sleeping**

Accommodations in Joseph are expensive; Enterprise (6 miles north) has budget choices. Reserve ahead in summer, especially during festivals.

TOP CHOICE Bronze Antler B&B
B&B $$

(☎541-432-0230, 866-520-9769; www.bronzeantler.com; 309 S Main St; d $129-250; ❁❋☎) This restored Craftsman home offers three elegant rooms, each with private bathroom, plus one luxurious suite with steam shower and jets in the tub. There's also a bocce court in the yard, and your friendly hosts know the area well. A cat roams the premises.

Belle Pepper's B&B
B&B $$

(☎541-432-0490, 866-432-0490; www.bellepeppersbnb.com; 101 S Mill St; d $95-150; ❁❋☎) Off the main street and on an acre of grounds is this colonial-style, no-nonsense B&B that embraces green practices such as recycled building materials, composting, low-flow faucets and local products. There are three comfy rooms (all with private bath) and a nice garden with goats and chickens out back.

Chandler's Inn
B&B $$

(☎541-432-9765; www.josephbedandbreakfast.com; 700 S Main St; d $85-160; ❁❋☎) With more of a lodge feel than a typical B&B, this homely and casual spot offers a variety of rooms, including a couple of two-bedroom suites and a small cabin. Breakfast is country-style, and your hosts are an American-English couple.

Indian Lodge Motel
MOTEL $

(☎541-432-2651; www.indianlodgemotel.com; 201 S Main St; d $90-100; ❁❋☎) This is Joseph's only motel, with 16 neat plain rooms and a great downtown location. Off-site cottages ($109 to $185) also available. Reserve well in advance.

Hurricane Creek Campground
CAMPGROUND $

(Mile 7, Hurricane Creek Rd; campsites $6) In summer the action is at Wallowa Lake, but campers seeking peace should try this primitive but beautiful campground about 7 miles south of Enterprise. Bring water or a filter.

✖ Eating

If you like vodka, check out the tasting room of family-run **Stein Distillery**, next door to Mutiny Brewing; they make handcrafted spirits, including fruit cordials.

Caldera's
AMERICAN $$

(☎541-432-0585; www.calderasofjoseph.com; 300 N Lake St; mains $11-27; ☺10am-9pm Wed-Mon) This small but interesting restaurant

is gorgeously decorated in an art-nouveau style. Salads and meat dishes dominate the dinner menu; lunch is more limited but also more affordable. Don't miss the stunning glass-tiled bathrooms.

Embers Brewhouse
BREWPUB $$

(206 N Main St; mains $8-15; ☺11am-9pm) Pizza, sandwiches, salads and microbrews all go down easy in this relaxed pub. On summer evenings the place to be is on the front deck, with people-watching opportunities and views of the Wallowas.

Mutiny Brewing Company
BREWPUB $$

(www.mutinybrewing.blogspot.com; 600 N Main St; mains $8-16; ☺11am-9pm Tue-Thu, till 10pm Fri, 8am-10pm Sat & Sun) Joseph's newest brewery is a casual place with pleasant front garden tables, excellent on warm days. The lunch menu's highlights are burgers, while dinner means fancier offerings such as bacon-wrapped scallops.

Wallowa Mountains

Rising precipitously from the flatlands in Oregon's far northeastern corner, the Wallowas have 19 peaks over 9000ft. Ice Age glaciers carved sharp crags and deep canyons into the mountains, and the moraines of one such glacier now impound Wallowa Lake. Much of the high country, including the only remaining glacier (Alpine Glacier) and Eastern Oregon's highest peak (the 9838ft Sacajawea), is part of Eagle Cap Wilderness Area, a 715-sq-mile natural area studded with alpine meadows and lakes.

Trails, campgrounds and fishing holes are popular during the high season. In particular, the lovely state park at Wallowa Lake takes on a carnival atmosphere on summer weekends. Some secondary roads over the Wallowa Mountains are closed between November and May, so check ahead.

WALLOWA LAKE

Located 6 miles from Joseph, Wallowa Lake was formed when glaciers plowed down out of the Wallowas, pushing huge piles of displaced rock. These rock moraines eventually stopped the progress of the glacier, which melted, creating a lake basin. Today the lake is surrounded by dramatic peaks, including the 9617ft Chief Joseph Mountain. Speaking of Chief Joseph, his gravesite is located near the north shore of Wallowa Lake, just a mile south of Joseph and right on the highway.

JOSEPH TO HALFWAY – OR BUST

From Joseph, paved USFS Rd 39 skirts the eastern Wallowas and heads south to Hwy 86, just east of Halfway. Part of the Hells Canyon Scenic Byway, this drive links the northern and southern halves of the Wallowas. It also provides access to Hells Canyon Overlook, 3 miles off USFS Rd 39 on USFS Rd 3965, the only canyon viewpoint you can drive to over a paved surface.

It's 73 miles between Joseph and Halfway along this route. USFS Rd 39 is usually closed November to May (though it's groomed for snowmobiles and cross-country skiing). There are trailheads and campsites along the way, but no gas stations or other services.

This road was closed in 2010 due to severe flood damage; check to see if it's been repaired.

Pretty **Wallowa Lake State Park** (☎541-432-4185; 72214 Marina Lane) is the center of activities at the lake's south end. A swimming beach and a boat launch bustle madly in summer, and you can rent a variety of boats at the marina here, along with fishing gear (www.wallowalakemarina.com). The best hiking is from the end of Wallowa Lake Rd.

The **Wallowa Lake Tramway** (☎541-432-5331; www.wallowalaketramway.com; 59919 Wallowa Lake Hwy; adult/child $24/15; ☉10am-5pm late May-Sep) leaves from Wallowa Lake and climbs 3700ft to the top of 8150ft Mt Howard. The 15-minute ride is thrilling enough, but the real rewards are the easy alpine hikes around Mt Howard's summit, with views onto Hells Canyon, the Wallowas and Idaho's Seven Devils. A restaurant serves food at the summit.

🛏 Sleeping & Eating

Reserve in summer.

Flying Arrow Resort   CABINS $$
(☎541-432-2951; www.flyingarrowresort.com; 59782 Wallowa Lake Hwy; cabins $90-450; ☺❈🛜▦) This friendly resort is awesome, boasting 36 spacious cabins of all sizes, each with its own kitchen and many with a deck overlooking the Wallowa River. One six-bedroom lodge that sleeps 14 is available.

Wallowa Lake Lodge   LODGE $$
(☎541-432-9821; www.wallowalake.com; 60060 Wallowa Lake Hwy; d $99-180, cabins $160-255; ☺) This 1923 lodge, on the shores of the lake, has both charming lodge rooms and rustic but comfortable lakeside cabins. Two-bedroom units are available. There's a great stone fireplace in the lobby, and a restaurant on the premises.

Eagle Cap Chalets   CABINS/ROOMS $$
(☎541-432-4704; www.eaglecapchalets.com; 59879 Wallowa Lake Hwy; RV sites $29, d $75-100, cabins $75-150; ☺❈▦) Choose from simple and unpretentious motel rooms, cabins or condos. RV sites are also available. There's a mini-golf course for the kids, and an indoor pool and spa for everyone.

Wallowa Lake State Park   CAMPGROUND $
(☎541-432-4185, 800-452-5687; 72214 Marina Lane; tent/RV sites $20/25, yurts $38) This popular lakeside state park offers more than 200 campsites, along with two yurts. Flush toilets and showers are available.

🔝 **Vali's Alpine Restaurant** HUNGARIAN $$
CHOICE (☎541-432-5691; 59811 Wallowa Lake Hwy; mains $11-15; ☉5pm & 7pm seatings Wed-Sun Memorial Day-Labor Day, Sat & Sun only rest of year) Hungarian specialties such as cabbage rolls, chicken paprika, beef kabobs and schnitzel are all excellent here, though dishes change daily. Do not miss dessert. Credit cards are not accepted, and reservations are required.

Wallowa Lake Lodge Dining Room
                                        AMERICAN $$
(☎541-432-9821; www.wallowalakelodge.com/menu.htm; 60060 Wallowa Lake Hwy; mains $19-28; ☉7:30-11am & 5:30-8pm Fri-Tue) This old-fashioned dining room serves up fancy dishes such as rib-eye steak, baked trout and Mediterranean pasta. For breakfast ($7 to $10) there are hazelnut pancakes, blintzes and biscuits with gravy.

EAGLE CAP WILDERNESS

Glacier-ripped valleys, high mountain lakes and marble peaks are some of the rewards that long-distance hikers find on overnight treks into the beautiful Eagle

Cap Wilderness, nicknamed 'America's Little Switzerland.'

A major trailhead starts at the south end of Wallowa Lake Rd. One popular trail is the 6-mile one-way jaunt to the gorgeous Aneroid Lake, where you can camp; hike 2½ miles further to reach Tenderfoot Pass. A longer trek is the West Fork Trail, which follows the Wallowa River to the Lakes Basin area (9 miles one way). From the upper Lostine Valley, or from USFS Rd 39's Sheep Creek Summit, there's easier day-hike access to the Eagle Cap's high country.

For easier, organized hiking, consider using horses or llamas to help out. **Eagle Cap Wilderness Pack Station** (541-432-4145; www.eaglecapwildernesspackstation.com; 59761 Wallowa Lake Hwy) offers a variety of horseback trips, from hour-long rides to extended pack tours. For llama excursions, contact **Wallowa Llamas** (541-742-2961; www.wallowallamas.com; 36678 Allstead Lane, Halfway). It runs multiday trips in the region.

Go skiing in the backcountry with **Wing Ridge Ski Tours** (800-646-9050; www.wingski.com; 65113 Hurricane Creek Rd, Enterprise). It supplies guides and hut stays, though you'll need to bring your own food.

Hells Canyon

Over its 13-million-year life span, the Snake River, which neatly straddles the border between Oregon and Idaho, has carved out the deepest river gorge in North America – yes, at 8000ft from highest peak to river, it's deeper even than the Grand Canyon (though not nearly as dramatic). The river originates in Yellowstone National Park and ends at the Columbia River near Pasco, Washington – running more than 1000 miles in total.

The prehistoric people who dwelled along Hells Canyon left pictographs, petroglyphs and pit dwellings. The Shoshone and Nez Perce tribes battled for dominance along this stretch of the Snake, with the Nez Perce winning out.

Relics of the mining era, from the 1860s to the 1920s, are also found throughout the canyon, and tumbledown shacks remain from the unlikely settlement attempts of turn-of-the-century homesteaders.

◉ Sights

Hat Point   VIEWPOINT
High above the Snake River, the Hat Point fire lookout tower (elevation 6982ft) offers

great views. On each side of the canyon, mountains soar toward 10,000ft, with the Seven Devils on the Idaho side and the towering Wallowas on the Oregon side.

From Hat Point, a hiking trail edges off the side of the canyon. It's a steep 2 miles to another vista from the top of the river cliffs, then another 4 miles down to the river itself.

To reach Hat Point from Joseph, follow Hwy 350 about 30 miles to the little hamlet of Imnaha. From here, a gravel road climbs up the Imnaha River canyon to Hat Point. Allow about 1½ hours each way for the 24-mile drive from Imnaha to Hat Point; you'll be stopping for photos along the way. The road is generally open from June until October.

There are no services at Hat Point.

Imnaha River Valley   VALLEY
Just west of Hells Canyon, the Imnaha River digs a parallel canyon that offers pastoral scenery in addition to astounding cliff faces.

The gravel Imnaha River Rd follows this narrow valley between Imnaha and the junction of USFS Rd 39 for about 40 miles. The northern end is very dramatic, as the river cuts more and more deeply through stair-stepped lava formations. The southern end is bucolic, with meadows and old farmhouses flanking the river.

North of Imnaha, a gravel road continues for 20 miles to Cow Creek Bridge, where the Imnaha River Trail begins (4.5 miles one way). Two miles beyond the bridge is the start of the Nee-Me-Poo Trail (which traces the path of Chief Joseph and the Nez Perce); it climbs 3.5 miles to a viewpoint over the Snake River. The road ends 5 miles later at Dug Bar, where the 56-mile (one way) Snake River Trail begins.

Hells Canyon Dam   CANYON
Hells Canyon's most spectacular scenery is perhaps along the Snake River itself, following 25 miles of paved road (Idaho's Rte 454) towards Hells Canyon Dam; here dramatic canyon walls loom almost vertically. The road goes up the Idaho border but is accessed via the southern end of the Wallowa Mountain Loop, near Oxbow (previously known as Copperfield, in Oregon). Just past the dam the road ends at the **Hells Canyon Visitors Center** (541-785-3395; ⊗8am-4pm summer) and boat launch. Miles beyond here, the Snake drops 1300ft in elevation through wild scenery and equally wild rapids, and the area can only be accessed via jet boat or raft.

There's also a gravel road that goes up the Snake River on the Oregon side, but it stops short of the dam. It accesses Bureau of Land Management (BLM) land, and some trailheads and rustic campgrounds. There's no bridge linking this gravel road to Rte 454 over the Snake.

Hells Canyon Adventures (☑541-785-3352, 800-422-3568; www.hellscanyonadventures.com; 4200 Hells Canyon Dam Rd, Oxbow) is the area's main tour outfitter, running a variety of raft and boat trips from May through September. Reservations are required.

There are several good hiking trails on the way to the dam; Allison Creek (on the Idaho side), about 4.5 miles round trip, is an especially good one (watch for rattlesnakes though). Longer trails are possible; check with the Hells Canyon Visitors Center, from where there's also the mile-long Stud Creek hike downriver.

🛏 Sleeping

Enterprise, Joseph and Halfway are all day trips away from Hells Canyon, but you also have closer options.

There's a free primitive campsite near Hat Point. Imnaha has food and water (and some basic RV sites), but for gas you'll have to go to Joseph. There's plenty of camping in the Hells Canyon Dam area, and B&Bs near Oxbow.

Imnaha River Inn   INN **$$**
(☑541-577-6002, 866-601-9214; www.imnahariverinn.com; d $120) Fine inn 5 miles north of Imnaha.

River House   HOUSE **$$**
(☑541-432-4075; www.wallowascenicrentals.com; per day $130) Three miles south of Imnaha; a three-bedroom house that requires a three-night minimum stay.

FREE **BLM campsites**   CAMPGROUND
Rustic campsites on the Oregon side of the Snake River.

Hells Canyon Park   CAMPGROUND **$**
(☑800-422-3143; tent/RV sites $10/16) Pretty campsite on the Idaho side of Snake River.

Copperfield Park   CAMPGROUND **$**
(☑800-422-3143; tent/RV sites $10/16; ⊙Apr-Oct; 🛜) Pleasant campsite at Oxbow.

Hells Canyon B&B   B&B **$**
(☑541-785-3373; www.hellscanyonb-b.com; d $70; ⊜❀🛜) Great-value B&B in the Oxbow area.

Hillside B&B   B&B **$$**
(☑541-785-3389; d $115; ⊜❀) Homey and casual B&B in the Oxbow area.

Ollokot (campsites $8) and **Blackhorse** (campsites $8), are two campgrounds at the southern end of the canyon, right on USFS Rd 39, midway between Halfway and Joseph.

Halfway
POP 450

An idyllic little town, Halfway lies on the southern edge of the Wallowa Mountains and is surrounded by beautiful meadows dotted with old barns and hay fields. It's a friendly spot with just enough tourist services to make it a decent base to explore the Hells Canyon Dam area. The **Pine Ranger Station** (☑541-742-7511; 38470 Pine Town Lane; ⊙7:30-11:45am & 12:30-4:30pm Mon-Thu, till 3:30pm Fri) is 1 mile south of Halfway and acts as the region's tourist information.

The **Pine Valley Museum** (☑541-742-5346; admission by donation; ⊙10am-4pm Sat & Sun summer) is located right in the middle of town and has a few of the region's old photos and relics. It's open on weekdays and by request for a $5 fee.

🛏 Sleeping & Eating

Halfway has very limited dining options – for average fare, head to **Wild Bill's** or **Stockman's**, both on the main drag. If you want something a bit more special, drive about 15 miles northeast to **Hells Canyon Inn** (☑541-785-3383) in Oxbow.

TOP CHOICE **Pine Valley Lodge**   LODGE **$$**
(☑541-742-2027; www.pvlodge.com; 163 N Main St; d incl breakfast $85-140; ⊜❀🛜) Halfway's fanciest accommodation, with seven lovely and very comfortable rooms in three buildings, all surrounded by flowery gardens. There's a great porch with wicker rocking chairs, and one cabin is also available (from $150). Continental breakfast included.

Inn at Clear Creek Farm   B&B **$$**
(☑541-742-2238; www.clearcreekinn.com; 48212 Clear Creek Rd; d $95-150; ⊜❀🛜) This gorgeous inn, 4 miles north of Halfway, is also a working cattle ranch with a small pear orchard. It offers six elegant rooms, including a suite that sleeps five; meals (except for the included breakfast) are extra. No shoes are allowed inside, so bring your slippers!

Halfway Motel MOTEL $

(☑541-742-5722; 170 S Main St; RV sites $20, d $55-65; ❄) Both old and new rooms are available at this reasonable motel. Go for the newer ones on the 2nd floor (facing the back) to enjoy peaceful meadow views. Rustic older rooms are smaller and cheaper. RV hookups are available.

Baker City

POP 10,000

Back in the old days, Baker City was the largest metropolis between Salt Lake City and Portland, and was also the commercial and cultural capital of Eastern Oregon. The 1860s gold rush helped establish the town, enriching its coffers while making it party central for the region – a heady mix of miners, cowboys, shopkeepers and loggers kept the city's many saloons, brothels and gaming halls boisterously alive.

The good old times are long gone now, but the city's wide downtown streets and historical architecture recall its rich bygone days. Today, travelers come not only for a peek at the city's swaggering history, but to explore the area's outdoor attractions. There's good skiing in winter, while fishing, hiking and boating are great in summer – and the Eagle Cap Wilderness and Wallowa Mountains aren't too far away.

Area events include the **Miners Jubilee** in mid-to-late July, with art and quilt shows, and a rodeo. In June there's the **Hells Canyon Rally** (www.hellscanyonrally. com), bringing hundreds of motorcycle aficionados into town for a motorcycle show and rides into the scenic surrounding region.

☉ Sights & Activities

Old Downtown Area NEIGHBORHOOD

The old downtown retains much of its late-19th-century Victorian Italianate architecture. A brochure describing a **walking tour** of historic buildings in the city center is available from the visitors bureau. To ogle at the 80.4oz Armstrong Nugget, found in the area in 1913, visit the **US Bank** (2000 Main St) during regular banking hours.

Housed in a 1921 natatorium (indoor swimming pool) is the **Baker Heritage Museum** (☑541-523-9308; 2480 Grove St; adult/child $6/5; ⊙9am-4pm late Mar-Oct). On display are machinery and antiques from Baker City's frontier days, along with plenty of semiprecious stones, fossils and petrified wood. Don't miss the fluorescent rock room and 950lb crystal.

Historic Adler House (☑541-523-9308; 2305 Main St; admission $6; ⊙10am-2pm Fri-Mon Apr-Oct) is great if you like old houses full of original fixtures and antiques. Planning to visit both this museum and the Baker Heritage Museum? Buy a $10 ticket for both.

National Historic Oregon Trail Interpretive Center INTREPRETIVE CENTER

(☑541-523-1843; www.oregontrail.blm.gov; 22267 Hwy 86; adult/senior $8/4.50; ⊙9am-6pm Apr-Oct, 9am-4pm Nov-Mar) This excellent interpretive center is the nation's foremost memorial to the pioneers who crossed the West along the Oregon Trail. Lying atop a hill 7 miles east of Baker City, it contains interactive displays, artifacts and films that stress the day-to-day realities of the pioneers. Outside you can stroll along the 4.2-mile interpretive path system and spot the actual Oregon Trail.

WORTH A TRIP

THE BLUE MOUNTAINS

Rising to the west from ranchland near Baker City, the Blue Mountains were responsible for the 1860s gold strikes that established towns such as Sumpter, Granite and Baker City. Ghost-town enthusiasts will find the Blue Mountains dotted with old mining camps, but there are also high mountain lakes, river canyons and hiking trails. And if you're crazy about trains, don't miss the narrow-gauge **Sumpter Valley Railroad** (www.svry.com).

A good way to explore the Blue Mountains is via the **Elkhorn Drive Scenic Byway**, which circles Elkhorn Ridge. It takes all day to properly explore this 106-mile loop that includes Baker City, Phillips Reservoir, Sumpter, Granite and Haines; it also skirts the Anthony Lakes area, which offers camping, fishing and hiking. Part of the loop (between Granite and Anthony Lakes) is often closed from late October to mid-June, so call or visit the Baker Ranger District in Baker City for road conditions.

Anthony Lakes
HIKING, SKIING

Anthony Lakes, some 30 miles northwest of Baker City, offers great scenery, along with camping and fishing. Several hiking trails lead to other small lakes, including a short but steep climb up Parker Creek to Hoffer Lake (1 mile one way). Another short hike goes from Elkhorn Crest Trail up to Black Lake (1 mile one way). In winter, ski-heads should make a beeline to nearby **Anthony Lakes Mountain Resort** (☑541-856-3277; www.anthonylakes.com; 47500 Anthony Lakes Hwy), which offers dry, fluffy powder and the highest base elevation in Oregon (7100ft). The resort grooms nearly 20 miles of cross-country trails.

🛏 Sleeping

A Beaten Path B&B
B&B $

(☑541-523-9230; www.abeatenpathbb.com; 2510 Court Ave; d $85; ⊜❈🐾) Located in a residential district, this friendly and eclectic B&B is in an 1888 historical home. Two large, comfortable Victorian-style rooms are available, but only one is rented at a time since there's one bathroom (unless you're willing to share the bathroom). Gourmet breakfast.

Bridge St Inn
MOTEL $

(☑541-523-6571, 800-932-9220; www.bridgestreetinn.net; 134 Bridge St; d $42-58; ❈🐾) The motel rooms here are nothing special and their layout is a bit eccentric, but the Nitty Gritty Dirt Band once slept here and that's worth something. And part of the cast and crew of *Paint Your Wagon* also stayed here. Get a room facing the back for peace.

Union Creek Campground
CAMPGROUND $

(☑541-894-2393; Hwy 7 at Phillips Reservoir; tent sites $12, RV sites $18-20; ☺May-Sep) Located 19 miles southwest of Baker City is this pleasant campground in a conifer forest around a reservoir popular with fishermen and boaters.

Anthony Lakes Campground
CAMPGROUND $

(☑541-894-2393; 47500 Anthony Lakes Hwy; campsites $8-12) Though it's 35 miles from town, this rustic but splendid campground is worth the drive (bring mosquito repellent!). It's high up and opens only after the snow melts, so call first.

🍴 Eating

The Geiser Grand Hotel has a fancy dining room.

GEISER GRAND HOTEL

Baker City's downtown landmark and fanciest **lodging** (☑541-523-1889, 888-434-7374; www.geisergrand.com; 1996 Main St; d $99-139; ⊜❈🐾) is this meticulously restored Italian Renaissance Revival building. The elegant rooms are spacious and decorated with old-style furniture, while the restaurant offers fine food and has a stunning stained-glass ceiling. There's a great old saloon, too. Cupola (ie huge) suites run $229.

Barley Brown's Brewpub
BREWPUB $$

(www.barleybrowns.com; 2190 Main St; mains $9-18; ☺4-10pm Mon-Thu, till 11pm Fri & Sat) Baker City's only microbrew pub, with comfortable atmosphere boasting tin ceilings and plenty of wooden booths. The regular pub menu features more than just pub food – think Kobe burgers, eggplant parmesan, jalapeno chicken pasta. Wash it all down with one of the eight brews on tap.

Haines Steak House
AMERICAN $$

(☑541-856-3639; www.hainessteakhouse.com; 910 Front St, Haines; mains $8-25; ☺5-9pm Mon, Wed & Thu, till 10pm Fri, 4-10pm Sat, 1-9pm Sun) Exceptional steaks are grilled up at this Western-themed restaurant, located 10 miles north of town in Haines. Good options are the T-bone, rib-eye or top sirloin; there's also prime rib and seafood. Vegetarians are plumb out of luck, other than the chuck-wagon salad bar and some sides.

Coffee Corral
COFFEE $

(1706 Campbell St; drinks $2-5; ☺5:30am-6pm Mon-Sat) Some of the best java in town is served at this drive-thru shack, located kitty-corner from the Baker Heritage Museum. If you need a serious buzz, ask for four shots in your espresso. A few pastries available.

Mad Matilda's Coffeehouse
COFFEEHOUSE $

(☑541-523-4588; 1917 Main St) This café – a community touchstone – was closed at research time, but there were plans to reopen it (possibly with a bakery). Check its status during your time in town, as it might well be worth a stop.

ℹ Information

Baker Ranger District Office (☑541-523-4476; 3285 11th St; ☺7:45am-4:30pm Mon-Fri) For info on nearby hiking trails.

Visitors Bureau (☏541-523-3356, 800-523-1235; www.visitbaker.com; 490 Campbell St; ☺8am-5pm Mon-Fri, 9am-5pm Sat, 9am-2pm Sun) Has good information

🅘 Getting There & Away

Baker Truck Corral (☏541-523-5011; 515 Campbell St) Greyhound bus stop.

John Day

POP 1,500

Smack near the middle of Eastern Oregon, this unpretentious, one-stoplight town strings along a narrow passage of the John Day River Valley. It's a utilitarian but decent enough place to base yourself while exploring the scenic region, and hosts a few interesting museums as well.

◉ Sights & Activities

FREE **Kam Wah Chung State Heritage Site** HISTORICAL SITE
(☏541-575-2800; 125 NW Canton St; ☺9am-5pm May-Oct) Don't miss this site, located in a building that served primarily as an apothecary for the noted Chinese herbalist and doctor Ing Hay. But it was also a community center, temple, general store and opium den for the Chinese population that reworked the area's mine tailings. A nearby interpretive center offers a 19-minute video; free tours of the heritage site leave from here.

Grant County Ranch & Rodeo Museum
MUSEUM
(☏541-575-5545; 241 E Main St; adult/child $3/free; ☺10am-4pm Thu & Sat) Rodeo lovers should visit this small museum, which showcases fine saddles and lots of rodeo photos. The friendly guys there really know the local rodeo and ranch scene. Call for off-hours visits.

Grant County Historical Museum MUSEUM
(☏541-575-0362; 101 S Canyon City Blvd; adult/child $4/2; ☺9am-4:30pm Mon-Sat May-Sep) Located 2 miles south of downtown John Day, in the center of tiny Canyon City, this museum houses gold-rush memorabilia, lots of polished agates and some stuffed two-headed calves. Outside is frontier poet Joaquin Miller's cabin.

🛏 Sleeping & Eating

See John Day Fossil Beds National Monument for other accommodation in the area.

Dreamers Lodge MOTEL $
(☏541-575-0526, 800-654-2849; 144 N Canyon Blvd; d $63-66; ❀❃☎) One of John Day's better-value places, this decent motel offers good-sized rooms (the ones with two beds are huge) - and it's off the main drag. Reserve in summer.

Sonshine B&B B&B $
(☏541-575-1827; www.sonshinebedandbreakfast. com; 210 NW Canton St; d $85; ❀❃☎) This small, friendly B&B is located right across from the Kam Wah Chung site and has two homey rooms that share a bathroom (or pay $120 for a private bathroom).

Hotel Prairie HOTEL $
(☏541-820-4800; www.prairiecityoregon.com/ prairie-city-oregon-hotel-prairie.html; 112 Front St; d $75-135; ❀❃) Located in Prairie City is this historic 1905 hotel with nine suites, most with private bathroom. There's a subdued, classy atmosphere and rooms are simple but comfortable; out back is a nice modern patio for hanging out. Prairie City is 13 miles east of John Day.

Strawberry Mountain Inn B&B B&B $$
(☏800-545-6913; www.strawberrymountaininn. com; 710 NE Front St; d $95-125; ❀❃☎) Located just east of Prairie City near the Strawberry Mountain Wilderness, this beautiful B&B offers five romantic rooms (most with private bath) and great meadow views. There's also a nice grassy garden out the back.

Clyde Holliday State Park CAMPGROUND $
(☏541-932-4453, 800-452-5687; www.oregon stateparks.org; Hwy 26 milepost 155, Mt Vernon; tent & RV sites $22, teepees $39) Six miles west of John Day, this pleasant, shady campground (with teepees) lies next to the John Day River, though it's also close to the road.

Snaffle Bit AMERICAN $$
(830 S Canyon City Blvd; mains $8-23; ☺11:30am-9pm Wed-Fri, 4-9pm Sat) John Day's best hamburgers are at this no-nonsense restaurant with a nice fountain patio. Also on the menu are salads, pasta, Mexican specialties, lots of steaks and decent margaritas.

The Outpost AMERICAN $
(www.gooutpost.com; 201 W Main St; mains $7-17; ☺6am-9pm) There's something for everyone at this Western-style joint, from soups and salads to sandwiches and pizzas to burgers and steaks. To pasta and fajitas. And breakfast too! Good atmosphere with rustic decor.

Information

Chamber of Commerce (☎541-575-0547; www.gcoregonlive.com; 301 W Main St; ☺9am-4pm Mon-Fri)

Malheur National Forest Ranger Station (☎541-575-3000; www.fs.fed.us/r6/malheur; 431 Patterson Bridge Rd; ☺7:45am-4:30pm Mon-Fri)

Getting There & Around

People Mover bus (☎541-575-2370; 229 NE Dayton) Services to Bend.

Strawberry Mountain Wilderness

Named for the wild strawberries that thrive on its mountain slopes, the Strawberry Range is covered with ponderosa and lodgepole pines growing on glacier-chiseled volcanic peaks that are 15 million years old. The Strawberry Mountains contain deceptively high country: much of the wilderness is above 6000ft, and the highest peak – Strawberry Mountain – rises to 9038ft.

A popular and rewarding 2.8-mile round-trip hike winds up a steep valley to **Strawberry Lake**. About 1.4 miles past the lake is **Strawberry Falls**. To reach the trailhead, follow the signs 11 miles south from Prairie City.

Circle around to the south side of the wilderness area on Hwy 14 and paved USFS Rds 65 and 16, past old ponderosa pines and wide meadows, to find more trails. Hike into **High Lake Basin** (2.6 miles round trip) from a trailhead high up the mountainside. From USFS Rd 16, turn on USFS Rd 1640 toward **Indian Springs Campground**. The trailhead is 11 miles up a steep gravel road.

There are several good campgrounds, including **Trout Farm** (☎541-820-3861; County Rd 62; campsites $8), a lovely stream-side spot 15 miles south of Prairie City. Water is available.

For more information, contact the **Prairie City Ranger District** (☎541-820-3800; 327 Front St; ☺8am-4:30pm Mon-Fri) in Prairie City.

John Day Fossil Beds National Monument

Within the soft rocks and crumbly soils of John Day country lies one of the world's greatest fossil collections. Discovered in the 1860s by clergyman and geologist Thomas Condon, these fossil beds were laid down between six and 50 million years ago, when this area was a coastal plain with a tropical climate. Roaming the forests at the time were saber-toothed, feline-like nimravids, bear-dogs, pint-sized horses and other early mammals.

The fossils of more than 2200 different plant and animal species have been found here. The national monument includes 22 sq miles at three different units: Sheep Rock Unit, Painted Hills Unit and Clarno Unit. Each has hiking trails and interpretive displays. To visit all of the units in one day requires quite a bit of driving, as more than 100 miles separate the fossil beds – it's best to take it easy and spend the night somewhere.

Visit the excellent **Thomas Condon Paleontology Center** (☎541-987-2333; www.nps.gov/joda; 32651 Hwy 19, Kimberly; ☺9am-5pm) 2 miles north of US 26. Displays include a three-toed horse and petrified dung-beetle balls, along with many other fossils and geologic history exhibits. It offers ranger-guided trips in summer.

The nearby **Cant Ranch House** offers a peek into settlers' early lives, and has picnic grounds and a riverside trail.

Note that this is a National Monument, and no fossil, rock or plant collecting is allowed.

Sights & Activities

Sheep Rock Unit   GEOLOGICAL DESTINATION
Featuring the most walks and hikes, this unit is also closest to the Paleontology Center. Above loom majestic, layered mountains tilted and eroding into spectacular formations that date back 28 million years. Fossils are continually being exposed here.

From the **Blue Basin Trailhead** there are several hikes that lead out to the fossil formations. The **Island in Time Trail** is a well-maintained, mile-long path that climbs up a narrow waterway to a badlands-basin of highly eroded, uncannily green sediments. Fossils can be seen along the trail. Several other overlook trails lead to amazing vistas of the John Day Valley.

Painted Hills Unit   GEOLOGICAL DESTINATION
Because no cap rock protects them from erosion, the Painted Hills have eroded into low-slung, colorfully banded hills that were originally formed about 30 million years ago. A series of eruptions drifted into beds hundreds of feet deep, layering the brick-red, yellow, black, beige and ochre-hued ash that you now see. It's a fabulous, uncommon sight.

RAFTING THE JOHN DAY

From Clarno Bridge (on Hwy 218) to Cottonwood Bridge (on Hwy 206), a distance of 70 miles, the John Day River cuts a deep canyon through basaltic lava flows on its way to the Columbia River. No public roads reach the canyon here; along the river are the remains of homesteads, Native American petroglyphs and pristine wildlife habitats.

Plan to float the John Day in spring or early summer, when the toughest rapids are class III or IV, depending on the water levels. Most trips take four days and some rafters float the John Day on their own. Shuttle service and raft rentals are available from **Service Creek Stage Stop** (☑541-468-3331; www.servicecreeklodge.com; 38686 Hwy 19).

Among the companies that run trips are:

Oregon Whitewater Adventures (☑800-820-7238; www.oregonwhitewater.com)

Ouzel Outfitters (☑800-788-7238; www.oregonrafting.com)

Oregon River Experiences (☑800-827-1358; www.oregonriver.com)

For specific advice, contact the **Prineville BLM office** (☑541-416-6700; 3050 NE 3rd St).

Interpretive walks include the easy half-mile (round trip) **Leaf Hill Trail**, which winds over the top of a banded hill, and the 1.5-mile (round trip) **Carroll Rim Trail**, which goes to the top of a high bluff for great views.

Clarno Unit   GEOLOGICAL DESTINATION
The oldest, most remote fossil beds in the area are at the base of the John Day River's canyon. The 40-million-year-old Clarno Unit exposes mud flows that washed over an Eocene-era forest. The **Clarno Formation** eroded into white cliffs topped with spires and turrets of stone. Several half-mile (round trip) interpretive trails: one passes through large boulders containing fossils of logs, seeds and other remains of an ancient forest, and another leads to the base of **Palisades Cliff** and some petrified logs.

🛏 Sleeping & Eating

The town (and nearby environs) of John Day itself has a few good accommodation choices.

Historic Hotel Oregon   HOTEL $
(☑541-462-3027; 104 E Main St, Mitchell; d $39-89; 🖴) This lovely old hotel is an insanely good-value place. It's in the little Western town of Mitchell, about 10 miles southeast of the Painted Hills Unit. Comfortable, homey rooms are featured, most with shared bathroom; dorm bunks are available for $15 each. Continental breakfast is included.

🛶 **Lands Inn B&B**   B&B $
(☑541-934-2333; www.landsinn.net; 45457 Dick Creek Lane; campsites $25, cabins $45-95; ☉Jun-Sep) Possibly the world's only B&B with its own airstrip, this mountain hideaway – 13 miles south of Kimberly and 5 miles up a dirt road – has several different cabins (most with outside bathroom), plus campsites. It's a great place to get away from it all. Breakfast is extra ($12), however, and all electricity is solar (so they occasionally 'run out'). Reservations are required.

Fish House Inn   INN $
(☑541-987-2124; www.fishhouseinn.com; 110 Franklin St, Dayville; tent/RV sites $15/25, d $50-70; 🖴❄) Five nice rooms (two with shared bathroom) are available at this inn in Dayville, less than 10 miles east of the Sheep Rock Unit. There's also a pleasant area for tents and RVs. Three-bedroom house available ($125). Note that no breakfast is served.

Service Creek Lodge   GUESTHOUSE $
(☑541-468-3331; www.servicecreeklodge.com; 38686 Hwy 19; d $75-95; 🖴❄📶) Twenty miles southeast of Fossil (which is near the Clarno Unit), this fine lodge has six awesome, comfortable rooms with country quilts, plus a restaurant and rafting services. Rates include breakfast; reception is at the restaurant.

Wilson Ranches Retreat B&B   B&B $
(☑866-763-2227; www.wilsonranchesretreat.com; 16555 Butte Creek Rd, Fossil; d $79-109;🖴❄) Six homey and comfortable guestrooms of different sizes (and all sharing bathrooms) are available at this good B&B, which is also a working ranch. There are pleasant common spaces, and horseback riding is available. It's located 2.5 miles northwest of Fossil.

Bridge Creek Flora Inn   B&B $
(☑541-763-2355; 828 Main St; d $85; 🖴) Located in Fossil, this very casual and eclectic B&B is located in two buildings. Don't

expect luxury – it's not a fancy place and is casually run. Two buildings hold 12 rooms in all; one two-bedroom suite with private bathroom available ($105).

There are several public campgrounds in the region in addition to the private listings given. Public campgrounds include **Lone Pine** (campsites $5; no water) and **Big Bend** (campsites $5; no water); both are nice riverside places on Hwy 402, north of the Sheep Rock Unit and 2 to 3 miles east of Kimberly. Over towards the Clarno Unit and 7 to 10 miles south of Fossil are **Bear Hollow** (campsites free; no water) and **Shelton Wayside** (campsites $10 1st night, $5 after), both with woodsy campsites.

Ontario

POP 11,000

Oregon's most easterly city, Ontario and its environs are often considered to be an extension of Idaho's fertile Snake River valley. The Malheur, Payette and Owyhee Rivers join the Snake's wide valley here, with irrigated farms producing a variety of crops – the region's economic backbone. The city itself is a bit homely and not worth more than a brief stop on your way somewhere more exciting.

Ontario shares the same time zone, Mountain Standard Time, with Idaho (it's one hour ahead of Pacific Standard Time). For tourist information visit the **Chamber of Commerce** (☑541-889-8012; www.ontario chamber.com; 876 SW 4th Ave; ☉8am-5pm Mon-Fri); it's located near the Four Rivers Cultural Center in a strip mall.

No car? There's **Greyhound** (☑541-823-2567; 191 SE 3rd St).

◉ Sights & Activities

Four Rivers Cultural Center MUSEUM
(☑541-889-8191; www.4rcc.com; 676 SW 5th Ave; adult/child $4/3; ☉10am-5pm Mon-Sat) A far cry from your typical small-town museum, this center celebrates the region's diversity, focusing on Paiute Native Americans, Basque sheep-herders, and Japanese- and Mexican-American farm workers.

🛏 Sleeping & Eating

Virtue House B&B B&B $$
(☑541-889-1996; www.virtuehouse.com; 788 SW 2nd St; cottage $100; ❄❂@) For something a little different, rent out this darling one-bedroom cottage in a residential area. You'll get all the benefits of your own private little house, and the 'hosts' (who live nearby) will cook you a full breakfast in the morning. Call ahead.

Lake Owyhee State Park CAMPGROUND $
(☑541-339-2331; www.oregonstateparks.org; 1298 Lake Owyhee Dam Rd; tent/RV sites $17/20, tee-pees $36) Some 40 miles south of Ontario is this desert-y state park, on the shores of Lake Owyhee. It's at the end of a long, one-way road, but getting here is half the fun – and there are teepees to rent.

Ontario Inn MOTEL $
(☑541-823-2556; www.ontarioinnmotel.com; 1144 SW 4th Ave; d $50-60; ❄❂) Pleasant, friendly, family-run motel with nothing-special but clean rooms. One big plus: bagels and fruit for breakfast.

Farewell Bend State Recreation Area CAMPGROUND $
(☑541-869-2365; www.oregonstateparks.org; I-84 exit 353; tent/RV sites $15/17, cabins $38) A good camping spot relatively close to Ontario is this large oasis at the Snake River's Brownlee Reservoir, 25 miles northwest of town.

Romio's Pizza and Pasta ITALIAN $$
(www.romios-pizza.com; 375 S Oregon St; pizzas $11-22; ☉11am-9pm Mon-Fri, noon-8pm Sun) Locals recommend this joint for great pizzas, topped with treats such as fresh garlic, artichoke hearts, feta cheese and bacon. Eight kinds of salads and plenty of sandwiches too, along with a few calzones.

Brewsky's Broiler AMERICAN $$
(23 SE 1st Ave; mains $7-15; ☉10am-midnight Mon-Sat) Experience family-friendly dining at this restaurant near the tracks. Burgers, sandwiches and Mexican specialties dominate the menu, and there's airy outside seating out front.

Jolts & Juice COFFEEHOUSE $
(cnr SW 3rd Ave & S Oregon Sts; drinks $1.50-4; ☉6am-7pm Mon-Fri, 7am-6pm Sat, 7am-4pm Sun) Ontario's most pleasant coffee shop. Order your favorite specialty coffee drink, fresh juice or smoothie (coffee, green tea or fruit-based). There are even plans to serve wine and beer.

There is a natural foods store in Ontario (really!); just point your Prius to **Oregon Natural Market** (☑541-889-8714; 373 SW 1st St; ☉9am-6pm Mon-Sat).

Jordan Valley

POP 125

The closest thing to civilization in the southeastern corner of Oregon is tiny Jordan Valley (Mountain Standard Time). Known for its Basque heritage, this pit stop has an interesting rebuilt *frontón,* a stone ball court used for playing the traditional Basque game of *pelota.* There is a motel (with check-in at a gas station) and a surprisingly good restaurant-inn.

Basque Station Motel (☑541-586-2244; 801 Main St; d $55-65; ❋) is nothing fancy, with large rooms overlooking a serene meadow out back.

Order *bacaloa* (dried salt cod), Basque-style chorizos or just broiled lamb chops at **Old Basque Inn** (☑541-586-2800; 306 Wroten St; mains $7-19; ❂7am-10pm), an old Basque boarding house. There are five homey rooms upstairs with shared bathrooms (doubles $65, including breakfast).

Burns

POP 3000

Named by a wistful early settler for Scottish poet Robert Burns, this isolated high-desert town was established in 1883 as the watering hole and social center for incoming settlers and roving cowhands. Today, Burns (don't mistake it for Burns *Junction* – essentially just a highway junction southwest of Jordan Valley) has plenty of services and is a convenient jumping-off point for trips south into the Malheur National Wildlife Refuge and Steens Mountain area.

◉ Sights & Activities

Harney County Historical Museum MUSEUM
(☑541-573-5618; www.burnsmuseum.com; 18 West D St; adult/child $4/1; ❂10am-4pm Tue-Sat Apr-Sep) Lots of historical relics – from photos to coins to guns to a document sentencing a hanging – are on exhibit at this museum; if you're a couple, the admission is $5 for you both.

Crystal Crane Hot Springs HOT SPRINGS
(☑541-493-2312; www.cranehotsprings.com; 59315 Hwy 78; ❂9am-9pm) This rustic resort, 25 miles southeast of Burns and 3 miles west of Crane, is a little oasis and worth a stop. The springs flow into a large pond ($3.50 day use) and are also piped into tubs in small private bathhouses ($7.50 per person per hour; reserve on weekends).

🛏 Sleeping

Crystal Crane Hot Springs CABINS $
(☑541-493-2312; 59315 Hwy 78; tent sites $15, RV sites $18-20, cabins $45-60; ❂❂) It's 25 miles from Burns, but the atmosphere is family-friendly and very casual – and like an oasis in the desert. Accommodation is rustic; the cabins are simple and share outside bathrooms. Hot-spring and kitchen use are included, and there's a common room in which to hang. You can even stay in teepees ($30 to $40).

Sage Country Inn B&B $$
(☑541-573-7243; www.sagecountryinn.com; 351½ W Monroe St; d $100; ❂❋❂) Burns' most charming lodging by far, this beautiful old house has three well-furnished rooms, each with its own bathroom. Grassy gardens surround the place, and it's located right near downtown.

Silver Spur Motel MOTEL $
(☑541-573-2077; www.silverspurmotel.com; 789 N Broadway Ave; d $49-56; ❋@❂) Your typical budget motel, with plain, small and clean rooms. If you want a pool, head to the **Days Inn** (577 W Monroe) – it's similar, and just a few bucks more.

Burns RV Park CAMPGROUND $
(☑541-573-7640; www.burnsrvpark.com; 1273 Seneca Dr; tent sites $18, RV sites $31-33) Just a quarter-mile north of Burns is this pleasant RV and camping park, just off the main road. Sites are decent, some with shade.

Idlewild Campground CAMPGROUND $
(☑541-573-4300; Hwy 395; campsites $10) North of town 17 miles, just off on Hwy 395, this public campground is in the Malheur National Forest. It's nice and peaceful, with sites among Jeffrey pines.

✗ Eating

TOP CHOICE **Meat Hook** STEAKHOUSE $$
(☑541-573-7698; 673 W Monroe St; mains $7-23; ❂4-9pm Mon-Sat) The region's best steaks can be had at this restaurant – they're surprisingly good for such a small town. Maybe it's because this place raises its own cows without steroids or hormones. And if you really like its stuff, you can order a half-cow to go – it sells in bulk.

Rhojo's AMERICAN $$
(☑541-589-1034; 314 N Broadway; mains $16-18; ❂6-9pm Thu & Fri) If you're here on a Thursday or Friday night and want an exceptional dinner, ring ahead to reserve your seat

SUCCOR CREEK & LESLIE GULCH

It takes a little doing to get to the wildly eroded Owyhee River country, but sections of this 35-mile gravel route (and its 14.5-mile side branch) are unforgettable. Running between Adrian and a junction with US 95, 18 miles north of Jordan Valley, this scenic route passes grand desert landscapes and spectacular rock peaks.

Take the gravel road eight miles south of Adrian; the sign should say 'Succor Creek State Park.' You'll drive through sagebrush and rolling hills for about 10 miles, then start descending. A couple of miles later are amazing vertical walls of volcanic tuff hundreds of feet high. The **Succor Creek State Natural Area** sits at the other end of the canyon, with basic campsites (no water), wildlife-watching opportunities and stunning vistas.

The scenery is even more spectacular at **Leslie Gulch**, located 26 miles further south on a 14.5-mile dead-end side branch off the main gravel road. A narrow creek channel goes through vividly colored volcanic rock eroded into amazing pinnacles and turreted formations, at last reaching Lake Owyhee Reservoir. Rock climbing (trad) is possible, and there's primitive camping at Slocum Creek campground (covered picnic tables, fire pits, gravel sites). Watch for rattlesnakes.

Driving on gravel roads is slow going, so leave yourself plenty of time and take food, lots of water and a full tank of gas.

here. There are just a few choices – from roast duck to pork tenderloin to whatever is on tap that night – but all will send you away happy.

Broadway Deli CAFÉ-DELI **$**
(530 N Broadway Ave; sandwiches $6-9; ⊘8am-4pm Mon-Fri, 11am-3pm Sat) Good sandwiches and salads are sold at this small, simple deli. Soups, smoothies and homemade pies and cakes are also available, and the service is old-fashioned.

Bella Java & Bistro COFFEEHOUSE **$**
(314 N Broadway; drinks $2-4; ⊘7:30am-3pm Mon-Fri, 9am-3pm Sat) Get your caffeine jolt at this pleasant coffee shop, decorated with tin ceilings and a couple of sofas. There's espresso or mocha, along with chai, Italian sodas and smoothies.

❶ Information

BLM office (☑541-573-4400; www.blm.gov/or/districts/burns; 28910 US 20W, Hines; ⊘7:45am-4:30pm Mon-Fri)

Chamber of Commerce (☑541-573-2636; www.harneycounty.com; 484 N Broadway; ⊘9am-5pm Mon-Fri)

Immigrant Creek Ranger District (☑541-573-4300; 265 US 20S, Hines; ⊘8am-4:30pm Mon-Fri)

❶ Getting There & Away

Porter Stage Lines (☑541-573-5500; 63 N Buena Vista Ave) Runs out of Figaro's Pizza.

Malheur National Wildlife Refuge

South of Burns, covering 290 sq miles of lake, wetland and prairie, is this important breeding and resting refuge for birds traveling along the Pacific Flyway. Six miles east of Hwy 205 on a side road is the **Refuge Headquarters & Visitors Center** (☑541-493-2612; www.fws.gov/malheur; 36391 Sodhouse Lane; ⊘8am-4pm, limited hours outside summer), which has information, maps, a little museum and good bird-watching on Malheur Lake.

◎ Sights & Activities

The refuge's two big, shallow lakes attract waterfowl, but the best place for wildlife-viewing is often south along the Donner und Blitzen River, where wide, grassy marshes and ponds shelter many animals. The gravel Central Patrol Rd runs between the refuge headquarters and Frenchglen, paralleling the river and providing some 40 miles of good access into the backcountry. A few walks (most of them short) lead to ponds, a canal and reservoir; many are along the Central Patrol Rd. Snag a brochure at the refuge headquarters for details.

Waterfowl migration at Malheur peaks in March, shorebirds arrive in April, and songbirds wing-in during May. During summer, waterfowl families skim across the ponds and lakes. In fall, birds come through on their way south. Mosquitoes are around most of the time, so bring repellant.

Adjacent to the wildlife refuge, 55 miles south of Burns and east of Hwy 205, is **Diamond Craters**, a slightly underwhelming area of volcanic craters, cinder cones and other lava formations that were formed about 2500 years ago. Pick up a brochure for a self-guided tour from the BLM office in Hines to sniff out the highlights.

Northeast of the Diamond Craters area and a mile off Lava Bed Rd is **Pete French's Round Barn**, an impressive (though a bit decrepit) 100ft-wide structure used to buck out broncos in the glory days of the open range. A nearby fancy **gift shop** (☑888-493-2420; ☺9am-5pm, limited hours outside summer) provides a commercial angle to this unique attraction. You can also ask here about **Jenkins Historical Tours** (www.roundbarn. net), a variety of tours that offer background and transport in the area.

🛏 Sleeping & Eating

Hotel Diamond   B&B $
(☑541-493-1898; www.central-oregon.com/hotel diamond; 10 Main St; d $75-97; ☻✿) This small but beautiful hotel, located in the hamlet of Diamond, is decorated with antiques and offers eight lovely rooms with quilt bedspreads. Both new and older rooms are available, and some share bathrooms. Continental breakfast is included, and dinners ($17 to $23) are available to guests and visitors alike (reservations required).

The Narrows RV Park   CAMPGROUND $
(☑541-495-2006; www.thenarrowsrvpark.com; 33468 Sodhouse Lane; tent sites $12, RV sites $26-28; ☎) At the junction of Hwy 205 and Sodhouse Lane is this cheery RV park offering campers a desert refuge. There's a restaurant, 'saloon,' convenience store, espresso shop and gas. You can even stay in a yurt ($33; reserve in advance).

Malheur Field Station   TRAILERS, DORMS $
(☑541-493-2629; www.malheurfieldstation.org; 34848 Sodhouse Lane; RV sites $19, dm $22-30, trailers d $70-90; ☻✿) About 4.5 miles west of the refuge headquarters, this collection of rustic buildings offers RV hookups, simple dormitories, kitchenette trailers and no-nonsense meals (reserve a week ahead). Bring your own bedding, a towel, toiletries and flashlight – lights out at 10pm!

Steens Mountain

The highest peak in southeastern Oregon, Steens Mountain (9773ft) is part of a massive, 30-mile-long fault-block range that was formed about 15 million years ago. On the western slope of the range, Ice Age glaciers bulldozed trenches that formed massive U-shaped gorges and hanging valleys. To the east, 'the Steens' – as the range is usually referred to – drop off to the Alvord Desert, 5000ft below.

Guided tours of the region are available; check out **Jenkins Historical Tours** (☑888-493-2420; www.roundbarn.net).

◉ Sights & Activities

Beginning in Frenchglen, the 56-mile, gravel **Steens Mountain Loop Rd** is Oregon's highest road and offers the range's best sights, with awesome overlooks and access to camping and hiking trails. You'll see sagebrush, bands of junipers and aspen forests, and finally fragile rocky tundra at the top. **Kiger Gorge viewpoint** is especially stunning; it's 25 miles up from Frenchglen.

The gravel loop road is open as weather allows, July through October – check road conditions with the Burns BLM office, or ask in Frenchglen. Much of the road (and highlights) is usually accessible to regular cars, but you might need a high-clearance vehicle if you want to do the whole loop – east of the South Steens campground the road becomes bumpy dirt. Making it all the way around in a non-high-clearance vehicle all depends on the road conditions.

The loop takes about three hours all the way around if you're just driving through, but if you include stops (and you'll be stopping for sure) give yourself much more time.

You can also see the eastern side of the Steens via the flat gravel road through the Alvord Desert. This is a well-maintained road, but take a full gas tank and water, and be prepared for weather changes at any time of year.

🛏 Sleeping & Eating

Frenchglen (population 12) has one charming hotel with dining room, a small store with seasonal gas pump and not much else. There are camping options on the Steens Mountain Loop Rd, such as the BLM's pretty Page Springs. A few other campgrounds, further into the loop, are very pleasant but accessible in summer only; Page Springs is

One of the highlights you might experience while exploring the Steens could be spotting a herd of wild mustangs. Descended from domesticated horses that escaped from Native Americans, early Spanish explorers and pioneers, these free-roaming herds are managed by the BLM, who cull the animals (usually for adoption) to keep them healthy, maintain desired characteristics and prevent overpopulation.

Several different herds can be seen, each with their own distinctive markings. The most famous – and rarest – bunch are the Kiger mustangs, who were discovered in 1977 during a round-up and are considered to have descended directly from original Spanish stock. They number less than 100 and are generally dun in color, sometimes sporting a dark dorsal stripe and zebra-like markings on their legs. Their rugged handsomeness and vitality attracted the attention of DreamWorks, whose animated 2003 film *Spirit: Stallion of the Cimarron* was based on a Kiger mustang.

One of the best places to spot these animals is on the southern leg of the Steens Mountain Loop Rd. Keep your eyes peeled as you explore this area – if luck is on your side, you may get a glimpse of these wild symbols of the West.

open year-round. Water is available at all of these campgrounds (sites $6 to $8). Free backcountry camping is also allowed in the Steens.

TOP CHOICE **Frenchglen Hotel**   HOTEL **$**
(☑541-493-2825; fghotel@yahoo.com; 39184 Hwy 205, Frenchglen; d $70-110; ⊘Mar 15-Oct 31; ⊜❋) This historic hotel dates from the 1910s and features eight small but cute rooms, all sharing outside bathrooms. A newer section of the hotel (called the 'Drovers' Inn') has five rooms, each with private bathroom. Dinners ($20 to $23, reservations required) are family style and served promptly at 6:30pm. Breakfast and lunch is also available, without reservations.

Steens Mountain Resort CAMPGROUND, CABINS **$**
(☑800-542-3765; www.steensmountainresort.com; 35678 Resort Lane, off Steens Mountain Loop Rd; tent sites $15, RV sites $25-30, cabins $65-160; ⊜❋) Three miles from Frenchglen, just before Page Springs campground, this 'resort' has nine decent single-wide trailers ('modular cabins') of various sizes spread out over a sparse hillside with low trees. All have kitchen areas; most require that you bring linens and bedding. Campsites and RV sites available.

Alvord Desert

Once a large, 200ft-deep lake, the stunning Alvord Basin is now a series of playas – beige-white alkali beds that have resulted from centuries of evaporation. They alternate startlingly with sagebrush prairies

and old ranches, while Steens Mountain looms dramatically to the west. The 66-mile, mostly gravel Fields–Denio Rd, between the hamlet of Fields and Hwy 78, is well maintained and open year-round.

About 23 miles north of Fields is rustic but worthy **Alvord Hot Springs**; look for the small metal shelter 100 yards off the road. Some 30 miles north of Fields, a side road goes a few miles to **Mickey Hot Springs**, a miniature Yellowstone with bubbling mud pots, steam vents and – beware – pools too hot for bathing. **Mann Lake**, 42 miles north of Fields, offers fishing, bird-watching and primitive campsites (no water).

There's free backcountry camping around the edge of the Alvord Desert (windy). There's also camping down a dirt road directly across from Alvord Hot Springs, or go 2 miles further up the main road from here to a very rough (ie high-clearance vehicles only) side road; after about a mile, it ends at a camping area and the start of a good 3-mile hiking trail. Bring food, water and sun protection; there are no services along the Fields–Denio Rd.

For more details, contact the BLM in Hines.

In the hamlet of Fields, **Fields Station** (☑541-495-2275; 22276 Fields Dr) is a small **store** (⊘8am-6pm Mon-Sat, 9am-5pm Sun) and **café** (⊘8am-4:30pm Mon-Sat, 9am-4:30pm Sun). It's a near-mandatory stop for gas, snacks, good burgers and sublime milkshakes. Rooms are available to rent here ($65), along with a house ($90) and basic camping/RV sites ($20). There's also a tiny **inn** (☑877-225-9424; www.alvordinn.com; d $60-80).

Hart Mountain National Antelope Refuge

From the tiny town of Plush, Hart Mountain Rd crosses the Warner Lakes Basin, climbs into the spectacular, near-vertical Hart Mountain fault block (peak elevation over 8000ft) and emerges onto the prairie-like expanses of the Hart Mountain National Antelope Refuge. Roughly 2500 pronghorn antelope are protected within the refuge's 435 sq miles – a shadow of the millions of pronghorns that once roamed North America, but at least the population has remained steady.

Pronghorns are not true antelopes, and have horns rather than antlers, shedding only the outer hairy sheath and growing a new covering each year. Pronghorns are the world's second-fastest land animal (after the cheetah), having been clocked at over 60mph.

The refuge also protects bighorn sheep, reintroduced to Hart Mountain in the 1950s and now living on the steep western side of the refuge. Cougar, bobcat, coyote, mule deer and a wide variety of birds (including sage grouse) inhabit the area.

Hart Mountain has an extensive network of 4WD trails and single-tracks through isolated areas, making for good hiking and mountain biking. At **Petroglyph Lake**, a short loop around the lake makes for great petroglyph-spotting, or hike along **Skyline Drive** (open in summer; 4WD vehicles only), where you have a decent chance at spotting antelope or sage grouse.

At the often unstaffed refuge **headquarters** (☑541-947-2731; ⏱7am-4:30pm) you can pick up brochures any time and use the area's only potable water and toilet facilities. Pitch a tent at the free **Hot Springs Campground**, about 4 miles south of HQ. There's a lovely wooded creek plus an open-air bathhouse that traps a hot spring – just the thing after a dusty day of exploring. There's an undeveloped hot-spring pool nearby.

If you're just passing through, allow two to three hours to travel the 75 miles between Plush and Frenchglen (about 50 miles is on a slow gravel surface); make sure you have plenty of gas. Call in winter or after heavy rains to check the refuge's roads are passable.

Lakeview

POP 2700

There's no longer any lake in view here, but at an elevation of 4800ft, homely Lakeview is 'the tallest town in Oregon.' It's also known as the 'hang-gliding capital of the west,' with surrounding towering fault-block rims and prevailing westerly winds bringing hundreds of aficionados for summertime hang-gliding and paragliding events.

There are hot springs just outside town, and there's also the **Schminck Memorial Museum** (☑541-947-3134; 128 South E St; admission $4; ⏱11am-4pm Wed-Sat Jun-Aug), which holds pioneer relics including pressed-glass goblets, china dolls and a few Native American artifacts. Opening days are limited outside summer.

🛏 Sleeping & Eating

Lakeview Lodge   MOTEL $
(☑541-947-2181; www.lakeviewlodgemotel.com; 301 NG St; d $65-70; ❋🐾) Run by a British couple, this comfortable motel has good, spacious rooms, some featuring sofas. All have fridge and microwave, and there's a Jacuzzi for all guests to use.

Hunter's Hot Springs Resort   RESORT $
(☑541-947-4142; www.huntersresort.com; 18088 US 395 N; d $65-75; ➿❋🐾⛱) This homespun resort, 1.5 miles north of town, offers a hot mineral swimming pool ($10 for nonguests) and unpretentious, motel-like rooms. The Pacific Northwest's only hot-water geyser used to erupted here every few minutes, but due to a low water table in 2010 it stopped. This may change in the future, however.

Goose Lake State Park   CAMPGROUND $
(☑541-947-3111; www.oregonstateparks.org; US 395 at the state line; tent & RV sites $20) This fine campground, with shady, grassy sites, is 14 miles south of Lakeview (right on the Californian border) and offers bird-watching and boating opportunities.

Eagle's Nest   AMERICAN $$
(117 North E St; mains $6-13; ⏱11am-2pm & 5-9pm Mon-Fri, 5-9pm Sat) This old-time locals' spot serves up sandwiches, salads and 10 kinds of burgers. Occasional steak specials run over $20. The attached lounge next door has longer hours and also serves food.

ℹ Information

Chamber of Commerce (☑541-947-6040; www.lakecountychamber.org; 126 North E St; ⏱9am-5pm)

Lakeview Ranger District office (☑541-947-2151; www.fs.fed.us/r6/frewin; 1301 SG St; ⏱7:45am-4:30pm Mon-Fri). The BLM office is at the same telephone and address.

Vancouver, Whistler & Vancouver Island

Best Places to Eat

» C Restaurant (p367)
» Araxi Restarant & Lounge (p377)
» Raincity Grill (p367)
» Red Fish Blue Fish (p387)
» Tojo's (p369)

Best Places to Stay

» Free Spirit Spheres (p396)
» Wickaninnish Inn (p398)
» Spinnakers Guesthouses (p385)
» Nita Lake Lodge (p376)

Why Go?

British Columbia visitors are never short of superlatives when writing their postcards home. It's hard not to be moved by looming mountain ranges, wildlife-packed forests and uncountable kilometers of pristine coastline that slow your heartbeat like a sigh-triggering spa treatment. But Canada's westernmost province is much more than a nature-hugging diorama.

Cosmopolitan Vancouver is an animated fusion of cuisines and cultures from Asia and beyond, while historic Victoria and resort town Whistler have their own vibrant and alluring scenes. And for sheer character, it's hard to beat the province's kaleidoscope of quirky little communities, from the rustic Sunshine Coast to the laid-back Southern Gulf Islands.

Wherever you head, of course, the great outdoors will always be calling your name. Don't just point your camera at it. BC is unbeatable for the kind of life-enhancing skiing, kayaking, hiking and biking that you'll be bragging about to everyone back home.

When to Go
Vancouver, BC

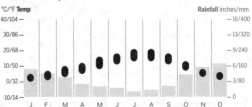

December–March	July & August	September & October
Powder action on the slopes of Whistler and Blackcomb Mountains	Beaches, barbecues and a plethora of overlapping festivals in Vancouver	Great surfing and the start of the storm-watching season in Tofino

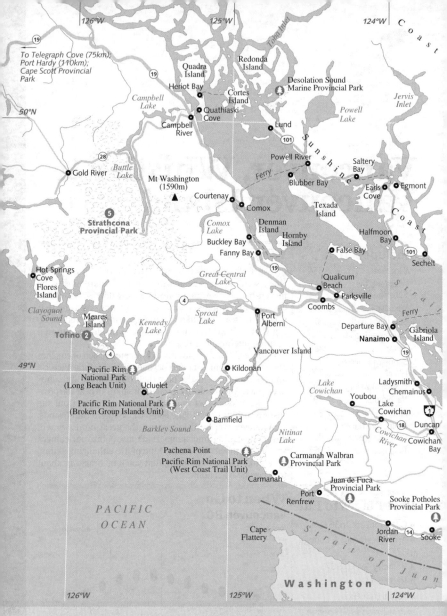

Vancouver, Whistler & Vancouver Island Highlights

❶ Stretch your legs on a seawall stroll around Vancouver's **Stanley Park** (p355), then enjoy a relaxing Third Beach sunset

❷ Surf up a storm (or just watch a storm) in **Tofino** (p398) on Vancouver Island's wild west coast

❸ Knock back some lip-smacking beers at a **Victoria** (p370) brewpub

❹ Ski the Olympian slopes at **Whistler** (p375) and enjoy a warming après beverage while

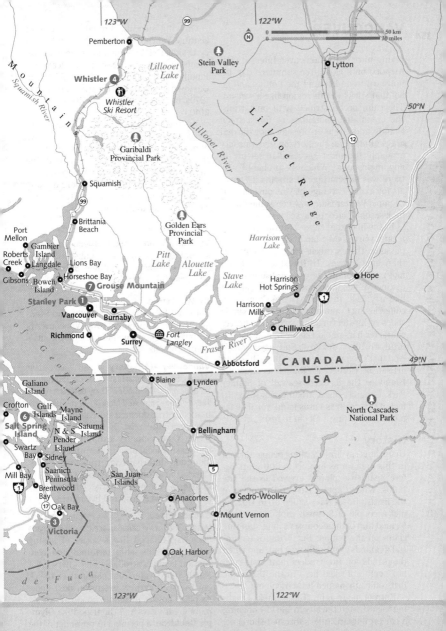

123°W

99

122°W

Pemberton

N

0   50 km
0   30 miles

Lillooet Lake

Stein Valley Park

Lytton

Whistler 4

50°N

Whistler Ski Resort

Lillooet River

Lillooet Range

12

Garibaldi Provincial Park

Squamish

99

Brittania Beach

Golden Ears Provincial Park

Harrison Lake

Hope

Port Mellon

Gambier Island

Roberts Creek

Langdale

Lions Bay

Pitt Lake

Alouette Lake

Stave Lake

Harrison Hot Springs

Gibsons

Horseshoe Bay

Bowen Island

7 Grouse Mountain

Harrison Mills

1

Stanley Park 1

Vancouver

Burnaby

Fort Langley

Chilliwack

Richmond

Surrey

Fraser River

Abbotsford

CANADA

49°N

USA

Galiano Island

Blaine

Lynden

Crofton

Gulf Islands

Mayne Island

6

Salt Spring Island

N & S Pender Island

Saturna Island

Bellingham

North Cascades National Park

Swartz Bay

Sidney

Mill Bay

Saanich Peninsula

San Juan Islands

1

Brentwood Bay

17

Oak Bay

Anacortes

Sedro-Woolley

3

Victoria

Mount Vernon

Oak Harbor

de   Fuca

123°W

122°W

you rub your aching muscles in the village

5 Hug the ancient trees in **Strathcona Provincial Park** (boxed text, p402) on a drive across Vancouver Island

6 Putter around the lively Saturday Market on **Salt Spring Island** (p405) and scoff more than a few fruit and bakery treats

7 Peer down over the twinkling Vancouver cityscape from the top of **Grouse Mountain** (p362), then hit the Eye of the Wind tower for an even higher vantage point

VANCOUVER

POP 578,000

Flying into YVR (Vancouver International Airport) on a cloud-free summer's day, it's not hard to understand the Lotus Land label that sticks to this region like a wetsuit. The calm ocean striped with boat trails, the crenulated shorelines of forest-green islands and the ever-present snow-dusted crags glinting on the horizon give this city arguably the most spectacular setting of any metropolis. Which is probably why there was no shortage of stirring TV visuals for global coverage of Vancouver's 2010 Olympic Winter Games, when some events took second place to the scenery.

But while the city's natural backdrop means you're never far from great outdoor pursuits, there's much more to Vancouver than appearances. Hitting the streets on foot means coming across a kaleidoscope of distinctive neighborhoods, each one almost like a village in itself. There's bohemian, coffee-loving Commercial Dr; the cool indie shops of hipster-hugging SoMa; the hearty character bars of old Gastown; and the colorful streets of the West End 'gayborhood.' And that's before you even get to the bustling artisan nest otherwise known as Granville Island or the forested seawall of Stanley Park, Canada's finest urban green space. In fact, if this really is Lotus Land, you'll be far too busy checking it all out to rest.

History

Historians say First Nations people thrived in this area for as long as 16,000 years before Spanish explorers arrived in the late 1500s. When Captain George Vancouver of the British Royal Navy sailed up in 1792, he met a couple of Spanish captains who informed him of their country's long-standing claim on the region. But Britain's territorial demands eventually won out, and when thousands of fur traders and gold-rush prospectors flocked here in the 1850s, the Brits officially named it their colony.

Entrepreneur John 'Gassy Jack' Deighton kick-started the city in 1867 by opening a bar on Burrard Inlet's forested shoreline, triggering a rash of development called 'Gastown' that eventually became modern-day Vancouver. Not everything went to plan for the fledgling city: it was almost completely destroyed in an 1886 fire. A prompt rebuild followed and a new downtown soon took shape.

Growing steadily throughout the 20th century, Vancouver added a National Hockey League (NHL) team and other accoutrements of a midsized North American city. Finally reflecting on its heritage, old-school Gastown was saved by gentrification in the 1970s, becoming a National Historic Site in 2010.

In 1986, Vancouver hosted a successful Expo World's Fair, sparking a massive wave of new development and adding the first of the mirrored skyscrapers that now define the downtown core. The Olympic and Paralympic Winter Games, staged here in 2010, aimed for a similar economic lift by showcasing the city to the world.

◉ Sights

Vancouver's most popular attractions are in several easily walkable neighborhoods, especially Gastown, Chinatown, Stanley Park and Granville Island.

DOWNTOWN

Bordered by water on two sides and Stanley Park on its tip, downtown Vancouver is centered on shop-lined Robson St, the city's main promenade.

Vancouver Art Gallery ART GALLERY
(Map p358; www.vanartgallery.bc.ca; 750 Hornby St; adult/child C$22.50/7.50, by donation 5-9pm Tue; ⊙10am-5pm Wed-Mon, to 9pm Tue) Dramatically transformed since 2000, the VAG is now a vital part of the city's cultural scene. Contemporary exhibitions – often showcasing local photoconceptualists – run alongside international traveling shows. Check out **Fuse** (admission C$19.50), a quarterly late-night party where young arties chill over wine and live music.

Canada Place NOTABLE BUILDING
(Map p358; www.canadaplace.ca; 999 Canada Place Way) Shaped like a series of jutting sails, this cruise-ship terminal and convention center's strollable pier offers great North Shore waterfront panoramas. Check out the swanky new extension next door: its plaza houses dramatic public artworks, more great views and the tripodlike **Olympic Cauldron**, a permanent reminder of the 2010 games.

BC Place Stadium NOTABLE BUILDING
(Map p358; www.bcplacestadium.com; 777 Pacific Blvd) Site of the Olympic opening and closing ceremonies, the city's main arena was having a new retractable lid fitted during

BRITISH COLUMBIA FAST FACTS

» **Population** 4.5 million

» **Area** 944,735 sq km

» **Capital City** Victoria

» **Other Cities** Vancouver

» **Sales Tax** 12%

» **Birthplace of** artist Emily Carr (1871–1945), celebrity Pamela Anderson (b 1967), musician Diana Krall (b 1964), actor-screenwriter Seth Rogen (b 1982), singer Nelly Furtado (b 1978)

» **Home of** Stanley Park, Douglas Coupland, Vancouver Canucks, Lululemon, Kermode Bears, Bard on the Beach Shakespeare Festival, world's largest hockey stick (Duncan)

» **Famous for** breathtaking mountain and ocean landscapes, the 2010 Olympic and Paralympic Winter Games and the world's largest public ferry system

» All prices in this chapter are in Canadian dollars (US1$ = C$1.02 at press time)

research for this book. On completion, it will host football's BC Lions and soccer's Vancouver Whitecaps. The **BC Sports Hall of Fame & Museum** (www.bcsportshalloffame.com) – a kid-friendly celebration of the province's sporting achievements – is also expected to reopen post-refurb.

Bill Reid Gallery of Northwest Coast Art
ART GALLERY

(Map p358; www.billreidgallery.ca; 639 Hornby St; adult/child C$10/5; ⊙11am-5pm Wed-Sun) Showcasing carvings, paintings and jewelry from Canada's most revered Haida artist, this is a comprehensive intro to Reid and his First Nations co-creators.

Vancouver Lookout
NOTABLE BUILDING

(Map p358; www.vancouverlookout.com; 555 W Hastings St; adult/child C$15/7; ⊙8:30am-10:30pm mid-May–Sep, 9am-9pm Oct–mid-May) Atop this 169m needle-like viewing tower – accessed via twin glass elevators – you'll enjoy 360-degree vistas of city, sea and mountains unfurling around you.

STANLEY PARK

This magnificent 404-hectare park combines excellent attractions with a mystical natural aura. Don't miss a stroll or cycle (rentals near the W Georgia St entrance) around the breathtaking 8.8km seawall.

Vancouver Aquarium
AQUARIUM

(www.vanaqua.org; adult/child C$27/17, reduced in winter; ⊙9:30am-7pm Jul & Aug, 9:30am-5pm Sep-Jun) Home to 9000 water-loving critters – think wolf eels, beluga whales and mesmerizing jellyfish – there's also a walk-through a rain-forest area of birds, turtles and a statue-still sloth. Check for feeding times and consider an Animal Encounter **trainer tour** (from C$24) or the 4D Experience: a 3D movie theater with added wind, mist and aromas.

Miniature Railway
RAILWAY

(☏604-257-8531; adult/child C$6.19/3.10; ⊙10am-6pm Jul-early Sep, reduced hours off-season) Families looking for a charming alternative to the city's bigger kid-friendly attractions should head to the heart of the park for a 15-minute railway trundle through the trees. This is also one of Vancouver's fave Christmas lures, when the grounds are decorated with Yuletide decorations and dioramas.

Second Beach & Third Beach
BEACH

Second Beach is an ever-busy, family-friendly area on the park's western side, with a grassy playground, snack bar and a pitch-and-putt golf course. Its main attraction is the seasonal outdoor swimming pool on the waterfront. Third Beach is more laid-back, with plenty of large logs to sit against and catch possibly Vancouver's best sunset.

Lost Lagoon
NATURE RESERVE

Originally an extension of Coal Harbour, this tranquil watery oasis is now colonized by indigenous plants and beady-eyed birdlife accessed via a shoreline trail. Drop into the **Nature House** (www.stanleypark ecology.ca; admission free; ⊙10am-7pm Tue-Sun May-Sep) for an introduction to the park's ecology and ask about area walks (adult/child C$10/5).

Vancouver

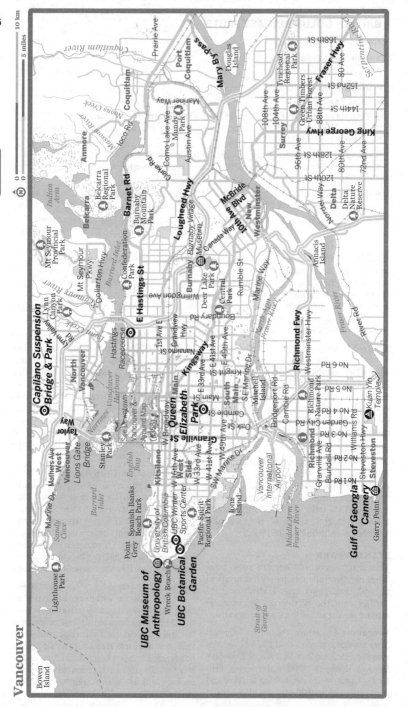

10 km
5 miles
0
0

Ⓝ

Bowen Island

Strait of Georgia

Lighthouse Park

Sandy Cove

Marine Dr

West Vancouver

Mathers Ave

Lions Gate Bridge

Burrard Inlet

Point Grey Spanish Banks Beach Park

Wreck Beach

UBC Museum of Anthropology

University of British Columbia

UBC Botanical Garden

UBC Winter Sports Center

Pacific Spirit Regional Park

Iona Island

Middle Arm Fraser River

Capilano Suspension Bridge & Park

Mt Seymour Provincial Park

Lynn Canyon Park

Seymour River

Seymour PKWY

Mt Seymour PKWY

Dollarton Hwy

North Vancouver

Taylor Way

Stanley Park

English Bay

Vancouver Harbour

First Narrows

See Downtown Vancouver & Around Map (p363)

Kitsilano

Hastings

West Side

W 16th Ave

W Broadway

W 33rd Ave

W 41st Ave

SW Marine Dr

Granville St

Queen Elizabeth Park

Main St

South Main

Cambie St

Oak St

W 49th Ave

Richmond

Granville Ave

Blundell Rd

No 2 Rd

No 1 Rd

Williams Rd

Steveston Hwy

Steveston

Gulf of Georgia Cannery

Garry Point

No 3 Rd

Garden City Rd

No 4 Rd

No 5 Rd

No 6 Rd

Bridgeport Rd

Cambie Rd

Richmond Westminster Hwy

Richmond Fwy

Kuan Yin Temple

Indian Arm

Belcarra

Belcarra Regional Park

Anmore

Ioco Rd

Missouri River

Noons Creek

Sasamat Lake

Barnet Rd

Burnaby Mountain Park

Barnet Hwy

Coquitlam

Port Coquitlam

Prairie Ave

Coquitlam River

Mariner Way

Como Lake Ave

Austin Ave

Clarke Rd

Mundy Park

Mary Hill By-Pass

Douglas Island

Lougheed Hwy

Burnaby

Burnaby Village Museum

Confederation Park

E Hastings Ave

E Hastings St

Willingdon Ave

Deer Lake Park

Central Park

Canada Way

Rumble St

Marine Way

Boundary Rd

Grandview Hwy

1st Ave E

Nanaimo St

Knight St

E 41st Ave

E 49th Ave

SE Marine Dr

Kingsway

E 33rd Ave

E 1st Ave

Mitchell Island

Annacis Island

North Arm Fraser River

River Rd

Fraser River

McBride Blvd

10th Ave

New Westminster

Delta

Nordel Way

Delta Nature Reserve

Surrey

King George Hwy

96th Ave

88th Ave

80th Ave

72nd Ave

120th St

128th St

104th Ave

108th Ave

144th St

152nd St

168th St

80 Ave

Fraser Hwy

Green Timbers Urban Forest

Tynehead Regional Park

Serpentine River

Hastings Racecourse

Burrard Inlet

WEST END

Dripping with wooden heritage homes and well-maintained older apartment blocks, this bustling residential neighborhood – home of Vancouver's gay community – combines seawall promenades and a myriad of midrange dining options.

Roedde House Museum   MUSEUM
(Map p358; www.roeddehouse.org; 1415 Barclay St; admission C$5; ⊙10am-5pm Tue-Sat, 2-4pm Sun) For a glimpse of pioneer town Vancouver, drop by this handsome 1893 timber-framed mansion. Packed with antiques, it's a superb re-creation of how well-heeled locals used to live. Sunday entry includes tea and cookies (for C$1 extra). Also check out the surrounding preserved homes in **Barclay Heritage Square**.

English Bay Beach   BEACH
(Map p358; cnr Denman & Davie Sts) Whether it's a languid August evening with buskers, sunbathers and volleyballers, or a blustery November day with the dog-walkers, this sandy curve is an unmissable city highlight. Snap photos of the beach's towering *inukshuk* First Nations sculpture or continue along the bustling seawall into neighboring Stanley Park.

YALETOWN

An old brick warehouse district transformed into swanky restaurants and boutiques, pedestrian-friendly Yaletown is where the city's beautiful people come to be seen, especially at night when the bars are full of designer trendies.

Roundhouse Community Arts
& Recreation Centre   NOTABLE BUILDING
(Map p358; www.roundhouse.ca; 181 Roundhouse Mews, cnr Davie St & Pacific Blvd) Yaletown's main cultural space occupies a refurbished historic railway shed. Train-flavored heritage is recalled in its small on-site **museum** (www.wcra.org/engine374; admission free) housing one of the city's most important artifacts: Engine No 374, the locomotive that pulled the first passenger train into Vancouver in 1887.

David Lam Park   PARK
(Map p358; www.vancouverparks.ca; cnr of Drake St & Pacific Blvd) A crooked elbow of landscaped waterfront at the neck of False Creek, this popular hangout is the perfect launch point for a 2km stroll along the north bank of False Creek. You'll pass public artworks, slick glass towers and visiting birdlife – including blue herons.

Contemporary Art Gallery   ART GALLERY
(Map p358; www.contemporaryartgallery.ca; 555 Nelson St; admission free; ⊙noon-6pm Wed-Sun) Focused on modern art – photography is particularly well represented – this small gallery showcases local and international works.

GASTOWN & CHINATOWN

Now a National Historic Site, the cobbled streets of Gastown are where the city began – look for the jaunty bronze of early resident Gassy Jack teetering on his whiskey barrel. Many heritage buildings remain, most now housing cool bars, restaurants or trendy shops.

Steam Clock   HISTORIC CLOCK
(Map p358) The landmark in Gastown is halfway along Water St. A snapshot favorite, it's actually powered by electricity.

Chinatown Millennium Gate   MONUMENT
(Map p358; W Pender & Taylor Sts) Gastown is adjoined by North America's third-largest Chinatown: check out the towering gate, the area's monumental entry point, and don't miss the bustling summer **night market**. For Chinatown information, see www.vancouver-chinatown.com.

Science World at TELUS World of
Science   MUSEUM
(Map p358; www.scienceworld.ca; 1455 Quebec St; adult/child C$21/14.25; ⊙10am-5pm Mon-Fri, 10am-6pm Sat & Sun) The hands-on science and natural-history exhibits here bring out the kid in everyone. An ideal place to entertain the family, it also has an **Omnimax Theatre** screening large-format documentaries. Explore without the kids at the regular adults-only After Dark events (C$19.75). During research, an upgrade and an outdoor science park expansion were under way.

Vancouver Police Museum   MUSEUM
(Map p358; www.vancouverpolicemuseum.ca; 240 E Cordova St; adult/student C$7/5; ⊙9am-5pm) Charting the city's murky criminal past – via confiscated weapons, counterfeit currencies and a mortuary exhibit lined with tissue samples – this excellent little museum also runs evocative Sins of the City walking tours (adult/child C$15/12) plus after-hours Forensics for Adults (C$12) workshops.

Dr Sun Yat-Sen Classical Chinese
Garden   GARDEN
(Map p358; www.vancouverchinesegarden.com; 578 Carrall St; adult/child C$14/10; ⊙9:30am-7pm mid-Jun–Aug, 10am-6pm Sep & May–mid-Jun,

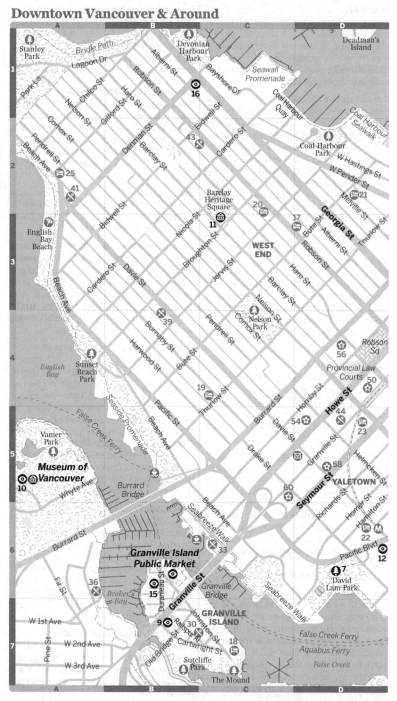

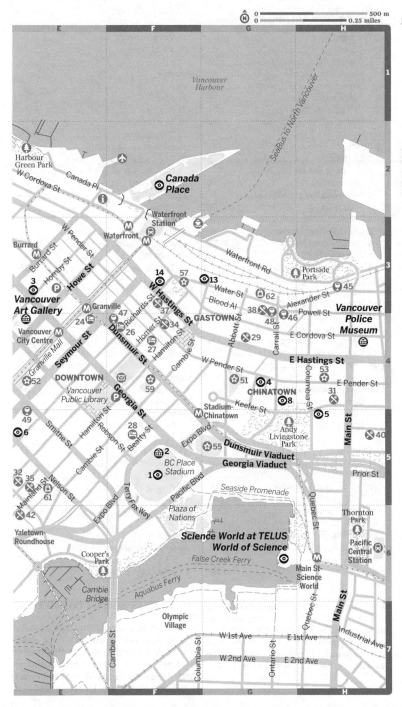

0   500 m
0   0.25 miles

Vancouver
Harbour

Harbour
Green Park

W Cordova St

Canada Pl

**Canada
Place**

SeaBus to North Vancouver

Waterfront
Station

Waterfront

Burrard

W Pender St

Burrard St

Hornby St

Howe St

Waterfront Rd

Portside
Park

45

**Vancouver
Police
Museum**

3

**Vancouver
Art Gallery**

Granville

Richards St

W Hastings St

14   57   13

Water St

Blood Al

GASTOWN

62

38   46

Alexander St

Powell St

E Cordova St

Vancouver
City Centre

24

47

26

Homer St

Hamilton St

37

34

27

Seymour St

Dunsmuir St

Cambie St

Abbott St

Carrall St

29

48

52

DOWNTOWN

Granville Mall

Vancouver
Public Library

Georgia St

59

W Pender St

51   4

E Hastings St

53

E Pender St

31

49

6

Smithe St

Hamilton St

Robson St

Beatty St

28

Stadium-
Chinatown

CHINATOWN

8

Keefer St

5

Columbia St

Main St

40

32   35

Mainland St

Nelson St

61

42

2

1

**BC Place
Stadium**

55

Expo Blvd

Dunsmuir Viaduct

Georgia Viaduct

Andy
Livingstone
Park

Pacific Blvd

Seaside Promenade

Prior St

Yaletown-
Roundhouse

Cooper's
Park

Cambie
Bridge

Terry Fox Way

Plaza of
Nations

Aquabus Ferry

**Science World at TELUS
World of Science**

False Creek Ferry

Quebec St

Thornton
Park

Pacific
Central
Station

6

Main St-
Science
World

Olympic
Village

Cambie St

Columbia St

W 1st Ave

W 2nd Ave

Ontario St

E 1st Ave

E 2nd Ave

Quebec St

Main St

Industrial Ave

E   F   G   H

Downtown Vancouver

VANCOUVER, WHISTLER & VANCOUVER ISLAND VANCOUVER

10am-4:30pm Oct-Apr) A tranquility break from clamorous Chinatown, this intimate 'garden of ease' reveals the Taoist symbolism behind the placing of gnarled pine trees and ancient limestone formations. Check out the less elaborate but free-entry park next door.

SOUTH MAIN (SOMA) & COMMERCIAL DRIVE

Eschewing the fake tans of Robson St's mainstream shoppers, Vancouver's indie crowd has colonized an area of town that used to be a byword for down-at-heel. Radiating from the intersection of Main St and Broadway, South Main – also known as SoMa – is home to the city's young alternative crowd: think skinny jeans and plaid shirts for guys; vintage chic and thick-framed spectacles for girls. Independent coffee shops, cool-ass bars, vegetarian eateries and one-of-a-kind boutiques abound – especially past the 20th Ave intersection.

In contrast, Commercial Dr is the city's bohemian hang-out. Urban adventurers should alight from the Broadway-Commercial SkyTrain station for a stroll north along the drive, where decades of European immigrants – especially Italians, Greeks and Portuguese – have created a funky United Nations of restaurants, coffee bars and exotic delis. It's the best spot in town to watch international soccer games among passionate fans, and it's also a promenade of espresso-supping patio dwellers on languid afternoons.

GRANVILLE ISLAND

Tucked under the looming Granville Bridge, this gentrified former industrial peninsula – not actually an island – is one of Vancouver's best lazy-afternoon haunts. Studded with restaurants, bars, theaters and artisan studios, it's crowded on summer weekends as visitors chill out with the buskers and wrestle the seagulls for their fish 'n chips. For information, see www.granvilleisland.com.

Public Market　　　　　　　　MARKET
(Map p358; Johnston St; ⊙9am-7pm) Granville Island's highlight is the covered Public Market, a multisensory smorgasbord of fish, cheese, fruit and bakery treats. Pick up fixings for a picnic at nearby Vanier Park or hit the international food court (dine off-peak to snag a table). **Edible BC** (www.edible -britishcolumbia.com; tours C$49) offers great market tours for the foodie-inclined.

Granville Island Brewing　　MICROBREWERY
(Map p358; www.gib.ca; 1441 Cartwright St; tours C$9.75; ⊙noon, 2pm & 4pm) A tour of Canada's oldest microbrewery ends with four sample beers in the Taproom – often including summer-favorite Hefeweizen, mildly hopped Brockton IPA or the recommended Kitsilano Maple Cream Ale. Buy takeout in the adjoining store and look for special-batch tipples like Ginger Ale.

KITSILANO

A former 1960s hippy haven, 'Kits' is now a pleasant neighborhood of heritage homes and browsable shops. Take a lazy afternoon stroll along store-lined W 4th Ave or sunbather-packed Kitsilano Beach, or hit the triumvirate of Vanier Park museums.

HR MacMillan Space Centre　　MUSEUM
(Map p358; www.hrmacmillanspacecentre. com; 1100 Chestnut St; adult/child C$15/10.75; ⊙10am-5pm daily Jul & Aug, 10am-3pm Mon-Fri, 10am-5pm Sat & Sun Sep-Jun) Popular with kids, this high-tech space center offers the chance to battle aliens, design spacecraft and take a Mars-bound simulator ride. There's an additional free-entry **observatory** (open most weekends) and a **planetarium** running weekend music-themed laser shows (C$10.75).

Museum of Vancouver　　MUSEUM
(Map p358; www.museumofvancouver.ca; 1100 Chestnut St; adult/child C$12/8; ⊙10am-5pm Tue-Sun, to 8pm Thu) The recently rebranded MOV has upped its game with cool exhibitions and late-opening parties aimed at an adult crowd. There are still colorful displays on local 1950s pop culture and 1960s hippie counterculture – plus plenty of hands-on kids stuff, including weekend scavenger hunts.

Vancouver Maritime Museum　　MUSEUM
(www.vancouvermaritimemuseum.com; 1905 Ogden Ave; adult/child C$11/8.50; ⊙10am-5pm daily May-Aug, 10am-5pm Tue-Sat & noon-5pm Sun Sep-Apr) Combines dozens of intricate model ships with detailed re-created boat sections and a few historic vessels; the highlight here is the *St Roch,* an arctic patrol vessel that was the first to navigate the Northwest Passage in both directions.

UNIVERSITY OF BRITISH COLUMBIA

West from Kits on a 400-hectare forested peninsula, **UBC** (www.ubc.ca) is the province's largest university, complete with a surprising number of visitor attractions.

Botanical Garden　　GARDEN
(www.ubcbotanicalgarden.org; 6804 SW Marine Dr; adult/child C$8/4; ⊙9am-4:30pm Mon-Fri, 9:30am-4:30pm Sat & Sun, reduced hours off-season) A giant collection of rhododendrons, a fascinating apothecary plot and a winter green space of off-season bloomers are highlights of this 28-hectare themed garden complex. The additional **Greenheart Canopy Walkway** (www.greenheartcanopy walkway.com; adult/child C$20/6; ⊙9am-5pm; ⊕) lifts visitors 17m above the forest floor on a 308m guided eco tour. Combined entry with Nitobe Memorial Garden is adult/child C$12/6.

DON'T MISS

THE RETURN OF VANCOUVER'S BEST MUSEUM

Recently reopened after an extensive C$55-million reno that doubled its size, the **Museum of Anthropology** (www.moa.ubc.ca; 6393 NW Marine Dr; adult/child C$14/12; ⊙10am-5pm Wed-Mon, 10am-9pm Tue, closed Mon mid-Oct–mid-Jan) is Vancouver's best museum. It houses Canada's most important northwest coast aboriginal artifact collection, including full-size Haida houses and a spectacular array of totem poles set against a dramatic cliffside window. The expansion enables many non-First Nations exhibits to finally see the light of day, including jaw-dropping European ceramics and Cantonese opera costumes (no, you can't try them on). There's such depth here that taking one of the free guided tours – there are three per day – is highly recommended. Also check out the gift shop and its lovely First Nations arts and crafts.

Nitobe Memorial Garden   GARDEN
(www.nitobe.org; 1895 Lower Mall; adult/child C$8/4; ⊙10am-4pm, reduced hours off-season) Designed by a top Japanese landscape architect, this lovely green space is a perfect example of the Asian nation's symbolic horticultural art form. Aside from some traffic noise and summer bus tours, it's a tranquil retreat, ideal for quiet meditation. Combined entry with botanical garden is adult/child C$12/6.

WEST SIDE

Covering City Hall and the heritage homes of Fairview – plus the strollable stores and restaurants of South Granville – this area gives you several good reasons to visit. And with the opening of the Canada Line SkyTrain link, it's now easy reachable from downtown.

VanDusen Botanical Garden   GARDEN
(www.vandusengarden.org; 5251 Oak St; adult/child C$9.75/5.25; ⊙10am-4pm Nov-Feb, 10am-5pm Mar & Oct, 10am-6pm Apr, 10am-8pm May, 10am-9pm Jun-Aug, 10am-7pm Sep) A highly ornamental confection of sculptures, Canadian heritage flowers, rare plants and a popular hedge maze, this garden is also one of Vancouver's top Christmastime destinations: think thousands of twinkling fairy lights.

Queen Elizabeth Park   PARK
(www.vancouverparks.ca) This 52-hectare park is a local favorite. Check out the formal gardens, great hilltop views and synchronized fountains, where you'll also find a hulking Henry Moore bronze called *Knife Edge – Two Piece*.

Bloedel Floral Conservatory   GARDEN
(www.vancouverparks.ca; adult/child C$4.76/2.43; ⊙9am-8pm Mon-Fri & 10am-9pm Sat & Sun May-Aug, 10am-5pm daily Sep-Apr) Cresting the hill in Queen Elizabeth Park, this domed conservatory has three climate-controlled zones

housing 400 plant species, dozens of koi carp and many free-flying tropical birds, including parrots and macaws.

NORTH VANCOUVER & WEST VANCOUVER

Accessed from downtown via the Lions Gate Bridge or the SeaBus service, the North Shore comprises the commuter city of North Vancouver and chichi 'West Van.'

Capilano Suspension Bridge   BRIDGE
(www.capbridge.com; 3735 Capilano Rd, North Vancouver; adult/child C$29.95/10; ⊙8:30am-8pm Jun-Aug, 9am-7pm May & Sep, reduced hours off-season) This 140m-long pedestrian walkway sways over tree-lined Capilano Canyon, an awesome visual even for the most jaded traveler. The surrounding park houses totem poles, rain-forest walks and a network of smaller cable bridges between the trees.

Grouse Mountain   VIEWS, SNOW SPORTS
(www.grousemountain.com; 6400 Nancy Greene Way, North Vancouver; adult/child C$39/13.95; ⊙9am-10pm; ⊞) The mountain offers smashing views of downtown Vancouver. In summer, Skyride gondola tickets to the top include access to lumberjack shows, alpine hiking trails and a grizzly-bear refuge. Pay extra for the zipline course (C$105) or new Eye of the Wind tour (C$25) which takes you up a 20-story wind turbine tower for some spectacular views. In winter, Grouse is also a magnet for skiers and snowboarders.

Cypress Provincial Park   PARK
(www.bcparks.ca; Cypress Bowl Rd, West Vancouver) This park, 8km north of West Van via Hwy 99, offers excellent summertime hiking trails. In winter, the park's **Cypress Mountain** (www.cypressmountain.com) attracts sporty types with its 38 ski runs and popular snowshoe trails – this was the site of snow-

board and freestyle skiing events at the 2010 Olympic and Paralympic Winter Games.

 Activities

With a reputation for outdoorsy locals who like nothing better than an early-morning 10km jog and a lip-smacking feast of rice cakes for breakfast, Vancouver is all about being active.

Hiking & Running

For an arm-swinging strolls or a heart-pounding run, the 8.8km Stanley Park seawall is mostly flat – apart from a couple of uphills where you could hang onto a passing bike. UBC's Pacific Spirit Regional Park is also a popular running spot, with tree-lined trails marked throughout the area.

Grouse Grind RUNNING

If you really want a workout, try North Vancouver's Grouse Grind, a steep, sweat-triggering slog up the side of Grouse Mountain that's nicknamed 'Mother Nature's Stairmaster.' Reward yourself at the top with free access to the resort's facilities – although you'll have to pay C$10 to get down via the Skyride gondola.

Cycling

Sharing the busy Stanley Park seawall with cyclists (and in-line skaters), joggers can take sidelong glances at some breathtaking sea-to-sky vistas. Since camera-wielding tourists crowd the route in summer, it's best to come early in the morning or later in the afternoon.

After circling the park to English Bay, continue along the north side of False Creek toward Science World, where the route heads up south False Creek toward Granville Island, Vanier Park, Kitsilano Beach and, finally, UBC. This extended route, including Stanley Park, is around 25km. If you still have some energy, UBC's Pacific Spirit Regional Park has forested bike trails, some with challenging uphills.

There's a plethora of bike and blade rental stores near Stanley Park's W Georgia St entrance, especially around the intersection with Denman St. Also, pick up the *Greater Vancouver Cycling Map* (C$3.95) from local convenience stores. It highlights bike routes around the region.

Spokes Bicycle Rentals CYCLING
(Map p358; www.vancouverbikerental.com; 1798 W Georgia St) The biggest cycling shop.

On the Water

It's hard to beat the joy of an early-evening paddle around the coastline here, with the sun sliding languidly down the mirrored glass towers that forest the city like modern-day totems.

Ecomarine Ocean Kayak Centre KAYAKING
(Map p358; www.ecomarine.com; 1668 Duranleau St; rentals per 2hr/day C$36/69; ⊙9am-6pm Sun-Thu & 9am-9pm Fri & Sat Jun-Aug, 10am-6pm

---

WHERE BC BEGAN

Little Fort Langley's tree-lined streets and 19th-century storefronts make it an ideal day out from Vancouver. Its main historic highlight is the colorful **Fort Langley National Historic Site** (www.pc.gc.ca/fortlangley; 23433 Mavis Ave; adult/senior/child C$7.80/6.55/3.90; ⊙9am-8pm Jul & Aug, 10am-5pm Sep-Jun), perhaps the region's most important old-school landmark.

A fortified trading post since 1827, this is where James Douglas announced the creation of BC in 1858. With costumed re-enactors, re-created artisan workshops and a gold-panning area that's very popular with kids – who'll also enjoy charging around the wooden battlements – this is a recommended spot for families who want to add a little education to their vacation.

If you need an introduction before hitting the buildings, there's a surprisingly entertaining time-travel-themed movie presentation on offer. And make sure you check the website before you arrive: there's a wide array of events that bring the past evocatively back to life, including a summer-evening campfire program that will take you right back to the pioneer days.

From Vancouver, drive Hwy 1 east for 40km, then take the 232nd St exit north. Follow the signs along 232nd St until you reach the stop sign at Glover Rd. Turn right here, and continue into the village. Turn right again on Mavis Ave, just before the railway tracks. The fort's parking lot is at the end of the street.

Sep-May) Headquartered on Granville Island, it offers rentals and tours. Its Jericho Beach **branch** (Jericho Sailing Centre, 1300 Discovery St; ⊙9am-dusk May-Aug, 9am-dusk Sat & Sun Sep) organizes events where you can hang with local paddle nuts.

Windsure Adventure Watersports
WATER SPORTS

(www.windsure.com; Jericho Sailing Centre, 1300 Discovery St; surfboard/skimboard rentals per hr C$18.58/4.64; ⊙9am-8pm Apr-Sep) specializes in kiteboarding, windsurfing and skimboarding, offering lessons and rentals from its Jericho Beach base.

Tours

Architectural Institute of BC
WALKING

(☑604-683-8588/333; www.aibc.ca; tours C$5; ⊙1pm Tue-Sat Jul & Aug) Two-hour guided walks around the buildings and history of historic neighborhoods. Six tours available.

Vancouver Trolley Company
BUS

(☑604-801-5515, 888-451-5581; www.vancouvertrolley.com; adult/child C$38/20) Red replica trolley buses offering hop-on-hop-off transportation around popular city stops.

Vancouver Tour Guys
WALKING

(☑604-690-5909; www.tourguys.ca) The scheduled walking tours of three area

neighborhoods are free but gratuities (in the C$5 to C$10 range) are highly encouraged. Check the website for the ever-changing itinerary.

Harbour Cruises & Events
BOAT

(☑604-688-7246, 800-663-1500; www.boatcruises.com; adult/child C$30/10; ⊙May-Oct) View the city – and some unexpected wildlife – from the water on a 75-minute harbor boat tour. Dinner cruises also available. Located at the north foot of Denman St.

⭐ Festivals & Events

Chinese New Year
COMMUNITY

(www.vancouver-chinatown.com) This festive kaleidoscope of dancing, parades and great food is held every January or February.

Vancouver Playhouse International Wine Festival
WINE

(www.playhousewinefest.com) The city's oldest and best annual wine celebration takes place in late March.

Vancouver International Children's Festival
CHILDREN

(www.childrensfestival.ca) Storytelling, performance and activities at venues across Granville Island in early June.

VANCOUVER FOR CHILDREN

Family-friendly Vancouver is stuffed with things to do with vacationing kids. Grab a copy of the free *Kids' Guide Vancouver* flyer from racks around town or visit www.kidsvancouver.com for tips and resources. If you're traveling without a car, hop on the SkyTrain or SeaBus transit services or the miniferry to Granville Island: kids love 'em – especially the new SkyTrain cars, where they can sit up front and pretend they're driving. Under-fivess travel free on all transit.

Childcare equipment – strollers, booster seats, cribs, baby monitors and toys etc – can be rented from the friendly folk at **Wee Travel** (☑604-222-4722; www.weetravel.ca). Hotels can also usually recommend licensed and bonded babysitting services.

Stanley Park (p355) can easily keep most families occupied for a day. If it's hot, hit the water park at Lumberman's Arch or try the swimming pool at Second Beach; also consider the miniature railway. The park is a great place to bring a picnic, and its beaches – especially Third Beach – are highly kid-friendly. Save time for the **Vancouver Aquarium** (p355) and, if your kids have been good, consider a behind-the-scenes trainer tour. The city's other educational attractions include **Science World** (p357) and the **HR MacMillan Space Centre** (p361).

If you time your visit right, the city also has an array of family-friendly festivals, including the **Pacific National Exhibition** (p365), the **Vancouver International Children's Festival** (p365) and the fireworks fiesta known as the **Celebration of Light** (p365).

📶**Little Nest** (www.littlenest.ca; 1716 Charles St) is worth a visit if you'd like to have a meal with your kids without worrying about other diners. This family-friendly joint, just off Commercial Dr, is a home-away-from-home hang-out and does a great line in local and organic nosh for even the pickiest of eaters.

BC'S BEST BIRD-WATCHING

Reifel Migratory Bird Sanctuary (www.reifelbirdsanctuary.com; 5191 Robertson Rd; adult/child C$5/3; ⊙9am-4pm), southwest of Vancouver, is small-town Ladner's main attraction, operating like a wetland nature stroll for visiting ornithologists. It's an important stopover for migrating birds – it's at its most cacophonous in the fall – and the flying critters to watch out for include the Russian lesser snow goose, the yellow-breasted chat and the boreal owl. Off Hwy 17, turn right on Ladner Trunk Rd and follow it through Ladner to River Rd. Turn right on Westham Island Rd, go over the bridge and follow it to the sanctuary.

Bard on the Beach THEATRE
(www.bardonthebeach.org) A season (June to September) of four Shakespeare-related plays in Vanier Park tents.

Vancouver International Jazz Festival MUSIC
(www.coastaljazz.ca) City-wide cornucopia of superstar shows and free outdoor events from mid-June.

Celebration of Light FIREWORKS
(www.celebration-of-light.com) Free international fireworks extravaganza in English Bay from late July.

Pride Week COMMUNITY
(www.vancouverpride.ca) From late July, parties, concerts and fashion shows culminating in a giant pride parade.

Pacific National Exhibition COMMUNITY
(www.pne.bc.ca) Family-friendly shows, music concerts and a fairground from mid-August.

Vancouver International Fringe Festival THEATER
(www.vancouverfringe.com) Wild and wacky theatricals at mainstream and unconventional Granville Island venues in mid-September.

Vancouver International Film Festival FILM
(www.viff.org) Popular two-week showcase (from late September) of Canadian and international movies.

🛏 Sleeping

Vancouver room rates peak in summer, but great deals are available in fall and early spring when the weather can be almost as good. **Tourism Vancouver** (www.tourismvancouver.com) and the province's **Hello BC** (www.hellobc.com) provide listings and booking services.

DOWNTOWN

TOP CHOICE **Loden Vancouver** BOUTIQUE HOTEL **$$$**
(Map p358; ☑604-669-5060, 877-225-6336; www.theloden.com; 1177 Melville St;

r from C$249; ✸⊛) The definition of class, the stylish Loden is the real designer deal. Its 70 rooms combine a knowing contemporary élan with luxe accoutrements like marble-lined bathrooms and those oh-so-civilized heated floors. The attentive service is top-notch, while the glam Voya is one of the city's best hotel bars. Hit the town in style in the hotel's complimentary London taxicab.

Urban Hideaway Guesthouse GUESTHOUSE **$$**
(Map p358; ☑604-694-0600; www.urban-hideaway.com; 581 Richards St; d/tw/loft C$109/129/149; ⊛) This supremely cozy spot is a good-value word-of-mouth favorite. Tuck yourself into one of the seven comfy rooms (the loft is our favorite) or spend your time in the lounge downstairs. Breakfast fixings (eggs, bacon etc) are provided: you cook it yourself in the well-equipped kitchen. Bathrooms are mostly shared, although the loft is ensuite.

Victorian Hotel HOTEL **$$**
(Map p358; ☑604-681-6369, 877-681-6369; www.victorianhotel.ca; 514 Homer St; r with shared/private bathroom from C$129/149; ⊛) Housed in a pair of renovated older properties, the high-ceilinged rooms here combine glossy hardwood floors, an occasional bay window and plenty of antique-style charm. Most are ensuite – with TVs and summer fans provided – but the best rooms are in the newer extension, complete with marble-floored bathrooms.

St Regis Hotel BOUTIQUE HOTEL **$$**
(Map p358; ☑604-681-1135, 800-770-7929; www.stregishotel.com; 602 Dunsmuir St; r from C$220; ✸⊛⊛) The rooms at this art-lined boutique sleepover in the heart of downtown exhibit a loungey atmosphere, with leather-look wallpaper, earth-tone bedspreads, flat-screen TVs and multimedia hubs. Check out the furniture, too: it's mostly reclaimed

and refinished from the old Hotel Georgia. Rates include breakfast, a business center with free-use computers and access to the nearby gym.

Samesun Backpackers Lodge HOSTEL **$**
(Map p358; ☎604-682-8226, 877-972-6378; www.samesun.com; 1018 Granville St; dm/r C$29.50/71; ❂❖) Expect a party atmosphere at this lively hostel in the heart of the Granville nightclub area – there's also a hopping onsite bar if you don't quite make it out the door. The dorms, complete with funky paint jobs, are comfortably small and there's a large kitchen plus a strong lineup of social events. Free continental breakfast.

WEST END

Sylvia Hotel HOTEL **$$**
(Map p358; ☎604-681-9321; www.sylviahotel.com; 1154 Gilford St; s/d/ste from C$110/165/195; ❖) Generations of guests keep coming back to this ivy-covered gem for a dollop of old-world charm and a side order of first-name service. The lobby resembles a Bavarian pension – stained-glass windows and darkwood paneling – and there's a wide array of comfortable room configurations. The best are the 12 apartment suites, which include full kitchens and English Bay panoramas.

Listel Vancouver BOUTIQUE HOTEL **$$**
(Map p358; ☎604-684-8461, 800-663-5491; www.thelistelhotel.com; 1300 Robson St; d from C$169; ❂) Vancouver's self-described 'art hotel' is a cut above the other properties at this end of Robson St. Attracting sophisticates with its gallery-style art installations (check the hidden art space just off the lobby), its mood-lit rooms are suffused with a relaxing West Coast ambience. Adding to the artsy appeal, the on-site resto-bar hosts nightly live jazz.

HI Vancouver Downtown HOSTEL **$**
(Map p358; ☎604-684-4565, 888-203-4302; www.hihostels.ca/vancouver; 1114 Burnaby St; dm/r C$33.50/83.25) Quiet, purpose-built hostel with a more institutional feel than its Granville St brother. Dorms are small and rates include continental breakfast.

Blue Horizon Hotel HOTEL **$$$**
(Map p358; ☎604-688-1411, 800-663-1333; www.bluehorizonhotel.com; 1225 Robson St; d from C$159; ❂❖❂) Sleek and comfortable, this slender tower-block property has business-hotel-like rooms. All are corner suites with balconies.

YALETOWN

Opus Hotel Vancouver BOUTIQUE HOTEL **$$$**
(Map p358; ☎604-642-6787, 866-642-6787; www.opushotel.com; 322 Davie St; d & ste from C$280; ❂❖) Celebs looking for a place to be seen should look no further: the city's original designer sleepover has been welcoming the likes of Justin Timberlake and that bald bloke from REM for years. The paparazzi magnets come for the chic suites, including feng-shui bed placements and luxe bathrooms with clear windows overlooking the streets (visiting exhibitionists take note). There's a stylish onsite resto-bar and a small gym.

YWCA Hotel HOSTEL **$**
(Map p358; ☎604-895-5830, 800-663-1424; www.ywcahotel.com; 733 Beatty St; s/d/tr C$69/86/111; ❂❖❂) One of Canada's best Ys, this popular tower near Yaletown is a useful option for those on a budget. Accommodating men, women, couples and families, it's a bustling place with a communal kitchen on every other floor and rooms ranging from compact singles to group-friendly larger quarters. All are a little institutional – think student study-bedroom – but each has a sink and refrigerator.

GRANVILLE ISLAND & KITSILANO

Granville Island Hotel BOUTIQUE HOTEL **$$$**
(Map p358; ☎604-683-7373, 800-663-1840; www.granvilleislandhotel.com; 1253 Johnston St; d from C$159; ❂❂) Hugging the quiet eastern tip of Granville Island, it's a five-minute walk from shops, theaters and the public market here. Characterized by contemporary West Coast decor, rooms feature exposed wood and soothing earth tones. There's also a cool rooftop Jacuzzi, plus an onsite brewpub (Jamaican Lager recommended).

Mickey's Kits Beach Chalet B&B **$$**
(☎604-739-3342, 888-739-3342; www.mickeysbandb.com; 2142 W 1st Ave; d C$135-175; ❖❂) This modern, Whistler-style chalet has three rooms and a tranquil, hedged-in garden terrace. Rooms – including the gabled, top-floor York Room – are decorated in a comfortable contemporary style, but only the York has an ensuite bathroom. It's a family-friendly place: the hosts can supply toys and cribs and help arrange babysitters. Includes continental breakfast.

HI Vancouver Jericho Beach HOSTEL **$**
(☎604-224-3208, 888-203-4303; www.hihostels.ca/vancouver; 1515 Discovery St; dm/r C$20/76.25; ◷May-early Oct; ❂❖) Resembling a Victorian

hospital from the outside, this large hostel has a great outdoorsy location – especially if you're here for the sun-kissed Kitsilano vibe and the activities at nearby Jericho Beach (downtown is a 20-minute bus ride away). Rooms are basic, but extras include a large kitchen, licensed café and bike rentals. Book ahead for a sought-after private room.

UBC & WEST SIDE

Shaughnessy Village   HOTEL **$$**
(☎604-736-5511; www.shaughnessyvillage.com; 1125 W 12th Ave; s/d C$79/101; ⊠) This entertainingly kitsch sleepover – pink carpets, flowery sofas and nautical memorabilia – describes itself as a tower-block 'B&B resort.' Despite the old-school approach, it's perfectly shipshape, right down to its well-maintained rooms, which, like boat cabins, are lined with wooden cupboards and include microwaves, refrigerators and tiny ensuites.

University of British Columbia Housing   HOSTEL, HOTEL **$-$$**
(☎604-822-1000, 888-822-1030; www.ubcconferences.com; hostel r from C$35, apt r from C$49, ste from C$179; ☏) Pretend you're still a student by staying at UBC. The wide variety of room types includes good-value one- or two-bed spots at the Pacific Spirit Hostel; private rooms in shared four- to six-bed apartments at Gage Towers (most with great views); and the hotel-style West Coast Suites with flat-screen TVs and slick wood and stone interiors. Mostly available May to August only.

Plaza 500   HOTEL **$$**
(☎604-873-1811, 800-473-1811; www.plaza500.com; 500 W 12th Ave; r from C$159; ⊠☏) With some great mountain-baked city views available, rooms at the Plaza 500 have a contemporary business-hotel feel. It's a mod look that's taken to the max in Fig-Mint, the property's lobby resto-bar. Rates include local gym passes, while the nearby Canada Line SkyTrain station can whisk you downtown in minutes.

✗ Eating

Vancouver is celebrated for its international diversity; visitors can fill up on great ethnic dishes before they even start on the region's flourishing West Coast cuisine. Whatever you choose, don't miss the seafood, BC's greatest culinary asset. Tap into the foodie vibe via www.urbandiner.ca or pick up a free copy of *Eat Magazine*.

DOWNTOWN

Templeton   BREAKFAST, BURGERS **$$**
(Map p358; www.thetempleton.blogspot.com; 1087 Granville St; mains C$8-12; ⊛) A funky chrome-and-vinyl '50s diner with a twist, Templeton chefs up plus-sized organic burgers, addictive fries, vegetarian quesadillas and perhaps the best hangover cure in town – the 'Big Ass Breakfast.' Sadly, the mini jukeboxes on the tables don't work, but you can console yourself with a waistline-busting chocolate ice-cream float. Beer here is of the local microbrew variety. Avoid busy weekend peak times or you'll be queuing for ages.

C Restaurant   SEAFOOD **$$$**
(Map p358; ☎604-681-1164; www.crestaurant.com; 1600 Howe St; mains C$28-40) This pioneering sustainable seafood restaurant overlooking False Creek isn't cheap (lunch is cheaper, though) but its revelatory approach to fish and shellfish makes it the city's best seafood dine-out. You'll be hard-pressed to find smoked salmon with cucumber jelly served anywhere else, but there's also a reverence for simple preparation that reveals the delicate flavors in dishes such as local side-stripe prawns and northern BC scallops.

Finch's   CAFÉ **$**
(Map p358; www.finchteahouse.com; 353 W Pender St; mains C$3-8) Arrive off-peak and you might find a seat at one of the dinged dining tables studding this buzzing corner café which has a 'granny-chic' look of creaky wooden floors and junkshop bric-a-brac. You'll be joining in-the-know locals who've been hanging out here for years. They come for the good-value breakfasts (egg and soldiers from C$2.50) and fresh-prepared baguette sandwiches with house-made soups.

Gorilla Food   VEGETARIAN **$**
(Map p358; www.gorillafood.com; 436 Richards St; mains C$4-7.50; ✓) This smashing little subterranean eatery is lined with woodsy flourishes and the kind of fresh-faced, healthy-living vegans who will make you want to adopt a new lifestyle. Organic raw food is the approach, which means treats such as seaweed wraps or pizza made from a dehydrated seed crust topped with tomato sauce, tenderized zucchini and mashed avocado.

WEST END

TOP CHOICE **Raincity Grill**   WEST COAST **$$$**
(Map p358; ☎604-685-7337; www.raincitygrill.com; 1193 Denman St; mains C$17-30)

This excellent English Bay restaurant was sourcing and serving unique BC ingredients long before the fashion for Fanny Bay oysters and Salt Spring Island lamb took hold. It's a great showcase for fine West Coast cuisine: the C$30 three-course tasting menu (served between 5pm and 6pm) is a bargain and the weekend brunch is a local legend. If you're on the move, drop by the takeout window and pick up gourmet fish 'n chips for C$10, then head to English Bay Beach for a picnic. Great wine list.

Lolita's   MEXICAN $$
(Map p358; www.lolitasrestaurant.com; 1326 Davie St; mains C$18-25) This lively cantina is ever popular with in-the-know West Enders for good reason: its warm and mellow party vibe makes you feel like you're hanging out with friends in a bar at the beach. Turn your taste buds on with a few rounds of gold tequila or a fruity cocktail, then take a booze respite with some spicy, fusionesque fare including the wonderful halibut tacos.

Sushi Mart   JAPANESE $
(Map p358; www.sushimart.com; 1686 Robson St; mains C$6-10) You'll be rubbing shoulders with chatty young Asians at the large communal dining table here, one of the best spots in town for a sushi feast in a casual setting. Check the fresh-sheet blackboard showing what's available and then tuck into expertly prepared and well-priced shareable platters of all your fave nigiri, maki and sashimi treats.

YALETOWN

Blue Water Café   SEAFOOD $$$
(Map p358; ☎604-688-8078; www.bluewatercafe.net; 1095 Hamilton St; mains C$22-44) Vancouver's best posh oyster bar, this high-concept seafood restaurant is the pinnacle of Yaletown fine dining. House music gently percolates through the cobalt-blue interior, while seafood towers, arctic char and BC sablefish grace the tables inside and on the patio. If you feel like an adventure, head for the semicircular raw bar and watch the whirling blades prepare delectable sushi and sashimi, served with the restaurant's signature soy-seaweed dipping sauce.

Glowball Grill Steaks & Satay   FUSION $$
(Map p358; www.glowbalgrill.com; 1079 Mainland St; mains C$17-40) Casting a wide net that catches the power-lunch, after-work and late-night fashionista crowds, this hip but unpretentious joint has a comfortable, lounge-like feel. Its classy dishes fuse West Coast ingredients with Asian and Mediterranean flourishes – the prawn linguine is delicious and the finger-licking satay sticks always recommended. Check the glass-walled meat cellar and choose your desired steak cut.

Regional Tasting Lounge   FUSION $$
(Map p358; www.r.tl; 1130 Mainland St; mains C$16-26) An intimate, mood-lit dining room with an innovative menu approach: every three months they add a new regional focus, which brings tastebud-hugging treats from different parts of the world. Foodie focuses have included Italy, Spain, Greece and New Orleans, but there's always a selection of Pacific Northwest classics if you want to taste-trip BC, too. There's a three-course C$29 tasting menu available daily.

GASTOWN & CHINATOWN

Acme Café   CAFÉ $
(Map p358; www.acmecafe.ca; 51 W Hastings St; mains C$8-13; 🖪) The black-and-white deco interior here is enough to warm up anyone on a rainy day – or maybe it's the retro-cool U-shaped counter. But it's not just about looks at this new neighborhood fixture. The hipsters flock here for good-value hearty breakfasts and heaping comfort-food lunches with a gourmet flourish: meatloaf, chicken club and shrimp guacamole sandwiches are grand but why not drop by for an afternoon coffee and some house-baked fruit pie?

Judas Goat   FUSION $$
(Map p358; www.judasgoat.ca; 27 Blood Alley; small plates C$6-10) This 28-seat mosaic-and-marble nook is a local foodie favorite. Named after the goats used to lead sheep off slaughterhouse trucks, it's nailed the art of small, simply prepared but invitingly gourmet tapas treats like beef brisket meatballs, lamb cheek wrapped in savoy cabbage and scallop tartare with pork rinds. Arrive off-peak to avoid lineups: there's a 90-minute time limit for diners.

Bao Bei   ASIAN FUSION $$
(Map p358; www.bao-bei.ca; 163 Keefer St; mains C$10-18) This chic Chinese brasserie quickly hooked the hipsters when it opened in 2010. From its prawn and chive dumplings to its addictive short-rib-filled buns, it's brought a unique contemporary flair to Chinatown dining, combined with an innovative approach to ingredients: top-of-the-range organic meat and sustainable seafood is used throughout.

Phnom Penh
VIETNAMESE **$$**

(Map p358; 244 E Georgia St; mains C$8-18) Arrive early or late to avoid the queues at this locals' favorite eatery. The dishes here are split between Cambodian and Vietnamese soul-food classics, such as crispy frogs legs, spicy garlic crab, and prawn- and sprout-filled pancakes. Don't leave without sampling a steamed rice cake, stuffed with pork, shrimp, coconut and scallions.

SOUTH MAIN (SOMA) & COMMERCIAL DRIVE

Chutney Villa
INDIAN **$$**

(www.chutneyvilla.com; 147 E Broadway; mains C$8-18) This warmly enveloping South Indian restaurant lures savvy SoMa-ites with its lusciously spiced curries (lamb *poriyal* – pan-fried with coconut and spices – is a favorite), best scoffed with some fluffy dosas. There's an outstanding Sunday brunch combo of veggie curries and piping-hot Indian coffee, plus a drinks list of bottled Indian beers, on-tap BC brews and fresh lime cordial. Come hungry, expect to share and stay long.

Foundation
VEGETARIAN **$$**

(2301 Main St; mains C$6-14; 🖉) This lively vegetarian (mostly vegan) noshery is where artsy students and chin-stroking young intellectuals like to hang. Despite the clientele, it's not at all pretentious (apart from the philosophical quotes on the walls) and its mismatched Formica tables are often topped with dishes like heaping Utopian Nachos, spicy black bean burgers or hearty house-made curries. Vancouver's Storm Brewing beers are also served.

Havana
LATIN, FUSION **$$**

(www.havanarestaurant.ca; 1212 Commercial Dr; mains C$10-20) The granddaddy of Drive dining has still got it, hence its buzzing patio on most summer nights. Combining a rustic Latin American ambience – peruse the graffiti signatures scratched into the walls – with a roster of satisfying Afro-Cuban-Southern soul-food dishes, its highlights range from yam fries to slow-roasted lamb curry and perfect platters of clams, mussels and oysters.

GRANVILLE ISLAND

Go Fish
SEAFOOD **$$**

(Map p358; 1505 W 1st Ave; mains C$8-13) A two-minute walk west along the seawall from the Granville Island entrance, this popular seafood shack is one of Vancouver's best joints for fish 'n chips. The smashing (and lighter) fish tacos are also highly recommended, while the ever-changing daily specials often include praiseworthy scallop burgers or ahi tuna sandwiches. There's not much seating, so pack your grub along the seawall to Vanier Park for a picnic.

Agro Café
CAFÉ **$$**

(Map p358; www.agrocafe.org; 1363 Railspur Alley; mains C$6-10) Seemingly known only to locals, this slightly hidden Railspur Alley café is a smashing coffee stop with a fairtrade commitment. But there's much more on offer here: tuck into a BC-brewed Back Hand of God Stout or a bulging ciabatta sandwich. And if you're hungry for a good start, the heaping breakfasts are a great fill-up. In summer, sip your Americano outside and watch the Granville Island world go by.

KITSILANO & WEST SIDE

Maenam
THAI **$$**

(www.maenam.ca; 1938 W 4th Ave; mains C$15-18) A swish, contemporary reinvention of the Thai restaurant model, this is probably unlike any Thai eatery you've been to. Sophisticated, subtle and complex traditional and international influences flavor the menu in a room with a laid-back modern lounge feel. Inviting exploration, try the *geng panaeng neua* beef curry – a sweet, salty and nutty treat suffused with aromatic basil.

Tojo's
JAPANESE **$$$**

(📞604-872-8050; www.tojos.com; 1133 W Broadway; mains C$19-26) Hidekazu Tojo's legendary skill with the sushi knife has created one of North America's most revered sushi restaurants. Among his exquisite dishes are favorites like lightly steamed monkfish, sautéed halibut cheeks and fried red tuna wrapped with seaweed and served with plum sauce. The maplewood sushi bar seats here are more sought-after than a couple of front-row Stanley Cup tickets, so reserve ahead.

Naam
VEGETARIAN **$$**

(www.thenaam.com; 2724 W 4th Ave; mains C$8-14; 🖉) Luring city vegetarians for 30 years, this casual 24-hour eatery still has the ambience of a cozy hippie hang-out. But the menu and weekend brunch queues show that these guys mean business, encouraging legions of repeat diners who keep coming back for stuffed quesadillas, hearty farmers breakfasts and sesame-fried potatoes with miso gravy. Live music is a nightly fixture and there's a convivial covered patio.

🍷 Drinking

Granville St, from Robson to Davie Sts, is a party district of mainstream haunts, but Gastown is your best bet for brick-lined character bars. Try the region's excellent craft brews, including tipples from Driftwood Brewing, Howe Sound Brewing and Central City Brewing.

TOP CHOICE Alibi Room   PUB
(Map p358; www.alibi.ca; 157 Alexander St) This hopping contemporary tavern stocks an ever-changing roster of around 25 mostly BC beers from celebrated breweries like Phillips, Driftwood, Old Yale, Crannog, Central City and beyond. Adventurous taste-trippers – Main St hipsters and old-lag CAMRA (Campaign for Real Ale) drinkers alike – enjoy the C$9 'frat bat' of four sample tipples: choose your own or ask to be surprised.

Six Acres   BAR
(Map p358; www.sixacres.ca; 203 Carrall St) Perfect for a shared plate of finger food, it's just as easy to cover all the necessary food groups with the extensive bottled beer selection here. There's a small patio out front but inside is great for hiding in a candlelit corner and working your way through brews like London Porter and the rather marvelous Draft Dodger from Phillips Brewing.

Railway Club   PUB
(Map p358; www.therailwayclub.com; 579 Dunsmuir St) Accessed via an unobtrusive wooden door next to a 7-Eleven, this is one of the city's friendliest drinkeries and you'll fit right in as soon as you roll up to the bar – unusually for Vancouver, you have to order at the counter. Expect regional microbrews from the likes of Tree Brewing and Central City (go for their ESB). There's also an eclectic roster of live music every night.

Cascade Room   BAR
(www.thecascade.ca; 2616 Main St, South Main) A warm and chat-noisy spot that's the perfect contemporary reinvention of a trad neighborhood bar. Choice bottled beers feature but the excellent 50-strong cocktail list is recommended: try a Cascade Room cocktail of bourbon, pressed apple, lime juice, vanilla bean, bitters and egg white. Food is of fine gastropub quality, with the wine-braised beef and bubble and squeak recommended.

UVA   BAR
(Map p358; www.uvawinebar.ca; 900 Seymour St) Possibly the city's best wine bar, this little nook combines a heritage mosaic floor and swanky white vinyl chairs that add a dash of mod class. But despite the cool look, there's a snob-free approach that will have you happily taste-tripping through a boutique drinks list carefully selected from old and new world delights. Combine with tasting plates from charcuterie to tangy cheese.

Diamond   BAR
(Map p358; www.di6mond.com; 6 Powell St) Look for the unassuming entrance and head upstairs and you'll suddenly find yourself in one of Vancouver's best cocktail bars. This high-ceilinged heritage room is popular with local hipsters but it's never pretentious. Try the list of perfectly nailed cocktails plus some intriguing, Asian-focused tapas plates.

☆ Entertainment

Pick up the *Georgia Straight* or 'West Coast Life' section of the *Vancouver Sun* – both out on Thursdays – to tap into local happenings.

Nightclubs

Fortune Sound Club   NIGHTCLUB
(Map p358; www.fortunesoundclub.com; 147 E Pender St) The city's best club has transformed a grungy old Eastside location into a slick space with the kind of genuine staff and hipster-cool crowd rarely seen in Vancouver nightspots. Slide inside and you'll find a giant dancefloor bristling with party-loving locals out for a great time. Expect a long wait to get in on weekends.

Caprice   NIGHTCLUB
(Map p358; www.capricenightclub.com; 967 Granville St) Originally a movie theater, this cavernous two-level venue is a thumping magnet for local preppies and their miniskirted girlfriends, while the adjoining resto-lounge is great if you need to rest your eardrums and grab a restorative cocktail and bite to eat. Expect to line up here on weekends when the under-25s visiting from the suburbs dominate.

Shine   NIGHTCLUB
(Map p358; www.shinenightclub.com; 364 Water St) With music from electro to funky house and hip-hop, Gastown's sexy subterranean Shine attracts a younger crowd and is divided into a noisy main blue room and an intimate cozy cave red room with a 12m chill-out sofa. The club's Bonafide Saturday indie disco and electro rave night is justi-

fiably popular, while Wednesday's reggae, glitch and dubstep is slightly more chill.

Live Music

Biltmore Cabaret
LIVE MUSIC

(www.biltmorecabaret.com; 395 Kingsway) One of Vancouver's best alt venues, the SoMa crowd comes for the nightly changing smorgasbord of local and visiting indie bands. When there are no bands, DJ, poetry and film nights keep things lively, as does Sunday's highly popular burlesque show.

Commodore
LIVE MUSIC

(Map p358; www.livenation.com; 868 Granville St) Up-and-coming local bands know they've finally made it when they play the city's best midsized music venue, a lovingly restored art-deco ballroom that still has the bounciest dance floor in town – courtesy of stacks of tires placed under its floorboards.

Yale
LIVE MUSIC

(Map p358; www.theyale.ca; 1300 Granville St) Blues fans should head along Granville to the Yale, a blowsy, unpretentious joint with a large stage, devoted clientele and a beer-sticky dance floor. Many shows are free – check the website for details.

Cellar Restaurant & Jazz Club
LIVE MUSIC

(www.cellarjazz.com; 3611 W Broadway, West Side) Chin-stroking jazz nuts might find themselves drawn to the subterranean Cellar Restaurant & Jazz Club where serious tunes are reverentially performed. Tuesday entry is free and there are good beer specials.

Theater & Cinemas

Scotiabank Theatre
CINEMA

(Map p358; www.cineplex.com; 900 Burrard St) Modern, nine-screen multiplex.

Cinemark Tinseltown
CINEMA

(www.cinemark.com; 88 W Pender St) Popular multiplex combining blockbusters and art-house films.

Pacific Cinémathèque
CINEMA

(Map p358; www.cinematheque.bc.ca; 1131 Howe St) Art-house cinema screening foreign and underground movies.

Vancity Theatre
CINEMA

(Map p358; viff.org; 1181 Seymour St) State-of-the-art facility screening festival and art-house fare.

Vancouver Playhouse
THEATER

(Map p358; www.vancouverplayhouse.com; cnr Hamilton & Dunsmuir Sts) Presenting a six-play season at its large civic venue.

Arts Club Theatre Company
THEATER

(www.artsclub.com) Popular classics and works by contemporary Canadian playwrights are at three venues around town.

Sports

Vancouver Canucks
HOCKEY

(www.canucks.com) The city's NHL hockey team is Vancouver's leading sports franchise. Book ahead for games at downtown's Rogers Arena (Map p358), also known as GM Place.

Vancouver Whitecaps
SOCCER

(www.whitecapsfc.com) Playing at the temporary Empire Field stadium until BC Place is renovated, the city's professional soccer team hits the MLS big-league in 2011.

BC Lions
FOOTBALL

(www.bclions.com) Also playing at Empire Field until BC Place is ready, Vancouver's Canadian Football League (CFL) side is ever-hungry for Grey Cup triumph.

Vancouver Canadians
BASEBALL

(www.canadiansbaseball.com) Playing at Nat Bailey Stadium on the West Side, watching this fun baseball team is all about hanging out in the sun with beer and a hotdog.

Shopping

While Robson St is fine for chain fashion stores, it's hard to beat the edgier SoMa boutiques between 19th and 23rd Aves, plus the similar mix of stores radiating from Gastown's Maple Tree Sq. For window shopping, Granville Island and Kitsilano's 4th Ave are ideal.

Regional Assembly of Text
ACCESSORIES

(www.assemblyoftext.com; 3934 Main St) The epitome of South Main eccentricity, this ironic antidote to the digital age was founded by pen-and-paper-loving art-school grads. Ink-stained fans flock here to stock up on Little Otsu journals, handmade pencil boxes and American Apparel T-shirts printed with typewriter motifs. Don't miss the monthly letter-writing club (7pm, first Thursday of every month), where you can sip tea, scoff cookies and hammer away on those vintage typewriters.

John Fluevog Shoes
CLOTHING

(Map p358; www.fluevog.com; 65 Water St) The cavernous Gastown flagship of Vancouver's fave shoe designer (the smaller original store still operates on Granville); Fluevog's funky shoes, sandals and thigh-hugging boots have been a fashion legend since

1970. It's tempting to try something on – some of the footwear looks like Doc Martens on acid, while others could poke your eye out from 20 paces – but beware: falling in love can happen in an instant.

Mountain Equipment Co-op OUTDOOR GEAR
(www.mec.ca; 130 W Broadway) Cavernous granddaddy of Vancouver outdoor stores, with an amazing selection of mostly own-brand clothing, kayaks, sleeping bags and clever camping gadgets: MEC has been turning campers into full-fledged outdoor enthusiasts for years. You'll have to be a member to buy, but that's easy to arrange and only costs C$5. Equipment – canoes, kayaks, camping gear etc – can also be rented here.

Smoking Lily CLOTHING
(www.smokinglily.com; 3634 Main St) Quirky art-school cool is the approach at this SoMa store, where skirts, belts and halter tops are whimsically accented with prints of ants, skulls or the periodic table. Men's clothing is slowly creeping into the mix, with some fish, skull and tractor T-shirts and ties. A fun spot to browse (the staff is friendly and chatty), and it's hard to imagine a better souvenir than the silk tea cozy printed with a Pierre Trudeau likeness.

Gravity Pope CLOTHING
(www.gravitypope.com; 2205 W 4th Ave) One of a clutch of cool clothing stores strung along Kitsilano's highly browsable W 4th Ave, this unisex shop includes ultra-cool footwear on one side and designer clothing for the pale and interesting set (think ironic tweed ties and printed halter tops) on the other. Don't spend all you dosh here, though: check out nearby Vivid and Urban Rack, too.

Rubber Rainbow Condom Company
ACCESSORIES
(3851 Main St) Doing brisk business in its Main St location, this fun, funky condom and lube store serves all manner of experiment-inviting accessories, including studded, vibrating and 'full-fitting strawberry fla-vored' varieties. Ask for a selection pack if you're going to be in town for a while – you never know how lucky you might get.

Coastal Peoples Fine Arts Gallery
SOUVENIRS
(Map p358; www.coastalpeoples.com; 1024 Mainland St) This sumptuous Yaletown gallery showcases a fine selection of Inuit and Northwest Coast aboriginal jewelry, carv-

ings and prints. It focusesg on the high-art side of native crafts; you'll find some exqui-site items here that will likely have your credit card sweating within minutes.

Red Cat Records MUSIC STORE
(www.redcat.ca; 4332 Main St) High Fidelity–style record store that's a 101 intro to Vancouver's underground music scene.

Wanderlust BOOKSTORE
(www.wanderlustore.com; 1924 W 4th Ave, Kitsilano) Extensive travel guides, maps and accessories.

ℹ Information

Internet Access

Internet Coffee (1104 Davie St; per hr C$3.25; ⊘9am-1:30am) Twenty terminals plus fax, CD-burning and printing services.

Vancouver Public Library (www.vpl.vancouver.bc.ca; 350 W Georgia St; ⊘10am-9pm Mon-Thu, 10am-6pm Fri & Sat, noon-5pm Sun; 🛜) Free internet access on library computers plus free wi-fi access with a guest card from the information desk.

Media & Internet Resources

City of Vancouver (www.vancouver.ca) Resource-packed official city site with down-loadable maps.

CKNW 980AM (www.cknw.com) News, traffic and talk radio station.

Georgia Straight (www.straight.com) Free listings newspaper.

Inside Vancouver (www.insidevancouver.ca) Stories on what to do in and around the city.

Miss 604 (www.miss604.com) Vancouver's favorite blogger.

Tyee (www.thetyee.ca) Local online news source.

Vancouver Sun (www.vancouversun.com) The city's main daily newspaper.

Medical Services

Shoppers Drug Mart (www.shoppersdrugmart.ca; 1125 Davie St; ⊘24hr) Pharmacy chain.

St Paul's Hospital (1081 Burrard St; ⊘24hr) Downtown accident and emergency.

Ultima Medicentre (www.ultimamedicentre.ca; Bentall Centre, Plaza Level, 1055 Dunsmuir St; ⊘8am-5pm Mon-Fri) Walk-in clinic, appoint-ments unnecessary.

Money

RBC Royal Bank (www.rbc.com; 1025 W Geor-gia St; ⊘9am-5pm Mon-Fri) Main bank branch with money exchange services.

Vancouver Bullion & Currency Exchange
(www.vbce.ca; 800 W Pender St; ⊘9am-5pm Mon-Fri) Often the best exchange rates in town.

Post

Canada Post main outlet (Map p358; 349 W Georgia St; ⊙8:30am-5:30pm Mon-Fri)

Howe St postal outlet (Map p358; 732 Davie St; ⊙9am-7pm Mon-Fri, 10am-5pm Sat)

Tourist Information

Tourism Vancouver Visitor Centre (Map p358; www.tourismvancouver.com; 200 Burrard St; ⊙8:30am-6pm daily Jun-Aug, 8:30am-5pm Mon-Sat Sep-May) Free maps, city and wider BC visitor guides and a half-price theater ticket booth.

Getting There & Away

Air

Vancouver International Airport (www.yvr.ca) is the main West Coast hub for airlines from Canada, the US and international locales. It's in Richmond, a 13km, 30-minute drive from downtown.

Intra-Canada flights arriving here include regular **Westjet** (www.westjet.com) and **Air Canada** (www.aircanada.com) services. Linked to the main airport by free shuttle bus, the South Terminal receives BC-only flights from smaller airlines and floatplane operators.

Several handy floatplane services can also deliver you directly to the Vancouver waterfront's Seaplane Terminal. These include frequent **Harbour Air Seaplanes** (www.harbour-air.com) and **West Coast Air** (www.westcoastair.com) services from Victoria's centrally located Inner Harbour.

Boat

BC Ferries (www.bcferries.com) services arrive at Tsawwassen – an hour south of downtown – from Vancouver Island's Swartz Bay (passenger/vehicle C$14/46.75, 90 minutes) and Nanaimo's Duke Point (passenger/vehicle C$14/46.75, two hours). Services also arrive here from the Southern Gulf Islands.

Ferries also arrive at West Vancouver's Horseshoe Bay – 30 minutes from downtown – from Nanaimo's Departure Bay (passenger/vehicle C$14/46.75, 90 minutes), Bowen Island (passenger/vehicle C$9.75/27.90, 20 minutes) and Langdale (passenger/vehicle C$12.85/43.20, 40 minutes) on the Sunshine Coast.

Bus

Most out-of-town buses grind to a halt at Vancouver's **Pacific Central Station** (1150 Station St). **Greyhound Canada** (www.greyhound.ca) services arrive from Whistler (from C$25, 2¾ hours), Kelowna (from C$48, six hours) and Calgary (from C$79, 14 to 17 hours) among others. Traveling via the BC Ferries Swartz Bay-Tsawwassen route, frequent **Pacific Coach Lines** (www.pacificcoach.com) services trundle in here from downtown Victoria (from C$28.75, 3½ hours). PCL also operates services between

Whistler, Vancouver and Vancouver International Airport (from C$35, from 3½ hours).

Snowbus (www.snowbus.com) also offers a winter-only ski bus service to and from Whistler (C$30.95, three hours).

Quick Coach Lines (www.quickcoach.com) runs an express shuttle between Seattle and Vancouver, departing from downtown Seattle (US$40.85, four hours) and the Seattle's Sea-Tac International Airport (US$54.15, 3½ hours).

Car & Motorcycle

If you're coming from Washington State in the US, you'll be on the I-5 until you hit the border town of Blaine, then on Hwy 99 in Canada. It's about an hour's drive from here to downtown Vancouver. Hwy 99 continues through downtown, across the Lions Gate Bridge to Horseshoe Bay, Squamish and Whistler.

Coming from the east, you'll probably be on the Trans-Canada Hwy (Hwy 1), which snakes through the city's eastern end, eventually meeting with Hastings St. If you want to go downtown, turn left onto Hastings and follow it into the city center, or continue on along the North Shore toward Whistler.

If you're coming from Horseshoe Bay, Hwy 1 heads through West Vancouver and North Vancouver before going over the Second Narrows Bridge into Burnaby. If you're heading downtown, leave the highway at the Taylor Way exit in West Vancouver and follow it over the Lions Gate Bridge toward the city center.

All the recognized car-rental chains have Vancouver branches. Avis, Budget, Hertz and Thrifty also have airport branches.

Train

Trains trundle in from across Canada and the US at **Pacific Central Station** (1150 Station St). The Main St-Science World SkyTrain station is just across the street for connections to downtown and the suburbs.

VIA Rail (www.viarail.com) services arrive from Kamloops North (C$86, 10 hours), Jasper (C$179, 20 hours) and Edmonton (C$241, 27 hours), among others.

Amtrak (www.amtrak.com) US services arrive from Eugene (from US$67, 13½ hours), Portland (from US$50, eight hours) and Seattle (from US$35, 3½ hours).

Getting Around

To/From the Airport

SkyTrain's 16-station **Canada Line** (adult one-way fare to downtown C$7.50 to C$8.75) operates a rapid-transit train service from the airport to downtown. Trains run every eight to 20 minutes and take around 25 minutes to reach downtown's Waterfront Station.

If you prefer to cab it, budget C$30 to C$40 for the 30-minute taxi ride from the airport to your downtown hotel. For C$10 to C$20 more, consider arriving in style in a limo from **Aerocar Service** (www.aerocar.ca).

Bicycle

With routes running across town, Vancouver is a relatively good cycling city. Pick up a *Greater Vancouver Cycling Map* (C$3.95) at convenience stores. Cyclists can take their bikes for free on SkyTrains, SeaBuses and rack-fitted transit buses. Additional maps and resources are available via the **City of Vancouver** (www.vancouver.ca/cycling) website.

Boat

Running mini vessels (some big enough to carry bikes) between the foot of Hornby St and Granville Island, **Aquabus Ferries** (www.theaquabus.com) services spots along False Creek as far as Science World. Its cutthroat rival is **False Creek Ferries** (www.granvilleislandferries.bc.ca), which operates a similar Granville Island service from the Aquatic Centre, plus additional ports of call around False Creek.

Car & Motorcycle

The rush-hour vehicle lineup to cross the Lions Gate Bridge to the North Shore frequently snakes far up W Georgia St. Try the alternative Second Narrows Bridge. Other peak-time hot spots to avoid are the George Massey Tunnel and Hwy 1 to Surrey.

Parking is at a premium downtown: there are few free spots available on residential side streets and traffic wardens are predictably predatory. Some streets have metered parking but pay-parking lots (from C$4 per hour) are a better proposition – arrive before 9am at some for early-bird discounts. Underground parking at either Pacific Centre shopping mall or the Vancouver Public Library will have you in the heart of the city.

Public Transportation

The website for **TransLink** (www.translink.bc.ca) bus, SkyTrain and SeaBus services has a useful trip-planning tool, or you can buy the handy *Getting Around* route map (C$1.95) from convenience stores.

A ticket bought on any of the three services is valid for 90 minutes of travel on the entire network, depending on the zone you intend to travel in. The three zones become progressively more expensive the further you journey. One-zone tickets are adult/child C$2.50/1.75, two-zone tickets C$3.75/2.50 and three-zone tickets C$5/3.50. An all-day, all-zone pass costs C$9/7. If you're traveling after 6:30pm or on weekends or holidays, all trips are classed as one-zone fares and cost C$2.50/1.75. Children under five years travel free on all transit services.

The bus network is extensive in central areas and many vehicles have bike racks. All are wheelchair accessible. Exact change (or more) is required since all buses use fare machines and change is not given.

The aquatic SeaBus shuttle operates every 15 to 30 minutes throughout the day, taking 12 minutes to cross the Burrard Inlet between Waterfront Station and Lonsdale Quay. At Lonsdale there's a bus terminal servicing routes throughout North Vancouver and West Vancouver. Vessels are wheelchair accessible and bike-friendly.

The SkyTrain rapid-transit network consists of three routes. The original 35-minute Expo Line runs between downtown Vancouver and Surrey, via stops throughout Burnaby and New Westminster. The Millennium Line alights near shopping malls and suburban residential districts in Coquitlam and Burnaby. Opened in late 2009, the new Canada Line links the city to the airport and Richmond. If you're heading for the airport from the city, make sure you board a YVR-bound train – some are heading to Richmond but not the airport.

Taxi

Flagging a downtown cab shouldn't take too long, but it's easiest to get your hotel to call you one. Operators include **Vancouver Taxi** (☑604-871-1111), **Black Top & Checker Cabs** (☑604-731-1111) and **Yellow Cab** (☑604-681-1111). Taxi meters start at C$3.05 and add C$1.73 per kilometer.

WHISTLER & THE SUNSHINE COAST

The winding Sea to Sky Hwy (Hwy 99) delivers spectacular cliff-top views of idyllic Howe Sound en route to Whistler, around 90 minutes from big-city Vancouver. The celebrated ski resort is a hive of snow-based activity in winter, when it can be just as much fun hanging with the beautiful people in the bars as actually hitting the slopes. For those who prefer toasty temperatures, the resort in summer is also a popular hiking and biking magnet.

Travelers who like to keep their tans topped up should consider the Sunshine Coast, which reputedly receives more rays than Hawaii. This 139km stretch of crenulated, mostly forested waterfront northwest of Vancouver is accessible via a 40-minute ferry ride from the outskirts of the city. Many Vancouverites have little idea just how close they are to a region renowned for diving, kayaking and an independent islandlike feel.

Whistler

Host mountain at the 2010 Winter Olympics and nestled in the shade of the formidable Whistler and Blackcomb Mountains, this gabled village has a frosted, Christmas-card look from November to April. In summer, its outdoor expanses become an alpine treat for hikers and bikers, while ziplining and rafting also lure the T-shirt crowd.

Centered on four main neighborhoods – approaching via Hwy 99 from the south, you'll hit Creekside first – Whistler Village is the key hub for hotels, restaurants and shops. You'll find humbler B&B-type accommodations in the quieter Village North, while the Upper Village is home to some swanky hotels, clustered around the base of Blackcomb.

Sights

Squamish Lil'wat Cultural Centre CULTURAL CENTER
(www.slcc.ca; 4854 Blackcomb Way; adult/youth/child C$18/11/8; 9:30am-5pm) The dramatic, wood-beamed cultural center showcases two quite different First Nations groups – one coastal and one interior-based – with museum exhibits and artisan presentations. Entry starts with a 15-minute movie and includes a self-guided tour illuminating the heritage and modern-day indigenous communities of the region. There's a wealth of arts and crafts on display – check out the amazing sea serpent carving near the entrance.

Whistler Sliding Centre OLYMPICS CENTER
(www.whistlerslidingcentre.com; 4910 Glacier Lane; adult/child C$7/free; 10am-5pm) Perched just above the village on Blackcomb, this center hosted Olympic bobsled, luge and skeleton events and is now open to the public. You can wander exhibits and check out video footage from the track or take a general tour (adult/child C$15/free) or behind-the-scenes tour (adult/child C$69/59).

Activities

Skiing & Snowboarding

Whistler-Blackcomb SKIING
(www.whistlerblackcomb.com; 1-day lift ticket adult/youth/child C$93/78/46) Comprising 38 lifts and almost 3280 hectares of skiable terrain crisscrossed with over 200 runs (more than half aimed at intermediate level skiers), the sister mountains of Whistler-Blackcomb were physically linked for the first time in 2009. The resort's mammoth 4.4km **Peak 2 Peak Gondola** includes the world's longest unsupported span and takes 11 minutes to shuttle wide-eyed powder hogs between the two high alpine areas, so you can hit the slopes on both mountains on the same day.

The winter season kicks off in late November and runs to April on Whistler and June on Blackcomb – December to February is the peak. If you want to emulate your fave Olympic ski heroes, Whistler Creekside was the setting for all the 2010 downhill skiing events.

You can beat the crowds with an early-morning **Fresh Tracks ticket** (adult/child C$17.25/12.60), which must be bought in advance at Whistler Village Gondola Guest Relations. The price includes a buffet breakfast at the Roundhouse Lodge up top. Night owls might prefer the evening **Night Moves** program (adult/child C$18/12) operated via Blackcomb's Magic Chair lift after 5pm.

Cross-Country Skiing & Snowshoeing

Lost Lake SKIING
(www.crosscountryconnection.bc.ca; day pass adult/youth/child C$17/10/8.50; 8am-9pm) A pleasant stroll or free shuttle bus away from the village, Lost Lake is the hub for 22km of wooded cross-country ski trails, suitable for novices and experts alike. Around 4km of the trail is lit for additional nighttime skiing until 10pm and there's a handy 'warming hut' providing lessons and equipment rentals. Snowshoers are also well served in this area: you can stomp off on your own on 10km of trails or rent equipment and guides.

Outdoor Adventures Whistler SNOWSHOEING
(www.adventureswhistler.com; 4205 Village Sq; tours adult/child from C$69/39) For snowshoeing tours – including a three-hour fondue excursion – check in here. Prices include equipment rentals and the company also offers a wide array of other tours and activities.

Mountain Biking

Whistler Mountain Bike Park MOUNTAIN BIKING
(www.whistlerbike.com; 1-day pass adult/youth/child C$53/47/29; 10am-8pm mid-Jun–Aug, 10am-5pm May–mid-Jun & Sep–mid-Oct) Taking over the melted ski slopes in summer and accessed via the lift at the village's south end, this bike park offers barreling downhill runs and an orgy of jumps, beams and bridges twisting through 200km of well-maintained forested trails.

Outside the park, winding trails around the region include **Comfortably Numb** (a tough 26km with steep climbs and bridges); **A River Runs Through It** (suitable for

DON'T MISS

WIRED FOR FUN

Stepping out into thin air 70m above the forest floor might seem like a normal activity for a cartoon character but ziplining turns out to be one of the best ways to encounter the Whistler wilderness. Attached via a body harness to the cable you're about to slide down, you soon overcome your fear of flying solo. By the end of your time in the trees, you'll be turning midair somersaults and whooping like a banshee. The two cool courses operated by **Ziptrek Ecotours** (www.ziptrek.com; adult/child from C$99/79) are strung between Whistler and Blackcomb Mountains and operate in both winter and summer seasons. Its newer **TreeTrek guided canopy walk** (adult/child C$39/29) is a gentle web of walkways and suspension bridges for those who prefer to keep their feet on something a little more solid than air. It's ideal for families.

all skill levels, it has teeter-totters and log obstacles); and the gentle **Valley Trail**, an easy 14km loop that encircles the village and its lake, meadow and mountain chateau surroundings – this is recommended for first-timers.

Hiking

With more than 40km of flower-and-forest alpine trails, most accessed via the Whistler Village Gondola, the region is ideal for those who like nature of the strollable variety. Favorite routes include the **High Note Trail** (8km), which traverses pristine meadows and has stunning views of the blue-green waters of Cheakamus Lake. Route maps are available at the visitor centre.

Whistler Alpine Guides Bureau   HIKING
(www.whistlerguides.com; guided hikes adult/child from C$79/59) Guided treks are offered by the friendly folk here, who can also help with rock-climbing and rap-jumping excursions.

🛏 Sleeping

Winter is the peak for prices here, but last-minute deals can still be had if you're planning an impromptu overnight from Vancouver – check the website of **Tourism Whistler** (www.whistler.com) for room sales and packages. Most hotels charge parking fees (up to C$20 daily) and some also slap on resort fees (up to C$25 daily) – confirm these before you book.

TOP CHOICE   **Nita Lake Lodge**   HOTEL $$$
(📞604-966-5700, 888-755-6482; www.nitalakelodge.com; 2135 Lake Placid Rd; r from C$250; 🛜) Adjoining Creekside train station – handy if you're coming up on the Rocky Mountaineer Sea to Sky Climb – this swanky timber-framed lodge is perfect for a pampering retreat. Hugging the lakeside, the chic but cozy rooms feature individual

patios, rock fireplaces and bathrooms with heated floors and large tubs – they also have little kitchenettes with microwaves and fridges. There's a good onsite restaurant but a free shuttle can whisk you to the village if you want to dine further afield. Creekside lifts are a walkable few minutes away.

HI Whistler Hostel   HOSTEL $
(📞604-962-0025; www.hihostels.ca; 1035 Legacy Way; dm/r C$39/153; @🛜) Replacing Whistler's former too-small HI, this smashing new hostel repurposes part of the 2010 Olympic athletes village near Function Junction – it's 7km south of town with transit bus access. The large, lodgelike building with its IKEA-esque furnishings includes 188 beds in four-bed dorms as well as 14 sought-after ensuite private rooms. There's a well-equipped kitchen plus a barbecue deck and café.

Adara Hotel   HOTEL $$
(📞604-905-4665, 866-502-3272; www.adarahotel.com; 4122 Village Green; r from C$160; ❄🛜) Unlike all those smaller lodges now claiming to be boutique hotels, the sophisticated and centrally located Adara was built from scratch as the real deal. Lined with sparse but knowing designer details – including fake antler horns in the lobby – the accommodations have spa-like bathrooms, flat-screen TVs and iPod docking stations (the front desk will loan you an iPod if you've left yours at home).

Riverside RV Resort & Campground
   CAMPGROUND $$
(📞604-905-5533; www.whistlercamping.com; 8018 Mons Rd; tent site/cabin/yurt C$35/159/99; 🐕) This warm and friendly RV property a few minutes' drive past Whistler on Hwy 99 recently restored its tent camping spots and

has also added some cool new yurts to its cozy cabin properties. The yurts have basic furnishings and electricity (bring your own sleeping bag) and they also have a dedicated service block with hot showers. The resort's onsite Junction Café serves great breakfasts (try the salmon eggs benedict).

Crystal Lodge
HOTEL **$$**

(☑604-932-2221, 800-667-3363; www.crystal
-lodge.com; 4154 Village Stroll; d/ste from C$130/
175; ✳✲📶) Not all rooms are created equal at the Crystal, a central sleepover forged from the fusion of two quite different hotel towers. Cheaper rooms in the South Tower are standard motel-style – baths and fridges are the highlight – but those in the Lodge Wing match the splendid rock-and-beam lobby, complete with small balconies. Both share excellent proximity to village restaurants and are less than 100m from the main ski lift.

Chalet Luise
B&B **$$**

(☑604-932-4187,800-665-1998;www.chaletluise
.com; 7461 Ambassador Cres; r from C$125; 📶) A five-minute trail walk from the village, this recently renovated Bavarian-look pension has eight bright and sunny rooms – think pine furnishings and crisp white duvets – and a flower garden that's ideal for a spot of evening wine-quaffing. Or you can just hop in the hot tub and dream about the large buffet breakfast coming your way in the morning. Free parking.

UBC Whistler Lodge
HOSTEL **$**

(☑604-822-5851; www.ubcwhistlerlodge.com; 2124 Nordic Dr; dm summer/winter C$30/40) Up a steep hill in the Nordic residential neighborhood, facilities are basic and quirky (bunks are built into the walls; rooms are separated by curtains) but the rates are a bargain.

Fairmont Chateau Whistler
HOTEL **$$$**

(☑604-938-8000, 800-606-8244; www.fair
mont.com/whistler; 4599 Chateau Blvd; r from C$350) Dramatic baronial lodge lobbies and comfortably palatial rooms, many with mountain views. Close enough to enjoy ski-in/ski-out privileges on Blackcomb.

Whistler Village Inn & Suites
HOTEL **$$**

(☑604-932-4004, 800-663-6418; www.whis
tlervillageinnandsuites.com; 4429 Sundial Pl; d/ste C$119/139; ✲📶) Recently renovated twin-lodge sleepover with rustic chic rooms and a free breakfast buffet. Good central location.

✗ Eating

Araxi Restaurant & Lounge
WEST COAST **$$$**

(☑604-932-4540; www.toptable.ca; 4222 Village Sq; mains C$30-45) Whistler's best splurge restaurant, Araxi dishes up an inventive and exquisite Pacific Northwest menu plus charming and courteous service. Try the exquisite BC halibut and drain the 15,000-bottle wine selection, but save room for a dessert: a regional cheese plate or the amazing Okanagan apple cheesecake….or both.

Christine's Mountain Top Dining
CANADIAN **$$**

(☑604-938-7437; Rendezvous Lodge, Blackcomb Mountain; mains C$12-22) Among the handful of places to eat while you're enjoying a summertime summit stroll or winter ski day on the slopes at Blackcomb Mountain, Christine's is the best mountaintop meal you'll have here. Try for a view-tastic patio table and tuck into a seasonal seafood grill or a lovely applewood smoked-cheddar grilled-cheese sandwich. Reservations recommended.

Crepe Montagne
FRENCH **$$**

(www.crepemontagne.com; 4368 Main St; mains C$8-14) This small, authentic creperie – hence the French accents percolating among the staff – offers a bewildering array of sweet and savory buckwheat crepes with fillings including ham, Brie, asparagus, banana, strawberries and more. Good breakfast spot: go the waffle route and you'll be perfectly set up for a day on the slopes.

Beet Root Café
CAFÉ **$**

(29-4340 Lorimer Rd; light mains C$6-11) The best home-style hang-out in town – pull up a cushion by the window, make yourself at home and tuck into fresh-made soup, bulging sandwiches or the excellent breakfast burritos. Stick around until you smell the cookies emerging from the oven, then scoff yourself into a happy stupor.

Sachi Sushi
JAPANESE **$$**

(106-4359 Main St; mains C$8-22) Whistler's best sushi spot doesn't stop at California rolls. Serving everything from crispy popcorn shrimp to seafood salads and stomach-warming udon noodles (the tempura noodle bowl is best), this bright and breezy eatery is a relaxing après hang-out. Consider a glass of hot sake on a cold winter day.

21 Steps Kitchen & Bar
CONTEMPORARY COMFORT **$$**

(www.21steps.ca; St Andrews House; mains C$14-22) With small plates for nibblers, the main dishes at this cozy upstairs spot have a high-end comfort-food approach. Not a great place for vegetarians – unless you like stuffed portobello mushrooms – as steak, chops and seafood feature heavily.

 Drinking & Entertainment

Garibaldi Lift Company PUB
(Whistler Village Gondola) The closest bar to the slopes – watch the powder geeks or bike nuts on Whistler Mountain skid to a halt from the patio – the GLC is a rock-lined cave of a place. It's the ideal spot to absorb a Kootenay Mountain Ale and a bulging GLC burger while you rub your muscles and exchange exaggerated stories about your epic battles with the mountain.

Whistler Brewhouse BREWERY
(www.markjamesgroup.com; 4355 Blackcomb Way) This lodgelike drinkery crafts its own beer on the premises and, like any artwork, the natural surroundings inspire the masterpieces, with names like Lifty Lager and Twin Peaks Pale Ale. It's an ideal pub if you want to hear yourself think – or if you just want to watch the game on one of the TVs. The food, including pasta, pizza and fish 'n chips, is superior to standard pub grub.

Longhorn Saloon & Grill PUB
(www.longhornsaloon.ca; 4290 Mountain Sq) Fanning out near the base of Whistler Mountain with a patio that threatens to take over the town, this local legend feels like it's been here since the first skier turned up. The pub food is nothing special but it's hard to beat the atmosphere here on a hopping winter evening.

Garfinkel's NIGHTCLUB
(www.garfswhistler.com; 1-4308 Main St) Mixing mainstream dance grooves with a few live bands, Whistler's biggest club is ever-popular. Arrive early on weekends when it's especially packed.

Moe Joe's NIGHTCLUB
(www.moejoes.com; 4155 Golfer's Approach) More intimate than Garfinkel's, this is the best place in town if you like dancing yourself into a drooling heap. It's always crowded on Friday night.

 Information

Pick up *The Pique* or *Whistler Question* newspapers for local insights.

Armchair Books (www.whistlerbooks.com; 4205 Village Sq; 9am-9pm) Central bookstore with strong travel section.

Custom House Currency Exchange (4227 Village Stroll; 9am-5pm May-Sep, 9am-6pm Oct-Apr) Handy central exchange.

Northlands Medical Clinic (www.northlands clinic.com; 4359 Main St; 9am-5:30pm) Walk-in medical center.

Post Office (106-4360 Lorimer Rd; 8am-5pm Mon-Fri, 8am-noon Sat)

Public Library (www.whistlerlibrary.ca; 4329 Main St; 11am-7pm Mon-Sat, 11am-4pm Sun; Internet free, C$1 guest library card required.

Whistler Activity Centre (4010 Whistler Way; 10am-6pm) Recommendations and bookings for local activities.

Whistler Visitor Centre (www.whistler.com; 4230 Gateway Dr; 8am-8pm) Flyer-lined visitor center with friendly staff.

 Getting There & Around

While most visitors arrive by car from Vancouver via Hwy 99, you can also fly in on a **Whistler Air** (www.whistlerair.ca) floatplane to Green Lake (from C$149, 30 minutes, two daily from May to September).

Greyhound Canada (www.greyhound.ca) bus services arrive at Creekside and Whistler Village from Vancouver (from C$25, 2¾ hours, seven daily) and Squamish (C$14, one hour, eight daily).

SkyLynx motor coach services from **Pacific Coach Lines** (www.pacificcoach.com) also arrive from Vancouver (from C$35, 3½ hours, six daily) and Vancouver International Airport and drop off at Whistler hotels. **Snowbus** (www.snowbus.com) operates a winter-only service from Vancouver (C$21, three hours, two daily).

Trainspotters can trundle into town on Rocky Mountaineer Vacations' **Whistler Sea to Sky Climb** (www.rockmountaineer.com), which winds along a picturesque coastal route from North Vancouver (from C$129, three hours, daily May to mid-October).

Whistler's **WAVE** (www.busonline.ca) public buses (adult/child/one-day pass C$2/1.50/5) are equipped with ski and bike racks. In summer, there's a free service from the village to Lost Lake.

Sunshine Coast

Stretching 139km from Langdale to Lund, the Sunshine Coast has an independent mentality that belies the fact that it's only a 40-minute ferry ride from West Vancouver's Horseshoe Bay. With Hwy 101 linking key communities like Gibsons, Sechelt and Powell River, it's an easy region to explore with plenty of activities to keep things lively: think kayaking and scuba diving with a side order of artists' studios. Check the website of **Sunshine Coast Tourism** (www. sunshinecoastcanada.com) for information.

GIBSONS

Your first port of call after docking in Langdale and driving on to town, Gibsons' pretty waterfront strip is named Gibsons Landing and it's a rainbow of painted wooden buildings perched over the marina. Head up the incline from the water and you'll hit the shops on the main drag of Upper Gibsons and Hwy 101. Drop by the **Visitor Centre** (☑604-886-2374, 866-222-3806; www.gibsonschamber.com; 417 Marine Dr; ⊙9am-5pm Jul & Aug, reduced hours off-season) for information.

Kayak rentals and tours are available from the friendly folk at **Sunshine Kayaking** (www.sunshinekayaking.com; Molly's Lane; rentals 4/24hr C$40/75; ⊙9am-6pm Mon-Fri, 8am-6pm Sat & Sun). Their guided sunset (C$65) tours are especially recommended.

Your best bet for a bed is **Soames Point B&B** (☑604-886-8599, 877-604-2672; www.soamespointbb.com; 1000B Marine Dr; d from C$159), an immaculate and tranquil sleepover with breathtaking waterfront views. The large suite has a private entrance, vaulted ceilings and its own deck – a great spot for breakfast.

While the best spot in town for a hearty breakfast and comfort food of the fish 'n chips variety is **Molly's Reach** (www.mollysreach.ca; 647 School Rd; mains C$7-12), gourmet seafood fans shouldn't miss **Smitty's Oyster House** (www.smittysoysterhouse.com; 643 School Rd; mains C$12-26). Regionally sourced and perfectly prepared treats include Fanny Bay oysters and golden halibut fritters.

SECHELT

A useful base for active travelers, with plenty of hiking, biking, kayaking and diving opportunities, Sechelt is the Sunshine Coast's second-largest town, with useful pit-stop amenities if you're just passing through. For information, drop by the **Visitors Centre** (☑604-885-1036, 877-885-1036; www.secheltvisitorcentre.com; 5790 Teredo St; ⊙9am-5pm Jul & Aug, 9am-5pm Mon-Sat Jun & Sep, 10am-4pm Mon-Sat Oct-May).

With a good kayak launch site and a sandy, stroll-worthy beach, fir-and-cedar-forested **Porpoise Bay Provincial Park** (www.bcparks.ca) is 4km north of Sechelt via East Porpoise Bay Rd. There are trails throughout the park and an 84-site **campground** (www.discovercamping.ca; campsite C$24) with handy hot showers.

For visiting paddlers (and peddlers), **Pedals & Paddles** (www.pedalspaddles.com; Tillicum Bay Marina; rentals 4/24hr C$40/75) organizes kayak rentals and tours of the inlet's wonderfully tranquil waters.

Alternatively, chat with local artists and growers at the summertime **Sechelt Farmers & Artisans Market** (www.secheltmarket.com; ⊙8:30am-1:30pm Sat Apr-Sep) in the parking lot of the Raven's Cry Theatre, or stick around for the mid-August **Sunshine Coast Festival of the Written Arts** (www.writersfestival.ca).

If you feel like a sleepover splurge, continue on Hwy 101 past Sechelt to **Rockwater Secret Cove Resort** (☑604-885-7038, 877-296-4593; www.rockwatersecretcoveresort.com; 5356 Ole's Cove Rd; r/ste/cabin/tent C$209/249/209/419; 🖱🐾), where highlight accommodations are luxury tent suites perched like nests on a steep cliff. About as far from camping as you can get, each canvas-walled cabin has a heated rock floor, Jacuzzi tub and private deck overlooking the bay.

The resort has a good West Coast restaurant (mains C$16 to C$28), but if you want to hang with the locals, try the **Lighthouse Pub** (5764 Wharf Rd; mains C$8-16), a lively neighborhood haunt where you can feast on hearty pub grub and boat-bobbing vistas.

POWELL RIVER

A short ferry hop along Hwy 101 brings you to this vibrant former resource town. Funkier than Sechelt and busier than Gibsons, Powell River is worth a sleepover and is a hot spot for outdoor activities – drop by the **Visitors Centre** (☑604-485-4701, 877-817-8669; www.discoverpowellriver.com; 111-4871 Joyce Ave; ⊙9am-9pm Mon-Fri, 10am-6pm Sat & Sun May-Sep, 9am-5pm Mon-Fri Oct-Apr) for tips.

West of downtown, **Willingdon Beach City Park** is ideal for a waterfront picnic. The fascinating **Powell River Museum** (www.powellrivermuseum.ca; 4798 Marine Ave; adult/child C$2/1; ⊙9am-4:30pm daily Jun-Aug, Mon-Fri Sep-May) nearby houses a shack once occupied by Billy Goat Smith, a hermit who lived here (with his goats) in the early 1900s. Alternatively, hit the water – with a kayak – from **Powell River Sea Kayak** (www.bcseakayak.com; 3/12hr rental C$35/44).

For a quirky sleepover, the character-packed **Old Courthouse Inn** (☑604-483-4000, 877-483-4777; www.oldcourthouseinn.ca; 6243 Walnut St; s/d C$94/109) occupies the town's former court chambers and police

SUNSHINE COAST GALLERY CRAWL

While you're pootling along Hwy 101, keep your eyes peeled for a jaunty purple flag or two fluttering in the breeze. The flags indicate that an artist is at work on the adjoining property. Pick up the *Sunshine Coast Purple Banner* flyer from area visitor centers and galleries and it will tell you where the artists are located, just in case you miss the flags, and if they're available for a drop-in visit – some prefer that you call ahead. The region is studded with arts and crafts creators, working with wood, glass, clay, jewelry and just about everything else. For further information, check www.suncoastarts.com.

station. Rooms are handsomely decorated with antiques.

At the end of a long day, it's hard to beat a brew and a hearty meal at the **Shinglemill Pub & Bistro** (www.shinglemill.net; 6233 Powell Pl; mains C$8-16). If you're looking for something fancier, the **Alchemist Restaurant** (www.alchemistrestaurant.com; 4680 Marine Ave; mains C$19-33) fuses local seasonal ingredients with French Mediterranean flourishes.

❶ Getting There & Around

BC Ferries (www.bcferries.com) services arrive at Langdale, 6km northeast of Gibsons, from West Vancouver's Horseshoe Bay (passenger/vehicle C$12.85/43.20, 40 minutes, eight daily). Reservations recommended in summer. **Sunshine Coast Transit System** (www.busonline.ca; adult/child C$2.25/1.75) runs bus services from the terminal into Gibsons, Roberts Creek and Sechelt.

Malaspina Coach Lines (www.malaspina coach.com) buses arrive twice daily (once a day off-season) from Vancouver, via the ferry, in Gibsons (C$30, two hours), Roberts Creek (C$32, 2½ hours), Sechelt (C$40, three hours) and Powell River (C$58, five to six hours). Rates include the ferry fare.

VANCOUVER ISLAND

The largest populated landmass off the North American coast – it's around 500km long and 100km wide – Vancouver Island is laced with colorful, often quirky communities, many founded on logging or fishing and featuring the word 'Port' in their name.

Despite the general distaste among residents for the 'too busy' mainland, the locals are friendly and welcoming, proud of their region and its distinct differences. If you want to make a good impression, don't refer to the place as 'Victoria Island,' a frequent mistake that can provoke involuntary eye-rolls and an almost perceptible downgrading of your welcome.

While Victoria itself – the history-wrapped BC capital – is the first port of call for many, it should not be the only place you visit here. Food and wine fans will enjoy weaving through the Cowichan Valley farm region; those craving a laid-back family-friendly enclave should hit the twin seaside towns of Parksville and Qualicum; outdoor activity enthusiasts shouldn't miss surf-loving Tofino; and those who fancy an escape far from the madding crowds should make for the North Island, one of BC's most rewarding wilderness areas.

For further information, contact **Tourism Vancouver Island** (☎250-754-3500; www.van couverisland.travel).

Victoria

POP 78,000

With a population approaching 350,000 when you add in the suburbs, this picture-postcard provincial capital was long-touted as North America's most English city. This was a surprise to anyone who actually came from Britain, since Victoria promulgated a dreamy version of England that never really was: every garden (complete with the occasional palm tree) was immaculate; every flag pole was adorned with a crisp Union Jack; and every afternoon was spent quaffing tea from bone-china cups.

Thankfully, this theme-park Olde England has been superseded in recent years. Fueled by a younger demographic, a quiet revolution has seen lame tourist pubs, eateries and stores transformed into bright-painted bohemian shops, wood-floored coffee bars and surprisingly innovative restaurants. It's worth seeking out these enclaves on foot but activity fans should also hop on their bikes: Victoria has more cycle routes than any other Canadian city. Once you've finished exploring, there's also BC's best museum, a park licked with a windswept seafront and a doorstep of outdoor activities from whale-watching to kayaking.

⊙ Sights

Parliament Buildings HISTORICAL BUILDING
(www.leg.bc.ca; 501 Belleville St; admission free;
⊘8:30am-5pm daily May-Sep, Mon-Fri Oct-Apr)
Across from the museum, this handsome
confection of turrets, domes and stained
glass is the province's working legislature
but it's also open to history-loving visitors. Peek behind the facade on a colorful
30-minute **tour** led by costumed Victorians, then stop for lunch at the 'secret' politi-
cians' restaurant (p389).

Art Gallery of Greater Victoria ART GALLERY
(www.aggv.bc.ca; 1040 Moss St; adult/child
C$13/2.50; ⊘10am-5pm Mon-Wed, Fri & Sat, 10am-
9pm Thu, noon-5pm Sun) Head east of downtown on Fort St and follow the gallery signs
to find one of Canada's best Emily Carr collections. Aside from Carr's swirling nature
canvases, you'll find an ever-changing array
of temporary exhibitions. Check online for
events including lectures, presentations and
even singles nights for lonely arts fans.

Craigdarroch Castle MUSEUM
(www.thecastle.ca; 1050 Joan Cres; adult/child
C$13.75/5; ⊘9am-7pm mid-Jun–Aug, 10am-
4:30pm Sep–mid-Jun) If you're in this part of
town checking out the gallery, don't miss
this elegant turreted mansion a few minutes' walk away. A handsome, 39-room landmark built by a 19th-century coal baron with
money to burn, it's dripping with period architecture and antique-packed rooms. Climb
the tower's 87 steps (check out the stained-
glass windows en route) for views of the
snowcapped Olympic Mountains.

Victoria Bug Zoo ZOO
(www.bugzoo.com; 631 Courtney St; adult/youth/
child C$9/8/6; ⊘10am-5pm Mon-Sat, 11am-5pm
Sun, reduced hours off-season) The most fun
your wide-eyed kids will have in Victoria;
step inside the bright-painted main room

for some show-and-tell insect encounters.
The excellent guides handle and talk about
critters like frog beetles, dragon-headed
crickets and the disturbingly large three-
horned scarab beetles, before releasing their
audience (not the insects) into the gift shop.

Beacon Hill Park PARK
Fringed by the crashing ocean, this dramatic green space is a great spot to weather a
wild storm – check out the windswept trees
along the cliff top. You'll also find one of the
world's tallest totem poles, a marker for Mile
0 of Canada's Hwy 1, and a statue of Terry
Fox, the one-legged runner whose attempted
cross-Canada trek gripped the nation. Here
with kids? Check out the **Children's Farm**
with its baby goats and wandering peacocks.

Emily Carr House MUSEUM
(www.emilycarr.com; 207 Government St; admission by donation; ⊘11am-4pm Tue-Sat May-Sep)
The birthplace of BC's best-known painter,
this yellow, gingerbread-style house has plenty of period rooms and displays on the artist's life and work. There's an ever-changing
array of contemporary works on display but
head to the Art Gallery of Greater Victoria
(p381) for more of Carr's paintings.

🏃 Activities
Whale-Watching

Raincoat-clad tourists head out by the boat-
load from Victoria throughout the May-to-
October viewing season. The whales don't
always show, so most excursions also visit the
local haunts of elephant seal and sea lions.

Prince of Whales WHALE-WATCHING
(☑250-383-4884, 888-383-4884; www.
princeofwhales.com; 812 Wharf St; adult/child
C$100/80) Long-established local operator.

Springtide Charters WHALE-WATCHING
(☑250-384-4444, 800-470-3474; www.spring
tidecharters.com; 1111 Wharf St; adult/child
C$99/69) Popular local operator.

DON'T MISS

Victoria's **Royal BC Museum** (www.royalbcmuseum.bc.ca; 675 Belleville St; adult/child
C$14.29/9.06; ⊘10am-5pm) is the best spot in the province to dip into the region's natu-
ral, social and political history. Start at the 2nd-floor natural history showcase fronted
by a beady-eyed wooly mammoth and lined with realistic dioramas – the forest of
elk and grizzlies peeking from behind trees is highly evocative. Then peruse the First
Peoples exhibit and its deep exploration of indigenous culture, including a fascinating mask gallery (look for the ferret-faced white man). The best area, though, is the
walk-through re-created street that reanimates an early colonial city, complete with
a chatty Chinatown, highly detailed stores and a little movie house showing Charlie
Chaplin films. The museum also has an IMAX Theatre.

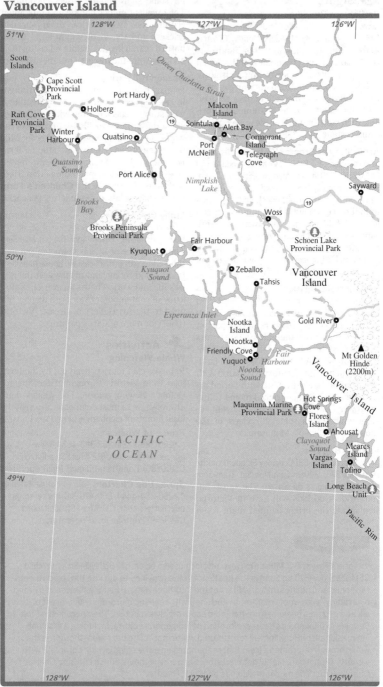

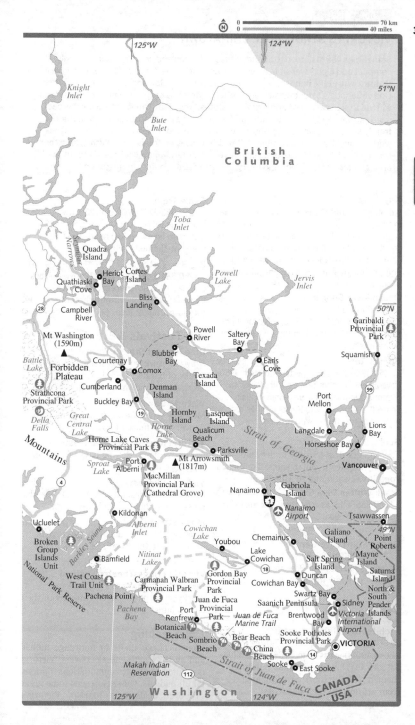

DON'T MISS

VICTORIA'S STROLLABLE CHINATOWN

Sometimes you just need to abandon the guidebook and go for a wander. Luckily, compact and highly walkable downtown Victoria is ideal for that. Start your amble in **Chinatown**, at the handsome gate near the corner of Government and Fisgard Sts. One of Canada's oldest Asian neighborhoods, this tiny strip of businesses is studded with neon signs and traditional grocery stores, while **Fan Tan Alley** – a narrow passageway between Fisgard St and Pandora Ave – is a miniwarren of traditional and trendy stores hawking cheap and cheerful trinkets, cool used records and funky artworks. Consider a guided amble with **Hidden Dragon Tours** (www.oldchinatown.com; adult/child C$29/14.50). Its three-hour evening lantern tour will tell you all about the area's historic opium dens and the hardships of 19th-century immigration.

Kayaking

Ambling around the coast of Vancouver Island by kayak is the perfect way to see the region, especially if you come across a few soaring eagles, lolling seals and an occasional starfish-studded beach. You can rent equipment for your own trek or join a tour of the area's watery highlights.

Ocean River Sports KAYAKING
(☎250-381-4233; www.oceanriver.com; 1824 Store St; rental 2/24hr C$30/48; ☺9:30am-6pm Mon-Wed & Sat, 9:30am-8pm Thu & Fri, 10am-5pm Sun) Runs 2½-hour harbor tours (C$65).

Sports Rent KAYAKING
(☎250-385-7368; www.sportsrentbc.com; 1950 Government St; canoe rental 5/24hr C$39/49; ☺9am-5:30pm Mon-Thu, 9am-6pm Fri, 9am-5pm Sat, 10am-5pm Sun) Rents canoes as well as bikes, tents, wetsuits etc.

Scuba Diving

The region's dive-friendly underwater ecosystem includes popular spots like Ogden Point Breakwater and 10 Mile Point.

Frank Whites Dive Store SCUBA DIVING
(☎250-385-4713; www.frankwhites.com; 1620 Blanshard St; ☺9am-5:30pm) Scuba equipment rentals and courses.

Ogden Point Dive Centre SCUBA DIVING
(☎250-380-9119, 888-701-1177; www.divevictoria.com; 199 Dallas Rd; ☺9am-6pm) Courses, rentals etc a few minutes from the Inner Harbour.

☞ Tours

Architectural Institute of BC WALKING
(☎604-683-8588/333, 800-667-0753; www.aibc.ca; 1001 Douglas St; tours C$5; ☺1pm Tue-Sat Jul & Aug) Five great-value, building-themed walking tours covering angles from art deco to ecclesiastical.

Cycle Treks BIKE
(☎250-386-2277, 877-733-6722; www.cycletreks.com; 1000 Wharf St; tours from C$99; ☺9:30am-6pm Mon-Sat) Leads six-hour seafront-themed cycling tours.

Big Bus Victoria BUS
(☎250-389-2229, 888-434-2229; www.bigbusvictoria.ca; 811 Government St; adult/child C$35/17) Offers 90-minute hop-on-hop-off tours around 22 local points of interest.

✸ Festivals & Events

Dine Around Stay in Town FOOD
(www.tourismvictoria/dinearound) Three weeks of bargain prix-fixe meals at restaurants around the city; mid-February.

Victoria Day Parade COMMUNITY
Mid-May street fiesta shenanigans with dancers and marching bands.

Victoria International Jazzfest MUSIC
(www.jazzvictoria.ca) Nine days of jazz performance in late June.

Victoria SkaFest MUSIC
(www.victoriaskafest.ca) Canada's largest ska music event, held in mid-July.

Moss Street Paint-In ART
(www.aggv.bc.ca) In mid-July 100 artists demonstrate their skills at this popular one-day community event.

Victoria Fringe Theatre Festival THEATER
(www.victoriafringe.com) Two-weeks of quirky short plays staged throughout the city in late August.

⌂ Sleeping

From heritage B&Bs to midrange motels and swanky high-end sleepovers, Victoria is stuffed with accommodations options for all budgets. Off-season sees some great sleepover deals and Tourism Victoria's room reservation service (☎250-953-2033, 800-663-3883; www.tourismvictoria.com) can let you know what's available.

Spinnakers Guesthouses
B&B $$$

(☎250-384-2739; www.spinnakers.com; 308 Catherine St; r/ste from C$159/259; 🛜) A short stumble from its own celebrated brewpub (p389), this clutch of adult-oriented guesthouses combines luxury details with pampering home comforts. The Heritage House is a restored 1884 family home with antiques, fireplaces and private patios. The larger Garden Suites have a contemporary feel and a smattering of Asian design flourishes. Gourmet continental breakfast included.

Swans Suite Hotel
HOTEL $$$

(☎250-361-3310, 800-668-7926; www.swanshotel .com; 506 Pandora Ave; d/ste C$199/289; 🛜) Across the street from the tiny railway station – you'll hear the train toot into town twice a day – this former old brick warehouse has been transformed into an art-lined boutique sleepover. Most rooms are spacious loft suites where you climb upstairs to bed in a gabled nook, and each is decorated with a comfy combination of wood beams, rustic chic furniture and deep leather sofas.

Fairmont Empress Hotel
HOTEL $$$

(☎250-384-8111, 866-540-4429; www.fairmont .com/empress; 721 Government St; r from C$189; ❄@≋) Rooms at this ivy-covered, century-old Inner Harbour landmark are elegant but conservative and some are quite small, but the overall effect is grand and classy – from the Raj-style curry restaurant to the high tea sipped while overlooking the waterfront. Even if you don't stay, make sure you stroll through and soak up the ambience.

Parkside Victoria Resort & Spa
HOTEL $$$

(☎250-716-2651, 866-941-4175; www.parkside victoria.com; 810 Humboldt St; ste from C$269; 🛜≋) A slick new apartment-style hotel a couple of blocks from the Inner Harbour; the comfortable, well-equipped rooms here are ideal if you want a home-style base steps from the city center. Full kitchens, balconies and a gym might make you want to move in permanently. There's also an onsite mini cinema screening nightly free flicks.

Hotel Rialto
HOTEL $$

(☎250-382-4157, 800-332-9981; www.hotelrialto .ca; 653 Pandora Ave; r C$139-249; 🛜) Completely refurbished from the faded former budget hotel it used to be, the new Rialto is a well-located downtown option in an attractive century-old heritage building. Each of the 38 mod-decorated rooms has a fridge, microwave and flat-screen TV and some rooms have bath tubs as well as showers. The lobby's tapas lounge is justifiably popular, whether or not you're staying here.

James Bay Inn
INN $$

(☎250-384-7151, 800-836-2649; www.jamesbay inn.bc.ca; 270 Government St; r from C$129) A few minutes from the Emily Carr House, this quirky charmer has a well-maintained, retro feel. The charm might wear off when you realize there's no elevator, but once you've lugged your bags up the stairs you'll find a vast array of room types: most have busy-patterned carpets and furniture that's old but not quite antique. Some rooms have kitchenettes.

Ocean Island Inn
HOSTEL $

(☎250-385-1788, 888-888-4180; www.ocean island.com; 791 Pandora Ave; dm/s/d from C$27.50/30/55; @🛜) This funky, multicolored sleepover is a labyrinth of dorms and private rooms – ask for one with a window. There's a large communal kitchen on the ground floor and a licensed lounge for quiz nights and open mic nights. Also offers private **self-catering suites** (www.oisuites. com; from C$128) across town in a James Bay character house.

HI Victoria Hostel
HOSTEL $

(☎250-385-4511, 888-883-0099; www.hihos tels.ca; 516 Yates St; dm/d C$31.50/78; @🛜) A well-located, quiet hostel with two large single-sex dorms, three small co-eds and a couple of private rooms. An extensive reno is being planned in coming years.

Abbeymoore Manor
B&B $$

(☎250-370-1470, 888-801-1811; www.abbey moore.com; 1470 Rockland Ave; r from C$165; 🛜) A romantic 1912 Arts and Crafts mansion, Abbeymoore has a handsome colonial exterior hiding seven antique-lined rooms furnished with Victorian knick-knacks. Some rooms have kitchens and jetted tubs.

Queen Victoria Hotel
HOTEL $$

(☎250-386-1312, 800-663-7007; www.qvhotel. com; 655 Douglas St; d/ste from C$133/152; ❄≋) A well-maintained tower-block property near the Inner Harbour; rooms here have a business-hotel feel. All have balconies and handy fridges; some also have kitchenettes.

🍴 Eating

Formerly dominated by tourist traps serving nothing but poor-quality fish 'n chips,

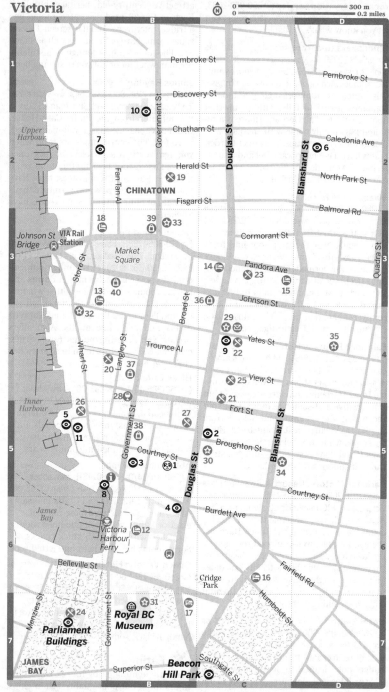

VANCOUVER, WHISTLER & VANCOUVER ISLAND VANCOUVER ISLAND

Victoria

0 — 300 m
0 — 0.2 miles

Pembroke St
Pembroke St
Discovery St
Chatham St
10
Herald St
7
19
CHINATOWN
Fan Tan Al
Fisgard St
18
39 **33**
Cormorant St
Johnson St Bridge
VIA Rail Station
Market Square
14
Pandora Ave
23
15
13
40
Broad St
Johnson St
36
32
29
Trounce Al
9 **22**
Yates St
35
Langley St
20 **37**
View St
25
28
21
Fort St
26
27
5
11
38
2
Broughton St
Courtney St
3
1
30
34
8
4
Burdett Ave
James Bay
Victoria Harbour Ferry
12
Belleville St
Cridge Park
16
Fairfield Rd
31
17
24
Royal BC Museum
Parliament Buildings
JAMES BAY
Superior St
Beacon Hill Park
Southgate St

Douglas St
Douglas St
Blanshard St
Blanshard St
Store St
Wharf St
Government St
Government St
Menzies St
Government St
Humboldt St
Quadra St

Caledonia Ave
6
North Park St
Balmoral Rd

Upper Harbour

Inner Harbour

VANCOUVER, WHISTLER & VANCOUVER ISLAND VICTORIA

Victoria's dining scene has been radically transformed in recent years. Pick up *Eat Magazine* (free) to see what's on the menu and keep in mind that hours are often extended ad hoc in summer.

TOP CHOICE **Fort Café**   CANADIAN **$**
(742 Fort St; mains C$6-10; 🐶) This warm and inviting subterranean hipster haunt offers the perfect combination of great comfort food and cool digs. Among the heaping fresh-made nosh, the turkey avocado wraps and hot pepper beef sandwiches are standouts, while there's also a rare offering of all the Salt Spring Brewing beers on draft. Check out the Atari game system around the corner at the back or drop in for Friday's massively popular quiz night (doors open 7:30pm).

Hernande'z   MEXICAN **$**
(www.hernandezcocina.com; off 750 Yates St; mains C$5-8; 🍴) Inauspiciously hidden in a covered passageway between Yates and View Sts, Victoria's best Mexican hole-in-the-wall has a queue of slavering locals as soon as it opens. Vegetarian options abound but the *huarache de pollo* (thick tortilla with chicken) is legendary and goes perfectly with a local Phillips Brewing beer. There are never enough available tables, so consider packing your butchers paper parcel and heading to Beacon Hill Park for a picnic. Cash only.

Red Fish Blue Fish   SEAFOOD **$**
(www.redfish-bluefish.com; 1006 Wharf St; mains C$6-10) On the waterfront boardwalk at the foot of Broughton St, this freight container takeout shack serves a loyal clientele that just can't get enough of its fresh-made sustainable seafood. Highlights like scallop tacones (tortilla hand-rolls), wild salmon sandwiches, tempura battered fish 'n chips and the signature chunky Pacific Rim Chowder all hit the spot: find a waterfront perch to enjoy your nosh but watch for hovering seagull mobsters.

Camille's
WEST COAST $$$

(☎250-381-3433; www.camillesrestaurant.com; 45 Bastion Sq; mains C$18-26) A charming subterranean dining room with a lively, ever-changing menu reflecting whatever the chef can source locally and seasonally, perhaps ranging from pan-seared BC duck and sweet spot prawns to breathtaking desserts packed with local fruits and berries. With a great wine menu, this spot invites adventurous foodies to linger. Recommended for a romantic night out.

John's Place
BREAKFAST, CANADIAN $$

(www.johnsplace.ca; 723 Pandora Ave; mains C$7-17; ⊕) Victoria's best weekend brunch spot, this wood-floored, high-ceilinged heritage room is lined with funky memorabilia and the menu is a cut above standard diner fare. They'll start you off with a basket of addictive house-made bread, but save room for heaping pasta dishes or a Belgian waffle breakfast. And don't leave without trying a thick slab of fruit pie.

Pig BBQ Joint
SANDWICH SHOP $

(www.pigbbqjoint.com; 749 View St; mains C$5-6) This vegetarian-free hole-in-the-wall is all about the meat, specifically bulging, Texas-style pulled-pork sandwiches (beef brisket and smoked-chicken variations are also offered). Expect lunchtime queues (better to arrive early or late) and consider perking up your order with a side of succulent cornbread and house-made ice tea. Plans were afoot to open a second, larger venue around the corner on our visit – stay tuned.

Tibetan Kitchen
ASIAN FUSION $

(www.tibetankitchen.ca; 680 Broughton St; mains C$7-15; ✐) Lunch specials are an excellent deal (check the board outside) at this cozy, wood-lined South Asian eatery. Start with some shareable openers like veggie pakoras and paneer poppers, then move on to fresh-made noodle and curry mains; there are plenty of vegetarian options but the slow-cooked, ginger-infused Shepta beef is highly recommended.

Legislative Dining Room
WEST COAST $$

(Room 606 Parliament Buildings; mains C$6-16) One of Victoria's best-kept dining secrets, the Parliament Buildings has its own subsidized restaurant where MLAs (and the public) can drop by for a silver-service menu of regional dishes, ranging from smoked tofu salads to velvety steaks and shrimp quesadillas. It's cash only and entry is via the security desk just inside the building's main entrance.

Brasserie L'Ecole
FRENCH $$$

(☎250-475-6260; www.lecole.ca; 1715 Government St; mains C$20-24) This country-style French bistro has a warm, casual atmosphere and a delectable menu. Locally sourced produce is *de rigueur,* so the dishes constantly change to reflect seasonal highlights like figs, salmonberries and heirloom tomatoes. We recommend the lamb shank, served with mustard-creamed root vegetables and braised chard.

Drinking

Spinnakers Gastro Brewpub
PUB

(www.spinnakers.com; 308 Catherine St) A pioneering craft brewer, this wood-floored smasher is a short hop from the Inner Harbour and it's worth it for tongue-ticklers like copper-colored Nut Brown Ale and hoppy Blue Bridge Double IPA – named after the sky-blue span that delivers most quaffers to the door. Save room to eat: the seasonal dishes are often designed for beer pairing.

Big Bad John's
PUB

(www.strathconahotel.com; 919 Douglas St) Easily missed from the outside, this evocative little hillbilly theme bar feels like you've stepped into the backwoods. But rather than some dodgy banjo players with mismatched ears, you'll find good-time locals enjoying the cavelike ambience of peanut shell–covered floors and a ceiling dotted with grubby bras.

Bard & Banker
PUB

(www.bardandbanker.com; 1022 Government St) This cavernous Victorian repro pub is handsomely lined with cut-glass lamps, open fireplaces and a long granite bar topped with 30 brass beer taps. Pull up a stool and taste-test Phillips Blue Buck, Nova Scotia's Alexander Keiths and the house-brand Robert Service Ale. There's nightly live music plus a nosh menu of elevated pub classics.

☆ Entertainment

Check the freebie *Monday Magazine* weekly for listings or head online to www.livevictoria.com.

Live Music & Nightclubs

Lucky Bar
NIGHTCLUB, LIVE MUSIC

(www.luckybar.ca; 517 Yates St) A Victoria institution, downtown's eclectic Lucky Bar offers live music from ska and indie to electroclash. There are bands here at least twice a week, while the remaining evenings are occupied by dancefloor club nights, including Wednesday's mod fest and Saturday's mix night.

Logan's Pub
LIVE MUSIC

(www.loganspub.com; 1821 Cook St) A 10-minute walk east from downtown along North Park St, this sports pub in Cook St Village looks like nothing special from the outside, but its roster of shows is a main fixture of the local indie scene. Friday and Saturday are your best bet for performances but other nights are frequently also booked – check online to see what's coming up.

Sugar
LIVE MUSIC, NIGHTCLUB

(www.sugarnightclub.ca; 858 Yates St) A popular, long-standing club that's been hosting a wide array of local and visiting bands for years. Expect everything from Bob Marley tribute acts to a thundering visit from the Dayglo Abortions. Usually only open Thursday to Saturday, the two-floor joint hosts DJ club nights when there's no live act on board.

Element
NIGHTCLUB

(www.elementnightclub.ca; 919 Douglas St) Conveniently located under the Sticky Wicket and Big Bad John's, Elements is a mainstream club hang-out known for its Saturday Top 40, hip-hop and R&B night. Friday is also popular and there are additional fairly regular live acts.

Theater & Cinemas

Victoria's main stages, **McPherson Playhouse** (www.rmts.bc.ca; 3 Centennial Sq) and the rococo-interior **Royal Theatre** (www.rmts.bc.ca; 805 Broughton St), each offer mainstream visiting shows and performances. The latter is also home of the **Victoria Symphony** (www.victoriasymphony.bc.ca) and **Pacific Opera Victoria** (www.pov.bc.ca).

Belfry Theatre
THEATER

(www.belfry.bc.ca; 1291 Gladstone Ave) A 20-minute stroll from downtown, the city's celebrated Belfry showcases contemporary plays in its lovely former church building venue.

Cineplex Odeon
CINEMA

(www.cineplex.com; 780 Yates St) The city's main first-run cinema.

Cinecenta
CINEMA

(www.cinecenta.com; University of Victoria) Arthouse flicks at UVic's.

IMAX Theatre
CINEMA

(www.imaxvictoria.com) The Royal BC Museum shows larger-than-life documentaries and Hollywood blockbusters.

 Shopping

While Government St is a magnet for souvenir shoppers, those looking for more original purchases should head to the Johnson St stretch between Store and Government Sts. Now designated as 'LoJo' (Lower Johnson), this old-town area is a hotbed of independent stores.

Smoking Lily
CLOTHING

(www.smokinglily.com; 569 Johnson St) LoJo's signature shop is an almost too-tiny boutique stuffed with eclectic garments and accessories that define art-school chic. Tops and skirts with insect prints are hot items, but there are also lots of cute handbags, socks and brooches to tempt your credit card.

Ditch Records
MUSIC

(www.ditchrecords.com; 635 Johnson St) This narrow, High Fidelity–style shop is lined with tempting vinyl and furtive musos perusing the homemade racks of releases by bands like the Meatmen and Nightmares on Wax. With its threadbare carpet and cave-like feel, it's an ideal wet Monday afternoon hang-out. And if it suddenly feels like time to socialize, you can book gig tickets here, too.

Munro's Books
BOOKSTORE

(www.munrobooks.com; 1108 Government St) Like a cathedral to book reading, this high-ceilinged local legend lures browsers who just like to hang out among the shelves. There's a good array of local-interest tomes as well as a fairly extensive travel section at the back on the left. Check the racks of bargain books, too – they're not all copies of *How to Eat String* from 1972.

Rogers' Chocolates
FOOD, DRINK

(www.rogerschocolates.com; 913 Government St) This charming, museumlike confectioners has the best ice-cream bars in town, but repeat offenders usually spend their time hitting the menu of rich Victoria Creams, one of which is just about enough to substitute for lunch. Flavors range from peppermint to chocolate nut and they're good souvenirs, so long as you don't scoff them all before you get home.

Silk Road
FOOD, DRINK

(www.silkroadtea.com; 1624 Government St) A pilgrimage spot for regular and exotic tea fans; you can pick up all manner of leafy paraphernalia here. Sidle up to the tasting bar to quaff some adventurous brews. There's also a small onsite spa where you can indulge in oil treatments and aromatherapy.

Information

Downtown Medical Centre (622 Courtney St; ⊗8:30am-5pm) Handy walk-in clinic.

Main Post Office (706 Yates St; ⊗9am-5pm Mon-Fri) Near the corner of Yates and Douglas Sts.

Stain Internet Café (609 Yates St; per hr C$3.50; ⊗10am-2am) Central and late-opening internet spot.

Visitor Centre (www.tourismvictoria.com; 812 Wharf St; ⊗8:30am-8:30pm Jun-Aug, 9am-5pm Sep-May) Busy, flyer-lined visitors center overlooking the Inner Harbour.

Getting There & Away

Air

Victoria International Airport (www.victoria airport.com) is 26km north of the city via Hwy 17. **Air Canada** (www.aircanada.com) services arrive here from Vancouver (from C$73, 25 minutes, up to 21 daily) while **Westjet** (www.westjet.com) flights arrive from Calgary (from C$129, 90 minutes, six daily). Both airlines offer competing connections across Canada.

 Harbour Air Seaplanes (www.harbour-air.com) arrive in the Inner Harbour from downtown Vancouver (C$145, 35 minutes) throughout the day. Similar **Helijet** (www.helijet.com) helicopter services arrive from Vancouver (from C$149, 35 minutes).

Boat

BC Ferries (www.bcferries.com) arrive from mainland Tsawwassen (adult/child/vehicle C$14/7/46.75, 90 minutes) at Swartz Bay, 27km north of Victoria via Hwy 17. Services arrive hourly throughout the day in summer but are reduced off-season.

 Victoria Clipper (www.clippervacations.com) services arrive in the Inner Harbour from Seattle (adult/child US$93/46, three hours, up to three a day). **Black Ball Transport** (www.ferrytovictoria.com) boats also arrive from Port Angeles (adult/child/vehicle US$15.50/7.75/55, 90 minutes, up to four daily) as do **Victoria Express** (www.victoria express.com) services (passenger US$10, one hour, up to three daily).

Bus

Services terminating at the city's main **bus station** (700 Douglas St) include **Greyhound Canada** (www.greyhound.ca) routes from Nanaimo (C$23.30, 2½ hours, four daily) and Port Alberni (C$40.30, four to five hours, two daily), along with frequent **Pacific Coach Lines** (www.pacificcoach.com) services from Vancouver (from C$28.75, 3½ hours) and Vancouver International Airport (C$40.25, four hours).

Train

The charming **VIA Rail** (www.viarail.com) *Malahat* train arrives in the city on the Johnson St Bridge from Courtenay (C$53, five hours, daily), with additional up-island stops in Nanaimo, Parksville and Chemainus, among others.

Getting Around

To/From the Airport

AKAL Airporter (www.victoriaairporter.com) minibuses run between the airport and area hotels (C$19, 30 minutes). The service meets all the airport's incoming and outgoing flights. In contrast, a taxi to downtown costs around C$50, while transit bus 70 takes around 35 minutes, runs throughout the day and costs C$2.50.

Bicycle

Victoria is a great cycling capital with plenty of routes crisscrossing the city and beyond. Bike rentals are offered by **Cycle BC Rentals** (www.cyclebc.ca; 685 Humboldt St; per hr/day C$7/24; ⊗9am-6pm).

Boat

Victoria Harbour Ferry (www.victoriaharbour ferry.com; tickets from C$5) covers the Inner Harbour, Songhees Park (for Spinnakers Brewpub), Reeson's Landing (for the LoJo shopping area) and other stops along the Gorge Waterway with its colorful armada of bath-sized little boats.

Public Transportation

Victoria Regional Transit (www.busonline.ca; tickets adult/child C$2.50/1.65) buses cover a wide area from Sidney to Sooke, with some routes served by modern double-deckers. Day passes (adult/child C$7.75/5.50) are also available from convenience and grocery stores. Children under five years travel free.

Southern Vancouver Island

Not far from Victoria's madding crowds, Southern Vancouver Island is a laid-back region of quirky towns, tree-lined cycling routes and rocky outcrops bristling with gnarly Garry oaks. The wildlife here is abundant and impressive; you'll likely spot bald eagles swooping overhead and sea otters cavorting on the beaches.

SAANICH PENINSULA & AROUND

Home of Vancouver Island's main airport and ferry terminal, this peninsula north of Victoria has more to offer than just a way to get from here to there. On a languid day out from Victoria, you'll find waterfront Sidney and BC's most popular garden attraction.

At the northern end of Saanich Peninsula, seafront **Sidney** is studded with a dozen used bookstores, enabling it to call itself the region's 'Booktown.' Drop by the **Visitor Centre** (☏250-656-7102; www.sidney. ca; 2295 Ocean Ave; ◷10am-4pm) for bookish and nonbookish tips.

The cracking **Shaw Ocean Discovery Centre** (www.oceandiscovery.ca; 9811 Seaport Pl; adult/child C$12/6; ◷noon-5pm) is the town's kid-luring highlight. Enter through a dramatic Disney-style entrance that makes you think you're descending below the waves, then step into a world of iridescent jellyfish, spiky sea cucumbers and a touch tank brimming with starfish and anemones.

If the sight of fish just makes you hungry, head to the end of the town's short pier and tuck into some halibut and chips at **Pier Bistro** (2550 Beacon Ave; mains C$10-16), which serves lovely waterfront views along with its nosh. Or try an authentic Mexican alternative – the C$9.95 three-part taco plate is best – at the cheery **Carlos Express** (2527 Beacon Ave; mains C$8-10) nearby.

Sleep it off at the swanky new **Sidney Pier Hotel and Spa** (☏250-655-9445, 866-659-9445; www.sidneypier.com; 9805 Seaport Pl; d/ste C$159/299; @) on the waterfront.

Victoria Regional Transit (www.busonline. ca) bus 70 trundles into Sidney from Victoria (C$2.50, one hour) throughout the day.

The rolling farmlands of waterfront **Brentwood Bay** are chiefly known for **Butchart Gardens** (www.butchartgardens. com; 800 Benvenuto Ave; adult/youth/child C$28.10/14.05/2.86; ◷9am-10pm mid-Jun–Aug, reduced hours off-season), Vancouver Island's top visitor attraction and just a 30-minute drive from the city via West Saanich Rd. The immaculate grounds are divided into separate gardens where there's always something in bloom. Summer is crowded, with tour buses rolling in relentlessly, but evening music performances and Saturday-night fireworks (July and August) make it all worthwhile. Tea fans take note: the **Dining Room Restaurant** serves a smashing afternoon tea, complete with roasted vegetable quiches and Grand Marnier truffles... leave your diet at the door.

If you have time, also consider nearby **Victoria Butterfly Gardens** (www.butterflygardens .com; 1461 Benvenuto Ave; adult/youth/child C$12.50/11.50/6.50; ◷9am-5:30pm May-Aug, reduced hours off-season), which offers a kaleidoscope of thousands of fluttering critters

(from around 75 species) in a free-flying environment. As well as watching them flit about and land on their heads, visitors can learn about ecosystem life cycles, and eyeball exotic fish, plants and birds. Look out for Spike, the red-crowned puna ibis that likes strutting around the trails as if he owns the place.

SOOKE & AROUND

Rounding Vancouver Island's rustic southern tip toward Sooke (a 45-minute drive from Victoria), Hwy 14 is lined with twisted Garry oaks and unkempt hedgerows, while the houses – many of them artisan workshops or homely B&Bs – seem spookily hidden in the forest shadows. For information, chat up the friendly folk at **Sooke Visitor Centre** (☏250-642-6351, 866-888-4748; www. sooke-portrenfrew.com; 2070 Philips Rd; ◷9am-5pm, closed Mon in winter).

Sharing the same building (and hours) as the visitors center, **Sooke Region Museum** illuminates the area's rugged pioneer days. Check out **Moss Cottage** in the museum grounds: built in 1869, it's the oldest residence west of Victoria.

If you're craving a few thrills, find your inner screamer on the eight-run forested zipline course (plus two suspension bridges) operated by **Adrenaline** (www.adrenaline zip.com; 5128 Sooke Rd; adult/child C$95/85). The monthly full-moon zips are the most fun and if you don't have your own transport, they'll pick you up from Victoria.

For a more relaxed way to encounter nature, drop into **Sooke Potholes Provincial Park** (www.bcparks.ca), a 5km drive from Hwy 14 (the turnoff is east of Sooke). With rock pools and potholes carved into the river base during the last ice age, it's a popular spot for swimming and tube floating and is ideal for a summer picnic.

You'll find B&Bs dotted along the route, but for one of BC's most delightful sleepovers consider **Sooke Harbour House** (☏250-642-3421, 800-889-9688; www.sookeharbourhouse. com; 1528 Whiffen Spit Rd; ste from C$399). Paintings, sculptures and carved wood line its interiors, while some of the 28 rooms have fireplaces and steam showers and all have views across the waterfront – look for gamboling sea otters and swooping cranes.

You won't be disappointed with the hotel's celebrated eatery, but the town's **Edge Restaurant** (6686 Sooke Rd; mains C$9-19) is also excellent. The menu is ever-changing – spend some time perusing the chalkboard – but it often includes delectables like crispy

DON'T MISS

ON YER BIKE

Bring your bike across on the ferry from the mainland and when you hop off in Swartz Bay you can hop on to the easily accessible and well-marked **Lochside Regional Trail** to downtown Victoria. The 29km mostly flat route is not at all challenging – there are only a couple of overpasses – and it's an idyllic, predominantly paved wind through small urban areas, waterfront stretches, rolling farmland and forested countryside. There are several spots to pick up lunch en route and, if you adopt a leisurely pace, you'll be in town within four hours or so. If you've been bitten by the biking bug, consider extending your trek past Victoria on the 55km **Galloping Goose Regional Trail**. Colonizing a former 1920s railway line, it's one of the island's most popular bike routes and it will take you all the way to rustic, waterfront Sooke. While longer than its sibling, it's similarly flat most of the way which makes it popular with the not-quite-so-hardcore biking fraternity. You can access the trail by crossing over the Johnson St Bridge from downtown Victoria; the trailhead is on your right.

tuna or braised beef short rib. The desserts (think apple spring rolls with whipped cream cheese) are dangerously alluring.

The 47km **Juan de Fuca Marine Trail** (www.juandefucamarinetrail.com) in **Juan de Fuca Provincial Park** (www.bcparks.ca) rivals the West Coast Trail (p398) as a must-do trek for outdoorsy visitors. From east to west, its trailhead access points are China Beach, Sombrio Beach, Parkinson Creek and Botanical Beach.

It takes around four days to complete the route – the most difficult stretch is between Bear Beach and China Beach – but you don't have to go the whole hog. Be aware that some sections are often muddy and difficult to hike, while bear sightings and swift weather changes are common.

The route has several basic campsites and you can pay your camping fee (C$5 per person) at any of the trailheads. The most popular tent spot is the slightly more salubrious **China Beach Campground** (☎604-689-9025, 800-689-9025; www.discovercamping.ca; tent site C$24); it has pit toilets and cold-water taps but no showers. Book ahead in summer.

Booking ahead is also required on the **West Coast Trail Express** (☎250-477-8700, 888-999-2288; www.trailbus.com) minibus that runs between Victoria, the trailheads and Port Renfrew (from C$55; daily from May to September in each direction).

Port Renfrew, located between the Juan de Fuca and West Coast Trails, is a great access point for either route. Quiet and stormy during the off-season, it's usually dripping with preparing or recuperating hikers in summer. There are several spots to stock up on supplies and fraternize with

other trekkers, and it's also worth dropping by the **Visitor Centre** (www.portrenfrew.com; ⊙10am-6pm May-Sep) on your left as you enter town.

If you've had enough of your sleeping bag, try **Port Renfrew Resorts** (☎250-647-5541; www.portrenfrewhotel.ca; 17310 Parkinson Rd; d from C$159), a recently refurbished waterfront mini-resort with motel-style rooms plus luxurious, wood-lined cabins.

And for a respite from campground mystery-meat pasta, the nearby **Coastal Kitchen Café** (17245 Parkinson Rd; mains C$8-14) serves fresh salads and sandwiches, plus burgers and pizzas. The seafood is the star attraction – especially the Dungeness crab and chips. Hikers are often found lolling around outside on the picnic tables here.

Cowichan Valley

A swift Hwy 1 drive northwest of Victoria is verdant Cowichan Valley, ripe for discovery, especially if you're craving some outdoor activities. Contact **Tourism Cowichan** (☎250-746-1099, 888-303-3337; www.tourism cowichan.com) for information.

DUNCAN

Originally an isolated logging-industry railroad stop – the gabled station now houses a little museum – Duncan is the Cowichan Valley's main town (officially, it's a city).

Quw'utsun' Cultural & Conference Centre (www.quwutsun.ca; 200 Cowichan Way; adult/child C$13/6; ⊙10am-4pm Mon-Sat Jun-Sep) is the place to head if your First Nations curiosity has been piqued by the dozens of totem poles dotting the town. Here you can learn about carving, beading and traditional salmon runs.

Alternatively, drive 3km north of town to the **BC Forest Discovery Centre** (www.discoveryforest.com; 2892 Drinkwater Rd; adult/child C$15/10; ☺10am-4:30pm Jun-early Sep, reduced hours off-season), complete with its pioneer-era buildings, logging machinery and a working steam train.

The area's chatty hub, **Duncan Garage** (3330 Duncan St; mains C$4-9) is a refurbished heritage building housing a bookstore, an organic grocery store and a lively café. For more substantial fare, **Craig Street Brewpub** (www.craigstreet.ca; 25 Craig St; mains C$11-15) serves quality comfort food like jambalaya pizza and excellent own-brewed beer – try the Shawnigan Irish Ale.

COWICHAN BAY

'Cow Bay' to the locals, the region's most attractive pit stop is a colorful string of wooden buildings perched on stilts over a mountain-shadowed ocean inlet. It's well worth an afternoon of your time, although it might take that long to find parking on a busy weekend day. Arrive hungry and drop into **Hilary's Artisan Cheese** (www.hilaryscheese.com; 1737 Cowichan Bay Rd) and **True Grain Bread** (www.truegrain.ca; 1725 Cowichan Bay Rd) for the makings of a great picnic.

After you're fully fueled, duck into the **Maritime Centre** (www.classicboats.org; 1761 Cowichan Bay Rd; admission by donation; ☺9am-dusk) to peruse some salty boat-building exhibits and intricate models.

CHEMAINUS

After the last sawmill shut down in 1983, tiny Chemainus became the model for BC communities dealing with declining resource jobs. Instead of submitting to a slow death, town officials commissioned a giant wall mural depicting local history. More than three-dozen additional artworks were later added and a tourism industry was born.

Stroll the Chemainus streets on a mural hunt and pass artsy boutiques and tempting ice-cream shops. In the evening, the surprisingly large **Chemainus Theatre** (www.chemainustheatrefestival.ca; 9737 Chemainus Rd) stages professional productions – mostly popular plays and musicals to keep you occupied.

You can chat with the locals over coffee at the **Dancing Bean Café** (www.dancingbean.ca; 9885 Maple St; mains C$6-9.50), an animated hangout with light meals (chicken sandwich recommended) and a good-value C$2.22 breakfast special.

Nanaimo

POP 79,000

Maligned for years as Vancouver Island's grubby second city, Nanaimo will never have the allure of tourist-magnet Victoria. But the 'Harbour City' has undergone its own quiet renaissance since the 1990s, with the downtown emergence of some good shops and eateries and a slick new museum. With its own ferry service from the mainland, the city is also a handy hub for exploring. Connect with **Tourism Nanaimo** (☏250-754-8141; www.tourismnanaimo.com; 2290 Bowen Rd; ☺9am-6pm May-Aug, reduced hours off-season) for further information.

◉ Sights & Activities

Nanaimo Museum   MUSEUM
(www.nanaimomuseum.ca; 100 Museum Way; adult/youth/child C$2/1.75/0.75; ☺10am-5pm daily mid-May–Aug, Tue-Sat Sep–mid-May) Just off the Commercial St main drag, this shiny new museum showcases the region's heritage, from First Nations to colonial, maritime, sporting and beyond. Highlights include a strong Coast Salish focus and a walk-through evocation of a coalmine that's popular with kids. Ask at the front desk about summertime pub and cemetery tours. It also overseas the nearby **Bastion** (www.nanaimomuseum.ca; cnr Front & Bastion Sts; adult/child C$1/free; ☺10am-3pm Jun-Aug, reduced hours May & Sep) historic tower.

Newcastle Island Marine Provincial Park   PARK
(www.newcastleisland.ca) Nanaimo's rustic outdoor gem offers tranquil hiking and cycling, as well as beaches and wildlife-spotting opportunities. Settled by the Coast Salish – and still part of their traditional territory – it was the site of shipyards and coalmines before becoming a popular short-hop summer excursion in the 1930s, when a teahouse was added. Accessed via a 10-minute ferry from the harbor (adult/child C$4/3), it has a seasonal eatery and regular First Nations dancing displays.

Just Dive In Adventures   DIVING/SNORKELING
(☏250-754-2241; www.justdiveinadventures.com; dive excursions C$95, boat tours C$79) Possibly the most fun you'll have in the water, snorkeling with seals is this operator's most

WEAVING AROUND WINE (AND CIDER) COUNTRY

Eyebrows were raised when the Cowichan Valley region proclaimed itself Vancouver Island's version of Provence a few years back, but the wine snobs have been choking on their words ever since. Slow down your trip and take in a few tasty pit stops.

Favorites include **Cherry Point Vineyards** (www.cherrypointvineyards.com; 840 Cherry Point Rd, Cobble Hill; ☺10am-5pm) with its lip-smacking blackberry port; **Averill Creek** (www.averillcreek.ca; 6552 North Rd, Duncan; ☺11am-5pm May-Oct) with its view-tastic patio and lovely pinot noirs; and the ever-popular **Merridale Estate Cidery** (www.merridalecider.com; 1230 Merridale Rd, Cobble Hill; ☺10:30am-4:30pm), an inviting apple-cider producer offering six varieties as well as a new brandy-distilling operation.

For more information on the wineries of this area and throughout Vancouver Island, check www.wineislands.ca.

popular excursion. You'll likely spot dozens of the playful critters and – possibly – a killer whale or two. Scuba diving is also offered: the regional waters are among the best in Canada for diving, and wolf eels and Pacific octopus sightings are common.

Wild Play Element Parks   AMUSEMENT PARK (www.wildplayparks.com; 35 Nanaimo River Rd; adult/child from C$40/20; ☺10am-6pm mid-Jun–Aug, reduced hours off-season) This former bungee-jumping site has reinvented itself with five obstacle courses strung between the trees. Once you're harnessed, you can hit ziplines, rope bridges, tunnels and Tarzan swings, each aimed at different ability levels.

🛏 Sleeping

Painted Turtle Guesthouse   HOSTEL $-$$ (☏250-753-4432, 866-309-4432; www.painted turtle.ca; 121 Bastion St; dm C$26.12, r C$45-98; @☎) This exemplary budget property in the heart of downtown combines four-bed dorms with family and private rooms. Hardwood floors and Ikea-esque furnishings abound while facilities range from a large and welcoming kitchen to a laundry room and ensuite showers. You can book local activities through the front desk.

Kennedy House B&B   B&B $$ (☏250-754-3389, 877-750-3389; www.kennedy house.ca; 305 Kennedy St; r C$85-125) Uphill from the waterfront, this is one of the few Nanaimo B&Bs nearish to the city center – it's also close to the VIA Rail stop and the Old City Quarter. A restored and outwardly imposing 1913 heritage mansion, it has two lovely rooms, combining antique knick-knacks and contemporary flourishes. Elegant, quiet and adult-oriented.

Coast Bastion Inn   HOTEL $$ (☏250-753-6601, 800-663-1144; www.coasthotels. com; 11 Bastion St; r from C$139; ☎) Downtown's leading hotel has an unbeatable location overlooking the harbor and most rooms have good views. Rooms have been refurbished with a lounge-modern élan in recent years, adding flat-screen TVs and (in most rooms) small fridges. The lobby resto-bar is a popular hang-out and there's also an onsite spa.

🍴 Eating

Gabriel's Café   FUSION $
TOP CHOICE (183 Commercial St; mains C$4-8; ✐) This well-located hole-in-the-wall is a revelation. Chat with the man himself behind the counter, then tuck into made-from-scratch treats like pulled-pork sandwiches with apple cider barbecue sauce or the popular Thai green chili coconut curry, inspired by the owner's global travels. Vegetarians are well-looked after – try the black bean burger – while off-menu vegan dishes can be made on request.

Wesley Street Restaurant   WEST COAST $$ (www.wesleycafe.com; 321 Wesley St; mains C$15-29; ☺11:30am-2:30pm & 5:30-10pm Tue-Sat) Like a transplant from Victoria, Nanaimo's best splurgeworthy dine-out showcases BC-sourced ingredients prepared with contemporary flair. The oft-changing menu is seasonal, but look out for Haida Gwaii salmon, Qualicum Bay scallops and Cowichan Valley duck. Check out the Tuesday to Thursday three-course C$30 dinner special.

Penny's Palapa   MEXICAN $$ (10 Wharf St H Dock; mains C$8-12; ☺Apr-Oct) This tiny, flower-and-flag-decked floating hut and patio in the harbor is a lovely spot for an al fresco meal among the jostling boats. An inventive, well-priced menu of Mexican delights includes seasonal seafood specials – the signature halibut tacos are recommended – plus some good vegetarian options. Drinks-wise: it's all about the margaritas.

🍷 Drinking & Entertainment

Longwood Brewpub   BREWERY
(www.longwoodbrewpub.com; 5775 Turner Rd) Incongruously located in a new strip mall development, this handsome stone and gabled resto-pub combines a surprisingly good food menu with some lip-smacking own-brewed beers. Try for a deck table and consider the four-beer sample selection for C$6.63 – make sure one of them is Russian Imperial Stout.

Dinghy Dock Pub   PUB
(www.dinghydockpub.com; 8 Pirates Lane) This lively pub and restaurant combo floating offshore from Protection Island is an ideal place to rub shoulders with salty locals. The menu doesn't stretch far beyond classic pub fare but there's live music on weekends to keep your toes tapping. To get there, take the 10-minute ferry (return C$9) from the harbor.

Queen's Hotel   LIVE MUSIC
(www.thequeens.ca; 34 Victoria Cres) The city's best live music and dance spot, hosting an eclectic roster of performances and club nights, ranging from indie to jazz and country.

Port Theatre   THEATER
(www.porttheatre.com; 125 Front St) Presenting local and touring live-theater shows.

❶ Getting There & Away
Air

Nanaimo Airport (www.nanaimoairport.com) is 18km south of town via Hwy 1. **Air Canada** (www.aircanada.com) flights arrive here from Vancouver (from C$98, 25 minutes) throughout the day.

Frequent **Harbour Air Seaplanes** (www.harbour-air.com) services arrive in the inner harbor from downtown Vancouver (C$79, 25 minutes) and Vancouver International Airport (C$67, 20 minutes).

Boat

BC Ferries (www.bcferries.com) from Tsawwassen (passenger/vehicle C$14/$46.75, two hours) arrive at Duke Point, 14km south of Nanaimo. Services from West Vancouver's Horseshoe Bay (passenger/vehicle C$14/$46.75, 95 minutes) arrive at Departure Bay, 3km north of the city center via Hwy 1.

Bus

Greyhound Canada (www.greyhound.ca) buses arrive from Victoria (C$23.30, 2½ hours, four

daily), Campbell River (C$30.80, three hours, two daily), Port Alberni (C$25.80, 90 minutes, two daily) and Tofino (C$46.30, four hours, two daily).

Train

The daily **VIA Rail** (www.viarail.com) *Malahat* train trundles in from Victoria (C$27, 2½ hours), Parksville (C$20, 35 minutes) and Courtenay (C$27, two hours), among others.

❶ Getting Around

Downtown Nanaimo around the harbor is highly walkable, but after that the city spreads out and a car or strong bike legs are required. Be aware that taxis are expensive here.

Nanaimo Regional Transit (www.busonline.ca) buses (one trip/day pass C$2.25/5.75) stop along Gordon St, west of Harbour Park Mall. Bus 2 goes to the Departure Bay ferry terminal. No city buses run to Duke Point.

Nanaimo Airporter (www.nanaimoairporter.com; C$26) provides door-to-door service to downtown from both ferry terminals.

Parksville & Qualicum

Previously called Oceanside, this mid-island region has reverted to using its twin main towns as its moniker, mainly because no one could tell where Oceanside was just by hearing its name. Find out more about this family-friendly region – which also includes rustic Coombs – by checking in with the local **tourism board** (☑250-248-6300, 888-799-3222; www.visitparksvillequalicumbeach.com).

◉ Sights & Activities

Coombs Old Country Market   MARKET
(www.oldcountrymarket.com; 2326 Alberni Hwy, Coombs; ⊘9am-7pm Jul & Aug, reduced hours off-season) The mother of all pit stops, this ever-expanding menagerie of food and crafts is centered on a large store stuffed with bakery and produce delectables. It attracts huge numbers of visitors on balmy summer days, when cameras are pointed at the grassy roof where a herd of goats spends the season. Nip inside for giant ice-cream cones, heaping pizzas and the deli makings of a great picnic.

Horne Lake Caves Provincial Park   PARK
(www.hornelake.com; tours adult/child from C$20/17; ⊘10am-5pm Jul & Aug, reduced hours off-season) Horne Lake Caves Provincial Park is a 45-minute drive from Parksville (take Hwy 19 toward Courtenay, then exit 75 and proceed for 12km on the gravel road) but it's worth it for BC's best spelunking spot. Two caves are open to the public for

self-exploring, or you can take a guided tour of the spectacular Riverbend Cave – look out for the 'howling wolf' and 'smiling Buddha' formations.

🛏 Sleeping & Eating

TOP CHOICE **Free Spirit Spheres** CABIN $$
(☑250-757-9445; www.freespiritspheres.com; 420 Horne Lake Rd, Qualicum Bay; cabin from C$125) Suspended by cables in the trees, this clutch of three spherical tree houses enables guests to cocoon themselves in the forest canopy. Compact inside, Eve is smaller and basic, while Eryn and Melody are lined like little boats with built-in cabins, nooks and MP3 speakers. Sleeping here is all about communing with nature but there's also a ground-level facilities block with sauna, barbecue and hotel-like showers.

Fish Tales Café SEAFOOD $$
(www.fishtalescafe.com; 336 W Island Hwy, Qualicum Beach; mains C$8-21) This Qualicum fixture has the look of an old-school English teashop but it's been reeling in visitors with its perfect fish 'n chips for years. It's worth exploring the non-deep-fried dishes – the two-person platter of scallops, shrimp, smoked salmon and mussels is recommended – and if you arrive early enough, you can grab a table in the garden.

❶ Getting There & Away

Greyhound Canada (www.greyhound.ca) services arrive in Parksville from Victoria (C$35.80, three to four hours, five daily), Nanaimo (C$14.90, 40 minutes, four daily) and Campbell River (C$27.30, two hours, two daily), among others. The same buses, with similar times and rates, serve Qualicum Beach.

The daily **VIA Rail** (www.viarail.com) *Malahat* train arrives in Parksville from Victoria (C$34, 3½ hours), Nanaimo (C$20, 40 minutes) and Courtenay (C$20, 80 minutes), among others. The same train, with similar times and rates, serves Qualicum Beach.

Pacific Rim National Park Reserve

A wave-crashing waterfront and brooding, mist-covered trees ensure that the **Pacific Rim National Park Reserve** (www.pc.gc.ca/pacificrim; park pass adult/child C$7.80/3.90) is among BC's most popular outdoor attractions. The 50,000-hectare park comprises the northern Long Beach Unit, between Tofino and Ucluelet; the Broken Group Islands in Barkley Sound; and, to the south, the ever-popular West Coast Trail.

Drop by the **Pacific Rim Visitor Centre** (☑250-726-4600; www.pacificrimvisitor.ca; 2791 Pacific Rim Hwy; ◷10am-4pm, reduced hours off-season) for information.

❶ Getting There & Around

Tofino Bus (www.tofinobus.com) runs a 'Beach Bus' service linking points throughout the area (one-way/return/all-day pass C$10/15/21).

LONG BEACH UNIT

Attracting the lion's share of visitors, Long Beach Unit is easily accessible by car along the Pacific Rim Hwy. Wide sandy beaches, untamed surf, lots of beachcombing nooks and a living museum of old-growth rain forest are the main reasons for the summer tourist clamor.

Wickaninnish Interpretive Centre (Wick Rd; admission incl with park user fee) was being redesigned during our visit to the region: check ahead and consider a visit if it's open, since it's a great introduction to the park.

If you're inspired to take a stroll, try one of the following trails, keeping your eyes peeled for swooping bald eagles and shockingly large banana slugs. Safety precautions apply on all trails in the region: tread carefully over slippery surfaces and never turn your back on the mischievous surf.

Long Beach Great scenery along the sandy shore (1.2km; easy).

Rainforest Trail Two interpretive loops through old-growth forest (1km; moderate).

Schooner Trail Through old- and second-growth forests with beach access (1km; moderate).

🛏 Sleeping & Eating

Green Point Campground CAMPGROUND $
(☑250-689-9025, 877-737-3783; www.pccamping.ca; campsites C$34.40; ◷mid-Mar–mid-Oct) Between Ucluelet and Tofino on the Pacific Rim Hwy, Green Point Campground encourages lots of novice campers to try their first night under the stars. Extremely popular in the summer peak (book ahead); its 105 basic tent sites are located on a forested terrace, with trail access to the beach.

Wickaninnish Restaurant WEST COAST $$
(www.wickaninnish.ca; mains C$16-28) You can make up for roughing it with a rewarding meal in the interpretive centre at the Wickaninnish Restaurant, where the crashing surf views are served with fresh-catch lo-

cal seafood. If you're just passing through, drop by the complex's **Beachfront Café** (snacks C$3-5; ⊗9am-6pm Mar-Sep) for a snack or an ice-cold Wickaccino.

BROKEN GROUP ISLANDS UNIT

Comprising some 300 islands and rocks scattered across 80 sq km around the entrance to Barkley Sound, the Broken Group is a serene natural wilderness beloved of visiting kayakers – especially those who enjoy close-up views of gray whales, harbor porpoises and multitudinous birdlife. Compasses are required for navigating here, unless you fancy paddling to Hawaii.

If you're up for a trek, **Lady Rose Marine Services** (www.ladyrosemarine.com) will ship you and your kayak from Port Alberni to its Sechart Whaling Station Lodge (three hours away) in Barkley Sound on the *MV Francis Barkley*. The lodge also rents kayaks (per day C$40 to C$60) if you'd rather travel light and it offers accommodations (singles/doubles C$150/235, including all meals).

From there, popular paddle destinations include Gibraltar Island, a one-hour kayak away, with its sheltered campground (fees C$9.80) and explorable beaches and tidal pools. Willis Island (90 minutes from Sechart) is also popular. It has a campground and, at low tide, you can walk to the surrounding islands. Remote Benson Island (four hours from Sechart) has a campground, grazing deer and a blowhole.

WEST COAST TRAIL UNIT

The 75km West Coast Trail is BC's best-known hiking route. It's also one of the toughest and is not for the uninitiated.

Winding along the wave-licked rainforest shoreline between trailhead information centers at **Pachena Bay**, 5km south of Bamfield on the north end, and **Gordon River**, 5km north of Port Renfrew on the southern tip, the entire stretch takes between six or seven days to complete. Open May to September, access to the route is limited to up to 60 overnight backpackers each day. All overnighters must pay a trail user fee (C$127.50) plus C$30 to cover the two short ferry crossings on the route. **Reservations** (⊠250-387-1642, 800-435-5466; www.parkscanada.gc.ca/pacificrim; nonrefundable reservation fee C$24.50) are required for the mid-June to mid-September peak season but not for the off-peak periods. All overnighters must attend a 90-minute orientation session before departing.

If you don't have a reservation, some permits are kept back for a daily wait-list system: six of each day's 26 available spaces are set aside at 1pm to be used on a first-come, first-served basis at each trailhead. If you win this lottery you can begin hiking that day, but keep in mind that you might wait a day or two to get a permit this way in peak season.

If you don't want to go the whole hog (you wimp), you can do a day hike or even hike half the trail from Pachena Bay, considered the easier end of the route. Overnight hikers who only hike this end of the trail can leave from Nitinat Lake. Day hikers are exempt from the large trail user fee but they need to get a free day-use permit at one of the trailheads.

West Coast Trail Express (www.trailbus.com) runs a daily shuttle between May and September to Pachena Bay from Victoria (C$85, six hours) and Nanaimo (C$95, four hours). It also runs a service to Gordon River from Victoria (C$60, 2½ hours) and Bamfield (C$75, 3½ hours). Check the website for additional stops and reserve ahead in summer.

Tofino

POP 1650

Transforming in recent years from a sleepy hippie hang-out into a popular eco destination with high-end resorts, Tofino is like the Whistler of Vancouver Island. A short drive south of town, the **Visitor Centre** (⊠250-725-3414; www.tourismtofino.com; 1426 Pacific Rim Hwy; ⊗10am-6pm May-Sep, reduced hours off-season) has detailed information on area accommodations, hiking trails and hot surf spots. There's also a satellite branch in town at 455 Campbell St.

⊙ Sights

Tofino Botanical Gardens   GARDEN
(www.tbgf.org; 1084 Pacific Rim Hwy; 3-day admission adult/youth/child C$10/6/free; ⊗9am-dusk) Check out what coastal temperate rain forests are all about by exploring the flora and fauna at the Tofino Botanical Gardens, complete with a frog pond, forest boardwalk, native plants and an ongoing program of workshops and field trips. There's a C$1 discount for car-free arrivals. This is also the new home of the **Raincoast Interpretive Centre** (www.raincoasteducation.org).

Maquinna Marine Provincial Park
PARK

(www.bcparks.ca) One of the most popular day trips from Tofino, the highlight here is Hot Spring Cove. Tranquility-minded trekkers travel to the park by Zodiac boat or seaplane, watching for whales and other sea critters en route. From the boat landing, 2km of boardwalks lead to the natural hot pools.

Meares Island
PARK

Visible through the mist and accessible via kayak or tour boat from the Tofino waterfront, Meares Island is home to the Big Tree Trail, a 400m boardwalk through old-growth forest that includes a stunning 1500-year-old red cedar. The island was the site of the key 1984 Clayoquot Sound antilogging protest that kicked off the region's latter-day environmental movement.

Activities

Surfing

Live to Surf
SURFING

(www.livetosurf.com; 1180 Pacific Rim Hwy; board rental 6hr C$25) Tofino's original surf shop also supplies skates and skimboards.

Pacific Surf School
SURFING

(www.pacificsurfschool.com; 430 Campbell St; board rental 6/24hr C$15/20) Offering rentals, camps and lessons for beginners.

Surf Sister
SURFING

(www.surfsister.com; 625 Campbell St) Introductory lessons for boys and girls plus women-only multiday courses.

Kayaking

Rainforest Kayak Adventures
KAYAKING

(www.rainforestkayak.com; 316 Main St; multiday courses & tours from C$685) Specializes in four- to six-day guided tours and courses.

Remote Passages
KAYAKING

(www.remotepassages.com; Wharf St; tours from C$64) Gives short guided kayaking tours around Clayoquot Sound and the islands.

Tofino Sea Kayaking Co
KAYAKING

(www.tofino-kayaking.com; 320 Main St; tours from C$60) Offers short guided paddles, including a popular four-hour Meares Island trip. Plus rentals (from C$40).

Tours

Jamie's Whaling Station
BOAT

(www.jamies.com; 606 Campbell St; adult/child C$99/65) Whale, bear and sea-lion spotting tours.

Ocean Outfitters
BOAT

(www.oceanoutfitters.bc.ca; 421 Main St; adult/child C$79/59) Popular whale-watching tours, with bear and hot-springs treks also offered.

Tla-ook Cultural Adventures
BOAT

(www.tlaook.com; tours from C$44) Learn about aboriginal culture by paddling an authentic dugout canoe.

Sleeping & Eating

Wickaninnish Inn
HOTEL $$$

(250-725-3100, 800-333-4604; www.wickinn.com; Chesterman Beach; r from C$399) Cornering the market in luxury winter storm-watching packages, 'the Wick' is worth a stay anytime of year. Embodying nature with its recycled wood furnishings, natural stone tiles and the ambience of a place grown rather than constructed, the sumptuous guest rooms have push-button gas fireplaces, two-person hot tubs and floor-to-ceiling windows. Excellent waterfront restaurant.

Inn at Tough City
HOTEL $$

(250-725-2021; www.toughcity.com; 350 Main St; d C$169-229;) Near the heart of the action and monikered after the town's old nickname, this quirky brick-built waterfront inn offers eight wood-floored ensuite rooms, most with balconies and some with those all-important Jacuzzi tubs. Room five has the best views – look out for the bright-red First Nations longhouse across the water. Built from recycled wood, bricks and stained-glass windows from as far away as Scotland.

Whalers on the Point Guesthouse HOSTEL $

(250-725-3443; www.tofinohostel.com; 81 West St; dm C$32, r C$85-135;) Close to the center of town but with a secluded waterfront location, this excellent HI hostel is a comfy wood-lined joint where the lounge overlooks the shoreline. The dorms are mercifully small and some doubled-bed private rooms are also available. Facilities include a granite-countered kitchen, barbecue patio, games room and a wet sauna. Reservations essential in summer.

TOP CHOICE TacoFino
MEXICAN $

(www.tacofino.com; 1180 Pacific Rim Hwy; mains C$4-10) Arrive off-peak at this massively popular orange-painted taco truck or you'll be waiting a while for your made-from-scratch nosh. It's worth it, though: these guys have nailed the art of great Mexican comfort food. Pull up an upturned yellow bucket – that's the seating – and tuck into sustainable fish tacos or bulging burritos stuffed with chicken. Even better are the tasty pulled-pork gringas and ever-popular taco soup, washed down with a zinging lime-mint freshie.

Sobo SEAFOOD **$$**
(www.sobo.ca; 311 Neill St; mains C$6-14) Before TacoFino ruled the vending-cart world, Sobo – it means 'sophisticated bohemian' – were the kings with their legendary purple truck. They were so successful they've now upgraded to their own wildly popular bistro-style restaurant. Fish tacos and crispy shrimp cakes remain, but new treats at the table include Vancouver Island seafood stew and roasted duck confit pizza.

Shelter WEST COAST **$$$**
(www.shelterrestaurant.com; 601 Campbell St; mains C$25-39) An exquisite West Coast eatery with international accents. Our menu favorite here is the shrimp and crab dumplings. There's a strong commitment to local, sustainable ingredients – the salmon is wild and the sablefish is trap-caught – and there are plenty of non-fishy options for traveling carnivores, including a delectable char-grilled pork chop dish.

❶ Getting There & Around

Orca Airways (www.flyorcaair.com) flights arrive at Tofino Airport from Vancouver International Airport's South Terminal (C$206, 55 minutes, one to four daily).

Greyhound Canada (www.greyhound.ca) buses arrive from Port Alberni (C$29.40, two hours, two daily), Nanaimo (C$46.30, four hours, two daily) and Victoria (C$70.70, six to seven hours, three daily), among others.

Tofino Bus (www.tofinobus.com) 'Beach Bus' services roll in along Hwy 4 from Ucluelet (C$15, 40 minutes, up to three daily).

Ucluelet

POP 1500

Driving on Hwy 4's winding mountain stretch to the west coast, you'll suddenly arrive at a junction sign proclaiming that Tofino is 33km to your right, while just 8km to your left is Ucluelet (yew-klew-let). Most still take the right-hand turn, which is a shame because sleepier 'Ukee' has more than a few charms and is a good reminder of what Tofino used to be like. For information, head to the **Visitor Centre** (☑250-726-2485; www.ucluelet.travel; 200 Main St; ◷9:30am-4:30pm), up the ramp at the back of the building.

◎ Sights & Activities

Ucluelet Aquarium AQUARIUM
(www.uclueletaquarium.org; Main St Waterfront Promenade; adult/child C$5/2; ◷10am-6pm Mar-Oct) Tucked in a little waterfront cabin is this excellent small attraction, often crammed with wide-eyed kids. The emphasis is on biodiversity education using pinkie-finger touch tanks teeming with colorful local marine life, including purple starfish and alienlike anemones – the octopus is the star attraction, though. All the critters are here temporarily on a catch-and-release program. Bold plans are afoot for a much bigger facility – watch this space.

Majestic Ocean Kayaking KAYAKING
(www.oceankayaking.com; 1167 Helen Rd; tours from C$67) Can lead you around the harbor or Barkley Sound on a bobbling kayak trek.

Relic Surf Shop SURFING
(www.relicsurfshop.com; 1998 Peninsula Rd; 3hr lesson C$74, rentals per day from C$40) Offers lessons and rentals.

🛏 Sleeping & Eating

Surf's Inn Guesthouse HOSTEL **$**
(☑250-726-4426; www.surfsinn.ca; 1874 Peninsula Rd; dm/ste/cottage C$28/159/259; ☜) While this blue-painted clapboard house on a small hill contains three homely little dorm rooms, a well-equipped kitchen and is high on the friendly approach, it's the two refurbished cabins out back that attract many: one is larger, self-contained and great for groups of up to six, while the other is divided into two suites with kitchenettes. Surf packages are also available.

Black Rock Oceanfront Resort HOTEL **$$$**
(☑250-726-4800, 877-762-5011; www.blackrockresort.com; 596 Marine Dr; r from C$179) Just to prove that Tofino doesn't have all the swanky resorts, this slick new sleepover combines lodge, cottage and beach-house accommodations all wrapped in a contemporary wood-and-stone West Coast look. Many rooms have great views of the often dramatically stormy surf and there's a vista-hugging restaurant specializing in regional nosh.

Ukee Dogs CANADIAN **$$**
(1576 Imperial Lane; mains C$4-7) Focused on home-baked treats and comfort foods, this bright and breezy good-value eatery offers hotdogs of the gourmet variety (go for the Canuck dog) and great pies from steak and curry to salmon wellington. Drop by in the afternoon for coffee and sprinkle-topped

cakes and come back for the best breakfast in town: the sausage scrambler. Cash only.

ⓘ Getting There & Around

Greyhound (www.greyhound.ca) buses arrive from Port Alberni (C$27.30, 90 minutes, two daily), Nanaimo (C$46.30, three to four hours, two daily) and Victoria (C$64.70, five to seven hours, three daily), among others.

Tofino Bus (www.tofinobus.com) 'Beach Bus' services roll in along Hwy 4 from Tofino (C$15, 40 minutes, up to three daily).

Comox Valley

Comprising the towns of Comox, Courtenay and Cumberland, this rolling region of mountains, alpine meadows and colorful communities is a good base for outdoor adventures. Drop by the **Visitor Centre** (☎250-334-3234, 888-357-4471; www.discovercomoxvalley.com; 2040 Cliffe Ave, Comox; ◷9am-5pm daily mid-May–Aug, Mon-Sat Sep–mid-May) for tips.

◉ Sights & Activities

Mt Washington Alpine Resort   SKIING
(www.mountwashington.ca; lift ticket adult/child winter C$59/31, summer C$37.50/25) The main reason for winter visits is the island's skiing mecca, with its 60 runs, snowshoeing park and 55km of cross-country ski trails. But there are also great summer activities here, including horseback riding, alpine hiking and mountain biking. Visit www.discovermountwashington.com for more suggestions.

Miracle Beach Provincial Park
                                            HIKING, BEACHES
(www.bcparks.ca) Home to some excellent hiking trails and tranquil beaches.

Pacific Pro Dive & Surf   DIVING, SURFING
(www.scubashark.com; 2270 Cliffe Ave, Courtenay) Can help with scuba lessons and equipment rentals.

Simon's Cycles   BIKE
(www.simoncycle.com; 1841 Comox Ave, Comox) Offers bike rentals.

⌂ Sleeping & Eating

Riding Fool Hostel   HOSTEL $
(☎250-336-8250, 888-313-3665; www.ridingfool.com; 2705 Dunsmuir Ave, Cumberland; dm/r C$23/55; @⑆) One of Vancouver Island's best backpacker joints, Riding Fool is a restored heritage building with immaculate wooden interiors, large kitchen and lounge

area and the kind of neat and tidy private rooms often found in small hotels. Bicycle rentals available at the downstairs shop.

Mad Chef Café   CANADIAN, FUSION $$
(www.madchefcafe.net; 492 Fitzgerald Ave, Courtenay; mains C$8-20) Bright and colorful neighborhood eatery serving a great selection of made-from-scratch meals: this is a good place for a salad; they're heaping and crispy-fresh. Sharers should go for the Mediterranean plate, piled high with olives, hummus, pita and lovely own-made bruschetta. Gourmet burgers of the duck or salmon variety are also popular.

Kingfisher Oceanside Resort   HOTEL $$
(☎250-338-1323, 800-663-7929; www.kingfisherspa.com; 4330 Island Hwy, Courtenay; r/ste C$145/220; @⑆) Comfortable waterfront lodge property with spa. Many rooms have full kitchens and shoreline balconies.

Waverly Hotel Pub   BURGERS $
(www.waverlyhotel.ca; 2692 Dunsmuir Ave, Cumberland; mains C$8-14) Come for hearty pub grub and stick around for live bands on the kick-ass little stage.

Campbell River

POP 29,500

Southerners will tell you this marks the end of civilization on Vancouver Island, but Campbell River is a handy drop-off point for wilderness tourism in Strathcona Provincial Park and is large enough to have plenty of attractions and services of its own. The **Visitor Centre** (☎250-830-1115, 877-286-5705; www.campbellriver.travel; 1235 Shoppers Row; ◷9am-6pm Mon-Sat, 10am-4pm Sun) can fill you in.

◉ Sights & Activities

Museum at Campbell River   MUSEUM
(www.crmuseum.ca; 470 Island Hwy; adult/child C$6/4; ◷10am-5pm May-Sep, noon-5pm Tue-Sun Oct-Apr) Showcases aboriginal masks, an 1890s pioneer cabin and video footage of the world's largest-ever artificial, non-nuclear blast: an underwater mountain in Seymour Narrows that caused dozens of shipwrecks before it was blown apart in 1958.

Discovery Pier   FISHING
(rod rentals per day C$6) Since locals claim the town as the 'Salmon Capital of the World,' you should wet your line off the downtown pier, or just stroll along with the crowds and see what everyone else has caught.

Much easier than catching your own lunch, you can also buy fish 'n chips here.

🛏 Sleeping & Eating

Heron's Landing HOTEL **$$**
(☑250-923-2848, 888-923-2849; www.herons landinghotel.com; 492 S Island Hwy; r from C$145; @☎) Superior motel-style accommodations with renovated rooms, including large loft suites ideal for families.

Heritage River Inn MOTEL **$$**
(☑250-286-6295, 800-567-2007; www.heritage riverinn.com; 2140 N Island Hwy; r from C$80; ❄) Quiet motel north of downtown with sauna, Jacuzzi and gazebo-covered barbecues. Rates include continental breakfast.

Royal Coachman Inn BURGERS **$$**
(84 Dogwood St; mains C$8-18) Brit-style pub serving BC and cross-Canada brews and a large array of grub from burgers to Thai ginger salad.

❶ Getting There & Around

Campbell River Airport (www.crairport.ca) receives **Pacific Coastal Airlines** (www.pacific -coastal.com) flights from Vancouver International Airport (C$208, 45 minutes, up to seven daily).

Greyhound Canada (www.greyhound.ca) services arrive from Port Hardy (C$48.30, 3½ hours, daily), Nanaimo (C$35.80, three hours, two daily), Victoria (C$57.60, six to 10 hours, three daily) and beyond.

Campbell River Transit (www.busonline.ca; adult/child C$1.75/1.50) operates local buses throughout the area.

North Vancouver Island

Down-islanders (anyone below Campbell River) will tell you, 'There's nothing up there worth seeing,' while locals here will respond, 'They would say that, wouldn't they?' Parochial rivalries aside, what this giant region covering half the island lacks in towns, infrastructure and population, it more than makes up for in rugged natural beauty.

Spotting black bears feasting on roadside berries soon becomes commonplace up here, but you'll also appreciate the quirky locals who color the region: northerners have a hardy, independent streak that marks them out from the south-island softies. For further information, check in with the folks at **Vancouver Island North** (www. vancouverislandnorth.ca).

❶ Getting There & Around

Pacific Coastal Airlines (www.pacific-coastal. com) services arrive from Vancouver (C$235, 75 minutes, up to three daily).

Greyhound Canada (www.greyhound.ca) buses roll in from Port McNeill (C$14.90, 45 minutes, daily), Campbell River (C$48.30, 3½ hours, daily) and Nanaimo (C$73, seven hours, daily).

BC Ferries (www.bcferries.com) arrive from Prince Rupert (passenger/vehicle C$170/390, 15 hours, schedules vary) via the spectacular Inside Passage route.

North Island Transportation (nit@island.net) operates a handy shuttle (C$8) to and from the ferry terminal via area hotels.

TELEGRAPH COVE

Originally a one-shack telegraph station, charming Telegraph Cove has successfully reinvented itself as a visitor magnet. Its outpost feel is enhanced by the dozens of wooden buildings standing around the marina on stilts, but the place can get ultra-crowded in summer.

Head first along the boardwalk to the smashing **Whale Interpretive Centre** (www.killerwhalecentre.org; suggested donation C$2; ☺May-Sep), bristling with hands-on artifacts and artfully displayed skeletons of cougar, sea otter and a giant fin whale.

You can also see whales of the live variety: this is one of the island's top marine-life viewing regions and **Stubbs Island Whale Watching** (www.stubbs-island.com; tours adult/child C$94/84; ☺May-Sep) will get you up close with the orcas on a boat trek – you might also see humpbacks, dolphins and sea lions. Its sunset cruise is a highlight. For a bear alternative, **Tide Rip Grizzly Tours** (www.tiderip.com; tours C$288; ☺mid-May–Sep) leads full-day trips to local beaches and inlets in search of the area's furry residents.

The established **Telegraph Cove Resorts** (☑250-928-3131, 800-200-4665; www. telegraphcoveresort.com; campsite/cabin from C$27/115) provides accommodations in forested tent spaces and a string of rustic cabins overlooking the marina. The nearby and much newer **Dockside 29** (☑250-928-3163, 877-835-2683; www.telegraphcove.ca; r C$140-175) is a good, motel-style alternative. Its rooms have kitchenettes with hardwood floors and waterfront views.

The **Killer Whale Café** (mains C$14-18; ☺May-Sep) is the cove's best eatery – the salmon, mussel and prawn linguini is recommended. The adjoining **Old Saltery Pub** is an atmospheric, wood-lined nook with

WORTH A TRIP

VAN ISLE'S ANCIENT WILDERNESS

Strathcona Provincial Park (www.bcparks.ca), BC's oldest protected area and Vancouver Island's largest park, is inland from Campbell River on Hwy 28. Centered on Mt Golden Hinde, the island's highest point (2200m), Strathcona is a magnificent pristine wilderness crisscrossed with trail systems that deliver you to waterfalls, alpine meadows, glacial lakes and looming mountain crags.

On arrival at the main entrance, get your bearings at **Strathcona Park Lodge & Outdoor Education Centre** (www.strathcona.bc.ca). A one-stop-shop for park activities, including kayaking, guided treks, yoga camps, ziplining and rock climbing (all-in adventure packages are available, some aimed specifically at families), this is a great place to rub shoulders with other outdoorsy types – head to the **Whale Dining Room** or **Canoe Club Café** eateries for a fuel up. The lodge also offers good accommodations (rooms/cabins from C$136/175) which, in keeping with its low-impact approach to nature and commitment to eco-education, is sans telephones and TVs.

Notable park hiking trails include **Paradise Meadows Loop** (2.2km), an easy amble in a delicate wildflower and evergreen ecosystem, and **Mt Becher** (5km), with its great views over the Comox Valley and mountain-lined Strait of Georgia. The 9km **Comox Glacier Trail** is quite an adventure but is only recommended for advanced hikers.

---

a cozy central fireplace and tasty Killer Whale Pale Ale.

PORT HARDY
POP 3800

Settled by Europeans in the early 1800s, this small north-island settlement is best known as the arrival and departure point for BC Ferries Inside Passage trips. It's also a handy gear-up spot for the North Coast Trail.

Head to the **Visitor Centre** (250-949-7622; www.porthardy.travel; 7250 Market St; 9am-5pm daily Jun-Aug, Mon-Fri Sep-May) for information, including comprehensive North Coast Trail maps (C$9.95).

Quatse Salmon Stewardships Centre (www.thesalmoncentre.org; 8400 Byng Rd; adult/child C$5/2; 10am-5pm Wed-Sun mid-May–Sep) is worth checking out before you leave town on a long hike – here you can learn all about the life cycle of local salmon. The kid-friendly facility has lots of critters in tanks and was also working on a new theater room on our visit. The friendly staff will answer all your salmon-related questions.

Port Hardy is a great access point for exploring the north island wilderness and hikers can book a customized guided tour with the friendly folk at **North Island Daytrippers** (www.islanddaytrippers.com). For those who prefer to paddle, **Odyssey Kayaking** (www.odysseykayaking.com; rentals/tours from C$40/99) can take you on guided tours around Malei Island, Bear Cove and Alder Bay or leave you to your own devices with a full-day rental.

The immaculate little clutch of cedar-wood cabins on offer at **Ecoscape Cabins** (250-949-8524; www.ecoscapecabins.com; 6305 Jensen Cove Rd; C$125-175;) are divided between three compact units – with flat-screen TVs, microwaves and sunny porches (ideal for couples) – and three roomier hilltop units with swankier furnishings, barbecues and expansive views. There's a tranquil retreat feel here – expect to see eagles swooping around the trees. For a hostel alternative in the center of town, consider **North Coast Trail Backpackers Hostel** (250-949-9441, 866-448-6303; www.northcoasthostel.com; 8635 Granville St; dm/r from C$24/58), combining a friendly welcome and a labyrinth of clean and comfortable rooms.

Food-wise, the town's highlight is **Escape Bistro & Gallery** (8405 Byng Rd; mains C$16-22), just across from the Salmon Stewardships Centre. The old-school dining room (try for a booth) has been reinvented with local artworks and there's live Friday and Saturday guitar music to keep things animated. The menu combines simple home-cooked dishes with lip-smacking European fare like Hungarian goulash and Vienna schnitzel – go for Friday's pork roast special.

CAPE SCOTT PROVINCIAL PARK

It's more than 550km from the comparatively metropolis-like streets of down-island Victoria to the nature-hugging trailhead of this remote **park** (www.bcparks.ca) on Vancouver Island's crenulated northern tip. But if you really want to experience the raw, ravishing beauty of BC – especially its unkempt shorelines, breeze-licked rain forests and stunning sandy bays animated with tumbling waves and beady-eyed seabirds – this should be your number-one destination.

Hike the well-maintained, relatively easy 2.5km San Josef Bay Trail and you'll stroll from the shady confines of the trees right onto one of the best beaches in BC; a breathtaking, windswept expanse of roiling water, forested crags and the kind of age-old caves that could easily harbor lost smugglers. You can camp right here on the beach or just admire the passing ospreys before plunging back into the trees.

With several wooded trails to tempt you – most are aimed at well-prepared hikers with plenty of gumption – the forest offers moss-covered yew trees, old-growth cedars that are centuries old and a soft carpet of sun-dappled ferns covering every square centimeter.

Raft Cove Provincial Park   NATURE PARK
(www.bcparks.ca) One of the area's shortest trails (2km), adjoining Cape Scott Provincial Park, brings you to the wide, crescent beach and beautiful lagoons of Raft Cove. You're likely to have the entire 1.3km expanse to yourself, although the locals also like to surf here (it's their secret, so don't tell anyone).

North Coast Trail   HIKING
Hiking much further in the region is not for the uninitiated or unprepared. But if you really want to go for it, consider hitting the relatively new 43km North Coast Trail. It features sandy coves, deserted beaches and dense, wind-whipped rain-forest woodland, as well as a couple of river crossings on little cable cars.

SOUTHERN GULF ISLANDS

Stressed-out Vancouverites tired of languishing on their favorite Stanley Park beach often seek solace in the restorative, rustic Southern Gulf Islands, handily strung like a necklace of enticing pearls between the mainland and Vancouver Island. Once colonized by hippie-dippy Canadian dropouts and fugitive US draft dodgers, Salt Spring, Galiano, Mayne, Saturna and the North and South Penders are the natural retreat of choice for many in the region. Whichever island you choose, the soothing relaxation begins once you step on the ferry to get here: time suddenly slows, your heart rate drops to hibernation level and the forested isles and glassy waters slide by like a slow-motion nature documentary.

During your ferry trip, pick up a free copy of the *Gulf Islands Driftwood* (www.gulfislandsdriftwood.com) newspaper for local info, listings and happenings.

ℹ Getting There & Around

Serving the main Southern Gulf Islands, **BC Ferries** (www.bcferries.com) operates direct routes from Vancouver Island's Swartz Bay terminal to Salt Spring and North Pender. From North Pender, you can connect to Mayne, Galiano or Salt Spring. From Mayne, you can connect to Saturna.

From the mainland, there is a direct service from Tsawwassen to Galiano, which then connects to North Pender. There are also direct weekend services from Tsawwassen to both Mayne (Sunday only) and Salt Spring (Friday to Sunday). For more frequent services to these and the other islands, you will need to travel from Tsawwassen to Swartz Bay, then board a connecting ferry. For island hopping, consider a handy **SailPass** (4/7-day pass C$199/239). It covers ferry travel around the region on 20 different routes.

Gulf Islands Water Taxi (www.saltspring.com/watertaxi) runs walk-on ferries between Salt Spring, North Pender and Saturna (one way/return C$15/25) and between Salt Spring, Galiano and Mayne (one way/return C$15/25), twice daily from September to June and once a day in July and August.

Salt Spring Air (www.saltspringair.com) floatplane services arrive throughout the Southern Gulf Islands from downtown Vancouver and Vancouver International Airport. Check the website for the myriad of schedules and fares. Similar services are offered by **Seair Seaplanes** (www.seairseaplanes.com).

Salt Spring Island

POP 10,500

A former hippie enclave that's now the site of many rich vacation homes, pretty Salt Spring justifiably receives the majority of Gulf Island visitors. The heart of the community is Ganges, also the location of the **Visitor Centre** (✆250-537-5252; www.saltspringtourism.com; 121 Lower Ganges Rd; ⊗9am-5pm Jul & Aug, reduced hours off-season).

◉ Sights & Activities

Saturday Market   MARKET
(www.saltspringmarket.com; Centennial Park, Ganges; ⊗8am-4pm Sat Apr-Oct) If you arrive

on a summer weekend, the best way to dive into the community is at the thriving market, where you can tuck into luscious island-grown fruit and piquant cheeses while perusing locally produced arts and crafts. Visit some of these artisans via a free downloadable Studio Tour Map (www.saltspringstudiotour.com). One of the best is the rustic **Blue Horse Folk Art Gallery** (www.bluehorse.ca; 175 North View Dr; ◷10am-5pm Sun-Fri Mar-Dec), with, among other cool creations, funky carvings of horses. The friendly owners recently opened an on-site **B&B** (www.bloomorganicbandb.com; d C$150) if you feel like sticking around.

 Salt Spring Island Cheese

CHEESE TASTING

(www.saltspringcheese.com; 285 Reynolds Rd) Can be visited for a self-guided tour of its facilities – worthwhile indeed if you haven't eaten your fill at the market. Be sure to check out the miniature ponies before sampling up to 10 curdy treats in the winery-style tasting room.

Ruckle Provincial Park   PARK

(www.bcparks.ca) Pack up your picnic and head over to this southeast gem with its ragged shorelines, gnarly arbutus forests and sun-kissed farmlands. There are trails here for all skill levels, with Yeo Point making an ideal pit stop.

Salt Spring Adventure Co   KAYAKING

(www.saltspringadventures.com; 124 Upper Ganges Rd; tours from C$50) Can kit you out for a Ganges Harbour kayak tour.

Sleeping & Eating

Love Shack   CABIN **$$**

(☑250-653-0007, 866-341-0007; www.oceanside cottages.com; 521 Isabella Rd; cabin C$135) If Austin Powers ever comes to Salt Spring, this is where he'll stay. A groovy waterfront nook where the hardest part is leaving, this cozy cottage has a lava lamp, collection of vintage cameras and a record player plus albums (Abba to Stan Getz). With plenty of artsy flourishes, the kitchen is stocked with organic coffee and the private deck is ideal for watching the sunset in your velour jumpsuit.

Lakeside Gardens   CABIN **$$**

(☑250-537-5773; www.lakesidegardensresort .com; 1450 North End Rd; cabana/cottage C$75/135; ◷Apr-Oct) A rustic wooded retreat where nature is the main attraction, this tranquil, family-friendly clutch of cottages and cabanas is ideal for low-key fishing,

swimming and boating. The cabanas are basic – think camping in a cabin – with fridges, outdoor barbecues and solar-heated outdoor showers, while the larger cottages have TVs, ensuites and full kitchens.

Tree House Café   CAFE **$$**

(www.treehousecafe.com; 106 Purvis Lane; mains C$11-18) A magical outdoor café in the heart of Ganges; you'll be sitting in the shade of a large plum tree here as you choose from a menu of comfort pastas, Mexican specialties and gourmet burgers – the teriyaki salmon burger is recommended, washed down with a hoppy bottle of Salt Spring Pale Ale. Live music every night in summer.

Raven Street Market Café   CANADIAN **$$**

(www.ravenstreet.ca; 321 Fernwood Rd; mains C$8.50-18) A favorite haunt of north island locals, this daily neighborhood eatery has a comfort-food menu with a gourmet twist. Adventurous pizzas include herbed lamb and artichoke, while the awesome seafood-and-sausage gumbo combines mussels, tiger prawns and chorizo sausage with a secret Creole recipe.

ⓘ Getting There & Around

BC Ferries, Gulf Island Water Taxis and Salt Spring Air operate services to Salt Spring (see p406). The island's three ferry docks are at Long Harbour, Fulford Harbour and Vesuvius Bay. Water taxis and floatplanes arrive in Ganges Harbour.

If you don't have your own car, **Salt Spring Island Transit** (www.busonline.ca; adult/under 5yr C$2/free) runs a five-route mini shuttle service around the island, connecting to all three ferry docks. Bus 4 runs from Long Harbour to Ganges. Alternatively, **Amber Taxi Co** (☑250-537-3277) provides a local cab service.

North & South Pender Islands

POP 2200

Once joined by a sandy isthmus, the North and South Penders are far quieter than Salt Spring and attract those looking for a low-key retreat. With pioneer farms, old-time orchards and almost 40 coves and beaches, the Penders – now linked by a single-lane bridge – are a good spot for bikers and hikers. For visitor information check www.penderislandchamber.com.

◉ Sights & Activities

Dozens of artists call Pender home and you can chat with them in their galleries and studios by downloading a pair of free maps from Pender Creatives (www.pendercreatives. com) that reveal exactly where they're all at. Not surprisingly most are on North Pender.

Enjoy the sand at **Medicine Beach** and **Clam Bay** on North Pender as well as **Gowlland Point** on the east coast of South Pender.

Farmers Market MARKET
(⊘Apr-Nov) There's a regular Saturday market in the community hall.

Mt Norman Regional Park PARK
Just over the bridge to South Pender and complete with a couple of hikes that promise grand views of the surrounding islands.

Pender Island Kayak Adventures KAYAKING
(www.kayakpenderisland.com; Otter Bay Marina; tours adult/child from C$45/30) You can hit the water with a paddle (and hopefully a boat) with the friendly team here.

Morning Bay Vineyard WINE TASTING
(www.morningbay.ca; 6621 Harbour Hill; ⊘10am-5pm Wed-Sun, reduced hours off-season) If you prefer recreation of the bottled variety, consider a tasting at Morning Bay.

🛏 Sleeping & Eating

Poet's Cove Resort & Spa HOTEL $$$
(☑250-629-2100, 888-512-7638; www.poets cove.com; 9801 Spalding Rd, Bedwell Harbour, South Pender; r from C$250; 🕸) A luxurious harborfront lodge with Arts and Crafts–accented rooms, most with great views across the glassy water. Chichi extras include a full-service spa and an activity center that books eco-tours and kayaking and fishing excursions around the area. The resort also offers a full-treatment spa, complete with that all-important steam cave.

Inn on Pender Island HOTEL $$
(☑250-629-3353, 800-550-0172; www.innon pender.com; 4709 Canal Rd; r/cabin C$99/149) A rustic lodge with motel-style rooms and a couple of cozy, wood-lined cabins. You're surrounded here by verdant woodland, which explains the frequent appearance of wandering deer. The lodge rooms are neat and clean and share an outdoor hot tub, while the waterfront cabins have barrel-vaulted ceilings, full kitchens and little porches out front.

Pender Island Bakery Café BAKERY $
(Driftwood Centre, 1105 Stanley Point Dr; mains C$6-16) The locals' fave coffeehouse, there's much more to this chatty nook than regular joe. For a start, the java is organic, as

are many of the bakery treats, including some giant cinnamon buns that will have you wrestling an islander for the last one. Gourmet pizzas are a highlight – the Gulf Islander (smoked oysters, anchovies, spinach and three cheeses) is best.

Aurora WEST COAST $$$
(www.poetscove.com; Poet's Cove Resort; mains C$18-34) Seasonal and regional are the operative words at this Poet's Cove fine-dining eatery. Allow yourself to be tempted by a Salt Spring goat-cheese tart starter but save room for main dishes like the local seafood medley of crab, scallops and mussels. Dinner reservations are recommended.

ℹ Getting There & Around

BC Ferries, Gulf Island Water Taxis and Salt Spring Air operate services to Pender (see p406). Ferries stop at North Pender's Otter Bay, where most of the islands' population resides. If you don't have a car, and your accommodations can't pick you up, catch a **Pender Island Taxi** (☑250-629-3555).

Saturna Island

POP 325

Small and suffused with tranquility, Saturna is a lovely nature retreat that's remote enough to deter casual visitors. Almost half the island, laced with curving bays, stunning rock bluffs and towering arbutus trees, is part of the Gulf Islands National Park Reserve and the only crowds you're likely to come across are the feral goats that have called this their munchable home for decades. If you've had enough of civilization, this is the place to be. The **Saturna Island Tourism Association** (www.saturna tourism.com) website has a downloadable map. Bring cash with you – there are no ATMs (and only two shops) here.

On the north side of the island, **Winter Cove Park** has a white-sand beach that's popular for swimming, boating and fishing. If you're here for Canada Day (July 1), you should also partake of the island's main annual event in the adjoining Hunter Field. This communal **Lamb Barbeque** (www.saturn alambbarbeque.com; adult/child C$20/10), complete with live music, sack races, beer garden and a smashing meat-lovers feast, is centered on a pagan fire pit surrounded by dozens of staked-out, slow-roasting sheep.

Walk off your meat belly the next day with a hike up **Mt Warburton Pike** (497m) where you'll spot wild goats, soaring eagles and restorative panoramic views of the surrounding islands: focus your binoculars and you might catch a whale or two sailing quietly along the coast.

If you've been inspired by the gentler pace of life to stick around, **Breezy Bay B&B** (250-539-5957; www.saturnacan.net/breezy; 131 Payne Rd; d C$95) is a century-old stillworking farmhouse property with its own private beach. The main house has wooden floors, stone fireplaces and even an old library, while your room – with shared bathroom – will be fairly basic but clean and comfortable. Breakfast is in a window-lined room overlooking a garden. Alternatively, **Saturna Lodge** (250-539-2254, 866-539-2254; www.saturna.ca; 130 Payne Rd; d C$119-149; ⊛) is an elegant, six-room country inn, combining landscaped gardens with close proximity to the waterfront. Rates include breakfast.

ⓘ Getting There & Around

BC Ferries, Gulf Island Water Taxis and Salt Spring Air operate services to Saturna (see p406). The ferry docks at Lyall Harbour on the west of the island. A car is not essential here since some lodgings are near the ferry terminal, but there are no taxis or shuttle services to get you around. Only bring your bike if you like a challenge: Saturna is a little too hilly for casual peddlers.

Mayne Island

POP 900

Once a stopover for gold-rush miners on their way to the mainland, who nicknamed it 'Little Hell,' Mayne is the region's most historic island. Long past its importance as a commercial hub, it now houses a colorful clutch of resident artists. For further information, visit www.mayneislandchamber.ca.

The heritage **Agricultural Hall** in Miners Bay hosts the lively **Farmers Market** (10am-1pm Sat Jul-Sep) of local crafts and produce, while the nearby **Plumper Pass Lock-up** (11am-3pm Fri-Mon late Jun-early Sep) is a tiny museum that originally served as a jailhouse.

Among the most visit-worthy galleries and artisan studios on the island is **Mayne Island Glass Foundry** (www.mayneisland glass.com; 10am-5pm Jun-Sep, reduced hours off-season), where recycled glass is used to fashion new jewelry and ornaments – pick up a cool green-glass slug for the road.

The south shore's **Dinner Bay Park** has a lovely sandy beach, as well as a **Japanese Garden**. Built by locals to commemorate early-20th-century Japanese residents, it's immaculately landscaped and is lit up with fairy lights at Christmas.

For paddlers and peddlers, **Mayne Island Kayaking** (www.kayakmayneisland.com; 563 Arbutus Dr; rentals 2/8hr from C$40/60, tours from C$50) offers rentals and tours.

If it's time to eat, head to **Wild Fennel Restaurant** (574 Fernhill Rd; mains C$16-20) which specializes in seasonal fresh ingredients. The menu changes constantly, but hope for the Crab Three Ways – crab served in salad, bisque and lollipop form.

If you're just too lazy to head back to the mainland, **Mayne Island Resort** (866-539-5399; www.mayneislandresort.com; 494 Arbutus Dr; r/cottage from C$99/225; ⊛⊠) combines ocean-view rooms in a century-old inn with swanky new luxe beach cottages. There's also a large resto-bar and a new spa.

ⓘ Getting There & Around

BC Ferries, Gulf Island Water Taxis and Salt Spring Air operate services to Mayne (see p406). For transportation around the island, call **MIDAS Taxi** (250-539-3132).

Galiano Island

POP 1100

Named after a Spanish explorer who visited in the 1790s, the bustling ferry end of Galiano is markedly different to the rest of the island, which becomes ever more forested and tranquil as you continue your drive from the dock. Supporting the widest ecological diversity of the Southern Gulf Islands – and regarded by some as the most beautiful – this skinny landmass offers a bounty of activities for visiting marine enthusiasts and landlubbers alike.

The main clutch of businesses and services is around the ferry dock at Sturdies Bay and includes a garage, post office, bookstore and **Visitor Info Booth** (www.galianois land.com; 2590 Sturdies Bay Rd; Jul & Aug).

Once you've got your bearings – ie driven off the ferry – head for **Montague Harbour Marine Provincial Park** for trails to beaches, meadows and a cliff carved by glaciers. In contrast, **Bodega Ridge Provincial Park** is renowned for its eagle, loon and cormorant birdlife and has some spectacular drop-off viewpoints.

The protected waters of **Trincomali Channel** and the more chaotic waters of **Active Pass** satisfy paddlers of all skill levels. **Gulf Island Kayaking** (www.seakayak.ca; rental per 3hr/day from C$38/75, tours from C$55) can help with rentals and guided tours.

If you're without a car or you just want to stretch your legs, you can explore the island with a bike from **Galiano Bicycle** (www.galianoisland.com/galianobicycle; per 4hr/day C$25/30).

Fuel up on food and local gossip at **Daystar Market Café** (96 Georgeson Bay Rd; mains C$4-10), a funky hang-out that serves hearty salads, thick sandwiches and fruit smoothies. Alternatively, down a pint or three at the venerable **Hummingbird Pub** (www.hummingbirdpub.com; 47 Sturdies Bay Rd; mains C$8-12) where pub grub on the patio is always a good idea.

Among the places to sleep on the island, sophisticates will enjoy **Galiano Inn** (☎250-539-3388; 877-530-3939; www.galianoinn.com; 134 Madrona Dr; r C$249-299; ☎), a Tuscan-style villa with 10 elegant rooms, each with a fireplace and romantic oceanfront terrace. Adult, sophisticated and soothing, it's close to the Sturdies Bay ferry dock. Those craving a nature-hugging retreat will likely enjoy **Bodega Ridge** (☎250-539-2677, 877-604-2677; www.bodegaridge.com; 120 Manastee Rd; d C$200; ☎), a tranquil woodland clutch of seven cabins at the other end of the island. Each has three bedrooms and is furnished in rustic country fashion.

ⓘ Getting There & Around

BC Ferries, Gulf Island Water Taxis and Salt Spring Air operate services to Galiano (see p406). Ferries arrive at the Sturdies Bay dock.

Understand the Pacific Northwest

population per sq mile

WASHINGTON   OREGON   USA

≈ 40 people

Pacific Northwest Today

Recent Times

Since the bursting of Silicon Forest's high-tech bubble in 2000, the Pacific Northwest has had ups and downs trying to regain a foothold is this now-fickle field. In recent years, many companies of all kinds have either shut down, moved away or laid off workers. As an example, Boeing – the world's number-one aircraft manufacturer – moved its corporate offices to Chicago in 2001, but despite layoffs has fortunately remained responsible for thousands of Seattle-area jobs. Unemployment has always been an issue, especially in Oregon, and the recent world economic crisis has certainly not spared this region.

At least the seriously dampened real estate market has cut over-inflated housing prices down to size, making it more affordable for young people to buy a house – *if* they've managed to get and keep their job. And transplants from the north, south and east continue to journey westward, as the pioneers did hundreds of years ago, looking for a higher quality of life – even if it means taking a serious pay cut and dealing with gloomy weather more attractive to vampires than sun-worshippers.

The Pacific Northwest keeps exerting a strong pull on the adventurous of spirit. And though today's Northwest populations tend to be driven by espresso rather than the desire to chart new territory, there remains a culture founded on restless idealism and the sense that there's still more prospecting to do – and always the hope that the economy will once again head north.

What You Talkin' About?

Mention the Northwest to folks outside this area and you'll start a conversation on the region's lush forests, snow-dusted volcanic mountains and amazing waterways and coastlines. Then you might gab about the

> The highest point in the Pacific Northwest is Mt Rainier at 14,410ft.

Top Films

One Flew Over the Cuckoo's Nest (1975) Oscar-winning movie about a mental institution and its inhabitants, filmed in Salem, Oregon (where the novel was based).

Sleepless in Seattle (1993) Romantic comedy that highlighted Seattle's Space Needle and its houseboat communities.

Twilight (2008) Highly popular vampire saga that catapulted sleepy Forks, Washington (as well as other Pacific Northwest locations) onto the world's center stage.

78 would be white
11 would be Latino
6 would be Asian

3 would be black
2 would be Native American

74 would be white
20 would be Asian
3 would be Native American

2 would be Latino
1 would be black

not-so-vibrant economy, high unemployment rates and the computer industry (that's the 'Silicon Forest' to the uninitiated). And certainly you'll discuss the rain, but locals don't mind – it keeps everyone else from moving in.

But what are the real hot-button issues that people love to discuss? Politics is always a good one – the trials and tribulations of Portland's gay mayor Sam Adams have been very entertaining, as sex scandals usually are (it certainly helped that nearly everyone involved had porn names, from Beau Breedlove to Mark Weiner). Up north, British Columbia's new Harmonized Sales Tax riled up Canadian consumers in 2010 by taxing previously untaxed goods and services. (Oregonians, meanwhile, continue to consistently vote down statewide sales tax referendums – nine times in the past.) And in Seattle, folks are bantering about the likely replacement to their aging Alaskan Way Viaduct – a 2-mile tunnel that would run under the city (and cost over 4 billion dollars).

Sustainability is such a presence in this region that people at parties might be chatting about hot composting, keeping chickens and/or goats, city growth boundaries and – of course – the environment and what to do about it; paper or plastic? Local or organic? Hydroelectric power or salmon migration?.

Sports talk is a no-brainer in this outdoor-loving region, even though Washington and Oregon only have a few major-league teams: the Seattle Seahawks (football) and Mariners (baseball), the Oregon Trailblazers (basketball) and the Portland Timbers (soccer). Hockey-loving BC, meanwhile, loves to gab about its Canucks.

Vancouver, BC's Asian population is over 45% – the highest in continental North America.

ASIAN VANCOUVER

Top Books

The Good Rain: Across Time and Terrain in the Pacific Northwest by Timothy Egan. One man's narrative on the land he loves, with social, economic and political perspectives.

The Pacific Northwest: An Interpretive History by Carlos Arnaldo Schwantes. A historical focus on the Pacific Northwest's environment, economic development and urbanization.

Field Guide to the Pacific Northwest by National Audubon Society. A comprehensive guide to the region's flora, fauna and diverse habitats, plus much more.

CHRISTMAS TREES

Economic Biggies

Once covered in lush forests, it's no surprise that the Northwest, with its rich natural resources, invited colonization. Today Oregon and Washington continue to lead the USA in lumber production, while British Columbia (BC) contains most of the marketable timber in Canada.

The Columbia and other Northwest rivers were once teeming with salmon, but overfishing, dam building and deforestation have nearly wiped out the species. Though much diminished, commercial and sport fishing still plays an important role in the regional economy.

The high-tech industry has redefined the region's personality by creating jobs and enriching support industries. The Seattle area continues to be headquarters for many big companies like Microsoft, Nintendo and Amazon.com, while Oregon's 'Silicon Forest' is supported by campuses and branches of Intel, Tektronix and Google. BC has its own high-tech niches, but Vancouver's vibrant film industry tends to steal the economic spotlight. Outdoor clothing and shoe companies like Nike, Columbia Sportswear and Adidas (North America office) are all based here, and – with its high precipitation – hydroelectric power is another big industry in the Pacific Northwest.

Agriculture flourishes along the moist valleys of the Rogue, Umpqua, Skagit and Fraser Rivers. Cattle and sheep graze the eastern uplands, and golden wheat fields stretch across volcanic plateaus. The rain-swept valleys along the Pacific Coast are famous for their dairy farms, and along the Columbia and Okanogan Rivers are vast orchards of apples, cherries, peaches and pears. Finally, let's not forget the grape – Oregon's fertile Willamette Valley yields its famous pinot noir, while the irrigated vineyards of Washington's Columbia, Walla Walla and Yakima Valleys produce world-class chardonnays and merlots.

Oregon produces more Christmas trees than any other US state.

Fun Oregon Facts

Oregon claims the deepest river gorge in North America (Hells Canyon) and the deepest lake in the US (Crater Lake). It's also the only US state with a two-sided flag, and it grows 99% of the country's hazelnuts.

Faux Pas

» Washington – Flaunting that you moved here from California because real estate is cheaper.

» Oregon – Trying to pump your own gas at a service station.

» British Columbia – Mistaking a Canadian for an American.

Rain, Go Away

When people think of the Pacific Northwest, they think of rain. But in terms of annual rainfall, Hawaii and Louisiana top the list; Washington and Oregon don't even make top 10! (Cloudy skies and drizzle are another matter, however.)

History

The human history of the Pacific Northwest started about 20,000 years ago, when people first stepped into North America via a land bridge from Siberia to Alaska. This area, now underwater, is known as the Bering Strait. These early hunter-gatherers, the ancestors of Native Americans, spread down through the Americas over millennia, and a multitude of tribes, each with its own culture and language, flourished around the Pacific Northwest.

In the mid-16th century, however, white men came knocking, which spelled the gradual demise of the First Nations. Explorers from Portugal, Spain, Britain and Russia all sought territorial claims, but it was the famed expedition of Lewis and Clark that first seriously mapped out the region and later nabbed an American foothold. A wealth of beaver and otter brought riches to many in the fur trade, and the principal British trading post of Fort Vancouver became an agricultural hub. Soon after, Oregon City was established, becoming the first incorporated city west of the Rockies.

The Northwest's population continued to thrive with trading posts, farming and missionary work, and in 1843 the region's first government was voted into existence. There now existed opportunities for whole families to stake out new land and settle down. Thousands loaded up their possessions in covered wagons and headed west, following the sometimes treacherous Oregon and Applegate Trails, and often traveling up to eight months to reach their destinations.

By the 1880s the abundant land yielded fortunes in agriculture, fishing and logging. Railroads were built, making access and trading even easier. With the discovery of more gold in the Klondike, Seattle flourished, and the two World Wars' demands on lumber and shipbuilding brought more industry to the area. Later in the 20th century the local economy shifted to high-tech and gave the area its 'Silicon Forest' nickname.

During the last ice age, so much water was trapped in huge glaciers that sea levels were 300ft lower than today. This created a land bridge between Alaska and Asia thought to have been over 1000 miles wide. Today the Bering Strait, at its narrowest, is 53 miles wide.

LAND BRIDGE

TIMELINE

20,000 BC	c 13,000 BC	c 5600 BC
Nomadic people cross a land bridge connecting Asia and North America and disperse southward, becoming the ancestors of today's Native Americans.	Epic glacial floods carve out 4000ft cliffs along an 80-mile section of the Columbia River Gorge. Eventually the river will stretch to 1243 miles long.	Mt Mazama erupts in an explosion estimated to be over 40 times more powerful than Mt St Helens' in 1980. The subsequent caldera creates what is now Crater Lake.

Just like the intrepid explorers before them, people are still drawn to the Pacific Northwest. There isn't much virgin land to settle, but these new travelers come for most of the same reasons – to be surrounded by natural beauty and grand opportunities.

Native Americans

Native People of the Northwest: A Traveler's Guide to Land, Art and Culture, by Jan Halliday and Gail Chehak, is a hands-on guide to Native American hot spots like galleries, museums and historical sites.

Early coastal inhabitants – who tramped up and down the Pacific Coast, around Puget Sound and along river valleys – went out to sea in pursuit of whales or sea lions, or depended on catching salmon and cod and collecting shellfish. On land they hunted deer and elk while gathering berries and roots. Plenty of food was stored for the long winters, when free time could be spent on artistic, religious and cultural pursuits like putting on potlatches (ceremonial feasts), taking part in 'vision quests' (spiritual trances) or carving dancing masks and totem poles. The construction of ornately carved cedar canoes led to extensive trading networks among the permanent settlements that stretched along the coast.

Inland, on the arid plateaus between the Cascades and the Rocky Mountains, a regional culture based on seasonal migration between rivers and temperate uplands developed among tribes including the Nez Perce, Cayuse, Spokane, Yakama and Kootenai. During salmon runs, the tribes gathered at rapids and waterfalls to net or harpoon fish, which they then dried or smoked. Most transportation was overland, with large dogs serving as pack animals until horses arrived in the 18th century.

In the harsh landscapes of Oregon's southern desert, yet another native culture evolved. Tribes such as the Shoshone, Paiute and Bannock were nomadic peoples who hunted and scavenged in the northern reaches of the Great Basin desert. Berries, roots and small game such as gophers and rabbits constituted their meager diet. Clusters of easily transported, woven-reed shelters made up migratory villages, while religious and cultural life focused on shamans, who could tap into the spirit world to heal sickness or bring success in hunting.

Today, Oregon has nine federally recognized Native American tribes, while Washington has nearly 30 and British Columbia over a hundred.

Europeans Take a Look

The first Europeans to clap eyes on the area were the crew of Portuguese explorer Juan Rodríguez Cabrillo. In 1542 his ships sailed from Mexico and, under the command of Bartolomé Ferrelo (Cabrillo died along the way), reached the mouth of the Rogue River in 1543. English explorer Sir Frances Drake checked out the region in 1579; and by the 18th century, the Spanish had colonized the southern parts of California and begun to explore the northern Pacific Coast in earnest. They were looking for the Northwest Passage, a fabled direct water route from the Pacific Ocean to the Atlantic Ocean. By 1774, Spanish frig-

1543	**1792**	**1804**
Juan Rodríguez Cabrillo's crew are the first Europeans to sight the Pacific Northwest coast. Cabrillo himself didn't see it, having died along the way.	American Robert Gray finds the elusive mouth of the Columbia River and sails upstream, becoming the first non-Native American to do so. He names the river after his ship, the *Columbia Rediviva*.	The Lewis and Clark Expedition – which consisted of 33 members, including Sacagawea – leaves St Louis, Missouri on its journey toward the Pacific Ocean.

RICHARD CUMMINS

» Columbia River

ates reached as far north as the Queen Charlotte Islands, claiming the Northwest coast for the Spanish crown.

The British, not to be outdone, were also looking for the Northwest Passage. In 1778, Captain James Cook explored the coast of present-day Oregon, Washington and British Columbia, landing at Nootka Sound on Vancouver Island. With him was George Vancouver, who in 1792 became the first European explorer to sail and chart the waters of Puget Sound. The Spanish attempted to build colonies along the Northwest coast; however, European politics forced Spain to give up its Northwest claim to Britain in 1792.

The Americans entered the scene in 1792, when Captain Robert Gray spotted the mouth of the Columbia River through obscuring sandbars and hazardous currents. He sailed up the great waterway, traded with the Native Americans and named his discovery the Columbia, in honor of his ship. The true importance of his discovery would be realized later, when it supported US territorial claims to the area.

Lewis & Clark

Like European explorers before them, Lewis and Clark came to the Pacific Northwest in search of adventure – and the fabled Northwest Passage. It started in 1801, when US president Thomas Jefferson enlisted his personal secretary, Meriwether Lewis, as leader of an expedition to chart North America's western regions. The goal was to find a waterway to the Pacific while exploring the newly acquired Louisiana Purchase and establishing a foothold for American interests. Lewis, then 27, had no training for exploration, but couldn't resist this grand opportunity. He convinced his good friend, 33-year-old William Clark, an experienced frontiersman and army veteran, to tag along. In 1804, the party left St Louis, Missouri, heading west with an entourage of 40 adventurers.

The Corps of Discovery – the expedition's official name – fared relatively well, in part because of the presence of Sacagawea. This young Shoshone woman had been sold to, and become the wife of, Toussaint Charbonneau, a French-Canadian trapper who was part of the entourage. Sacagawea proved invaluable as a guide, translator and ambassador to the area's Native Americans. York, Clark's African American servant, also softened tensions between the group and the Native Americans.

The party traveled some 8000 miles in about two years, documenting everything they came across in their journals with such bad spelling that it must have taken historians a few extra years just to sort out what they wrote. Meticulous notes were made on 122 animals and 178 plants, with some new discoveries being made along the way. In 1805 the party finally reached the mouth of the Columbia River and the Pacific Ocean

In 1793 Scottish fur trader Alexander Mackenzie became the first European to reach the Pacific Ocean (north of Mexico) via an overland route. He followed Native American trails across the Canadian Rockies to arrive at present-day Bella Coola, in British Columbia, where an inscribed rock marks his arrival.

The Northwest Passage, a sea route connecting the Pacific and Atlantic Oceans through Canada's northern islands, is blocked by thick ice nearly year round. However, scientists predict that in a few decades the passage may be much more easily passable due to global warming.

1805	1811	1825	1829
Lewis and Clark finally reach the Pacific Ocean after a year and six months of traveling. They lay groundwork that immensely aids future US expansion toward the West.	Pacific Fur Company mogul John Jacob Astor establishes Fort Astoria, the first permanent US settlement on the Pacific Coast. He later becomes the country's first millionaire.	Hudson's Bay Company establishes Fort Vancouver, which becomes the most prominent European presence in the Northwest. Today, Washington state's Vancouver is located here.	Oregon City becomes the first established city west of the Mississippi and the pot-of-gold destination for early pioneers traversing the Oregon Trail.

at Cape Disappointment, and bedded down for the winter nearby, thus establishing Fort Clatsop.

Lewis and Clark returned to a hero's welcome in St Louis in 1806. Lewis was later appointed governor of the Louisiana Territory but he died a year later; possibly murdered, but more likely by suicide. Clark became governor of the Missouri Territory, living to be 68.

The daily logs of Lewis and Clark, as presented in Bernard DeVoto's carefully edited *Journals of Lewis and Clark*, are full of wild adventures, misspellings and wonderful candor.

Otters & Beavers Lose Out

The British and Americans soon tapped into the Northwest's bounty of fur-bearing wildlife. While in the Northwest in 1778, Cook's crew traded with Native Americans for animal pelts, of which sea otter and beaver were the most valuable. This trade dominated British and US economic interests in the northern Pacific for the next 30 years, until the War of 1812 stuck a thorn in the side of relations between the two countries.

Trappers from two competing British fur-trading companies – the Hudson's Bay Company (HBC) and the North West Company – began to expand from their bases around Hudson's Bay and the Great Lakes, edging over the Rocky Mountains to establish fur-trading forts. These trading posts were quite successful, each linked to eastern markets by an 1800-mile overland trail. The forts were given goods to trade with local Native Americans for beaver, otter, fox, wolf or whatever other fur-bearing animal had yet to be wiped out. Forts edged closer to the Pacific, and in 1811 the American fur magnate, John Jacob Astor, established a post in Astoria, at the mouth of the Columbia River. During the War of 1812, however, it was sold to the North West Company, which merged with the HBC in 1821. With the Americans out of the way, the HBC created a network of relationships with Native American tribes throughout the region, establishing headquarters at Fort Vancouver, which straddled the Willamette and Columbia Rivers.

Undaunted Courage, by Stephen Ambrose, is a compelling account of the Lewis and Clark expedition; it follows the footsteps of their extraordinary journey to the Pacific and back again.

By 1827 the Northwest's borders were becoming more defined. Spain had withdrawn its claim, establishing the northern border of New Spain at the 47th parallel (the current Oregon–California border). Russian ambitions were limited to the land north of the 54°40' parallel, at the start of the Alaska panhandle, near Prince Rupert, BC. The USA, through the Louisiana Purchase, owned all land south of the 49th parallel and east of the Rocky Mountains, while Britain controlled the territory north of this line. This left a vast territory of present-day BC – the states of Oregon, Washington and Idaho and parts of western Montana and Wyoming – open to claims by both Britain and the USA.

The Treaty of Ghent, which ended the War of 1812, included an amendment that declared a joint custody (of sorts) of the Pacific Northwest: Britain and the USA could continue economic development in the area, but neither could establish an official government.

1836	1843	1846	1847
The Whitman Party (which includes the first two women to travel the Oregon Trail) establishes a mission near Walla Walla, Washington. Their adventures would end in tragedy 11 years later.	A slim-margin vote at Champoeg (30 miles south of current-day Portland) establishes Oregon's first independent government, weakening the British hold on the region.	The Oregon Treaty brings an end to land disputes between the US and Britain. Both countries had jointly occupied the region since the Treaty of 1818.	The Whitman Massacre starts the Cayuse War, resulting in the decimation of the Cayuse people and their forced relocation onto a reservation.

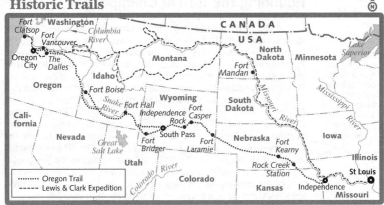

The Americans Settle In

Unlike most other early trading posts, which were basically repositories for goods, Fort Vancouver became a thriving, nearly self-sufficient agricultural community complete with mills, a dairy, gardens and fields.

Canadian-born Dr John McLoughlin, often called the 'father of Oregon,' was the capable steward of this post. He encouraged settlement beyond the precincts of the fort, and allowed retired HBC trappers to settle along the Willamette River in an area still called French Prairie. By 1828 these French Canadians, with their Native American wives, began to clear the land and build cabins. McLoughlin established a mill and incorporated the first town in the Northwest in 1829, at Oregon City. He later built a house there, which today is a museum (see p231).

The eventual decline of the fur trade, along with an influx of American farmers, traders and settlers from the east, all helped loosen the weakening British Empire's grip on the Pacific Northwest. But it was the missionaries who probably played the biggest role. In 1834 New England Methodists Daniel and Jason Lee founded a mission just north of present-day Salem. Other missionaries arrived in 1836, establishing missions near today's Walla Walla in Washington, and Lewiston in Idaho.

Losing ground despite the Treaty of Ghent, the HBC hedged its bets and established another center of operations further north at Fort Victoria, on Vancouver Island. But the federal government did not offer military intervention to rid the area of British stragglers. If the settlers wanted an independent civil authority, they would have to do the dirty work themselves.

The oldest commercial corporation in North America is the Hudson's Bay Company, which once controlled the Pacific Northwest fur trade, conducted early exploration of the region and even functioned as a de facto government before the US took over.

1848	1851	1853	1858
The Oregon territory officially becomes US land, with its capital at Oregon City. The territory's borders encompass today's Oregon, Washington and Idaho, plus parts of Wyoming and Montana.	The first significant gold deposits are discovered near Jacksonville, starting a gold rush in Oregon. Thousands of fortune seekers pour into the state, creating new settlements and small towns.	The Washington Territory is created from the northernmost half of the Oregon Territory. Its borders later change, but become permanent when Washington state is created in 1889.	Cascade Railroad Company is the region's first railroad and begins operations in the Columbia River Gorge. It will take 25 years for transcontinental rail lines to finally reach the Pacific Northwest.

Rounding the Turn at Champoeg

By the early 1840s the Willamette Valley had become home to a rag-tag mix of 700 French-Canadian farmers, retired trappers, Protestant missionaries and general adventurers. Eager to establish some order to the region, the settlers created the framework for a budding government. Meetings led to an 1843 vote at Champoeg, along the Willamette River about 30 miles south of Portland (now Champoeg State Heritage Area). By a razor-thin 52-to-50 margin, a measure was passed to organize a provisional government independent of the HBC. The land north of the Columbia, however, would remain in control of the British – for a bit longer.

Meanwhile, the USA–Canada boundary dispute became a hotbed of contention. There was a fervent settler movement to occupy the Northwest all the way up to present-day Alaska. The 1844 presidential campaign slogan became '54/40 or fight' (referring to the geographical parallel). The bickering finally ended in 1846 when the British and Americans negotiated the Treaty of Oregon, and agreed to today's present USA–Canada border, which runs along the 49th parallel.

Accepting its inevitable fate, the HBC gave up its headquarters at Fort Vancouver and high-tailed it north to Fort Victoria on Vancouver Island (many British citizens followed, and Vancouver Island was designated a crown colony in 1849). In 1848 Oregon officially became a US territory.

In Chinese markets, an exceptional sea-otter pelt could fetch the equivalent of a year's pay for a fur-company laborer.

In 1859 Oregon became the 33rd state of the union. It voted to outlaw slavery, but free blacks still couldn't settle here, and only white men over 21 were allowed to vote.

Follow the Oregon Trail

The party was now just getting started. In the Willamette Valley, nearly 900 new settlers arrived in one go, more than doubling the area's population. They were a trickle in what became a flood of migrants following the 2170-mile Oregon Trail, which edged south around the footsteps of the explorers before them – first Lewis and Clark, then adventurous fur trap-

NORTHERN GOLD

Nothing draws fortune seekers more than the lure of riches. In 1851, gold was discovered in southern Oregon near the Rogue River valley. Prospectors and scoundrels flooded in, boomtowns popped up overnight and native populations were brushed aside. A year later gold was discovered near Scottsburg along the Umpqua River, while along the coast miners washed gold dust out of sands near Coos Bay.

In 1861 the Blue Mountains of eastern Oregon became the next target for gold seekers, but violent clashes ensued between Native Americans and the newcomers. The result for most Native Americans was forced relocation to reservations, some as far away as Oklahoma. Meanwhile, the rush kept moving north into British Columbia's Fraser River and, over the next few decades, beyond into the Yukon Territory.

1859	1871	1889	1899
On February 14, Oregon is admitted into the union and becomes the USA's 33rd state, about nine months after Minnesota achieves its own statehood.	British Columbia, Canada's third-largest province in area and population, becomes the country's sixth province to join into Confederation.	On November 11, President Benjamin Harrison signs a bill making Washington the USA's 42nd state.	Mt Rainier National Park is established on March 2, becoming the USA's fifth national park. It contains the highest point in the Cascade Range (over 14,000ft) and encompasses 368 sq miles.

pers and intrepid missionaries. Between 1843 and 1860, over 50,000 fresh faces arrived to a brand-new future in the gorgeous Pacific Northwest.

Spanning six states, the Oregon Trail sorely tested the families who embarked on this perilous trip. Their belongings were squirreled away under canvas-topped wagons, which often trailed livestock. The journey could take up to eight months, and by the time the settlers reached eastern Oregon their food supplies were running on fumes. And there was one last challenge; when the weary parties arrived at the Columbia River in the Dalles, they had to choose between rafting themselves and all their belongings through the rapids in the Columbia River Gorge or struggling up the flanks of Mt Hood and descending via the precipitous Barlow Trail.

The journey ended at Oregon City, at the base of the falls of the Willamette River, which became the region's early seat of government. Above the falls, in the river's broad agricultural basin, small farming communities sprang up. Not far away, Portland, near the Willamette's confluence with the Columbia River, took on an early importance as a trade center.

After Fort Vancouver fell to the Americans in 1846, explorers began to mosey up the Cowlitz River into the Puget Sound area, initially planting roots at Tumwater near Olympia. By 1851 a group of Oregon Trail pioneers, led by brothers Arthur and David Denny, set their sights on Elliott Bay and founded the port city of Seattle.

In 1846, seeking a route around the daunting Columbia River Gorge, a party of pioneers began to blaze a southern route into the Willamette Valley. This new Applegate Trail cut through the deserts of Nevada and California before turning north through the valleys of southern Oregon. Immigrants along this route established towns such as Eugene, and scouted the land in the Rogue, Umpqua and Klamath River valleys.

By the late 1850s settlers had staked claims to the best land in the western valleys. Some folks began looking east of the Cascades, particularly to the Grande Ronde River valley of present-day Oregon and Walla Walla River valley of what would be Washington. Eastern Oregon didn't become a hot spot until the discovery of gold there in the 1860s.

Decimation of Native Americans

By 1860 the Pacific Northwest's coast was strung with white settlements, and most major cities had been founded. The area's wildlife, especially the beaver and otter populations, had been nearly extinguished. European diseases had devastated whole Native American communities, while alcoholism took its own insidious toll on their cultures.

Missionaries eventually delivered the final blow. In 1847, near Walla Walla, the Whitman mission's attempts to bring Christianity to eastern Washington tribes ended in tragedy. The Cayuse Native Americans slew over a dozen missionaries in revenge for a measles epidemic. Settlers

Among the provisions recommended for those traveling the Oregon Trail were coffee (15lb per person), bacon (25lb per person), 1lb of castile soap, citric acid to prevent scurvy and a live cow for milk and emergency meat.

In 1850 Congress passed the Donation Land Act, which granted every white European settler and 'American half-breed Indian' 320 acres. Married couples could claim 640 acres.

1937

After three years and $88 million, Bonneville Dam is completed on Oregon's Columbia River. The construction provides 4000 crucial jobs during the Great Depression.

1962

Seattle hosts the second major World's Fair since WWII and offers a glimpse of what the future might hold. The Space Needle opens on the first day of the fair, April 21.

» Mt Rainier

now felt justified in removing Native Americans from their land and incarcerating them on reservations. Coastal Native Americans were marched or shipped to reservations in 1855 and 1856, where increased illness, starvation and dislocation led to the complete extinction of many tribal groups. Even on Vancouver Island, where British policies were generally more enlightened most arable land was given to European settlers. Missionaries worked to make illegal the traditional potlatches that formed the nucleus of coastal Native American religion and social life.

East of the Cascades, Native Americans were more resistant to the US military and settlers. Fierce battles were fought between the US Army and various tribes from 1855 to 1877. Especially bloody were the Rogue River and Modoc Wars, in southern Oregon, and the Cayuse War, near Walla Walla. However, these Native American groups also ended up on reservations, dependent upon the federal government for subsistence.

The incidents leading up to, during and after the tragic Whitman Massacre, which had wide-ranging repercussions in Oregon's history, are detailed at www.oregonpioneers.com/whitman.htm.

More Recent Times

By the 1880s the Northwest's port cities boomed with the region's rich agricultural, fishing and logging resources. The Northern Pacific Railroad linked the Northwest to the eastern USA, making national markets more accessible and bringing in more settlers. Seattle became the area's most important seaport in 1897 when gold was discovered in the Canadian Klondike and prospectors poured into the city.

The World Wars brought further economic fortune to the Pacific Northwest, when the area became the nation's largest lumber producer and both Oregon's and Washington's naval yards bustled, along with William Boeing's airplane factory. The region continued to prosper through the second half of the 20th century, attracting new migrations of educated, progressively minded settlers from the nation's east and south. In the 1980s and '90s the economy shifted to the high-tech industry, embodied by Microsoft in Seattle and Intel in Portland.

But growth has not come without cost. The production of cheap hydroelectricity and massive irrigation projects along the Columbia have led to the near-irreversible destruction of the river's ecosystem. Dams have all but eliminated most runs of native salmon and have further disrupted the lives of remaining Native Americans who depend on the river. Logging of old-growth forests has left ugly scars, while 'silicon forest' had its own economic collapse at the turn of the 21st century. And Washington's Puget Sound area and Portland's extensive suburbs are groaning under the weight of rapidly growing population centers.

Still, the Pacific Northwest's inhabitants generally manage to find a reasonable balance between their natural resources and continued popularity. The region continues to be one of the USA's most beautiful places to visit...and settle down.

In 1990 the northern spotted owl was declared a threatened species, barring timber industries from clear-cutting certain old-growth forests. The controversy sparked debate all across the Pacific Northwest, pitting loggers against environmentalists.

OWL

1980	1988	1995	2010
Mt St Helens blows her top, killing 57 people and destroying 250 homes. Her elevation is cut from 9677ft to 8365ft, and where a peak once stood, a mile-wide crater is born.	Nirvana records 10 demos in just six hours, leading to the band being signed to the Sub Pop label. Later in the year they play their first Seattle show.	Amazon, one of the first major companies to sell products online, is launched in Seattle. Originally started as a bookseller, it will not become annually profitable until 2003.	Vancouver hosts the Olympic winter games and wins 14 gold medals, including in men's and women's ice hockey. It is Canada's third time hosting, and Vancouver's first.

Life as a Pacific Northwesterner

People in the Pacific Northwest are some pretty cool cats, living a relatively laid-back lifestyle. But this doesn't mean Northwesterners don't care about what's going on around them. Quite the opposite: they're highly attuned to the economy and political bubble of the region, as well as to whatever might be going on outside it. And folks here aren't complacent either – everyone is quick to voice their own opinion, whether it's about the right to own guns, 'local' versus 'organic' produce, Oregon's 'Death with Dignity' act or spotted owls. Here in the Northwest, people are deeply concerned about their communities, the environment and what's happening in the world that might affect their valued and independent lives.

The People

A Texan, a Californian and an Oregonian were sitting around a campfire drinking. The Texan took a swig of whiskey, threw the bottle in the air and shot it with his pistol while yelling 'We have lots more whiskey where I come from!' The Californian sipped his zinfandel, grabbed the Texan's pistol, threw the wine bottle in the air, and shot it while yelling 'We have lots more wine where I come from!' The Oregonian guzzled his microbrew, grabbed the Texan's pistol, threw the empty in the air but caught the bottle and shot the Californian. He said 'We have lots of Californians where I come from, but I need to recycle this beer bottle.'

While not everyone in the Pacific Northwest is a tree-hugging hipster with activist tendencies and a penchant for latte, many locals are proud of their independent spirit, profess a love for nature and yes, will separate their plastics when it's time to recycle. They're a friendly lot and, despite the common tendency to denigrate Californians, most are transplants themselves. Why did they all come here, from all edges of the globe? Among other things, for the lush scenery, the good quality of life and the lack of pretension that often afflicts bigger, more popular places. Primping up and putting on airs is not a part of Northwestern everyday life, and wearing Gore-Tex outerwear to restaurants, concerts or social functions will rarely raise an eyebrow.

In a broad sense the Northwest shares the general cultures of the US and Canada, but adds its own personal twist. In rural parts of eastern Oregon and Washington, the personality of the Old West is still very much alive. Fishing towns have a distinctive and often gritty sensibility that comes from making a living on the stormy Pacific Ocean. Urban centers have a reputation for progressive, somewhat maverick politics. Also, some folk do put emphasis on 'old family' legitimacy and connections, boasting of ancestors who came across

Oregon is the home to Nike and Columbia Sportswear, while Washington boasts Starbucks and REI. Vancouver doesn't care – it scored the 2010 Winter Olympics.

Washington and Oregon are the only US states with a 'Death with Dignity' act, by which some terminally ill patients are allowed to voluntarily end their lives.

Outdoor-loving Pacific Northwesterners like to commute to work by bike: it's 3% in Seattle and 6% in Portland (the highest in the nation, whose average is a paltry 0.5%). Vancouver, however, is seriously thinking about establishing a public bike-share program – it wants 10% of all trips to be by bicycle.

OFFBEAT BELIEFS

Only a quarter of Pacific Northwesterners have a religious affiliation, and a good chunk of those bow to Christianity, Judaism and the Mormon Church. Asians have brought Buddhism, Hinduism, Sikhism and Islam – especially to Vancouver – and New Age spirituality isn't a stranger here. However, some even stranger and more exotic beliefs and religions have claimed footholds in the Northwest.

Ramtha's School of Enlightenment, known for channeling and out-of-body experiences, is headquartered in Yelm, Washington (the movie *What the Bleep Do We Know* was filmed in Portland's Bagdad Theatre, and its three directors were devotees). The Living Enrichment Center was a large 'New Thought' church located in Wilsonville, Oregon; it closed in 2004 because of a financial scandal. Bhagwan Shree Rajneesh – an Indian spiritual leader who started the Osho movement – created a community in Antelope, Oregon, which voted the city council out of office and legalized public nudity (among other things). He was deported in 1985. Witchcraft-practicing Wiccans, despite their positive exposure on popular TV shows like *Buffy the Vampire Slayer* and *Charmed,* fear persecution and continue their tradition of secrecy; in fact, revealing oneself to others is called 'coming out of the broom closet.'

the Oregon Trail or who were early Brits in Victoria. And while most urban Americans and Canadians are tolerant of individual eccentricities, rural Northwesterners tend to be conservative and perhaps a little skeptical of strangers.

There is indeed a wide mix of peoples in this great region, but they do tend to share several things in common: a do-it-yourself ethic, a respect for the outdoors, and the desire to keep frills to a minimum. And a certain affableness – if you're friendly to a local, whether they're a city slicker or country bumpkin, they often can't help but to be friendly right back.

Livin' the Life

The region's gorgeous waters, forests and mountains certainly help define the lifestyle of Northwesterners. Here, people can be close to nature without sacrificing the comforts of a sophisticated metropolis. During the week they'll work in city centers, dine at world-class restaurants and take in fine theatrical productions or cutting-edge live music. Then on weekends they'll head to the beach or ski slopes, or hike to the nearest mountaintop. And while they love their outdoors, Northwesterners can be just as happy inside their warm homes – especially when snow, drizzly rain and gray skies take over in winter. Reading, watching movies and drinking (both microbrew and coffee) are a few popular indoor pastimes, and the area is known for its bookstores, funky cinemas, breweries and cafés.

The Pacific Northwest lifestyle is generally relaxed, and a certain degree of eccentricity is even expected – that shabbily dressed, green-haired woman next to you at the coffee shop might be a tattoo artist – or a software developer at Microsoft. Portland's unofficial motto is 'Keep Portland Weird,' while Seattle's popular Fremont neighborhood proclaims the 'freedom to be peculiar.' And let's not forget gays and lesbians, who are widely accepted and especially attracted to the Northwest's liberal cities. Girls, forget San Francisco – lesbians *love* Portland.

However, not everything is perfect in paradise; in big cities, urban sprawl and rising real-estate prices are a problem. And despite the large percentage of bicycle commuters, as well as great public transportation systems, freeways will get jammed during rush hours. Plus, unemploy-

GAY RIGHTS

Gays living in the Pacific Northwest have more rights than in most other states. Oregon and Washington recognize same-sex domestic partnerships, and in Canada, same-sex marriage is legal.

ment continues to be a big problem, as more and more people continue to be attracted to the region. Northwesterners are an adaptable lot, however. Like their ancestors, who came over the Oregon Trail (or from California, the East Coast or Hong Kong), they've learned to change with the times – even as they voice their opinions and complain the whole way.

Multiculturalism

Combined, the current population of Oregon and Washington is about 10.4 million, which amounts to about 3.8% of the total US population. By far the greatest concentrations of people huddle in Washington's Puget Sound area and Oregon's Willamette Valley. Oregon and Washington are among the fastest-growing states in the USA.

With a population of 4.5 million, BC is the fastest-growing Canadian province, due both to immigration largely from Hong Kong and to movement within Canada. The greater Vancouver area is home to about half those people.

Most US Northwesterners are white; minority groups include Latinos, Asians and African Americans. BC, while largely founded by British settlers, has a much more racially mixed population. Nearly half of Vancouver's population is made up of minority groups – most with an Asian background.

The US government recognizes around three dozen Pacific Northwestern Native American tribes, for whom reservations or trust lands

The Pacific Northwest's spirit of independence is most extremely exemplified by the 'Republic of Cascadia' movement, which calls for Oregon, Washington and British Columbia to secede from the US and Canada. Currently however, there's no danger of this happening.

LIFE AS A PACIFIC NORTHWESTERNER

THE SPORTING LIFE

Outdoor-loving Pacific Northwesterners cherish their sports, whether they're players themselves or just watching their favorite teams go at it.

The Pacific Northwest's only National Football League (NFL) franchise is the Seattle Seahawks, owned by Microsoft cofounder Paul Allen (who also owns the Portland Trail Blazers and part of the Seattle Sounders). They played their first game in 1976, but only made it to the Super Bowl once – in 2006. The American football regular season runs from September to December or early January.

Generating nearly as much enthusiasm are contests between university teams, most notably the University of Washington Huskies, the Washington State University Cougars, the University of Oregon Ducks and the Oregon State University Beavers. The season runs from September to February.

Vancouver is home to the Canadian Football League's (CFL) BC Lions, who won the 2006 Grey Cup against the Montreal Alouettes (who probably deserve to lose based on their name alone). Their season runs from July to early November.

The Seattle Mariners is the region's only professional baseball team, and likely owes a big chunk of its popularity to star right-fielder Ichiro Suzuki. Minor league baseball has its fans as well, and is played by teams that include the Vancouver Canadians, Spokane Indians, Yakima Bears and Eugene Emeralds.

Portland's Trail Blazers are currently the only National Basketball Association (NBA) basketball team; the season runs from late October until mid-April.

Visiting Vancouver during the October-to-April hockey season? Catch Canada's favorite sport, pastime and religion. The National Hockey League's (NHL) Vancouver Canucks have never won the Stanley Cup, but they did come close in 1994 – and their loss to the New York Rangers sparked a riot in downtown Vancouver. Seattle's Thunderbirds and Portland's Winter Hawks are a couple of the region's other ice-hockey teams.

Soccer isn't a major spectator sport in the US, but the United Soccer League (USL) does have its fervent fans. The Seattle Sounders, the Portland Timbers and the Vancouver Whitecaps are the Pacific Northwest's teams, kicking it from May to mid-September.

Pacific Northwest has lost some sports teams lately; the Seattle Supersonics moved to Oklahoma in 2009 and the Portland Beavers lost their stadium in 2010. Vancouver is still mourning their loss of the Grizzlies...in 2001!

SPORTS

have been set aside. A number of other Native American groups in the region have no federally recognized status – without which they are ineligible for government assistance to support tribal schools and cultural centers. Moreover, without legal recognition, it is difficult for tribes to maintain cultural identity. The total Native American population of Oregon and Washington is around 176,000 (or 1.7% of the population).

In Canada, tribal bands control small tracts of land called reserves, the parameters of which were determined through treaties with Great Britain prior to independence (though only about a quarter of the country's native people actually inhabit these lands). First Nations inhabitants of BC number roughly 196,000 (4.8% of BC's population).

Music & the Arts

Blame it on the weather, or maybe it's all that natural beauty, but the Pacific Northwest is ground zero for right-brain thinkers and mind-blowing art. From music-makers to famous writers to glassblowers and cutting-edge architecture, you'll find creativity galore in this progressive and inspiring region.

The Seattle Sound: Then & Now

No other music genre is associated with the Pacific Northwest like grunge – that angst-driven, heavily riffed and distorted sound born in the late 1980s out of Seattle's garages and cherished by Generation X. Evolved from music to a lifestyle (flannel shirt and ripped jeans anyone?), grunge became a way to voice cynicism and disillusionment in a society of vanity and materialism.

Grunge started in the mid-1980s and was heavily influenced by a cult group called the Melvins, inspiring Seattle bands with their sludgy and aggressive mix of hardcore punk and heavy metal. Alternative rock band Green River also had a heavy hand in the genre's beginnings – vocalist Mark Arm even coined the term 'grunge' (and its members later went on to start Mudhoney and Pearl Jam). Distorted guitars, strong riffs, heavy drumming and gritty styles defined the unpolished musical style.

The real success of grunge, however, didn't explode until the record label Sub Pop – which signed up many of the bigger grunge band names – put out Nirvana's *Nevermind* in 1991, skyrocketing the 'Seattle Sound' into mainstream music. True purists, however, shunned Nirvana for what they considered selling out to commercialism while overshadowing equally worthy bands like Soundgarden and Alice in Chains. In fact, some grunge bands even renounced their own fame and fortune, claiming it went against the spirit of the movement.

The general popularity of grunge continued through the early 1990s, but the very culture of the genre took part in its downfall. Bands lived hard and fast, never really taking themselves seriously: playing to friends for fun was more important than being successful in business. Many eventually succumbed to internal

Early January
River City Bluegrass Festival
Highlights mostly bluegrass but also features country, folk, swing and even gospel; held in Portland.

February
Portland Jazz Festival
Big-name national and international artists from American jazz saxophonist Pharoah Sanders to Brazilian singer/composer Luciana Souza.

Late May
Sasquatch Music Festival
Gorgeous location at the gorge amphitheater in George, Washington, this festival has headlined fine indie and alternative acts.

Late May
Northwest Folklife Festival
Vibrant folk music, as well as dance, visual arts, workshops, exhibits and films. One of the largest folk-oriented celebrations in North America.

June–July
Vancouver International Jazz Festival Showcasing regional and international artists like Miles Davis, Wynton Marsalis and Tito Puente.

Mid-July
Vancouver Folk Music Festival Everything from Utah Phillips to hip-hop to Tuvan throat singers. Great location on the beachy sands of Jericho Beach Park.

strife and drug abuse. The final blow was in 1994, when Kurt Cobain – the heart of Nirvana – found peace with a shotgun.

In the mid-1990s, post-grunge was born. It was a commercially friendly, more accessible version of grunge, borrowing the sounds and aesthetics of its predecessor but with an uplifting spirit. Popular bands showcasing this new genre were Foo Fighters (with ex-Nirvana drummer Dave Grohl), Creed, Bush, Candlebox and Matchbox Twenty.

Beyond Grunge

Rock music wasn't born in the Pacific Northwest, but the region has certainly attracted more than its share of creative musicians. Jimi Hendrix, Anthony Ray (Sir Mix-a-Lot) and the Wilson sisters (of Heart) all grew up in the Seattle area. Bryan Adams, Sarah McLachlan and Nelly Furtado have BC associations. Even Courtney Love (of Hole) was a teenage rockster in Oregon.

A few cities, however, have especially connected with indie music. Seattle was the original stomping grounds for Modest Mouse, Death Cab for Cutie and The Postal Service. Olympia (WA) has been a hotbed of indie rock and riot grrrls, and birthplace of the now-defunct groups Sleater-Kinney and Beat Happening (see box p116). BC, meanwhile can claim popular indie bands like The New Pornographers, Black Mountain and Hot Hot Heat, as well as the punksters Subhumans. It's Portland, Oregon, however, which has really attracted indie bands in the past decade: the city has boasted such diverse groups as folktronic hip-hop band Talkdemonic, alt-band The Decemberists and multi-genre Pink Martini, not to mention The Shins, The Dandy Warhols, Blind Pilot and Elliot Smith.

Meanwhile, jazz is alive and seriously kicking in the major cities, thanks to the region's early African American inhabitants. Seattle jazz was raging back in the 1930s and '40s, but today avant-garde artists like Bill Frisell and Wayne Horvitz hold their own. The cities also host major operas and symphonies.

Pacific Northwest By the Book

Many great writers have either grown up in the Pacific Northwest, or now call this region home. Washington's late Raymond Carver, known for his grim vision of working-class angst, has a collection of best stories in the volume *Where I'm Calling From* (1988). Novelist Mary McCarthy (1912–89) inspired the play *Imaginary Friends* by Nora Ephron and was known for her satirical, semi-autobiographical prose. David Guterson is famous for his award-winning *Snow Falling on Cedars* (1994), a vivid tale of prejudice in a San Juan Island fishing community. Popular author Tom Robbins, a La Conner resident, has won numerous devotees for his wacky, countercultural novels, including *Even Cowgirls Get the Blues* (1976).

Jon Krakauer is the award-winning author of *Into Thin Air* (1997) and *Under the Banner of Heaven* (2003), while Sherman Alexie is a Native American author who adapted his short story *This is What It Means to Say Phoenix, Arizona* into the excellent movie *Smoke Signals* (1998).

Oregon's biggest literary name is the late Ken Kesey, whose *One Flew Over the Cuckoo's Nest* (1962) became a textbook of 1960s nonconformity and inspired a movie that won five Oscars; Kesey also penned the brilliant *Sometimes a Great Notion* (1971). Novelist Chuck Palahniuk, best known for *Fight Club* (1996), lives in Portland and writes about it in *Fugitives and Refugees: A Walk in Portland, Oregon* (2003). Portland also boasts two novelists with a bent towards science fiction and fantasy: the prolific and multi-award-winning Ursula LeGuin is responsible for *The Left Hand of Darkness* (1969) and *The Farthest Shore* (1972),

You can see the handwritten lyrics of Nirvana singer/songwriter Kurt Cobain (born in Aberdeen, Washington) at the Experience Music Project in the Seattle Center.

Powell's Books claims to be the largest independent new and used bookstore in the world. The main store takes up a whole city block, and it's been a part of Portland book culture since the early 1970s.

Top Film Festivals
» Portland International Film Festival, February
» Seattle International Film Festival, May-June
» Vancouver International Film Festival, September-October
» Northwest Film and Video Festival (Portland), November

while Jean Auel is best known for her widely read *Clan of the Cave Bear* series.

BC's ever-active literary scene has cultivated a wide range of talent. The English novelist and poet Malcolm Lowry, who's best known for his semi-autobiographical *Under the Volcano* (1947), lived in BC for many years before his death in Sussex. BC resident WP Kinsella's award-winning novel *Shoeless Joe* (1982) was adapted for the film *Field of Dreams* (1989). Douglas Coupland (*Generation X,* 1991) makes his home in Vancouver, as does science-fiction guru William Gibson, who coined the term 'cyberspace' in his 1984 novel *Neuromancer.*

The Pacific Northwest's First Art...

The first artists drawn to the Northwest's beauty were Coastal Native Americans, whose tribes included the Haida, Salish, Tlingit and Tsimshian. The most well-known form of art in this region is the totem pole, clan symbols which denote wealth and prestige. Made of Western red cedar, these totems used stylized geometric shapes and the motifs of sacred animals (such as eagles, ravens and bears). They could reach 80ft in length and take up to a year to complete.

Carved wooden masks are another popular form of Northwest Coast art. These were originally used in dances, traditional ceremonies and even wars, often depicting supernatural beings or animal heads. They'd often be painted in red and black, and decorated with hair, feathers, fur and shells. Valued highly by private collectors, these Native American masks can go for tens of thousands of dollars today.

The fanciest Haida dugout canoes, which could be up to 60ft long, sometimes boasted carved prows and were decorated with beautiful animal images. Some other art forms practiced by the region's native peoples are basketry and blanket weaving.

...and Artists

Well-known Northwest Coast artists include Bill Reid (1920–98), an outstanding Haida artist who acquired his skills from Mungo Martin, a Kwakiutl master carver of totem poles. He's a descendant of Charles Edenshaw, another legendary carver and silversmith. Robert Davidson, a contemporary BC craftsman also of Haida descent, is a master mask and totem-pole carver who has been highly awarded for his interpretation of traditional Haida forms. Yet another BC resident is Susan Point, who has combined personal style with traditional Salish art elements in a variety of artistic mediums; many of her works can be seen in public areas, such as at the Vancouver International Airport.

Architecture & Notable Buildings

Architecture in the Pacific Northwest is as progressive and eclectic as in any other modern region of the world. There are historic brick structures, tall skyscrapers, lofty bridges and super-modern buildings that could be classified as either cutting-edge or downright ugly, depending on who you ask. Outside the big cities you can find architecturally quirky places like Leavenworth (boasting Bavarian buildings), Winthrop (with its Wild West feel) and Port Townsend (a Victorian-lover's dream).

August
Blue Waters Bluegrass Festival Takes place at Medical Lake in eastern Washington; enjoy world-class line-ups and fun workshops.

Mid-September
MusicfestNW Indie, hip-hop and punk bands play at this successful music fest in Portland.

Mid-October
Earshot Jazz Festival Seattle's three-week, eclectic jazz concert series that highlights the work of innovative jazz names who are redefining the genre.

Early September
Bumbershoot Fun and famous music festival drawing up to 150,000 people. Fifteen stages showcase top-shelf music acts of all kinds.

Top Native Art

» Seattle Art Museum

» University of Washington's Burke Museum

» University of Oregon Museum of Natural History

» UBC Museum of Anthropology

» Royal British Columbia Museum

MUSIC & THE ARTS THE PACIFIC NORTHWEST'S FIRST ART...

MUSIC & THE ARTS ARCHITECTURE & NOTABLE BUILDINGS

Black Mountain (Vancouver, BC) *Black Mountain* (2005)
The Dandy Warhols (Portland, OR) *Thirteen Tales From Urban Bohemia* (2000)
Death Cab for Cutie (Bellingham, WA) *Plans* (2005)
The Decemberists (Portland, OR) *The Crane Wife* (2006)
Foo Fighters (Seattle, WA) *One By One* (2002)
Hot Hot Heat (Victoria, BC) *Make Up The Breakdown* (2004)
Modest Mouse (Issaquah, WA) *Lonesome Crowded West* (1997)
The New Pornographers (Vancouver, BC) *Mass Romantic* (2000)
Pearl Jam (Seattle, WA) *Ten* (1991)
Pink Martini (Portland, OR) *Sympathique* (1997)
The Postal Service (Seattle, WA) *Give Up* (2003)
The Shins (Portland, OR) *Chutes Too Narrow* (2003)
Sleater-Kinney (Olympia, WA) *Call The Doctor* (1996)
Talkdemonic (Portland, OR) *Beat Romantic* (2006)

Glassmaster Dale Chihuly is known for his blown-glass sculptures, infused with lush color and sensual textures. His installations are scattered around the Seattle area, but Tacoma has the lion's share.

DALE CHIHULY

Modern Art

» Seattle Art Museum

» Roq la Rue Gallery

» Portland Art Museum

» Schneider Museum of Art

» Vancouver Art Gallery

» Contemporary Art Gallery

Buildings

Seattle's 605ft Space Needle (p64) is likely the Pacific Northwest's most famous structure. Completed in 1961 for the world's fair, this landmark can withstand 200-mile-an-hour winds and has had several people jump off the top – with parachutes on. The emerald city also boasts the Columbia Center, the region's tallest building at 937ft; head to the observation deck on the 73rd floor for an awe-inspiring view of the city. The cutting-edge Central Library and Experience Music Project (p64) are other noteworthy buildings here.

Portland's controversial Portland Building (p203), designed by Michael Graves, is a great example of the postmodern period. Out front is Portlandia, the second-largest hammered-copper statue in the world (after the Statue of Liberty). The glassy twin towers of the city's Oregon Convention Center (p208) are hard to miss from the freeway as you enter town; inside is the world's largest foucault pendulum. And outside Salem is the Mount Angel Abbey (p240), which boasts a modernist library designed by Finnish architect Alvar Aalto.

Vancouver's most notable structures include its huge, coliseum-like public library building and concrete-and-glass Museum of Anthropology (p362), inspired by Native American dwellings.

Bridges

With all those rivers, the Pacific Northwest is also famous for its bridges. Seattle's Spokane Street Bridge is a concrete, double-leaf swing bridge and has received awards for its innovative design – and it claims to be the only one of its kind in the world. The city's Elliot Avenue Helix (pedestrian) bridge is a stunner, with its DNA ladder–like good looks.

Portland has 10 bridges spanning the Willamette River. The lovely St John's is the city's only suspension bridge, while the Hawthorne is the world's oldest vertical-lift bridge and the Steel's lower and upper decks can move independently of each other – a unique trait among the world's bridges.

Meanwhile, Vancouver's landmark Lions Gate Bridge connects the city to the north shore, and is a look-alike to San Francisco's Golden Gate.

Possibly the area's most infamous bridge was the 1940 Tacoma Narrows Bridge (aka 'Galloping Gertie') in Puget Sound, which existed for only four months. It collapsed spectacularly in a windstorm due to structural flaws; its replacement was designed much more carefully.

Beervana & Beyond

By Lucy Burningham
Lucy Burningham (www.lucyburningham.com) is a food,
drink and travel writer based in Portland, Oregon

Pacific Northwesterners like to say that surviving the long, gray, rainy winters hinges on two things: beer and coffee. But what people drink here is just as important as where the stuff comes from, and thanks to a long lineage of fiercely independent pioneers, the Northwest has become a prime source for great wines, distilled spirits, and of course, sudsy craft brews and carefully roasted coffee beans.

Beer

While many West Coast breweries claim rights to the early roots of the craft brewing movement, there's no doubt Northwest brewers greatly influenced the evolution of craft beer. Starting in the early 1980s, a few intrepid home brewers in Portland started selling their beer commercially, including the McMenamin brothers, who opened the first post-Prohibition brewpub in Oregon in 1985 (they now operate 60 hotels, bars and restaurants, including 24 brewpubs, in the Northwest). Other still-operating pioneers include BridgePort Brewing and Widmer Brothers Brewery in Portland and Elysian Brewing, Pike Brewing and Hale's Ales in Seattle – all of which made small batch beers in a variety of styles, a strong deviation from the bland, mass-produced commercial beers that dominated the market at the time.

Craft brewing allowed brewers to get creative, and many of them started making beer inspired by traditional European styles before creating riffs of their own. Take the English-styled India Pale Ale (IPA), which once included hops as a preservative to keep beer fresh aboard long sea voyages between England and India. Northwest brewers added copious amounts of hops to create IPAs that include flavors and aromas reminiscent of everything from pine to grapefruit. High-hopped beers have come to define regional beers of all kinds; many Northwestern craft beer drinkers proudly call themselves Hop Heads, which is appropriate considering 90% of the nation's hops are grown in Oregon and Washington.

Local brewers say the secret to their good beers lies in the access to good ingredients: pure water, locally malted barley and locally cultivated yeasts. During late summer and early fall, during four weeks of hop harvest, many brewers head to local hops farms to pick up supplies of fresh, or wet, hops, which go into special 'fresh hop' beers. It's a tradition that can't be duplicated in other parts of the country, as the hops must be added to a beer-in-progress within 24 hours of being picked.

BEERVANA

Affectionately known as 'Beervana,' Portland boasts more than 30 breweries, more than any other city in the world.

Oregon and Washington grow 90% of the country's hops, one of the four main ingredients in beer.

STARBUCKS

Today, beer aficionados (otherwise known as beer geeks) sip and savor beer as they would wine, and some urban restaurants even have beer 'programs,' 'sommeliers' and cellars. Many brewpubs and restaurants host beer dinners, a chance to experience just how beers pair with different foods. But the heart of Northwest beer culture still rests squarely inside the basic brewpub, a place where beers are brewed onsite. Stroll through a local grocery store to see the scope of what local brewers are producing, or ask where locals consume craft beer. Most likely, you'll find a pint of fresh, small-batch beer brewed fresh in a place where you can pull up a chair, even if you're in tiny towns, including Twisp, Washington, and Baker City, Oregon. To learn more about the beer-making process, tour larger local breweries, including BridgePort in Portland (p223; scheduled tours on Saturday at 1pm, 3pm and 5pm or by appointment) and at Pike Pub & Brewery in Seattle (p77; by appointment only).

Coffee

The Northwest's progressive coffee culture was born in 1971, when Starbucks opened its first location across from Pike Place Market in Seattle. The idea, to offer a variety of roasted beans from around the world in a comfortable café, helped start filling the American coffee mug with more refined, complicated (and expensive) drinks compared to the ubiquitous Folgers and diner cups of joe. Specialty coffeehouses started springing up in Seattle and Portland during the 1980s, the foundation for today's burgeoning coffee culture.

Not only can you find Starbucks on every corner today, just like in almost every place in the US, but in the Northwest, independently owned coffeehouses occupy just as much real estate. Coffeehouse culture in the Pacific Northwest encourages lingering; think free wi-fi, comfortable indoor and outdoor seating, and little pressure to buy more food and drink even after camping out at a table for hours. But the desire to caffeinate extends beyond the café; you can't escape coffee shacks and cafés, even in rural areas.

Locals take coffee just as seriously as beer, and for the most part, they prefer dark roasts. But ultimately the quality of the beans and the roast determines a coffee's popularity. As with most food and drink in these parts, consumers demand to know details about what they're consuming—the wheres, hows and whys of harvests, roast times and bean grinders. That attention to detail has led to extensive coffee-sourcing programs at Northwest roasteries, and many coffee roasters personally travel around the globe to source their beans. That way they can describe how certain coffee farmers in Guatemala treat their workers and their coffee trees. At the most high-level cafés, experienced baristas will happily banter about the origins of any roast and will share their ideas about bean grinds and more.

Stumptown Coffee Roasters, which started in Portland with one roastery and café in 1999, helped small-batch roasting go mainstream (the company now has a location in New York City). These days, 'micro roasters,' who roast blends and single-origin coffees to precise specifications in garages, metal shops and basements of cafés, brown some of the best coffee beans in the world. Many Northwest cafés now feature beans from multiple micro roasters or they roast their own batches onsite.

Wine

Many Northwesterners can remember a time when 'local wine' meant a varietal from northern California. That's because wine growing in the Pacific Northwest is a relatively new phenomenon within the grand global tradition of wine making – most vines were planted in the past couple of decades. Recent successes have spurred a boom in grape

The Starbucks coffee chain now operates more than 16,000 stores in more than 50 countries.

planting and wine production. For the visitor, the burgeoning wine industry can mean an odd mixture of hole-in-the-wall tasting rooms and sprawling new hotels with wine-themed spa treatments, and it's easy to find people who will tout the non-Napa nature of the local wine regions or reminisce about the simpler times of days gone by.

Oregon's modern wine movement began in the 1960s, most notably when a handful of Californians made their way north to Oregon's Willamette Valley and planted pinot noir grapes, a delicate and difficult-to-grow variety. Oregon's hot, dry summers, cool, wet winters and rich volcanic soils mimic conditions in Burgundy, one of the few places in the world where the grape thrives. Pioneers David Lett, Dick Erath and Charles Coury planted the first pinot grapes – along with pinot gris, Chardonnay and Riesling – and today the grape has come to signify Oregon wines. In 2009, the state boasted 387 wineries and more than 19,000 acres of planted grapes everywhere from the dry, eastern Snake River Valley AVA (American Viticulture Area) to the Rogue and Applegate valleys in Southern Oregon.

Washington, which shares the same latitude as the French Burgundy and Bordeaux regions, has become the second-largest wine-producing region in the country (after California). Fans of the state's wines say it's all about the soil, which was enriched over 15,000 years ago when the Missoula floods deposited a thick layer of sediment around the Columbia River Gorge. The dry climate and long hours of daylight help produce Washington's eclectic mix of wines, 80% of which are red: merlot, cabernet sauvignon and syrah. The Columbia Valley AVA covers more than a third of the state and produces 99% of the state's wine, and a small part of that area, the Walla Walla region, has become the state's 'Napa Valley,' with a plethora of tasting rooms, wine shops and B&Bs. Other good bets include Yakima, Ellensburg and Spokane.

And don't forget BC, which has 192 wineries that straddle both sides of the Cascades: on Vancouver Island, the Gulf Islands and Fraser Valley and in the Okanagan Valley. These regions are known for crisp, fruity white and dessert wines, but reds, including cabernet sauvignon, cabernet franc, merlot and pinot noir, are just starting to catch up in number.

Spirits

Ever pioneering when it comes to imbibing, many inventive small-batch distilleries are popping up in Oregon. Look for bottles of delicious, unique specialty liquors, such as Eau de Vie of Douglas Fir and lava-filtered vodka from Clear Creek Distillery, a 20-year-old business started by Stephen McCarthy, who invented a creative use for the crop from his family's pear orchard in Hood River. Other distillers have emerged during the past decade, including Brandy Peak, Bendistillery and House Spirits Distillery. Even beer brewery Rogue Ales now offers its own line of spirits: try the hazelnut-spiced rum and wasabi vodka.

In Portland, five east-side distillers make up Distillery Row, one of the only concentrations of artisan distillers in the country. These craft distillers offer tasting-room hours, when visitors can sample everything from hazelnut vodka and absinthe to aquavit and fruit brandies. And in the tradition of artisan craftsmanship, the owners are the distillers, and they're frequently on hand during tastings to explain the distilling process and share their passion for the craft.

After California, Washington produces the most wine in the US, with over 650 registered wineries in 11 American Viticulture Areas.

Biodynamics, one of the new buzzwords in the wine world, focuses on the health of the soil by using organic and sustainable practices. For example, farmers deter pests by planting flowers or distributing bark chips rather than using pesticides.

BIODYNAMICS

BEERVANA & BEYOND

Pacific Northwest Cuisine

By Lucy Burningham
Lucy Burningham (www.lucyburningham.com) is a food,
drink and travel writer based in Portland, Oregon

Try to think of a food that isn't grown, raised or harvested in the Pacific Northwest, and you'll realize why in-the-know foodies have been putting down roots in the region for decades. Outsiders, who have been slower to discover the abundance, now flock here for the food, seeking a taste of Northwest cuisine prepared by talented chefs who cook local, seasonal foods with an alluring simplicity.

The late James Beard (1903–85), an American chef, food writer and Oregon native, believed foods prepared simply, without too many ingredients or complicated cooking techniques, allowed their natural flavors to shine. This philosophy has greatly influenced modern Northwest cuisine.

In some of Beard's writings, he describes his first tastes of wild mushrooms, herbs, truffles, berries and seafood, both in his hometown of Portland and on the coast, at Gearhart, where he spent his childhood summers. Those tastes of foods at their seasonal prime shaped his reverence for quality ingredients.

In the spirit of James Beard, Pacific Northwesterners don't like to think of their food as trendy or fussy, but at the same time, they love

> 'I don't like gourmet cooking or 'this' cooking or 'that' cooking. I like good cooking.' James Beard, American chef, food writer and native Oregonian (1903–85).

FUNGI FANATICS

Some people go out of their way to take advantage of local wild foods. While living in the Pacific Northwest means finding mushrooms growing in unexpected places, like car trunks and manicured lawns, it also means eating an amazing array of wild mushrooms, including the yellow-fluted chanterelle, bolete (otherwise known as porcini), morel and matsutake fresh from the forest.

While it's easy to walk into most woods and find mushrooms ripe for the picking, don't plan to eat just anything you find. Always show an experienced mushroom picker the fruits of your foray – many toxic mushrooms look identical to edible ones. Mycological societies have sprouted up around the region and welcome visitors to meetings and 'field trips.'

There you may encounter a burgeoning group of truffle enthusiasts. While Europeans have been sniffing out the expensive underground fungi with pigs and dogs for hundreds of years, Americans are newer to the hunt – three new varieties of truffles were discovered in Oregon just 30 years ago. To go on a bona fide truffle hunt or learn more about the mysterious edibles, contact the Oregon-based **North American Truffling Society** (www.natruffling.org), or attend the annual Truffle Festival in Eugene, Oregon, for dog-training workshops, elaborate truffle dinners and more.

to be considered innovative, especially when it comes to 'green,' hyperconscious eating. Don't be surprised if, when sharing a meal with locals, the conversation turns to how the food was prepared, grown, harvested, slaughtered or caught, which inevitably leads to conversations about the morals and ethics of its consumption. These are people who love to show off their homegrown vegetables, neighborhood-picked fruit, eggs gathered from backyard chickens and honey from nearby hives.

Bounty

The diverse geography and climate – a mild, damp coastal region with sunny summers and arid farmland in the east – foster all types of farm-grown produce. Farmers in these parts grow plenty of fruit, from melons, grapes, apples and pears to strawberries, cherries and blueberries. Veggies thrive here too: potatoes, lentils, corn, asparagus and Walla Walla sweet onions, all of which feed local and overseas populations.

Other well-known farmed products include hazelnuts (also known as filbert nuts; Oregon produces 99.9% of the hazelnuts grown in the US), in addition to herbs for harvest, especially lavender and spearmint. Hops farming also stands out as a regional specialty – the Northwest is the only region of the country with large-scale hops farms, which provide the sticky, fragrant cones that help add flavor, aroma and bitterness to many beers around the world.

Many wild foods thrive here as well, especially in the damper regions, such as the Coast Range. Foragers there seek out year-round wild mushrooms, as well as summertime huckleberries and blackberries.

With hundreds of miles of coastline and an impressive system of rivers, Northwest folk have access to plenty of fresh seafood. Depending on the season, specialties include razor clams, mussels, prawns, albacore tuna, Dungeness crab and sturgeon. Salmon remains one of the region's most recognized foods, whether it's smoked, grilled, or in salads, quiches and sushi. On the coast you can always find good seafood, and can often buy directly from the boat if you're willing to take the time to ask around. Of course, the closer you are to the source, the better the quality, so don't expect inland towns to express the same passion for seafood.

While the Northwest has a reputation for vegetarian and vegan eating, the past few years have spawned a meat backlash, and in true Northwest style, the carnivore craze has involved sourcing top-quality meats locally (one chef even started raising pigs who were fed hazelnuts during their final days). Small-scale meat farmers who raise cattle, lamb, pigs, chickens and goats have formed relationships with urban chefs, who will sometimes visit farms to participate in slaughter. Also, many meat farmers sell everything from grass-fed beef to pigs' feet and livers at farmers markets. Other evidence of meat mania? Butchering classes for the public as well as restaurants with their own 'house cured' meats, such as pancetta, sopressata and sausage.

January

Oregon Truffle Festival (www.oregontrufflefestival.com) – Eugene, OR

February

Chinese New Year – Vancouver, BC

March

Razor Clam Festival (www.oceanshores.org/clams.html) – Ocean Shores, WA

April

Crab, Seafood & Wine Festival (www.oldoregon.com/events) – Astoria, OR

May

Seattle Cheese Festival (www.seattlecheesefestival.com)

Portland Indie Wine Festival (www.indiewinefestival.com)

June

Comox Valley Shellfish Festival (www.comoxvalleyshellfishfestival.ca) – Vancouver Island, BC

Strawberry Festival (www.lebanonstrawberryfestival.com) – Lebanon, OR

Washington Brewers Festival (www.washingtonbeer.com) – Kenmore, WA

July

Oregon Brewers Fest (www.oregonbrewfest.com) – Portland, OR

International Pinot Noir Celebration (www.ipnc.org), McMinnville, OR

Local Leanings

Finding local products has become a popular pursuit for an increasingly food-aware, eco-minded population (most of whom believe that shipping food long distances wastes precious resources). The year-round availability of fresh produce has helped spawn the food-obsessed masses; unlike in other parts of the country, Northwesterners can always find some fruit or vegetable growing in season, outside a greenhouse. Many of those same food fanatics prefer organic, sustainably produced edibles, and conventional farmers and vintners are working to meet the demand by undergoing the two-to-three-year organic certification process.

Farmers markets have become the best examples of this new hyperawareness of food sourcing, and a handful even operate year-round. Some of the most popular markets go beyond offering produce, with everything from stalls selling pastries, artisan cheeses, honey and jam to hot foods like wood-fired pizzas, roasted peppers, and biscuits and gravy.

If you miss the markets, don't worry. Many grocery stores and specialty food stores prominently label locally made foods. Large-scale brands like Tillamook Cheese, which makes cheese, yogurt and ice cream in the coastal town of Tillamook, Oregon, have a devoted customer base that enjoys supporting local economies. So does the fast-food chain Burgerville, which buys ingredients for its menus from local sources (think Walla Walla onion rings, blackberry or hazelnut milkshakes and Tillamook cheddar burgers).

More upscale restaurant menus also reflect the public's passion for local foods. Some menus name the farms and harvesters who supplied specific ingredients. Others ask that servers mention the source of certain ingredients when naming the specials. If you're curious, ask servers for details about a restaurant's sourcing practices – most likely they'll be used to such requests.

Created by amateur foodies, food blogs and forums can help you sort through the numerous choices for dining out. Visit **An Exploration of Portland Food & Drink** (www.portlandfoodanddrink.com), the **Chowhound board for the Pacific Northwest** (www.chowhound.com/boards/4) and **Food Carts Portland** (www.foodcartsportland.com) for ideas.

Regional Cuisines

The further you head inland, away from the region's biggest cities, the less you'll find things like pork finished on hazelnuts and discussions about organic produce. Expect more 'traditional' meat and potato dish-

CART CULTURE

What do fried pies, burgers pressed between grilled cheese sandwiches, waffles slathered with Nutella, Thai street food, Italian-style espressos and poutine have in common? They're dishes served from some of Portland's most popular food carts. During the past few years, the number of food carts on the west coast has exploded as creative professional chefs and amateur home cooks have looked for cheap and easy ways to serve their creations to the masses. The public has hungrily sopped up cart food, especially in Portland, where more than 500 carts now operate citywide.

Cart culture thrives late at night, during the after-hours hunger period, and at lunchtime, although it's not hard to find carts open for business during other times of the day (don't ever give up hope of finding an early-morning pastry or afternoon plate of huevos rancheros). Most cart owners cook the food served there, and visiting carts will help you appreciate their efforts, which require long hours in tiny kitchens and a willingness to feed hungry people in a highly competitive marketplace.

While carts are required to have the capability of being mobile by law (all have wheels even if they're cosmetic), most park in permanent locations – in empty parking lots, driveways and street corners. In Portland, many carts are arranged in 'pods,' clusters that allow cart operators to share resources like dining tables, electricity and water. Find maps and descriptions of Portland's individual carts and pods on www.portlandfoodcarts.com; see p218 for our top choices.

es, pizzas and burgers, and fewer ethnic restaurants, with the exception of Mexican food. Thanks to a large immigrant population, you can find many excellent, authentic Mexican restaurants in unexpected places, like the Yakima Valley.

In the cities, you'll discover diverse ethnic cuisine, from Ethiopian to Ecuadorian, but it's Asian foods that really shine. Vancouver (see p367), in particular, offers a high concentration of Japanese, Thai, Chinese and Asian fusion restaurants, but it's easy to find all manner of Asian food everywhere in the Northwest.

As for 'Northwest cuisine,' the nebulous, all-encompassing term doesn't really mean much. Try asking a local, 'What exactly *is* Northwest cuisine?' and you might experience an uncomfortable pause followed by, 'local, seasonal and fresh,' or 'organic and sustainable.' While those words won't conjure up an image of a specific dish or narrow to a section of the spice rack, they hint at what truly defines the regional fare – simplicity.

Vegetarians, Vegans & Special Diets

More than in any other part of the country, vegetarians and vegans will discover plenty of food made just for them. So many people practice animal-free eating that even the smallest cafés and restaurants will frequently carry vegan pastries or desserts. Even if you're not dining at a strictly vegan or vegetarian restaurant (there are a handful in larger cities), you'll discover vegetarian-friendly menus at most eateries in the metropolitan areas. Ethnic cuisine, such as Thai and Indian, usually includes many vegetarian items, and there's no shortage of delicious main-dish meat-free dishes in cafés, restaurants and food carts.

Outside the cities vegetarians have fewer choices, and vegans even fewer still. Avoid Mexican restaurants, which usually cook seemingly meat-free dishes in lard, and opt for pasta and pizza joints, although restaurants of every kind usually have at least one vegetarian main meal. Don't be surprised if small towns in the eastern parts of Washington and Oregon (prime cattle country) don't have veggie burgers on the menu.

People with other types of dietary restrictions, including those who are gluten-free or lactose intolerant, will find friendly foods everywhere from restaurants to grocery stores, especially in the cities. If you're looking to avoid specific ingredients, be sure to ask. Most restaurants are happy to accommodate, and some already identify these types of foods on their menus.

Garlic Fest (www.chehalisgarlicfest.com) – Chehalis, WA

September

Wenatchee River Salmon Festival (www.salmonfest.org) – Leavenworth, WA

October

Fresh Hop Ale Festival (www.freshhopalefestival.com) – Yakima, WA

Wild Mushroom Celebration (www.funbeach.com/mushroom) – Long Beach Peninsula, WA

November

Wine Country Thanksgiving (www.willamettewines.com/events/thanksgiving-weekend) – Willamette Valley, OR

December

Winter Beer Fest (www.washingtonbeer.com) – Seattle, WA

Wild Things

The Pacific Northwest is home, sweet home to a wide range of spectacular wildlife. The region's mix of ocean, forests, grasslands, deserts and mountains creates a great diversity of habitats for both animals and plants; fortunately a number of these environments are protected within national wildlife refuges and parks. And while many animals can be relatively easily spotted from the shoreline or a vehicle, like grey whales or Roosevelt elk, others are much better at hiding in dense vegetation and rugged terrain. Be patient, and perhaps with a bit of luck you may be able to spot a bald eagle, pronghorn antelope or even a killer whale. Just remember to bring your binoculars and a sense of discovery, and start seeking them out!

Animals

Elk & Land Mammals

Among the Pacific Northwest's signature animals is the Roosevelt elk, whose eerie bugling courtship calls can be heard each September and October in forested areas throughout the region. Full-grown males may reach 1100lb and carry 5ft racks of antlers, so you won't soon forget catching sight of these creatures. During winter, large groups gather in lowland valleys and can be observed at a number of well-known sites such as Jewell Meadows Wildlife Area (about 65 miles northwest of Portland), Dean Creek Elk Viewing Area (p299) and along the Spirit Lake Memorial Highway in Mt St Helens National Volcanic Monument (p166). Also, Olympic National Park (p116) is home to the world's largest unmanaged herd of Roosevelt elk.

The open plains of eastern Oregon and Washington are the playing grounds of pronghorn antelope, curious-looking deer-like animals with two single black horns instead of antlers. Pronghorns belong to a unique antelope family and are only found in the American west, but they are more famous for being able to run up to 60mph for long stretches – they're the second-fastest land animal in the world. Boasting keen eyesight and an acute sense of smell, pronghorns keep their distance from humans, though they are sometimes spotted along highways, especially in the Hart Mountain National Antelope Refuge (p350) in southeast Oregon.

One of the elusive animals in Mt Rainier and other parks is the white mountain goat, which lives on high peaks and alpine meadows. Black bears and mountain lions also inhabit Mt Rainier and other Pacific Northwest forests, but their encounters with humans are rare. The beaver is another little-seen creature, but in the late 18th century they were so numerous that fur trading essentially started the exploration of the Pacific Northwest. It's also North America's largest rodent.

The marmot, another big rodent (which looks more like a fuzz ball), is often seen around mountain parking lots and campgrounds, espe-

Seasonal Guide to the Natural Year: A Month By Month Guide to Natural Events by James Luther Davis presents a seasonal breakdown and reveals the premier places to view wildlife in the Pacific Northwest.

The adorable American pika is quickly becoming an endangered species. Pikas live mostly in alpine environments, and these are being lost to global warming. For your chance to spot one, keep your eyes peeled on Mt Rainier or at Crater Lake.

PIKA

cially in popular places such as Olympic National Park (p116) or Manning Provincial Park. Marmots are adorable and might beg for food scraps, but no matter how lovingly they gaze into your eyes, resist the temptation to feed it – or any other wild creature.

If you're very lucky, you might spot wild mustangs in southeast Oregon's Steens Mountain Range (p349).

Fish

The rich ocean environment of the Pacific Northwest creates ideal conditions for a tremendous variety of fish and for the marine mammals that feed on them. There are plenty of harbors and small fishing towns lining the coast, proving this point.

Although salmon could be considered the very lifeblood of the Pacific Northwest, even locals can be forgiven for having a hard time keeping the names of different species straight. Not only do scientists argue over how to name and separate the seven species of salmon that are currently recognized, but these important fish have been given dozens of confusing common names such as king, coho, chinook sockeye and pink, to name but a few.

Salmon have a unique lifestyle of migrating out to sea as juveniles, then returning to the stream of their birth to breed and die as adults. The annual run of returning salmon used to be one of the greatest wildlife spectacles on the planet, with 11 to 16 million salmon in the Columbia River alone. Dams, habitat destruction, overfishing and hatcheries have reduced these majestic runs to mere shadows of their former selves, but it is still possible to view spawning salmon in sizable numbers each October.

You may also glimpse the odd-looking white sturgeon at one of the hatcheries or salmon viewing sites along the Columbia River, such as the Bonneville Fish Hatchery (p252). This monster fish can weigh up to 1800lb and is a living fossil from the time of the dinosaurs. Found only in the Columbia River system, it has been overfished for its delicious flesh – and adversely impacted by the river's many dams.

If you want to fish, see p41 for general information and the index for specific places where you can toss a line in.

Orcas & Marine Mammals

The aptly named 'killer whale' or orca is one of the few predators capable of attacking adult seals. This fierce predator is the largest dolphin in the world and the undisputed spirit animal of Pacific Northwest waters. Spending their entire lives in pods led by dominant females, orcas have

---

SALMON

WILD THINGS ANIMALS

Salmon conservation includes protecting populations around the entire Pacific Rim from the Russian Far East to northern California. Learn more at www.wild salmoncenter.org.

THE BANANA SLUG: DON'T TREAD ON ME

While walking down a forest path in one of the Pacific Northwest's many woodsy parks, you might come across a large, yellow slug sliming slowly along the trail and minding its own business. Don't panic and smash it underfoot; this isn't your typical garden pest, but rather the Pacific banana slug – a native slug usually found in damp, coastal coniferous forests from California to Alaska. Banana slugs are part of healthy forest ecosystems, and their food sources include decaying plants, seeds, mushrooms and dead animals.

The official mascot of at least one university, the banana slug can come in several colors, from yellow to green to brown; many have black markings too. These gastropods can grow up to 10in long and are hermaphroditic (both male and female). Perhaps the most bizarre part of their mating ritual is that they often have to gnaw off each other's penises to separate after doing the deed. Then they keep crawling along their merry way – as newly formed females.

TOP TIDE POOLS

Who doesn't like exploring tide pools? These miniature, fun-filled ecosystems are home to pretty starfish, colorful anemones, prickly sea urchins and secretive abalone. You can see hermit crabs scuttling about, small fishes darting around and mussels snapping shut. One or two hours before low tide is the best time for tide pooling; this gives you some time to explore before the tide comes back in.

Some words of warning, however: be aware of incoming tides and never get so absorbed in watching tide pools that you forget about the ocean. Sneaker waves are a serious danger and have swept away unwary beachgoers. Also, don't remove anything from a tide pool (it could be illegal!), and remember to watch where you step – hundreds of little lives will thank you.

Some exceptional places in the Pacific Northwest for exploring tide pools:

» **Haystack Rock, Cannon Beach, Oregon** (p284) Lots of critters in the pools, and there are often docents to explain what you're seeing. Also, keep a lookout for puffins, those comical-looking birds.

» **Yaquina Head Outstanding Nature Area, Oregon** (p291) Fabulous pools, and rangers often guide tours to them. These tide pools are actually an old abandoned rock quarry.

» **Yachats, Oregon** (p293) A couple miles of rocky shore to explore, all along the town. Watch the waves though. Also head south towards Florence and look for potential tide pools, as there are many in the area.

» **Rialto Beach, Olympic National Park, Washington** (p132) Head less than a mile north of the parking area, through 'Hole-in-the-Wall' (a hole in a rock) and seek out the tide pools. A beautiful, rugged beach too.

» **Beach 4 near Kalaloch, Olympic National Park, Washington** (p124) Great tide pools, and large sandstone rocks with starfish and anemones clinging to their bases at low tide. Rangers here give nature talks too.

» **Botanical Beach, Juan de Fuca Provincial Park, Vancouver Island BC** (p392) Host to one of the richest tidal zones on the west coast. Granite and sandstone rocks shelter pools and their inhabitants.

Orcas have pretty long life spans: on average, males can live 30 to 60 years, while females can live 50 to 80 years. While in captivity, however, most orcas live less than six years.

ORCAS

complex societies and large brains that rival those of humans. Several resident pods live around the San Juan Islands and prey on fish, while transient pods migrate along the outer coast and hunt seals, sea lions and sometimes whales. While on a ferry around Washington's Puget Sound, keep your eyes peeled – if you're lucky you may spot a dorsal fin or two; Vancouver's Telegraph Cove (p401) is another orca hot spot.

Anywhere on the Pacific Coast, it's hard to miss seals and sea lions. Most numerous are small, leopard-spotted harbor seals that drape themselves awkwardly over rocky headlands. From April to July harbor seal pups may be found resting on beaches while their mothers are hunting at sea. Well-intentioned people often take these pups to animal shelters without realizing that their mothers are nearby, so it's best to leave them alone.

The much larger and darker sea lions, with external ears and the ability to 'walk' on land by shuffling on their flippers, are renowned for the thick manes and roaring cries that give them their name. Sea lions easily adapt to human presence and can be common around docks and jetties, where they are sometimes blamed for stealing fish from fishermen.

Other famous marine mammals include gray and humpback whales, which make the longest migrations of any mammals in the world. The best time to view them offshore is November to December and April to May. Once hunted to near extinction, these majestic creatures have made a comeback and are a major reason for visiting the Pacific Northwest coast. See p42 for the best places to spot whales.

Birds

The Pacific Northwest is a stronghold for bald eagles, who feast on the annual salmon runs and nest in old-growth forests. With a 7.5ft wingspan, these impressive birds gather in huge numbers in places like Washington's Upper Skagit Bald Eagle Area (p145) and Oregon's Klamath Basin National Wildlife Refuges (p326). Other raptors include ospreys, often seen along large bodies of water like the Columbia River; peregrine falcons, happy to nest along sheer cliffs or under urban bridges; and the northern spotted owl, which can only live in old-growth forests. Common coastal birds include pelicans, cormorants, sandpipers and puffins.

The region's two prominent jay species include the dark-blue, black-crested Steller's jay, which occupies conifer forests throughout the Pacific Northwest and is notable for its loud screeching calls as it swoops down on picnickers, eagerly seeking out food scraps. Meanwhile, hikers and skiers in the high mountains may encounter the gray jay (or 'camp robber'), with its soft cooing whistles and gentle demeanor; these inquisitive jays are fearless in taking food from people's hands.

Clark's nutcracker, first observed by William Clark (of Lewis and Clark fame), is often found in high-altitude pine forests. Crows and ravens are other very commonly seen members of the corvid family; they're happy in both wild and more urban environments throughout the region. Sandhill cranes can sometimes be seen in fields, such as those on Sauvie Island (p213) near Portland.

In a more urban setting, Vaux's swifts put on an unforgettable show every September in northwest Portland, when up to 35,000 individuals (the largest congregation in the world) spiral down into Chapman school's old chimney to roost for the night. The event has become a popular local attraction, and hundreds of people take blankets and snacks to watch the phenomenon occur at sunset. See http://audubonportland.org/local-birding/swiftwatch.

Plants & Trees

The west and east sides of the Cascade Range are like day and night when it comes to geographical differences. The wet and wild west side captures most rain clouds coming in from the ocean, relieving them of their moisture and creating humid forests full of green life jostling for space. Meanwhile, the dry, deserty east side – robbed of rains by the tall Cascades – is mostly the stomping grounds for sagebrush and other semi-arid-loving vegetation. Don't fret, however; there are still plenty of lush pockets here and there in this region, especially along the foothills of several beautiful mountain ranges.

West of the Cascades

An abundance of rainfall on the west side supports the most impressive gathering of conifer trees anywhere in the world, with individual trees from six of the 30 or so species exceeding 500 years in age and reaching heights of over 195ft and diameters around of 6ft to 10ft. This lofty and grand forest is not only home to many creatures but also the foundation for a vast logging economy that props up countless small rural towns throughout the region.

The most ecologically and economically significant conifers are the Douglas fir, western hemlock and western red cedar, with Sitka spruce being dominant in the coastal fog zone. Taken together, these four trees account for the majority of the forested landscapes from ocean edge to high Cascades peak.

Bird-watchers in the Pacific Northwest have a unique online resource at http://thebirdguide.com.

Top Bird-Watching

» Klamath Basin National Wildlife Refuges (p326)

» Malheur National Wildlife Refuge (p347)

» Sauvie Island Wildlife Area (p213)

» Bald Eagle Interpretive Center (p145)

» Reifel Migratory Bird Sanctuary (p365)

Redwood trees outside California? Yes there are: *Sequoia Sempervirens'* northernmost distribution is near Brookings, Oregon's southernmost coastal town.

WILD THINGS PLANTS & TREES

WILD THINGS PLANTS & TREES

FIRE AND ICE: A GEOLOGIC HISTORY

From 16 to 13 million years ago, eastern Oregon and Washington witnessed one of the premier episodes of volcanic activity in Earth's history. Due to shifting stresses in the earth's crust, much of interior western North America began cracking along thousands of lines and releasing enormous amounts of lava that flooded over the landscape. On multiple occasions, so much lava was produced that it filled the Columbia River channel and reached the Oregon coast, forming prominent headlands like Cape Lookout. Today, the hardened lava flows of eastern Oregon and Washington are easily seen in spectacular rimrock cliffs and flat-top mesas.

Not to be outdone, the ice ages of the past two million years created a massive ice field from Washington to BC – and virtually every mountain range in the rest of the region was blanketed by glaciers. Even more dramatically, tongues of ice extending southward out of Canada prevented the 3000-sq-mile glacial Lake Missoula in present-day Montana from being able to drain. Consequently, on about 40 separate occasions, these massive ice dams burst, releasing more water than all the world's rivers combined and flooding much of eastern Washington up to 1000ft deep. Grand Coulee and Dry Falls of northeastern Washington are remnants of these spectacular floods, as are the crowd-pleasing waterfalls of the Columbia River Gorge that plummet over cliffs carved by the floods.

Top Five Geographic Wonders

The Great Bear Rain Forest of coastal BC is the largest intact temperate rain forest in the world and many environmental groups are working to keep it that way. See www.savethegreatbear.org.

On the west side of the Olympic Peninsula and in other coastal areas where rainfall may surpass 195in per year, these same trees reach incredible sizes and become engulfed in thick carpets of bright-green moss. These are the world-famous temperate rain forests of the Pacific Northwest.

Anyone hiking in these forests will soon come to recognize a common group of plants that form the typical understory. Included in this group are densely clumped sword ferns that cover entire hillsides, as well as taller thickets of small-leaved huckleberries bearing heavy loads of delicious fruits. The state flower of Washington, the pink-flowered rhododendron, and the state flower of Oregon, the holly-leaved Oregon grape, are abundant in these areas and add much color when in bloom.

East of the Cascades

For an entirely different experience, journey over the Cascades to a landscape many people think of as desert. Technically, the parched regions of eastern Oregon and Washington are semi-arid grassland or sagebrush steppe, but, terminology aside, they are still dry places. Forest cloaks some of the higher slopes and mountains, but the most common plant at lower elevations is the pungent sagebrush, the ubiquitous plant of the arid American west. Native grasses, cleared for crops or grazed out by cattle, are being replaced by an aggressive alien species called cheatgrass that leaves spiky seeds in your socks.

Common trees east of the Cascades include the stately ponderosa pine with its orange bark and sweet vanilla smell. A grove of ancient unlogged ponderosa pines is one of the most beautiful habitats in the Pacific Northwest. Unfortunately, most of these trees have been logged. In drier areas pines are replaced by densely foliaged western junipers, whose scaly needles look like miniature lizard tails. Junipers produce crops of attractive blue-gray berries, which provide the major food for half a dozen types of birds.

A surprising sight east of the Cascades is the fall colors displayed by cottonwoods. These trees require a lot of water to survive, so look for patches of golden yellow and orange along rivers and streams – and enjoy a bit of color in this mostly dry region.

Sustainable Pacific Northwest

The Pacific Northwest is one of the most progressive regions in the world when it comes to sustainability. Seattle, Portland and Vancouver all lead US and Canadian cities in recycling, bike friendliness, public transportation, storm-water management, renewable-energy use and green architecture. In Seattle, eco-roofs adorn City Hall and the Ballard Library; Portland's many street swales filter stormwater that would otherwise run off into the Willamette River; and in Vancouver, electric vehicle stalls are now required in all new condominium complexes. These are just a few examples of the culture of sustainability that has permeated this region. Being green isn't just the right thing to do here; it's the norm.

Of course, there's a flip side to every story. Urban sprawl is a problem in the suburbs of Seattle and Portland, and – despite a network of good public transportation – rush hour is a very real problem in big cities. Clear-cut forests cause hillsides to erode and fill streams with silt, which, along with the hundreds of hydroelectric dams in the area, impact wild salmon populations. And global climate change is occurring faster in the Pacific Northwest than in many other places in the world, affecting snow packs, melting glaciers and raising water levels in Puget Sound.

But at least most people living in this beautiful region realize that protecting what they have is a key to their future. They'll keep recycling, biking to work and doing whatever else they can to keep their environment as 'sustainable' as possible – and enjoy their glorious surroundings as reward.

> Over 6% of Portlanders bike to work – the highest percentage in the US. Seattle's figure is about 3%. What's the national average? That would be 0.5%.

What's the Alternative?

Renewable energy is big – really big – in the Pacific Northwest. The region leads North America in green power sales, and Oregon and Washington states both want 20% of their energy to come from renewable sources within a decade (BC has even loftier ambitions). Nuclear power is yesterday's news – in 2006, the Trojan Nuclear power plant in Rainier, Oregon was imploded to great fanfare.

Hydroelectric energy is huge in the Pacific Northwest, helped by all the rain feeding streams and rivers, which in turn power dams. In fact, the region gets nearly 70% of its power needs from hydroelectric – more than any other region in the US. Some of the biggest systems in the region are the Grand Coulee Dam (p191; itself the largest power generator in North America), the Bonneville Dam (p249) and the Bridge River Power Project in BC. The Grand Coulee and Bonneville dams lie on the Columbia River, which is North America's largest power-producing waterway.

These days, however, dams aren't all fine and dandy; one of their downsides is that they're highly detrimental to salmon migrations. This has become such as issue that many smaller dams have been or are being removed from various rivers in Washington, Oregon and BC.

Building new dams is becoming a thing of the past, but the demand for power is not backing down. Enter wind power, which has huge potential in the region – especially on the Columbia River Gorge. Inland heat draws air from the coast through the narrow gorge, creating a tunnel that produces reliable and forceful winds. Currently, Oregon and Washington are in the top five for states producing wind power, and more wind farms are being planned – including one of the world's largest in Oregon. The region is, quite literally, throwing its energy future into the wind.

Solar energy is, surprisingly, alive and well in the drizzly Pacific Northwest. This ain't Arizona, but the region does get enough sun to make this alternative energy viable – and even popular. Solar panels are becoming more and more common on rooftops here, both on homes and businesses, and the region boasts multiple leading solar-energy manufacturing companies.

Wave, tide and geothermal energies are other potential sources of energy in this geologically active area.

DAMS

The Columbia River system has more than 400 dams – more than any other river system in the world.

Eco-Cities of the Future

Seattle, Portland and Vancouver consistently top the 'Greenest Cities in the US' (or Canada) lists. With good public transportation, hundreds of miles of bike lanes and high-density population neighborhoods, these urban centers have made it a priority to live respectably within their natural surroundings.

And they're getting better. Vancouver wants to become the world's 'greenest city' by the year 2020; it already uses less energy and land per resident than its southerly big-city neighbors. Seattle recently completed its light-rail connection from downtown to Sea-Tac airport, and Portland has nudged its carbon emissions to below-1990 levels – the first of any US city. The region also has more than its share of green public spaces and community gardens.

The 'New Urbanism' or 'Urban Village' concepts are also popular in the Pacific Northwest, and emphasize compact, walkable communities that cut down the need to drive everywhere for work, schools and shopping. These neighborhoods also help facilitate a strong community feel to bring people together, a trait that has been lost in this era of modernism and urban sprawl.

DON'T DAM THE SALMON

Salmon depend on cold, clear waters during the early stages of their development – their eggs can't tolerate warm, silted waters. Unfortunately, logging (which creates erosion) and global warming are two strikes against them. A third is dams – and the Pacific Northwest has lots of them.

Dams hurt young salmon because they slow down water, which increases its temperature and the travel time for fish to get to the ocean. Many are also killed by hydroelectric turbines. And on the way back – going upstream – adult salmon have a hard time getting through dams, even with fish ladders to help them.

But things are slowly changing. Dams have been taken down on many rivers that salmon depend on throughout the Pacific Northwest, and more are slated for removal. Even though some of these barriers aren't huge – sometimes the dams are only a few feet high – every bit makes a difference when you're a small fish fighting your way upstream.

Seattle, Portland and Vancouver are some of the top cities embracing the Leadership in Energy and Environmental Design (LEED) certification system for 'green' buildings. These buildings use safe, sustainable building materials and incorporate water- and energy-efficient systems. Local examples include Seattle's Justice Center and Hyatt Hotel at Olive 8, Portland's Ecotrust building and Avalon Hotel & Spa, and Vancouver's Port Authority. Also keep an eye out for eco-roofs, which are covered with soil and living plants. These green (literally!) roofs absorb and filter rainwater, provide insulation, create wildlife habitats and lower surrounding air temperatures – and look ubercool.

Some people dislike wind power because of its association with bird and bat deaths. But when you take into account the wildlife killed by electric transmission lines, oil spills and pollution created by dirty energy, the figures pale in comparison.

Vancouver's Convention Centre is one of the world's greenest buildings. It features a gray- and black-water recycling system, seawater heat pump to provide heating and cooling, artificial reef as foundation (it's built over water) and six-acre green roof – the largest in Canada.

Survival Guide

Directory A–Z

Accommodations

Accommodations in this book fall into one of three categories:

		less than $100
budget	$	(double room)
mid-range	$$	$100 to $175
top end	$$$	more than $175

We have marked exceptional picks with a [TOP CHOICE] icon, but every property we recommend meets a certain baseline standard for quality within its class.

Room prices listed in this guidebook are high-season rates, excluding local taxes. Prices vary widely depending on the season, festivals and holidays, whether it's a weekend and sometimes even vacancy rates. Prices are generally highest in summer (or in winter at ski resort towns), and some places have two- or three-night minimum stays. Always ask about discounts, packages and promotional rates, especially in low seasons. Some places give better rates if you book online.

It's always a good idea to see a room before paying for it. Rooms can vary widely within an establishment. Reserve ahead during festivals and holidays, or in summer (especially on the coast). If you plan on arriving late, let your hotel know or it might give away your room.

Many lodgings have only nonsmoking rooms, but you can usually smoke outdoors. Air-conditioning is common in inland places but nearly nonexistent along the coast, which is much cooler. Some hotels take pets, but always ask beforehand. Internet computers or wi-fi access are commonplace except in backcountry towns. Children (defined as anything from under six to under 18) can often stay free with their parents.

B&Bs

If you want an intimate alternative to impersonal hotel rooms, stay at a B&B. They're typically in large historical or country homes with charm-ing furnishings and just a few rooms – usually with private bathrooms. The owners tend to be friendly and are happy to offer advice on the area. Most B&Bs appreciate advance reservations, though some will take the occasional drop-in. Nearly all prohibit smoking and many don't allow young children. Substantial breakfasts are nearly always included in the price, which is usually between $90 and $200.

B&Bs abound throughout Oregon and Washington, but are particularly concentrated on the islands of Puget Sound and along the Oregon coast. Countless B&B websites compile lists and photos, including:

BC Innkeepers (www.bcsbestbnbs.com)

Bed & Breakfast Explorer (www.bbexplorer.com)

Oregon B&B Guild (www.obbg.org)

Washington Bed & Breakfast Guild (www.wbbg.com)

Camping & Recreational Vehicles (RVs)

Camping is a wonderful, cheap way to appreciate the outdoors, especially in summer. The Pacific Northwest is strewn with campgrounds, both public and private, and pitching a tent usually costs $15 to $20. RV site costs depend on hookups, but generally run from $20 to $30.

Campground facilities vary widely. Basic or primitive campgrounds usually have vault toilets, fire pits and (sometimes) drinking water, and are most common in national forests and on Bureau of Land

Management (BLM) land. The state- and national-park campgrounds tend to be the best equipped, featuring picnic benches, flush toilets, hot showers and RV hook-ups. Private campgrounds are usually close to town and tend to cater to RVers, with good services and facilities such as full hookups, showers, coin laundry, swimming pools, play areas and even small convenience stores.

Most campgrounds along the coast are open year-round, but inland where it snows they close in winter. Dispersed (or backcountry) camping is only permitted in national parks with a permit. It's a good idea to reserve campsites in summer.

Yurts, found mostly at state parks, are Mongolian-style round houses with a canvas shell; see p281 for details. Reserve yurts as far in advance as you can in summer.

Hostels

Hostels are an excellent budget option; what they lack in amenities and privacy they make up for in savings and a ready-made travelers' community. Most have cooking facilities, common lounges, information boards, tour services and computer access. Dormitory beds (sometimes segregated by sex) average from $20 to $26, with private rooms priced similarly to a budget hotel. Some hostels have a small charge for sheet and towel rental.

Hostelling International (HI; www.hiusa.org in the US, www.hihostels.ca in Canada) lists member hostels. Independent hostels have comparable rates and conditions to HI/AYH hostels. During high seasons, reserve ahead.

Lodges

The word 'lodge' is used with great latitude in the Northwest. Places such as Timberline Lodge on Mt Hood and Paradise Inn on Mt Rainier are magnificent old log structures boasting dozens of woods-infused, comfortable rooms with handcrafted details. Most other lodges are more modest. Those on the lakes of the Cascades have cabin accommodations, campsites, boat rentals and at least a small store if not a café. Some of these are just fine; others are quite unspectacular. If your standards are exacting, check websites and make careful inquiries before heading up long mountain roads to marginal accommodations best suited to hardened anglers.

Motels & Hotels

Motels are cheaper than hotels, with rooms that open to the outside and often surround a parking lot. Hotels have inside hallways, nicer lobbies and provide extra services.

As a rule, motels offer the best lodging value for the money. Rooms are unmemorable but usually comfortably furnished and clean. Amenities vary, but expect a private bathroom, cable TV, telephone with free local calls, heating and air-conditioning. Many have small refrigerator, coffeemaker and microwave. Some have kitchenette, coin laundry and swimming pool.

Rental Accommodations

In many coastal areas and in Central Oregon and Washington, owners of weekend or vacation homes depend on occasional rentals to help pay the mortgage. Most of these well-maintained, furnished homes have at least three bedrooms. For a family or a group of friends these homes may represent some of the best-value lodgings in the area.

Descriptions of rental properties can usually be found on the internet. Local visitors centers should also be able to supply informa-tion. Some restrictions apply: houses are often occupied by the owners on major holidays and summer weekends, there's usually a minimum stay of two nights and there may be a housekeeping fee.

Resorts

Certain parts of Oregon and Washington are home to huge resort communities offering diverse rental options such as condominiums, apartments, lodge rooms, cottages and houses. These are usually privately owned and rented out for supplemental income. More upscale versions boast amenities such as golf courses, tennis courts, swimming pools and guided outdoor activities.

Business Hours

Exceptions to standard opening hours have been specifically noted in the reviews in this book. For Sights, Activities and Information, we've mostly listed high-season hours. Mid- or low-season hours vary throughout the year.

TYPE OF BUSINESS	STANDARD OPENING HOURS
businesses	9am-5pm
post offices & banks	8am or 9am-5pm Mon-Fri, some 8am or 9am-2pm Sat
restaurants	7-11am breakfast, 11:30am-2:30pm lunch, 5-10pm dinner
shops	9am or 10am-5pm or 6pm (malls 9pm) Mon-Sat, noon-5pm Sun
supermarkets	24hr in large cities

Discount Cards

Many hostels in the Pacific Northwest are members of **HI-USA** (www.hiusa.org), which is affiliated with **Hostelling International** (www. hihostels.com). You don't need a HI-USA card to stay at these hostels, but having one saves you a few bucks per night. You can buy one at the hostel when checking in. If you're a student, bring along your student ID, which can get you discounts on transportation and admission to sights and attractions.

People over the age of 65 (or sometimes younger) often qualify for the same discounts as students; any identification showing your date of birth should suffice. Contact the **American Association of Retired Persons** (AARP; ☎888-687-2277; www.aarp.org), an advocacy group for Americans 50 years and older and a good resource for travel discounts.

Electricity

120V/60Hz

120V/60Hz

Gay & Lesbian Travelers

As elsewhere in North America, gay life in the Pacific Northwest is most tolerated in urban centers, while attitudes tend to be far less accepting in the hinterlands. In the major cities of Seattle, Vancouver and Portland, and even some smaller towns, such as Eugene and Victoria, travelers will find everything from gay religious congregations to gay hiking clubs, while in the rural areas they may want to keep their orientation to themselves.

The Capitol Hill neighborhood is the center of gay life in Seattle. Helpful websites include:

Gay/Lesbian Business Association (www.thegsba. org)

Lesbian Resource Center (www.lrc.net)

Pride Parade (www.seattle pride.org) Late June.

Seattle Gay News (www. sgn.org)

Be proud in Oregon – Portland's mayor, Sam Adams, is openly gay. Useful contacts include:

Gay & Lesbian Community Yellow Pages (www. pdxgayyellowpages.com)

Just Out (www.justout.com) Biweekly newspaper.

Pride Festival (www.pride nw.org) Mid to late June.

On Vancouver Island:

Pink Pages (www.gayvictoria .ca/pinkpages)

Vancouver Pride Parade & Festival (www.vancouverpride. ca) Late July/early August.

Health

Altitude Sickness

Acute Mountain Sickness (AMS), aka 'Altitude Sickness,' may develop in those who ascend rapidly to altitudes greater than 8000ft (2400m), but sometimes less. Being physically fit offers no protection. Those who have experienced AMS in the past are prone to future episodes. The risk increases with faster ascents, higher altitudes and greater exertion. Symptoms may include headaches, nausea, vomiting, dizziness, malaise, insomnia and loss of appetite. Severe cases may be complicated by fluid in the lungs (high-altitude pulmonary edema) or swelling of the brain (high-altitude cerebral edema).

The best treatment for AMS is descent. If you are exhibiting symptoms, do not ascend. If symptoms are severe or persistent, descend immediately. When traveling to high altitudes, avoid overexertion, eat light meals and abstain from alcohol. If your symptoms are more than mild or don't resolve promptly, see a doctor. Altitude sickness should be taken seriously; it can be fatal when severe.

Heat Exhaustion or Heatstroke

Dehydration is the main contributor to heat exhaustion. Symptoms include weakness, headache, irrita-

PRACTICALITIES

» **Time zones** Pacific Standard Time zone – GMT -0800 (-0700 during daylight savings). A tiny sliver along the Oregon-Idaho border lies in the Mountain Standard Time zone – GMT -0700 (-0600 during daylight savings).

» **Distances** In the US, for distance use feet, yards and miles; for weight use ounces, pounds and tons. Canada officially uses the metric system.

» **Radio** National Public Radio (www.npr.org) – a progressive yet impartial approach to news and talk radio.

» **Post** US Postal Service (www.usps.com) and Canada Post (www.canadapost.ca) provide dependable, timely service.

» **Laundry** Self-service, coin-operated laundries are widely available.

» **Smoking** Smoking is banned in all indoor public spaces throughout the Pacific Northwest, including bars and restaurants. Some bars have patios where smoking is allowed.

bility, nausea or vomiting, sweaty skin, a fast but weak pulse and a normal or slightly elevated body temperature. Treatment involves getting out of the heat, fanning the victim and applying cool wet cloths to the skin, laying the victim flat with their legs raised and rehydrating with water containing a quarter of a teaspoon of salt per liter. Recovery is usually rapid and it is common to feel weak for some days afterwards.

Heatstroke is a serious medical emergency. Symptoms come on suddenly and include weakness, nausea, a hot, dry body with a body temperature of over 106°F, dizziness, confusion, loss of coordination, fits and eventually collapse and loss of consciousness. Seek medical help and commence cooling by getting the person out of the heat, removing their clothes, fanning them and applying cool, wet cloths or ice to their body, especially to the groin and armpits.

Hypothermia

To prevent hypothermia, keep all body surfaces cov-

ered, including the head and neck. Synthetic materials such as fleece or Gore-Tex provide excellent insulation. Because the body loses heat faster when it is wet, stay dry at all times. Change inner garments promptly when they become moist. Keep active, but get enough rest. Consume plenty of food and water. Be especially sure not to have any alcohol. Caffeine and tobacco should also be avoided.

Watch for the 'umbles' – stumbles, mumbles, fumbles and grumbles – which are important signs of impending hypothermia. If someone appears to be developing hypothermia, you should insulate them from the ground, protect them from the wind, remove wet clothing or cover them with a vapor barrier such as a plastic bag, and transport them immediately to a warm environment and a medical facility. Warm fluids (but not coffee or tea – noncaffeinated herbal teas are OK) may be given if the person is alert enough to swallow.

Ocean Waves & Riptides

Never turn your back on the ocean when beachcombing or examining tide pools. Large 'sneaker waves' often catch the unwary and sweep them out to sea. If you're swimming and get caught in a riptide, which pulls you away from shore, don't fight it – even expert swimmers can get exhausted and drown. Instead, swim parallel to the shoreline, and once the current stops pulling you out, swim back to shore.

Wildlife

BEARS & MOUNTAIN LIONS

It's unlikely that you'll run into a bear or mountain lion while hiking or camping. Talking or making noise (to avoid surprising them) usually scares them off. Bears are attracted to campgrounds, where they may find accessible food in bags, tents, cars or picnic baskets. Get advice from the local ranger station or follow posted instructions; never feed bears or other wildlife!

You'd be very lucky to even glimpse a mountain lion (also called a cougar or puma). Adult travelers aren't much at risk of an attack, but unattended children and pets can be. Loud noises and making yourself appear bigger (hold open your jacket) will usually scare them off.

TICK BITES

Ticks are parasitic arachnids that may be present in brush, forest and grasslands, where hikers often get them on their legs or in their boots. Adult ticks suck blood from hosts by burrowing into the skin and can carry infections such as Lyme disease.

Always check your body (or pet) for ticks after walking through high grass or thickly forested area. If you find an attached tick, grab its head with tweezers as close to the skin as possible and gently pull it backwards – do not twist it. (If no tweezers are

Entering the USA

Getting into the United States can be a bureaucratic nightmare, depending on your country of origin, as the rules keep changing. For up-to-date information about visas and immigration, check the website of the **US Department of State** (http://travel.state.gov/visa/visa_1750.html) and the travel section of the **US Customs & Border Protection** (www.cbp.gov).

In 2004 the US Department of Homeland Security introduced a new set of security measures called US-VISIT. Upon arrival in the US, all visitors are photographed and have their index fingers scanned. Eventually, this biometric data will be matched when you leave the US. For full details about US-VISIT, check with a US consulate or online at www.dhs.gov/us-visit.

Entering Canada

Visitors to Canada from major Western countries need no visa, but citizens of more than 150 nations do. Visa requirements change frequently, so check **Citizenship & Immigration Canada** (http://www.cic.gc.ca/english/visit/visas.asp) before you leave.

Officially, US citizens don't need a passport or visa to enter Canada by land; some proof of citizenship, such as a birth certificate along with state-issued photo identification, will ordinarily suffice. However, since the introduction of tighter border security, officials recommend that US citizens carry a passport to facilitate entry.

Customs

US customs allows each person over the age of 21 to bring 200 cigarettes or 100 cigars (non-Cuban unless from an authorized Cuba trip) or 2kg (4.4lbs) of smoking tobacco duty free into the country, plus 1L of liquor. US citizens and permanent residents are allowed to import, duty free, $800 worth of gifts from abroad, while non-US citizens are allowed to bring in $100 worth. US law permits you to bring in, or take out, up to $10,000 (cash, travelers checks etc); greater amounts must be declared to customs.

Canadian Customs in BC allows visitors 19 years and older to bring in 1.14L of liquor or 1.5L of wine or a case of beer (24 cans or bottles), plus 200 cigarettes, duty-free. You can bring in gifts up to C$60 in value without being taxed.

Consulates in the Pacific Northwest

Australia Washington (☑206-575-7446; 401 Andover Park East, Tukwila); British Columbia (☑604-684-1177; 1075 West Georgia St, Suite 2050, Vancouver)

Canada Oregon (☑503-417-2166; 805 SW Broadway, Suite 1900, Portland); Washington (☑206-443-1777; 1501 4th Ave, Suite 600, Seattle)

France Oregon (☑503-725-5298; 1721 SW Broadway, 141F Cramer Hall at Portland State University, Portland); Washington (☑206-256-6184; 2200 Alaskan Way, Suite 490, Seattle); British Columbia (☑604-637-5300; 1130 Pender St, Suite 1100, Vancouver)

Germany Oregon (☑503-222-0490; 200 SW Market St, Suite 1695, Portland); British Columbia (☑604-684-8377; 999 Canada Pl, Suite 704, Vancouver)

New Zealand (☑604-684-7388; 888 Dunsmuir St, Suite 1200, Vancouver, BC)

UK Oregon (☑503-227-5669, calls only); British Columbia (☑604-683-4421; 1111 Melville St, Suite 800, Vancouver)

USA (☑604-685-4311; 1095 W Pender St, Vancouver, BC)

---

available, use your fingers, but protect them from contamination with a piece of tissue or paper.) Do not burn or smother the tick as it may release infected fluids. Wash your hands, bite site and tweezers after this procedure.

If you suspect Lyme disease, you might want to keep the tick. Place it in a vial after removal and make a note of the date and where on the body the tick was found. If you get sick in the following

couple of weeks, consult a doctor.

SNAKE BITES

There are several varieties of venomous snakes in the Pacific Northwest, but none are likely to cause instantaneous death – and antivenins are available. It's a good idea to wear sturdy, protective footgear where snakes are active; watch especially for rattlesnakes in dry desert country, where they like to bask on trails.

First aid is to place a light constricting bandage over the bite, keep the wounded part below the level of the heart and move it as little as possible. Don't overreact, stay calm and get to a medical facility as soon as possible. Bring the dead snake for identification if you can, but don't risk being bitten again. Do not use the mythic 'cut an X and suck out the venom' trick; this causes more damage to snakebite victims than the bites themselves.

Legal Matters

If you are stopped by the police for any reason in the USA, there is no system of paying fines on the spot. Attempting to pay the fine to the officer may lead to a charge of attempted bribery. Most matters can be handled by mail.

If you are arrested for more serious offenses, you have the right to remain silent and are presumed innocent until proven guilty. There is no legal reason to speak to a police officer if you don't wish to. All persons who are arrested are legally allowed the right to make one phone call. If you don't have a lawyer, friend or family member to help you, call your embassy. The police will give you the number upon request. If you don't have a lawyer, one will be appointed to you free of charge.

You must be at least 16 years old to drive in Oregon, Washington or BC. The drinking age is 21 in Washington and Oregon, and 19 in BC, and you need photo identification that proves your age. Stiff fines, jail time and other penalties can be incurred for driving under the influence

(DUI) of alcohol or drugs. It is also illegal to carry open containers of alcohol inside a vehicle. Containers that are full and sealed may be carried, but if they have been opened or are empty put them in the trunk.

The age of consent in Washington and BC is 16. In Oregon it's 18. Travelers should note that they can be prosecuted under the law of their home country regarding age of consent, even when abroad.

Possessing illegal drugs is always a bad idea, and if you're caught expect fines, lengthy jail sentences and/ or deportation (if you're a foreigner).

Public Holidays

Holidays falling on a weekend are usually observed the following Monday.

New Year's Day January 1 (USA & Canada)

Martin Luther King Jr Day Third Monday in January (USA)

Presidents' Day Third Monday in February (USA)

Good Friday Friday before Easter Sunday (Canada)

Easter Sunday in late March or early April (USA & Canada)

Easter Monday Monday after Easter (Canada)

Victoria Day Monday preceding May 24 (Canada)

Memorial Day Last Monday in May (USA)

Canada Day July 1 (Canada)

Independence Day July 4 (USA)

Labor Day First Monday in September (USA & Canada)

Columbus Day Second Monday in October (USA)

Thanksgiving Day Second Monday in October (Canada); fourth Thursday in November (USA)

Veterans' Day November 11 (USA)

Remembrance Day November 11 (Canada)

Christmas Day December 25 (USA & Canada)

Boxing Day December 26 (Canada)

Tipping

Tipping for certain services is the norm in the US and Canada. If service is truly appalling, however, don't tip. Customary tipping amounts:

SERVICE	USUAL TIP
bartenders	15% of the bill
bellhops, skycaps in airports	$1-2 per bag
housekeeping staff	$2 daily, left on the pillow each day
parking valets	$1-2
restaurant servers	15-20% of the pretax bill (no tax in Oregon)
taxi drivers	10-15% of metered fare

Tourist Information

Oregon, Washington and BC have state and provincial tourist bureaus that offer glossy guides, maps and plenty of other pertinent travel information. Individual cities and regions also maintain visitors centers, which are often run by the local chamber of commerce; contact details for these are in the regional chapters.

Oregon Tourism Commission (☎800-547-7842; www.traveloregon.com)

Tourism British Columbia (☎800-435-5622; www.hellobc.com)

Washington State Tourism (☎800-544-1800; www.experiencewa.com)

Travelers With Disabilities

If you have a physical disability, travel within the Pacific Northwest won't be too difficult. The Americans with Disabilities Act (ADA) requires all public buildings in the US – including most hotels, restaurants, theaters and museums – to be wheelchair accessible. Most sidewalks in the Pacific Northwest are wide and smooth and many intersections have curb cuts and sometimes audible crossing signals.

Lift-equipped buses are the norm in Washington, Oregon and BC, and many taxi companies have wheelchair-accessible cabs. Some municipal bus networks provide door-to-door service for people with disabilities. Disabled travelers using Washington State Ferries can phone ☎206-515-3460 for a copy of *The Accessible Ferry, a Guide for Disabled Passengers* (also available in Braille). Most car-rental franchises are able to provide hand-controlled models at no extra charge – but reserve well ahead. All major airlines, Greyhound buses

and Amtrak trains allow service animals to accompany passengers (bring documentation for them). Airlines will also provide assistance for connecting, boarding and disembarking if requested with your reservation.

Many state and national parks in the Northwest maintain a nature trail or two for use by wheelchair-using travelers. For a list of accessible trails in Washington State, see www.parks.wa.gov/ada-rec. A relatively new website for accessible trails in the US is www.greatwheelchairaccessiblehikes.com; check out its 'other resources' link for more websites.

The America the Beautiful Access Pass (previously known as the Golden Access Passport; these are still honored) is available free to blind or permanently disabled US travelers with documentation. It gives free lifetime access to US national parks and wildlife refuges and 50% off campground use. For more information see http://www.nps.gov/fees_passes.htm.

Organizations & Resources

A number of organizations and tour providers specialize in serving disabled travelers:

Access-Able Travel Source (www.access-able.com) Excellent website with good links.

Disabled World (www.disabled-world.com/travel) Click on 'Canada' or 'United States' for general information.

Emerging Horizons (www.emerginghorizons.com) The website of a magazine about accessible travel.

Mobility International USA (www.miusa.org) Advises travelers with disabilities on mobility issues; runs educational exchange programs.

MossRehab ResourceNet (www.mossresourcenet.org) Lists extensive web contacts.

New Directions (www.newdirectionstravel.com) Specializes in developmentally challenged travelers.

Society for Accessible Travel & Hospitality (www.sath.org) Useful links and information specifically about travel.

Flights, tours and rail tickets can be booked online at www.lonely planet.com/bookings.

Transportation

GETTING THERE & AWAY

Air

Domestic airfares fluctuate significantly depending on the season, day of the week, length of stay and flexibility of the ticket for changes and refunds. Still, nothing determines fares more than demand, and when business is slow, airlines drop fares to fill seats. Airlines are competitive and at any given time any one of them could have the cheapest fare.

Most air travelers to the Pacific Northwest will arrive at one of the three main airports in the region:

Seattle-Tacoma International (SEA; www.portseattle. org) Known locally as 'Sea-Tac'.

Portland International Airport (PDX; www.flypdx. com)

Vancouver International Airport (YVR; www.yvr.ca) All offer a good selection of regularly scheduled flights to both domestic and international destinations.

Land

Border Crossings

The main overland point of entry from Washington to Vancouver, BC, is at the Blaine/Douglas (aka Peace Arch) crossing, on the northern end of I-5, which continues as Hwy 99 on the Canadian side. This crossing has the longest lines.

Commercial trucks (and regular vehicles) use the Pacific Hwy crossing, 3 miles (5km) east of Blaine/Douglas; from I-5, take exit 275 (the one before Blaine). If you're entering Canada with duty-free goods, you'll need to cross here.

A good choice during busy times is the little-known Lynden/Aldergrove crossing, about 30 miles (50km) east of Blaine/Douglas. Take exit 256 off I-5, just north of Bellingham, and follow Hwy 539.

Lastly there's Sumas/Huntingdon, 62 miles (100km) east of Blaine/Douglas. It's best for heading to BC's interior; take exit 255 off I-5, just north of Bellingham, and follow Hwy 542 and then Hwy 9.

All crossings are open 24 hours except Lynden/Alder-

grove, which is open 8am to midnight. During the week, expect to wait five to 20 minutes; on weekends and holidays, an hour or more. For details check www.van couver.hm/border.html (tips and directions) or www.bor derlineups.com (wait times, web cams and hours).

Many travelers also cross the border by ferry, principally on journeys from Anacortes to Sidney, BC (near Victoria) and from Port Angeles to Victoria. See p455 for details.

Both US citizens and foreigners should check the 'International Visitors' box on p451.

Bus

In car-oriented societies like the USA and Canada, bus travel takes second place. Service is infrequent or inconvenient, networks are sparse and fares can be relatively high. Air travel is often cheaper on long-distance routes, and it can even be cheaper to rent a car, especially for shorter routes. However, very long-distance bus trips can be available at decent prices if you purchase or reserve tickets in advance.

The largest nationwide bus company in the USA and Canada, **Greyhound** (☑800-231-2222; www.greyhound. com) operates to major and minor cities throughout the Pacific Northwest; check its website for destinations and schedules. Tickets can be purchased by phone or online with a major credit card and mailed to you if purchased 10 days in advance, or picked up at the terminal with proper identification. Buying tickets in advance will save you money, as will traveling during weekdays and nonholiday times. Children, students, military personnel, veterans and seniors are eligible for discounts as well; check Greyhound's website for specifics.

Car & Motorcycle

Although the quickest way to get to the Pacific Northwest is usually by plane, the best way to get around is by car. If you have time, it can be less expensive to drive to the Pacific Northwest than to fly and rent a car. And the region is blessed with many scenic highways that make driving long distances a feasible alternative.

Note that driving regulations, such as speed limits and the permissibility of right turns on red lights or making U-turns, can vary somewhat from state to state. Also, Oregon law prohibits you from pumping your own gasoline – all stations there are full service.

Train

The Pacific Northwest is well served by **Amtrak** (☎800-872-7245; www.amtrak. com) in the USA and **VIA Rail** (☎888-842-7245; www. viarail.ca) in Canada. Trains are comfortable, if slow, and equipped with dining and lounge cars on long-distance routes.

Amtrak's *Coast Starlight* links Los Angeles to Portland and Seattle via Oakland and other West Coast cities. The *Empire Builder* runs from Chicago to the Pacific Northwest via Minneapolis and Spokane, where it separates to reach Portland and

Seattle. VIA Rail's *Canadian* runs between Vancouver and Toronto. Schedules can be very fluid: arrival and departure times become less reliable the further you are from the starting point.

Fares on Amtrak vary greatly, depending on the season and what promotions are going. You can beat the rather stiff full-price fares by purchasing in advance – the sooner you buy, the better the fare. Round trips are the best deal, but even these can be more expensive than airfares. Children, students, veterans, military personnel, seniors and even AAA members are eligible for discounts; check Amtrak's website for details, and for Rail Passes, which are a good option for longer travel periods.

GETTING AROUND

Air

Seattle, Portland and Vancouver are the principal hubs for flights to outlying Pacific Northwest cities, which include (but are not limited to) Klamath Falls, Eugene, Medford, Salem, Yakima, Walla Walla, Spokane, Bellingham and Wenatchee. Seattle also has air destinations in the San Juan Islands and Victoria.

Bicycle

Cycling is a very popular recreational activity in the Pacific Northwest, and an interesting, inexpensive and environmentally friendly way to travel. Roads are good, shoulders are usually wide, and there are many decent routes for bikes. Summer is best; during other seasons, changeable weather can be a drawback, especially at high altitudes where thunderstorms are frequent. In some areas, the wind can slow your progress to a crawl (traveling west to east and north to south is generally easier than the opposite), and water sources can be far apart. Spare parts are widely available and repair shops are numerous, but it's still important to know some basic mechanical work, such as fixing a flat tire.

Seattle, Portland and Vancouver all have great bike paths, and many streets have bike lanes. Some local buses in these cities provide bike racks, and you can also take your bikes on light-rail systems, trains and ferries. On the road, cyclists are generally treated courteously by motorists. Bicycles are prohibited on interstate highways if there is a frontage road; however, where a suitable frontage road or other alternative is lacking, cyclists are permitted on some interstates.

Bicycles can be transported by air, usually in a bike bag or box, although

---

CLIMATE CHANGE & TRAVEL

Every form of transport that relies on carbon-based fuel generates CO_2, the main cause of human-induced climate change. Modern travel is dependent on aeroplanes, which might use less fuel per mile per person than most cars but travel much greater distances. The altitude at which aircraft emit gases (including CO_2) and particles also contributes to their climate change impact. Many websites offer 'carbon calculators' that allow people to estimate the carbon emissions generated by their journey and, for those who wish to do so, to offset the impact of the greenhouse gases emitted with contributions to portfolios of climate-friendly initiatives throughout the world. Lonely Planet offsets the carbon footprint of all staff and author travel.

BIKE RENTALS & CO-OPS IN THE BIG CITIES

If you are thinking of buying a bicycle, consider patronizing bike cooperatives (co-ops) – worker-owned, nonprofit organizations that repair bikes and/or take in donated bikes and refurbish them for sale. They often encourage cycling by renting bikes, supporting community biking events and organizing work-for-trade programs. Try the following:

Bike Kitchen (604-827-7333; www.thebikekitchen.com; 6138 Student Union Blvd, Vancouver) Student-run, full-service co-op that sells and rents refurbished bikes.

BikeWorks (206-725-9408; www.bikeworks.org; 3709 S Ferdinand St, Seattle) Not really a co-op but a nonprofit organization with an 'earn-a-bike' youth program; offers maintenance classes and donates bikes to needy communities.

City Bikes (503-239-0553; www.citybikes.coop; 1914 SE Ankeny, Portland) Worker-run co-op that fixes bikes, and sells and rents them from its annex on 734 SE Ankeny.

Community Cycling Center (503-287-8786; www.communitycyclingcenter.org; 1700 NE Alberta St, Portland) Helps cyclists – especially youths – through educational bike programs and services.

airlines often charge an additional fee. Check this with the airline in advance, preferably before you pay for your ticket. You can hire bikes in most cities for reasonable prices; you'll find places that rent them throughout this guide. Buying a bicycle is another option, and the Pacific Northwest has lots of bike shops with a wide range of choices. For used bikes check www.craigslist.com, but beware of stolen bikes.

In Oregon, it's a state law that children under 16 years old must wear helmets. In Washington mandatory helmet use varies, but most major cities or counties require helmet use for all ages; check www.wsdot.wa.gov/bike/helmets.htm for details. In BC all cyclists are required to wear a helmet. In any case, helmets are easy to wear and reduce the risk of head injury.

Wearing highly reflective clothing makes you much more visible to cars, as do nightlights, which are required by law throughout most of the Pacific North-

west. Also, using the best lock you can get is a must, as bike theft is fairly common; consider using two kinds of locks at the same time. Adding stickers and painting over expensive brand names to make your bike less desirable is another option.

For more on cycling in the region and bike tour companies, see p38.

Boat

Washington and BC have two of the largest state-owned ferry systems in the world; these ferries access some of the most rewarding destinations in the Pacific Northwest. Some boats are passenger-only, while others take both vehicles and passengers. Be aware that some summertime ferry routes can have long waits if you're in a car, and bring snacks, as ferry offerings are limited and expensive. For good general information on the area's schedules and routes, check www.youra.com/ferry.

BC Ferries (888-223-3779; www.bcferries.com) Operates most of the ferries in BC. Primary links are between Tsawwassen (south of Vancouver) and Swartz Bay (on Vancouver Island), and to Nanaimo from Tsawwassen and Horseshoe Bay. BC Ferries services also link Gulf Islands to Tsawwassen.

Black Ball's Coho Ferry (360-457-4491 in Washington, 250-386-2202 in BC; www.cohoferry.com) Privately operated; connects Victoria, BC with Washington's Port Angeles (on the Olympic Peninsula).

Clipper Navigation (206-448-5000, 800-888-2535; www.clippervacations.com/ferry_schedule) Privately operated; operates the *Victoria Clipper*, a passenger ferry that connects Seattle with Victoria, BC. Stops at San Juan Islands in summer.

Washington State Ferries (WSF; 206-464-6400; www.wsdot.wa.gov/ferries) Operates most of the ferries that run in the Puget Sound area. Popular routes go to Bremerton and to Bainbridge and Vashon Islands from Seattle. WSF also operates the ferry system through the San Juan Islands and on to Sidney (near Victoria, on Vancouver Island) from Anacortes. Check its website for fares, schedules, route maps and tourist information, plus links to other ferry services.

Bus

Greyhound (800-231-2222; www.greyhound.com) generally serves the less affluent strata of American society – those without private vehicles. Service is relatively good but infrequent, especially in more remote areas. Greyhound largely sticks to the interstate freeway system, while regional carriers provide service to outlying areas. In almost all cases, these smaller bus lines share

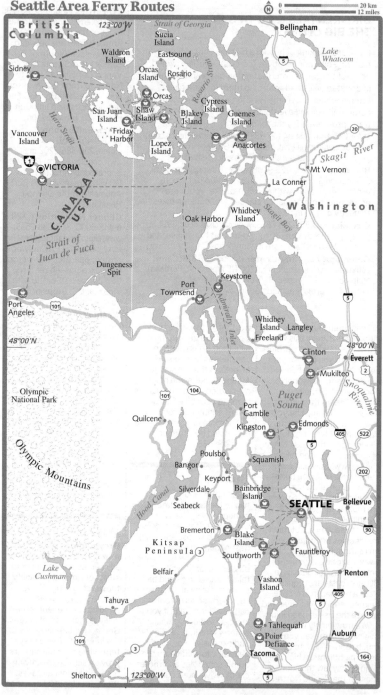

Seattle Area Ferry Routes

British Columbia

Strait of Georgia

Bellingham

Lake Whatcom

123°00'W

Sucia Island

Waldron Island

Eastsound

Orcas Island

Rosario

Cypress Island

Guemes Island

Sidney

Orcas

Rosario Strait

San Juan Island

Shaw Island

Blakey Island

Anacortes

Friday Harbor

Vancouver Island

Lopez Island

Haro Strait

Skagit River

Mt Vernon

20

VICTORIA

La Conner

CANADA USA

Washington

Oak Harbor

Whidbey Island

Skagit Bay

Strait of Juan de Fuca

48°00'N

Dungeness Spit

Keystone

Port Townsend

Admiralty Inlet

Whidbey Island

Langley

Freeland

Clinton

48°00'N

Port Angeles

101

Everett

2

Olympic National Park

Snoqualmie River

Mukilteo

101

104

Puget Sound

Port Gamble

Edmonds

405

522

Quilcene

Kingston

5

Poulsbo

202

Bangor

Squamish

Keyport

Olympic Mountains

Silverdale

Bainbridge Island

SEATTLE

Bellevue

Hood Canal

Seabeck

90

Bremerton

Blake Island

Kitsap Peninsula 3

Southworth

Fauntleroy

Lake Cushman

Belfair

Renton

Vashon Island

405

Tahuya

5

18

Tahlequah

Auburn

101

3

Point Defiance

164

Shelton

Tacoma

123°00'W

5

0 20 km
0 12 miles

depots and information services with Greyhound.

Generally, buses are clean, comfortable and reliable. Amenities include onboard lavatories, air-conditioning and slightly reclining seats. Smoking is not permitted. Buses break for meals every three to four hours, usually at fast-food restaurants or cafeteria-style truck stops. When you buy tickets a week in advance, discounts apply.

Bus stations are often dreary places. In small towns, where there is no station, buses stop in front of a specific business; in these cases, be prepared to pay the driver with exact change.

Car & Motorcycle

When you're traveling around the most car-oriented societies on the planet, auto transportation is well worth considering. A car is much more flexible than public transportation (especially if you're camping), and in a region where gas is still a relatively inexpensive commodity, it's likely to be cheaper. Use of seat belts is mandatory in the USA and Canada.

For tips and rules on driving in the USA, get an Oregon or Washington Driver Handbook at any Department of Motor Vehicles (DMV) office; you can also check online at www.drivershandbook.com. For Canada read or download the *RoadSense for Drivers* manual at http://www.llbc. leg.bc.ca/public/pubdocs/ bcdocs/371018/index.htm.

Keep in mind that Oregon law prohibits you from pumping your own gasoline – all stations are full service, so just sit back and enjoy it.

Automobile Associations

The **American Automobile Association** (AAA; ☑800-444-8091; www.aaa.com) and **Canadian Automobile Association** (CAA; ☑604-268-5500 in BC; www.caa.ca)

provide useful information, free maps, travel discounts and routine road services such as tire repair and towing (free within a limited radius) for their members. Similar benefits or discounts are extended to the members of foreign affiliates, such as the Automobile Association in the UK; bring your membership card from your country of origin.

To become a member of AAA, call or visit the website. The basic membership fee is $66 per year – a good investment for the maps alone. For roadside assistance, call the AAA's **toll-free number** (☑800-222-4357).

For CAA membership, call or visit the website. The basic CAA plan costs C$93 (plus tax); for roadside assistance call the **toll-free number** (☑800-222-4357).

Driver's Licenses

Foreigners driving in the Pacific Northwest officially need an International Driving Permit (IDP) to supplement their national or state driver's license; note that the IDP is only valid if issued in the same country as your driver's license. Local traffic police are more likely to accept an IDP than an unfamiliar foreign license as valid identification. Your national automobile association can provide one for a small fee, and they're usually valid for one year.

Insurance

Auto insurance is obligatory for car owners in the Pacific Northwest. Rates fluctuate widely, depending on where the car is registered; it's usually cheaper if registered at an address in the suburbs or in a rural area, rather than in a central city. Male drivers under the age of 25 will pay astronomical rates. Collision coverage has become very expensive, with high deductibles, and is generally not worthwhile unless the car is somewhat valuable.

Obtaining insurance, however, is not as simple as walking into an agency, filling out a form and paying for it. Many agencies refuse to insure drivers who have no car insurance – a classic catch-22. Those agencies that will do so often charge much higher rates because they presume a higher risk. The minimum term for a policy is usually six months, but some insurance companies will refund the difference on a prorated basis if the car is sold and the policy voluntarily terminated. Shop around. If you're planning to drive in both the USA and Canada, make sure your insurance is valid on both sides of the border.

Motorcycles & Scooters

With its beautiful coastline, national parks and backcountry deserts, there are some great opportunities for motorcycling in the Pacific Northwest. For foreigners, an IDP endorsed for motorcycles will simplify the rental process. You can download USA motorcycle manuals at www.dmv.org/ motorcycle-manual.php. To drive on freeways, you must have at least a 150cc engine. Helmets are mandatory for both drivers and passengers.

Rentals are not cheap – motorcycles start at about $140 per day and scooters about $75 per day. Insurance is extra. Hire companies to try include:

Columbia Scooters (☑503-872-8565; www.co lumbiascooters.com; Portland) Scooter and electric bike rentals.

Cycle BC Rentals (☑866-380-2453; www.cyclebc.ca; Vancouver) Rents a good selection of motorcycles and scooters.

Mountain to Sound Motorcycle Adventures (☑425-222-5598; www.mtsma.com; Seattle) Rentals and tours.

ROAD DISTANCES (MILES)

	Seattle	Portland	Vancouver	Spokane	Eugene	Ashland	Seaside	Bend	ONP	Walla Walla	Whistler
Portland	172										
Vancouver	141	315									
Spokane	280	351	410								
Eugene	283	110	424	462							
Ashland	460	285	599	637	180						
Seaside	194	80	334	432	181	356					
Bend	330	159	470	396	120	186	247				
ONP	90	146	128	370	265	425	150	305			
Walla Walla	270	245	408	158	352	470	322	286	350		
Whistler	215	390	70	495	498	675	409	640	305	485	
Mt Rainer	85	136	179	212	204	325	279	195	175	173	300

Northwest Motorcycles Adventures (☎360-241-6500; www.northwestmotor cycleadventures.com; Portland) Rentals and tours.

Scoot About (☎206-407-3362; www.scootabout.biz; Seattle) Scooter rentals. For more information about motorcycling in the region, check out www.soundrider. com, www.pnwriders.com and www.roadsnw.com.

Purchase

If you're spending a few months in the USA and Canada, a car may be a good investment, particularly if you're splitting the expense with others. Keep in mind, however, that it can be complicated and requires plenty of research.

It is possible to purchase a viable used car for less than $2000, but it might eventually need repair work that could cost several hundred dollars or more. It doesn't hurt to spend more to get a quality vehicle – you can sometimes sell it for close to what you paid. It's also worth having a mechanic check over the vehicle for problems; AAA has diagnostic centers that can do this for members.

Check the official value of a used car by looking it up in the **Kelley Blue Book** (www. kbb.com), which is a listing of cars by make, model and year that gives the average resale price. Local public libraries have copies.

Recreational Vehicles (RVs)

You can drive, eat and sleep in a recreational vehicle (RV). It's easy to find campgrounds with hookups for electricity and water, but in big cities RVs are a nuisance, since there are few places to park or plug them in. They're cumbersome to navigate and they burn fuel at an alarming rate, but they solve transportation, accommodations and cooking needs in one fell swoop.

For a state-by-state list of dealers, rentals and repairs check www.koa.com/rvfinder, which also lists its excellent campgrounds. Another good campground list is at www.woodalls.com; while a great source for general RV-travel tips is www.rvtravel.com.

Rental

Major international rental agencies have offices throughout the Pacific Northwest. To rent a car, you must have a valid driver's license, be at least 21 years of age and present a major credit card or a large cash deposit. Drivers under 25 must pay a surcharge over the regular rental.

Agencies often have bargain rates for weekend or week-long rentals, especially outside the peak seasons or in conjunction with airline tickets. Prices vary greatly depending on the type or size of car, pick-up and drop-off locations, number of drivers etc. In general, expect to pay from $30 to $60 per day for a midsize car, more in peak seasons. Rates usually include unlimited mileage, but not taxes or insurance.

You may get better rates by prebooking from your home country. If you get a

NORTH TO ALASKA

Waaay at the northwest tip of North America lies the USA's 49th state, Alaska. It's the biggest state by far, and home to stupendous mountains, massive glaciers and amazing wildlife. Mt McKinley (the continent's highest peak) is here, as are huge numbers of humpback whales and bald eagles.

Thinking of stopping in? There are daily flights from Seattle to Juneau, and you could always drive (and drive and drive) – but the best way to reach Alaska is probably by ferry. Think of it as like taking a cruise ship through the inside passage, but cheaper and more interesting. The trip from Bellingham to Juneau takes nearly three days, but other routes are available. For more information see www.dot.state.ak.us/amhs.

fly-drive package, local taxes may be an extra charge when you collect the car. Several online travel reservation networks have up-to-the-minute information on car-rental rates at all the main airports. Compare their rates with any fly-drive package you're considering.

Basic liability insurance covers damage you may cause to another vehicle. Rental companies are required by law to provide the minimum level set by each state, but it usually isn't enough in the event of a serious accident. Many Americans already have enough insurance coverage under their personal car-insurance policies; check your own policy carefully. Foreign visitors should check their travel-insurance policies to see if they cover foreign rental cars. Rental companies charge about $15 per day for this extra coverage.

Insurance against damage or loss to the car itself, called Collision Damage Waiver (CDW) or Loss Damage Waiver (LDW), can cost up to around $25 per day (and may have a deductible). The CDW may be voided if you cause an accident while breaking the law, however. Again, check your own coverage to see if you have comprehensive and collision insurance.

Some credit cards cover CDW for rentals up to 15 days, provided you charge the entire cost of the rental to the card. Check with your credit-card company to determine the extent of coverage.

Most of the big international rental companies have desks at airports, in all major cities and some smaller towns.

For rates and reservations, check the internet or call toll-free:

Alamo (☑800-327-9633; www.alamo.com)

Avis (☑800-230-4898; www.avis.com)

Budget (☑800-527-0700; www.budget.com)

Dollar (☑800-800-3665; www.dollar.com)

Enterprise (☑800-261-7331; www.enterprise.com)

Hertz (☑800-654-3131; www.hertz.com)

National (☑877-222-9058; www.nationalcar.com)

Rent-A-Wreck (☑877-877-0700; www.rentawreck.com)

Thrifty (☑800-847-4389; www.thrifty.com)

Road Hazards

A few backcountry roads of the Pacific Northwest region are in open-range country where cattle forage along the highway. Deer and smaller wildlife are more of a road hazard on roads all around the region, however. Pay attention to the roadside, especially at night.

During winter months – especially at the higher elevations – there will be times when tire chains are required on snowy or icy roads. Sometimes such roads will be closed to cars without chains or 4WD, so it's a good idea to keep a set of chains in the trunk. Make sure they fit your tires, and practice putting them on *before* you're out there next to the busy highway in the cold and dirty snow. Also note that many car-rental companies specifically prohibit the use of chains on their vehicles. Roadside services might be available to attach chains to your tires for a fee.

Local Public Transport

Though local bus networks are minimally developed in the hinterlands, the bigger cities have extensive services; with some planning, you can usually get wherever you want by bus. Because these systems are aimed at the commuting workforce rather than tourists, outside of peak commuting hours service may be sparse.

Portland boasts one of the country's best public-transportation systems, with an efficient light-rail system, extensive bus service and downtown streetcars. Within the city center, these services are free all day! Seattle also has an excellent transit system, with underground bus tunnels, light rail, a monorail and ferries; it also has free downtown bus rides during the day. And Vancouver is no slouch either, with great bus, train and streetcar services. All three cities have direct public-transport connections from their city centers to their airports.

Train

Amtrak (USA) and VIA Rail (Canada) trains provide an attractive, if costly, alternative to buses for travel between major points. Amtrak's *Cascades* train links Vancouver, BC, to Eugene, Oregon – via Seattle, Portland and Salem. This connects with Amtrak Thruway buses (actually a regional bus line under contract with Amtrak) to reach other destinations such as the Oregon coast.

A branch of Amtrak's daily *Empire Builder* leaves Portland and crosses to Vancouver (in Washington, not BC) before making its scenic run up the north side of the Columbia River Gorge to meet the other eastbound half of the train in Spokane. The Seattle branch of the *Empire Builder* heads north to Everett before winding east to Spokane. Note that the westbound *Empire Builder* divides in Spokane for Portland and Seattle: make sure you're sitting in the correct portion of the train!

One thing to know about these trains – delays can be very frequent, so don't plan on getting anywhere exactly on time.

behind
the
scenes

SEND US YOUR FEEDBACK

We love to hear from travelers – your comments keep us on our toes and help make our books better. Our well-traveled team reads every word on what you loved or loathed about this book. Although we cannot reply individually to postal submissions, we always guarantee that your feedback goes straight to the appropriate authors, in time for the next edition. Each person who sends us information is thanked in the next edition – and the most useful submissions are rewarded with a free book.

Visit **lonelyplanet.com/contact** to submit your updates and suggestions or to ask for help. Our award-winning website also features inspirational travel stories, news and discussions.

Note: We may edit, reproduce and incorporate your comments in Lonely Planet products such as guidebooks, websites and digital products, so let us know if you don't want your comments reproduced or your name acknowledged. For a copy of our privacy policy visit lonelyplanet.com/privacy.

OUR READERS

Many thanks to the travelers who used the last edition and wrote to us with helpful hints, useful advice and interesting anecdotes:

Martin Bergman, Laura Corcoran, Jill Dieterich, Caroline Hay, Cheryl Hill, Abid Kagalwalla, Nigel Reilly, Brian Santiago, Kristine K Stevens, Pierre Tissot van Patot, Carol Williams

AUTHOR THANKS

Sandra Bao

I couldn't have done this book without the companionship and masterful driving abilities of my husband, Ben. He makes life on the road more interesting for me, and I enjoyed looking at Oregon through his eyes. My coauthors have been patient and helpful with my requests; a more experienced bunch I couldn't have asked for. Editor extraordinaire Suki Gear has been awesome to work with, and thanks also to Kate and Dan, plus Todd, for their local Oregon knowledge.

Brendan Sainsbury

Thanks to all the untold bus drivers, tourist info volunteers, restaurateurs, national park rangers, weather forecasters, enologists and innocent bystanders who helped during my research. Thanks also to Suki Gear for offering me the gig, and Sandra Bao for being a supportive coordinating author. Special thanks to Andy McKee for his fast-paced hiking in the North Cascades. Thanks also to my wife, Liz, and four-year-old son, Kieran, for their company on the road.

John Lee

I'd like to send hearty thanks to those locals and friendly visitor-centre staff who took the time to stop, chat and help me at various points around the province. Thanks also to my nephew, Christopher, for joining me on the Vancouver Island portion of the trip and making it a lot more fun. Finally, thanks to my brother Michael and my Dad for coming out from the UK to test-drive the book: they get the first copy.

Becky Ohlsen

I'd like to thank Sandra Bao for doing all the hard work, and John Graham, Abby Margulies, Richard Rose, Maureen O'Hagan, AP Kryza, Jason Simms, Janice Logan, Heidi Messer, Deb Raftus, Matthew Stearns and Tom Burnett for their help in gathering local intel during the research of this book.

ACKNOWLEDGMENTS

Climate map data adapted from Peel MC, Finlayson BL & McMahon TA (2007) 'Updat-

ed World Map of the Köppen-Geiger Climate Classification', *Hydrology and Earth System Sciences*, 11, 163344.
Cover photograph: Mt Rainier from Spray Park, Mt Rainier National Park/George Ostertag/Photolibrary. Many of the images in this guide are available for licensing from Lonely Planet Images: www.lonelyplanet images.com.

THIS BOOK

This 5th edition of Lonely Planet's *Washington, Oregon & the Pacific Northwest* guidebook was researched and written by Sandra Bao (coordinating author), Brendan Sainsbury, John Lee and Becky Ohlsen. Lucy Burningham wrote the Beervana & Beyond and Pacific Northwest Cuisine chapters. The same authors also wrote the previous edition, along with David Lukas and Ellee Thalheimer.

This guidebook was commissioned in Lonely Planet's Oakland office, and produced by the following:

Commissioning Editors
Suki Gear, Catherine Craddock-Carrillo

Coordinating Editors
Charlotte Harrison, Kate James
Coordinating Cartographer Anthony Phelan
Coordinating Layout Designer Jacqui Saunders
Managing Editor Sasha Baskett
Senior Editors Helen Christinis, Katie Lynch
Managing Cartographers Alison Lyall, Adrian Persoglia
Managing Layout Designers Indra Kilfoyle, Celia Wood
Assisting Editors Carly Hall, Anne Mulvaney, Helen Yeates

Assisting Cartographer Julie Dodkins
Cover & Internal Image Research Sabrina Dalbesio

Thanks to Mark Adams, Imogen Bannister, Valeska Canas, David Connolly, Stefanie Di Trocchio, Janine Eberle, Bruce Evans, Joshua Geoghegan, Mark Germanchis, Michelle Glynn, Lauren Hunt, Laura Jane, David Kemp, Lisa Knights, Nic Lehman, John Mazzocchi, Wayne Murphy, Adrian Persoglia, Piers Pickard, Kirsten Rawlings, Raphael Richards, Lachlan Ross, Michael Ruff, Julie Sheridan, Laura Stansfeld, John Taufa, Sam Trafford, Juan Winata, Emily Wolman, Nick Wood

how to use this book

These symbols will help you find the listings you want:

◉	Sights	🎏	Festivals & Events	☆	Entertainment
🏃	Activities	🛏	Sleeping	🛍	Shopping
🍽	Courses	🍴	Eating	ℹ	Information/Transport
☞	Tours	🍷	Drinking		

Look out for these icons:

TOP CHOICE — Our author's recommendation

FREE — No payment required

🌱 — A green or sustainable option

Our authors have nominated these places as demonstrating a strong commitment to sustainability – for example by supporting local communities and producers, operating in an environmentally friendly way, or supporting conservation projects.

These symbols give you the vital information for each listing:

☏	Telephone Numbers	🛜	Wi-Fi Access	🚌	Bus
⊙	Opening Hours	🏊	Swimming Pool	⛴	Ferry
P	Parking	🥗	Vegetarian Selection	M	Metro
⊖	Nonsmoking	📖	English-Language Menu	S	Subway
❋	Air-Conditioning	👪	Family-Friendly	⊖	London Tube
@	Internet Access	🐾	Pet-Friendly	🚋	Tram
				🚆	Train

Reviews are organised by author preference.

Map Legend

Sights
- ◎ Beach
- ▲ Buddhist
- ◎ Castle
- ◎ Christian
- ◎ Hindu
- ◐ Islamic
- ◎ Jewish
- ◎ Monument
- ⊕ Museum/Gallery
- ◎ Ruin
- ◎ Winery/Vineyard
- ◎ Zoo
- ◎ Other Sight

Activities, Courses & Tours
- ◎ Diving/Snorkelling
- ◎ Canoeing/Kayaking
- ◎ Skiing
- ◎ Surfing
- ◎ Swimming/Pool
- ◎ Walking
- ◎ Windsurfing
- • Other Activity/Course/Tour

Sleeping
- ◎ Sleeping
- ◎ Camping

Eating
- ● Eating

Drinking
- ◎ Drinking
- ◎ Cafe

Entertainment
- ◎ Entertainment

Shopping
- ◎ Shopping

Information
- ◎ Post Office
- ◎ Tourist Information

Transport
- ◎ Airport
- ◎ Border Crossing
- ◎ Bus
- ⊹◎⊹ Cable Car/Funicular
- ◎ Cycling
- ◎ Ferry
- Ⓜ Metro
- ◎ Monorail
- P Parking
- S S-Bahn
- ◎ Taxi
- ◎ Train/Railway
- ◎ Tram
- ◎ Tube Station
- ◎ U-Bahn
- • Other Transport

Routes
- Tollway
- Freeway
- Primary
- Secondary
- Tertiary
- Lane
- Unsealed Road
- Plaza/Mall
- Steps
- ⊣ ⊏ Tunnel
- Pedestrian Overpass
- Walking Tour
- Walking Tour Detour
- Path

Boundaries
- International
- State/Province
- Disputed
- Regional/Suburb
- Marine Park
- Cliff
- Wall

Population
- ◎ Capital (National)
- ◉ Capital (State/Province)
- ◎ City/Large Town
- ◎ Town/Village

Geographic
- ◎ Hut/Shelter
- ◎ Lighthouse
- ◎ Lookout
- ▲ Mountain/Volcano
- ◎ Oasis
- ◎ Park
-)(Pass
- ◎ Picnic Area
- ◎ Waterfall

Hydrography
- River/Creek
- Intermittent River
- Swamp/Mangrove
- Reef
- Canal
- Water
- Dry/Salt/Intermittent Lake
- Glacier

Areas
- Beach/Desert
- + + + Cemetery (Christian)
- × × × Cemetery (Other)
- Park/Forest
- Sportsground
- Sight (Building)
- Top Sight (Building)

Becky Ohlsen

Seattle Becky has lived in the Pacific Northwest for 15 years. Drawn here from her native Colorado by the promise of great music and the ocean, she discovered that the area also provides excellent beer, a wide variety of pinball machines, cute skater boys and lots of rainy days for reading moodily in coffee shops. She lives in Portland. In addition to covering Seattle and elsewhere for Lonely Planet, she works as a freelance writer and copy editor, reviewing films, books and restaurants. When she's not traveling, Becky races vintage motorcycles very, very tentatively. Her favorite bar in Seattle is Shorty's and her favorite Nirvana album is *Bleach*.

Read more about Becky Ohlsen at:
lonelyplanet.com/members/beckyohlsen

EXPERT AUTHOR

Lucy Burningham (www.lucyburningham.com) is a food, drink and travel writer based in Portland, Oregon. Lucy wrote the Beervana & Beyond and Pacific Northwest Cuisine chapters of this book.

OUR STORY

A beat-up old car, a few dollars in the pocket and a sense of adventure. In 1972 that's all Tony and Maureen Wheeler needed for the trip of a lifetime – across Europe and Asia overland to Australia. It took several months, and at the end – broke but inspired – they sat at their kitchen table writing and stapling together their first travel guide, *Across Asia on the Cheap*. Within a week they'd sold 1500 copies. Lonely Planet was born.

Today, Lonely Planet has offices in Melbourne, London and Oakland, with more than 600 staff and writers. We share Tony's belief that 'a great guidebook should do three things: inform, educate and amuse'.

OUR WRITERS

Sandra Bao

Coordinating Author, Portland, The Willamette Valley & Wine Country, Columbia River Gorge, Central Oregon Cascades, Oregon Coast, Ashland & Southern Oregon, Eastern Oregon Sandra has lived in Buenos Aires, New York and California, but Oregon has become her final stop. Researching the Beaver state has been a highlight of Sandra's 10-year-long Lonely Planet career. She's come to appreciate the beauty of her home state, how much it has to offer and how friendly people are in tiny towns in the middle of nowhere.

Sandra lives in Portland with her husband Ben Greensfelder. They've embraced the local green culture by installing rain barrels and solar panels, recycling and running a community compost bin. When Sandra's not traveling she's obsessed with laying brick paths, working on her perennials and growing the perfect tomato.

Read more about Sandra Bao at:
lonelyplanet.com/members/sandrabao

Brendan Sainsbury

Northwest Washington & the San Juan Islands, Olympic Peninsula & Washington Coast, Washington Cascades, Central & Eastern Washington UK-born Brendan first discovered Washington State through a well-worn copy of the album *Nevermind* by Aberdeen-raised grunge merchants Nirvana. A decade later he visited again in person, from his new home in White Rock, BC, less than 2 miles from the US–Canadian border at Blaine. These days he lives within sight of the Evergreen state (Orcas Island is visible from his kitchen window) and makes regular sorties across the 49th parallel to visit the North Cascades, the San Juan Islands and Seattle.

Read more about Brendan Sainsbury at:
lonelyplanet.com/members/brendansainsbury

John Lee

Vancouver, Whistler & Vancouver Island Born in St Albans in southeast England, John moved to Canada's West Coast to study in the 1990s, relocating to Vancouver and launching an independent travel-writing career in 1999. Since then, he's been covering the region (and beyond) for major newspapers and magazines around the world. Becoming a Lonely Planet author in 2005, he has contributed to 18 titles, including writing recent editions of the *Vancouver* city guide, and penning a daily blog for the LP website from the 2010 Olympic Winter Games. To read his latest stories and see what he's up to, visit www.johnleewriter.com.

Read more about John Lee at:
lonelyplanet.com/members/johnlee

OVER PAGE | MORE WRITERS

Published by Lonely Planet Publications Pty Ltd
ABN 36 005 607 983
5th edition – April 2011
ISBN 978 1 74179 329 1
© Lonely Planet 2011   Photographs © as indicated 2011
10 9 8 7 6 5 4 3 2 1
Printed in Singapore

Although the authors and Lonely Planet have taken all reasonable care in preparing this book, we make no warranty about the accuracy or completeness of its content and, to the maximum extent permitted, disclaim all liability arising from its use.